EU External Relations Law and Policy in the Post-Lisbon Era

Paul James Cardwell
Editor

EU External Relations Law and Policy in the Post-Lisbon Era

T·M·C·ASSER PRESS

Springer

Dr. Paul James Cardwell
School of Law, University of Sheffield
Bartolomé House, Winter Street
Sheffield, S3 7ND
UK
e-mail: p.cardwell@sheffield.ac.uk

ISBN 978-90-6704-822-4 e-ISBN 978-90-6704-823-1
DOI 10.1007/978-90-6704-823-1

Library of Congress Control Number: 2011940204

Published by T.M.C. ASSER PRESS, The Hague, The Netherlands www.asserpress.nl
Produced and distributed for T.M.C. ASSER PRESS by Springer-Verlag Berlin Heidelberg

Cover design: eStudioCalamar, Berlin/Figueres

Printed on acid-free paper

Springer is part of springer Science+Business Media (www.springer.com)

Foreword

The growth of the European Union (EU) from a small regional coordinating organisation devoted to the management of coal and steel resources into a global political actor with a full range of power resources and unique responsibilities represents one of the most remarkable achievements in the history of international organisation. No other regional organisation on the planet has managed to take on so many of the traditional governing functions of its Member States while simultaneously developing its own power projection capabilities, involving trade policy, development and humanitarian aid, economic and financial sanctions, diplomacy and good offices, policing forces, and military forces.

This achievement is even more remarkable when one considers the uneven and even disorganised institutional history of European integration, which involves numerous actors with a wide range of power resources, policy interests and institutional preferences for various forms of European integration. These actors involve not just institutions in Brussels and Luxembourg, such as the Commission and the European Court of Justice, but also national governments and policy-makers, private firms, academics and think-tanks, concerned citizens and other interested players, all organised in dense webs of formal and informal networks across the EU and beyond.

Despite this diffusion of actors, or perhaps because of it, European integration is critically dependent on the emergence of rules to govern the activities of these players, in the form of customs, norms, international treaties, regulations and other laws at the EU and national levels. This system of law has been associated primarily with, and instigated by, the steady development of the single European market since the 1950s. However, as the EU's global ambitions have increased, so has its concern with the overall purpose and effectiveness of its various international activities. The EU is paying more attention than ever before to the external impact of European integration, and in areas well beyond the more traditional—for the EU—trade and economic development policy domains. This concern to improve the overall coherence of the EU's foreign policies was a major impetus behind the failed effort to produce a constitution for the EU, followed by the more successful effort to reform various EU policy domains under the Treaty of Lisbon.

Now that the Treaty of Lisbon has finally entered into effect, the time is ripe for a comprehensive analysis of how the Treaty reforms will impact on the EU's external relations policy ambitions. As with most major Treaty reforms in the EU, the general blueprint for Lisbon was finalised in a series of complicated intergovernmental conferences and periodic negotiations, yet the true impact of the Treaty will only be known after policymakers at the EU and national levels attempt to put its various provisions into practice. This process has now begun, and it is already clear that the Treaty reforms have created numerous challenges and opportunities for revising EU policy-making procedures, and for both internal and external policies. As always, these challenges and opportunities have inspired a range of interesting solutions in the form of informal and formal norms, soft law, socialisation processes, network-building and other 'behind the scenes' institutional reforms as various policy experts and legal officials attempt to put flesh on the bones of the Lisbon Treaty.

This volume provides us with a wide range of analyses targeted at these law-making and law-following efforts in the realm of European foreign policy. Together, they can help us determine whether the Lisbon Treaty will work as intended, and whether another round of institutional reform is necessary in the EU. Towards this end, the volume covers topics such as the principle of coherence in EU foreign policy, the creation of the new European External Action Service, the Common Foreign and Security Policy, the role of the High Representative of the Union for Foreign Affairs and Security Policy, the role of the European Court of Justice, networking mechanisms in the realm of EU foreign policy, the EU's efforts regarding weapons proliferation, European Neighbourhood Policy, relations across the Atlantic and with NATO, the Area of Freedom, Security and Justice, EU climate change policy, Common Commercial Policy and new provisions on investment and other critical issues regarding the EU's increasingly prominent role as a global actor.

The specific theories, methodologies, and arguments presented in these chapters vary widely, yet taken as whole they clearly indicate that the EU possesses nearly as many foreign policy competencies as those of a nation-state, and that legal procedures—involving national, EU-level, and international law—are absolutely critical in the way that the EU develops and pursues these competencies. However, this wide range of competencies, and the complex interactions among (at least) three major legal jurisdictional levels, make it extremely difficult for scholars to compare and generalise their findings beyond their specific cases. This is why it is so critical for volumes such as this, based as it was on a very stimulating interdisciplinary conference held at the University of Sheffield, to offer insights drawn from a range of viewpoints but always with an eye towards the creation of cumulative knowledge about one of the most important and theoretically interesting actors in the international system, the European Union.

Prof. Michael E. Smith
University of Aberdeen
m.e.smith@abdn.ac.uk

Preface

The present volume originates from a two-day conference, *EU External Relations Law and Policy in the Post-Lisbon Era*, hosted by the Sheffield Centre for International and European Law (SCIEL) at the School of Law, University of Sheffield on 13 and 14 January 2011. The conference was generously funded by the *Modern Law Review* and the University Association for Contemporary European Studies (UACES).

Participants at the conference were invited to consider the scope, nature and practice of EU External Relations Law and Policy in the Post-Lisbon Era. At the time of the conference, the Treaty had entered into force some 13 months earlier, so authors were able to reflect on some of the immediate consequences—both theoretically and practically—brought about by the Treaty as well as some of the incremental changes occurring during the period of Treaty reform. The response and the breadth of papers discussed was testament to the healthiness of EU external relations as a research area. The approach taken was deliberately interdisciplinary in order to promote a wide understanding of the contemporary nature of this dynamic field of study.

Sheffield, August 2011 — Paul James Cardwell

Acknowledgments

I am extremely grateful to the Modern Law Review and UACES for their generous financial support. I would also like to thank all the participants in the conference and contributors to this collection for helping make it such a successful event and making this book one of the first substantial publications about EU external relations since the Treaty entered into force. My thanks also go to the editors of the *European Foreign Affairs Review and Studia Diplomatica* for permitting the inclusion of previously published articles.

At Sheffield, I am especially grateful to Duncan French, Director of SCIEL, for his support as well as my colleagues in the School of Law and the Department of Politics who were in involved in the conference and the production of this volume: Diego Acosta, Estella Baker, Russell Buchan, Simon Bulmer, Richard Collins, Tamara Hervey and Emma Nesbit, as well as Tawhida Ahmed (University of Reading) and Daniel Wunderlich (University of Bath). Sarah Beedham, Harriet Godfrey and Audrey Pang provided their excellent skills in helping organise the conference and I am grateful to them. I would also like to express my sincere gratitude to Katie Tunstall for her research assistance in the preparation of the manuscript; Philip van Tongeren, Marjolijn Bastiaans and Antoinette Wessels at TMC Asser Press; Ursula Gramm and Arul Johny Marcus at Springer, and Seethalakshmi S at SPS. Finally, my eternal gratitude for love and support goes to Etienne Dunant.

Contents

Contributors

Dr. rer. pol. Annegret Bendiek Stiftung Wissenschaft und Politik, German Institute for International and Security Affairs, Berlin, Germany

Prof. Dr. Steven Blockmans T.M.C. Asser Institute, The Netherlands and University of Leuven, Leuven, Belgium

Dr. Maja Brkan European Court of Justice, Luxembourg, Luxembourg

Prof. Morten P. Broberg University of Copenhagen, Copenhagen, Denmark

Dr. Paul James Cardwell Sheffield Centre for International and European Law (SCIEL) at the School of Law, University of Sheffield, Sheffield, UK

Dr. Angelos Dimopoulos Tilburg Law School, Tilburg, The Netherlands

Dr. Rilka Dragneva School of Law, University of Manchester, Manchester, UK

Prof. Dr. Simon Duke European Institute of Public Administration (EIPA), Maastricht, The Netherlands

Dr. Nariné Ghazaryan Brunel Law School, Brunel University, Uxbridge, UK

Lisanne Groen Department of Political Science, Institute for European Studies (IES), Vrije Universiteit Brussel, Brussels, Belgium

Marja-Liisa Laatsit European University Institute, Florence, Italy

Elitsa Mincheva Department of EU General Studies, College of Europe, Bruges, Belgium

Pol Morillas European Institute of the Mediterranean (IEMed), Barcelona, Spain

Prof. Dr. Arne Niemann Department of Political Science, University of Mainz, Mainz, Germany

Dr. Maria O'Neill Dundee Business School, University of Abertay Dundee, Scotland, UK

Prof. Uwe Puetter Department of Public Policy, Center for European Union Research, Central European University, Budapest, Hungary

María Quesada Gámez Department of EU International Relations and Diplomacy Studies, College of Europe, Bruges, Belgium

Dr. Aurel Sari School of Law, University of Exeter, Exeter, UK

Julia Schmidt School of Law, University of Edinburgh, Edinburgh, UK

Prof. Michael E. Smith Department of Politics and International Relations, University of Aberdeen, Aberdeen, UK

Bettina Trueb Center for Doctoral Studies in Social and Behavioral Sciences (CDSS), University of Mannheim, Mannheim, Germany

Dr. Kataryna Wolczuk Centre for Russian and East European Studies, University of Birmingham, Birmingham, UK

Dr. Chien-Huei Wu Institute of European and American Studies, Academia Sinica, Taipei, Taiwan

Dr. Kamil Zwolski Department of History, Politics and Philosophy, Manchester Metropolitan University, Manchester, UK

Abbreviations

AAU	Assigned Amount Units
ACP	African, Caribbean and Pacific states
AETR/ERTA	European Road Transport Agreement
AFET	Foreign Affairs Committee of the European Parliament
AFSJ	Area of Freedom, Security and Justice
AG	Advocate General at the Court of Justice of the European Union
AMM	Aceh Monitoring Mission
ASEAN	Association of Southeast Asian Nations
AU	African Union
BASIC	Brazil, South Africa, India, China
BIT	Bilateral Investment Treaty
BRICs	Brazil, Russia, India, China
CAP	Common Agricultural Policy
CBRN	Chemical, Biological, Radiological and Nuclear
CCP	Common Commercial Policy
CEDAW	Convention on the Elimination of All Forms of Discrimination Against Women
CEE/CEEC	Central and Eastern Europe/Central and Eastern European Countries
CEPOL	European Police College
CFI	Court of First Instance
CFP	Common Fisheries Policy
CFR	Charter on Fundamental Rights
CFSP	Common Foreign and Security Policy
CHOD	Chiefs of Defence
CITES	Convention on International Trade in Endangered Species of Wild Fauna and Flora
CJEF	Combined Joint Expeditionary Force
CJEU	Court of Justice of the European Union

COLAT	Council Working Group for Latin America
COP	Conference of the Parties
COREPER	Comité des représentants permanents (Permanent Representatives Committee of the Council)
COWEB	Council Working Group on the Western Balkans
CPM	Civil Protection Mechanism
CSDP	Common Security and Defence Policy
DCI	Development and Cooperation Initiative
DDA	Doha Development Agenda
DRC	Democratic Republic of Congo
EC	European Community
ECAP	European Capability Action Plan
ECFR	European Council on Foreign Relations
ECHR	European Convention on Human Rights
ECJ	European Court of Justice
ECOWAS	European Community of West African States
ECSC	European Coal and Steel Community
ECtHR	European Court of Human Rights
EDA	European Defence Agency
EDC	European Defence Community
EDF	European Development Fund
EEAS	European External Action Service
EEC	European Economic Community
EFP	European Foreign Policy
EMEA	Euro-Mediterranean Economic Area
EMU	Economic and Monetary Union
ENP	European Neighbourhood Policy
ENPI	European Neighbourhood Partnership Instrument
EP	European Parliament
EPC	European Political Cooperation
ESDP	European Security and Defence Policy
ESS	European Security Strategy
EU	European Union
EU SITCEN	EU Situation Centre
EUBAM	EU Border Assistance Mission
EUMC	European Union Military Committee
EUMS	European Union Military Staff
EURATOM	European Atomic Energy Community
Eurojust	The European Union's Judicial Cooperation Unit
EuroMed	Euro-Mediterranean Partnership
Europol	The European Police Office
FAC	Foreign Affairs Council
FAO	Food and Agricultural Organisation of the United Nations
FCO	Foreign and Commonwealth Office

FDI	Foreign Direct Investment
FET	Fair and Equitable Treatment
GAM	Free Aceh Movement
GATS	General Agreement on Trade in Services
GATT	General Agreement on Tariffs and Trade
GC	General Court of the European Union
GCC	Gulf Cooperation Council
GSC	General Secretariat of the Council
GSP	General System of Preferences
HLCG	High Level Contact Group (on Data Protection)
HR	High Representative of the Union for Foreign Affairs and Security Policy
HR/VP	High Representative of the Union for Foreign Affairs and SecurityPolicy/Vice-President (of the Commission)
ICJ	International Court of Justice
IfS	Instrument for Stability
IGC	Intergovernmental Conference
IIA	International Investment Agreement
ILO	International Labour Organisation
INSC	Instrument for Nuclear Safety Cooperation
ISAF	International Security Assistance Force
ISCID	International Centre for Settlement of Investment Disputes
ISTC	International Science and Technology Centre
JHA	Justice and Home Affairs
KEDO	Korean Peninsula Energy Development Organisation
LAC	Latin America and Caribbean
LAIF	Latin America Investment Facility
LIBE	Civil Liberties, Justice and Home Affairs Committee of the Parliament
LULUCF	Land Us, Land Use Change and Forestry
MEP	Member of the European Parliament
MERCOSUR	Mercado Común del Sur (Southern Common Market)
MFN	Most Favoured Natiom
MIC	Monitoring and Information Centre
MONUC	United Nations Organisation Mission in the Democratic Republic of Congo
MPoI	Minimum Platforms on Investment
NATO	North Atlantic Treaty Organisation
NGO	Non-Governmental Organisation
NSC	New Strategic Concept
OECD	Organisation for Economic Co-operation and Development
PCA	Partnership and Cooperation Agreement
PCIJ	Permanent Court of International Justice

PESCO	Permanent Structured Cooperation
PJCCM	Police and Judicial Cooperation in Criminal Matters
PNR	Passenger Name Record
PoCo	Political Committee
PSC	Political and Security Committee
QMV	Qualified Majority Voting
REIO	Regional Economic Integration Organisations
RPC	Rules of Procedure of the Council
RPCJEC	Rules of Procedure of the European Parliament
SALW	Small Arms and Light Weapons
SEA	Single European Act
SIRENE	Schengen Information System
SitCen	CFSP's Joint Situation Centre
SNE	Seconded National Experts
STCU	Science and Technology Centre in Ukraine
TACIS	Technical Aid to the Commonwealth of Independent States
TEU	Treaty on European Union
TFEU	Treaty on the Functioning of the European Union
TFTP	Terrorist Finance Tracking Programme
TLD	Transatlantic Legislators Dialogue
TRIMs	Trade-Related Investment Measures
TRIPS	Agreement on Trade-Related Aspects of Intellectual Property Rights
UK	United Kingdom
UMFA	Union Minister of Foreign Affairs
UN	United Nations
UNAMID	African Union/UN Hybrid operation in Darfur
UNCLOS	United Nations Convention on the Law of the Sea
UNFCCC	United Nations Framework Convention on Climate Change
UNITA	National Union for the Total Independence of Angola
UNSC	United Nations Security Council
USA	United States of America
WAEMU	West African Economic and Monetary Union
WEU	Western European Union
WHO	World Health Organisation
WMD	Weapons of Mass Destruction
WTO	World Trade Organisation

Chapter 1
EU External Relations Law and Policy in the Post-Lisbon Era

Paul James Cardwell

Contents

1.1 Introduction

The European Union (EU) institutions and Member States could be forgiven for giving a collective sigh of relief on 1 December 2009 when the decade-long process of constitutional reform of the EU finally reached its end. The entry into force of the Treaty of Lisbon, born from the ashes of the abandoned Treaty Establishing a Constitution for Europe, was a pivotal moment in the history of the European integration process and its external relations. But, as with any major constitutional change, its entry into force posed as many questions for the future of the EU as it gave responses to the need for the EU to have a new Treaty in the first place. If the political elites responsible for the text of the Treaty are allowed their sigh of relief, then the citizens of Europe (if not the world) should also be permitted to wonder why the Treaty took so long and what the point of it all was.

The need for strengthening the external relations of the EU was, from the start, a key driver in constitutional reform. Yet, the end result for external relations

P. J. Cardwell (✉)
School of Law, University of Sheffield, Bartolomé House,
Winter Street, S3 7ND, Sheffield, UK
e-mail: p.cardwell@sheffield.ac.uk

P. J. Cardwell (ed.), *EU External Relations Law and Policy in the Post-Lisbon Era*,
DOI: 10.1007/978-90-6704-823-1_1, © T.M.C. ASSER PRESS, The Hague,
The Netherlands, and the authors 2012

seems indicative of the wider result. The Treaty can perhaps best be characterised as a compromise solution which did not meet the grand expectations set out at the beginning of the reform process. It did not create a finalised constitutional template for what the EU stands for and continued in the tradition of piecemeal, if grand-scale, reforms but with an ever increasing number of opt-outs, conditions and qualifications to its principles, processes and aims. This included aspects of the external relations dimension.

But we should also not be too harsh in our evaluation of what the Treaty has done. The EU continues to navigate in unchartered waters: no other project of regional integration has so successfully put in place such grand ideas as a single currency, a huge increase in membership, nor moved forward into areas where many other states around the world would never dream of cooperating with their neighbours, including external relations of course, but also Justice and Home Affairs. But the problem with trailblazing in this way is that it requires a continued belief in the core aims and values of the Union. The debate over the 'constitutional symbols' of the Union to be included within the Treaty was not merely one of aesthetics, but one which pointed to the lack of a finalised, comprehensive constitutional settlement. Jo Shaw has commented on the 'uneasy shift which has occurred between "old" and "incremental" versions of European constitutionalism based on the classic law/integration interface and "newer" more formalised ones, epitomized by the grand and ultimately misplaced "dreams" of a "Constitution for Europe's citizens" trailed in the Laeken Declaration of December 2001'[1] which seems to go to the heart of the tensions over the direction of the EU. In the end, dropping the most symbolic 'constitutional' provisions was the most appropriate way forward: the EU has its flag and anthem but the European integration project is still open to interpretation as to its possible and eventual aims.

What cannot be disputed, however, is the continued centrality of external relations to the contemporary nature and work of the EU and the reforms introduced at Lisbon. With the exception of the domain of Justice and Home Affairs—which now carries an increasingly prominent external dimension—few substantive areas of the EU integration process were under such scrutiny during the decade-long search for change. Much of this was due to the continuation of the EU's evolving practices in external relations, which have developed incrementally: external commercial relations were established as a Community competence very early on, but political external relations ('foreign policy' proper, including defence policy) followed only later—and even then at a gradual pace. The Treaty of Lisbon, in one way, moved the EU along the road of bringing external relations more comprehensively within its scope and allowing the unfinished and unsatisfactory nature of the EU's institutional machinery, as created in the Treaty on European Union, the Treaty of Amsterdam and the Treaty of Nice, to meet the goals the EU had set itself. But the development in competences was matched by the nature of certain aspects of the text, which reveals even further the reticence of

[1] Shaw 2011, 583.

the Member States to allow the EU too much power and influence in this field in key aspects of external relations (notably the CFSP). There continues to be a mismatch between the aims the EU is supposed to meet, and the ability it has to meet them: the oft-quoted 'capability-expectations' gap.[2] The Common Foreign and Security Policy (CFSP) is often the focus of criticism by both scholars and practitioners, which is understandable since its name incorporates a vision of EU foreign policy which many do not see operating in reality. The complex workings of the EU institutions means that EU foreign policy may be more effective than we think, but we do not (yet) adjust our vision to see it.[3] Part of this is the reason why scholarly work on the EU's external relations, including this volume, is often more concerned with the internal workings of the EU rather than its actual effects on the world outside its borders.

The changing global context which the EU finds itself in has also provided at least some impetus to emphasising the importance of external relations within the governance structure of the EU and its projection outwards. In economic terms, China and India's rise to prominence has forced the EU to consider where it will fit into the global economy in the future, and to what extent its relations with other parts of the globe (Africa in particular) will be affected. Global financial instability since 2007 has shaken the foundations of the euro. Politically, the 2000s witnessed greater levels of EU involvement in two externally-focussed areas which had previously only been peripheral: security and migration. The Laeken Declaration was soon followed by the 9/11 attacks, and the following years were punctuated by terror attacks in Europe and Europe's near neighbours. The European Security Strategy 2003[4] was created to coordinate a response to the questions over the EU's role in this new world order. Assuring Europe's 'internal' security, the EU has engaged in external measures—perhaps most notably the freezing of assets, which has led to the European Court of Justice examining the relationship between EU Law and International Law in the *Kadi* cases.[5] Some perennial international issues from the 1990s and before—the Middle East conflict, instability in the Balkans—were joined by sporadic other international issues which demanded a strong response from the EU. Many of these issues—the Russia–Georgia conflict, the 'Arab Spring'—solicited responses from the EU which could be easily criticised for being incoherent or ineffective. Of course, there is almost universal agreement that if the EU is to meet its goals and be recognised as a fully-fledged international actor, with the capacity to pursue its aims to impose its norms and values beyond

---

[2] Hill 1993

[3] On this point see, for example, Cardwell 2009; Bickerton 2011.

[4] *European Security Strategy: A Secure Europe in a Better World*, Brussels, 12 December 2003, as complemented by the High Representative's *Report on the Implementation of the European Security Strategy—Providing Security in a Changing World*, doc. 17104/08 (S407/08), 11 December 2008, endorsed by the European Council, Presidency Conclusions, doc. 17271/08 (CONCL 5), 12 December 2008.

[5] Cardwell, French and White 2009.

its borders,[6] then it needs to be able to have the institutions and instruments to do so, backed up with the political ambition from the Member States too. This, however, is easier said than done. But it is also a truism that the EU's capacity as a foreign policy actor should not rely on its ability to merely respond to global events: as many of the chapters in this volume demonstrate, taking a long-term view of EU external relations is essential in evaluating the kind of actor it is and what is needed (legally or politically) to strengthen its capabilities. The Treaty has provided an opportunity to rethink some of these dimensions of its external relations.[7]

What started out therefore as a forward-looking project to make the EU a true 'global actor' in fact resulted in the Treaty-writing projects trying to catch-up with developments both inside and outside the EU. Even so, 2010 marked a busy year for the EU institutions as the entry into force of the Treaty finally allowed movement on several fronts. At the institutional level, the appointments of the permanent President of the Council and High Representative of the Union for Foreign Affairs and Security Policy were the headline grabbing issues (though accurately characterised by Panos Koutrakos as being viewed as 'distinctly underwhelming' choices)[8] and both were subject to scrutiny in the early stages of their new roles. For the High Representative, the creation of the European External Action Service (EEAS) was at the top of the in-tray,[9] and much of the other work to be done post-Lisbon was 'behind the scenes'. Elsewhere, the Commission brought forward proposals based on new, externally focussed areas including in investment policy[10] and aspects of Justice and Home Affairs[11] whereas the other actors (not least the rotating Member State presidencies) dealt with the questions of who-does-what. And at the same time, the world beyond the EU looked to see what changes, if any, could be expected from the EU.

---

[6] La 2008, 4.

[7] See, for example, Joint Communication to the European Council, the European Parliament, the Council, the European Economic and Social Committee and the Committee of the Regions—A Partnership for Democracy and Shared Prosperity with the Southern Mediterranean, COM (2011) 200.

[8] Koutrakos 2011, 236.

[9] Council Decision 2010/427/EU of 26 July 2010 establishing the organisation and functioning of the European External Action Service, *OJ* 2010 L 201/30.

[10] See, in particular, Communication from the Commission to the Council, the European Parliament, the European Economic and Social Committee and the Committee of the Regions 'Towards a comprehensive European international investment policy', Brussels 7.7.2010, COM (2010) 343; Proposal for a regulation of the European Parliament and of the Council establishing transitional arrangements for bilateral investment agreements between Member States and third countries, Brussels 7.7.2010, COM (2010) 344.

[11] See, for example, Commission (2010) Strategy for the effective implementation of the Charter of Fundamental Rights by the European Union, COM (2010) 573.

1.2 Scope and Objectives of the Book

Is it possible to state that the entry into force of the Treaty of Lisbon marks the beginning of a new 'era' in European integration? In some areas, the Treaty made few changes but this cannot be said to be the case for external relations. As mentioned above, some of the most visible changes to come into effect were the institutional modifications relating to the representation of the EU beyond its borders: the substantially altered role of the High Representative, the creation of the EEAS and the appointment of a permanent President of the European Council (who also has a representative role, albeit not fully defined). Alongside these developments, the acquisition of new competences (for example, in investment policy and Common Security and Defence Policy) and the establishment of cross-cutting requirements to ensure consistency/coherence can be said to reinvigorate the conduct and scope of external relations. The text of the Treaty therefore suggests that an important new chapter has begun in EU external relations but—and this is perhaps where the legal and political insights contained in this volume are most useful—to determine whether Lisbon really makes a difference is to assess whether the EU capitalises on these changes. Perhaps it is true that an 'era' can be properly coined as such only once it comes to an end, in which case we will need to see when the next major change—perhaps another comprehensive treaty revision process—occurs. What this book does show is that there is an incredible richness in the vast number of dimensions to the contemporary state of the EU's external relations, of which only a select few are covered here. EU external relations remain ripe for analysis from legal scholars, political scientists and those navigating the terrain between these disciplines.

The purpose of this book is to consider the state of play of the EU's external relations now that the Treaty has been in force for, at the time of writing, just over one year. This has allowed some contributors to examine a number of the immediate changes which have been brought about under the Treaty, in particular the creation of the new EEAS. Of course, it is not suggested that the full impact of the Treaty can be felt yet and much remains to be seen in terms of how the EU manages to capitalise on the Treaty's provisions. Hindsight will be essential to evaluate the extent to which, to take one recurring theme running through the book, the EU's various actions have reached a greater level of coherence.

Contributors have considered one of more of the following questions: how are the new institutional arrangements taking shape? What are the challenges, difficulties and opportunities created by the Treaty of Lisbon for the EU's institutional and constitutional arrangements? How are the arrangements being translated into the practice of external relations outside the EU? How are the different dimensions (for example, Common Commercial Policy, CFSP) of EU external relations evolving? Is increased consistency and coherence across the EU's external relations possible? How do theories of European integration, International Relations and legal theory inform our understanding of EU External Relations post-Lisbon?

With these questions in mind, the aim of the book has not been to analyse the terms of the Treaty in isolation, nor to only speculate or predict what these mean for the future—though both of these considerations do occur in the contributing chapters. Rather, the book casts a wide net to examine where EU external relations stand, how this situation was arrived at and what the future may hold. Contributions consider some direct changes brought about by the entry into force of the Treaty; for example, the new requirement for 'consistency/coherence' and the institutional changes to the role of the High Representative, and the EEAS and permanent President of the European Council. Others trace the development of different aspects of EU external relations which may be affected by the spirit of Lisbon (and the process by which it was created) if not the letter of the law. Taken together, the book aims to offer an insight into the multiple facets of the way in which the EU deals with the outside world—including, as will already be familiar to scholars of EU external relations—how it equips itself as a non-traditional actor in international affairs to overcome internal institutional challenges.

1.3 Overview

This book is divided into four parts, each aiming to examine a different aspect of EU external relations with a common thread. Each part includes contributions from legal and political science scholars.

It may be expected in a work consecrated to the External Relations of the EU, that considerable attention is devoted to the CFSP, since this is identified within the Treaties as the main vehicle for EU foreign policy and, as the EU has discovered since 1992, the provisions form the benchmark against which 'success' in EU foreign policy-making can/should be judged. In Part I, the four chapters consider the different theoretical and practical implications of the Treaty of Lisbon for the CFSP writ large. The first three chapters use different theoretical frameworks to explain the unique position the CFSP finds itself in within the Treaty, where as the fourth chapter considers the potentially important (though often overlooked) role of the Court of Justice.

In Chapter 2, Uwe Puetter uses a theoretical framework he has developed—'deliberative intergovernmentalism'—to characterise the workings of the CFSP. The main thrust of this theory, that the main actors in CFSP remain the EU's Member State governments, thus contends that CFSP governance represents a continuation of moves towards foreign policy coordination since 1992 rather than a break with the past. Insofar as the appointment of the High Representative and permanent President of the Council are concerned, the Treaty of Lisbon has 'engineered' these posts to facilitate closer policy and decision-making consensus. Therefore, despite the inherently intergovernmental settings (including the European External Action Service which, given the participation by national officials amongst in staff, has a very different institutional character to the EU institutions) the High Representative and permanent President may prove to be effective if they are skilled in being both pro-active and framing issues for debate as common problems needing solution. The Treaty text therefore only tells part of the story, and much will depend on the personalities and skills of the incumbents of these posts.

The alternative theoretical insights provided in Chapter 3, by Annegret Bendiek, partly shift the focus away from the EU institutions to the Member States and their role in and control over the CFSP. She examines the dominant theoretical approaches to the study of contemporary European foreign policy and makes the case for the use of European Realism as a means of understanding the 'two track' quality of foreign policy, i.e., the Member State level-track and the EU level-track. Bendiek critiques the existing theoretical approaches for failing to appreciate the dominant role played by Member States in the formation of European foreign policy, and argues that a European variant of Realism takes into account the dominant roles played by Member States (and in particular, France, Germany and the UK) over the supranational considerations at EU level. This is not to say that the voice of smaller states is never heard, but that we should not ignore the synergy between national interests—particularly in the field of security—and the formation of European foreign policy as based primarily on the interests of individual Member States. The thrust of Bendiek's chapter is that European Realism allows the 'politics' to be brought to the fore once again in the consideration of what Europe's foreign policy is. The Treaty of Lisbon has thus enhanced the need for a return to a serious consideration of the use of the theoretical tools offered by realism.

In contrast, Aurel Sari's contribution (Chapter 4) takes a very legal topic—the issue of the EU and its institutions' competence over the CFSP—but places it within an institutionalist frame of analysis which is useful for both legal and political science scholars alike. His starting point is that the Member States saw no need to define the EU's competence over the CFSP in express terms but in the long process of treaty reform during the 2000s, this changed. He explains this institutionalisation of the CFSP by what he calls the 'Goldilocks principle of institutional design': not too much, not too little, but just right. Member States have carefully segregated the CFSP away from other areas, despite its all-encompassing nature. Sari argues that the issue of delimiting CFSP competence only came during the reform process, not before, as a consequence of the decision to create a single legal personality for the Union. Therefore, the clarification 'was driven not by practical necessity, not by the need to resolve any real-life difficulties, but by the logic of the treaty reform process itself'. Analysis of the CFSP in this way opens the door to inviting more complex and refined insights into the workings of the CFSP than would be suggested by a legal approach which contends that since it is formally separate within the Treaty structure, then it can be treated as a purely intergovernmental form of cooperation.

In Chapter 5, Maja Brkan picks up on one aspect of the competence analysis covered by Sari in the previous chapter, that of the role of the European Court of Justice. Although the Treaty still excludes the Court of Justice from competence over the CFSP explicitly, her analysis reveals that the Treaty provision laying this down does not in itself tell the whole story. Rather, an analysis of the context of recent decisions by the EU's judicial arm, in addition to other provisions within the Treaties reveal that the Court of Justice does indeed continue to have a potentially important role to play. Brkan explains this by identifying the legal questions which are likely to arise in the post-Lisbon era. These include the role of the Court in policing the boundaries between the CFSP and other areas, which in the new Treaties brings a new dimension since the previously valid rule of absolute preference of Community law over the CFSP does not apply anymore. The Court may also have influence over the CFSP through the review of economic sanctions either against natural or legal persons or against third countries. The possibility of direct review by the Court of certain restrictive measures against natural or legal persons gives claimants more certainty and an opportunity to seek annulment of restrictive measures early in the process of adoption of these measures. As the Charter of Fundamental Rights is now part of the EU's legal order, the Court of Justice should also ensure that measures respect human rights. This chapter demonstrates, therefore, that there is more to the Court's role in CFSP than meets the eye and whilst the changes are not revolutionary, the post-Lisbon era of CFSP incorporates a potentially significant role for the Courts.

Part II expands the scope of inquiry beyond the CFSP to the wider institutional questions raised by the Treaty of Lisbon. The scene is set in this part of the book by a chapter which focuses in particular on the immediate period after the entry into force of the Treaty under the Spanish Council Presidency. This is followed by a detailed consideration of the developments in creating the EEAS before two chapters which each consider the potential longer-term impact of institutional changes, including the obligation to promote the EU's values.

Pol Morillas, in Chapter 6, discusses some of the main themes in this book resulting from the changes brought about by the Treaty, but focuses his attention on the six-month period immediately following its entry into force. The Spanish Presidency in the first half of 2010 was the first under the new Treaty and had to deal with the difficult issues of institutional arrangement alongside many aspects of the 'usual' work done by a Council Presidency. But in the realm of external relations, Morillas' analysis of the developments during the Spanish Presidency shows that rather than the Treaty ending debates about who-does-what, the discussions actually brought them to the fore in Council discussions. Member States, keen to ensure that foreign policy discussions retained their intergovernmental character, had to learn to co-exist with the High Representative's new powers of initiative. Since 'foreign policy' is rarely consigned to one particular political, economic or military dimension—as the crises of Gaza and Haiti during this period demonstrate—the different actors quickly developed a set of working practices initiated by the Spanish Presidency to ensure the functioning of the external relations machinery. What occurred in this short time period was a significant level of institutionalisation which provided the High Representative with room for manoeuvre in terms of her power of initiative, but with the Member States retaining their traditional grip on EU foreign policy.

In Chapter 7, Steven Blockmans and Marja-Liisa Laatsit examine the European External Action Service (EEAS) which was, in itself, one of the main externally focussed innovations in the Treaty, and one closely related to the creation of the post of High Representative. But the EEAS is also a case-study of the application of the principle of coherence in practice. In the relatively short period of operation of the EEAS, they contend that the diversity of the personnel involved (drawn from Commission and Council officials as well as seconded staff from Member States) is matched by the diversity of the political 'masters' that the EEAS serves. In this respect, the findings of this chapter reflect the general uncertainty over how the new institutional format will work in the future. Nevertheless, the authors point to the possibility that EEAS will be a very effective and influential policy actor, providing that the institutions whom it serves do not engage in institutional battles. However, since the EEAS is not a decision-making body per se (at least not in terms of having the power to take formal, legal measures) they also conclude that including 'action' in the title is potentially problematic and that its success might be better measured in terms of how it manages to fill the role of 'coordination' between the various actors instead.

In this part's penultimate chapter, Julia Schmidt takes the earlier analysis of the principle of coherence and the new institutional framework for dealing with the outside world a step further, in examining the case of crisis management. As Schmidt notes, the EU has been involved in 22 crisis management missions since 2003; a not inconsiderable total and one which is likely to continue to increase in the years to come. The chapter takes a wide approach to crisis management, which is not the subject of a single policy-making area but rather a collection of potential measures—legal, political and economic—which can be put to use on a differentiated basis. Since the Treaty of Lisbon has not adequately delimited the institutional competences between the different actors, this is likely to hinder a 'coherent' approach of both policy and on-the-ground reaction to crisis. Reflecting the concerns of other contributors to this volume, the potential confusion over who represents the Union in external relations is also highlighted as (potentially) problematic for the EU in the post-Lisbon era.

The following chapter by Morten Broberg covers one of the most notable changes to the text of the Treaty for both legal and political science scholars, namely the obligation to further its values in its external relations. The potential impact of this value-led approach has attracted less attention than the obligation on the EU institutions to ensure coherence between their different actions in the external sphere. But, as Broberg argues, when the two principles are considered together, they are a potentially powerful driver behind the future direction of EU external relations. This is particularly the case in the area of development cooperation, where the extent to which the EU seeks to further its values can justifiably lead to the EU being referred to as the 'missionary man'. For Broberg, the promotion of values (especially in the context of development policy) does not necessarily mean that the EU should be seen—as it is often assumed—as acting in a neo-colonial way. Nevertheless, the success of the EU in being able to act in a normative, value-led way—as the Treaties require it to do—is likely to be dependent on external factors including the need to act as an effective commercial player. It may be that the promotion of (non-economic) values by the EU in the wider world eventually takes second place behind the role the EU plays as a trade player.

Part III moves to considering the EU's relationship with states and groupings of states beyond the EU's the borders. There is not enough space to deal with the (potential) impact of the EU in the post-Lisbon era on all the regions around the world. However, the five chapters here cover a range of different types of relationships, which combine multilateral and bilateral aspects. Three of the regions under the microscope here, Eastern Europe, North Africa and the US have very deep (albeit very different) relationships with the EU. The EU's neighbourhood policies deserve a great deal of attention since the Treaty provisions have a direct influence on the aims the EU is supposed to pursue in its neighbourhood. The extent to which EU external relations can be studied beyond the provisions of the CFSP is in evidence in the two chapters devoted to North Africa and the transatlantic relationship which centre on the external dimension of Justice and Home Affairs (JHA) provisions. Latin America is an interesting case-study of a region the EU has traditionally placed less emphasis on developing its relationship with—but offers a rich example of an 'everyday' level analysis of EU external relations.

Two contributions consider the EU's relationship with neighbouring countries through the prism of the European Neighbourhood Policy (ENP). In Chapter 10, Nariné Ghazaryan examines the institutional trends since the putting into place of the ENP in 2004 and the entry into force of the Treaty of Lisbon. Aside from the general institutional issues arising from the Treaty—which are treated here as to their specific effects regarding the EU's neighbourhood—the Treaty provisions which explicitly relate to the neighbourhood are examined. Neighbourhood states are the subject of a new, specific provision in the form of Article 8 TEU, which states that the Union shall develop a special relationship with neighbouring countries, 'founded on the values of the Union'. This takes the value-led approach to foreign policy as discussed by Broberg to a deeper level insofar as the neighbourhood is concerned, though, as Ghazaryan explains, the text is ambiguous enough to leave open the question as to whether the enlargement process is merely an inspiration for neighbourly relations or a tantalising carrot for the states involved regarding future possible full membership. Returning to a discussion of the post-Lisbon era institutional structure, the chapter notes that ENP is in an unusual place being partly within the remit of the High Representative but also the Commissioner for Enlargement and Neighbourhood Policy.

Chapter 11, by Rilka Dragneva and Kataryna Wolczuk, turns attention to the countries covered by the ENP. They enquire into the nature and appropriateness of 'law export' to the countries in Eastern Europe who do not have full membership prospects. The export of law is thus a legal issue (to what extent can and should countries such as Ukraine incorporate different dimensions of EU law into its national legal order?) and also a political one, since the EU is employing many of the same techniques it has acquired during the enlargement processes in the region. Whereas the EU may not be as unique an actor as we may often think in terms of exporting law—a point they identify with reference to general literature on the subject of law export—its promotion as a law exporter is linked to its confidence gained from successive enlargements. As an exporter of law to countries in the neighbourhood which do not have the prospects for full EU membership, the ENP sits 'uneasily' between being a fully-fledged external policy or an internal policy. As such, it is also subject to the post-Lisbon institutional changes which affect both the internal divisions of power and competence identified in other chapters, as it is to the changes to the external representation of the Union. Although the Treaty does appear to place more emphasis on the ENP, the text incorporates the ambiguous nature of the ENP as being subject to institutional pushing and pulling rather than settling what purpose the ENP serves in the post-Lisbon era.

The neighbourhood countries are also the focus of Chapter 12, and Maria O'Neill considers the meeting place of several of the important themes covered in this collection. Relations with North African states are important for numerous reasons, but as the EU has in recent years intensified its internal Justice and Home Affairs/Freedom, Security and Justice policy-making, the North African states have been the focus of the 'external' dimension to Justice and Home Affairs/ Freedom, Security and Justice. This is particularly in evidence in the Stockholm Programme which was created as a direct consequence of the changes brought in by the Treaty of Lisbon. O'Neill discusses the place of cross-border law enforcement between the EU and the North African states, picking out where the tensions lie and (in the context of the 'Arab spring' and changes in many of the governments of the North African states) the future development of this cooperation. As with many of the issues surrounding the external relations of the EU in the post-Lisbon era, O'Neill also discusses the evolving internal competences in this rapidly developing area. She concludes that the lack of clarity over whether measures will be taken under the competences of the CFSP or Police and Judicial Cooperation in Criminal Matters (PJCCM) is likely to be problematic for the future development of both EU-North Africa relations and (from a judicial perspective) within the courts of the EU Member States.

The very different relationships the EU has across the Atlantic with North and South American states form the basis of the final two chapters in this part. In Chapter 13, Bettina Trueb examines the nature of EU relations with Latin America. This is an interesting case-study for two reasons: first, Latin America, in a similar way to the EU's neighbouring states, is taken to be an area where European influence has traditionally been strong via the links with Spain and Portugal. Yet, it is not a region which regularly appears at the top of the EU's foreign policy agenda. It is also neither very rich nor very poor and, as such, it constitutes (in Trueb's words) an 'everyday' example of EU foreign policy-making. Second, and a related point, is that relations with Latin America are not dominated by one particular aspect of EU external relations. Nevertheless, the increasing global economic importance of Latin America means that it has attracted interest from other parts of the globe (including China). Europe may therefore not be in a position to assume in the future that Latin America aspires to maintaining the strong links of the past. In terms of prospects for the post-Lisbon era, Trueb's position is that coherency of action is the key, but this also includes the coordination of actions between the Member States as well as the EU institutions. Latin America is not likely to suddenly become an economic or political 'priority' region for the EU, but if it wishes to remain an attractive partner for Latin America (in economic or other fields) then it will have to gain the confidence to act much more coherently.

María Quesada Gamez and Elitsa Mincheva (Chapter 14) find the focus of their examination of one aspect of the EU's external relations at the very heart of a political-legal conundrum with one of the EU's closest strategic partners. The long-running dispute with the US over transatlantic information exchange has involved almost all the key EU institutions, especially the Court of Justice in the light of its finding of the unlawfulness of the Passenger Name Record (PNR) agreement of 2006. The multitude of EU actors involved in forging an agreement with the US is one of the reasons why the EU has not been in the driving seat but has rather responded to the agenda of the US. The Treaty of Lisbon substantially alters the institutional balance, by strengthening the respective roles of the Commission and, notably, the Parliament, at the expense of the Council. The Commission has already acted on the strengthening of its role as initiator of legislation in this field since Lisbon entered into force. Although the strengthened position of the Parliament might suggest that transatlantic cooperation in this field may stall, due to the caution exercised by Parliament when considering issues of data protection, the authors of this chapter make the case that the EU as a whole may be in a stronger negotiating position. Greater flexibility, better knowledge of the EU decision-making machinery post-Lisbon on the part of the US and greater consideration for European standards of human rights protection, will be increasingly important factors for the success of EU–US cooperation in data exchange.

The final part of the book (IV) takes a number of key policy areas which have been affected both directly and indirectly by the entry into force of the Treaty. All these areas—climate change, defence, non-proliferation and commercial policy—have, to a greater or less extent, short and long-term implications for the way in which the EU is able to act in the post-Lisbon era. Alongside development (explored earlier in Chapter 9) and Freedom, Security and Justice (Chapter 12), these areas constitute some of the most dynamic (if occasionally contested) dimensions in contemporary European integration.

In Chapter 15, Lisanne Groen and Arne Niemann examine the EU's role at the Copenhagen climate change summit in 2009. The timing could not have been more significant as the summit took place just days after the entry into force of the Treaty of Lisbon. For the purposes of this volume, the subject is vital for three reasons. First, climate change is a pressing global issue and one which the EU has consistently stressed its leadership in combating through legal and political measures; second, the politicised (and public) nature of the summit is an important testing ground for the EU's ability to act. Finally, the EU's mandate is not derived from the main 'external' competences covered elsewhere in this book, including the CFSP and Common Commercial Policy (CCP) but under the environmental competences, making it an interesting case from an institutional perspective. Many of the findings by Groen and Niemann about why the EU failed to capitalise on its leadership role in the international arena during this summit resonate with points made in other chapters. In particular, although the EU is a unitary actor according to the Treaty (including having full legal personality) it is constantly required to seek the agreement—in this case unanimity—of all the Member States. This is not new, but what the chapter does argue is that in a fast-moving scenario being visibly played out in the public eye, the EU cannot necessarily keep up with other (state) actors when it cannot be afforded flexibility to negotiate by Member States.

Simon Duke considers, in Chapter 16, the relationship between the EU and NATO in the post-Lisbon era. The relationship is ill-defined and somewhat paradoxical given that both organisations appear to emphasise their importance to each other, while in recent years they have both taken on new tasks which appear to compete, albeit in different ways. As Duke points out, it cannot be said that the EU is merely a soft power any more so than NATO can be said to be purely a military alliance. With this in mind, both have identified their respective importance to each other, but there are key obstacles to overcome in order to fully realise a 'partnership' between them, not least the differences in membership and unresolved issue of Cyprus. Lisbon has introduced some potentially significant changes to the way the EU operates as a defence/security actor, but the chapter argues that EU–NATO relations are not undergoing fundamental realignment. Changes, if they occur, are most likely to do so over the longer term.

Rivalries between EU institutions and questions about respective competences are also at the heart of Kamil Zwolski's Chapter 17 on the EU and non-proliferation policy. Here, he examines the confusion over the content and nature of the EU's policy, given that the institutional format for dealing with this hugely importance global issue has been developed concurrently within the Council and the Commission. The Treaty of Lisbon does therefore offer an opportunity for the EU to play a far stronger role in setting the global agenda on WMDs as well as exerting influence in bilateral ties with certain states. This is dependent in particular on inter-institutional cooperation, but the establishment of the EEAS does offer a chance to do this in a bottom-up, organic way. As such, although non-proliferation policy will remain a contested issue between the Member States (and thus the link with the promotion of the EU's 'values' is a difficult one to establish) the Treaty offers an opportunity to capitalise on efforts to secure a stronger position on non-proliferation within the EU's external relations.

The final contributions to this collection concern the principal change to the EU's external economic competences and policy brought about by the Treaty of Lisbon, that of investment policy. Chien-Huei Wu, in Chapter 18, traces the recent development of the EU institutions' gradual involvement in investment issues, including the jurisprudence relating to Austria, Sweden and Finland on the validity of their national investment treaties prior to their accession. This is instructive in terms of the competences the Union has gained under the Treaty of Lisbon which suggest that the EU has exclusive competence to conclude Bilateral Investment Treaties (BITs) with third countries, but does not resolve the question of the numerous existing BITs that Member States hold with countries outside the EU.

Questions of legal certainty and coherent policy coordination are at stake if the Commission in particular tries to assume too much discretionary power too quickly. Wu also places the new competences on FDI within the context of the EU's external commercial policies and finds evidence that the EU is pursuing much more investment-focussed provisions in Free Trade Agreements (FTA) pursued with third countries including, for example, the recently concluded EU-Korea FTA. This, he states, could be a key way in which the EU's competitiveness as an international economic actor could be enhanced.

Finally, in Chapter 19, Angelos Dimopoulos also examines the development of EU investment policy in the post-Lisbon era. Building on the historical exploration and competence issues identified by Wu in the previous chapter, he examines in more detail the challenges for the EU, which arise from understanding the actual types of investment and objectives covered under Bilateral Investment Treaties. Given the wide concept of 'investment' and the different dimensions of it, Dimopoulos puts forward the view that if an EU-level approach to concluding investment agreements is envisaged (which is presumably behind the inclusion of investment in the CCP) then a high level of cooperation will be needed by the Member States and the EU institutions, in order to determine the exact scope of EU competence in the field and integrate comprehensive investment agreements within the framework of the new 'constitutional' objectives of EU external relations. This is likely to be extremely important given the diversity of BITs already in existence by the Member States and the complexities arising from their envisaged gradual phasing out. Therefore, although the inclusion of investment within CCP can be said to herald a new era in EU external economic policy, it is somewhat of a blunt instrument and great care will need to be taken to ensure that confusion or contradictions do not arise between the policies and measures taken at EU level and at Member State level.

References

Bickerton C (2011) European Union Foreign Policy from effectiveness to functionality. Palgrave, Basingstoke

Cardwell PJ (2009) EU external relations and systems of governance, the CFSP, Euro-Mediterranean partnership and migration. Routledge, Oxford

Cardwell PJ, French D,White ND (2009) Kadi: the Interplay between EU and international law. Int Comp Law Q 58:229–240

Hill C (1993) The capability-expectations gap, or conceptualizing Europe's international role. Journal of Common Market Studies 31:305–328

Koutrakos P (2011) The role of law in common security and defence policy. In: Koutrakos P (ed) European Foreign Policy: legal and political perspectives. Edward Elgar, Cheltenham, pp 235–260

La Z (2008) European preferences and their reception. In: La Z (ed) EU foreign policy in a globalized world: normative power and social preferences. Routledge, Oxford

Shaw J (2011) Citizenship: contrasting dynamics at the interface of integration and constitutionalism. In: Craig P, De Búrca G (eds) The evolution of EU law, 2nd edn. Oxford University Press, Oxford, pp 575–609

Part I
The Common Foreign and Security Policy in the Post-Lisbon Era

Chapter 2
The Latest Attempt at Institutional Engineering: The Treaty of Lisbon and Deliberative Intergovernmentalism in EU Foreign and Security Policy Coordination

Uwe Puetter

Abstract The Treaty of Lisbon is the latest in a series of attempts at institutional engineering seeking to enhance the EU's capability to act within a decentralised policy setting which is not governed through the classic Community method and in which Member States either cannot be at all formally sanctioned for non-compliance or only in very exceptional circumstances. More specifically, this chapter reviews the new role of the High Representative within the Common Foreign and Security Policy as well as the changed presidency regime of the European Council. It does so with a view to how these changes further consolidate a system of deliberative intergovernmentalism which is constituted by routinised and consensus-oriented policy dialogue and, thus, departs from previous notions of intergovernmentalism in EU policy-making. Similarly, the increased use of informal working methods as well as the repercussions of the creation of the

---

Uwe Puetter—Professor at the Department of Public Policy and Director of the Center for European Union Research at the Central European University in Budapest. Draft versions of this chapter have been presented at the UACES/Modern Law Review conference 'EU External Relations Law and Policy in the Post-Lisbon Era', University of Sheffield, 13–14 January 2011 and the UACES conference 'The Lisbon Treaty Evaluated', 31 January 2011. This chapter also has benefited from collaborative research carried out and directed by the author and Antje Wiener, University of Hamburg, in the context of the Commission sponsored FP6 RECON project, WP6. The author is grateful to Stiftung Wissenschaft und Politik in Berlin for hosting him as a visiting fellow in the second half of 2009 when he undertook research on the changing role of the European Council and the Council in European Union governance. Finally, the author wishes to thank Paul James Cardwell for his very helpful comments and suggestions.

U. Puetter (✉)
Department of Public Policy, Central European University,
Budapest, Hungary
e-mail: puetteru@ceu.hu

U. Puetter
Central European University, Budapest, Hungary

P. J. Cardwell (ed.), *EU External Relations Law and Policy in the Post-Lisbon Era*,
DOI: 10.1007/978-90-6704-823-1_2, © T.M.C. ASSER PRESS, The Hague,
The Netherlands, and the authors 2012

European External Action Service for enhanced administrative cooperation between national administrations are discussed.

Contents

2.1 Introduction

This chapter analyses the changes brought about by the Lisbon Treaty to the governance dimension of the European Union's (EU) Common Foreign and Security Policy (CFSP). It does so by highlighting that these changes reflect a more substantial adjustment to the respective role of the European Council and the Council in the overall EU governance architecture. Most importantly, CFSP governance is interpreted as a system of deliberative intergovernmentalism which is based on consensus-oriented and intensive policy dialogue among independent actors. This is a feature shared with another nascent field of intensive EU activity—the area of economic governance under Economic and Monetary Union.[1] As CFSP implementation requires the sharing and pooling of highly decentralised resources and the adjustment of national policy-making towards common guidelines and rules, policy-makers constantly struggle with rallying consensus behind common EU positions. Ever since its inception in the Maastricht Treaty, CFSP has led to the development of a series of procedures and practices which seek to address the challenge to govern in a predominantly intergovernmental setting.

In particular, the leadership role assumed by the European Council and the Council as well as the development of an underlying committee system headed by the Political and Security Committee (PSC) reflect this challenge. The Lisbon Treaty is the latest in a series of attempts of institutional engineering which seek to enhance the EU's capability to act within a decentralised policy setting which is not governed through the classic Community method[2] and in which Member States either cannot be at all formally sanctioned for non-compliance or only in

---

[1] Puetter 2012.

[2] The term 'Community method' is used throughout this chapter in order to highlight the substantive meaning of what has become the key decision-making method in the process of European integration. Its centrality for EU decision-making is reflected in Articles 288–292 TFEU.

very exceptional circumstances. More specifically, this chapter reviews the new role of the High Representative within CFSP as well as the changed presidency regime of the European Council. It does so with a view to how these changes further consolidate a system of deliberative intergovernmentalism which is constituted by routinised and consensus-oriented policy dialogue and, thus, departs from previous notions of intergovernmentalism in EU policy-making. Similarly, the increased use of informal working methods in the Council context as well as the repercussions of the creation of the European External Action Service (EEAS) for enhanced administrative cooperation between national administrations are discussed. The following sections are organised as a commentary of the relevant Lisbon Treaty provisions against the background of findings from new empirical research including a series of expert interviews with CFSP policy-makers in Brussels and Member State capitals, which have been carried out between 2008 and 2010.

The Lisbon Treaty is reviewed mainly from a political science perspective while specific links between the political science and legal studies literatures in this field are highlighted. To this end this chapter is organised as follows. The second section provides a brief overview on potential research perspectives applicable to the analysis of the changes brought about by the Lisbon Treaty and discusses why deliberative intergovernmentalism is chosen as the conceptual framework for this commentary. The third section reflects on how the new Treaty defines CFSP as a decentralised governance set-up. Sections four and five review the changes introduced by the Treaty regarding the role of the High Representative and the European Council respectively. The final section interprets the findings within the framework of deliberative intergovernmentalism and considers the Treaty changes as attempts at institutional engineering which yet have to materialise in the form of changed CFSP governance practices.

2.2 The Treaty of Lisbon as an Attempt at Institutional Engineering: Conceptual Perspectives

There is no straightforward recipe as to how to set up a conceptual framework for interpreting Treaty changes and their relevance for EU policy-making. Most importantly, there are different disciplinary and theoretical perspectives which inform research on Treaty changes. For example, lawyers may ask about the implications of Treaty changes for the EU's legal order[3] and engage in interpreting specific provisions and discuss their repercussions for the role of specific actors such as the Court, Member States or individual citizens. They may also reconsider

[3] On the institutional-level questions see, for example, the contributions to this collection by Brkan, Sari and Schmidt.

the very notion of EU law as a core aspect of EU governance in the light of Treaty change.[4]

Similarly, political scientists may focus on different sets of questions when analysing Treaty changes. Classical integration theory, for example, will ask in how far a particular Treaty alters the character of the EU as a supranational polity.[5] In short, does it lead to more or less integration? Others will discuss in how far a new Treaty empowers specific actors and deprives others from their influence. In addition, and partially related to this question, political scientists will also ask in how far a new Treaty changes the rules of the game[6] or the modes of interaction and policy practice in EU policy-making. Finally, there is a larger scholarship out there dealing with the question of the process of Treaty change itself.[7] This research is occupied with the questions of ‘How did we get here?’ and ‘Who got what?’. The latter perspective particularly gained ground in relation to the work of the Convention of the Future of Europe and the process of drafting the Constitutional Treaty.

This chapter concentrates on the question of what repercussions the Lisbon Treaty has for the overall *governance method* and the institutional set-up of CFSP. In doing so the chapter seeks to interpret both the formal legal framework constituted by the Treaty as well as established practices and routines in decision-making. Such a focus on both the *formal* and *informal* aspects of a given governance context is compatible with previous research in the legal studies and political science fields alike. In particular the large literature on the role of new modes of governance and soft law in EU policy-making has established such a dual perspective in contemporary EU studies.[8]

More specifically, CFSP is understood to constitute one of several new fields of EU activity which have been first introduced by the Maastricht Treaty and have evolved since then under the premise that they would not be governed through the traditional Community method for the foreseeable future. This means in particular that while Member States largely share the determination to develop common policies in these fields and to respond collectively to key policy challenges they remain reluctant to transfer ultimate decision-making competences to the EU level. Economic governance within EMU and CFSP are the most prominent examples for this institutional formula but they are by far not the only ones as the examples of employment and social inclusion policy coordination show.[9] This does not, however, imply that these policy fields have been immune to changes with regard to the way they are governed. All Treaties following the Maastricht Treaty have reflected this.

[4] Armstrong 2011.

[5] See Majone 1997; Mancini 1998; Moravcsik 1998; Schmitter 2004.

[6] See Héritier 2007; Tallberg 2006.

[7] Christiansen and Reh 2009.

[8] See e.g. Amstrong 2010; Trubek and Mosher 2003.

[9] Policy coordination in the latter two policy fields was introduced as the main governance method by the Treaties of Amsterdam and Nice, respectively.

Instead of uploading new ultimate decision-making competences to the EU level, Treaty changes have focused on regulating policy coordination procedures and reconfirmed the model of a decentralised decision-making system which is based on close intergovernmental policy coordination. In this context, Commission input is a crucial aspect of policy coordination but does not amount to the full right of legislative initiative, which the Commission enjoys under the Community method in other policy areas. Similarly, there are no sanctioning mechanisms for those Member States which do not comply with commonly defined policy objectives.

Given the decentralised nature of the decision-making process and the dispersed character of the resources for policy implementation, the generation of consensus over common policy action has become a constantly reoccurring challenge for CFSP decision-makers. As it is only through voluntary commitment that EU Member States can act collectively and (re-)orient their national policies towards commonly agreed objectives the emphasis is on refining working methods, coordination procedures and the administrative underpinnings of such a coordination process. This process is conceptualised here as *deliberative intergovernmentalism*. Instead of understanding intergovernmental relations in the EU primarily as a process of negotiation between Member States about the limited transfer of power to the EU level through the means of creating supranational competences in the tradition of the Community method,[10] intergovernmental relations in the field of CFSP are interpreted here as driven by the paradoxical struggle for policy consensus in a decentralised policy framework. As policy-makers cannot retreat to the instrument of integration through law[11] in the sense of binding and enforceable provisions, which would institutionalise their policy consensus for a longer period of time, the only alternative is to adjust the instruments for policy coordination with a view to improving their potential to foster consensus orientation and close intergovernmental coordination at all levels of bureaucracy. It is only this way that Member States can formally reserve the right to ultimate decision-making while making progress on joint policies in response to foreign and security policy challenges.

In short, the argument is that the Lisbon Treaty has not changed the fundamental character of CFSP governance as an area of intergovernmental policy coordination in which decision-making ultimately rests with the Member States. However, the Treaty brings about a series of changes as to how decision-making in these two policy fields is organised and carried out. The Lisbon Treaty is therefore understood as an attempt of *institutional engineering* in the sense that the new provisions are aimed at addressing dysfunctional aspects of the previously existing institutional framework without however changing the general character of the allocation of formal decision-making competences in this policy field.[12]

[10] Moravcsik 1993.

[11] Haltern 2003.

[12] The concept of institutional engineering is borrowed from and used by analogy with Giovanni Sartori's famous work on constitutional engineering and the context of comparative institutionalist scholarship on democratic institutions. See Sartori 1994.

The concept of deliberative intergovernmentalism can help to explain this particular institutional dynamic.[13] It implies that intergovernmental relations in key EU policy areas such as economic governance and CFSP evolve around the permanent search for policy consensus. The output efficiency of these settings may be considered to be limited by default when they are compared to a top-down hierarchical decision-making structure and the classic Community method. Deliberative intergovernmentalism holds that they nevertheless can be studied in terms of their evolution over time. Institutional change in this regard is understood as the adjustment of a given context's potential to foster consensus seeking and policy dialogue among formally independent actors. As a result policy consistency and the effectiveness of the decision-making process may increase. Moreover, deliberative intergovernmentalism expects a concentration of policy dialogue at the most senior levels of bureaucracy as common policies in such important fields like foreign and security policy can only be implemented provided that there is clear endorsement by the most senior members of the Member State governments. The European Council and the Council are therefore at the centre of political gravity and it is in these settings that we should expect to witness the increasing importance of policy deliberation as a key method of decision-making. Moreover, CFSP is an evolving policy field in which core policy norms are relatively broadly defined and remain inherently contested.[14] As long as these broad parameters apply, the evolution of CFSP governance mechanisms can be analysed in terms of their capacity to generate policy consensus among independent actors. Deliberative intergovernmentalism as an analytical framework provides a set of criteria for engaging in such a review of the CFSP governance framework and the changes brought to it by the Lisbon Treaty. Most importantly, deliberative intergovernmentalism distinguishes between the impact of the negotiation setting and the policy content.

The negotiation setting will be more conducive towards policy deliberation if informal settings which create room for frank and interactive policy dialogue complement formal decision-making procedures. The most prominent example for such an evolution so far has been the creation of the informal Eurogroup of finance ministers in the field of euro area economic governance.[15] Moreover, the degree of routinisation of policy review procedures, which address diverse national policy responses, matters as much as the socialisation of actors into the practice of open and consensus-oriented debate does. Similarly, deliberative intergovernmentalism assumes that the combination of technical knowledge and the ability to exercise political leadership is crucial. Therefore, group membership and the closeness of senior policy experts and the most high-ranking political representatives of Member State governments and the relevant EU institutions matter. These factors need to be considered together with more technical aspects such as the duration

[13] Puetter 2012.

[14] Puetter and Wiener 2009.

[15] Puetter 2006.

and frequency of negotiations. The content of policy debates will matter with regard to the question of whether and to what extent a specific policy challenge can be framed as a common problem by the involved actors. This essentially depends on individual actors and whether they can play a certain role under the above specified parameters of a given negotiation setting. However, some policy issues may be better suited than others for being framed in such way. For example, if Member States have experienced coordination failure regarding their responses to a particular problem or policy challenge in the past but were in agreement that it was necessary to avoid this in the future, the readiness to engage in coordination might be higher in a situation when a similar challenge reoccurs.

Thus, Treaty changes can only partially contribute to the creation of such an environment as it is essentially constituted through informal practices and routines which evolve over time. However, new or changed Treaty provisions may have significant repercussions for existing practices and routines as they may alter the conditions under which these have previously evolved. Treaty changes may also create new opportunities for further informal adjustments. This is particularly true for provisions defining certain decision-making procedures and assigning specific roles to individual actors therein. As it was the case with employment and social inclusion policy coordination in the Amsterdam and Nice Treaties, Treaty changes may also simply codify an informal or semi-formal practice which existed before.

2.3 How the Lisbon Treaty Defines CFSP as a Decentralised Governance Set-Up

Before actually looking at what changes the Lisbon Treaty introduced to the CFSP governance architecture it is worth recapturing in which context the Lisbon Treaty did emerge. As a slightly modified version of the original Constitutional Treaty the Lisbon Treaty can be considered as reflecting the outcome of the Convention process and the following Intergovernmental Conference. This is all the more important as the Convention was charged with reflecting on both the scope of EU policy competences and the appropriateness of governance mechanisms. Thus, the Lisbon Treaty can also be understood as a statement on where the EU stands and what institutional options do (or do not) exist in the foreseeable future.

The new Treaty essentially confirms the overall governance structure and policy orientation of CFSP as it was set out previously. This means that EU foreign and security policy is based on an underlying normative framework which highlights the fundamental norms of democracy, rule of law, human rights and international law as well as the principles of the United Nations Charter and is not limited to particular aspects of foreign and security policy.[16] Moreover, this

[16] Treaty on European Union, Article 21. For further exploration on the 'values' of EU foreign policy, see the chapter in this volume by Broberg.

normative framework is related to the EU's own history as a specific regional integration project among democratic states. In this sense the Lisbon Treaty does not change the fundamental policy orientation and thus the policy content dealt with under CFSP.[17] The Lisbon Treaty—as the preceding Treaties—refrains from specifying further policy objectives beyond these fundamental foreign policy norms. Concrete steps in the development of CFSP therefore need to be taken on the basis of case-by-case agreement among the Member States and the actors involved. In other words, CFSP remains based on a rather thin policy framework as regards the Treaty provisions related to this policy field. The fundamental norms specified under Article 21 (TEU) can be considered as inherently contested. Research shows that while they receive wide recognition and appraisal among core elites in EU foreign and security policy, policy-makers derive diverging policy options from them when it comes to actually adopting common positions and joint actions.[18] The observation that the Lisbon Treaty confirms the *status quo ante* is not trivial. The Treaty is the manifestation of a deliberate decision against a unified method of decision-making in EU governance. It confirms the deviation from the original Community method as far as it is understood as a mechanism to establish binding and enforceable provisions. This development path was first established with the Maastricht Treaty. This is all the more important as it comes at the expense of not having a unitary method of decision-making in all areas of EU activity. While on the one hand, the Lisbon Treaty advances the Community method more than any other Treaty before by firmly establishing co-decision and qualified majority voting (QMV) as the default decision-making mechanism for most areas of EU activity previously identified as first pillar policies it, on the other hand, consolidates notably CFSP and economic governance under EMU as policy areas governed through enhanced intergovernmental policy coordination.

For CFSP the Lisbon Treaty, thus, prescribes the concept of a decentralised policy framework in which independent actors agree on common policies based on a rather thin institutional framework. The real challenge for CFSP governance, therefore, continues to rest with foreign policy practice and the need to forge policy consensus in response to particular foreign policy scenarios. The reaffirmation of this particular governance method is reflected in smaller and mainly editorial changes to existing provisions which define the overall organisation of the CFSP governance set-up and the allocation of competences. In this context the new wording included in Article 24.1 (TEU) starting with the second sentence is noteworthy:

> The common foreign and security policy is subject to specific rules and procedures. It shall be defined and implemented by the European Council and the Council acting unanimously, expect where the Treaties provide otherwise. The adoption of legislative acts shall be excluded.

---

[17] This does not mean that there are no changes to the policy content dealt with in the CFSP arena. As CFSP practice shows an expansion of the scope of foreign and security policy activity this is certainly the case. However, this development is currently not determined by Treaty changes.

[18] Puetter and Wiener 2007.

The Lisbon Treaty confirms the principle of unanimity as well as the exclusion of legislative acts from the range of decision-making options. These are the key features of CFSP governance and correspond to the thin normative framework of CFSP as discussed above. As others in this volume have noted,[19] without enjoying legislative competences in the field of CFSP the EU lacks a mechanism to further specify binding policy objectives and legislation beyond the broad CFSP principles provided by the Treaty. CFSP governance is clearly distinguished from the classic Community method and is not designed to evolve based on the concept of integration through law. The European Council and the Council are the key institutions in this governance set-up. They represent those actors in the CFSP setting who have ultimate decision-making power. Only the heads of state and government and the foreign ministers are in a position to agree on common policy options and to ensure implementation with the help of the disperse and decentralised foreign and security policy resources of the Member States. In the absence of an instrument to introduce legally binding decisions the mobilisation of these resources can only come about through the voluntary commitment of the Member States. To the extent that the Commission commands relevant policy resources in this area it is equally involved in this process. Yet, it remains one among many actors sharing responsibility for policy execution and implementation. Compared to the previously applied wording the Lisbon Treaty is more pointed in summarising this key method of CFSP governance and its special character compared to other areas of EU activity. This in itself may be considered as an expression of the firm intention to govern CFSP in a particular way for the foreseeable future. Article 24.1 (TEU) continues:

> The common foreign and security policy shall be put into effect by the High Representative of the Union for Foreign Affairs and Security Policy and by Member States, in accordance with the Treaties. The specific role of the European Parliament and of the Commission in this area is defined by the Treaties. The Court of Justice of the European Union shall not have jurisdiction with respect to these provisions…

As previously discussed, the European Parliament is only assigned a limited role in CFSP governance.[20] The specific involvement of the Commission was outlined above. The special role of the two institutions is reflected in the above quote. In other words, the Treaty refrains from making a general statement on competence allocation—something one would expect in areas governed by the Community method. Crucially, the Court continues to be deprived of the role it plays in areas other than CFSP and economic governance under EMU.[21]

---

[19] See, in particular, the chapters by Sari and Brkan who explore the limits of the legal enforceability of CFSP instruments, and that lack of jurisdiction of the European Court of Justice (ECJ).

[20] This is not to say that the EP cannot use competences it enjoys in other areas to exercise pressure on the Council and the European Council to recognise more explicitly the parliament's point of view. The example of the discussion about the establishment of the EEAS was instructive in this regard.

[21] See, further, Brkan (in this volume) who analyses the reasons for the lack of jurisdiction and also identifies the ways in which the ECJ enjoys some competence over CFSP-related areas.

Again, with regard to these fundamental parameters the Lisbon Treaty does not change the previously existing institutional framework but is more pointed in distilling the essence of CFSP governance.

2.4 The New Role of the High Representative

After taking stock of how the Lisbon Treaty defines the overall CFSP governance framework this section turns to the more substantial changes—notably the increased role of the High Representative. Again, the last quote from Article 24.1 TEU in the previous section is instructive in the sense that it includes the High Representative alongside the Member States in being responsible for putting CFSP 'into effect'. The fact that the High Representative is mentioned on equal footing with the Member States constitutes a departure from the changes brought about by the Amsterdam and Nice Treaties. Here the role of the High Representative had been introduced as one of assisting the Council and the presidency in running CFSP. It is therefore worth looking into the new provisions concerning the High Representative in greater detail.

The above formula '[t]he Council and the High Representative' is now also used when describing the responsibility to 'ensure compliance' with the fundamental principles of CFSP.[22] Previously, only the Council was mentioned as being responsible for this task.[23] This joint responsibility is also emphasised later when the Treaty provisions stipulate that the Council and the High Representative shall ensure the unity, consistency and effectiveness of action by the Union'.[24] This shared responsibility is also related to the executive dimension of CFSP when the Treaty stipulates that the 'policy shall be put into effect by the High Representative and by the Member States, using national and Union resources'.[25]

The Lisbon Treaty ends the central role of the rotating Council presidency in CFSP governance. Previously the rotating presidency was in charge of chairing the Council meetings and representing the EU in CFSP matters to the outside world.[26] It was also responsible for the implementation of policy decisions.[27] Prior to the Lisbon Treaty the High Representative only 'assisted' the presidency in relation to these tasks.[28] The same applied to the 'formulation, preparation and implementation of policy decisions' and the task of 'conducting political dialogue with third

22 Treaty on European Union, Article 24.3.

23 Treaty on European Union (pre-Lisbon) Article 11.2.

24 Treaty on European Union, Article 26.2.

25 Treaty on European Union, Article 26.3. See further, in this volume, Schmidt and her discussion of how this is likely to function insofar as crisis management operations are concerned.

26 Treaty on European Union (pre-Lisbon), Article 18.1.

27 Treaty on European Union (pre-Lisbon), Article 18.2.

28 Treaty on European Union (pre-Lisbon), Article 18.3.

parties'.[29] Now the Treaty clearly assigns these functions to the High Representative.[30] Thus, the new provisions allow the High Representative to play a more pro-active role at all stages of the policy process.[31]

This means the entire field of CFSP governance is now removed from the immediate influence of the rotating Council presidency. The Treaty does not reserve any prerogatives for the rotating presidency of the Council which still exists as an institutional mechanism for organising the work of other Council formations. The High Representative can exercise all functions of an active chair of the Council including and has the right to table his/her own proposals as well as the responsibility to 'ensure implementation' of policy decisions taken by the European Council and the Council.[32] The High Representative also has the right to call extraordinary Council meetings.[33] Moreover, the Lisbon Treaty assigns the role of a mediator to the High Representative in cases of severe disagreement with a CFSP decision on the part of a Member State.[34] Previously such a case could only be resolved through transferring the matter to the European Council. Yet, the latter option still remains available under the Lisbon Treaty.

Finally, the Lisbon Treaty equips the High Representative with a separate administrative infrastructure: the European External Action Service (EEAS).[35] The institutional set-up of the service reflects the decentralised nature of CFSP as it is composed of officials from both the Commission and the General Secretariat of the Council as well as seconded diplomats from the Member States.[36] The service is also not supposed to act independently but in 'cooperation with the diplomatic services of the Member States'.[37] It can be best described as an integrated intergovernmental bureaucracy which further institutionalises the functional integration of decentralised resources without fully transforming them into a supranational and fully independent bureaucratic resource.

2.5 The European Council and CFSP Governance

Research on the changing character of intergovernmental relations in the EU shows the evolution of the European Council as the virtual centre of political gravity in EU governance.[38] Over the last 15 years or so the European Council has

---

[29] Treaty on European Union (pre-Lisbon), Article 26.

[30] Treaty on European Union, Article 27.

[31] See Sect. 2.6.

[32] Treaty on European Union, Article 27.1.

[33] Treaty on European Union, Article 30.

[34] Treaty on European Union, Article 31.2.

[35] See, further, the chapter in this volume by Blockmans and Laatsit.

[36] Treaty on European Union, Article 27.3.

[37] Treaty on European Union, Article 27.3.

[38] Puetter 2012.

become a major actor in day-to-day decision-making at the EU level as in particular the areas of CFSP and economic governance under EMU constantly require agreement at the highest political level. Otherwise policy decisions would lack the necessary political backing to be implemented at the national level- or risk not being reached at all. Foreign and security policy is an area which is considered to concern core aspects of national sovereignty. Member States have made clear that they are not ready to govern CFSP through the classic Community method for the foreseeable future. This means that in many instances only the most senior representatives of Member State governments can bring about final policy decisions and, thus, become involved in a routinised and intense policy dialogue about CFSP issues themselves. In many cases the foreign ministers cannot finalise decisions alone but only prepare them. It is often only after authorisation from the European Council that they can implement and operationalise major policy decisions. This is well reflected in the agenda, duration and frequency of European Council meetings which are not coincidentally overwhelmingly dominated by CFSP and economic governance issues—the two main areas governed through intergovernmental policy coordination. Thus, the European Council obtains a central role in the day-to-day decision-making process. The Lisbon Treaty acknowledges this central role by introducing new CFSP specific provisions related to the European Council as well as new general provisions regarding the functioning of the institution.

The Lisbon Treaty reconfirms the crucial role of the European Council in CFSP decision-making by reserving the institution the right to 'identify the Union's strategic interests, determine the objectives of and define general guidelines' for policy-making.[39] It reproduces almost entirely the language of the pre-Lisbon Article 13 TEU. However, the Lisbon Treaty adds to it the term 'the Union's strategic interests'.[40] The new Treaty also reproduces the definition of the division of labour between the Council and the European Council in CFSP by making clear that the Council acts 'on the basis' of political guidance provided by the European Council. It is up to the Council to 'frame' policy—a new term—and to take decisions regarding its definition and implementation.[41] As previously noted, the European Council appoints the High Representative but now does so in agreement with the Commission President.[42] Similarly, the European Council also has the right to dismiss the High Representative.[43]

The hierarchical relation between the European Council and the Council is also reflected in a catalogue of decisions the Council shall take by qualified majority. Although the field of CFSP in general is subject to the unanimity principle the Council decides (based on a qualified majority) whenever the European Council has established a clear framework for such decision-making in the first place.[44]

---

[39] Treaty on European Union, Article 26.

[40] Treaty on European Union, Article 26.1.

[41] Treaty on European Union, Article 26.2.

[42] Treaty on European Union, Article 18.

[43] Treaty on European Union, Article 18.

[44] Treaty on European Union, Article 31.

What is new is that the European Council can charge the High Representative with proposing a particular decision on an EU action or position to the European Council. Under the new provisions the European Council can also specify other cases in which the Council will act based on qualified majority decision-making. Once such a proposal is adopted by the European Council, the Council again operates under QMV rules regarding any further decision-making following from this act.

The Lisbon Treaty also provides for new provisions on the European Council outside Title V which have repercussions for CFSP governance. Most of these provisions take stock and codify the *de facto* role the European Council has acquired in EU policy-making ever since the entering into force of the Maastricht Treaty. In addition, the European Council itself has been subject to institutional engineering. Most importantly, the European Council is now chaired by an elected permanent president and thus operates the same presidency regime as the Foreign Affairs Council.[45] Moreover, the High Representative 'shall take part'[46] in the work of the European Council. In practice this arrangement implies that the High Representative plays a crucial role for linking the work of the European Council and the Council provided that the foreign ministers now no longer participate in European Council sessions unless they are explicitly required to do so. The participation of the High Representative in European Council meetings also shows the importance CFSP has gained with regard to the agenda of this forum.[47]

Similar to the High Representative, the President of the European Council enjoys the role of an active chair. The President has the authority to call extraordinary meetings and is in charge of ensuring 'the preparation and continuity of the work of the European Council'.[48] This may also imply an adjustment of the European Council's working methods. Indeed, in one of his first major programmatic speeches, the newly elected president of the European Council Herman Van Rompuy made it clear that he intends to use this instrument and that the adjustment of European Council working methods is a top priority for him. He highlighted that this is particularly relevant for the work of the European Council in the areas of CFSP and economic governance.[49] The procedure was used on 1 March 2011[50] to convene an extraordinary meeting of the European Council on 11 March to discuss

[45] Treaty on European Union, Article 15.5.

[46] Treaty on European Union, Article 15.2.

[47] The Lisbon Treaty does not foresee a similar arrangement for the President of the Eurogroup. However, the current President of the Eurogroup is Luxembourg's Prime Minister Jean-Claude Juncker who is a member of the European Council. He has been chairing the Eurogroup since 2005 when the office of an elected president was created for the first time. His appointment became possible because he also acted as Luxembourg's finance minister at the time.

[48] Treaty on European Union, Article 15.6.

[49] See Van Rompuy H (2010) The Challenges for Europe in a Changing World, European Council Press Release PCE 34/10.

[50] European Council (2011) President of the European Council convenes an extraordinary European Council on Friday 11 March 2011. Press Release PCE 055/11.

'developments in Libya and the Southern neighbourhood region and set the political direction and priorities for future EU policy and action'.[51]

The President of the European Council now formally represents the EU at the level of heads of state and government on CFSP matters[52]—a function which, as other contributors to this volume have found,[53] may overlap with the competences of the High Representative. The President of the European Council also can 'convene an extraordinary meeting of the European Council in order to define the strategic lines of the Union's policy'[54] in the light of specific foreign policy developments which may require so. Again, this prerogative will require close coordination with the High Representative. This procedure, however, also establishes a clear hierarchy between the President of the European Council and the High Representative as the former presides over the institution which defines the 'strategic lines' of CFSP.

2.6 What Next? The Lisbon Treaty as an Attempt at Institutional Engineering

The Lisbon Treaty did not alter the overall governance model which is applied in the field of CFSP. Nevertheless, the Lisbon Treaty adjusted individual features of the CFSP institutional set-up. Seen from the point of view of classical integration theory which would measure closer integration by the transfer of ultimate decision-making power to the supranational level, the Lisbon Treaty may appear as a total disappointment. In contrast to this the analytical concept of deliberative intergovernmentalism offers the opportunity to arrive at a more differentiated assessment of the modified CFSP governance architecture. Starting from the observation that governments are not ready to agree to a further substantial transfer of ultimate decision-making power to the EU-level within the area of foreign and security policy, CFSP is understood as a system of close intergovernmental policy coordination which is different from the traditional Community method. Its basis is the general desire on the part of the Member States to increase the ability to act collectively in this policy field while preserving ultimate decision-making authority at the national level. This increases the need to find mechanisms which actively encourage the constant generation of consensus and self-commitment. This is crucial for coherent collective policy action as Member States control most of the dispersed resources for CFSP implementation.

---

[51] European Council (2011) Declaration adopted by the extraordinary European Council, 11 March 2011. EUCO 7/11.

[52] Treaty on European Union, Article 15.6.

[53] See in particular Schmidt, who also notes the lack of clarity in dividing the tasks between the High Representative.

[54] Treaty on European Union, Article 26.1.

Thus, the strengthening of policy coordination is the key method through which CFSP is developed. In this context the notion of policy deliberation as the search for a reasoned consensus on common policy positions which is reached on the basis of initially diverging preferences is crucial. The evolution of the CFSP governance set-up can be conceptualised as increasing its potential to generate policy consensus under the condition that implementation cannot rely on the instruments of EU law. Consequently, deliberative intergovernmentalism expects that such a dependency on consensus generation translates into institutional adjustments which are aimed at enhancing the potential of core CFSP forums to generate consensus over policy. The review of the Lisbon Treaty in the previous sections was intended to demonstrate exactly this. In the following the main findings are briefly interpreted and summarised.

First, more clearly than any Treaty has done before, the Lisbon Treaty defines CFSP governance as being different from the Community method. Although the changes in the relevant Treaty provisions are essentially of an editorial nature these changes confirm the key premise of deliberative intergovernmentalism, i.e. that CFSP governance is confined to an inherently intergovernmental setting for the foreseeable future and shall continue to evolve within these parameters.

Second, the Treaty changes therefore concentrate on the adjustment of the working methods of key CFSP decision-making forums and do not focus on policy as such. Most importantly, they alter the way the Council and the European Council operate within CFSP. The key innovation in this regard is the transformation of the High Representative into a full-time chair of the Foreign Affairs Council. Given the competences assigned to the High Representative this means essentially the creation of the position of a pro-active chair who can structure the work of the Foreign Affairs Council internally and becomes the main spokesperson for CFSP externally. This constitutes an important change to the CFSP set-up. In a decentralised decision-making setting which relies on constant consensus formation and lacks legislative decision-making power a permanent and pro-active chair can make a difference. Such a chairperson can assume a crucial role in framing policy issues for debate and introducing them as common problems—a key precondition for successful policy deliberation. This also involves reminding Council members of previously reached agreements and discussion outcomes. It is noteworthy that the new Treaty provisions specify core tasks and responsibilities of the High Representative in relation to the concept of a pro-active chair. This includes in particular the responsibility to ensure compliance and consistency.

Indeed, expectations have been running high with regard to the new role envisaged for the High Representative under the Lisbon Treaty. Member States have emphasised this ever since the debates in the Convention and the negotiations leading to the Constitutional Treaty. The transformation of the position of High Representative the Lisbon Treaty provides for is, however, no guarantee that the above listed functions of a permanent chair will be actually performed in way that is conducive towards fostering consensus oriented policy dialogue among ministers. The example of the Eurogroup shows that such arrangements can give a mandate to a permanent president but they cannot engineer personal qualification and interaction dynamics among ministers. The recognition and general acceptance of the chair within the relevant setting is something which cannot be taken for granted but evolves through practice. Most importantly, successful presidents need to command respect among their group members and be considered to be impartial and/or particularly competent. They also need to be willing to actually act as a pro-active chair. Here, not only the individual commitment and qualification matters but also the behaviour of other influential group members. Such group members may prevent the chair from structuring internal policy dialogue and from asserting him/herself as the central spokesperson in relation to the outside world. Although it is important to have a formal endorsement of this function in the first place it does not hinder others to publicly contest or compete with the permanent chair.

It is beyond the scope of this contribution to review in greater detail how Catherine Ashton—as the first High Representative working under the new rules—has performed this task so far and how she is likely to perform in the future.[55] However, it should be stressed that from the perspective of deliberative intergovernmentalism the potential of the High Representative to further the evolution of CFSP is not related to her ultimate decision-making competences but to her ability to act as a pro-active chair of CFSP coordination who reminds actors of their previously made commitments, shapes their focus on common policy challenges and acts as a single spokesperson for the EU. Moreover, key aspects of these functions involve behind-the-scenes-activity which is difficult to assess from an outside perspective. Most importantly, the role of a pro-active chair needs to evolve over-time and through practice. It cannot be engineered solely by a Treaty mandate. Such a mandate can only provide the conditions for a change in CFSP practice. However, it can be said that the Lisbon Treaty has done this.

The enhanced role of the High Representative as a pro-active chair of the CFSP policy process is further emphasised by the creation of the EEAS. The service will certainly increase the High Representative's potential to issue policy proposals and structure the agenda. The model of the EEAS can again be best explained by deliberative intergovernmentalism.[56] The service is set-up as a hybrid model. It is best described as an integrated intergovernmental bureaucracy with supranational elements. This hybrid nature reflects again the key assumption that CFSP shall not evolve in the framework of the classic Community method. Rather it is developed on the basis of a closer integration of intergovernmental resources. Notably, this includes the secondment of civil servants from the diplomatic services of the Member States to the EEAS and the construction and entertainment of a network of pooled resources. Thus, the development and operation of the EEAS in itself involves similar features as the process of creating policy consensus at the level of Council decision-making. The High Representative needs to chair and structure such processes and will need to rely on permanent consensus-building activity. If well developed, the EEAS structures may be the key instrument for further developing a

[55] On the working of the High Representative within the context of the Spanish EU Presidency in 2011, see the chapter in this volume by Pol Morillas.

[56] See also Blockmans and Laatsit (this volume).

much more closely integrated intergovernmental bureaucracy by involving further levels of national bureaucracies into the CFSP process more systematically.

The other major institutional adjustment in CFSP governance concerns the European Council. The institution is now dealt with by the Treaty as a regular EU institution and receives full attention in the text. Previous Treaties have avoided further specifying the role of the European Council in EU governance more generally. For CFSP this meant that the role of the institution was mainly defined through the CFSP-specific Treaty provisions. The new wording on the European Council introduced by the Lisbon Treaty can be considered as codification of what for many years has already shaped EU governance practice: the European Council's central role in CFSP and economic governance. This senior policy-making forum is indispensable for processing day-to-day decision-making—a role not envisaged for the European Council under the classic Community method. Thus, the relevant editorial changes introduced by the Lisbon Treaty acknowledge more clearly than ever before the changed reality of EU decision-making.

As in the case of the new competences of the High Representative the creation of the office of a permanent President of the European Council by the Lisbon Treaty can be seen as an attempt to enhance the deliberative potential of the European Council as a forum for policy dialogue at the highest political level. Again, it remains to be seen how the respective individual holding the office will perform the role of a pro-active chair. However, there is no doubt that the Lisbon Treaty provides the European Council president with such a mandate. Herman Van Rompuy has made clear from the beginning that this may involve far-reaching adjustments to the European Council's own working methods. He has already convened informal meetings and announced a further extension of this working method.

Finally, there is now a clear hierarchy between the European Council on the one hand, and the Council, on the other hand. The CFSP provisions make it quite clear how and when the European Council instructs the foreign ministers and the High Representative. Moreover, it is worth considering the role of the European Council in CFSP governance in relation to other policy fields—notably economic governance. The Lisbon Treaty has created a troika of permanent presidents involving the European Council, the Foreign Affairs Council and the Eurogroup. This may foster policy coherence and coordination between the three bodies. However, the three office holders may also compete with each other depending on how each of them is able to fulfil his/her role in the relevant context. It is far too early to assess the repercussions the Lisbon Treaty may have with regard to such institutional dynamics but they may well be quite significant.

References

Amstrong K (2010) Governing social inclusion. Europeanization through policy coordination. Oxford University Press, Oxford

Armstrong K (2011) Law after Lisbon: legalization and delegalization of European governance. Biennial Conference of the European Union Studies Association, Boston, 3–5 March

Christiansen T, Reh C (2009) Constitutionalizing the European Union. Palgrave Macmillan, Houndmills, Basingstoke

Haltern U (2003) Integration through law. In: Diez T, Wiener A (eds) European integration theory. Oxford University Press, Oxford, pp 177–196

Héritier A (2007) Explaining institutional change in Europe. Oxford University Press, Oxford

Majone G (1997) From the positive to the regulatory state. Journal of Public Policy 17:139–167

Mancini GF (1998) Europe: the case for statehood. European Law Journal 4:29–42

Moravcsik A (1993) Preferences and power in the European Community: a liberal intergovernmentalist approach. Journal of Common Market Studies 31:473–524

Moravcsik A (1998) The choice for Europe. Social purpose and state power from Messina to Maastricht. Cornell University Press, Ithaca

Puetter U (2006) The Eurogroup how a secretive circle of finance ministers shape European economic governance. Manchester University Press, Manchester

Puetter U (2012) Europe's deliberative intergovernmentalism—the role of the Council and European Council in EU economic governance. Journal of European Public Policy (forthcoming)

Puetter U, Wiener A (2007) Accommodating normative divergence in European foreign policy co-ordination: the example of the Iraq crisis. Journal of Common Market Studies 45:1065–1088

Puetter U, Wiener A (2009) EU foreign policy elites and fundamental norms. Implications for governance, RECON Online Working Paper. www.reconproject.eu/main.php/RECON_wp_0917.pdf?fileitem=5456591. Last accessed 18 Apr 2011

Sartori G (1994) Comparative constitutional engineering: an inquiry into structures, incentives, and outcomes. New York University Press, New York

Schmitter P (2004) Neo-neofunctionalism. In: Diez T, Wiener A (eds) European integration theory. Oxford University Press, Oxford, pp 45–74

Tallberg J (2006) Leadership and negotiation in the European Union. Cambridge University Press, Cambridge

Trubek DM, Mosher JS (2003) New governance, employment policy, and the European social model. In: Zeitlin T (ed) Governing work and welfare in a new economy: European and American experiments. Oxford University Press, Oxford, pp 33–58

Chapter 3
European Realism in the EU's Common Foreign and Security Policy

Annegret Bendiek

Abstract Many authors analyse EU foreign policy in the post-Lisbon era as following a one-dimensional (stop-and-go) spill-over logic. European foreign policy is assumed to become, sooner or later, a truly supranational policy with broad competences held by the Commission and the European Parliament. This chapter proposes the idea that such expectations are misguided. European foreign policy does not follow the logic of ever-closer integration but is better understood as an intergovernmental opportunity structure for uploading national policies, for institutional forum-shopping and for strategically using the EU's political resources for national interests. The theoretical literature on the EU's foreign policies is in need of putting more emphasis on the interaction between the CFSP institutions and individual Member State policies. Realism is the proper candidate for theoretical guidance. Recent attempts to apply realism to the EU have used either an offensive or a defensive variant, speculated about the re-emergence of the unified Germany as a European hegemon (Mearsheimer, Int Secur 15(4):5–56, 1990) or explained why exactly this is unlikely to happen (Grieco, Br J Politics Int Relat 11(2):192–204, 2009). This project develops an innovative theoretical approach, which combines classical Realism with multi-level analysis. It explains both the fragmented institutional structure in European foreign policy-making. This chapter analyses the decision-making processes that underpin Europe's foreign policy in the 'post-Lisbon era'. It is built on the idea that European foreign

Dr. Rer. pol. Annegret Bendiek—Deputy Head of the Research Division EU External Relations at the Stiftung Wissenschaft und Politik.

A. Bendiek (✉)
Research Division EU External Relations, at the Stiftung Wissenschaft und Politik
(German Institute for International and Security Affairs), Berlin, Germany
e-mail: annegret.bendiek@swp-berlin.org

P. J. Cardwell (ed.), *EU External Relations Law and Policy in the Post-Lisbon Era*,
DOI: 10.1007/978-90-6704-823-1_3, © T.M.C. Asser press, The Hague,

policy should be understood as a fragmented intergovernmental opportunity structure.

Contents

3.1 Introduction: What is European Foreign Policy?

The analysis of the European Union's foreign policy has been dominated by supranational idealism and technocratic legalism. Its foreign policy has been equated with the output of the EU's Common Foreign and Security Policy (CFSP) and been applauded for its non-military character. The content of the EU's foreign policy has been described as that of a civilian or normative power[1] and some have even asked whether it should be seen as a 'force for good.'[2] None of this is adequate for understanding European foreign policy. The EU's foreign policy does not follow any normative logic—if that exists at all—but can better be understood in the categories of realism.

This chapter sets out to provide a theoretical frame for understanding European foreign policy and produces empirical evidence for underlining its relevance. In order to do so, I revive the long-standing tradition of political Realism, adapt it to the two-track logic of the European parallelism of supranational and Member States foreign policies and transform it into a specific European version of Realism. I start with introducing an understanding of EU foreign policy that takes its two-track character seriously. I use this concept for criticising the recent scholarly debate and argue that the main analytical approaches to understanding European foreign and security policy overlook both the close relation between national and European foreign policies, and the dominance of national over European foreign policies. The theoretical argument of the chapter is centred on adapting classical Realism to the conditions of the EU in the twenty-first century. I show that the explanatory power of Realism is not limited to explaining national foreign policies but can well be used for understanding the two-track foreign policy of Europe. The

[1] Duchêne 1973; Manners 2002.

[2] Sjursen 2006a.

central thrust of this chapter is theoretical, rather than empirical, however. It is about making the claim that Realism still provides many important insights into understanding European foreign policy.

3.1.1 The Two-Track Character of the EU's Foreign Policy

As opposed to most of the literature, I understand European foreign policy as encompassing all non-communitarised cross-border policies of the European Union institutions plus those of the Member States. European foreign policy covers the European Commission's policies (e.g., development cooperation policy, neighbourhood policy), the treaties, decisions and declarations concluded and adopted by the European Council and the Council, and the individual foreign polices of the Member States. It is about policies between the Member States and third countries, and between the European institutions and third countries.[3]

Such a broad understanding of EU foreign policy will sound unfamiliar to many EU scholars who are used to understanding EU foreign policy as comprising only those policies that are conducted under the legal and institutional umbrella of the CFSP. They might object that I analyse foreign policy *in* Europe rather than the foreign policy *of* the European Union. I submit, however, that the very nature of EU foreign policy defies any legalistic formalism. European foreign policy-making must be properly understood as a two-track process in which Member States deliberately choose whether to conduct a foreign policy at the European or at the national level. The Member States have over time established a *de facto* division of competences between the national and the European level which is easily overlooked by approaches that equate European foreign policy with the policies of the European institutions: the European institutions have been equipped with the competence only to develop and implement 'normative' policies with a strong foundation in universal values such as foreign aid and the promotion of human rights.[4] All these 'track one policies' emphasise 'positive conditionality', common norms and values and refrain from entertaining open economic or even military threats. They are evidence that the EU is established on a set of shared norms and values and that it is more than a technical problem-solving community or a purely functional regime.

Track one policies are, however, only a part of the story. The EU's foreign policies are simultaneously formulated on a second Member State track that is in charge of the 'non-normative' policies. Military interventions and alliance-building, the fighting of terrorism, or decision-making in the United Nations Security Council are not off the agenda of European politics. They are relegated to the

[3] Smith 2004; Hill 2004; Nuttall 2001.

[4] For further on the values-led approach to European foreign policy, in the context of development policy, see Broberg (this volume).

national and international realm and are conducted without supranational interference. It also militates against a neat separation of the European and the national level that many of the strategic partnerships and regional neighbourhood initiatives of the EU are de facto national or mini-lateral projects of a small group of Member States. European politics is often European only in name. Many of the initiatives and missions conducted under the European label are better understood as mini-lateral or even unilateral policies that are only tolerated by other Member States. Individual Member States, or small groups of Member States, use the opportunity to upload their national foreign policies onto the European level in order to strengthen own bargaining power via third countries.[5] This phenomenon of an instrumentalisation of the EU for national policies is easily overlooked by approaches that identify the output of the CFSP institutions with the European foreign policy as such.

3.1.2 From Idealism to Pragmatism

The development of the European two-track foreign policy over the last 20 years is a story of reducing overly ambitious aims and of realising that the Member States, and not the European institutions, are—and probably will remain—in the driver's seat. The main idea behind the launch of the CFSP in 1992 was to overcome the European foreign policy dissonance, to make Europe speak with one voice, and to enable the EU to secure peace in Europe and its neighbourhood. The summits of Cologne, Petersberg and St. Malo, and the European Security Strategy (ESS) were perceived as important milestones on that way. The EU would have a clear idea of its interests abroad and be equipped with the hard- and software to implement the necessary actions.[6] Thorough Treaty revision was suggested in order to streamline the institutions of the CFSP with a view to making the EU's actions more coherent and effective, and to provide the European partners with a single responsible contact person for all external affairs.[7]

Little of these high ambitions have been realised in the meantime.[8] The EU still has neither a single foreign policy voice nor the necessary institutional software for formulating a coherent foreign policy. The 15th United Nations Framework Convention on Climate Change (UNFCCC) Conference of the Parties (COP) meeting in Copenhagen in December 2009 made that painfully clear.[9] The Lisbon

5 Irondelle and Kempin 2008; Schmidt-Felzmann 2008.

6 Bendiek 2006, 3; Gosalbo Bono 2006.

7 Tomuschat 2010.

8 Biscop 2010; Majone 2009.

9 The disappointing role by played by the EU at the Copenhagen COP summit is the focus of the chapter by Groen and Niemann (this volume) who find that the EU's stance was weakened by an inflexibility in its negotiation position due to the requirement to seek unanimity on any changes in its position from all 27 Member States.

Treaty has done little to improve the international standing of the EU. It failed to establish a powerful institution with the competence to formulate and implement the EU's foreign policies. The pre-Lisbon idea to establish a single telephone number for third parties wanting to negotiate with Brussels has been realised; unfortunately, however, the telephone is answered by a President of the European Council who is more a chairman than a leader. He is in charge of reconciling points of view and of encouraging the emergence of consensus among the 27 Member States only. That includes working in harmony with the President of the Commission, and the newly appointed High Representative.[10] The newly appointed High Representative is also a rather weak actor who can speak for the Member States only if they have agreed on the policy in advance. Foreign policy competences in the EU are still divided among the European Council, the High Representative, the Commission, the Presidency of the EU, and—last but not least—the 27 Member States.

It is true that the institutional fragmentation of the EU's foreign policies is not a new phenomenon but has been criticised ever since the CFSP had been launched in 1993.[11] What is new, however, is that we are witnessing today a farewell to the very idea of a supranational institutionalisation of the Common Foreign and Security Policy (CFSP) of the EU. The old supranationalists' idea that the European institutions should provide the Member States' foreign policies with a strong institutional framework has turned from a compelling normative vision into a political anachronism. Today, the 27 Member States perceive and use the EU as an instrument for fostering national interests. A pragmatic understanding and use of the EU has become predominant.

3.2 The State of the Debate

Much of the recent theoretical literature on the EU's foreign policy does not take proper account of the European disillusionment with high-flying ideas. The most prominent contributions to the debate focus on the European institutional set-up and its normative ambitions but disregard national interests and Member State security concerns.

3.2.1 Supranational Institutionalism

Supranational institutionalism is probably the most common approach for analysing European foreign policy.[12] It is an approach that identifies the EU's policies

[10] Bendiek 2010.

[11] Hill 1993.

[12] Hill 1993; Meunier 2000, 103–135; Smith 2004; Caporaso and Jupille 1999.

with the output of the Commission, the Council and the European Council. An often-used distinction in supranational institutional analyses is that between intergovernmental and supranational institutions. The former are found ideal typically in the European Council. In the European Council, all states have the same right to veto a policy and no decision can be adopted which is rejected by any of the Member States.[13] In sharp contrast to intergovernmental decision-making, policies like the European Development Policy are in the competence of the supranational European Commission, which is supposed to be highly independent from the Member States individual development policies, and to autonomously propose and implement policies.[14]

An important difference between the two decision-making procedures, so many supranational institutionalists argue, is its implications for the European Union's policy coherence and its problem-solving capacity.[15] Only independent agents but not intergovernmental bodies can efficiently produce coherent policies and tackle effectively real-world problems without being handicapped by the need to integrate a disparate set of national interests and concerns.[16] The right to veto policies and the insistence of the Member States on their national sovereignty is understood to be a major factor prohibiting a coherent and effective EU foreign policy.[17]

Supranational Institutionalism has produced many important insights into the effects of decision-making procedures on European policy-making (Committee governance, Council Working Group on the Western Balkans (COWEB) etc.). The strength of Supranational Institutionalism, however, is also its major weakness. Due to its concentration on European decision-making procedures, it is conceptually blind to national policy-making and the growing emphasis of many Member States on their national interests.[18] A Supranational Institutionalist's account of the EU's foreign policy focuses on the new competences of the European Parliament to participate in the conclusion of international treaties, the establishment of a European Foreign Service, and the new 'double-hatted' post of the High Representative.[19] It submits an interpretation of the EU's foreign policy development that is often highly formalistic, focuses on legal norms and lacks the analytical categories for taking changes in the political climate into account. Its major shortcoming is that it is not only unable to account for the European disillusionment with supranational ambitions but that it fails to even realise its very occurrence.

[13] Tallberg 2008.

[14] Garrett and Tsebelis 2001.

[15] Meunier 2000; Dijkstra 2009.

[16] Bátora 2009.

[17] Dobbins et al. 2005.

[18] Toje 2008

[19] Maurer and Kietz 2010.

3.2.2 Supranational Idealism

Supranational Idealism has celebrated a forceful comeback in recent years in European foreign policy analysis. For some years now, researchers have put forth the theory that the EU should be seen as a 'normative power', which is attempting to communicate its model of integration to other parts of the world beyond its borders. Following the seminal article by Manners on 'normative power Europe,'[20] a large body of scholarly articles discusses the EU's foreign policy as fostering universal values.[21] It is argued that the EU is predisposed to normativity due to its historical development, its hybrid structure including supranational and intergovernmental elements, and its cumulative system of legal rules. In this respect, the EU cannot help but continue to spread its values and norms to the benefit of the international system. The EU is described as a 'force for good'[22] that acts in the global interest and abstains from using force or threats.[23] It is understood as a new type of polity that is established on the experiences of past wars and that has learnt its lessons that war and aggression do not pay out. The EU thus only engages in policies with universal appeal such as human rights policy, the abolition of the death penalty, sustainable environmental and development policies, but is deliberately short on military and security policies. Even if it deploys troops abroad, it only uses this instrument for promoting peace, democracy and human rights. The deployment of EU task forces to Congo in 2003 and again during the 2006 elections, for example, are interpreted as cases in which the EU accepted a post-conflict responsibility within EU-African cooperation. In Asia, the Aceh Monitoring Mission (AMM) is justified as serving the implementation of a peace agreement between the Free Aceh Movement (GAM) and the Indonesian government.[24]

Supranational Idealism rejects the idea of fixed state preferences (or even interests) and argues that Member State preferences have an intrinsically European flavour because they are subject to intense intergovernmental deliberation and discursive interaction between the supranational, the governmental and the domestic level of policy-making.[25]

Emphasising the normative character of the EU's foreign policies adequately highlights the shortcomings of the EU in terms of military hardware and its lack of institutional software for adopting controversial decisions. The EU has a mainly consensus-based institutional machinery with little capacity to make its Member States comply with inconvenient decisions such as imposing sanctions on third

---

20 Manners 2002; Manners 2010.

21 Sjursen 2006a, b; Pace 2007; Scheipers and Sicurelli 2007; Bicchi 2006; Lucarelli and Manners 2006; Diez 2005.

22 Sjursen 2006b.

23 Smith 2005.

24 Bersick 2009.

25 Smith 2004; Wiener and Puetter 2009.

countries[26] or even going to war. The EU neither has a budget for military missions nor a standing army or the tanks, planes and warships required for imperial policies. It is thus indeed a normative power, although, as some would add, probably not by intent but by defect.[27]

The related concept of 'civilian power' is used in many different ways. Early contributions highlighted the EU's innovative political structure, the voluntary transferral of national sovereignties to supranational institutions, and the EU's function as a role model for other regions. Maull[28] and Kirste[29] have later used it for analysing the limited range of means that the EU uses for projecting its interests abroad. The concept of civilian power is since then often used as both a descriptive and a normative concept. In both cases, the decisive criterion for being a civilian power is not whether or not the entity possesses weapons or whether it uses them, but rather the orientation of its foreign and security dealings in accordance with specific criteria. According to Jünemann and Schörnig,[30] these criteria include the conscious renunciation of classical power politics techniques, the active promotion of more civil intergovernmental relations, the integration and regulation of the international system by means of international regimes, and the promotion of democracy and human rights. Civilian powers, however, are not necessarily bound to behaving unselfishly. In fact, they follow their own interests—just like other states—and aspire to realise these interests internationally by exerting their influence. According to Tewes,

> [C]ivilian Power [is …] about exerting influence. Its objective is the civilization of the international environment, which means that […] the use of military force is tamed in order to guarantee the rule of law, prosperity and legitimate governance.[31]

In order to substantiate the claim that the EU has the character of a civilian power, common references are made to the so-called domestic analogy. According to this analogy, it is not just states, but also groups of states like the EU that want their international environment to be ordered according to the same values and principles as their own political and social system. Concepts of order and ideals such as economic liberalisation, juridification and rule of law as well as democracy and human rights are therefore the quintessential foundations of the EU's foreign relations across the world.[32]

The analytical problem of Supranational Idealism here becomes already apparent. Although the supranational layer of the EU may indeed abstain from imperial or other offensive policies and might well be called a normative or

---

[26] Brummer 2009.

[27] Matlary 2006.

[28] Maull 1997.

[29] Kirste and Maull 1996.

[30] Jünemann and Schörnig 2002.

[31] Tewes 2002, 11.

[32] On the EU's value-led approach within the context of development, see Broberg (this volume).

civilian power, the Member States of the EU are not less confrontational than any other states of comparable size. France and Britain have a long tradition of military interventions, and Germany has since some years started to rediscover the global range of its national interests. The justification of former German defence minister Struck for the Bundeswehr's intervention in Afghanistan has become famous: 'German security is defended at the Hindukuch'.[33] Member State troops today can be found in a great number of states in Africa, Asia and Europe and only sometimes use their missions for applying universal standards. In the same way as Supranational Institutionalism, Supranational Idealism does not dispute the data, but worse, ignores them. It is focused on the policies of the EU institutions as if they were not the product of the decisions of the very same governments as those who sent troops abroad and pursue traditional power politics.[34] Supranational Idealism thus deliberately overlooks a crucial element of European foreign policy.

3.2.3 Liberal Intergovernmentalism

Liberal Intergovernmentalism is increasingly being used for explaining European foreign policy.[35] The growing diversity of modern foreign policy and its relevance for many domestic policies has made the distinction between high and low politics much more difficult. Foreign policy is no longer conceived of as an area in which non-governmental actors, lobbies, and other domestic actors have little influence. Among the most important foreign policy concerns today are environmental policy, energy security, migration policy, trade policy and many other policies with a direct 'behind-the-border effect'.

The central argument of Liberal Intergovernmentalism maintains that supranational policy outcomes reflect the asymmetrical bargaining power of the Member States, which again reflect the interests of their strongest domestic pressure groups. Supranational institutions hardly ever have a significant autonomous impact on the EU's foreign policies and are incapable of realising even a modest degree of policy coherence. If the Member States do not agree, 'European institutions cannot do much more than paper over differences'.[36] Faced with the war in Iraq in 2002 for example, the EU experienced its greatest internal division since the inauguration of the Treaty on the European Union. A total of 18 out of the present 27 EU Member States supported the American position, while France and Germany led a minority of opponents.[37] The intergovernmental argument has

---

33 Press Conference with the German Minister of Defence Peter Struck (2002) 5 December, 2002, Berlin.

34 Asseburg and Kempin 2009; Treacher 2004.

35 Schimmelfennig 2001; Moravcsik 1999; Moravcsik 2010; Gordon 1997–1998.

36 Chopin and Lefebvre 2010.

37 Hill 2004.

proven to be a forceful explanatory tool in the EU's environmental policy, its enlargement policy[38] and many other policy areas.[39] Liberal Intergovernmental approaches have also produced important insights into understanding European trade policy and that the bargaining position of the EU in the World Trade Organization (WTO) is strongly influenced by strong domestic pressure groups in the big Member States.

Liberal Intergovernmentalism is less helpful, however, for understanding change. It explains policy outcomes basically as a function of economic preferences that are rather fixed over time.[40] Member States have followed a policy of market liberalisation since the beginning of the European Coal and Steel Community (ECSC). They differ only with regard to the conditions of liberalisation, which are for example transition periods for the liberalisation of certain products and rules or the insistence on side-payments for their acquiescence to the agenda of their more economically - advanced partners. Liberal Intergovernmentalism deals with processes of up- and downloading of economic policies but is rather insensitive to non-economic issues such as Member State security concerns.[41] The historically rooted fear of many Central and Eastern European (CEE) countries towards Russian influence in Eastern Europe[42] is missing from most intergovernmental accounts in the same way as Polish fears about being economically dominated by Germany, or French concerns about a new German 'Ostpolitik'.[43] The heated debates about the military and political support for the invasion of Iraq have made it clear, however, that the EU of today is politically split between a Western European continental camp that strives for closer political and foreign policy integration and an Eastern European camp which perceives American troops in Europe as the first best guarantee that Russian troops will stay out. Liberal Intergovernmentalism therefore has its strength in explaining the past of the economic integration of the EU-15 rather than understanding the post-enlargement politics of the EU of 27 Member States.

3.3 Bringing Realism Back in Practice

It becomes clear that the theoretical literature on the EU's foreign policies is in need of sharpening its awareness on the two-track character of the EU's foreign policy. It is only sometimes conducted by the CFSP institutions and more often than not dominated by individual national interests. Realism is the proper

[38] Moravcsik and Vachudova 2003.

[39] Finke 2009.

[40] Moravcsik 1998.

[41] Forster 1998.

[42] Rumer and Stent 2009; Jakniunaite 2009.

[43] Bendiek and Neyer 2009.

candidate for theoretical guidance. It is a theoretical approach that took many of its crucial empirical insights from analysing European politics.[44] Recent attempts to apply Realism to the EU have used either an offensive or a defensive variant, speculated about the re-emergence of the unified Germany as a European hegemon[45] or explained why exactly this is unlikely to happen.[46] Realism has also been applied to analysing the policies of the supranational layer of the EU. Zimmermann, for example, has shown that the EU's bargaining strategy in the WTO seeks relative rather than absolute gains.[47] Hyde-Price has criticised the idealism inherent in notions of 'normative power Europe' and stressed that 'the EU is used by its Member States as a collective instrument for shaping its external milieu by a combination of hard and soft power'.[48]

The variety in theoretical approaches already makes clear that Realism, similar to Constructivism or Institutionalism, is not a clear-cut theory but rather an umbrella term for a variety of approaches. Most realists, however, share the underlying concept of an international anarchy, the implication that politics is ultimately a zero-sum game about power and security, and the conviction that states are the most important actors in global politics. National interests and security concerns are emphasised and the role of international institutions and law is downplayed.[49]

All of these conceptual building blocs are refuted in most modern integration theory as inadequate for understanding the EU.[50] Critics of Realism hold that its central analytical categories capture the European war-torn past rather than the post-Westphalian European polity of today.[51] The EU is often portrayed as a constitutionalised polity, or even a Kantian paradise of eternal peace[52] in which transnational deliberation and the law give expression to a new type of political order beyond the nation-state.[53] Neither Poland and Germany, nor Germany and France perceive each other anymore as enemies or only as threats. Security concerns are no longer important issues, and war has become a highly remote phenomenon of—if at all—its post-Soviet periphery. Economic integration has led to an integrated economic space in which transnational linkages and interdependencies have made military adventures far too costly, and probably not even possible because important military equipment is produced in multi-national

44 Carr 1939; Morgenthau 1948.

45 Mearsheimer 1990.

46 Grieco 2009.

47 Zimmerman 2007.

48 Hyde-Price 2006.

49 Waltz 2000.

50 Wiener and Diez 2009.

51 Ruggie 1993.

52 Kagan 1993.

53 Eriksen 2010.

European companies like EADS.[54] Member States have become full-blown democracies with transparent decision-making procedures. They no longer distrust each other, have thus overcome the security dilemma and today maximise absolute economic gains rather than relative power gains. In addition, 50 years of cooperation and legal integration have established a thick layer of transnational trust, a feeling of belonging together and probably even the beginnings of a common identity. They have established amongst them an anarchical society[55] which has strong elements of a security community.[56]

All this would be hard to dispute. It is a powerful story that explains much of the success of the European project. Offensive neo-realism with its emphasis on states as status maximisers[57] is probably impossible to defend as an approach for understanding EU foreign policies. It would be a mistake, however, to take this as a convincing case against Realism as such. Many of the crucial building blocks of Realism can be reformulated and integrated into a specific European blend of realism.[58] European Realism is also sensitive to international power asymmetries. It is well aware that Britain and France are nuclear powers that hold permanent seats in the UN Security Council. They play, together with Germany, more important roles than all other Member States in the making of European foreign policy. This does not mean that the concerns of other Member States are not heard in the European Council but that nothing meaningful can be done without an agreement between these three states.[59]

European Realism is also in accordance with Realism in arguing that security concerns are driving forces of foreign policy. They are, however, dressed in wider clothes today. Modern security policy not only implies to safeguard against military aggression from neighbouring countries (although some Eastern European countries such as Lithuania would emphasise this aspect) but also refers to the so-called 'new risks' such as terrorism, migration, trafficking, environmental degradation, economic competitiveness, and many more.[60] The European Security Strategy (ESS) of 2003 and 2008 covers all these issues and makes it explicit that security issues—broadly understood—are on top of the foreign policy agenda of the EU. Zero-sum rationality is also still on the agenda. The launch of an 'Eastern Partnership' of the EU can well be interpreted as a response to the French initiative to establish a Union for the Mediterranean (which was originally intended to exclude non-Mediterranean Member States such as Germany).[61] The hard

---

[54] Eisenhut 2010.

[55] Bull 1977.

[56] Deutsch 1957.

[57] Mearsheimer 2001.

[58] Selden 2010.

[59] Tallberg 2008.

[60] Sjursen 2005.

[61] The role and influence of Member States in the creation of external frameworks, in particular in the EU's neighbourhood, is explored further in this volume by Ghazaryan, and Dragneva and Wolczuk.

bargaining about voting rights during the negotiations of the Lisbon Treaty between Poland and the rest of the EU is a case for the zero-sum logic in European politics just as the competition among the Member States for low corporate taxation. All Member States finally suffer from the economic downturn of the world economy and intensely compete abroad for export markets that can safeguard national employment.

This is not to suggest that all of European politics follows the logic of Realism, power-play and zero-sum rationality. It also is surely true that European Realism is a far cry from the Realism of the first half of the twentieth century. Security issues today are for no Member State of the European Union a matter of life and death. The security dilemma in its traditional interpretation as an existential threat to the survival of the state has been overcome in the EU. European Realism therefore does not claim a universal applicability for all politics beyond the state. It is limited to explaining policy-making in the non-communitarised areas of European politics, and to those areas that fall under the new security agenda of politics. It accepts the insight that legal integration has transformed significant parts of Europe from an unregulated anarchy into a constitutionalised polity with strong elements of deliberative interaction.[62] European Realism thus is a theoretical approach that is conceptually limited to the non-legalised areas of European politics. It shares some features with Realism and differs with respect to others. European Realism submits three basic propositions about the interests, the ideas and the institutions of European foreign policy.

3.3.1 Interests: National Security and Governmental Autonomy

A Europeanised version of Realism holds that states have national interests that originate from own historical experiences and political cultures.[63] Polish, German, French or British foreign policy is impossible to understand without taking the presence of the past into account. Poland's century-long experience of being invaded by its neighbours is important for understanding its close relations with the US. The fact that Germany has started and lost two world wars is crucial for its hesitancy to engage today in military missions abroad. The long colonial histories of France and Britain and the fact that both countries still have territories and military bases around the world give them a national (or even international), but not a European approach to international issues. European Realism thus rejects the neorealists' suggestion that the non-existence of a monopoly of coercion in the EU forces the Member States to identify their national interest with an increase in power only.

---

[62] Neyer 2010.

[63] Carr 1939.

Interests have long been neglected in the analysis of European foreign policy. The dominant discourse on 'civil' or even 'normative power Europe' has distracted many scholars from realising that politics is ultimately about interests and not ideas. It is not easy, however, to apply the concept of interests to the supranational layer of the EU. The last years of debate on the ESS have exposed the Member States' inability to identify a European 'national' interest. By adopting the ESS, the Member States have tried to overcome the strategic dissonance of the EU's foreign policies by improving the EU's strategic clarity, providing a clear definition of its interests and identifying long-term policy objectives. Whilst most observers have welcomed that effort and applauded the document for its ambitions, its shortcomings are equally clear. The ESS says virtually nothing on energy security or climate change, on the division of tasks between the national and the European level, and it has very little to say about Russia. Most important questions either remain unaddressed, or are only insufficiently addressed. It is also telling that the European Council has failed to produce a program of how to implement the strategy. The ESS thus is a document that lacks any real bite.

A major reason why the ESS has remained stuck in ambition is that the EU suffers from a structural strategic dissonance. The EU is de facto divided in two camps with an antagonistic strategic orientation. A group of Western European Member States, which is centred around France and Belgium, is striving for military and political self-reliance and expects the CFSP and the European Security and Defence Policy (ESDP/CSDP) to deliver this good. The US is viewed as a strategic competitor with an incompatible idea of how the world should be ordered. The strategic orientation thus is to balance against the US.[64] Most of the new Eastern European Member States, especially Poland, the Czech Republic, and the Baltic States are directly opposed to this strategic orientation.[65] Centuries of military aggression from their Western and Eastern neighbours have made them aware that they need a strong ally in order to remain independent. The offer of the US to provide that guarantee is thus highly welcome and, by implication, excludes any support for a strategy of balancing against the US. Not balancing, but 'bandwagoning' is here the strategy of choice. The deep cleavage in the EU over the support of the US-led invasion in Iraq, the dispute on the establishment of an antiballistic missile defence system in Poland, the Czech Republic in 2006 and 2007 and now Romania, and the quarrel between France and some of the new Member States on the European reaction to the Russian invasion of Georgia in 2008 are only the most obvious examples of this deep strategic rift in the EU.

Whilst a unified European national interest does hardly exist, national interests do so and are even crucial for understanding European politics. They have neither disappeared in the process of Europeanisation nor are governments too fragmented

[64] Posen 2006.

[65] Longhurst 2003.

to identify them. European Realism rejects the suggestion that national interests have been diluted in processes of socialisation[66] and reflexive preference shaping[67] or are even subordinated to collective 'truth seeking.'[68] Most European states have a long-standing tradition of following well-established foreign policies that reflect deep-rooted national concerns much more thoroughly than European deliberative interaction. In the same way as 50 years ago, France still pursues its post-colonial policies in Africa and the Mediterranean, Germany looks again for close cooperation with Russia (even if it comes at the cost of a worsening relationship with Poland), and the UK emphasises its special relationship with the US. Similar continuities could be sketched for nearly all Member States. They all underline that the importance of European institutions must not be overestimated. International institutions such as the intergovernmental bodies of the CFSP do not produce policies but are the product of policies.[69]

It must be added, however, that governments, not nations, have founded the EU, and that they conduct its daily business. The distinction is important because governments have an overriding interest to stay in power, and need domestic support for that purpose. International politics among democracies is thus not following the nineteenth century 'Primat der Außenpolitik' (Leopold Ranke) but is better conceptualised as a two-level game.[70] Governments pursue the national interest only if that does not imply conducting policies that are domestically unwelcome and impossible to sell to their domestic principals at an acceptable cost. Put differently, we can also assume that governments have strong incentives to conduct foreign policies that simultaneously pursue the national and governmental interests, i.e., increase national security and governmental autonomy from domestic scrutiny. The more a foreign policy promises to contribute to both goals the more it will be welcomed by the Member States. The first-best foreign policy from any member government's perspective is thus a policy which pursues national interests while at the same time expanding governmental autonomy. The post-9/11 wave of international cooperation in security-enhancing policies is a perfect example for such a match of national and governmental interests. The terrorist attacks of New York and Washington provided fertile political ground for governmental efforts to 'securitize'[71] an ever-increasing range of political issues, thereby simultaneously expanding national security and governmental domestic autonomy. New institutional settings such as the Berner Club,[72] or other informal

---

[66] Checkel 1999.

[67] Wiener and Puetter 2009.

[68] Deitelhoff 2003.

[69] Mearsheimer 1994/1995.

[70] Putnam 1988.

[71] Buzan et al. 1998.

[72] The Berner Club (also known as Club de Berne) having been founded in 1972 is an intelligence sharing forum where the Heads of EU Member States' security and intelligence services (as well as Norway and Switzerland) meet on a regular basis to discuss intelligence and security matters. For further information see Scheren 2009.

meetings that are beyond parliamentarian scrutiny by either the European or national parliaments, are most cherished sites for policy-making. They open new opportunities for cooperation among the intelligence services and provide governments with policy-making tools that are far less transparent and inclusive than anything they have had access to in pre-9/11 domestic politics. The post-9/11 security discourse thus has had—and still has—the important effect of maximising the domestic leverage that European politics offers to governments. Because security today is perceived as a global issue, governments have little difficulty to justify the decoupling of sensitive policies from domestic scrutiny and to pool their respective policy-making capacities in European or international arenas. This new window of opportunity has made European foreign policy a phenomenon which stretches across the former 'pillars'[73] and has given governments an extended power to influence the domestic political agenda.

3.3.2 Ideas: The EU in the Service of National Interests

Classical Realism rightly attaches an important role to ideas. Although interests and not ideas directly effect political action, ideas about the identity of one's self and of others are crucial for determining one's interests. Tracing the changing Member State ideas of the telos of the European Union is an insightful way for understanding what the EU's foreign policy today is, and what it is not. Such an analysis can start with the post-1989 political enthusiasm that set in when the Wall came down. The goal to politically unify the continent turned from a vision into a project. The enthusiasm was strong enough to make the Member States agree in Maastricht in 1992 on the telos of an 'ever closer union'. This was probably the first time in the history of the integration project that the Member States—guided by the visionary president of the Commission Jacques Delors—were willing to concede political integration the status of a good in itself. Major European politicians such as De Gaulle, Adenauer or Thatcher had until then always followed a much more pragmatic approach to integration, emphasising its instrumental value for fostering the four freedoms, for putting reform pressure on domestic producers or for politically stabilising Europe. It was only in 1992 that the telos of an 'ever closer union' was adopted as a normative principle of the integration process.

The idea to make integration a goal in itself, however, came soon under pressure of reality. The negative referendum in Denmark, the near-rejection in France (both in 1992), and the unwillingness of the Member States to use the Treaties of Amsterdam (1997) and Nice (2001) for making the EU fit for enlargement made it plain clear that all efforts to decouple European integration from Member States interests would lead to nowhere. The Member States were not

[73] Stetter 2007.

ready to delegate the necessary competences to the EU but left a number of issues with high importance for the functioning of the EU of 27 unsolved (the so-called leftovers). The Convention on the Future of Europe with its ambitious goal to deliver a constitution for the EU was already past its time when it was launched in 2001. It aimed at overcoming the intergovernmental method of Treaty-making and to supplant that method with a European constitutional assembly that mimicked earlier constitutional conventions such as the American constitutional convention of 1787.

It is not surprising that the result was a complete failure. Its final outcome, the Constitutional Treaty was rejected first by the French and laters by the Dutch people (2005). Only after this double failure was the European political elite ready to accept that the political mood in the Member States had changed quite substantially since Maastricht. The Treaty of Lisbon can be seen as a codification of Europe's disillusionment and as a return to the interest-based pragmatism of pre-1989. The Member States have deleted all references that could be read as leading to supranational statehood. The European anthem and flag have been removed from the Treaty and the Member States have deliberately refrained from explicitly stating that European law is superior to Member State law. All in all, the EU has returned to an understanding of its mission as serving the national interests of its Member States.

The provisions on the CFSP in the new Treaty of Lisbon reflect the low salience given to supranational Institutionalisation. The Member States have deliberately chosen not to develop the CFSP into a strong and coherent voice of the Member States in the world but confirmed its intergovernmental nature. They have refused to combine all foreign policies of the EU under one institutional umbrella (with one telephone number) and reaffirmed the often-lamented division of competences between the Commission, the European Council and the Member States. It is rather unlikely that the new Permanent President of the European Council will have enough agenda-setting powers to limit its intergovernmental nature and to advance a truly common policy-making. Herman van Rompuy has been deliberately chosen for his qualities in fostering compromises and in striking agreements not to agree; but he does not have a reputation for strong leadership. The big European powers, France, Germany and the UK, will most probably dominate policy-making in the European Council in the future even stronger than in the past. Small states could in the past use the rotating presidency as a window of opportunity for promoting their foreign policy pet projects.[74] The most likely effect of the abolishment of this instrument and of the introduction of the Permanent Presidency will thus not be a strengthening of the supranational character of the European Council but rather a weakening of the influence of the smaller states.

[74] Tallberg 2006.

3.3.3 Institutions: Made by States and for States

The institutions of the CFSP have often been attributed a crucial importance for understanding European foreign policy.[75] Realism rejects this emphasis and treats international institutions as mere epiphenomena of underlying national and governmental interests. As opposed to supranational institutions, international institutions have hardly any autonomous impact on Member State decision-making.[76] They merely reflect the interests and the distribution of power among their Member States. Realism is thus highly sceptical concerning the suggestion that international institutions, once they are founded, assume a 'life of their own.' The argument made prominently by Keohane[77] holds that the transaction costs of establishing and changing institutions are so high that states have an interest in maintaining them even if they comply only suboptimally with national interests.[78] Historical Institutionalism has similarly argued that the sunk costs of past decisions about institutional choice may be so high that path-dependent institutional development is to be expected.[79]

As opposed to both approaches, Realism holds that both the transaction costs and the sunk costs of international institutions are far less significant than is assumed. To our knowledge, the claims made by Keohane and Pierson have not found any systematic empirical substantiation in the literature. The empirical evidence of European foreign policy points rather in the opposite direction. Member States permanently invent new institutions in areas covered by all three of the former pillars of the EU and are quick to change old ones if they fail to meet the expectations. The recent innovations in the foreign policy-making process of the EU with the introduction of a Permanent Presidency and a High Representative for Foreign Affairs are cases in point. The institutions of European foreign policy can thus be assumed to either provide the Member States with proper arenas for maximising national security and governmental autonomy, or be subject to innovation, reinterpretation and—if they resist reform—decay into irrelevance. The unfortunate fate of the Weimar Triangle underlines this point. It was established in 1991 as a symbol of the process of reconciliation between France Germany and Poland. It foresaw annual consultations to be held on a large range of issues of European policy and aimed at establishing a permanent, although informal, forum for coordinating the foreign policies of the three Member States. Trilateral cooperation in the Weimar Triangle did not lead too far, however. It soon became evident that the interests of Poland, France and Germany differ in crucial aspects. The disagreements between Poland and France on the issue of intervening in Iraq, the German–Polish disputes over expellees and the debate on

[75] Hill 1993; Hill and Smith 2005.

[76] Moravcsik 1997.

[77] Keohane 1984.

[78] Keohane 1984.

[79] Pierson 2004.

the Treaty of Lisbon are only three examples from a long list. The Weimar Triangle thus decayed quickly into irrelevance.

Realism also rejects the suggestion that a unified Europe that speaks with one voice is a good in itself. Collective foreign policy-making always involves a trade-off between the benefits of increased bargaining power via third countries on the one hand and the costs of facilitating internal cooperation among the coalition on the other hand. Such costs can mean (1) a difficult process of facilitating internal agreement on the goals and strategies, will often (2) imply painful compromises, and may sometimes (3) even necessitate sharing the benefits of cooperation. All three issues can involve significant costs.

Facilitating internal cooperation is a cumbersome process among 27 Member States. The EU has had to learn the hard way since 2003 that the costs of internal agreement have been to high for either developing a coherent approach towards security cooperation with the US. In areas where internal cooperation is regularly achieved, such as in trade policy, it is often only possible because Member States make painful compromises. The insistence of France and other Southern European Member States, for example, to uphold the European agricultural protectionism has come at the cost of export-oriented Member States such as Germany or the Netherlands. Further steps towards liberalising global trade have become very difficult with negotiations stalled between the EU and other exporters of agricultural products.

Sharing of the benefits is also a relevant issue. National foreign ministers regularly equip their delegations with the CEOs of major national exporters. Most European foreign ministers use their visits abroad for advertising their national portfolio of high-tech goods and for trying to conclude as many sales as possible. It has hardly been heard, however, that a German foreign minister was advertising British products or vice versa. Foreign policy has become increasingly an instrument of promoting national exports and for opening foreign markets. Cooperation in the promotion of European goods abroad would mean that the national foreign ministers would lose a highly valued competence which is good for much domestic credit-claiming.

3.4 Conclusion

All this underlines that a common European foreign policy is not a good in itself for the Member States. It is a costly product and emerges only as the product of a deliberate calculation of the Member States on single issues. Realism thus predicts that the policy will define the coalition, and not the coalition the policy. This idea is the major reason behind the introduction of Article 23 TEU and Articles 326–334 TFEU. So-called enhanced cooperation allows for conducting mini-lateral cooperation under the umbrella of the EU and thus for the Member States to remain as flexible as possible in choosing the adequate coalition which suits their national interests.

References

Asseburg M, Kempin R (eds) (2009) Die EU als strategischer Akteur in der Sicherheits-und Verteidigungspolitik?: Eine systematische Bestandsaufnahme von ESVP-Missionen und Operationen, Stiftung Wissenschaft und Politik, Berlin (SWP-Studie S32)

Bátora J (2009) European defence agency: a flashpoint of institutional logics. West European Politics 32(6):1075–1098

Bendiek A (2006) Cross-pillar security regime building in the European Union: effects of the European security strategy of December 2003, European Integrration Online Papers 10, pp 1–17

Bendiek A (2010) Neuer Europäischer Realismus, Stiftung Wissenschaft und Politik (SWP-Aktuell 10) February 2010

Bendiek A, Neyer J (2009) La nouvelle Ostpolitik allemand et la politique européenne de voisinage. Friedrich Ebert Stiftung, Paris, pp 1–7

Bersick S (2009) Die EU und Ostasien. In: Bendiek A, Kramer H (eds) Globale Außenpolitik der Europäischen Union: interregionale Beziehungen und 'strategische Partnerschaften. Nomos Verlagsges, Baden-Baden, pp 94–111

Bicchi F (2006) 'Our size fits all': normative power Europe and the Mediterranean. Journal of European Public Policy 13(2):286–303

Biscop S, Weiss T (2010) A realistic ambition: setting priorities for CSDP. In: Fabry E, Ricard-Nihoul G (eds) Think Global–Act European. The contribution of 14 European think tanks to the Spanish, Belgian and Hungarian trio Presidency of the European Union, Notre Europe, Paris, 164–168

Brummer K (2009) Imposing sanctions: the not so, normative power Europe. European Foreign Affairs Review 14:191–207

Bull H (1977) The anarchical society: a study of world politics. Columbia University Press, New York

Buzan B, Waever O, De Wilde J (1998) Security: a new framework for analysis. Lynne Rienner, Boulder

Caporaso JA, Jupille J (1999) Institutionalism and the European Union: beyond international relations and comparative politics. Annual Review of Political Science 2(2):429–444

Carr EH (1939) The Twenty Years' Crisis, 1919–1939. Perennial, New York (2001 edition)

Checkel JT (1999) Norms, institutions, and national identity in contemporary Europe. International Studies Quarterly 43(1):84–114

Chopin T, Lefebvre M (2010) Three phone numbers for Europe: will the Lisbon Treaty make the European Union more effective abroad? Center on the United States and Europe at Brookings, Washington/DC (U.S.–Europe Analysis Series, No. 43)

Deitelhoff N (2003) Talking states into persuasion. Norm-entrepreneurs and the manipulation of discursive settings in norm-construction instances, Mimeo

Deutsch KW et al (1957) Political community and the North Atlantic area: international organization in the light of historical experience. Princeton University Press, Princeton

Diez T (2005) Constructing the self and changing others: reconsidering, normative power Europe. Millennium – Journal of International Studies 33:13–636

Dijkstra H (2009) Commission versus Council Secretariat: an analysis of Bureaucratic Rivalry in EFP. European Foreign Affairs Review 14:431–450

Dobbins M, Schneider G, Zimmer C (2005) The contested council: conflict dimensions of an intergovernmental EU institution. Political Studies 53(2):403–422

Duchêne F (1973) The European community and the uncertainties of interdependence. In: Kohnstamm M, Hager W (eds) A nation writ large? Foreign-policy problems before the European community. Macmillan, London, pp 1–21

Eisenhut D (2010) Europäische Rüstungskooperation: zwischen Binnenmarkt und zwischenstaatlicher Zusammenarbeit, Nomos, Baden–Baden

Eriksen EO (2010) A state-less vanguard for a rightful world order. In: Neyer J, Wiener A (eds) Political theory of the European Union. Oxford University Press, Oxford, pp 69–88

Finke D (2009) Challenges to intergovernmentalism: an empirical analysis of EU treaty negotiations since Maastricht. West European Politics 32(3):466–49

Forster A (1998) Britain and the negotiation of the Maastricht treaty: a critique of liberal intergovernmentalism. Journal of Common Market Studies 36(3):347–368

Garrett G, Tsebelis G (2001) The institutional foundations of intergovernmentalism and supranationalism in the European Union. International Organization 55(2):357–390

Gordon PH (1997–1998) Europe's uncommon foreign policy. International Security 22(3): 74–100

Gosalbo Bono R (2006) Some reflections on the CFSP legal order. Common Market Law Review 43:337–394

Grieco JM (2009) Liberal international theory and imagining the end of the Cold War. The British Journal of Politics and International Relations 11(2):192–204

Hill C (1993) The capability-expectations gap, or conceptualizing Europe's international role. Journal of Common Market Studies 31(3):305–328

Hill C (2004) Renationalising or regrouping: EU foreign policy since 11 September 2001. Journal of Common Market Studies 42(1):143–163

Hyde-Price A (2006) Normative power Europe: a realist critique. Journal of European Public Policy 13(2):217–234

Irondelle B, Kempin R (2008) La coopération franco-allemande à l'épreuve, 64 Défense Nationale 8–9, pp 29–36

Jakniunaite D (2009) Neighbourhood politics in Baltic states: between the EU and Russia. In: Berg E, Ehin P (eds) Identity and foreign policy: Baltic–Russian relations and European integration. Ashgate, Farnham, pp 117–129

Jünemann A, Schörnig N (2002) Die Sicherheits- und Verteidigungspolitik der 'Zivilmacht Europa 'Ein Widerspruch in sich? Frankfurt a.M.: Peace Research Institute Frankfurt (PRIF), PRIF Report 13/2002

Kagan R (1993) Paradise and power. America and Europe in the New World order, London

Keohane RO (1984) After hegemony. Princeton University Press, Princeton

Kirste K, Maull HW (1996) Zivilmacht und Rollentheorie. Zeitschrift für Internationale Beziehungen 3(2):283–312

Longhurst K, Zaborowski M (2003) America's Protégé in the East? The emergence of Poland as a regional leader. International Affairs 79(5):1009–1028

Lucarelli S, Manners I (2006) Values and principles in European foreign policy. Routledge, Abingdon

Majone G (2009) Europe as the would-be world power: the EU at fifty. Cambridge University Press, Cambridge

Manners I (2002) Normative power Europe: a contradiction in terms? Journal of Common Market Studies 40(2):235–258

Manners I (2010) Global Europa: mythology of the European Union in world politics. Journal of Common Market Studies 48(1):67–87

Matlary JH (2006) When soft power turns hard: is an EU strategic culture possible? Security Dialogue 37(1):105–121

Maull H (1997) Zivilmacht Deutschland. Vierzehn Thesen für eine neue deutsche Außenpolitik. In: Senghaas D (ed) Frieden machen, Frankfurt a.M, 63–76

Maurer A, Kietz D (2010) Interinstitutional agreements: the unnoticed parliamentarisation of the CFSP. In: Kietz D, Maurer A and others (eds) Interinstitutionelle Vereinbarungen in der Europäischen Union: Wegbereiter der Verfassungsentwicklung, Baden–Baden, 199–224

Mearsheimer JJ (1990) Back to the future: instability in Europe after the Cold War. International Security 15(4):5–56

Mearsheimer JJ (1994/1995) The false promise of international institutions. International Security 19(3):5–49

Mearsheimer JJ (2001) The tragedy of great power politics. Norton, New York

Meunier S (2000) What single voice? European institutions and EU–U.S. trade negotiations. International Organization 54(1):103–135
Moravcsik A (1997) Preferences seriously: a liberal theory of international politics. International Organization 51(4):513–553
Moravcsik A (1998) The choice for Europe: social purpose and state power from Messina to Maastricht. Ithaca, New York
Moravcsik A (1999) Is something rotten in the state of Denmark? Constructivism and European integration. Journal of European Public Policy 6(4):669–681
Moravcsik A (2010) Europe, the second superpower, Current History 1:91–98
Moravcsik A, Vachudova MA (2003) National interests, state power and EU enlargement, archive of European integration, CES Working Paper No 97
Morgenthau HJ (1948) Politics among nations: the struggle for power and peace. McGrawHill, New York
Neyer J (2010) Justice, not democracy: legitimacy in the European Union. Journal of Common Market Studies 48(4):903–921
Nuttall SJ (2001) Consistency and the CFSP: a categorization and its consequences. Department of International Relations, London School of Economics and Political Science, London, November 2001 (EFPU Working Paper 2001/3), www2.lse.ac.uk/internationalRelations/centresandunits/EFPU/EFPUworkingpaperseries.aspx (consolidated on 26.10.2010). Last accessed 3 June 2011
Pace M (2007) The construction of normative power. Journal of Common Market Studies 45(5):1041–1064
Pierson P (2004) Politics in time. Princeton University Press, NJ
Posen B (2006) European Union security and defense policy: response to unipolarity? Security Studies 15(2):149–186
Putnam RD (1988) Diplomacy and domestic politics: the logic of two-level games. International Organization 42(3):427–460
Ruggie JG (1993) Multilateralism matters. The theory and praxis of an institutional form. Columbia University Press, New York
Rumer E, Stent A (2009) Russia and the west. Survival 51(2):91–104
Scheipers S, Sicurelli D (2007) Normative power Europe: a credible utopia? Journal of Common Market Studies 45(2):435–457
Scheren M (2009) Vernetzte Sicherheit—Zusammenarbeit der Inlandsnachrichten- und Sicherheitsdienste in Europa. In: Jäger T, Daun A (eds) Geheimdienste in Europa: transformation. Kooperation und Kontrolle, Wiesbaden, pp 168–181
Schimmelfennig F (2001) The community trap: liberal norms, rhetorical action, and the Eastern enlargement of the European Union. International Organization 55(1):47–80
Schmidt-Felzmann A (2008) Editorial: the European Union's external energy policy. Journal of Contemporary European Research 4(2):67–70
Selden Z (2010) Power is always in fashion: state-centric realism and the European security and defence policy. Journal of Common Market Studies 48(2):397–416
Sjursen H (2005) Security and defence. In: Carlsnaes W, Sjursen H, White B (eds) Contemporary European foreign policy. Sage Publications, London, pp 59–74
Sjursen H (2006a) The EU as a 'normative power': How can this be? Journal of European Public Policy 13(2):235–251
Sjursen H (2006b) What kind of power? Journal of European Public Policy 13(2):169–181
Smith ME (2004) Toward a theory of EU foreign policy-making: multi-level governance, domestic politics, and national adaptation to Europe's common foreign and security policy. Journal of European Public Policy 11(4):740–758
Smith KE (2005) Beyond the civilian power EU debate. Politique européenne 1(17):63–82
Stetter S (2007) EU Foreign and interior policies: cross-pillar politics and the social construction of sovereignty. Routledge, London/New York
Tallberg J (2006) Leadership and negotiation in the European Union: the power of the presidency. Cambridge University Press, Cambridge

Tallberg J (2008) Bargaining power in the European Council. Journal of Common Market Studies 46(3):685–708

Tewes H (2002) Germany civilian power and the New Europe. Enlarging NATO and the European Union. Palgrave Macmillan, Chippenham

Toje A (2008) The Consensus-Expectations gap: explaining Europe's ineffective foreign policy. Security Dialogue 39(1):121–141

Tomuschat C (2010) Guest editorial: calling Europe by phone. Common Market Law Review 47:3–7

Treacher A (2004) From civilian power to military actor: the EU's resistable transformation. European Foreign Affairs Review 9:49–66

Waltz KN (2000) Structural realism after the Cold War. International Security 25(1):5–41

Wiener A, Diez T (2009) European integration theory, 2nd edn. Oxford University Press, Oxford

Wiener A, Puetter U (2009) The quality of norms is as good as what actors make of them: critical constructivist research on norms. Journal of International Law and International Relations 5(1):1–15

Zimmerman H (2007) Realist power Europe? The EU in the negotiations about China's and Russia's WTO accession. Journal of Common Market Studies 45:813–832

Chapter 4
Between Legalisation and Organisational Development: Explaining the Evolution of EU Competence in the Field of Foreign Policy

Aurel Sari

Abstract The absorption of the European Community by the European Union has laid the foundations for the Union to become a more coherent and effective international actor. At the same time, the merger of the previously separate legal orders of the Community and the Union has put the intergovernmental character of the Common Foreign and Security Policy under considerable strain. The nature and extent of the Union's competences in foreign policy matters constitute one of the areas where this tension is particularly acute. The present chapter investigates why the question of Union competence in the field of foreign policy was not the subject of concern before the Treaty of Lisbon and what prompted the Member States to address this question during the treaty reform process. The chapter develops an answer to these questions by relying on two concepts borrowed from International Relations scholarship, legalisation and organisational development, and argues that the institutional design of European foreign policy cooperation is governed by what we may term the Goldilocks Principle.

Aurel Sari—Lecturer in Law, University of Exeter. Earlier versions of this paper have been presented at the EUI and in Sheffield. I am grateful to the participants of these events, in particular Marise Cremona, Christiaan Timmermans, Pascal Vennesson, and Joris Larik, for their helpful comments and suggestions. The usual disclaimer applies.

A. Sari (✉)
School of Law, University of Exeter, Exeter, UK
e-mail: A.Sari@exeter.ac.uk

P. J. Cardwell (ed.), *EU External Relations Law and Policy in the Post-Lisbon Era*,
DOI: 10.1007/978-90-6704-823-1_4,

Contents

4.1 Introduction

For some time now, foreign policy analysts and political scientists have concurred that the EU is an actor on the international stage,[1] but have disagreed about how the Union's actorness should be defined and measured.[2] Lawyers, by contrast, have long agreed on what constitutes a legal actor[3] or person under international law,[4] but have quarrelled for more than a decade over whether or not the EU in fact qualifies as an international legal person.[5] This question has become moot as a result of the entry

---

[1] Academic works studying the Union in terms of its 'actorness' abound. For some examples, see Taylor 1982; Cameron 1998; Ginsberg 1999; Bretherton and Vogler 2006; Greiçevci et al. 2007; Smith 2008, 25.

[2] According to the influential scheme proposed by Jupille and Caporaso 1998, the Union's capacity as an actor should be assessed with reference to four components: *recognition* by other actors, *authority* or legal competence to act, *autonomy* conceived as institutional distinctiveness and independence, and *cohesion*, meaning the ability to formulate internally consistent policy preferences. A different analytical framework is offered by Bretherton and Vogler 2006, who argue that the EU's actorness is determined by its ability to exert influence as measured in terms of opportunity, presence and capability.

[3] The notion of actorness has been imported into legal writing where it has mostly, although not exclusively, been treated as synonymous with legal personality. See Cremona 1998; Lenaerts and De Smijter 1999–2000; Editorial Comment 2001; Cannizzaro 2002; Tomuschat 2003.

[4] The leading case on the notion of international legal personality is *Reparation for Injuries Suffered in the Service of the United Nations* (Advisory Opinion) (1949) ICJ Rep. 174. In line with the *Reparation* case, most contemporary commentators derive the legal personality of international organisations from their constituent instruments and thus ultimately from the consent and will of their creators, whether manifested expressly or by implication. See Amerasinghe 2005, 77–86; White 2005, 68–69; Akande 2006, 282; Klabbers 2009, 46–51; Sands and Klein 2009, 473–480. See also Rama-Montaldo 1970, 111–131 and Bederman 1995–1996, passim.

[5] Those denying that the EU has acquired legal personality under international law include Neuwahl 1998; de Zwaan 1999; Denza 2002, 176, whilst those arguing in favour of this view include Wessel 1997; Tizzano 1998; Gütt 2003. For an overview of the opposing positions with extensive references to the literature, see Sari 2008, 71–80.

into force of the Lisbon Treaty,[6] since Article 47 TEU now confers legal personality upon the EU in express terms.[7] Although this provision does not endow the Union with legal personality under public international law in so many words,[8] the fact that EU enjoys extensive capacities to act on the international level and has replaced and succeeded the European Community (EC),[9] which itself was a subject of international law,[10] means that there can be no doubt that the Union possesses legal personality under both domestic and international law.[11]

The absorption of the EC and the express conferral of legal personality onto the EU has major implications for the Union's ability to act on the international stage. As an independent subject of international law, the EU constitutes an entity possessing the 'capacity to operate upon an international plane',[12] in particular the capacity to enter into relations with other international actors. The Treaty on the Functioning of the European Union (TFEU) has thus empowered the EU to conclude international agreements with one or more third countries or international organisations,[13] to establish and maintain appropriate forms of cooperation with other international organisations, including the UN and the Council of Europe,[14] and to send delegations to third countries and international organisations.[15] Most importantly, these powers now pertain to the EU alone[16]: as the legal successor to the EC, the Union's international action combines the external relations of the EC and its own Common Foreign and Security Policy (CFSP), leaving it with only one

[6] It should be noted that in recent years a consensus has emerged in the literature to the effect that the EU has evolved into a separate legal person of international law even before the entry into force of the Treaty of Lisbon as a result of its extensive treaty practice under the second pillar. See Thym 2006, 870–875; Naert 2007, 101; Grard 2006, 352–354.

[7] Papathanasiou 2009.

[8] Treaty on the European Union, Article 47 simply declares that '[t]he Union shall have legal personality'. Cf. MacLeod et al. 1996, 29–36.

[9] Treaty on the European Union, Article 1 provides that '[t]he Union shall replace and succeed the European Community'. This is not the first time the EU has taken on the functions of another international organisation: see Wessel 2001.

[10] ECJ, Case C- 22-70, *Commission v. Council (European Agreement on Road Transport)* [1971] ECR 263, paras 13–14. See Koutrakos 2006, 7–8.

[11] Indeed, this is how Treaty on the European Union, Article 47 is commonly understood: see Cremona 2008, 38; Wessel 2008, 152; Papathanasiou 2009, 37.

[12] ICJ, *Reparation for Injuries Suffered in the Service of the United Nations* (Advisory Opinion) (1949) ICJ Rep. 174, 178–179. On the consequences of legal personality, see Rama-Montaldo 1970, 131–147.

[13] Treaty on the Functioning of the European Union, Article 216.

[14] Treaty on the Functioning of the European Union, Article 220.

[15] Treaty on the Functioning of the European Union, Article 221.

[16] Görlitz 2004, 376.

set of international relations to maintain. The TEU accordingly directs the Union to pursue a single set of objectives in all areas of its international activities.[17]

In principle, these developments should render the EU's external action more coherent and thereby increase its effectiveness as an international actor.[18] However, while increased coherence and effectiveness have long been regarded as the holy grail of European foreign policy cooperation,[19] these are not the only considerations that motivate cooperation between the Member States in this area. Until now, steps towards closer foreign policy cooperation have always been tempered by the need to accommodate the continued existence of the Member States' national foreign policies. Since 1993, this interplay between increased cooperation and continued independence has manifested itself most visibly in the pillar structure of the EU, which was designed to safeguard the special character of the CFSP as an intergovernmental form of cooperation distinct from Community external relations. As long as the EU and the Community co-existed as 'integrated but separate legal orders',[20] a presumption prevailed that the CFSP did not share the normative qualities of the supranational Community legal order, such as the doctrine of supremacy and direct effect.[21] The creation of a single legal entity through the absorption of the EC into the EU has now reversed this presumption[22]: as a matter of principle, the internal law of the Union should be considered

[17] Treaty on the European Union, Article 21. This contrasts with the legal framework in place before Lisbon, where EC external relations and the CFSP pursued distinct, albeit in part overlapping, objectives. In the past, this has led to difficulties in the horizontal delimitation of competences, as seen in particular in ECJ, Case C-91/05, *Commission v. Council (Small Arms)* [2008] ECR I-3651. See Heliskoski 2008; van Vooren 2009.

[18] As Pernice 2008–2009 points out, the overarching aim of the Lisbon Treaty in the field of external action was to ensure that 'the Union shall be perceived as one unit, speak with one mouth, and implement consistent policies in external matters' (398). Of course, the conferral of legal personality in itself guarantees neither consistency nor effectiveness. Appropriate decision-making processes, amongst other things, are equally important. See Afionis 2008–2009.

[19] For some examples from the literature, see Krenzler and Schneider 1994; Schmalz 1998; Wessel 2000; Gauttier 2004; Blockmans and Wessel 2009.

[20] CFI, Case T-315/01, *Kadi v. Council and Commission* [2005] ECR II-3649, para 120; ECJ, Joined Cases C-402/05 P and C-415/05 P, *Kadi and Al Barakaat v. Council and Commission* [2008] ECR I-6351, para 202. Not all commentators have accepted the notion that the CFSP and Community law constitute separate legal orders. See in particular von Bogdandy and Nettesheim 1996.

[21] Gosalbo Bono 2006; Hermann 2008. On the legal character of Community law, see Denza 1999 and with reference to external relations, de Baere 2008, in particular 73–158. More recently, several commentators have detected signs of a gradual conversion between the CFSP and Community external relations: see Wessel 2009; de Baere 2008, 205–209.

[22] See also Bribosia 2007, 203–204.

identical in its character and legal effects across the entire field of its applicability, unless the Treaties provide otherwise.[23]

This new presumption in favour of legal uniformity[24] puts the intergovernmental character of the CFSP under considerable strain.[25] This was not lost on the Member States. To avoid a radical break with the established principles of European foreign policy cooperation, the Treaty of Lisbon draws three distinctions: it sets apart the Union's competence in the CFSP from its competences in other policy areas,[26] declares that the CFSP is 'subject to specific rules and procedures'[27] and provides that the implementation of Union's other policies must not affect the 'application of the procedures and the extent of the powers of the institutions laid down by the Treaties for the exercise of the Union competences' under the CFSP.[28] On its face, the traditional distinction between the CFSP and other policy areas thus seems to remain intact, leading some commentators to conclude that the Lisbon Treaty has retained the Union's pillar structure 'in all but name.'[29] Indeed, rather than demolishing the pillars, it appears that the Lisbon Treaty has left them standing and simply built up the gaps between them. It is not immediately obvious, however, whether in doing so the Treaty has preserved the CFSP as a distinct structural element of the redesigned European house or whether it has kept it simply as a period feature.[30]

One of the key questions in this respect concerns the delimitation of powers between the EU and the Member States in the area of the CFSP. For the first time, the Treaty of Lisbon has defined the scope of the EU's competence over foreign policy matters in express terms: Article 24 TEU declares that the Union's competence covers 'all areas of foreign policy and all questions relating to the Union's security, including the progressive framing of a common defence policy that might lead to a common defence.' This provision is remarkable for at least two reasons. First, the material scope of the EU's competence could hardly be broader, considering that it covers every aspect of foreign and security policy. Given its all-encompassing scope, it is imperative to better understand what restrictions the existence and exercise of Union competence imposes on the Member States' continued right to conduct their national foreign policies in parallel with the CFSP.

---

[23] Support for this view may be derived from Treaty on the European Union, Article 1 which provides that the Treaties have the same legal value, and from a general presumption (cf. Amerasinghe 2005, 17) in favour of the coherence and integrity of the internal law of any international organisation. Cf. Curtin and Dekker 1999, 89–90; Amerasinghe 2005, 24–65.

[24] Cf. Bast 2005, albeit in relation to the failed Constitutional Treaty. See also Trüe 2004, 410.

[25] For a powerful argument to this effect, see Denza 2004.

[26] Treaty on the Functioning of the European Union, Article 2.

[27] Treaty on the European Union, Article 24(1).

[28] Treaty on the European Union, Article 40.

[29] Koutrakos 2008, 669. See also Streinz 2005, 116–117; Karolewski 2005, 1657; Thym 2009, 336. On the initial workings of the Member State Council Presidencies immediately after the entry into force of Lisbon, see Morillas (this volume).

[30] For further on this point insofar as the new structure can be said to retain a system of 'deliberative intergovernmentalism', see Puetter (this volume).

Second, the express definition of the EU's competence in the field of foreign policy under Article 24 TEU contrasts starkly with the lack of concern, even indifference, with which the Member States have treated this question in the past. Indeed, before the entry into force of the Lisbon Treaty, one well-placed commentator has gone as far as to suggest that the CFSP '[did] not have the Community law principle of conferral of powers (*compétence d'attribution*)'.[31] Although technically not entirely correct, the notion that the CFSP did not involve a conferral of power onto the Union underlines that before the Lisbon Treaty, few have thought about the CFSP in terms of a competence.

The present chapter addresses this latter question and seeks to explain, first, why the Member States saw no need to define the EU's competence over the CFSP in express terms until the treaty reform process launched by the Laeken European Council 2001 and, second, what prompted them to change course. This chapter develops an answer with reference to International Relations scholarship on new institutionalism. Section 4.2 sets out the framework for analysis by developing two key concepts used in this chapter: legalisation and organisational development. Section 4.3 applies these concepts to the evolution of European foreign policy cooperation, while Sect. 4.4 studies the reform process that led to the adoption of the Treaty of Lisbon. Finally, Sect. 4.5 sets out the conclusions.

4.2 A Framework for Analysis

4.2.1 The Promise of New Institutionalism

It has often been pointed out that European foreign policy cooperation has developed in an incremental fashion.[32] In what has become an influential account of this process, Michael E. Smith has suggested that the evolution of European foreign policy is best explained in terms of the progressive institutionalisation of cooperation between the Member States.[33] According to Smith, a two-fold process was at work here. European Political Cooperation (EPC), the predecessor of the CFSP, provided the Member States with a framework for the articulation of functional goals and behavioural norms, that is a framework for institutionalisation,[34] which in turn prompted them to engage in closer cooperation in a way that reinforced the underlying process of institutionalisation. In essence, the Member

---

[31] Gosalbo Bono 2006, 393. This view is not an isolated one: see also Thym 2009, 337 and Görlitz 2004, who suggests that the EU enjoyed no competences in CFSP because of its lacking legal personality (369–370).

[32] For example, Koutrakos 2001, 15.

[33] See Smith 2001b and, more extensively, Smith 2004.

[34] Smith 2004, 38–39.

States entered into a virtuous circle where institutionalisation not only sustained their cooperation over time, but also drove its gradual expansion.

This account of the development of European foreign policy cooperation relies on what is known as new institutionalism in the social sciences. New institutionalism spans across a range of disciplines and comes in a variety of shapes and flavours.[35] In the field of International Relations, what unites the different strands of institutionalism and sets them apart from other theories, such as realism,[36] is their shared belief that institutions have a profound effect on the behaviour of states and therefore constitute an important aspect of International Relations which merits detailed study.[37]

For lawyers, in particular international lawyers, this premise has obvious appeal.[38] Most lawyers will share institutionalism's positive assessment of the impact of international institutions on state behaviour and their significance as a means for regulating international relations.[39] Even more so, considering that institutionalism and legal thought are concerned with broadly the same subject matter. As Stephen D. Krasner points out, the institutionalist perspective assumes that certain behavioural patterns, roles and rules exist over time and that these patterns structure human interaction.[40] Given this perspective, it is not surprising to find that many if not most brands of institutionalism adopt a decidedly normative or rule-based understanding of institutions.[41] Political scientists, for instance, have described institutions as 'rules and practices which are socially constructed, publicly known, anticipated and accepted',[42] while sociologists have defined institutionalisation as 'the processes by which social processes, obligations, or actualities come to take on a rule-like status in social thought and action'.[43] Referring to International Relations scholarship, Simmons and Martin note that 'most scholars have come to regard international institutions as sets of

[35] See March and Olsen 1984; Hall and Taylor 1996 ; Lowndes 1996 for some general overviews of the field.

[36] For realist responses to institutionalism, see Grieco 1988; Mearsheimer 1994.

[37] Generally, see Keohane 1982.

[38] On the conceptual affinities between institutionalism and international law, see Slaughter Burley 1993, especially 217–222.

[39] Henkin 1979; Kennedy 1986–1987; Koskenniemi 2002.

[40] Krasner 2009, 95–96.

[41] For the purposes of this chapter, the term norm covers both legal and non-legal rules. The different schools of institutionalism do not adopt a single approach in this regard. In particular, rational choice institutionalism focuses on rules, whereas constructivism operates with a broader understanding of norms: see Duffield 2007, 4–7. On the related concept of international regimes, see Hasenclever et al. 1997, 8–22.

[42] March and Olsen 1984, 249.

[43] Meyer and Rowan 1977, 341. Cf. Young 1982, who defines the 'conjunction of convergent expectations and patterns of behavior or practice' as the distinguishing feature of all social institutions (278).

rules meant to govern international behavior'.[44] The definition offered by Robert O. Keohane, who employs the term institution to mean 'related complexes of rules and norms, identifiable in space and time',[45] illustrates the point. In line with these normative approaches, international law itself may be seen as a particular form of social institution,[46] namely one that motivates human behaviour out of a sense of legal obligation,[47] whether at the level of individuals or that of states.[48]

Despite these commonalities, institutionalism suffers from certain ambiguities which undermine its usefulness for the purposes of legal analysis. Even a brief glimpse at the literature demonstrates the extraordinary elasticity of the term institution.[49] At one end, writers such as Hedley Bull define international institutions broadly to include concepts such as 'the balance of power, international law, the diplomatic mechanism, the managerial system of the great powers and war'.[50] Other commentators adopt a narrower understanding, even to the point of equating institutions with international organisations.[51] While all of these definitions still view international institutions from a normative perspective,[52] they evidently adopt very different levels of analysis.[53] For instance, diplomacy, the law of diplomatic relations, the person of the diplomatic agent, diplomatic immunity or even the Vienna Convention on Diplomatic Relations of 1961 could all conceivably be described as institutions. Yet none of this is particularly instructive from the lawyer's point of view. On the contrary, it muddies the waters by masking the distinctions that international law normally draws between diplomacy as a peaceful form of state interaction, the law of diplomatic relations as a field of public international law, the diplomatic agent as a specific state organ benefiting from a certain defined status, diplomatic immunity as a legal principle and the

---

[44] Simmons and Martin 2002, 194.

[45] Keohane 1988, 383. Many similar definitions can be found in the literature. Young 1986, for example, defines institutions as 'recognized practices consisting of easily identifiable roles, coupled with collections of rules or conventions governing relations among the occupants of these roles' (107).

[46] For example, Abbott 2008, 6, describing international law as a 'unique international institution'. In addition, legal concepts within a legal system may be conceived in institutional terms. See MacCormick and Weinberger 1985; Ruiter 1993.

[47] Cf. Hart 1997, 79–99.

[48] On the international level, one may point to the concept of customary international law as a pattern of State behaviour existing over a period of time and followed out of a sense of legal obligation. For a brief account of customary international law, see Müllerson 1997. For more detailed discussions, see Mendelson 1998; Roberts 2001; Kammerhofer 2004; Lepard 2010.

[49] Susan Strange's famous remark that the term regime 'is yet one more woolly concept that is a fertile source of discussion simply because people mean different things when they use it' also applies to the notion of international institutions; Strange 1982, 484–485.

[50] Bull 1995, 71. Similarly, Young 1989 counts among his list of institutions war, the State system and the order of the oceans (33).

[51] For example, Chimni 2004.

[52] Cf. Onuf 2002, 224. See also Haggard and Simmons 1987, 493–496.

[53] Setear 2003–2004, 743.

Vienna Convention as the codification of a 'self-contained regime'[54] of international law.

Trading in well-established terms of art for the more ambiguous concept of an institution offers no analytical benefit. The utility of institutionalism lies elsewhere. International Relations scholars rely on the concept of institutions to explain patterns of global governance over time: institutionalism is essentially concerned with the study of stability and change in international relations.[55] Since the primary concern of legal analysis is to provide an account of the law as it is, legal doctrine is somewhat ill-equipped to explain the evolution of legal norms and must therefore rely on other disciplines, including History and International Relations, for assistance.[56] One of the benefits of relying on institutionalism for the purposes of legal analysis is that doing so offers an opportunity to see law in its historical evolution, to watch it as a movie rather than look at it as a photograph.[57]

4.2.2 Institutions, Rules, Organisations

The foregoing points still leave us with the problem of multiple levels of analysis. To make institutionalism fruitful in the present context, it is necessary to draw certain distinctions. In recent years, a number of writers have sought to develop a richer understanding of norms and their role in sustaining international institutions. For example, in an article published in 1998, Finnemore and Sikkink argued that one of the key differences between norms and institutions is aggregation: 'the norm definition isolates single standards of behavior, whereas institutions emphasize the way in which behavioral rules are structured together and interrelate (a "collection of practices and rules").'[58] Finnemore and Sikkink also differentiated between different types of norms, recalling the distinction commonly drawn in the literature between regulative norms, which impose constraints on behaviour, and constitutive norms, which create new actors, interests or categories of action.[59] Of course, this distinction sounds familiar to students of law well-versed in the writings of H. L. A. Hart: regulatory norms correspond to what Hart called primary rules of law imposing obligations, while constitutive norms correspond to

[54] ICJ, *Case concerning the United States Diplomatic and Consular Staff in Tehran (USA v. Iran)*, (1980) ICJ Rep. 41, para 86.

[55] Yet institutionalism's ability to account for change has not gone without criticism, e.g., Gorges 2001.

[56] For example, Simpson 2004. Similarly, decision about the future development of the law must have recourse to extra-legal considerations, e.g., Higgins 1994, 2–12.

[57] On other uses of international relations theory by international lawyers, see Abbott 1992; Slaughter et al. 1998, 373–378. For a word of caution on the limits of inter-disciplinary rapprochement, see Simmons 2001, 276–278.

[58] Finnemore and Sikkink 1998, 891.

[59] Finnemore and Sikkink 1998, 891. See also Duffield 2007, 6–7.

what he termed secondary rules conferring powers.[60] Building on these ideas, in 2000, a group of scholars introduced the concept of legalisation in a series of articles published in a special issue of *International Organization* devoted to the theme of *Legalization and Word Politics*.[61] They defined their core concept as follows[62]:

> Legalization refers to a particular set of characteristics that institutions may (or may not) possess. These characteristics are defined along three dimensions: obligation, precision, and delegation. *Obligation* means that states or other actors are bound by a rule or commitment or by a set of rules or commitments. Specifically, it means that they are legally bound by a rule or commitment in the sense that their behavior thereunder is subject to scrutiny under the general rules, procedures, and discourse of international law, and often of domestic law as well. *Precision* means that rules unambiguously define the conduct they require, authorize, or proscribe. *Delegation* means that third parties have been granted authority to implement, interpret, and apply the rules; to resolve disputes; and (possibly) to make further rules.[63]

Accordingly, the authors distinguish between weakly legalised and highly legalised international institutions, depending on the degree or extent of legal obligation, precision and delegation they have attained.

In his analysis of European foreign policy cooperation, Michael E. Smith too relies on the concept of legalisation. However, unlike the authors of the *Legalization* issue,[64] he understands legalisation primarily as a process and employs it to explain how mutual expectations of consultation and coordination between the Member States in the context of the EPC have gradually hardened into binding rules of law.[65] Since institutionalisation as a process describes the emergence and consolidation of behavioural standards, while legalisation as a process refers more narrowly to the progressive development and codification of rules of law, it follows that legalisation constitutes one particular form of institutionalisation, as Smith and others have in fact pointed out.[66] However, this presents a methodological challenge in the present context: the fact that European foreign policy cooperation has become institutionalised first and foremost through incremental legalisation means that in this instance the two concepts overlap and depend on the

[60] Hart 1997, 81.

[61] See in particular Abbott et al. 2000. For an earlier account of the concept of legalisation, see Abbott 1998.

[62] For alternative uses of the term legalisation, see Scott et al. 2002, 291–292.

[63] Abbott et al. 2000, 401.

[64] Cf. the criticism on this point by Finnemore and Toope 2001, 750–751.

[65] Smith 2001b; Smith 2004, 117–144. Smith is not the first to study the evolution of international norms from an institutionalist perspective, see Finnemore and Sikkink 1998, 894–909.

[66] Abbott 1998, 59; Smith 2001b, 82.

same variables.[67] This is more of a problem for International Relations scholars than international lawyers, though. Given that the concept of an institution is of limited value to strict legal analysis,[68] it is immaterial whether European foreign policy cooperation is characterised as an institution, a regime,[69] a practice or a policy area for these purposes. The critical concept is that of legalisation.[70]

Broadly speaking, legalisation conceived as a process refers to the increasing legal density of a set of norms. In this sense, comparing the same set of norms at different points in time using the three variables proposed by the authors of the *Legalization* issue, namely obligation, precision and delegation, should provide a fairly detailed picture about the normative evolution of a particular institution, such as European foreign policy cooperation.[71] However, this picture can be brought into even sharper focus by distinguishing between different types of delegation. According to the authors of the *Legalization* issue, delegation measures the extent to which states have empowered third parties to 'implement, interpret, and apply the rules; to resolve disputes; and (possibly) to make further rules.'[72] Evidently, this is a rather broad unit of measurement which pays no attention to the purpose served by the delegation. In particular, it conflates adjudication with other forms of legal decision-making. Yet there are important differences between, say, the interpretation of an existing rule and the creation of a new one, even if one accepts that judges do not simply apply the law as they find it.[73] Judicial independence is not the same as political autonomy, nor does adjudication serve the same function as the exercise of legislative, executive or administrative responsibilities. Bearing in mind that the primary purpose of judicial bodies is the authoritative settlement of legal disputes and that, consequently, they are concerned with the existence, meaning and application of legal rules, it seems more appropriate to consider their contribution to institutionalisation primarily under the

[67] Cf. Setear 2003–2004, 742–747. This is so partly because legalisation is understood to encompass, at one end, the complete absence of law (Abbott 1998, 59). In other words, legalisation as a process may well start with the emergence of non-legal patterns of behaviour, just like institutionalisation.

[68] Of course, this does not mean that the concept is of no interest at all to international lawyers: for instance, it may be usefully employed to identify and describe consistent patterns of practice which have not attained the status of a rule of customary international law and to distinguish the former from the latter.

[69] For example, Wagner 2003, 37.

[70] For examples of the use of the term in international law scholarship, see Barker 2007; Øhlenschlæger Buhl 2009.

[71] Indeed, adopting such a comparative perspective provides the otherwise potentially abstract notion of precision with concrete meaning. Cf. the remarks by Friedrich Kratochwil in Scott et al. 2002, 297.

[72] Abbott et al. 2000, 401.

[73] As Hart 1997 has eloquently put it, legal rules limit the discretion of judges, although they do not exclude it altogether (147).

heading of obligation and precision,[74] rather than treat it principally or even exclusively as a question of delegation.[75]

Another blind-spot of the delegation concept employed in the *Legalization* issue concerns the constitutive function of delegation.[76] States confer powers onto third parties to varying degrees and the legal effects that such conferrals have on the parties concerned also differ considerably from one case to the other. Significantly, states not only confer powers onto existing international actors, for instance other states,[77] but they also create new legal entities, in particular international organisations, by way of endowing them with certain legal capacities and investing them with rights and responsibilities.[78] Since such new international actors are formally constituted through international legal processes, mostly in the form of an international agreement, the authors of the *Legalization* issue treat the delegation of authority as a variable of legalisation.[79] This makes sense from the narrow perspective of legalisation. However, considering that legalisation is merely an aspect of institutionalisation, it is more appropriate to treat the creation of formal international bodies and organisations as a separate variable of institutionalisation, alongside legalisation. The benefit of this approach is that it emphasises more prominently the possibility that an institution may attain a high degree of legalisation at the level of primary rules of obligation without necessarily achieving a similar measure of organisational identity through the conferral of state powers. In this way, one might describe the conduct of diplomatic relations as a highly legalised institution lacking a formal organisational existence.[80] Distinguishing more sharply between legalisation at the level of primary rules and organisational development at the level of secondary rules by treating them as separate variables

[74] Thus, even Abbott and Snidal 2000 seem to imply that the main purpose of delegating authority to judicial bodies is to achieve greater precision (433).

[75] This is not to deny the relevance of delegation in this context. Clearly, delegation of authority *is* involved in the creation of judicial organs and bodies, in particular where these constitute international organisations in their own right, such as the International Criminal Court. Rather, the point is that such delegation serves the purpose of determining the existence of legal obligations and increasing their precision.

[76] The term is borrowed from Duffield 2007, 12–13.

[77] For example, Lichtenstein's conferral of powers onto Switzerland in relation to the policing of third country nationals: see EComHR, *X and Y v. Switzerland*, App. No. 7289/75 and 7349/76 (1977) 9 D.R. 57, 14 July 1977.

[78] A fine example of such a norm is Treaty on the European Union, Article 1, which provides as follows: 'By this Treaty, the HIGH CONTRACTING PARTIES establish among themselves a EUROPEAN UNION, hereinafter called 'the Union', on which the Member States confer competences to attain objectives they have in common.' See Abbott and Snidal 1998.

[79] Abbott et al. 2000, 415–418.

[80] Care must be taken in choosing the level of analysis. In particular, difficulties arise where organisational development is not confined to a single institution. For example, treating the Coalition Provisional Authority created by the US and the UK in 2003 as the organisational dimension of belligerent occupation conceived as an institution may obscure the fact that the powers of the Authority were not solely derived from the law of armed conflict. See Kaikobad 2005.

should also enable us to better understand the mutual relationship between these two processes and their distinct contribution to institutionalisation.

It is tempting to label the establishment and subsequent growth of international bodies and organisations as a process of institutionalisation, in particular in this context given that the main organs of the EU are known as institutions.[81] In fact, institutionalisation is frequently used in this narrower sense to describe the development of formal international bodies and organisations,[82] including by students of European integration and European foreign policy.[83] However, if the notion of institutionalisation is to serve as a macro-level concept,[84] with legalisation and organisational development serving as variables, such terminological overlaps should be avoided.[85] Accordingly, for present purposes the process of creating international bodies and organisations through the conferral of state powers will be referred to as 'organisational development' or 'organisation' (see Fig. 4.1).[86] Let us now turn to the evolution of European foreign policy cooperation to see how this framework applies in that context.

4.3 The Evolution of European Foreign Policy Cooperation

The desire to create a common European foreign policy has been a recurring theme of European integration.[87] Initial attempts at European foreign policy cooperation after the Second World War were inspired by the supranational idea. In the early 1950s, the Member States of the European Coal and Steel Community made

[81] Treaty on the European Union, Article 13.

[82] For example, Wessel 1996 defines institutionalisation as a process of increasing collaboration leading to the creation of an international organisation (43). See also Bolleyer 2009, who uses institutionalisation as a descriptor for organisational autonomy (23–28). These terminological dilemmas are not new. The words international organisation and institution have been used more or less interchangeably for some time. See Potter 1945; Kratochwil and Ruggie 1986, 754–763.

[83] Rieber 1976 refers to the 'institutionalization of policy formulation' through the European Council (225); Philippart 2003 mentions the deliberate 'non-institutionalization' of political dialogue (202); Juncos and Reynolds 2007 suggest that the creation of the Political and Security Committee brought about 'the greater institutionalization of European foreign and security policy' (147); while Blockmans and Wessel 2009 describe permanent structured cooperation under Treaty on the European Union, Article 42(6) as a form of institutionalisation (303). See also Smith 2001a; Duke 2008.

[84] Cf. Stone Sweet et al. 2001, 7.

[85] Oran Young has thus distinguished sharply between institutions/regimes on the one hand and formal organisations on the other: see Young 1986, 108; Young 1989, 25–27.

[86] Although it is not necessary to measure organisational development for the purposes of the present article, one convenient way of doing so would be to rely on the tripartite typology of conferrals of power by States onto international organisations developed by Sarooshi 2005.

[87] For a brief overview of this chapter of European integration, see Keukeleire and MacNaughtan 2008, 35–64; Bindi 2010. For a more detailed narrative focusing on post-war European security cooperation, see Duke 2000.

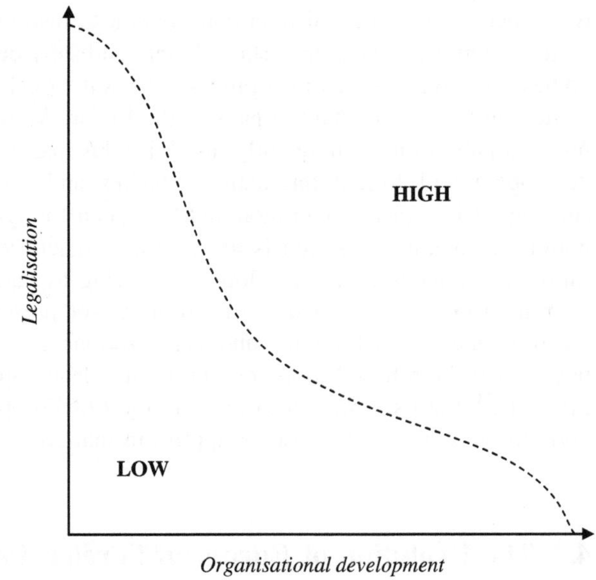

Fig. 4.1 Institutionalisation. The dotted line is meant to symbolise that the dividing line between low and high institutionalisation is not a rigid one. The dip in the middle represents the idea that legalisation and organisational development lead to high institutionalisation more quickly when they occur in conjunction rather than on their own

serious efforts to combine their armed forces under the military authority of a European Defence Community[88] and to establish a European Political Community to provide overall political direction to European integration.[89] However, these grand organisational designs, which would have seen the transfer of significant military and political powers onto the international level,[90] failed to muster sufficient support and did not bear fruit.[91] French initiatives in the early 1960s to develop a common foreign policy along more intergovernmental lines suffered a similar fate.[92] Thus, it was not before 1970 that the Member States finally agreed to cooperate in the field of foreign policy by launching the EPC.

4.3.1 European Political Cooperation

Until its codification in 1987, the EPC consisted of a set of informal rules and arrangements designed to ensure regular consultation and coordination between the Member States on matters of common interest in the field of foreign policy.[93]

---

[88] On the background and institutional features of the EDC, see Fursdon 1980; Ruane 2000.

[89] Griffiths 2000.

[90] See Berthold 2003; Bindschedler 1954, 263–331.

[91] For a detailed account of the domestic and international processes leading to the failure of the EDC and the EPC, see Lerner and Aron 1957; Noack 1977.

[92] Silj 1967. See also Wood 1977–1978.

[93] Among the extensive literature on the EPC, see Nuttall 1992; Gröne 1993.

To preserve its intergovernmental character, the Member States conducted the EPC outside the legal and institutional framework of the European Economic Community (EEC), emphasising that their cooperation was 'distinct from and additional to the activities of the institutions of the Community which are based on the juridical commitments undertaken by the member states in the Treaty of Rome.'[94] Nor did the Member States provide the EPC with any decision-making organs of its own.[95] The EPC thus lacked an independent corporate identity and remained, in the words of one of its practitioners, 'essentially an exercise in co-operation among sovereign governments'.[96] Whereas initially the Member States insisted on the strict separation of EPC and EEC business,[97] in practice they soon began to discuss foreign policy matters in the margins of the meetings of the EEC Council and started to utilise the powers and legal instruments of the Community to support the policies pursued in the context of the EPC, in particular through the adoption of economic sanctions.[98]

The Single European Act (SEA), which in 1987 provided the EPC with a treaty basis in the form of Article 30 SEA,[99] amplified these tendencies. Whereas early proposals aimed to codify the rules governing the EPC in a separate treaty, the Member States eventually decided to combine the draft provisions on the EPC and the draft provisions amending the Community Treaties they negotiated separately as two distinct parts of a single text.[100] This arrangement was something of a diplomatic masterstroke. On the one hand, concluding a single treaty enabled the Member States to emphasise that the EPC and the Communities served the same objective of contributing towards the establishment of a European Union.[101] To enhance the relationship between the EPC and the EEC, Article 30 SEA provided for the association of the European Commission and the European Parliament with the process of the EPC,[102] declared that the EPC and the external policies of the EEC had to be consistent[103] and conceded that the Council of the EEC could serve as a setting for meetings between the representatives of the Member States on EPC matters.[104] On the other hand, providing Article 30 SEA with its own distinct treaty section in the guise of Title III of the SEA allowed the

[94] Second Report of the Foreign Ministers to the Heads of State and Government of the Member States of the European Community (The Copenhagen Report), Copenhagen, 23 July 1973. In Hill and Smith 2000, 88.

[95] Stein 1983, 52.

[96] Hurd 1981, 386.

[97] See Ifestos 1987, 50.

[98] Holland 1991. More generally, see Nuttall 1987.

[99] Nuttall 1986.

[100] Lak 1989, 287–293. The structure of the SEA thus foreshadowed the pillar structure of the TEU (cf., Nutall 1986, 289).

[101] Single European Act, preamble paras 1 and 2 and Article 1.

[102] Single European Act, Articles 30(3)(b) and 30(4).

[103] Single European Act, Article 30(5).

[104] Single European Act, Article 30(3)(a).

Member States to detach the rules governing the EPC from the rest of the SEA and thereby preserve their legal character as rules of international, as opposed to Community, law.[105] The Preamble of the SEA further underlined this difference by distinguishing between the 'Communities operating in accordance with *their own rules*' and 'European Cooperation among the Signatory States in the sphere of foreign policy'.[106] As if to be on the safe side, the Member States concluded the provisions on the EPC in their capacity as High Contracting Parties, rather than as Member States of the EEC, and explicitly excluded the jurisdiction of the European Court of Justice (ECJ) from the EPC.[107]

Overall, Article 30 SEA initiated closer links between the EPC and the EEC on the organisational level, paving the way for the creation of a single institutional framework under the Maastricht Treaty several years later, but set the legalisation of European foreign policy cooperation on a trajectory of specificity. It is notable that even this limited involvement of the Community institutions in foreign policy matters prompted the Member States to address the scope of their powers under the EPC. The second subparagraph of Article 30(5) SEA entrusted the Presidency and the Commission with special responsibility to maintain consistency, but insisted that each should do so 'within its own sphere of competence'. Article 3 SEA, which formed part of the SEA's common provisions applicable both to the Community and the EPC, laid down a more general principle by declaring that '[t]he institutions and bodies responsible for [the EPC] shall exercise their powers and jurisdiction under the conditions and for the purposes laid down in Title III'. A closer look at Article 3 SEA shows that it was not an enabling provision: Its purpose was not to confer any substantive competences upon the institutions and bodies responsible for the EPC, but simply to limit the exercise of their powers to the terms of Article 30 SEA.[108] Despite strengthening the organisational aspects of the EPC, including through the creation of a permanent secretariat to provide greater policy continuity,[109] the Member States did not in fact confer any independent decision-making powers upon the institutions and bodies involved in the implementation of the EPC and consequently remained its sole legal actors.[110] Accordingly, Article 3 SEA is best understood as a safeguard provision adopted *ex abundanti cautela* and aimed at preserving the *status quo*: the minimal involvement of the Community institutions in the EPC and its normative character as a regime of international law.

---

[105] While some have questioned the legal quality of the Single European Act, Article 30, e.g., Ifestos 1987, 56–57, the limited nature of the commitments undertaken by the Member States should not detract from the fact that they were still legal commitments under international law. Cf. Dehousse and Weiler 1991.

[106] Preamble para 2 (emphasis added).

[107] Single European Act, Article 31. See Murphy 1989, 349–351.

[108] In other words, the Single European Act, Article 3 recalled the principle of conferral (see Treaty on the European Union, Article 5) whereby the competences of the institutions are limited to those powers which have been conferred upon them.

[109] de Costa Pereira 1988.

[110] See also Gosalbo Bono 2006, 339–340.

4.3.2 The Common Foreign and Security Policy

The launch of the Common Foreign and Security Policy (CFSP), which replaced the EPC in 1993, marked a milestone in the institutionalisation of European foreign policy cooperation.[111] Whereas under the EPC, the role of the Community institutions was confined to facilitating intergovernmental decision-making,[112] Title V of the Treaty on European Union adopted at Maastricht now entrusted the Council with various responsibilities in relation to the CFSP,[113] including the authority to adopt legally binding decisions.[114] As a result, the Council no longer served simply as a convenient institutional backdrop for the meetings of national representatives, but for the first time assumed an independent institutional role in the formulation of European foreign policy alongside the Member States.[115] Contrary to what has been suggested by some commentators,[116] the Council's newfound role clearly entailed a conferral of power by the Member States. This conclusion neither implies nor requires that the EU should have been a subject of international law itself: states may authorise entities or individuals to act on their behalf in the context of an agency relationship[117] even where these entities or individuals have no independent status under international law.[118] Consequently, nothing prevented the Member States from authorising the Council to assist them in the formulation of common policies and to adopt the necessary decisions in this regard, even if the EU was not, to use the words of the German Constitutional Court, a bearer of proper organisational competences itself.[119]

The Council's empowerment to act on behalf of the Member States represented an important landmark in the evolution of European foreign policy cooperation not only because it ushered in a new phase of formal organisational development, but also because by adopting hundreds of acts pursuant to the powers conferred upon it, the Council over the coming years created a dense web of legal rules governing the

---

[111] On the legal framework of the CFSP under Maastricht, see Edwards 1993; Fink-Hooijer 1994; Jürgens 1994.

[112] See Bonvicini 1988, 53–59.

[113] Murphy 1998, 885–886.

[114] Treaty on European Union (Maastricht) Articles J.2(2), J.3(1), J.8(2) and J.11(2).

[115] Cf. Jürgens 1994, 353.

[116] See *supra* note 31.

[117] See Sereni 1940.

[118] The appointment of arbitrators and expert committees provides one example; see for example, Exchange of Letters between the Government of New Zealand and the Government of France concerning the Implementation of the Ruling of 6 July 1986 by the Secretary-General of the United Nations Pertaining to the Differences between the two Government Arising from the *Rainbow Warrior* Affair, 9 July 1986, (1990) XIX RIAA 216.

[119] *Maastricht-Urteil* (1993) BVerfGE 89, 155, 195. See also Pechstein 1996.

activities of the Union and the Member States in this area.[120] The conferral of decision-making powers upon the Council thus significantly increased the intensity of the CFSP's legalisation. In addition, the Maastricht Treaty also tightened the treaty framework, among other things by imposing stricter obligations on the Member States[121] and by defining in more detail the procedures governing the implementation of the CFSP.[122] Notwithstanding these steps towards increased legalisation, the Member States' enthusiasm for more obligation and precision stopped short at integrating the CFSP into the Community legal order. Instead, they decided to maintain the separation between the CFSP and Community law in the form of the EU's pillar structure, which moreover enabled them to exclude the CFSP provisions from the jurisdiction of the ECJ.[123] The Maastricht Treaty thus continued along the lines drawn by the SEA: it relied on the institutional structure of the Community to strengthen the organisational dimension of European foreign policy cooperation, but increased its legal density in a way that preserved its legal specificity.[124]

The Treaty of Amsterdam, which entered into force in 1999, completely recast Title V of the TEU.[125] Although at the time of their adoption these changes were perceived to be modest at best and insufficient at worst,[126] their long-term impact has turned out to be rather more significant. On the organisational side, the Amsterdam Treaty authorised a second institution, the European Council, to adopt legally binding acts in the context of the CFSP and created the post of the High Representative to improve the CFSP's external representation.[127] It also expressly authorised the Council to enter into international agreements with third parties in the implementation of the CFSP,[128] although doubts remained whether the Council was meant to conclude these agreements on behalf of the Member States or on behalf of the EU as an independent legal person.[129] On the legalisation front, the Amsterdam Treaty increased both the obligation and precision dimensions of the treaty framework by distinguishing more clearly between the legal instruments of the CFSP, by introducing a new measure, common strategies, in order to increase

---

120 Many of these legal acts imposed what were earlier termed regulatory norms. Other acts, in particular joint actions, provided a framework for collective action and played an enabling rather than constraining role. For more details on this function of joint actions, see Sari 2011.

121 Pescatore 1987 dismissed the commitments undertaken by the Member States in the Single European Act, Article 30 as pretentious and coming close to ridicule (16). Compared to the mainly hortatory language of the Single European Act, Article 30, the Maastricht provisions on CFSP imposed more tangible and more precisely formulated obligations on the Member States. See Denza 2002, 55.

122 Treaty on European Union (Maastricht) Articles J.2 and J.3.

123 Treaty on European Union (Maastricht) Article L.

124 Of course, this dualism did little to clarify the legal status of the EU: see Sari 2008, 71–73.

125 See Monar 1997; Dashwood 1998b; Langrish 1998 for analysis.

126 'Some small steps in the right direction' was the verdict of Dehousse 1998, 530.

127 Treaty on European Union (post-Amsterdam) Articles 13(2) and 18(3).

128 Treaty on European Union (post-Amsterdam) Article 24.

129 See Sari 2008, 73–80, with further references.

the coherence of the Union's external activities[130] and by gathering the decision-making procedures of the CFSP into a single provision.[131] It also included the development of a common defence policy within the scope of the CFSP and incorporated the so-called Petersberg Tasks to indicate what kind of operations may be undertaken in the context of that policy.[132]

Looking at these amendments it is striking, at least with the benefit of hindsight, just how critical a role the Amsterdam Treaty has played in enabling the EU to raise its international profile over the last decade. While the Treaty of Nice has made certain adjustments to Title V of the TEU in 2003,[133] these largely technical changes were far eclipsed by the policy developments initiated by the Amsterdam Treaty, in particular the launch of the European Security and Defence Policy (ESDP) in 1999.[134] To bolster the EU's operational capabilities, the Member States created various bodies and agencies within the framework of the EU so as to enable it to conduct crisis management operations in third countries using military and civilian assets. In doing so, the Member States conferred additional powers onto the organs of the CFSP. For example, they authorised the Political and Security Committee to 'exercise, under the responsibility of the Council, political control and strategic direction of crisis management operations.'[135] The launch of the ESDP has also had a very significant impact on the EU as a formal international organisation: the Council's extensive treaty practice in this area since 2003 is widely understood to have confirmed the Union as an independent subject of international law even before the Lisbon Treaty recognised the EU as a legal person in express terms.[136]

4.3.3 Sovereignty Costs, Equilibrium and the Goldilocks Principle

Returning to the analytical framework sketched earlier, the first point to note is that the institutionalisation of European foreign policy cooperation took place in three stages. The process began in the early 1970s with the formulation and subsequent

---

130 Treaty on European Union (post-Amsterdam) Article 13(2).

131 Treaty on European Union (post-Amsterdam) Article 23.

132 Treaty on European Union (post-Amsterdam) Article 17. See Grassi 1998; Pagani 1998.

133 Amongst other things, the Treaty of Nice increased the scope of qualified majority voting (Treaty on European Union (post-Nice) Article 23), revised the procedure governing the conclusion of international agreements (Treaty on European Union (post-Nice) Article 24) and introduced enhanced cooperation into the CFSP (Treaty on European Union (post-Nice) Articles 27a–27e).

134 On the ESDP and its contribution to the EU's international identity, see Salmon and Shepherd 2003; Anand 2009. The founding document of the ESDP, the Anglo-French Declaration of St. Malo, specifically notes that enabling the EU to play its full role on the international stage 'means making a reality of the Treaty of Amsterdam, which will provide the essential basis for action by the Union.' See Rutten 2001, 8.

135 Treaty on European Union (post-Nice) Article 25.

136 In addition to the literature cited *supra* note 6, see Verwey 2004, 60–61; Sari 2008, 80–82.

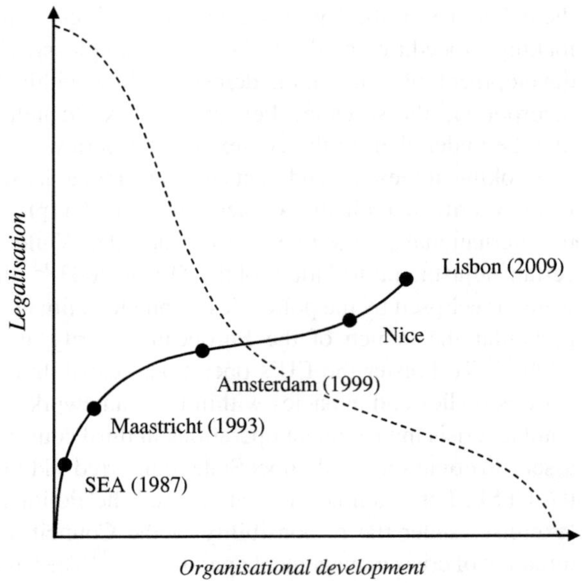

Fig. 4.2 The institutionalisation of European foreign policy cooperation

legalisation of a set of commitments undertaken by the Member States. Although the EPC soon shed its exclusively intergovernmental character when two non-state actors, the Council and the Commission, began to participate in the policy process in an auxiliary role, the organisational development of European foreign policy cooperation nevertheless remained modest at this stage, since the relevant bodies enjoyed no independent powers of their own. This changed with the entry into force of the Maastricht Treaty, when European foreign policy cooperation entered a phase of formal organisational growth with the creation of the CFSP and the express conferral of decision-making powers onto the Council. Finally, the amendments introduced by the Amsterdam Treaty brought the growth of legalisation and organisational development into line and paved the way for a rapid expansion on both fronts. Figure 4.2 charts this process and shows how legalisation and organisational development have promoted increased institutionalisation at different speeds over time.

Second, legalisation and organisational development are mutually reinforcing processes: their interaction has visibly increased the pace, intensity and complexity of the institutionalisation of European foreign policy cooperation. In line with the responsibilities assigned to it by the Maastricht Treaty, the Council has served as the engine for continued legalisation by adopting secondary acts on the basis of the Treaty. In doing so, the Council not only imposed new obligations on the Member States, but it also increased the precision of the treaty framework by giving concrete meaning to its often hortatory provisions.[137] Moreover, the refinement of the

[137] Cf. Koskenniemi 1998, 28–29.

treaty framework at Amsterdam, particularly in the area of defence policy, permitted the Council to achieve further organisational growth by adopting a series of legal acts creating several new bodies for the purposes of the ESDP. Accordingly, we witness an almost cyclical relationship between increased legalisation and organisational development, oscillating between primary law and secondary law.

Third, treating legalisation and organisational development as two distinct variables has also revealed that the institutionalisation of European foreign policy cooperation proceeded along two separate tracks: *specificity* in the case of legalisation, as reflected in Article 30 SEA and the pillar structure subsequently established by the Maastricht Treaty, and *unity* in the case of organisational development, as reflected in the concept of the single institutional framework of the EU. The reason for this twin-track approach becomes obvious when considering its theoretical alternatives: complete isolation from the Community legal order or full integration with it. On one hand, turning the initial separation of the EPC from the EC into a permanent feature of European foreign policy cooperation was never going to be a viable long-term option. Not only was the EPC intended as a contribution to European integration from the very start,[138] but the failure to adequately resource the EPC left the Member States with no alternative but to turn to the EC to provide the EPC with teeth. On the other hand, integrating European foreign policy cooperation fully into the Community legal order would have meant endowing the Community institutions, including the Commission, the European Parliament and the ECJ, with various powers and responsibilities in relation to the EPC, something that the majority of Member States were not prepared to do.

The twin-track approach of institutionalisation essentially allowed the Member States to steer a middle course: unity in organisational development provided them with a platform for cooperation and access to resources, while specificity in legalisation permitted them to avoid the sovereignty costs associated with Community law.[139] Faced with the need to cooperate in order to preserve their independence on the international stage, but also the realisation that increased cooperation implied a certain loss of that very independence, this twin-track approach enabled the Member States to maintain a suitable equilibrium between independence and cooperation. The institutionalisation of European foreign policy cooperation is therefore governed by what we may call the Goldilocks Principle of Institutional Design: not too much, not too little, but just right.

Finally, the foregoing also explains why the extent and nature of the EU's competence in the field of foreign policy was not a question of critical importance to the Member States, or indeed to anyone else it seems, before the Treaty of Lisbon. While the CFSP saw the transfer of significant powers upon the Council and the gradual emergence of the EU as a separate legal actor in the field of foreign

[138] See Communiqué of the Conference of the Heads of State and Government of the Member States of the European Community (The Hague Summit Declaration), The Hague, 2 December 1969. In Hill and Smith 2000, 72.

[139] The term sovereignty costs in this context refers to the loss of decision-making autonomy experienced by states as a result of institutionalisation, see Abbott and Snidal 2000, esp. 436–441.

policy and security matters, the Member States were careful to retain control over the CFSP both collectively and individually: only the intergovernmental institutions of the EU, namely the Council and the European Council, were empowered to adopt binding acts,[140] while the principle of unanimity as the prevailing mode of decision-making and the right to veto decisions taken by qualified majority voting safeguarded the interests of the individual Member States.[141] Despite the politically sensitive nature of the CFSP, the risks associated with organisational development in this area remained relatively low, since the formulation of new substantive policies required the approval of the Member States. The price of disagreement among the Member States was simply no new substantive policy.[142] The exclusion of the ECJ also meant that the sanctions for non-compliance with already agreed policies were political, not legal, in character and that further legalisation through the jurisprudence of the Community courts was excluded.[143]

The development of the EPC and the CFSP until the Lisbon Treaty therefore suggests that the progressive institutionalisation of European foreign policy cooperation through the organisational structure of the Community was possible only because legalisation had already taken a separate path of specificity distinct from Community law. It is precisely for these reasons that the nature and extent of the conferral of competences upon the EU in the context of the CFSP was not a particularly contentious matter during this period. Rather, discussions revolved around the procedures governing decision-making, in particular the use of qualified majority voting.[144] What, then, prompted the Member States to address the question of CFSP competence in the Lisbon Treaty?

4.4 The Treaty Reform Process

In their Declaration on the Future of the Union adopted on 26 February 2001 at Nice, the representatives of the Member States called for a 'deeper and wider debate about the future of the European Union' as a way to prepare a new

[140] In this respect, it is important to note that organs such as the High Representative exercise their functions under the authority, and thus control, of the Council. Cf. Craig 2005, 431–432.

[141] Treaty on European Union (Maastricht) Article J.8(2); Treaty on European Union (post-Amsterdam) Article 23; Treaty on European Union (post-Nice) Article 23.

[142] For example, on Yugoslavia, Salmon 1992; on the Leila/Perejil Island incident, Monar 2002; on Iraq, Roloff 2006.

[143] On the jurisdiction of the ECJ after the Treaty of Lisbon, see Brkan (this volume). Although breaches by the Member States of their obligations under Title V may give rise to their international responsibility, it would be quite exceptional for another Member State to invoke that responsibility in the context of formal legal proceedings, whether before the Court of Justice or another judicial body.

[144] For example, Gourlay and Remacle 1998, 60 et seq.

intergovernmental conference convened to tackle some of the legal and political questions left unresolved by the Nice Treaty.[145] Although not phrased in constitutional terms, the Nice Declaration was widely perceived as an invitation to launch a constitutional debate about the Union's future,[146] not at least because one of the key questions it posed for debate was the more precise delimitation of powers between the EU and its Member States.[147] The Laeken Declaration on the Future of the Union subsequently adopted by the European Council on 15 December 2001 confirmed the importance of this question when it placed the better division and definition of competences high on the agenda of the European Convention convened to consider the Union's ongoing development.[148] The effect of these decisions was to focus attention on the nature and extent of the EU's competence in the field of the CFSP.

4.4.1 The European Convention

Early discussions in the European Convention revealed a broad consensus among its members on the need to clarify the system of Union competences, but also that such a clarification should neither extensively modify the existing system nor lead to the establishment of a positive or negative list of competences.[149] In this, the Convention faithfully followed the limited mandate laid down by the European Council in its Laeken Declaration, which called for the clarification, simplification and possible adjustment of the Union's competences whilst respecting the *acquis communautaire*.[150] The Convention's task therefore was primarily one of clarification and improvement, rather than a fundamental realignment of the political order of the EU.[151]

A closer analysis of the specific questions posed by the Laeken Declaration regarding the division of competences suggest that the European Council's

---

[145] Declaration on the Future of the Union, Final Act, Treaty of Nice, OJ [2001] C80/85.

[146] Cf. de Witte 2001.

[147] This call for a better division of competences was taken up enthusiastically by key players. See Mayer 2001, 626–631.

[148] Laeken Declaration on the Future of the Union, Annex I to Presidency conclusions, Laeken, 14 and 15 December 2001, 4–5. See Götz 2002, 83–85.

[149] Note on the plenary meeting—Brussels, 15 and 16 April 2002, 25 April 2002, CONV 40/02 5–6; Note on the plenary meeting—Brussels, 23 and 24 May 2002, 29 May 2002, CONV 60/02, para 7. See Ritzer 2006, 133 et seq.

[150] Laeken Declaration on the Future of the European Union, Annex I to the Presidency Conclusions, Laeken, 14 and 15 December 2001. See Nettesheim 2004, 526.

[151] Craig 2004, 325; Nettesheim 2004, 512–514. This partly explains why the delimitation of competences was not considered in a working group dedicated solely to this question.

primary concern lied with the delimitation of powers between the Community and the Member States.[152] The problems identified by the European Council—the overall lack of clarity in the division of authority, the wide-spread feeling that the Union has acquired a greater share of powers than was strictly necessary and the need to close the door on the creeping expansion of its competences—were all problems of the Community legal order, rather than of the CFSP.[153] Nevertheless, it is clear from the Laeken Declaration that the European Council had no intention to exclude the CFSP from the competence debate. On the contrary, the Declaration in fact held up the development of a more coherent common foreign and defence policies as one example for the possible reallocation of powers between the EU and the Member States.[154] Although it did not express a preference for extending the Union's competences in the field of the CFSP, the fact that the European Council queried whether a reallocation of competences may be required to achieve greater policy coherence is noteworthy, as this could have opened the way for more wide-ranging discussions about the legal nature and scope of the CFSP, and thus more radical reform proposals,[155] than what the limited mandated laid down in the Laeken Declaration seemed to envisage.[156]

Reading the Laeken Declaration, it is notable that the European Council consistently but rather loosely referred to the EU's competences in general terms, without distinguishing between the powers of the Community and those of the Union.[157] This lax approach led the European Convention to study the question of competences from a global perspective, covering all aspects of the Union's activities. This is apparent from the deliberations of the Working Group on Complementary Competences. Although strictly speaking this was not part of

[152] Specifically, the Laeken Declaration asked three sets of questions: how the current division of competences could be made more transparent, whether the existing competences needed to be reorganised whilst respecting the *acquis communautaire* and how to ensure that a redefined division of competence did not lead to a creeping expansion of the Union's powers.

[153] Craig 2004; Nettesheim 2004, 514–525. On the question of Community competences and their reform more generally, see Dashwood 1996; von Bogdandy and Bast 2002; Trüe 2004.

[154] Laeken Declaration on the Future of the European Union, 5. In this respect, the European Council asked whether the Petersberg Tasks listed in Article 17 TEU-Nice should be updated. This was a peculiar question to ask in the context of a possible re-allocation of competences, given that the crisis management tasks listed in that provision were merely indicative of the type of operations the EU was competent to undertake within the scope of its common security and defence policy. As von Kielmansegg 2007 suggests, the original Petersberg Tasks offered an important insight into Union competence in this field, but they did not exhaustively define the material scope of that competence (647).

[155] For instance, providing the EU with exclusive competence in the field of foreign policy could resolve most of the vertical and horizontal coherence problems experienced in the past. However, this solution is clearly not politically viable.

[156] Cf. Götz 2002, who notes that this question expanded the scope of the previous competence debate (95).

[157] Bearing in mind that the European Council did so whilst calling for greater clarity and transparency, some may sense a certain irony here.

its mandate,[158] the Working Group recommended that the future treaty should contain a separate title dealing with all competence matters. The purpose of this title would be to define the main types of competence, delimit the powers between the Union and the Member States in each policy area and identify the conditions governing their exercise.[159] Concerning the different types of competence, the Working Group distinguished between supporting measures, exclusive competence and shared competence, although interestingly it declined to express a view as to which heading the CFSP should fall under. While the Working Group's motives for refusing to classify the CFSP within its typology of competences are not particularly persuasive,[160] both its work and the deliberations in the Plenary show that it was considered self-evident by members of the Convention that the review of the delimitation of EU competences should include the CFSP.

This became practically inevitable with the acceptance of the proposal to merge the legal personalities of the EU and the European Communities. As the report of the Working Group on Legal Personality made clear, the logical consequence of merging these distinct legal personalities was the merger of the founding treaties into a single document, in particular as this was seen to serve the aim of simplification.[161] Once the merger of the existing treaties became the horizontal organising principle of the draft treaty to be prepared by the Convention, any comprehensive definition of the Union's competences had to include the CFSP.[162] Thus, the clarification of the Union's competences in the field of the CFSP was driven not by practical necessity, not by the need to resolve any real-life difficulties, but by the logic of the treaty reform process itself: the problem of CFSP competence was thus born during the reform process, not before.

4.4.2 Classifying CFSP Competence

This still left the Convention to grapple with the question of how the EU's competences in this area should be characterised. Given the Laeken Declaration's preoccupation with the traditional competence problems of the Community

[158] The Working Group's mandate was limited to considering questions related to the future of complementary competences. See Mandate of the working group on Complementary Competencies, 31 May 2002, CONV 75/02.

[159] Final report of Working Group V, 4 November 2002, 2. CONV 375/1/02 REV 1.

[160] The Working Group justified its reluctance by suggesting that 'any such classification would greatly depend on a number of policy choices belonging to other fora of the Convention', Final report of Working Group V, 4 November 2002, footnote 3, CONV 375/1/02 REV 1. This makes sense in so far as the Convention may have decided to revise the Union's CFSP competences, yet this clearly is not a valid reason for refusing to consider the nature of those competences *de lege lata*.

[161] Final report of Working Group III on Legal Personality, 1 October 2002, para 14, CONV 375/1/02 REV 1.

[162] Simplification of the Treaties and drawing up of a constitutional treaty, 10 September 2002, CONV 375/1/02 REV 1, 15.

legal order,[163] it is perhaps not surprising to find that the question of Union powers in the CFSP came to be discussed alongside the competences of the Community and in the same analytical terms. Thus, a discussion paper prepared by the Praesidium and circulated in advance of the plenary meeting held on 15 and 16 April 2002 stated that the 'Union/Community' enjoyed three types of legislative competence: 'exclusive, concurrent (or shared) and complementary'.[164] The paper went on to suggest that the Union's powers in the field of the CFSP, with the exception of defence, fell within the category of concurrent or shared competence.[165] The paper defined concurrent competence as follows:

> areas in which Member States may legislate until such time and insofar as the Union/Community has not legislated. Once the Union/Community has legislated in a given area, Member States may no longer do so in the field of Community legislation.[166]

This classification of the CFSP as a form of concurrent competence was repeated in another discussion paper distributed the following month, which declared that '[t]he powers of the Union in the CFSP area are "concurrent" with those of the Member States, except in the case of defence policy (the Petersberg tasks), where they are complementary.'[167]

This categorisation is misguided. For a start, the definition of concurrent competence proposed in the two discussion papers reads like an offhand summary of the *ERTA* line of cases of the European Court of Justice (ECJ),[168] according to which the Member States may not undertake obligations at the international level where doing so would affect 'common rules' adopted by the Community[169] or where those obligations relate to areas which are covered to a large extent by Community rules[170] or are subject to complete harmonisation.[171] More importantly, both discussion

---

163 This was echoed in the work of the Convention: cf. Delimitation of competence between the European Union and the Member States—Existing system, problems and avenues to be explored, 15 May 2002, CONV 47/02, 3–4.

164 Description of the current system for the delimitation of competence between the European Union and the Member States, 28 March 2002, CONV 17/02, 2.

165 Description of the current system for the delimitation of competence between the European Union and the Member States, 28 March 2002, CONV 17/02, 4.

166 Description of the current system for the delimitation of competence between the European Union and the Member States, 28 March 2002, CONV 17/02, 3.

167 Delimitation of competence between the European Union and the Member States—Existing system, problems and avenues to be explored, 15 May 2002, CONV 47/02, 20.

168 On this line of cases, see Koutrakos 2006, 77–134. See also Nettesheim 2009, 423–434. For a critical analysis of the notion of concurrent competence employed in the Treaty Establishing a Constitution for Europe, Article I-12, see Trüe 2004, 415–418.

169 ECJ, Case 22-70, *Commission v. Council (European Agreement on Road Transport)* [1971] ECR 263, para 17.

170 ECJ, Opinion 2/91, *Convention No 170 of the International Labour Organization concerning safety in the use of chemicals at work* [1993] ECR I-1061, para 25.

171 ECJ, Opinion 1/94, *Competence of the Community to conclude international agreements concerning services and the protection of intellectual property* [1994] ECR I-5267, para 96.

papers suggest that the adoption of legal acts by the EU in the area of the CFSP prevents the Member States from exercising their national foreign policy competences. The notion that the CFSP has a pre-emptive effect which renders the EU's competence exclusive as soon as it has exercised its powers under Title V of the TEU displays a remarkable degree of ignorance about the evolution of the legal framework of European foreign policy cooperation; needless to say, this idea finds no support whatsoever either in law or in practice.

Subsequent debates and documents reveal a more nuanced approach. A discussion paper on external action acknowledged that the CFSP operated in accordance with a 'specific legal framework, instruments and procedures' and identified the possible extension of the Community method, in particular the use of qualified majority voting, in this area as a possible question for reflection.[172] During the plenary discussion held on 11 and 12 July 2002, some members blamed the intergovernmental nature of foreign and security policy for its lack of effectiveness and called for the extension of the Community method to this field. These proposals to 'communitarise' the CFSP by subjecting it to the traditional decision-making and legislative procedures of the Community went far beyond the mere simplification and clarification of the Treaties.[173] They entailed a significant departure from the *status quo* and therefore would almost certainly not have commanded the political support of all Member States. Other members stressed the specific character of foreign policy cooperation and suggested that many shortcomings of the CFSP could be attributed to a lack of political will rather than any deficiencies in its instruments or procedures.[174]

Further discussions in the Convention thus led to a compromise: while the majority of members felt that it would have been anachronistic to maintain the pillar structure in the light of the merger of the legal personalities and founding Treaties of the EU and the EC, it was eventually accepted that special procedures should remain in place for the CFSP.[175] The first skeleton draft prepared by the

---

172 EU External Action, 3 July 2002, CONV 161/02, 13.

173 See European Parliament Committee on Constitutional Affairs, A5-0133/2002, Report on the division of competences between the European Union and the Member States (2001/2024(INI)), 24 April 2002, 20; Contribution from Mr Alain Lamassoure, member of the Convention, 14 May 2002, CONV 46/02; WG V—WD 20, Note by Mr Peter Altmaier "The Division of Competencies between the Union and the Member States" (revised version), 4 September 2002, 14; WG VII—WD11, "Promoting the community method in the External actions of the EU"—Paper by Mr Adrian Severin, alternate member of the Convention, 28 October 2002.

174 Summary Report of the Plenary Session—Brussels, 11 and 12 July 2002, 16 July 2002, CONV 200/02.

175 Summary report on the plenary session—Brussels, 3 and 4 October 2002, 11 October 2002, CONV 331/02, 2. In its final report, the Working Group on Legal Personality argued that the pillar structure was not only outdated, but that retaining it was also unnecessary, since 'all the institutional and procedural features specific to the two intergovernmental pillars (CFSP and cooperation in criminal matters) which the Convention considers appropriate to maintain could be preserved in the new constitutional treaty'; Final report of Working Group III on Legal Personality, 1 October 2002, CONV 305/02, 6.

Preasidium setting out the structure of the first part of the future treaty identified CFSP competence as a separate type of competence distinct from the traditional Community competences.[176] The explanatory note attached to a subsequent draft containing the first substantive provisions of the new treaty stated that this was to reflect the specific nature of the Union's powers in that area.[177] This solution later found its way into the final text submitted by European Convention to the European Council in Rome on 18 July 2003[178] and, after yet another round of negotiations, into the Treaty Establishing a Constitution for Europe adopted on 29 October 2004.[179] Article I-12 of the Constitutional Treaty thus distinguished between five different categories of competence: exclusive competence, shared competence, the Union's competence to provide arrangements for the coordination of national economic and employment policies, its competence to define and implement the CFSP and, finally, its competence to carry out actions to support, coordinate or supplement the actions of the Member States.[180] Following the failure of the Constitutional Treaty, the substance of Article I-12 was incorporated into Article 2 of the TFEU, which in its fourth paragraph now singles out the Union's competence to define and implement a common foreign and security policy, including the progressive framing of a common defence policy, as a separate form of EU competence.[181]

4.4.3 Making Sense of Lisbon

A number of commentators have suggested that the separate treatment accorded to CFSP competence under Article 2(4) TFEU means that the Union's competence in this area is best described as *sui generis*.[182] While the drafting history of the Constitutional Treaty certainly bears out this interpretation, characterising CFSP competence as *sui generis* is not particularly helpful in explaining what exactly distinguishes it from other forms of Union competence and, in particular, what the legal consequences of this distinction are. What Article 2(4) TFEU and the drafting history nevertheless do suggest very strongly, and this is also the critical message of the *sui generis* characterisation, is that the legal effects of the exercise of CFSP competences are special. In other words, Article 2(4) TFEU was designed

---

176 Preliminary draft Constitutional Treaty, 28 October 2002, CONV 369/02, 3.

177 Draft of Articles 1–16 of the Constitutional Treaty, 6 February 2003, CONV 528/03, 16.

178 Draft Treaty establishing a Constitution for Europe, 18 July 2003, CONV 850/03.

179 Treaty establishing a Constitution for Europe, OJ [2004] C310/1.

180 For a general assessment of the relevant provisions, see Mayer 2005.

181 The separate treatment of CFSP competence has not escaped criticism, e.g., Nettesheim 2004, 527–528.; Puetter (this volume) and, for an alternative analysis through the lens of 'European Realism', Bendiek (this volume).

182 For example, Cremona 2003, 1354.

to preserve at least some degree of specificity in the legalisation in the CFSP and should therefore be read to rebut the presumption in favour of legal uniformity under the new united legal order of the EU. However, what degree of specificity in fact remains, and where exactly the new equilibrium between independence and cooperation lies after Lisbon, is not immediately clear and requires further study.

4.5 Conclusion

This chapter has suggested that the progressive institutionalisation of European foreign policy cooperation from the 1970s onwards may be explained through the interaction of two mutually reinforcing variables, legalisation and organisational development. Whereas the organisational development of foreign policy cooperation has taken a course of unity with the Community institutional structure, legalisation has developed along a separate path of specificity so as to preserve the CFSP's normative character as a regime of international law. It is this twin-track approach which allowed European foreign policy cooperation to evolve from a purely intergovernmental process of consultation and coordination into a highly institutionalised field of activity over the last four decades. It also explains why the precise delimitation of the EU's competences in the field of the CFSP was not a matter of critical importance to the Member States before the Treaty of Lisbon. Rather, the problem of CFSP competence was born during the treaty reform process itself. Two broader points may be drawn from this analysis, both of which deserve further attention in a different context.

First, as Alan Dashwood has pointed out in an article published in 1998, 'a Union composed of States is condemned to flexibility.'[183] More than a decade later, that observation has lost none of its force: the special treatment accorded to CFSP competence under Article 2(4) TFEU is yet another sign of the continuing search for a balance between independence and cooperation in the field of European foreign policy—what I have called the Goldilocks Principle of Institutional Design. However, considering the extent of the changes introduced by the Lisbon Treaty, as well as the dynamic nature and ever continuing institutionalisation of the CFSP, identifying where that balance lies is becoming more difficult, despite the Member States' good intentions to increase the clarity and transparency of the Treaties. This outcome indicates a need to apply sharper analytical tools to the study of the CFSP than has been done in the past.

Second, the merger of the previously separate legal orders and personalities of the EU and the EC raises the question whether the Treaty of Lisbon still fits the traditional pattern of incrementalism that has characterised the evolution of European foreign policy cooperation over the last four decades. By treating the Union's competence in CFSP as *sui generis*, has the Lisbon Treaty opened the

---

183 Dashwood 1998a, 216.

door to competence creep and thereby possibly enhanced the pace of institutionalisation in this area? If so, is there a tipping point where the sovereignty costs incurred by the Member States in participating in the CFSP outweigh the benefits involved, at least for some of the Member States? Past practice suggests not only that maintaining an appropriate balance between independence and cooperation is key to further integration, but also that it is for the Member States themselves, not the institutions, to determine where that balance lies. Creeping competence may well turn out to be counterproductive.

References

Abbott KW (1992) Elements of a joint discipline. American Society of International Law Proceedings 86:167–175

Abbott KW (1998) The many faces of international legalization. American Society of International Law Proceedings 92:57–63

Abbott KW (2008) Enriching rational choice institutionalism for the study of international law. University of Illinois Law Review 5:5–46

Abbott KW, Snidal D (1998) Why states act through formal international organizations. Journal of Conflict Resolution 42:3–32

Abbott KW, Snidal D (2000) Hard and soft law in international governance. International Organization 54:421–456

Abbott KW et al (2000) The concept of legalization. International Organization 54:401–419

Afionis S (2008–2009) European Union coherence in UNFCCC negotiations under the new Treaty of Lisbon (Reform Treaty). Sustainable Development Law and Policy 9:43–47

Akande D (2006) International organizations. In: Evans MD (ed) International law, 2nd edn. Oxford University Press, Oxford, pp 277–306

Amerasinghe CF (2005) Principles of the institutional law of international organizations, 2nd edn. Cambridge University Press, Cambridge

Anand M (2009) Empowering paradise: the ESDP at ten. International Affairs 85:227–246

Barker JC (2007) The politics of international law-making: constructing security in response to global terrorism. Journal of International Law and International Relations 3:5–30

Bast J (2005) The constitutional treaty as a reflexive constitution. German Law Journal 6: 1433–1452

Bederman DJ (1995–1996) The souls of international organizations: legal personality and the lighthouse at Cape Spartel. Virginia Journal of International Law 36:275–377

Berthold C (2003) Die Europäische Politische Gemeinschaft (EPG) 1953 und die Europäische Union (EU) 2001: Eine rechtsvergleichende Betrachtung. Lang, Frankfurt am Main

Bindi FM (2010) European Union foreign policy: a historical overview. In: Bindi FM (ed) The foreign policy of the European Union: assessing Europe's role in the world. Brookings Institution Press, Washington, pp 13–40

Bindschedler RL (1954) Rechtsfragen der europäischen Einigung: Ein Beitrag zu der Lehre von den Staatenverbindungen. Verlag für Recht und Gesellschaft, Basel

Blockmans S, Wessel RA (2009) The European Union and crisis management: will the Lisbon treaty make the EU more effective? Journal of Conflict and Security Law 14(2):265–308

Bolleyer N (2009) Intergovernmental cooperation: rational choices in federal systems and beyond. Oxford University Press, Oxford

Bonvicini G (1988) Mechanisms and procedures of EPC: More than traditional diplomacy? In: Pijpers AE, Regelsberger E, Wessels W (eds) European Political Cooperation in the 1980s: a common foreign policy for western Europe? Nijhoff, Dordrecht, pp 49–70

Bretherton C, Vogler J (2006) The European Union as a global actor, 2nd edn. Routledge, London
Bribosia H (2007) De la simplification des traités au traité constitutionnel. In: Amato G, Bribosia H, de Witte B (eds) Genèse et destinée de la Constitution européenne/Genesis and destiny of the European constitution. Bruylant, Brussels, pp 187–222
Bull H (1995) The anarchical society: a study of order in world politics, 2nd edn. Macmillan, London
Cameron F (1998) The European Union as a global actor: far from pushing its weight around. In: Rhodes C (ed) The European Union in the world community. Lynne Rienner Publishers, Boulder, pp 19–44
Cannizzaro E (ed) (2002) The European Union as an actor in international relations. Kluwer Law International, The Hague
Chimni BS (2004) International institutions today: an imperial global state in the making. European Journal of International Law 15:1–37
Craig P (2004) Competence: clarity, conferral, containment and consideration. European Law Review 29:323–344
Craig P (2005) European governance: executive and administrative powers under the new constitutional settlement. International Journal of Constitutional Law 3:407–439
Cremona M (1998) The European Union as an international actor: the issues of flexibility and linkage. European Foreign Affairs Review 3:67–94
Cremona M (2003) The draft constitutional treaty: external relations and external action. Common Market Law Review 40:1347–1366
Cremona M (2008) Defining competence in EU external relations: lessons from the treaty reform process. In: Dashwood A, Maresceau M (eds) Law and practice of EU external relations: salient features of a changing landscape. Cambridge University Press, Cambridge, pp 34–69
Curtin DM, Dekker IF (1999) The EU as a 'layered' international organization: institutional unity in disguise. In: Craig P, de Búrca G (eds) The evolution of EU law. Oxford University Press, Oxford, pp 83–136
Dashwood A (1996) The limits of European community powers. European Law Review 21: 113–128
Dashwood A (1998a) States in the European Union. European Law Review 23:201–216
Dashwood A (1998b) External relations provisions of the Amsterdam Treaty. Common Market Law Review 35:1019–1045
de Baere G (2008) Constitutional principles of EU external relations. Oxford University Press, Oxford
de Costa Pereira PS (1988) The uses of Secretariat. In: Pijpers AE, Regelsberger E, Wessels W (eds) European Political Cooperation in the 1980s: a common foreign policy for western Europe? Nijhoff, Dordrecht, pp 85–103
de Witte B (2001) The nice declaration: time for a constitutional treaty of the European Union? International Spectator 36:21–30
de Zwaan JW (1999) The legal personality of the European Communities and the European Union. Netherlands Yearbook of International Law 30:75–113
Dehousse F (1998) After Amsterdam: a report on the common foreign and security policy of the European Union. European Journal of International Law 9:525–539
Dehousse R, Weiler JHH (1991) EPC and the single act: from soft law to hard law? In: Holland M (ed) The future of European Political Cooperation: essays on theory and practice. St. Martin's Press, New York, pp 121–142
Denza E (1999) Two legal orders: divergent or convergent? International and Comparative Law Quarterly 48:257–284
Denza E (2002) The intergovernmental pillars of the European Union. Oxford University Press, Oxford
Denza E (2004) Lines in the sand: between common foreign policy and single foreign policy. In: Tridimas T, Nebbia P (eds) European Union law for the twenty-first century: rethinking the new legal order. Hart, Oxford, pp 259–272

Duffield J (2007) What are international institutions? International Studies Review 9:1–22
Duke S (2000) The elusive quest for European security: from EDC to CFSP. Palgrave, Basingstoke
Duke S (2008) Peculiarities in the institutionalisation of CFSP and ESDP. In: Blockmans S (ed) The European Union and crisis management: policy and legal aspects. T.M.C. Asser, The Hague, pp 75–105
Editorial Comment (2001) The European Union—a new international actor. Common Market Law Review 38:825–828
Edwards G (1993) Common foreign and security policy. Yearbook of European Law 13:497–509
Fink-Hooijer F (1994) The common foreign and security policy of the European Union. European Journal of International Law 5:173–198
Finnemore M, Sikkink K (1998) International norm dynamics and political change. International Organization 52:887–917
Finnemore M, Toope SJ (2001) Alternatives to "legalization": richer views of law and politics. International Organization 55:743–758
Fursdon E (1980) The European defence community: a history. Macmillan, London
Gauttier P (2004) Horizontal coherence and the external competences of the European Union. European Law Journal 10:23–41
Ginsberg RH (1999) Conceptualizing the European Union as an international actor: narrowing the theoretical capability-expectations gap. Journal of Common Market Studies 37:429–454
Gorges MJ (2001) New institutionalist explanations for institutional change: a note of caution. Politics 21:137–145
Görlitz N (2004) Europäischer Verfassungsvertrag und künftige EU-Kompetenzen: Materielle Kompetenzverschiebungen zwischen Europäischer Union und EU-Staaten nach den Vorgaben des Konventsentwurfs eines künftigen EU-Verfassungsvertrags. Die Öffentliche Verwaltung 57:374–383
Gosalbo Bono R (2006) Some reflections on the CFSP legal order. Common Market Law Review 43:337–394
Götz V (2002) Die Abgrenzung der Zuständigkeiten zwischen der Europäischen Union und den Mitgliedstaaten nach dem Europäischen Rat von Laeken. In: Götz V, Martínez Soria J (eds) Kompetenzverteilung zwischen der Europäischen Union und den Mitgliedstaaten. Nomos, Baden–Baden, pp 83–102
Gourlay C, Remacle E (1998) The 1996 IGC: the actors and their interaction. In: Eliassen KA (ed) Foreign and Security Policy in the European Union. Sage, London, pp 59–93
Grassi S (1998) L'introduzione delle operazioni di peace-keeping nel Trattato di Amsterdam: profile giuridici ed implicazioni politiche. Comunità Internazionale 53:295–326
Grard L (2006) L'Union européenne, sujet de droit international. Revue générale de droit international public 110:337–372
Greiçevci L et al (2007) To build a state: Europeanization, EU actorness and state-building in Kosovo. European Foreign Affairs Review 12:219–238
Grieco JM (1988) Anarchy and the limits of cooperation: a realist critique of the newest liberal institutionalism. International Organization 42:485–507
Griffiths RT (2000) Europe's first constitution: the European Political Community, 1952–1954. Federal Trust, London
Gröne D (1993) Die Europäische Politische Zusammenarbeit (1970–1991). Schäuble, Rheinfelden
Gütt TM (2003) Die Gemeinsame Außen- und Sicherheitspolitik und ihre Bedeutung für die Europäische Union: Rechtspersönlichkeit und Rechtsnatur der EU. Herbert Utz, München
Haggard S, Simmons BA (1987) Theories of international regimes. International Organization 41:491–517
Hall PA, Taylor RCR (1996) Political science and the three new institutionalisms. Political Studies 44:936–957
Hart HLA (1997) The concept of law, 2nd edn. Oxford University Press, Oxford

Hasenclever A et al (1997) Theories of international regimes. Cambridge University Press, Cambridge
Heliskoski J (2008) Small arms and light weapons within the union's pillar structure: an analysis of Article 47 of the EU treaty. European Law Review 33:898–912
Henkin L (1979) How nations behave: law and foreign policy, 2nd edn. Columbia University Press, New York
Hermann C (2008) Much ado about Pluto? The 'unity of the legal order of the European Union' revisited. In: Cremona M, de Witte B (eds) EU Foreign Relations Law: constitutional fundamentals. Hart, Oxford, pp 19–51
Higgins R (1994) Problems and process: international law and how we use it. Oxford University Press, Oxford
Hill C, Smith KE (2000) European Foreign Policy: key documents. Routledge, New York
Holland M (1991) Sanctions as an EPC instrument. In: Holland M (ed) The future of European Political Cooperation: essays on theory and practice. St. Martin's Press, New York, pp 180–198
Hurd D (1981) Political co-operation. International Affairs 57:383–383
Ifestos P (1987) European Political Cooperation (EPC): its evolution from 1970 to 1986, and the single European act. Journal of European Integration 11:47–62
Juncos AE, Reynolds C (2007) The political and security committee: governing in the shadow. European Foreign Affairs Review 12:127–147
Jupille J, Caporaso JA (1998) States, agency, and rules: the European Union in global environmental politics. In: Rhodes C (ed) The European Union in the world community. Lynne Rienner Publishers, Boulder, pp 213–229
Jürgens T (1994) Die gemeinsame europäische Aussen- und Sicherheitspolitik. Heymann, Köln
Kaikobad KH (2005) Problems of belligerent occupation: the scope of powers exercised by the coalition provisional authority in Iraq, April/May 2003–June 2004. International and Comparative Law Quarterly 54:253–264
Kammerhofer J (2004) Uncertainty in the formal sources of international law: customary international law and some of its problems. European Journal of International Law 15:523–553
Karolewski IP (2005) Constitutionalization of the common foreign and security policy of the European Union: implications of the constitutional treaty. German Law Journal 6:1649–1666
Kennedy D (1986–1987) The move to institutions. Cardozo Law Review 8:841–988
Keohane RO (1982) The demand for international regimes. International Organization 36: 325–355
Keohane RO (1988) International institutions: two approaches. International Studies Quarterly 32:379–396
Keukeleire S, MacNaughtan J (2008) The foreign policy of the European Union. Palgrave Macmillan, New York
Klabbers J (2009) An introduction to international institutional law, 2nd edn. Cambridge University Press, Cambridge
Koskenniemi M (1998) International law aspects of the common foreign and security policy. In: Koskenniemi M (ed) International law aspects of the European Union. Kluwer Law International, The Hague, pp 27–44
Koskenniemi M (2002) The gentle civilizer of nations: the rise and fall of international law, 1870–1960. Cambridge University Press, Cambridge
Koutrakos P (2001) Trade, foreign policy and defence in EU constitutional law: the legal regulation of sanctions, exports of dual-use goods and armaments. Hart, Oxford
Koutrakos P (2006) EU international relations law. Hart, Oxford
Koutrakos P (2008) Primary law and policy in EU external relations: moving away from the big picture. European Law Review 33:666–686
Krasner SD (2009) Power, the state, and sovereignty: essays on international relations. Routledge, London

Kratochwil F, Ruggie JG (1986) International organization: a state of the art on an art of the state. International Organization 40:753–775

Krenzler HG, Schneider HC (1994) Die Gemeinsame Außen- und Sicherheitspolitik der Europäischen Union—Zur Frage der Kohärenz. Europarecht 29:144–160

Lak MWJ (1989) Interaction between European Political Cooperation and the European Community (external)—existing rules and challenges. Common Market Law Review 26: 281–299

Langrish S (1998) The Treaty of Amsterdam: selected highlights. European Law Review 23:3–19

Lenaerts K, De Smijter E (1999–2000) The European Union as an actor under international law. Yearbook of European Law 19:95–138

Lepard BD (2010) Customary international law: a new theory with practical applications. Cambridge University Press, Cambridge

Lerner D, Aron R (eds) (1957) France defeats EDC. Praeger, New York

Lowndes V (1996) Varieties of new institutionalism: a critical appraisal. Public Administration 74:181–197

MacCormick N, Weinberger O (1985) Grundlagen des institutionalistischen Rechtspositivismus. Duncker & Humblot, Berlin

MacLeod I et al (1996) The external relations of the European Communities: a manual of law and practice. Oxford University Press, Oxford

March JG, Olsen JP (1984) The new institutionalism: organizational factors in political life. American Political Science Review 78:734–749

Mayer FC (2001) Die drei Dimensionen der Europäischen Kompetenzdebatte. Zeitschrift für ausländisches öffentliches Recht und Völkerrecht 61:577–640

Mayer FC (2005) Competences—reloaded? the vertical division of powers in the EU and the new European constitution. International Journal of Constitutional Law 3:493–515

Mearsheimer JJ (1994) The false promise of international institutions. International Security 19:5–49

Mendelson MH (1998) The formation of customary international law. Recueil des Cours 272:155–410

Meyer JW, Rowan B (1977) Institutionalized organizations: formal structure as myth and ceremony. American Journal of Sociology 83:340–363

Monar J (1997) The European Union's foreign affairs system after the Treaty of Amsterdam: a "strengthened capacity for external action"? European Foreign Affairs Review 2:413–436

Monar J (2002) The CFSP and the Leila/Perejil island incident: the nemesis of solidarity and leadership. European Foreign Affairs Review 7:251–255

Müllerson R (1997) On the nature and scope of customary international law. Austrian Review of International and European Law 2:341–360

Murphy DT (1989) European political cooperation after the Single European act: the future of foreign affairs in the European Communities. Boston College International and Comparative Law Review 12:335–355

Murphy DT (1998) The European Union's common foreign and security policy: it is not far from Maastricht to Amsterdam. Vanderbilt Journal of Transnational Law 31:871–913

Naert F (2007) ESDP in practice: increasingly varied and ambitious EU security and defence operations. In: Trybus M, White ND (eds) European security law. Oxford University Press, Oxford, pp 61–101

Nettesheim M (2004) Die Kompetenzordnung im Vertrag über eine Verfassung für Europa. Europarecht 39:511–546

Nettesheim M (2009) Kompetenzen. In: von Bogdandy A (ed) Europäisches Verfassungsrecht: Theoretische und dogmatische Grundzüge, 2nd edn. Springer, Berlin, pp 389–439

Neuwahl NAEM (1998) A partner with a troubled personality: EU treaty-making in matters of CFSP and JHA after Amsterdam. European Foreign Affairs Review 3:177–195

Noack P (1977) Das Scheitern der Europäischen Verteidigungsgemeinschaft: Entscheidungsprozesse vor und nach dem 30. August 1954. Droste, Düsseldorf

Nuttall S (1986) European Political Co-operation and the Single European Act. Yearbook of European Law 5:203–232
Nuttall S (1987) Interaction between European Political Co-operation and the European Community. Yearbook of European Law 7:211–249
Nuttall SJ (1992) European Political Co-operation. Oxford University Press, Oxford
Øhlenschlæger Buhl K (2009) Legalization of civil wars: the legal institutionalization of non-international army conflicts. Journal on Ethnopolitics and Minority Issues in Europe 1:1–42
Onuf N (2002) Institutions, intentions and international relations. Review of International Studies 28:211–228
Pagani F (1998) A new gear in the CFSP machinery: integration of the Petersberg tasks in the treaty on European Union. European Journal of International Law 9:737–749
Papathanasiou I (2009) The European Union's identity as a subject of the international legal order: evolutions under the Treaty of Lisbon. Cambridge Student Law Review 5:22–39
Pechstein M (1996) Rechtssubjektivität für die Europäische Union? Europarecht 31:137–144
Pernice I (2008–2009) The Treaty of Lisbon: multilevel constitutionalism in action. Columbia Journal of European Law 15:349–408
Pescatore P (1987) Some critical remarks on the "Single European Act". Common Market Law Review 24:9–18
Philippart E (2003) The Euro-Mediterranean partnership: a critical evaluation of an ambitious scheme. European Foreign Affairs Review 8:201–220
Potter PB (1945) Origin of the term international organization. American Journal of International Law 39:803–806
Rama-Montaldo M (1970) International legal personality and implied powers of international organizations. British Yearbook of International Law 44:111–155
Rieber RA (1976) The future of the European Community in international politics. Canadian Journal of Political Science 9:206–226
Ritzer C (2006) Europäische Kompetenzordnung: Reform der Kompetenzverteilung zwischen der europäischen Union und den Mitgliedstaaten durch den Vertrag über eine Verfassung für Europa. Nomos, Baden–Baden
Roberts AE (2001) Traditional and modern approaches to customary international law: a reconciliation. American Journal of International Law 95:757–791
Roloff R (2006) Grundlagen und Grenzen der GASP: Der Fall Irak. In: Müller-Graff P-C (ed) Die Rolle der erweiterten Europäischen Union in der Welt. Nomos, Baden–Baden, pp 225–240
Ruane K (2000) The rise and fall of the European defence community: Anglo-American relations and the crisis of European defence, 1950-55. Macmillan, Basingstoke
Ruiter DWP (1993) Institutional legal facts: legal powers and their effects. Kluwer, Dordrecht
Rutten M (ed) (2001) From St-Malo to nice-European defence: core documents. EU Institute for Security Studies, Paris
Salmon TC (1992) Testing times for European Political Cooperation: the Gulf and Yugoslavia, 1990-1992. International Affairs 68:233–253
Salmon TC, Shepherd AJ K (2003) Toward a European army: a military power in the making? Lynne Rienner Publishers, Boulder
Sands P, Klein P (2009) Bowett's law of international institutions, 6th edn. Sweet & Maxwell, London
Sari A (2008) The conclusion of international agreements by the European Union in the context of the ESDP. International and Comparative Law Quarterly 56:53–86
Sari A (2011) Article 28. In: Blanke H-J, Mangiameli S (eds) Commentary on the treaty on European Union. Springer, Berlin
Sarooshi D (2005) International organizations and their exercise of sovereign powers. Oxford University Press, Oxford
Schmalz U (1998) The Amsterdam provisions on external coherence: bridging the union's foreign policy dualism? European Foreign Affairs Review 3:421–442
Scott S et al (2002) Legalization: interpreting the empirical evidence. American Society of International Law Proceedings 96:291–298

Sereni AP (1940) Agency in international law. American Journal of International Law 34: 638–660
Setear JK (2003–2004) Can legalization last?: whaling and the durability of national (executive) discretion. Vanderbilt Journal of International Law 44:711–757
Silj A (1967) Europe's political puzzle: a study of the fouchet negotiations and the 1963 veto. Center for International Affairs, Cambridge
Simmons BA (2001) International law and international relations: scholarship at the intersection of principles and politics. American Society of International Law Proceedings 95:271–279
Simmons BA, Martin LL (2002) International organizations and institutions. In: Carlsnaes W, Risse-Kappen T, Simmons BA (eds) Handbook of international relations. SAGE, London, pp 192–211
Simpson GJ (2004) Great powers and outlaw states: unequal sovereigns in the international legal order. Cambridge University Press, Cambridge
Slaughter A-M et al (1998) International law and international relations theory: a new generation of interdisciplinary scholarship. American Journal of International Law 92:367–397
Slaughter Burley A-M (1993) International law and international relations theory: a dual agenda. American Journal of International Law 87:205–239
Smith ME (2001a) The quest for coherence: institutional dilemmas of external action from Maastricht to Amsterdam. In: Stone Sweet A, Sandholtz W, Fligstein N (eds) The institutionalization of Europe. Oxford University Press, Oxford, pp 171–193
Smith ME (2001b) Diplomacy by decree: the legalization of EU foreign policy. Journal of Common Market Studies 39:79–104
Smith ME (2004) Europe's foreign and security policy: the institutionalization of cooperation. Cambridge University Press, Cambridge
Smith KE (2008) European Union foreign policy in a changing world, 2nd edn. Polity, Cambridge
Stein E (1983) European Political Cooperation (EPC) as a component of the European Foreign Affairs System. Zeitschrift für ausländisches öffentliches Recht und Völkerrecht 43:49–69
Stone Sweet A et al (2001) The institutionalization of European space. In: Stone Sweet A, Sandholtz W, Fligstein N (eds) The institutionalization of Europe. Oxford University Press, Oxford, pp 1–28
Strange S (1982) Cave! hic dragones: a critique of regime analysis. International Organization 36:479–496
Streinz R (2005) Was ist neu am Verfassungsvertrag? Zum Vertrag von Rom über eine Verfassung für Europa vom 29. Oktober 2004. In: Gaitanides C, Kadelbach S, Rodríguez Iglesias GC, Zuleeg M (eds) Europa und seine Verfassung: Festschrift für Manfred Zuleeg zum siebzigsten Geburtstag. Nomos, Baden–Baden, pp 108–127
Taylor P (1982) The European Communities as an actor in international society. Journal of European Integration 6:7–41
Thym D (2006) Die völkerrechtlichen Verträge der Europäischen Union. Zeitschrift für ausländisches öffentliches Recht und Völkerrecht 66:863–925
Thym D (2009) Foreign affairs. In: von Bogdandy A, Bast J (eds) Principles of European Constitutional Law, 2nd edn. Hart, Oxford, pp 309–343
Tizzano A (1998) La personnalité internationale de l'Union européenne. Revue du Marché Unique Européen 4:11–40
Tomuschat C (2003) Die Europäische Union als ein Akteur in den internationalen Beziehungen. In: Frowein JA, Scharioth K, Winkelmann I, Wolfrum R (eds) Verhandeln für den Frieden—Negotiating for Peace: Liber Amicorum Tono Eitel. Springer, Berlin, pp 799–821
Trüe C (2004) Das System der EU-Kompetenzen vor und nach dem Entwurf eines europäischen Verfassungsvertrages. Zeitschrift für ausländisches öffentliches Recht und Völkerrecht 64:391–427
van Vooren B (2009) EU–EC external competences after the small arms judgment. European Foreign Affairs Review 14:7–24

Verwey DR (2004) The European Community, the European Union and the international law of treaties. TMC Asser Press, The Hague

von Bogdandy A, Bast J (2002) The European Union's vertical order of competences: the current law and proposals for its reform. Common Market Law Review 39:227–268

von Bogdandy A, Nettesheim M (1996) Ex pluribus unum: fusion of the European Communities into the European Union. European Law Journal 2:267–289

von Kielmansegg SG (2007) The meaning of Petersberg: some considerations on the legal scope of ESDP operations. Common Market Law Review 44:629–648

Wagner W (2003) Die Konstruktion einer europäischen Außenpolitik. Deutsche, französische und britische Ansätze im Vergleich. Campus, Frankfurt a.M

Wessel RA (1996) Towards a united Europe? a legal perspective on European institutionalization and integration. In: de Wilde J, Wiberg H (eds) Organized anarchy in Europe: the role of states and intergovernmental organizations. Tauris Publishers, London, pp 39–64

Wessel RA (1997) The international legal status of the European Union. European Foreign Affairs Review 2:109–129

Wessel RA (2000) The inside looking out: consistency and delimitation in EU external relations. Common Market Law Review 37:1135–1171

Wessel RA (2001) The EU as a black widow: devouring the WEU to give birth to a European security and defence policy. In: Kronenberger V (ed) The European Union and the international legal order: discord or harmony? TMC Asser Press, The Hague, pp 405–434

Wessel RA (2008) The EU as a party to international agreements: shared competences, mixed responsibilities. In: Dashwood A, Maresceau M (eds) Law and practice of EU external relations: salient features of a changing landscape. Cambridge University Press, Cambridge, pp 152–187

Wessel RA (2009) The dynamics of the European Union legal order: an increasingly coherent framework of action and interpretation. European Constitutional Law Review 5:117–142

White ND (2005) The law of international organisations, 2nd edn. Manchester University Press, Manchester

Wood RS (1977–1978) Foreign policy and defense in the European Community. Virginia Journal of International Law 18:389–410

Young OR (1982) Regime dynamics: the rise and fall of international regimes. International Organization 36:277–297

Young OR (1986) International regimes: toward a new theory of institutions. World Politics 39:104–122

Young OR (1989) International cooperation: building regimes for natural resources and the environment. Cornell University Press, Ithaca

Chapter 5
The Role of the European Court of Justice in the Field of Common Foreign and Security Policy After the Treaty of Lisbon: New Challenges for the Future

Maja Brkan

Abstract The purpose of this chapter is to show the increasing importance of the role of the European Court of Justice (ECJ) in the field of Common Foreign and Security Policy (CFSP) after the entry into force of the Treaty of Lisbon. Although the Treaties expressly exclude the jurisdiction of the ECJ in this area, certain changes brought about by the Treaty in this field could significantly enhance its role in shaping the European foreign policy.The chapter is divided in three substantive parts. The first part will briefly analyse the general rule in the Treaty of the lack of the jurisdiction of the ECJ in the field of CFSP and the reasons for this. Whereas the sensitivity of the area and the willingness of the Member States to keep their sovereignty in this field is a legitimate reason for the lack of jurisdiction, it is less clear why the Court does not have jurisdiction to rule on actions for annulment for the breach of essential procedural requirements in the adoption of CFSP acts as well on questions of compatibility of CFSP acts with human rights. The second part will deal with the questions of delimitation between pillars/areas. Pre-Lisbon, the first pillar had absolute preference over the second and third pillar. Lisbon changes this approach: not only shall the implementation of the CFSP not affect the exercise of the Union competences under the Treaty on the Functioning of the European Union (TFEU), but the implementation of these policies shall not affect the exercise of the Union competences under CFSP. The third part will discuss restrictive measures. In this

---

Dr Maja Brkan—Référéndaire, European Court of Justice. The views expressed in this chapter are the personal views of the author and do not represent the views of the institution where the author is employed.

M. Brkan (✉)
European Court of Justice, Luxembourg, Luxembourg
e-mail: maja.brkan@curia.europa.eu

P. J. Cardwell (ed.), *EU External Relations Law and Policy in the Post-Lisbon Era*,
DOI: 10.1007/978-90-6704-823-1_5, © T.M.C. ASSER PRESS, The Hague,
The Netherlands, and the authors 2012

field, the Treaty now distinguishes between three types of restrictive measures: measures intended to prevent and combat terrorism, measures against third countries and restrictive measures against natural or legal persons. The review of the latter is subjected to the jurisdiction of the ECJ, which is a novelty under the Treaty. It will be analysed how this new exception to the non-jurisdiction rule could influence cases such as *Kadi and Al Barakaat*.

Contents

5.1 Introduction

In 1962, American constitutional law professor Alexander Bickel published his famous book 'The least dangerous branch'[1] in which he argued that the judicial branch in the USA is, or should be, 'the least dangerous' of all the three branches of power. In the field of the European Union (EU)'s Common Foreign and Security Policy (CFSP), one could, upon first glance, build on a similar premise, given the lack of jurisdiction of the European Court of Justice (ECJ) in this field. However, when the analysis delves deeper, it can be seen that the ECJ can have a certain degree of influence in this field. The purpose of this chapter is to demonstrate the particular role of the ECJ in the field of CFSP, as well as its possibility in influencing the content of the CFSP. In addition, the increasing importance of its role in the field of CFSP after the entry into the force of the Lisbon Treaty will also be investigated.

The chapter is divided into three substantive sections. The following section of the chapter analyses the general rule of the lack of the jurisdiction of the ECJ in the field of CFSP. This includes a critical analysis of the reasons for the lack of its jurisdiction. The subsequent section deals with one of the exceptions to the non-jurisdiction rule, namely the questions of delimitation between areas (former pillars) in the EU, together with the pertinent ECJ case-law in this regard. Section 5.3 of the chapter discusses the role of the ECJ in the field of restrictive measures. Differences with the previous legal regime as well as the question of

[1] Bickel 1962.

how the novelties could influence the case-law of the ECJ are also analysed. The final section of the chapter contains conclusive remarks on the role of the ECJ in the field of CFSP. It is argued that the ECJ can influence the CFSP in a twofold way: through delimitating the boundaries between the CFSP and other TFEU-areas and through the review of economic sanctions either against natural or legal persons or against third countries.

5.2 The General Rule: No Jurisdiction for the ECJ

The general rule that remained in force, even after the entry of the Treaty, is that the ECJ does not have jurisdiction in the field of CFSP. Already in the Single European Act, the ECJ did not have jurisdiction to judge on what was then European Political Cooperation (EPC). Even though the EPC developed into the CFSP with the Treaty of Maastricht in 1992, this rule remained the same. In the pre-Lisbon era, Article 46 of the Treaty on European Union (TEU) determined in which fields of European integration the ECJ had jurisdiction. The CFSP was not included among those fields. In the 1990s, the Court confirmed its lack of jurisdiction in this area in the case *Grau Gomis*.[2]

After the entry into the force of the Treaty of Lisbon, the provision of the lack of jurisdiction of the ECJ was no longer included in the TEU, but instead was moved to the Treaty on the Functioning of the European Union (TFEU). With similar consequences to the pre-Lisbon era, Article 275(1) TFEU expressly excludes the jurisdiction of the ECJ from the area of the CFSP:

> The Court of Justice of the European Union shall not have jurisdiction with respect to the provisions relating to the common foreign and security policy nor with respect to acts adopted on the basis of those provisions.

The reasons for the lack of jurisdiction of the ECJ in the field of CFSP are twofold and are due to both the Member States and the Union institutions. The reasoning on the side of the Member States centres around the political sensitivity of the area of foreign policy coupled with their desire to remain sovereign in this field. Generally speaking, Member States want to maintain the soft and intergovernmental characteristic of the CFSP and do not want to be subjected to the possibility of being forced to comply with foreign policy decisions, either through political pressure, or through the decisions of the ECJ.[3] For the same reasons, the Member States also do not want to provide the ECJ with the possibility of interpreting the CFSP acts.

---

[2] ECJ, Case C-167/94 *Grau Gomis and Others* [1995] *ECR* I-1023. For comments on this case in the literature see, for example, Chavrier et al. 1995; Simon 2010.

[3] For example, by virtue of an action for non-fulfilment of obligations (Treaty on the Functioning of the European Union, Article 258). See, in this sense, Garbagnati Ketvel 2006, 80 and cf. Cremona 2004, 571.

For the Union, the literature cites that the reasons include the vague nature and uncertain meaning of the Treaty provisions in the CFSP, the general formulation of the goals of the CFSP, as well as the short-term characteristics of the CFSP acts.[4] It is, however, unclear how any of these factors would prevent the judicial control of the CFSP acts or the determination of whether the Member State fulfilled its obligations from the CFSP or not. The goals of the CFSP are not less determinate from the other goals of the EU. Therefore, the jurisdiction of the ECJ and its possibility to interpret the Treaty provisions should not depend on the fact of whether the provisions are semantically open or not. The second potential reason on the side of the Union could be that the judicial review in the foreign policy field is limited, due to the political nature of the questions in this field. This is a valid argument, but it is not to be confused with the US doctrine of political questions, developed by the US Supreme Court.[5]

For the reasons stated, the lack of jurisdiction of the ECJ in the CFSP is, in principle, understandable. It is, however, less clear why Member States or other interested parties are not allowed to file an action for an annulment pursuant to Article 263 TFEU for the breach of procedural requirements for the adoption of CFSP acts.[6] Furthermore, it is also unclear why the ECJ should not have general jurisdiction to rule on the question of whether CFSP acts respect human rights.[7] Under Lisbon, the ECJ can only judge on this issue in regard to the economic sanctions against individuals, not in regard to other acts.

However, there are certain exceptions to the rule of non-jurisdiction. The most important exceptions are the jurisdiction of the ECJ concerning the delimitation between areas (formerly characterised as 'pillars' under the Union's pre-Lisbon constitutional structure), as well as the jurisdiction to review the legality of CFSP acts imposing restrictive measures against natural or legal persons. The latter is a new exception introduced by the Treaty of Lisbon. The ECJ plays an important role in the field of economic sanctions, which are, from their content, a mixture of trade and foreign policies. The following sections of the chapter analyse the exceptions regarding the jurisdiction of the ECJ in the field of the CFSP, both under the pre-Lisbon and post-Lisbon regimes.

---

[4] Garbagnati Ketvel 2006, 80.

[5] There is a conceptual difference between nonjusticiability (USA) and the lack of jurisdiction (EU). On this issue, see the judgment of the US Supreme Court in the case *Baker* v. *Carr,* 369 U.S. 186 (1962), For further theoretical discussion see Brkan 2009, 174 et seq.

[6] In this regard, a theoretical example can be given: if unanimity was not respected for the adoption of a CFSP act, whereas it should have been respected, it is unclear why a Member State that has voted against the act does not have a possibility to file an action against such an act. Cf. Canor 1998, 94.

[7] De Zwaan 1998, 188.

5.3 Delimitation Between the Areas/Pillars

Under the pre-Lisbon regime, according to Article 46 of the former TEU, the ECJ had jurisdiction to judge on the final provisions of the TEU. Among these provisions was also (former) Article 47 TEU, according to which, nothing in the TEU shall affect the Treaties establishing the European Communities (EC Treaty). Article 47 of the former TEU was interesting from three perspectives.

First, in the way Article 47 TEU was formulated, it gave absolute preference to the first pillar over the second (or third) pillar. This means, in the words of Weatherill, that if something *can* be done within the framework of the first pillar, it *must* be done within the framework of the first pillar.[8] This means that if the institutions wanted to adopt a 'hybrid act' in which the areas of the first and second pillar were involved, they had to adopt it within the first pillar. Such a clear-cut and one-sided rule left many questions unanswered. For example, if the institutions wanted to adopt a 'hybrid act', what should be the legal basis for such act? Would it need to be adopted in the framework of the first pillar in combination with Article 308 EC or, should it to be based on the two legal bases in the first and second pillar together? The dogmatically clearest possibility would be to search for the centre of gravity of the competence, but if the centre of gravity has the same weight for the first and the second pillar, then the rule from Article 47 TEU precludes the act to be adopted on two legal bases.

Second, Article 47 TEU created an exception from the general rule of public international law, according to which a later international treaty (in this case TEU) shall prevail over the earlier international treaties (in this case EC Treaty).[9] Article 30(2) of the Vienna convention on the Law of Treaties states that when a treaty specifies that it is subject to, or that it is not to be considered as incompatible with, an earlier or later treaty, the provisions of that other treaty shall prevail. Although the Maastricht Treaty introduced the pillar structure, the second and third pillars had to give way to the first pillar in all cases in which a measure can be adopted under the first pillar.[10]

Third, this delimitation of competence was significantly different from the delimitation of the competence between the Community and the Member States.[11] If the Community had exclusive competence in a field, the Member States were precluded from adopting measures in this field. If the competence was concurrent, the Member States could adopt measures as long as the Community has not adopted them. In this way, the field is 'pre-empted' and only the Community can adopt measures in this field. In the delimitation between the first and the second pillars, the rule on pre-emption, however, does not apply.

---

[8] Weatherill 1998, 160.

[9] Garbagnati Ketvel 2006, 86.

[10] It is to be added that for the purposes of delimitation between the second and third pillar, the principle of *lex specialis derogat legi generali* is to be applied; see Wessel 2000, 1148.

[11] Eeckhout 2004, 150.

The only case so far in which the ECJ has ruled on the delimitation between the first and the second pillar[12] is the so-called 'ECOWAS' case.[13] The background of this case is as follows: in 2000, the European Community and its Member States signed the Cotonou Agreement with the African, Caribbean and Pacific (ACP) group of states. This was a mixed agreement concluded within the first pillar in the field of development cooperation. One of the goals of the agreement was to reduce trafficking and the accumulation of small arms and light weapons. In 2002, prior to the Cotonou Agreement entering into force, the Union adopted, within the second pillar, a CFSP Joint Action on combating the accumulation and spread of small arms and light weapons.[14] The objective of this joint action was therefore the reduction of the accumulation and spread of small arms and light weapons. In order to implement this joint action, in 2004, the Council adopted a decision[15] with regard to the ECOWAS states.[16] The aim of this decision was for the Union to provide financial contributions and technical assistance to prevent the accumulation and spread of small arms and light weapons in these states.[17]

It is apparent that certain goals from the Cotonou Agreement and the second pillar measures are similar. Therefore, the Commission was of the view that all the measures had to be adopted within the first pillar and that the Council, by adopting second pillar measures, infringed upon Article 47 TEU. The Commission therefore filed an action for annulment pursuant to Article 230 EC (now Article 263 TFEU) in which it requested, first, that the ECJ annul the contested Council Decision 2004/833/CFSP, and second, that the ECJ declares illegal and inapplicable the Joint Action 2002/589/CFSP.[18]

In its reasoning regarding the Council decision, the ECJ closely followed a two-step test. It first proved the primary purpose of the contested decision; if its primary purpose is the implementation of the CFSP, then it should be adopted within the CFSP. Second, if the measure simultaneously pursues two or more

[12] Conversely, the Court has ruled several times on delimitation between the first and third pillar—for example, in ECJ, Case C-170/96 *Commission* v. *Council (Airport Transit Visas)* [1998] *ECR* I-2763, ECJ, Case C-176/03, *Commission* v. *Council* (*Criminal penalties for environment protection*) [2005] *ECR* I-7879 and ECJ, Case C-440/05 *Commission* v. *Council* (*Criminal penalties against ship-source pollution*) [2007] *ECR* I-9097.

[13] ECJ, Case C-91/05 *Commission* v. *Council* [2008] *ECR* I-3651. For the comments on the case see, for example, Karmali 2008; Broussy et al. 2008; Heliskoski 2008; Herlin-Karnell 2008; Wessel R 2008; Martínez Capdevila 2008.

[14] Council Joint Action 2002/589/CFSP of 12 July 2002 on the European Union's contribution to combating the destabilising accumulation and spread of small arms and light weapons and repealing Joint Action 1999/34/CFSP, OJ 2002 L 191, 1.

[15] Council Decision 2004/833/CFSP of 2 December 2004 implementing Joint Action 2002/589/ CFSP with a view to a European Union contribution to ECOWAS in the framework of the Moratorium on Small Arms and Light Weapons, OJ 2004 L 359, 65.

[16] The Economic Community of West African States (ECOWAS) is a regional group of West African countries whose mission is to foster economic integration of these countries.

[17] ECJ, *Commission* v. *Council (ECOWAS)* [2008], paras 2–24.

[18] ECJ, *Commission* v. *Council (ECOWAS)* [2008], para 25.

objectives then, according to the general rule, such a measure would have to be founded on various legal bases.[19] However, under Article 47 TEU, such a solution is impossible.[20] If the first and second pillar objectives are equally important, the measure has to be adopted within the first pillar.[21] It is also important to note that the ECJ stated that this rule applies notwithstanding of the type of Community competence (shared or exclusive).[22] Following this two-step test, the ECJ decided that the Council decision pursues a number of objectives, falling within the CFSP and development cooperation policy. Therefore, this decision should have been adopted within the development cooperation policy. Instead, the Council infringed Article 47 EU.[23] The ECJ therefore annulled the Council decision.[24]

The ECJ, however, did not analyse the pleas in regard to the joint action; it only stated that since the decision must be annulled because of its own defects, it is not necessary to examine the pleas in regard to the joint action.[25] An open question left is whether the annulment of the Council decision bears any legal consequences for the joint action. Since it was not annulled, it could be argued that it is still valid and that the Council could base itself directly on this joint action in order to continue its activities in regard to ECOWAS in the second pillar. Article 14 (3) TEU (now Article 28(2) TEU) states that joint actions shall commit the Member States in the positions they adopt and in the conduct of their activity. The ECJ however expressly stated that acts falling within the CFSP, and capable of having legal effects, should not encroach upon the Community.[26] Therefore, it could also be argued that the joint action, without the Council decision implementing it, cannot produce legal effects of its own because the implementing measure was annulled.

After the entry into force of the Treaty of Lisbon, the regulation of the delimitation between areas is slightly different. Article 40 TEU states that, on the one hand, the implementation of the CFSP shall not affect the exercise of the Union competences under the TFEU, and, on the other hand, the implementation of the policies in the TFEU shall not affect the exercise of the Union competences under the CFSP. Thus, it is obvious that, under the Treaty, the previous rule 'if an act can be adopted in the first pillar, it should be adopted in the first pillar' no longer applies. Rather, the CFSP and the rest of the Union law have an equal weight and the non-affecting rule is applicable in both directions. More specifically, the CFSP should not affect other Union policies and other Union policies

[19] ECJ, *Commission* v. *Council (ECOWAS)* [2008], para 75.

[20] ECJ, *Commission* v. *Council (ECOWAS)* [2008], para 76.

[21] ECJ, *Commission* v. *Council (ECOWAS)* [2008], para 77.

[22] ECJ, *Commission* v. *Council (ECOWAS)* [2008], paras 61–62.

[23] ECJ, *Commission* v. *Council (ECOWAS)* [2008], para 109.

[24] ECJ, *Commission* v. *Council (ECOWAS)* [2008], para 110.

[25] ECJ, *Commission* v. *Council (ECOWAS)* [2008], para 111.

[26] ECJ, *Commission* v. *Council (ECOWAS)* [2008], para 33.

should not affect the CFSP. This will have important consequences for the role of the ECJ and the content of its case-law in this area.

It is submitted that it is quite possible that the ECOWAS-type of case will be decided differently after the entry into force of the Treaty. In regard to the Council decision implementing a 'decision defining action' (a former 'joint action'), the ECJ would probably only determine the primary purpose of the measure. If the primary purpose of the measure was development cooperation, the ECJ would probably annul the Council decision. If, however, both objectives were equally important, then either the CFSP decision or the Council decision concluding the international agreement would need to be adopted on two legal bases. This could, however, cause difficulties in practice because the procedure for the adoption of these legal acts is different. CFSP acts need to be adopted with unanimity, whereas the acts in the field of development cooperation are adopted according to the ordinary legislative procedures (Article 209 TFEU). These are some open-ended questions that the ECJ will have to face in the future.

5.4 The Regime of Economic Sanctions

Another area where the ECJ has jurisdiction is the area of economic sanctions. As previously mentioned, economic sanctions are a hybrid between trade and foreign policy. Examples of sanctions include trade embargoes (e.g., prohibiting exports and imports), financial sanctions (e.g., prohibiting the transfer of funds or investments) and sanctions concerning transport services (e.g., prohibition of transport for state transport companies).[27]

5.4.1 The Pre-Lisbon Regime of Economic Sanctions

Before the changes introduced by Lisbon, economic sanctions were regulated by Articles 60 and 301 EC. Article 60(1) EC stated that, in the cases envisaged in Article 301 EC, the Community can take measures on the movement of capital and payments in regard to third countries. According to Article 301 EC, if a common position, or a joint action, is provided for by an action of the Community to interrupt or to reduce, in part or completely, economic relations with one or more third countries, the Council shall take, by a qualified majority on a proposal from the Commission, the necessary urgent measures.

Two brief comments are to be made in regard to these two articles. First, a measure imposing economic sanctions needed to be adopted on both legal bases (Articles 60 and 301 EC). Second, the particularity of the system of economic

[27] More on economic sanctions see Eeckhout 2004, 424 et seq.

sanctions was that, in order to impose any economic sanctions, the Union first needed to adopt a second pillar measure (e.g., a joint action) that needed to be followed by a first pillar measure (e.g., a regulation). This two-step system has a double significance. On the one hand, economic sanctions were a hybrid between a foreign policy and a commercial policy measure. A part of foreign policy therefore came into the framework of the first pillar through the back door. On the other hand, the ECJ had jurisdiction to interpret these measures and to rule on their validity. This meant that it indirectly reviewed the second pillar content of the measure. What is more, most of the EC economic sanctions implement United Nations Security Council (UNSC) Resolutions.[28] This means that when the ECJ interpreted or judged the validity of the EC measure on economic sanctions, it could indirectly interpret or judge the validity of the UNSC Resolution.

One of the most important and the most often discussed cases in regard to economic sanctions is the case of *Kadi and Al Barakaat*,[29] decided by the ECJ in 2008, in which the Court annulled, insofar as it concerns Mr Kadi and the Al Barakaat International Foundation, a Council Regulation[30] freezing their funds and assets. The purpose of this chapter is neither to repeat the facts or the argumentation in this case, nor to conduct an in-depth analysis of the significance of the case itself.[31] For the purposes of this chapter, it is sufficient to stress that the importance of the *Kadi* case can be analysed from four perspectives.

The first is the perspective of Community/Union law. One the one hand, the ECJ in the *Kadi* judgment expressly designated the Community legal order as an autonomous legal order,[32] a principle which can be recognised as a settled

[28] It is to be stressed that the EU can adopt a regulation that sanctions more than a Security Council Resolution. An example of such a regulation was sanctions against Iraq (Regulation 2340/90) where the SC resolutions regulated a general embargo (on imports, selling and supply on products from Iraq—with the exception for humanitarian and medical reasons) as well as the flights to Iraq (Resolutions 661 (1990), 666 (1990), 670 (1990)). The EU Regulation contained also the prohibition of any other services that could enhance economic development in Iraq.

[29] ECJ, Joined Cases C-402/05 P and C-415/05 P, *Kadi and Al Barakaat v. Council and Commission* [2008] ECR I-6351.

[30] Council Regulation (EC) No 881/2002 of 27 May 2002 imposing certain specific restrictive measures directed against certain persons and entities associated with Usama bin Laden, the Al-Qaeda network and the Taliban, and repealing Council Regulation (EC) No 467/2001 prohibiting the export of certain goods and services to Afghanistan, strengthening the flight ban and extending the freeze of funds and other financial resources in respect of the Taliban of Afghanistan, OJ 2002 L 139, 9.

[31] There is abundant literature in this regard. See, for example, Graf Vitzthum 2008, 375–429; Sauer 2008, 25–27; Heun-Rehn 2008, 322–338; Ohler 2008, 630–633; Cassia and Donnat 2008, 1204–1217; Komárek 2008, 428–430; Do 2008, 867–873; Ferrari 2009, 187–192; Rijken 2009, 140–146; Kämmerer 2009, 114–130.

[32] ECJ, *Kadi and Al Barakaat* [2008], para 317.

case-law.[33] On the other hand, the test used in *Kadi* is the logical continuation of the *Bosphorus*[34] case, where the Court proved whether a Community regulation was in breach of the fundamental right to the respect for property, notwithstanding the fact that the regulation was implementing a UNSC Resolution. The Court's judgment in *Kadi* is consistent with the *Bosphorus* case in the sense that it does not create a difference in the review of legality of regulations that implement UNSC Resolutions and all other regulations.[35]

The second is the perspective of international law.[36] The outcome in the *Kadi* case could potentially create a problematic situation for the Member States. If the ECJ found that the breaches of fundamental lights cannot be remedied, or if the EU institutions would not remedy these breaches and the funds of Kadi would not be frozen, the Member States would be bound by both the UNSC Resolution (freezing Kadi's funds) and EC law (not freezing Kadi's funds).

The third is the point of view of the protection of human rights. It could be argued that the ECJ, when deciding upon the *Kadi* case, was in a similar position as the German *Bundesgerichtshof* in the *Solange II* case.[37] Contrary to the *Bundesgerichtshof,* which decided to refrain from the control of the compatibility of EU acts with human rights as long as the EU guarantees adequate protection of those rights, the ECJ came to a different conclusion. As long as the UN does not provide for the adequate protection of human rights, the ECJ will ensure the protection of human rights in regard to implementing measures.[38] In this regard, the Court sees the re-examination procedure before the UN Sanctions Committee as insufficient, by stating that this procedure does not provide any guarantees of judicial protection and that the persons have no opportunity of asserting their rights.[39]

The fourth perspective is the importance of the *Kadi* case for the system of EU economic sanctions. As previously mentioned, Articles 60 and 301 EC only provided for one type of economic sanction, namely sanctions against third countries. Before entry into force of the Treaty, sanctions against natural or legal persons were not expressly provided for by the Treaties. However, the ECJ in the *Kadi* case confirmed that the adoption of the economic sanctions against natural or legal

---

33 The Court breaks away from public international law which is the continuation of the idea, developed already in ECJ, Case 26/62, *Van Gend en Loos* [1963] *ECR* 1. The principle that the Community legal order is an autonomous legal order was repeated by the CFI (now the General Court (GC)) for example in the case T-85/09, *Kadi v Commission (Kadi II)*, 30 September 2010, not yet reported, para 119.

34 ECJ, Case C-84/95, *Bosphorus* v. *Minister for Transport, Energy and Communications, Ireland and the Attorney General* [1996] *ECR* I-3953.

35 Cf. Eeckhout 2005, 26.

36 On the analysis of *Kadi* from the point of view of the relationship between EU law and public international law cf. Cardwell et al. 2009.

37 Beschluss vom 22. Oktober 1986, Az: 2 BvR 197/1983.

38 Cf. in this regard, Sandulli 2008, 513 et seq.

39 ECJ, *Kadi and Al Barakaat* [2008], paras 321–323.

persons was possible with recourse to an additional legal basis, Article 308 EC. The argumentation of the ECJ to reach this result was very teleological and result-oriented. Contrary to the view of the Court of First Instance (CFI),[40] the ECJ stressed that Article 308 EC specifically requires that the measure has to be intended to attain 'one of the objectives of the Community'.[41] It, however, stressed that Articles 60 and 301 EC do pursue an objective of the Community for the purpose of Article 308 EC, precisely because they provide for Community powers to impose economic sanctions. As such, they are 'the expression of an implicit underlying objective, namely, that of making it possible to adopt such measures through the efficient use of a Community instrument'.[42]

The last line of cases that should very briefly be mentioned is the *Modjahedines* line of cases.[43] For the purposes of this chapter, only one aspect of the *Modjahedines* cases should be illustrated, namely the application of the principle of loyal cooperation within the CFSP. The *Modjahedines* cases are important because the CFI confirmed that the principle of loyal cooperation applies to the second pillar by stating that this principle is of general application. After the *Pupino* judgment,[44] in which the Court confirmed that the principle of loyal cooperation also extends to the third pillar, it was questionable whether this principle also extends to the second pillar.[45]

Economic sanctions are not only an issue in the framework of the annulment actions, but also in the framework of the preliminary rulings. In this regard, two cases will be analysed.

In the case of *M and Others*,[46] the ECJ interpreted the same regulation as the issue in the *Kadi* case, Regulation No. 881/2002. The case concerned the question of whether it is prohibited, under Article 2(2) of the regulation, to pay social security or social assistance benefits to the spouse of a person that is included in

---

[40] CFI, Case T-315/01, *Kadi* v. *Council and Commission* [2005] ECR II-3649, paras 121–130.

[41] ECJ, *Kadi and Al Barakaat* [2008], paras 198–199. The ECJ stressed (point 199) that the position of the CFI -runs counter to the very wording of Article 308 EC.

[42] ECJ, *Kadi and Al Barakaat* [2008], para 226.

[43] There have been three Mojahedin cases before the CFI: CFI, T-228/02, *Organisation des Modjahedines du peuple d'Iran* v. *Council* (*Modjahedines I*) [2006] *ECR* II-4665; CFI, T-256/07, *Organisation des Modjahedines du peuple d'Iran* v. *Council* (*Modjahedines II*) [2008] *ECR* II-2312 and CFI, T-284/08, *Organisation des Modjahedines du peuple d'Iran* v. *Council* (*Modjahedines III*) [*2006*] *ECR* II-3487. The latter two cases have been subject to appeal, ECJ, C-576/08 P, *Organisation des Modjahedines du peuple d'Iran* v. *Council* and ECJ, C-27/09 P, France v *Organisation des Modjahedines du peuple d'Iran.*

[44] ECJ, Case C-105/03 *Criminal Proceedings against Maria Pupino* [2005] *ECR* I-5285.

[45] It also has to be taken into account that the ECJ later—in ECJ, Case C-354/04 P, *Gestoras Pro Amnistia and Others* v. *Council* [2007] (*not published in the ECR*), para 52 and ECJ, Case C-355/04 P, *Segi and Others* v. *Council* [2007] *ECR* I-1657, para 52—applied this principle for a common position that was adopted on the legal basis of the second and third pillar.

[46] ECJ, Case C-340/08, *M and Others v. Her Majesty's Treasury* [2010], 29 April 2010, not yet reported.

the annex of this regulation.[47] According to Article 2(2), no funds or economic resources shall be made available, directly or indirectly, to, or for the benefit of, natural or legal persons, entities, bodies or groups listed in Annex I of that regulation. The underlying premise of the question was that the spouse will, or may, pay for the goods or services of the person listed in Annex I of the regulation.

The ECJ decided, following the opinion of the AG Mengozzi, that Article 2(2) of Regulation No. 881/2002 does not apply to the provision of social security, or social assistance benefits, to the spouse of a person included in Annex I. It stressed that this article cannot be applicable to the present case only because the spouse lives with that person and will, or may, use some of those payments to pay for goods and services which the designated person also will consume, or from which, he/she also will benefit.[48] The ECJ compared different language versions stating that they could lead to different results, but they have to be given a uniform interpretation.[49] However, since the purpose of that regulation was to combat international terrorism, the measure freezing economic resources only applied to those resources that could be used to support terrorist activities.[50] Since the social security or social assistance benefits were not of that kind, the ECJ did not include them under Article 2(2) of Regulation No. 881/2002.[51]

The same regulation on economic sanctions, as in the *Kadi* case, was also an issue in the case of *Möllendorf* which raised the issue of the applicability of this regulation in the context of the transfer of ownership of immovable property. The facts of the case are the following. Sellers had an immovable property in Berlin that was sold to buyers whose funds were frozen by Regulation No. 881/2002. The contract of sale and the agreement on the transfer of ownership were concluded and the sale price was paid before their inclusion into Annex I of Regulation No. 881/2002. After that, the buyers wanted to register the transfer of ownership in the Land Register. This was rejected by the competent authorities due to their inclusion into the annex of that regulation.[52] The question that arose in the case was whether this rejection was justified.[53]

The Court answered by the affirmative; it decided that, in a case such as this one, the provisions of Regulation No. 881/2002 must be interpreted as prohibiting the final registration, in performance of that contract, of the transfer of ownership in the Land Register, subsequent to the date on which the buyer was included in the annex of that regulation.[54] Notwithstanding the fact that the contract of sale

---

[47] For preliminary question see the judgment C-340/08, *M* (point 32).

[48] ECJ, *M and Others* [2010], 29 April 2010, para 74.

[49] ECJ, *M and Others* [2010], 29 April 2010, paras 34–44.

[50] ECJ, *M and Others* [2010], 29 April 2010, paras 53, 56.

[51] For the comments on the judgment, see, for example, Simon 2010; Mok 2010; Murphy 2011.

[52] For the facts of the case see judgment ECJ, Case C-117/06, *Möllendorf* [2007] ECR I-08361, paras 22-39.

[53] ECJ, *Möllendorf* [2007], para 40.

[54] ECJ, *Möllendorf* [2007], para 80.

and agreement on the transfer of ownership were concluded and the sale price was paid before the inclusion in Annex I to Regulation No. 881/2002, the final registration in the Land Register took place subsequent to the date of the inclusion in the Annex and was therefore prohibited to effectively achieve the goals of Regulation No. 881/2002.[55]

5.4.2 The Post-Lisbon Regime of Economic Sanctions

Contrary to the EC Treaty, that expressly provided for only one type of economic sanctions (against third countries, adopted according to a two-step system), the Treaty of Lisbon provides for three different types of economic sanctions in which it integrates the solution adopted in the *Kadi* case concerning the possibility of economic sanctions against natural or legal persons.

The first type of economic sanctions is regulated in Article 75 TFEU, included in the TFEU chapter on the Area of Freedom, Security and Justice.[56] This type of restrictive measure has four main characteristics. First, the restrictive measure is directed against natural or legal persons, groups or non-state entities. Second, the goal of the measure is to prevent and combat terrorism. Third, its content is particularly the freezing of funds, financial assets or economic gains. Fourth, its form and procedure can be summarised in that the Parliament and the Council adopt a framework for such restrictive measures, according to the ordinary legislative procedure; these measures are then implemented by the Council on a proposal from the Commission.

Furthermore, Article 215 TFEU provides for two other types of economic sanctions. On the one hand, it provides for sanctions against third countries and, on the other hand, for sanctions against natural or legal persons. In regard to both types of sanctions, the TFEU maintains the same two-step system as was in force prior to the adoption of Lisbon. The first step is the adoption of the initial CFSP measure providing for economic sanctions (measure pursuant to Chapter 2 of Title V TEU). In the second step, the Council, acting by a qualified majority on a joint proposal from the High Representative and Commission, adopts necessary measures.

It is to be stressed that, by reading the provisions of the TEU and TFEU, it might not be readily apparent that the Treaties provide for two different types of economic sanctions against natural or legal persons. This conclusion can be reached with a systematic argument and by examining the procedure for the adoption of each of these sanctions. First, it is to be stressed that the measures

[55] For the comments on the judgment, see, for example, Bernard 2007; Donnat 2007–2008; Lavranos 2008; Schmucker 2008; Murphy 2011.

[56] More precisely, Chapter I (General provisions) of Title V (Area of Freedom, Security and Justice) of the Treaty on the Functioning of the European Union.

referred to in Article 215 TFEU, measures adopted pursuant to Chapter 2 of Title V TEU (CFSP chapter), should not be confused with the measures adopted on the basis of Article 75 TFEU, included in the *TFEU* chapter on Area of Freedom, Security and Justice. Furthermore, unlike the case of the previously valid Articles 60 and 301 EC, there is no cross-reference between Articles 75 and 215 TFEU. Second, the economic sanctions pursuant to Article 75 TFEU were adopted pursuant to the ordinary legislative procedure and implemented by the Council on a proposal from the Commission, whereas the measures pursuant to Article 215 TFEU need an initial CFSP decision followed by a Council decision adopted with a qualified majority on a joint proposal from the High Representative and the Commission. The European Parliament has also to be informed.

A question that remains open after the entry into force of Lisbon is why the Treaties provide for two different types of sanctions against natural or legal persons. The answer to this question can be partially deduced from the fact that the Article 75 TFEU type of sanctions are provided only in the framework of the fight against terrorism, whereas the sanctions provided for in Article 215 TFEU can be imposed in all other cases in which such sanctions are necessary. By creating a special set of sanctions against natural or legal persons just for the purposes of the fight against terrorism, the Union legislator desired to provide for a possibility of sanctions in a very specific type of situation, where measures need to be adopted fast and without delay. It should also be noted that the different types of sanctions are adopted according to different procedures. Sanctions pursuant to Article 75 TFEU are adopted according to the ordinary legislative procedure with the Council implementing measures. The sanctions pursuant to Article 215 TFEU, however, are adopted following a CFSP measure by the Council with a qualified majority on a joint proposal of the High Representative of the Union and the Commission.

A new exception to the non-jurisdiction rule of the ECJ introduced by the Treaty, partially as a result of the *Kadi* case-law, is the possibility of the direct review of legality of restrictive measures in the field of CFSP against natural or legal persons. According to Article 275(1) TFEU, the Court has jurisdiction to review the legality of Council decisions providing for restrictive measures against natural or legal persons, adopted on the basis of Chapter 2 of Title V TEU (the CFSP chapter). This rule applies provided that the conditions for *locus standi* pursuant to Article 263(4) TFEU are fulfilled. The novelty of this exception is that the ECJ can review the legality of a CFSP measure *directly;* it does not only have jurisdiction to review the legality of the measure that was adopted in the aftermath of a CFSP measure (e.g., regulation).

In relation to this newly established exception, two comments should be put forward. First, in regard to the standing requirement, the question may be raised as to whether these restrictive measures would fall under the category of acts for which the claimant needs to show that he/she is directly and individually concerned, or under the category of regulatory acts that do not entail implementing measures and for which the applicant only needs to show that he/she is directly concerned. In this regard, it should be stressed that CFSP measures entailing economic sanctions will be followed by a measure adopted pursuant to Article 215

TFEU. Therefore, it cannot be argued that it will suffice for the applicants to merely show that the measure is of direct concern to them.

Second, if it is accepted that the ECJ has jurisdiction for direct actions against restrictive measures, it is unclear why it would not have jurisdiction to rule on preliminary rulings on validity concerning these acts. In my view, such a jurisdiction would be problematic from a twofold perspective. On the one hand, a 'literal' argument can be invoked: since this type of jurisdiction is not expressly provided for in the Treaties, it cannot be assumed implicitly. Such a jurisdiction would amount to a revision of the Treaties. On the other hand, such a solution would run counter to the purpose of the EU legislator. It can be argued that the goal of the Treaty was that such acts can be attacked only by persons who fulfil the standing requirements from Article 263(4) TFEU, so that a general review of the legality of such acts that can arise under the preliminary rulings on validity should not be permitted.

The changes brought about with the Treaty, concerning the jurisdiction of the ECJ in the field of CFSP, might have an influence on the case-law of the ECJ. The cases decided in the framework of the preliminary reference procedures in the field of economic sanctions, such as the *M* and the *Möllendorf* case, would not be influenced by the new set of rules, however, the cases, such as *Kadi* and *Mojahedin*, could indeed be influenced.

If the General Court and the ECJ will have to decide on an annulment action of a natural or legal person against a CFSP act imposing economic sanctions, it is possible that such a case would be treated differently from the actual *Kadi* case in three ways. The first difference is that the applicants could seek annulment directly for the CFSP measure.[57] The second difference is that in its analysis, the ECJ could refer to the Charter of Fundamental Rights of the EU as a formal source of law.[58] Already in the *Kadi* judgment, the ECJ did make a reference to the Charter,[59] but at the time, it was not yet a formal legal source. Third, once the EU will have acceded to the European Convention on Human Rights (ECHR), the applicant could start the procedure before the ECHR against the Union.

It has to be stressed that in the aftermath of the ECJ decision on the *Kadi* case, Kadi again filed an action of annulment[60] against the regulation which supposedly

[57] Provided that the measure was adopted in the framework of the to two-step system under Treaty on the Functioning of the European Union, Article 215. If the measure was adopted according to Treaty on the Functioning of the European Union, Article 75, the applicants would, in any event, be able to challenge it.

[58] According to Article 6(1) of the post-Lisbon Treaty on the European Union, the Charter of Fundamental Rights of the EU shall have the same legal value as the Treaties.

[59] ECJ, *Kadi and Al Barakaat* [2008], para 335.

[60] GC, *Kadi* v. *Council and Commission* [2010].

remedied the breach of his fundamental rights, yet his funds were again frozen.[61] The General Court again annulled this regulation on the ground that it was adopted in breach of the applicant's rights of defence.[62] In the argumentation, the General Court stressed that the applicant's rights of defence were only observed in the most formal and superficial sense[63] that the Commission did not take due account of the applicant's comments[64] and that he did not even have the most minimal access to the evidence against him.[65] The case is currently under a three-fold appeal before the ECJ.[66] In regard to this case, it can be observed that the three potential changes mentioned previously did not yet find its way into the case-law.[67]

In regard to the question of whether the principle of loyalty also extends to the CFSP, raised in the *Mojahedin* line of cases, it has to be pointed out that Article 11(2) of the former TEU stated that the Member States 'shall support the Union's external and security policy…in a spirit of loyalty and mutual solidarity' and that they will refrain from any action contrary to the interests of the Union. The revised TEU is even clearer in this regard. Article 24(3) not only contains what the previous provision states, but also expressly stipulates that the Member States shall comply with the Union's action in this area. After the entry into force of the Treaty of Lisbon, it is clear that the principle of loyalty also extends to the CFSP.

5.5 Conclusion

As demonstrated in this chapter, the ECJ can play a double role in the field of CFSP. On the one hand, when deciding the questions of delimitation between areas (former pillars), it can indirectly determine the scope of the CFSP. Under the new Treaty, the boundaries between the CFSP and the TFEU-areas might be subject to interpretation by the ECJ because the previously valid rule of absolute preference of Community law over the CFSP does not apply anymore. This can enable the

---

[61] Commission Regulation (EC) No 1190/2008 of 28 November 2008 amending for the 101st time Council Regulation (EC) No 881/2002 imposing certain specific restrictive measures directed against certain persons and entities associated with Usama bin Laden, the Al-Qaida network and the Taliban, OJ L 322, 2.12.2008, 25.

[62] GC, *Kadi* v. *Council and Commission* [2010], para 179.

[63] GC, *Kadi* v. *Council and Commission* [2010], para 171.

[64] GC, *Kadi* v. *Council and Commission* [2010], para 172.

[65] GC, *Kadi* v. *Council and Commission* [2010], para 173.

[66] The following appeals have been filed against the judgment of the General Court in the Case T-85/09, *Kadi* v *Commission*: ECJ, C-584/10 P, *Commission* v. *Kadi* (appeal of 10 December 2010); ECJ, C-593/10 P, *Council* v. *Kadi* (appeal of 10 December 2010); ECJ, C-595/10 P, *United Kingdom* v. *Kadi* (appeal of 10 December 2010).

[67] The first issue (direct challenge of the CFSP measure) was not relevant in this case because Kadi challenged the regulation on the basis of which his funds were frozen. The General Court also did not refer itself to the Charter of Fundamental Rights of the EU. The third potential change is not yet relevant because the EU did not yet accede to the ECHR.

ECJ to extend or to contract the boundaries of this policy and thereby influence also its content. On the other hand, the ECJ can have influence on the field of the CFSP also through the review of economic sanctions either against natural or legal persons or against third countries. The possibility of direct review by the ECJ of certain restrictive measures against natural or legal persons gives claimants more certainty and an opportunity to seek annulment of restrictive measures early in the process of adoption of these measures. It also ensures that these measures respect human rights. Although this is an example of positive development regarding the jurisdiction of the ECJ in the field of the CFSP, it is to be stressed that certain aspects of the lack of ECJ's jurisdiction still remain unclear, such as the lack of possibility to review, in general, the compatibility of CFSP acts with human rights.

The area of the CFSP is an area where significant changes were expected with the revision of the Treaties. While the changes that were finally introduced with the Treaty are not revolutionary, they do bring about more coherence to the CFSP. One of the most important changes introduced with the Treaty is the formal abolition of the pillar structure. However, the regulation of the CFSP has remained very specific and maintains many of the characteristics of the former second pillar.[68] Along these lines, the role of different institutions was not fundamentally changed.[69] However, despite the lack of fundamental changes concerning the role of the institutions, it is submitted that the changes, although minor, brought about by Lisbon concerning the jurisdiction of the ECJ, can still enhance its role in the field of CFSP. In the introduction of this chapter, the question was asked as to whether the judicial branch is the least dangerous branch in the field of CFSP. This chapter advocates that this is clearly not the case. Despite the marginal role that the ECJ plays in the field of CFSP, we can agree with the former judge of the ECJ, Tim Koopmans, that—at least as regards the ECJ—'the expression the 'least dangerous' branch seems singularly ill chosen'.[70]

References

Bernard E (2007) Sanctions économiques dans le cadre de la lutte contre le terrorisme, Europe n° 332, p 18–19

Bickel A (1962) The least dangerous branch: the Supreme Court at the bar of politics, Bobbs-Merrill, Indianapolis

Brkan M (2008) Presekani (in spet zavezani) gordijski vozel. Pravna praksa 36:25–27

Brkan M (2009) Pravne razsežnosti zunanje politike EU. GV Založba, Ljubljana

[68] For example the adoption of legislative acts is excluded and the unanimous adoption of the acts is a rule except when the Treaties provide otherwise. See Treaty on the European Union, Article 31(1).

[69] An exception is the creation of a new post of High Representative for Foreign Affairs and Security Policy that merges the former post of the former Commissioner responsible for External Relations and European Neighbourhood Policy and the former post of High Representative with the goal of a greater coherence of the external action of the Union.

[70] Koopmans 2003, 271.

Broussy E, Donnat F, Lambert C (2008) Chronique de jurisprudence communautaire. Politique étrangère et de sécurité commune, L'actualité juridique; droit administratif, 1534–1535
Canor I (1998) The recommended limitations on the exercise of Judicial Discretion by the European Court of Justice, Security and Foreign Affairs Issues. Nomos Verlagsgeselschaft. Baden-Baden
Cardwell PJ, French D, White N (2009) Kadi: the Interplay between EU and International Law. International and Comparative Law Quarterly 58:229–240
Cassia P, Donnat F (2008) Terrorisme international et droits fondamentaux: les leçons du droit communautaire. Revue française de droit administratif, 1204–1217
Chavrier H, Honorat E, Pouzoulet P (1995) Le contentieux communautaire. La recevabilité des questions préjudicielles et la compétence de la Cour pour y répondre. L'actualité juridique: droit administratif, 708–711
Cremona M (2004) The Union as a global actor. Roles, models and identity. Common Market Law Review 41:571
De Zwaan JW (1998) Community dimensions of the second pillar. In: Heukels T, Blokker N, Brus M (eds) The European Union after Amsterdam a legal analysis. Kluwer Law International, The Hague, pp 179–193
Donnat F (2007–2008) CJCE, Möllendorf et Möllendorf-Niehuus, aff. C-117/06, Rec. p. I-8361, Revue des affaires européennes, 11 october 2007, p 453–458
Do TU (2008) La jurisprudence de la Cour de justice et du Tribunal de première instance. Chronique des arrêts. Arrêt 'Yassin Abdullah Kadi et al Barakaat International Foundation c. Conseil et Commission'. Revue du droit de l'Union Européenne 4:867–873
Eeckhout P (2004) External relations of the European Union. Oxford University Press, Oxford
Eeckhout P (2005) Does Europe's constitution stop at the water's edge? Law and policy in the EU's external relations (Walter van Gerven Lecture). Europa Law Publishing, Leuven
Ferrari GF (2009) Kadi: verso una Corte di giustizia costituzionale? Diritto pubblico comparato ed europeo 187–192
Garbagnati Ketvel M-G (2006) The jurisdiction of the European Court of justice in respect of the Common Foreign and Security Policy. International and Comparative Law Quarterly 55(1):80
Graf Vitzthum N (2008) Les compétences législatives et juridictionnelles de la Communauté européenne dans la lutte contre le terrorisme—l'affaire 'Kadi' 3: Zeitschrift für Europarechtliche Studien—ZeuS. 375–429
Heliskoski J (2008) Small arms and light weapons within the Union's pillar structure: an analysis of Article 47 of the EU Treaty. European Law Review 898–912
Herlin-Karnell E (2008) Light weapons' and the dynamics of Art 47 EU—The EC's armoury of ever expanding competences. The Modern Law Review 71:998–1008
Heun-Rehn SL-T (2008) Kadi und Al Barakaat—Der EuGH, die Gemeinschaft und das Völkerrecht. European Law Reporter, 322–338
Kämmerer JA (2009) Das Urteil des Europäischen Gerichtshofs im Fall 'Kadi': Ein Triumph der Rechtsstaatlichkeit? Europarecht, 114–130
Karmali A (2008) Annulment of Council decision supporting moratorium on arms and weapons in West Africa—Case C-91/05, Commission v Council. Bulletin of International Legal Development 14. 159–161
Komárek J (2008) Boj proti terorismu, ochrana základních práv a vztah mezinárodního a unijního, Soudní rozhledy: mesícník ceské, zahranicní a evropské judikatury: nová soudní rozhodnutí vydávaná redakcí casopisu Právní rozhledy ve spoluprác jednotlivymi soudci 428–430
Koopmans T (2003) Courts and Political Institutions. Cambridge University Press, Cambridge
Lavranos N (2008) The effect of UN sanctions on private party transactions, European Law Reporter, p 137–143
Martínez Capdevila C (2008) Sobre el reparto horizontal de competencias entre la CE y la UE (Comentario a la Sentencia del TJCE, de 20 de mayo de 2008, as. Comisión c. Consejo—Lucha contra la proliferación de armas ligeras —C-91/05). Revista española de Derecho Europeo 29:101–127

Mok MR (2010) Casenote: Hof van justitie van de Europese unie (vierde kamer), 29 April 2010, nr. Case C-340/08, Nederlandse jurisprudentie. Uitspraken in burgerlijke en strafzaken 414:4101–4110

Murphy CC (2011) Comments on ECJ Case C-117/06, Proceedings brought by Gerda Möllendorf and Christiane Möllendorf-Niehuus; ECJ Case C-340/08, M and Others v. Her Majesty's Treasury; ECJ Case C-550/09, Criminal Proceedings Against E and F. Common Market Law Review 48:243–264

Ohler C (2008) Gemeinschaftsrechtlicher Rechtsschutz gegen personengerichtete Sanktionen des UN-Sicherheitsrats. Europäische Zeitschrift für Wirtschaftsrecht, 630–633

Rijken CRJJ (2009) Het Hof als hoeder van de fundamentele rechten in de zaak Kadi en Al Barakaat, Nederlands tijdschrift voor Europees recht, 140–146

Sandulli A (2008) I rapporti tra diritto europeo ed internazionale. Il caso Kadi: un nuovo caso Solange?, Giornale di diritto amministrativo, 513 ff

Sauer H (2008) Rechtsschutz gegen völkerrechtsdeterminiertes Gemeinschaftsrecht? Neue juristische Wochenschrift, 3685–3688

Schmucker A (2008) Verordnung (EG) Nr. 881/2002 Article 2 Abs. 3 (Keine Eigentumsumschreibung auf gelistete Person), Deutsche Notar-Zeitschrift: Verkündungsblatt der Bundesnotarkammer, n° 09, p 695–703

Simon D (2010) Contentieux des mesures anti-terroristes, Europe, June 2010, n° 191 p 10

Weatherill S (1998) Safeguarding the acquis communautaire. In: Heukels T, Blokker N, Brus M (eds) The European Union after Amsterdam: a legal analysis. Kluwer Law International, The Hague

Wessel RA (2000) The inside looking out: consistency and delimitation in EU external relations. Common Market Law Review 37:1135–1171

Wessel RA (2008) Veiligheidsbeleid of toch ontwikkelingssamenwerking? De afbakening van de externe bevoegdheden tussen de EU, de EG en de lidstaten. Nederlands tijdschrift voor Europees recht 10:292–299

Part II
Perspectives on Institutional Developments

Chapter 6
Institutionalization or Intergovernmental Decision-Taking in Foreign Policy: The Implementation of the Lisbon Treaty

Pol Morillas

Abstract This chapter analyses the evolving nature of the foreign policy of the EU as a consequence of the set up of new structures such as the office of the High Representative/Vice President and the European External Action Service. It argues that while decision-taking in CFSP and CSDP remains intergovernmental for the most part, the strengthened power of initiative granted to the new services has introduced critical changes in EU foreign policy-making. The first developments under the Lisbon Treaty hint a process of institutionalisation by practice in EU foreign policy initiative, which relates to the personalities at the top of new EU structures, the changes of procedures in the elaboration of policy papers and meeting agendas and the management of crisis situations. This process of institutionalisation by practice, as well as the reaction of EU Member States to it, is examined particularly with regard to the working relations between the new foreign policy structures and the Political and Security Committee of the EU.

Pol Morillas—MSc International Relations, London School of Economics and Political Science. Pol Morillas is Coordinator of Euro-Mediterranean policies at the European Institute of the Mediterranean (IEMed), Barcelona, Spain. He was previously Coordinator at the Political and Security Committee of the EU during the Spanish Presidency of the Council of the EU (January–June 2010). This chapter was first published as an article in *European Foreign Affairs Review* [2011] volume 16 (2), pp. 243–257. The editor of this volume is extremely grateful to the *EFA Rev* editors for allowing it to be reproduced here. The author would like to thank Professor Michael E. Smith from the University of Aberdeen for his valuable comments on previous versions of this chapter. I am also grateful to Dr Paul James Cardwell for accepting my participation at the conference 'EU External Relations Law and Policy in the Post-Lisbon Era' held in the School of Law of the University of Sheffield in January 2011, where an earlier version of this chapter was presented. The views expressed here are only those of the author and do not represent the position of the Spanish Presidency or government. Any errors or omissions are the responsibility of the author.

P. Morillas (✉)
London School of Economics and Political Science, London, UK
e-mail: polmorillas@hotmail.com

P. J. Cardwell (ed.), *EU External Relations Law and Policy in the Post-Lisbon Era*,
DOI: 10.1007/978-90-6704-823-1_6, © T.M.C. Asser press, The Hague,
The Netherlands, and the authors 2012

Contents

6.1 Introduction

One year after the entry into force of the Lisbon Treaty, the foreign policy system of the European Union is undergoing major transformations. Of all areas of reform, Common Foreign and Security Policy (hereafter CFSP) is at the core of institutional novelty, especially with regard to the creation of the figure of the High Representative of the Union for Foreign and Security Policy and Vice-president of the European Commission (hereafter HR/VP). The person in charge of this office is responsible for enhancing the position of the EU in the world, now with more powerful foreign policy instruments and visibility.

Catherine Ashton, appointed HR/VP by the European Council right after the entry into force of the Lisbon Treaty, has a 'once-in-a-generation opportunity to build something that finally brings together all the instruments of our engagement in support of a single political strategy […] and to adapt to a world of growing complexity and fundamental power shifts',[1] as she stated before the European Parliament on March 2010. To do so, the powers of the HR/VP have been reinforced and the post backed with a new institution, the European External Action Service (hereafter EEAS).

Institutional reforms introduced in the Lisbon Treaty go hand-in-hand with changes in EU foreign policy-making. Decision-taking in CFSP and Common Security and Defence Policy (hereafter CSDP) remains intergovernmental for the most part, but the new services hold strengthened powers of initiative in foreign policy.[2] The semester of the Spanish presidency, when the set up of the Lisbon institutional architecture began, provides valuable indications on the evolving procedures of EU foreign policy-making. As this chapter will study, the implementation of the Lisbon Treaty between January and June 2010 reveals a process of institutionalisation by practice.

---

[1] Speech of the HR/VP to the Foreign Affairs Committee of the European Parliament, Brussels, 23 March 2010. europa.eu/rapid/pressReleasesAction.do?reference=SPEECH/10/120&format=HTML&aged=0&language=EN&guiLanguage=en. Accessed 25 July 2011.

[2] This chapter will use 'decision taking' to refer to the procedures by which decisions are taken in the main foreign policy committees of the Council of the EU, i.e. by unanimity and intergovernmentalism. 'Decision making' will be understood as a broader formulation including further elements of foreign policy-making such as the power of initiative.

Institutionalisation will be understood here as a process whereby there is a conferral of powers to the new common institutions and EU foreign policy leaders, in particular, the EEAS and the HR/VP. The power of initiative in EU foreign policy, formerly held by Member States and the rotating Presidency of the Council only, is now shared with the HR/VP. In line with institutionalism theories, initial policy choices (the set up of new foreign policy structures and the conferral of powers to them in our case) have an impact on further institutional evolution.[3] A process of institutionalisation by practice as described in the last part of this chapter could foster fundamental changes in the nature of EU foreign policy, extending some aspects of the Community method to CFSP and CSDP. Moreover, the EEAS could enhance the institutionalisation of EU foreign policy, formalising a process of rule-governed action within an organisation with budget, staff and permanent headquarters entirely dedicated to the external relations of the EU.[4]

This chapter will first analyse the long road towards foreign policy reform from the establishment of the European Convention until the entry into force of the Lisbon Treaty. It will study the upgrading of the functions of the HR/VP, with a particular emphasis on its enhanced power of initiative, and will also refer to the structuring of new working relations within the Political and Security Committee of the EU (hereafter PSC). The second part of the chapter provides the time frame of such developments. The Spanish Presidency of the Council of the EU can be considered a paradigmatic case study of the evolution of EU foreign policy-making. As the first implementation presidency, the policies of the Spanish semester provoked reactions by other Member States which perceived a process of institutionalisation by practice of the EU foreign policy system.

This process is reviewed in further detail in the third part of the chapter. Here, the analysis focus on the importance of the personalities at the top of new EU structures, the changes of procedures in the elaboration of policy papers and meeting agendas, and the management of crisis situations. The chapter ends with some concluding remarks on the process of institutionalisation by practice in foreign policy initiative, its implications for the nature of EU external relations and the effects of the policies of the Spanish presidency on the post-Lisbon institutional system.

6.2 The Long Road Towards Foreign Policy Reform

When the European Council met in Laeken in December 2001, the main concern of the Heads of State and Government was to put in place institutional reforms that would enable the EU to speak to the world with a single voice and to enhance the

---

[3] Vanhoonacker 2005, 70.

[4] Michael E. Smith's view of institutionalisation is particularly relevant to assess the transformation of EU foreign policy from 'an informal, intergovernmental 'gentleman's agreement' with unwritten rules into a system of formal and informal legal obligations'. See Smith 2004, 11. The EEAS could become the central actor of such system.

effectiveness of its external action. The European Council established the European Convention on the Future of Europe, chaired by Valéry Giscard d'Estaing and entrusted to write a Draft Treaty establishing a Constitution for Europe. The draft Constitution was signed in Rome on 24 October 2004, but was finally rejected by referendum in France and the Netherlands in May 2005.

The reform of EU foreign policy aimed to promote the 'convergence of views among Member States on the different matters of external policy' and 'to circumvent the constraints of unanimity in CFSP'.[5] Several proposals were discussed during the drafting exercises of the European Constitution, particularly with regard to the figure of the High Representative for the CFSP.

As set up in the Treaty of Amsterdam of 1997, the position of the High Representative was meant to assist the Presidency of the Council and to contribute to the formulation, preparation and implementation of policy decisions and to conduct political dialogue with third parties at the request of the Presidency.[6] The text of the European Constitution upgraded the position of the office held at that moment by Javier Solana, giving the High Representative the mandate to shape foreign policy and EU external action. The High Representative would now have a formal right of initiative, contributing with his proposals to the development of CFSP. With this objective, the so-called Foreign Minister would become a double-hatted official, exercising both the offices of the Commissioner for External Relations and the High Representative. The European Constitution, if adopted, would have succeeded in 'endowing the Union with an institutional 'centre of gravity' to conduct external relations',[7] transforming the Foreign Minister into a political figure implementing and shaping foreign policy through its formal right of initiative. During the debates of the European Convention, some representatives saw an opportunity for transferring the Community method to external policy, while others remained committed to intergovernmentalism.

The European Convention finally circumvented this debate by focusing on the improvement of decision-making procedures in the field of CFSP. As Grevi has noted, 'further extension of aspects of the Community method to CFSP [during the debates of the Convention] were simply not there'.[8] In practice that meant that the creation of a double-hatted Foreign Minister (vice-president of the Commission and president of the Foreign Affairs Council) would not threaten the prerogatives of the Council in the field of CFSP. Decision taking in the field of foreign and security policy would still require the agreement of all Member States, even if the Foreign Minister would be granted the power of initiative in view of reinforcing coherence, efficiency and leadership of EU external action.

The Treaty of Lisbon has not changed substantially the mechanisms to increase coherence, leadership and influence in EU foreign policy. Without a reference to

[5] Grevi 2007, 778.

[6] Grevi 2007, 775.

[7] Grevi 2007, 800.

[8] Grevi 2007, 804.

the Foreign Minister, the text which entered into force on 1 December 2009 gives the new HR/VP enhanced functions to make the Union 'more present in the world.'[9] The Lisbon Treaty has created a triple-hatted office, adding to the two functions of the former EU Foreign Minister the Presidency of the Foreign Affairs Council, which was formerly exercised for six months by the Minister of Foreign Affairs of the rotating presidency of the Council.[10] The HR/VP conducts CFSP and CSDP, 'as mandated by the Council' (Article 18 (2) Treaty of the European Union, hereafter TEU), and exercises the right of initiative by making proposals in the field of CFSP. It is also responsible for ensuring consistency of the Union's external action.[11] The HR/VP 'contributes through his/her proposals to the development of CFSP and ensures implementation of the decisions adopted by the European Council and the Council'.[12]

The long negotiations of the Lisbon Treaty witnessed the demands of several delegations that nothing in the Treaty should change the CFSP decision-making process or the (weak) powers conferred to other EU institutions. As a result, 'CFSP remains (…) largely in the hands of the Council, and of its members, the representatives of the governments of the Member States'.[13] Unanimity remains the standard decision-taking procedure for CFSP,[14] even if the Lisbon Treaty has given the HR/VP a formal right of initiative and introduced a few improvements regarding the use of qualified majority voting, legal instruments and the participation of other EU institutions.[15] Although the HR/VP carries out CFSP and CSDP as mandated by the Council, it contributes through its initiative to the configuration and development and of this policy.

As a result of the Lisbon Treaty, the office of the HR/VP also strengthens its links with the PSC, a key committee for the development of CFSP and CSDP. Established in 2001 and formalised by the Treaty of Nice, the PSC gathers twice a week in Brussels at the ambassadorial level. Its tasks include the monitoring of the international agenda, the contribution to the definition and implementation of policies and the political control over crisis management missions and operations. With the Lisbon Treaty, the HR/VP is now more involved in the responsibilities of the PSC. A permanent chair has been appointed by Catherine Ashton to ensure proper coordination between the new services and the representatives of the Member States. The monitoring role of the implementation of agreed policies in the field of CFSP, one of the key responsibilities of the PSC, must now be exercised without prejudice to the

9 The text of the Laeken Declaration on the Future of the European Union of 15 December 2001.

10 Some EU officials even refer to a fourth role exercised by the HR/VP, which is to ensure coherence of all EU external action.

11 For a full revision of the tasks of the HR/VP, see Piris 2010, 246.

12 Piris 2010, 257.

13 Piris 2010, 260.

14 Wessels and Bopp 2008, 23.

15 Piris 2010, 261–265; European Parliament (2008) The Lisbon Treaty and its Implications for CFSP/ESDP. www.europarl.europa.eu/document/activities/cont/200805/20080513ATT28796/20080513ATT28796EN.pdf. Accessed 25 July 2011.

powers of the High Representative. Also, the strategic guidance and control of CSDP must be implemented 'under the responsibility of the Council *and* of the High Representative' (Article 38 TEU, emphasis added). Officials from the EEAS will also chair the working groups of the Council, in order to strengthen the consistency among committees responsible for EU foreign policy.

6.3 Implementing the Lisbon Treaty During the First Semester of 2010

This section will review some practical developments of EU foreign policy-making during the Spanish Presidency of the Council of the EU between January and June 2010, right after the entry into force of the Lisbon Treaty and the immediate appointment of Catherine Ashton as the new HR/VP.

The six-monthly programme of the Spanish Presidency of the Council of the EU highlighted as its main objective the 'fast and full enforcement of the Treaty of Lisbon.'[16] This came first in the programme, even before economic recovery and job creation. As many officials put it, the fourth Spanish presidency of the EU was to be not a transition but an *implementation* presidency. If successful, the Presidency would make a difference in implementing the new EU structures and become an example for future presidencies. In more theoretical terms, the 'informal customs' of the Spanish presidency could end up having a demonstration effect for the future configuration of the EU foreign policy system.[17]

As part of the Trio of presidencies formed by Spain, Belgium and Hungary, Spain was the first country to recognise that setting into motion the new European institutions, particularly the EEAS, was crucial to enhance coherence and efficiency in Europe's foreign policy. On the basis of the Spanish experience, the Belgian presidency also stated on its programme that the implementation of the Lisbon Treaty was of paramount importance in the following six months, with a particular emphasis on the consolidation and stabilisation of working methods and sharing of responsibilities.[18]

Working for the full implementation of the Lisbon Treaty also involved acknowledging the leading policy role of the HR/VP in CFSP. The Spanish presidency outspoke its support to the new holder of the post and committed to contribute actively with 'a smooth and orderly transition to the Union's new model

[16] Programme of the Spanish Presidency of the Council of the EU, 5. www.eu2010.es/export/sites/presidencia/comun/descargas/Spanish_Presidency_Program.pdf, Accessed 25 July 2011.

[17] See Smith 2004 for a detailed analysis of 'informal customs' and their effect on the foreign policy system of the EU.

[18] Programme of the Belgian Presidency of the Council of the EU. www.eutrio.be/files/bveu/media/documents/Programme_EN.pdf. Accessed 25 July 2011, 11.

of external action.'[19] In practice, this involved trespassing all policy initiatives in external affairs to the HR/VP, despite the references to foreign policy objectives in the Spanish six-monthly programme. For many, Madrid was cast in the role of an 'institutional laboratory rat',[20] forced to accept the secondary role given to rotating presidencies by the new institutional framework.

The Spanish authorities took the political decision not to push for national policy initiatives in order not to hold up the work of the new foreign policy structures. During six months, the rotating presidency would lose its foreign policy initiative in favour of other Member States and the new institutional services. As a leading Spanish political analyst put it, Spain was 'preparing a final farewell to the six-month presidency system [and] that may be the only mention the Spanish presidency gets in the history books.'[21]

Success of the Spanish term could thus not be measured in relation to initiatives taken and achieved during the first six months of 2010. Despite some criticism,[22] most stakeholders in Brussels and other capitals acknowledged that Spain was the 'first country to swallow the bitter medicine of accepting the secondary role the treaty gave national capitals.'[23] Member States recognised the difficult position of this presidency, having prepared for a normal six-month term and forced to adapt its working methods a month after the entry into force of the Lisbon Treaty.

The Treaty had a direct impact on the PSC as a core committee of the EU foreign policy machinery. During the Spanish semester, the Ambassador of Spain to the PSC became the chair of this committee, chairing it under the authority of the HR/VP. In fact, that meant that Spain did not have an Ambassador sitting at this committee. The Belgian presidency suffered from a similar lack of foreign policy initiative at the PSC during the next six months, although both Spain and Belgium still chaired the working groups of the Council dedicated to foreign affairs. This transition period lasted until the appointment on 16 November 2010 of

---

[19] Programme of the Spanish Presidency, 20.

[20] European Voice (2010) Spain must show value of rotating presidency, 27 May 2010. www.europeanvoice.com/article/imported/spain-must-show-value-of-rotating-presidency/68062.aspx. Accessed 25 July 2011.

[21] Torreblanca J I (2010) Farewell, Presidencies, European Council on Foreign Relations. ecfr.eu/content/entry/commentary_torreblanca_on_presidencies/. Accessed 25 July 2011.

[22] Most of these comments referred to the fact that some Spanish authorities were seeking more visibility and presence during the presidency, as revealed in 'Spain's foreign policy push failing', European Voice. 27 May 2010. www.europeanvoice.com/article/imported/spain-s-foreign-push-failing/68061.aspx.; Strains are showing in the EU's new foreign policy structures, Financial Times, Brussels Blog, 24 January 2010, blogs.ft.com/brusselsblog/2010/01/strains-are-showing-in-the-eus-new-foreign-policy-structures/; and Spain ends invisible EU presidency. EU Observer, 30 June 2010. euobserver.com/9/30385. Accessed 25 July 2011.

[23] Torreblanca J I (2010) Foreign policy needs a rethink above and beyond Europe, European Council on Foreign Relations. ecfr.eu/content/entry/commentary_foreign_policy_needs_a_rethink_above_and_beyond_europe/. Accessed 25 July 2011.

former Ambassador of Sweden to the PSC, Olof Skoog, as permanent chair of this committee, who started chairing it on 1 January 2011.[24]

The secondary role of the Spanish presidency with regard to foreign policy initiative provoked some backlash reactions at decision-taking bodies such as the PSC. Some Member States feared that the Presidency's secondary role *vis-à-vis* the new foreign policy structures, and particularly the HR/VP, would translate into a radical change of EU foreign policy-making. According to these voices, decision-taking in CFSP remained intergovernmental and Spain's support to the role of the HR/VP could thwart the objective to strengthen the position of EU Member States during this transition period. Throughout several discussions on the responsibilities of this committee in EU foreign policy-making, some delegations insisted that the Lisbon Treaty and the appointment of the HR/VP had had no impact on CFSP decision-making procedures. This remained an intergovernmental EU policy and, as such, Member States should not be responsible for *shaping* policies but for *making* them.

Such observations also referred to the division of labour among committees of the Council responsible for EU foreign policy. If the PSC were to become a secondary body *vis-à-vis* the new structures, Member States could prefer referring controversial issues to purely intergovernmental bodies such as the Committee of Permanent Representatives (hereafter COREPER), where the Lisbon Treaty had introduced no change in foreign affairs matters. As the ultimate body reaching agreements on the agendas and conclusions of the Foreign Affairs Council (hereafter FAC), some national delegations threatened to use their veto power in this committee. All national voices would thus be respected and foreign policy would remain a purely intergovernmental policy.

As the Director of the EU Institute for Security Studies put it some time after the beginning of the Spanish Presidency, 'in the coming decade, the Union's external policy will either be forged by the Member States or it will not exist at all.'[25] This quote translates the policy debate into more theoretical discussions. Foreign policy-making after the entry into force of the Lisbon Treaty unveiled political discussions which reflected theoretical divergences on an increased institutionalisation of EU foreign policy versus the preservation of intergovermentalism. But the quote could also refer to the risk of bilateralisation of the foreign policies of EU Member States with world actors as a consequence of changes introduced by the new Treaty. Some diplomats alerted on the risk of big and medium Member States preferring to strengthen national ties with third actors at the expense of a perceived institutionalised EU foreign policy. The victory of UK conservatives in the general elections of 6 May 2010 and the intention of Foreign

[24] The announcement of the appointment of the Permanent Chair of the PSC by the HR/VP can be consulted here: www.consilium.europa.eu/uedocs/cms_data/docs/pressdata/EN/foraff/117740.pdf. Accessed 25 July 2011.

[25] de Vasconcelos 2010.

Secretary William Hague to strengthen UK's ties with world powers revealed some accuracy of these concerns.[26]

6.4 A Process of Institutionalisation by Practice

The Spanish government drafted the key elements of the presidency programme before the entry into force of the Lisbon Treaty. When its implementation started, the government decided to put all its people and means at the service of the new structures. This political decision involved turning the presidency into a testing ground for the implementation of the new foreign policy structures. It also involved the redefinition of the relationship between these structures and Member States. Consequently, the Spanish term witnessed vivid discussions about the role of each actor in EU foreign policy initiative and decision taking, bringing political discussions in Brussels back to theoretical debates on institutionalisation and intergovernmentalism in EU foreign policy.

This section will question whether the new structures of the Lisbon Treaty, in particular the set up of the office of the HR/VP, could foster a process of institutionalisation of EU foreign policy through daily working procedures. Institutional practice during the first six months of the Lisbon Treaty might have contributed to define institutionalised ways of functioning of the foreign policy system of the EU. Institutional novelties introduced by the Treaty such as the EEAS could also end up having a transformative effect over the nature of EU foreign policy, providing a paradigmatic case study for strengthened institutionalism in this EU policy.

On the basis of the distinction between initiative and decision taking in EU foreign policy, this section will identify three areas in which institutional practice has provoked significant changes in foreign policy-making. Systemic change towards more institutionalised practices can be noticed in procedural developments, initiative in crisis management situations and personalities at the top of the new institutional system. While decision-taking in EU foreign policy remains mostly intergovernmental, institutional practices hint an increased relevance of the Union foreign policy structures.

The set up of the EEAS represents a revolutionary change of EU foreign policy structures. The merging of EU services dealing with external relations, in particular the Directorate General for External Relations of the European Commission and the services of external relations of the Council of the EU, has created a brand-new institution under the control of the HR/VP and in charge of most aspects of EU external action. The Treaty leaves details on the structure, organisation and

[26] Hague the realist takes centre stage, Financial Times, 2 July 2010. UK's intention to strengthen bilateral ties with world powers such as the US, India and China went hand in hand with the government's will to engage more deeply with the EU and bolster UK's influence in key European bodies.

functioning of the EEAS to be determined at a later stage,[27] although negotiations already started during the Spanish presidency. The General Affairs Council of April 2010 reached political agreement on the draft decision on the establishment of the EEAS. The Council decision establishing the organisation and functioning of the EEAS was adopted on 26 July 2010 and the new service is fully operational since 1 January 2011.

Negotiations for the set up of the EEAS witnessed turf wars among institutions for the control of the new service. In particular, the European Parliament saw an opportunity for the progressive institutionalisation of foreign and security policy, in view of the final goal of European integration.[28] The Parliament also used the financial and personnel regulations of the new institution to make its voice heard in the negotiations.[29] Finally, it also requested to exercise political control over high officials of the service—for instance the new Heads of EU Delegations around the world— and to provide general guidance of foreign policy objectives, which was not accepted by EU Member States.

The influence of the EEAS and the new *de facto* powers of the European Parliament in foreign policy-making will need to be analysed in future studies, in particular regarding the theoretical impact of the new foreign policy structures and the creation of conditions for agreement between foreign policy actors and the emergence of a common political will in external policies.[30] So far, practices undertaken during the first months of 2010 hint at significant transformations in EU foreign policy initiative.

As many analysts foresaw, institutional practice has been crucial to establish the new EU foreign policy system as a consequence of the entry into force of the Lisbon Treaty.[31] Three elements advancing institutionalised practices during the first half of 2010 can be identified. These refer to the personality of the new foreign policy chief and its effects on the new machinery, the procedures in agenda setting and production of working papers for Council discussions and the handling of crisis management situations, in particular the earthquake of Haiti and the Flotilla crisis in Gaza. The last two, agenda setting and crisis management, reveal critical debates generated by the entry into force of the Lisbon Treaty with regards to EU foreign policy-making.

The first holder of the post of HR/VP, Catherine Ashton, entered European politics as the Commissioner for Trade. For two years, she negotiated trade deals on behalf of 27 Member States and represented the EU with a single voice at the World Trade Organization. When appointed by the Council as the first HR/VP, the diplomatic

---

[27] Piris 2010, 250

[28] Weiss 2010.

[29] As Piris notes, 'the organisation and functioning of the EEAS have to be laid down by a decision of the Council, acting by unanimity on a proposal from the High Representative, after *consulting* the European Parliament and obtaining consent from the Commission', Piris 2010, 250.

[30] Crowe 2008, 10.

[31] Grevi 2007; Piris 2010.

community of the Council feared that her previous position would reinforce the foreign policy powers of the Commission via Ashton's vice-president hat.

The director of a leading human rights NGO qualified the increased powers of the HR/VP and her team stating that 'we have created a monarch for EU foreign policy.' This referred to the working methods of Catherine Ashton regarding foreign policy initiatives, which also provoked harsh reactions at the main EU Council committees. As noted above, many Ambassadors revealed fears of their governments that the EU foreign policy machinery would seek to increase its powers over a traditionally intergovernmental policy.

However, as Giovanni Grevi already pointed out in 2007, 'the stronger the call for consistency between all external policies, the more pivotal is the figure that will ensure such consistency.'[32] The Lisbon Treaty gives enough room to the HR/VP to define by practice the potential of her position and the new institutional equilibriums in EU foreign policy. Her first public appearances revealed significant rapprochements to communitarian institutions such as the European Commission and the European Parliament.

The centrality of the new foreign policy chief's personality was evident when Catherine Ashton decided to build her team with former trade colleagues and to retain her office at the Berlaymont building, the headquarters of the European Commission.[33] Ashton's steering group for the creation of the EEAS also included a large representation of Commission officials, which triggered criticism among Member States when they saw that only the Spanish presidency and the Belgian and Hungarian permanent representative (as incoming presidencies) were represented in the group. According to a confidential document revealed by the newspaper The Guardian, Germany and France were 'anxious' to see that Ashton, but also the UK, were gaining 'excessive' EU powers.[34] Such fears became more intense when civil servants from the former DG Relex of the European Commission occupied an important number of the leading positions at the organigram of the EEAS.

Regarding the powers of the European Parliament, Ashton's first public appearances seemed to reinforce the foreign policy powers of this institution, especially when she declared herself ready to hold CFSP and CSDP accountable before the European Parliament.[35] Fears of a progressive institutionalisation of EU foreign policy became evident when a senior diplomat declared that 'Ashton is not an institution herself and cannot oppose what the Council has to say on foreign policy issues.'

---

[32] Grevi 2007, 801.

[33] See, for instance, the Charlemagne column, Too many cooks, The Economist, 19 December 2009. www.economist.com/node/15127624. Accessed 25 July 2011.

[34] Germany and France dispute Lady Ashton's 'excessive' EU powers, The Guardian, 28 February 2010. www.guardian.co.uk/world/2010/feb/28/germany-france-dispute-ashton-european-powers. Accessed 25 July 2011.

[35] Hearing of HR/VP Catherine Ashton at the Foreign Affairs Committee of the European Parliament, 2 December 2009.

Together with the personality of the new foreign policy chief, the setting of FAC and PSC agendas and the drafting of FAC conclusions and working papers for foreign policy discussions can also help to determine whether an increased institutionalisation by practice is taking place within the new EU foreign policy structures. Broad agenda-setting procedures and working methods are key elements of the institutionalisation of EU foreign and security policy.[36]

Agenda setting of the FAC during the first half of 2010 revealed interesting elements of the institutionalisation of foreign policy initiative and the intergovernmentalism of decision-taking. While the HR/VP and her cabinet tried in several occasions to limit the amount of items in the agenda so that Council meetings could be run in an orderly and effective manner, several Member States opposed that some items were not included in the agenda. For instance, the FAC of April 2010 ended up discussing Burma/Myanmar, even if the services had opposed this discussion to allow more time for the strategic debates on EU resource allocation and relations with strategic partners, an item put forward by the HR/VP.

This example shows that the Lisbon Treaty has strengthened the right of initiative of the HR/VP but also that decision-taking in foreign affairs remains mostly intergovernmental (an item cannot be removed from the FAC agenda if a Member State requests it). Indeed, the Treaty does not change decision-taking procedures in relation to the adoption of FAC agendas. After discussion at the PSC, these agendas are necessarily endorsed by the COREPER, where intergovernmentalism and right to veto reign on foreign policy issues and where the HR/VP has no formal presence.

PSC agenda setting also revealed the increased powers of the services put at the disposal of the HR/VP (General Secretariat of the Council and DG Relex at the European Commission). Former policy initiative held by the rotating presidency was replaced by agreement of the agendas between the head of the Policy Unit of the General Secretariat of the Council and the Chair of the PSC during the Spanish and Belgian Presidencies. During the Spanish Presidency, the leading voice in these meetings was that of the Head of the Policy Unit.

With the appointment of a permanent chair of the PSC, agenda setting will be fully decided by the services put at the disposal of the HR/VP (the chair of the PSC in this case). Initiative in this committee of the EU will be granted to the new foreign policy structures and Member States will be able to request the inclusion of a certain item once the agenda has been set. In short, Member States will adopt a reactive role rather than being the primary source of initiative with regard to PSC agenda setting.

During this transition period, FAC conclusions were drafted first in the offices of the European Commission and Council buildings. Member States received the papers once the cabinet of the HR/VP had given its green light for their distribution. The input by Member States only came at a later stage of the process. Something similar happened with working papers preparing the discussions of the

[36] Smith 2004.

PSC which feed the debates and conclusions of the FAC. The presentation of these working papers to Member States sometimes came a few hours before the FAC, which made it difficult for Member States to change their essence and key messages. As a senior diplomat put it, 'the PSC cannot be like the cabinet of the High Representative', referring to the prerogatives of this committee to discuss and take decisions on the contents of working documents and agendas of FAC meetings. To sum up, were working procedures of the first half of 2010 to consolidate over time, the foreign policy system of the EU would be adopting more institutionalised practices.

Finally, initiative in crisis management situations during the first half of 2010 also hinted at an institutionalisation process. The Haiti earthquake of 12 January 2010 was the first natural disaster faced by the new EU foreign policy structures. Their reaction was severely criticised due to the HR/VP's unwillingness to immediately visit the affected area. Ashton justified her position by arguing that 'I had nothing to contribute on the ground other than taking up valuable space when planes were unable to land because of the state of the airfield (…) I am not a doctor, nor a fire fighter. My place was to bring together co-ordination at EU level and with the UN.'[37]

Indeed, the HR/VP took a leading role in Brussels in coordinating the EU's response to the crisis. The first draft statement of the declaration of the HR/VP on the earthquake in Haiti included a reference to a launch of a CSDP operation. New CSDP missions and operations require the agreement of all Member States at the FAC. After long negotiations about how much military assets could contribute to the relief efforts in Haiti, the EU decided to create a cell within the Situation Centre (EU SITCEN) to assist in the coordination of military assets (EU Coordination Cell, EUCO Haiti).[38] The initiative to launch a CSDP operation as a response to the earthquake in Haiti clashed with the preferences of Member States in this crisis management situation.

Likewise, the debates on lessons learned from EU's response to the Haiti earthquake unveiled the difficulties of Member States to follow initiatives coming from the HR/VP in crisis management. Catherine Ashton and Commissioner for International Cooperation, Humanitarian Aid and Crisis Response, Kristalina Georgieva, presented a working paper which included references to the use of military means under CSDP in crisis situations. The willingness of the new structures and some Member States to move towards an EU comprehensive approach in crisis management (including the use of civilian and military assets) clashed with the difficulties of other Member States to welcome the recommendations by the HR/VP and Commissioner Georgieva. Some Member States reminded that an initiative to increase the

---

[37] European Parliament (2010) Haiti Needs Rapid Aid and Long-term Reconstruction, 19 January 2010, www.europarl.europa.eu/sides/getDoc.do?language=EN&type=IM-PRESS&reference=20100119IPR67605. Accessed 25 July 2011.

[38] For details of EU's reaction to the crisis in Haiti, see EU CSDP (2010) Newsletter 10, www.consilium.europa.eu/uedocs/cmsUpload/online_100818_CSDP_Newsletter_hw.pdf. Accessed 25 July 2011.

use of military means in crisis management requires discussion at intergovernmental bodies such as the PSC. According to these voices, decision-taking on crisis management under the Lisbon Treaty remains an intergovernmental policy and the HR/VP can only use her *Commission hat* on areas not belonging to CSDP.

The second crisis situation of 2010 which required close attention by the EU was the confrontation between Israel and a flotilla seeking to break Gaza's blockade in May 2010 which resulted in the death of several pro-Palestinian activists and sparked a diplomatic crisis in the region. In order to explore the EU's contribution to alleviate the blockade, the HR/VP decided to set up a Gaza Task Force with representation of France but not other Member States. The aim was to explore with like minded countries ways to reinforce the presence of the EU in the region (for instance by beefing up its CSDP contribution to monitor Gaza crossing points).

This initiative spread suspicions among other Member States with high stakes in the Israeli–Palestinian conflict, which saw how the new foreign policy structures could be shaping the EU's policy in the Middle East without their approval. In the event of a reinforcement of EU Border Assistance Mission (EUBAM) Rafah (the CSDP operation which monitors the Rafah crossing point between Israel and Egypt), all Member States should participate in decisions to be adopted by intergovernmental procedures. According to these Member States, the Gaza Task Force set up by the HR/VP could only be a consultative body and EU policy initiatives should be discussed at Council bodies such as the PSC, where all Member States are present.

As shown by the discussions on the EU's response to crisis situations, initiatives by the new foreign policy structures sometimes clashed with the unwillingness of Member States to relax their decision-taking prerogatives. The Haiti earthquake and the flotilla crisis in Gaza required rapid responses by the EU and the new structures responded to these challenges with policy initiatives that enhanced their leadership in EU foreign policy. However, Member States reminded that their participation and decisions were needed when CSDP actions were to be discussed. The set up of new foreign policy structures sped up the debate on CFSP and CSDP actions with the power of initiative of the HR/VP, but it did not replace the role of Member States in decision-taking.

6.5 Conclusions

The entry into force of the Lisbon Treaty has forced European foreign policy stakeholders to adapt to a new institutional framework. Member States share today their leading role in EU foreign policy with the new office of the HR/VP and the EEAS. Initiative in EU foreign policy has become a shared endeavour and the creation of new structures has had a remarkable impact upon foreign policy-making. As a consequence, Member States have reacted by making more explicit the distinction between initiative and decision-taking in EU foreign policy.

On one hand, foreign policy initiative during the first half of 2010 set off a process of institutionalisation by practice as a result of the personality of the holder of the top foreign policy post, the procedures in agenda setting and drafting of working papers and the response to crisis situations. On the other, Member States reacted to institutional novelty by reaffirming their position in the new institutional architecture. Although not seeking to undermine the new structures, they made clear that decision-taking in EU foreign policy still follows intergovernmental rules.

Working methods of foreign policy-making had to adapt to this new institutional environment. The role of the Spanish Presidency between January and June 2010 was critical in setting up the new foreign policy machinery. With its decision to put the new structures at the centre of policy-making, the Spanish presidency set important precedents for the evolution of the post-Lisbon foreign policy system.

Firstly, Member States reacted by making constant references to the rule of unanimity in EU foreign policy, which entailed the halt of some initiatives of the new foreign policy structures. Moreover, the risk of an increased bilateralisation of the foreign policy of EU Member States and the threat to deal with most controversial issues at intergovernmental bodies such as COREPER also spoke for the discontentment of some national capitals vis-à-vis the transition period and the role of the new foreign policy structures.

Secondly, the Spanish policies also raised expectations about the autonomy and reaction capability of these structures, being the HR/VP the main actor putting forward foreign policy initiatives. Hence the perception among diplomats and observers of a changing 'structure of command' in European foreign policy, even if the system still requires the agreement of all 27 Member States to put forward common policies and positions. The response by the EU to the crisis in Gaza and the lessons learned process on Haiti are particularly relevant in this regard.

The 'informal customs' of the Spanish term also had an immediate impact on the policies of the following rotating presidency. The Belgian authorities put a stronger emphasis on the relationship between Member States and the new foreign policy structures so that national capitals would not perceive the Lisbon structures as a threat to their prerogatives in foreign policy-making. As stated in the Belgian six-monthly programme, more efforts were devoted to the stabilisation of working methods and sharing of responsibilities between the new foreign policy structures and EU Member States. Had the Spanish presidency sought more adjustments between the new structures and Member States, national capitals would not have felt their prerogatives diminished by the implementation of the Lisbon foreign policy machinery. Member States would have watered down their calls to reaffirm their position in the system and discussions could have focused to a greater extent on foreign policy outputs and effective new working arrangements.

As previously noted, the policies of the Spanish presidency brought theoretical debates on the nature of EU foreign policy back to daily discussions of the key committees of the Council of the EU. Future policy-making is still likely to focus much attention on working methods and the relationships between the HR/VP and the EEAS and the Member States, as a consequence of the policies undertaken during the first months of the post-Lisbon era. An eventual change of the nature of EU foreign policy towards a more institutionalised system will need further re-evaluation once the new foreign policy machinery is fully operational, possibly enabling the 'informal customs' of the Spanish term to become actual institutional rules of EU foreign policy. So far, the first six months under Lisbon have given visibility to the new structures and have set up a process of institutionalisation by practice, although decision-taking has preserved its traditional intergovernmental nature.

References

Crowe B (2008) The European External Action Service. Roadmap for Success, Chatham House Papers, www.chathamhouse.org.uk/publications/papers/download/-/id/621/file/11583_0508eas_report.pdf. Accessed 25 July 2011

de Vasconcelos A (2010) After Lisbon: the states of the Union, issues. Institute for Security Studies of the European Union, Paris. www.iss.europa.eu/uploads/media/ISSues-31.pdf. Accessed 25 July 2011

Grevi G (2007) The institutional framework of external action. In: Amato G, Bribosia H, De Witte B (eds) Genesis and destiny of the European constitution. Commentary on the Treaty establishing a constitution for Europe in the light of the Travaux Préparatoires and future prospects. Bruylant, Brussels, pp 773–806

Piris J-C (2010) The Lisbon Treaty. A legal and political analysis. Cambridge University Press, Cambridge

Smith ME (2004) Europe's foreign and security policy. The institutionalization of cooperation. Cambridge University Press, Cambridge

Vanhoonacker S (2005) The institutional framework. In: Hill C, Smith ME (eds) International relations and the European Union. Oxford University Press, Oxford, pp 67–90

Weiss S (2010) External Action Service. Much ado about nothing. Spotlight Europe 5. www.bertelsmann-stiftung.de/cps/rde/xbcr/SID-3662273323E772BC/bst/spotlight_europe_European_External_Action_Service_KLEIN.pdf. Accessed 25 July 2011

Wessels W, Bopp F (2008) The institutional architecture of CFSP after the Lisbon Treaty. Constitutional breakthrough or challenges ahead? Centre for European Policy Studies Research Paper No 10

Chapter 7
The European External Action Service: Enhancing Coherence in EU External Action?

Steven Blockmans and Marja-Liisa Laatsit

Abstract In a rapidly changing world, the success of the European Union's institutions in effectively addressing challenges and seizing opportunities is helped by the constant revision of EU strategies, as well as the focused support of and provision of resources by the Member States to make a difference. Arguably, when these elements are absent, EU external action flounders. The Union's mixed performance in external action over the past few years illustrates the importance of the Lisbon Treaty, which was intended to create the tools for the EU to develop a more coherent, effective and visible foreign policy. One of the institutional innovations provided for in the Treaty on European Union to meet those ambitions is the creation of a European External Action Service (EEAS), which is intended to support the EU external action heroes. This contribution deals with the question whether the new EEAS is likely to enhance inter-institutional coherence in the Union's external action. In order to answer this question, both the raison d'être and the mandate of the EEAS are examined, as well as the organisational structure and aspects of internal coherence of the Service. This chapter attempts to answer the question whether the envisaged structure of the Service corresponds to its mandate

Prof. Dr. Steven Blockmans—Head of Research at the T.M.C. Asser Institute (The Hague) and Special Visiting Professor at the University of Leuven (Belgium).
Marja-Liisa Laatsit—Ph.D. candidate at the European University Institute (Florence).

S. Blockmans (✉)
T.M.C. Asser Institute, The Hague, The Netherlands
e-mail: s.blockmans@asser.nl

S. Blockmans
University of Leuven, Leuven, Belgium

M.-L. Laatsit
European University Institute, Florence, Italy
e-mail: Marja-Liisa.Laatsit@eui.eu

P. J. Cardwell (ed.), *EU External Relations Law and Policy in the Post-Lisbon Era*, DOI: 10.1007/978-90-6704-823-1_7, © T.M.C. Asser Press, The Hague, The Netherlands, and the authors 2012

and whether the EEAS is likely to live up to its expectations by enhancing coherence in EU external action.

Contents

7.1 Introduction

> The ambition to build a strong EU foreign policy received a major boost with the launch of the European External Action Service – the EEAS – on the 1st of January this year. The service will act as a single platform to project European values and interests around the world. And it will act as a one-stop shop for our partners.
>
> The aim of all this is to forge a better, more coherent policy, developing European answers to complex global problems, working with our partners around the world. It's something I know countries have long asked for – and that we can now deliver.
>
> Catherine Ashton, High Representative of the Union for Foreign Affairs and Security Policy, on the occasion of Europe Day, 9 May 2011[1]

European leaders in Member State capitals and at EU headquarters were caught completely by surprise by the unfolding of history in Tunisia, Egypt and Libya in early 2011. In its first-ever evaluation of Europe's performance in pursuing its interests and promoting its values in the world, the European Council on Foreign Relations (ECFR) found that, while 2010 was not a great year for European foreign policy, the performance of EU institutions and Member States was 'not uniformly mediocre'.[2] Among the most united EU responses in 2010, the ECFR

---

[1] Statement by High Representative Catherine Ashton on Europe Day, press release, Brussels, 7 May 2011, A 177/11, www.consilium.europa.eu/uedocs/cms_data/docs/pressdata/EN/foraff/121895.pdf.

[2] Vaisse and Kundnani 2011, 9. The assessment is of the collective performance of all EU actors rather than the action of any particular institution or country—either the High Representative, the European Council, the European Commission, a group of states like the EU3 (France, Germany and the UK), or an individual Member State.

counted stabilisation and state building in Iraq, relations with the US on climate change, relations with the Eastern neighbourhood on trade and energy, relations with China on Iran and proliferation, European policy in the World Trade Organization, and relations with the US on terrorism, information sharing and data protection. Unfortunately for the EU, the list of its most divisive issues in 2010 is both longer and more pertinent. The list includes European policy on the rule of law and human rights in China, bilateral relations with Turkey, relations with the US on NATO and NATO reform, relations with the US on global economic and financial reform, European policy in the G20 and G8 and the diversification of gas supply routes to Europe.[3] If anything, these lists show how plentiful and wide apart the foreign policy issues are that the EU has to deal with. To a certain extent, these challenges and opportunities have been outlined in the European Security Strategy (ESS) of 2003, which was reviewed in 2008.[4] But in a rapidly changing world, the success of the Union's institutions in effectively addressing challenges and seizing opportunities is helped by the constant revision of EU strategies, as well as the focused support of and provision of resources by the Member States to make a difference. Arguably, when these elements are absent, EU external action flounders.

The EU's slow and timid response to the dramatic events of the Arab Spring of 2011[5]—as indeed the Union's mixed performance in external action more widely—illustrate the importance of the Lisbon Treaty, which was intended to create tools for the EU to develop a more coherent, effective and visible foreign policy.[6] Various contributors to this volume have noted the theoretical and practical challenges in meeting these aims, in both sectoral policy areas and at the general institutional level. One of the institutional innovations provided for in the Lisbon Treaty is the creation of a European External Action Service (EEAS).[7] This

[3] Vaisse and Kundnani 2011, 11–12.

[4] *European Security Strategy: A Secure Europe in a Better World*, Brussels, 12 December 2003, as complemented by the High Representative's *Report on the Implementation of the ESS—Providing Security in a Changing World*, doc. 17104/08 (S407/08), 11 December 2008, endorsed by the European Council, Presidency Conclusions, doc. 17271/08 (CONCL 5), 12 December 2008, point 30.

[5] Compare, e.g. Statement by EU High Representative Catherine Ashton and European Commissioner for Enlargement Štefan Füle on the situation in Tunisia, Press release A 010/11, Brussels, 10 January 2011; 'EEAS' senior officials mission to Tunisia', Press Release A 029/11, 26 January 2011; and Statement by the EU High Representative Catherine Ashton on Tunisia, Press Release A 034/11, Brussels, 28 January 2011. See also T. Garton Ash, 'If this is young Arabs' 1989, Europe must be ready with a bold response', *The Guardian*, 2 February 2011: 'What happens across the Mediterranean matters more to the EU than the US. Yet so far its voice has been inaudible'.

[6] See 'Europe in the World—Some Practical Proposals for Greater Coherence, Effectiveness and Visibility), COM(2006) 278 final; the pre-Lisbon Draft IGC Mandate, annexed to the Presidency Conclusions of 22–23 June 2007; and the Annual Report from the Council to the European Parliament on the Main Aspects and Basic Choices of the CFSP (2008).

[7] Article 27(3) TEU.

contribution deals with the question whether the new European External Action Service is likely to enhance coherence in the EU's external action. In order to answer this question we will examine both the raison d'être (Section 2) and the mandate of the EEAS (Section 3), as well as the organisational structure of the Service (Section 4). We will ask ourselves whether the envisaged structure of the Service corresponds to its mandate and whether the EEAS as an entity is likely to enhance coherence in EU external action (Section 5). This contribution will therefore not deal with the other two overriding aims for the creation of the EEAS—effectiveness and visibility.[8]

Before embarking on our analysis, it is worth offering one further conceptual clarification. Rather confusingly, the Treaty on European Union speaks of the need to enhance *consistency* in EU external action.[9] Whereas legal scholarship is more or less united in drawing a distinction between the principles of coherence and consistency,[10] the drafters of the Treaties seem to have mistaken the one principle for the other. In the functional approach to the topics at hand, we understand the notion of consistency in primary law to mean the assurance that the different EU policies do not legally contradict each other. Moreover, synergies are sought in the implementation of these policies. The multi-layered concept of coherence is wider and relates to the construction of a united whole. For ease of distinction, we will focus here only the level of synergy between actors and instruments, a synergy which the EU system (in Articles 21(3), 4(3) and 13(2) TEU) aspires to promote through principles of cooperation and complementarity. For the purpose of this chapter, and in spite of the Treaty language, we have thus opted for the institutional use of the term coherence to gauge the potential impact of the EEAS on the level of coordination and cooperation in the formulation of EU external relations policy.

7.2 Reculer Pour Mieux Sauter: Changes Under the Treaty of Lisbon

In order to develop a more coherent, effective and visible EU foreign policy, the Lisbon Treaty has introduced fundamental changes at two levels.[11] Firstly, the objectives of the Union's external policies, from security over development to trade and environment, were merged in Article 21 TEU. This could, over time,

---

[8] For early findings on those ends, see Drieskens and Van Schaik 2010, and Emerson et al. 2011. These issues are dealt with by the contributions to this volume by Broberg and Schmidt.

[9] See Articles 18(4), 21(3) and 26(2) TEU.

[10] See, *inter alia*, Tietje 1997, Koutrakos 2001, 39–44, Hillion 2008, Cremona 2011 and, in this volume, Schmidt.

[11] For a more detailed review of the Lisbon changes with regard to EU external action, see the contributions to Koutrakos 2011.

lead to more policy coherence. Secondly, the architecture and procedural framework for EU external action were fundamentally amended so as to enhance coherence between the institutional actors. All these changes were introduced, however, without the simultaneous streamlining of the distribution of competences or decision-making procedures.[12] As has been observed, the Lisbon Treaty has not ended the first/second pillar dichotomy of late.[13] Due to their 'specific' character CFSP and CSDP remain located in the Treaty on European Union, under the umbrella of the general provisions of the Union's external action (Title V TEU) but nevertheless separate from the Union's other external relations policies in the Treaty on the Functioning of the EU (trade, development, cooperation with third countries, humanitarian aid, relations with international organisations). Arguably, it is the institutional innovation rather than the merging of objectives which will spur—in a practical sense—the drive for more coherence, effectiveness and visibility.[14] In that context, one can point to the institutionalisation of the European Council,[15] which has been tasked with the identification of the strategic interests and objectives of the Union,[16] as well as the external representation of the Union at Presidential level in the area of the CFSP.[17] Also, the European Parliament's role in EU decision-making in foreign affairs has been greatly enhanced, most notably with respect to the development of the Common Commercial Policy (CCP).[18]

The most important institutional changes in the Lisbon Treaty, however, relate to the position of the High Representative of the Union for Foreign Affairs and Security Policy (HR),[19] who 'conducts' the Union's foreign, security and defence policies,[20] contributes proposals to the development of those policies, and—together with the Council—ensures compliance by the Member States with their

---

[12] The most notable exception, however, is Article 216 TFEU, which provides Treaty foundation for the power to conclude international agreements, hitherto developed by the ECJ's case law.

[13] See, for example, Craig 2010, 380–381, Sari (this volume) and, insofar as the ECJ is concerned, Brkan (this volume).

[14] This tendency has been most vocally criticised by Kishore Mahbubani, in 'Europe's Errors', *TIME Magazine*, 8 March 2010: '(...) Europe's obsession with restructuring its internal arrangements is akin to rearranging the deck chairs of a sinking Titanic. The focus on internal challenges when the real threats are external is the first of three strategic errors Europe is making.'

[15] Article 13(1) TEU.

[16] Article 22(1) TEU.

[17] Article 15(6) TEU.

[18] Article 207(2) TFEU. On the post-Lisbon arrangements for the CCP generally (and the new provisions on investment), see the contributions in this volume by Wu and Dimopoulos.

[19] The name change (compare the title of the pre-Lisbon position) reflects the fact that it has become clear that the HR indeed represents the Union and not the (collective) Member States. Even the President of the European Council (note: not the European *Union*) exercises that position's external competences 'without prejudice to the powers of the High Representative of the Union for Foreign Affairs and Security Policy' (Article 15, para 6(d) TEU).

[20] Article 18(2) TEU.

CFSP obligations.[21] Primary authority for policy choices in these areas continues to rest with the European Council and the Council.[22] The Commission remains responsible for policy initiation, implementation and external representation in the other domains of EU external action.

To enhance coordination, the HR has been tasked to take part in the work of the European Council,[23] preside over the Foreign Affairs Council,[24] and hold the post of Vice-President of the European Commission (VP).[25] This new 'triple-hatted' person[26] is to take on the role of the big coordinator of the EU external policy: the HR/VP is to assist the Council and the Commission in ensuring consistency between the different areas of the Union's external action and between these and the EU's other policies.[27] When properly carried out, the upgraded position of HR/VP ought to allow for a stronger and more independent development and implementation of the Union's foreign, security and defence policy, which—potentially—would provide the EU with a more coherent and more effective role on the international scene.[28] To assist the HR/VP in what seems like a mission impossible, the EU Treaty foresees the creation of a brand new diplomatic service of the EU, the idea for which originated during the European Convention in the Working Group on External Action.[29]

The Lisbon Treaty provides for the creation of the diplomatic service in a short and rather open-ended manner. Article 27(3) TEU is the only Treaty basis for the establishment of the EEAS and stipulates:

> In fulfilling his mandate, the High Representative shall be assisted by a European External Action Service. This service shall work in cooperation with the diplomatic services of the Member States and shall comprise officials from relevant departments of the General Secretariat of the Council and of the Commission as well as staff seconded from national diplomatic services of the Member States. The organisation and functioning of the European External Action Service shall be established by a decision of the Council. The Council shall act on a proposal from the High Representative after consulting the European Parliament and after obtaining the consent of the Commission.

A single general procedural rule was provided for the establishment of the EEAS, i.e. the adoption of a Council Decision, proposed by the HR, with the

[21] Article 24(3) TEU.

[22] Articles 22–26 TEU, resp. Articles 26(2) and 28 TEU.

[23] Article 15(2) TEU.

[24] Article 18(2) TEU.

[25] Article 17(4) TEU.

[26] See Piris 2010, 243.

[27] See Articles 18(4), 21(3) and 26(2) TEU.

[28] It has been argued that the triple hats worn by the HR could lead to institutional schizophrenia, with the incumbent being subject to conflicting loyalties. See Devuyst 2008, 294–295. Indeed, the Member States of the EU may well have created an even more impossible job than that of the United Nations Secretary-General—a post often called the most difficult in the world.

[29] CONV 459/02, Final Report of Working Group VII on External Action, Brussels, 16 December 2002, at 6–7.

consent of the Commission after having heard the opinion of the European Parliament. In fact, most of the questions regarding the establishment of the EEAS were left open by the Treaty. It was up to the negotiators of the different parties involved to reach agreement on principles and technical issues.

The High Representative's initial proposal for a Council Decision on the set-up and functioning of the EEAS was drawn up in March 2010 and became subject to intense debates with Member States and, notably, the European Parliament. Much to her credit, the HR managed to navigate the high seas of inter-institutional politics and swiftly moved the legislative process towards adopting the constituent Council Decision on 26 July 2010.[30] This was followed by the adoption of three parallel legislative acts, which changed the EU's financial and staff regulations and established a start-up budget for the EEAS.[31] The completion of this complex process in barely 6 months triggered one insider to call it a 'Guinness record for speed'.[32] The EEAS was launched on 1 December 2010 and became operational a month later, on 1 January 2011 when 1643 permanent officials were transferred from the Council and the Commission.[33]

The key question now—the *internal* litmus test—is whether the EEAS will be able to provide the kind of assistance to its political master(s) that is needed to better coordinate external policies and thereby attain a higher level of coherence in EU external action.[34] To answer this question, we will first analyse the mandate of the EEAS and then its organisational structure. The mandate of the EEAS writ large entails two dimensions: coordination of EU external action at the levels of strategic planning (decision-shaping) and implementation. We will discuss each in turn, but first focus on the tasks which can be distilled from a combined reading of the EEAS Council Decision and the TEU.

---

[30] Council Decision 2010/427/EU of 26 July 2010 establishing the organisation and functioning of the European External Action Service, *OJ* 2010 L 201/30 (hereinafter: EEAS Council Decision).

[31] Regulation No 1081/2010 of the European Parliament and of the Council of 24 November 2010 amending Council Regulation No 1605/2002 on the Financial Regulation applicable to the general budget of the European Communities, as regards the European External Action Service, *OJ* 2010 L 311/9; Regulation No 1080/2010 of the European Parliament and of the Council of 24 November 2010 amending the Staff Regulations of Officials of the European Communities and the Conditions of Employment of Other Servants of those Communities, *OJ* 2010 L 311/1; and European Parliament resolution of 20 October 2010 on Council's position on Draft amending budget No 6/2010 of the European Union for the financial year 2010, Section II—European Council and Council; Section III—Commission; Section X—European External Action Service [13475/2010—C7-0262/2010—2010/2094(BUD)].

[32] Skytte Christoffersen 2010.

[33] See Press Release IP/10/1769, Brussels, 21 December 2010.

[34] For the EU as a whole, the *external* litmus test is the extent to which international partners find the EU to be more effective and visible. This point, however, is beyond the scope of the current chapter.

7.3 Mandate of the EEAS

7.3.1 *Inter-Institutional Coherence*

The EEAS Council Decision establishes the Action Service as a functionally autonomous body, separate from the General Secretariat of the Council and from the Commission, with the legal capacity necessary to perform its tasks and attain its objectives.[35] The Service has not been endowed, however, with the power to adopt individual and binding decisions vis-à-vis third parties.[36] It is placed under the authority of the HR,[37] and assists him/her in fulfilling his/her multiple mandates, as outlined, notably, in Articles 18 and 27 TEU:

> —in fulfilling his/her mandate to conduct the Common Foreign and Security Policy ('CFSP') of the European Union, including the Common Security and Defence Policy ('CSDP'), to contribute by his/her proposals to the development of that policy, which he/she shall carry out as mandated by the Council and to ensure the consistency of the Union's external action,
>
> —in his/her capacity as President of the Foreign Affairs Council, without prejudice to the normal tasks of the General Secretariat of the Council,
>
> —in his/her capacity as Vice-President of the Commission for fulfilling within the Commission the responsibilities incumbent on it in external relations, and in coordinating other aspects of the Union's external action, without prejudice to the normal tasks of the services of the Commission.[38]

As it turns out, the HR is only one of the EEAS' political masters. Article 2(2) of the EEAS Council Decision states that the 'EEAS shall assist the President of the European Council, the President of the Commission, and the Commission in the exercise of their respective functions in the area of external relations'. Thus, the EEAS is expected to serve multiple political masters. Considering that the EEAS was created as an inter-institutional body, it is indeed well placed to play a coordinating role and assist in efforts to ensure coherence between the different areas of the Union's external action and between those areas and its other policies. How this coordination is expected to play out in practice becomes clear from a close reading of Articles 3 ('Cooperation') and 4 ('Central administration of the EEAS') of the EEAS Council Decision.

Article 3(1) of the EEAS Council Decision specifically prescribes that the EEAS 'shall support, and work in cooperation with, the diplomatic services of the Member States, as well as with the General Secretariat of the Council and the

---

[35] Article 1(2) EEAS Council Decision. On the character of the EEAS, see Van Vooren 2001a, b.

[36] An exception could be provided by the inter-service 'arrangements' which the EEAS can conclude. (see below). These kinds of acts could potentially entail legal effects *vis-á-vis* third parties, within the meaning of Article 263 TFEU, and therefore could draw the EEAS into Court proceedings. See further Van Vooren 2001a, 493–496.

[37] Article 1(3) EEAS Council Decision.

[38] Article 2(1) EEAS Council Decision.

services of the Commission'. To start with the former: the success of the EEAS partly depends on national ownership, on Member States 'buying in' to the system. In this respect, a crucial but still uncertain factor is the willingness of the Member States to play an enabling role in the early functioning of the new Service, in terms of input (contributions by seconded national experts (SNEs)) and output (implementation), both in the capitals (foreign affairs and their line ministries) and the delegations abroad.[39] Through their membership of international decision-making organs, such as the UN Security Council, the G8 and G20, and their differentiated participation in several contact groups (e.g. France, Germany and the UK in the E3 group on Iran), individual Member States will continue to play a key role in EU foreign policy-making. Close interaction between the EEAS and the Member States' capitals—either through Brussels structures (COREPER, PSC and working groups) or key figures in the EEAS or in political cabinets—will therefore remain essential.[40] However, such coordination will not be sufficient to tame national ambitions, nor was it ever intended to.[41]

Insofar as cooperation between the EEAS and the General Secretariat of the Council (GSC), on the one hand, and between the Action Service and the Commission, on the other, is concerned, a key phrase mentioned twice in Article 2(1) of the EEAS Council Decision deserves attention: the EEAS shall assist the HR/VP in fulfilling his/her mandates 'without prejudice to the normal tasks' of the GSC and those of the services of the Commission. In the absence of an exhaustive *Kompetenzkatalog* of the EU and with the very idea of normality in EU external action having shifted dramatically with the entry into force of the Lisbon Treaty, it is not unlikely that the neutral phrase 'normal tasks' will be interpreted differently by persons with different institutional affiliations.[42] As indicated by Lefebvre and Hillion:

> Indeed, the functioning of the Service will probably remain determined by an invisible yet genuine distinction between two cultures: a Communitarian-like culture inherited from DG Relex (which will be numerically dominant in the EEAS, and which will most likely have the greatest influence on the geographic and thematic DGs, and on delegations); and

---

[39] See Vanhoonacker and Duke 2010, 6.

[40] See Lefebvre and Hillion 2010, 7.

[41] A. Rettman, 'UK champions own diplomacy over EU 'action service'', *EUObserver*, 5 May 2011. Compare also Declarations concerning the Common Foreign and Security Policy (Nos. 13 and 14) attached to the Lisbon Treaty which state, *inter alia*, that the CFSP, HR and EEAS provisions do not affect 'the responsibilities of the Member States, as they currently exist, for the formulation and conduct of their foreign policy nor of their national representation in third countries and international organisations' or 'the existing legal basis, responsibilities, and powers of each Member State in relation to the formulation and conduct of its foreign policy'. These disclaimers show that, indeed, there is still room for national diplomacy after Lisbon.

[42] According to one member of the Council Legal Service, the phrase should be interpreted in line with existing practice under Article 23(1) of the Council's Rules of Procedure: 'The Council shall be assisted by a General Secretariat…' Gilles Marhic at the DSEU Conference 'The Diplomatic System after Lisbon—Institutions Matter', 18–19 November 2010, Maastricht University.

a political culture inherited from the Council policy unit and crisis management structures, deemed to retain a certain autonomy within the Service. In this respect, the Council Decision suggests that the EEAS might well internalise past bureaucratic conflicts, rather than do away with them.[43]

The risk of classic turf wars rearing their ugly heads is also the consequence of the pre-Lisbon manoeuvring by then Commission President-designate José Manuel Barroso, who unveiled his new team of Commissioners in November 2009. By way of a simple asterisk behind the names of three designated Commissioners, Barroso indicated that the Commissioners responsible for 'International Cooperation, Humanitarian Aid and Crisis response', 'Development' and 'Enlargement and European Neighbourhood Policy' would exercise their functions 'in close cooperation with the High Representative/Vice-President in accordance with the Treaties.'[44] The requirement of close cooperation with the HR/VP and the condition to work closely with the EEAS (as provided in the Mission Letters) was later structured, under his ultimate leadership, by the President of the Commission so as to ensure the coherence of external policies.[45] It may be clear that this line of action curtails the HR/VP's responsibilities as entrusted to him/her by the Treaty. This is further enhanced by removing responsibility for the ENP from the portfolio External Relations to that of Enlargement. This (re-)reshuffling was not motivated by Barroso (II). Finally, the Trade Commissioner does not cooperate directly with the HR/VP or with the EEAS, notwithstanding the genuine international character of his portfolio. One could say that the High Representative's VP hat represents fewer portfolios and less coordinating powers then under Barroso (I). The 'normal tasks' of the Commission are therefore more expansive than a post-Lisbon coherence-driven process in EU external action would have tolerated.

One former 'normal task' of the GSC now entrusted to the EEAS is assisting the HR with exercising his/her responsibilities under the acts founding the European Defence Agency, the European Union Satellite Centre, the European Union Institute for Security Studies and the European Security and Defence College.[46]

[43] Lefebvre and Hillion 2010. For more on internal coherence, i.e. coherence within the confines of the organisational structure of the EEAS, see Sect. 7.4 of this chapter.

[44] Press release IP/09/1837 of 27 November 2009. The requirement of close cooperation was repeated in the Mission Letters of the same date from Barroso (II) to Andris Piebalgs and Stefan Füle, and of 27 January 2010 to Kristalina Georgieva, ec.europa.eu/commission_2010-2014/mission_letters/index_en.htm.

[45] See Article 17(6)(b) TEU, which states that the President of the Commission shall 'decide on the internal organisation of the Commission, ensuring that it acts consistently, efficiently and as a collegiate body'. On 22 April 2010, Barroso issued an Information Note from the President, 'Commissioners groups', SEC(2010) 475 final, in which the VP is tasked to chair the group of Commissioners responsible for 'External relations', a group further composed of Olli Rehn (economic and monetary affairs), Karel De Gucht (trade) and the three aforementioned Commissioners. The Note also says that 'the President can decide to attend any meeting, which he will then chair'.

[46] See the seventh recital of the Preamble of the EEAS Council Decision.

Other examples of such 'normal tasks' include the administrative tasks of preparing and holding Council meetings.[47]

With respect to the coordination and cooperation between the EEAS and the services of the Commission, the EEAS Council Decision specifically obliges the parties to consult each other on *all* matters relating to the external action of the Union in the exercise of their respective functions, except on matters of CSDP.[48] This far-reaching obligation stems, *inter alia*, from the quasi-blanket competence attributed to the Commission in Article 17(1), sixth sentence TEU to represent the Union externally 'with the exception of the common foreign and security policy, and other cases provided for in the Treaties'. As the Heads of the EU Delegations receive direct instructions from the HR, the EEAS and the Commission are effectively and legally bound to cooperate in the external representation of the Union.[49] On matters covered by the CSDP, simple coordination between the EEAS and the Commission will not do. In view of the competence distribution in the Lisbon Treaty, the EEAS is explicitly positioned to take part in the preparatory work and procedures relating to acts to be prepared by the Commission in the area of the CSDP.[50] In other words, the Commission relies on the HR and the EEAS in fielding proposals under Article 42(4) TEU.

At the same time, the EEAS is mandated to provide support for the HR/VP in his/her capacity as the Vice-President of the European Commission. The VP is responsible for the external relations of the EU and for coordinating other aspects of the Union's external action so as to ensure consistency in implementation.[51] The EEAS could be expected to operate in many ways like a service of the Commission, but this will require good will and cooperation on both sides. So far, however, the picture that has emerged from practice is rather mixed.[52]

Although not central to the equation, the European Parliament, European Council, Court of Justice and Court of Auditors are not left out. The EEAS shall extend 'appropriate support and cooperation to the other institutions and bodies of the Union, in particular to the European Parliament'.[53] What constitutes such

[47] See Council Rules of Procedure, Articles 3(2 & 5), 5(3–4), 7(3), 27(3–5).

[48] Article 3(2) EEAS Council Decision. This paragraph shall be implemented in accordance with Chapter 1 of Title V of the TEU, and with Article 205 TFEU.

[49] Article 5(3) EEAS Council Decision.

[50] Article 3(2) EEAS Council Decision.

[51] Article 18(4) TEU.

[52] European Commission President Barroso has been reported to take an uncooperative stance towards the difficulties which VP Ashton often faces to attend the Wednesday meetings of the College. Barroso has barred Ashton from participating via video conference or being deputised when abroad. See B. Waterfield, 'Is absent Ashton a part-timer?', *EUObserver*, 10 January 2011. On the other hand, cooperation between Ashton and individual Commissioners (Piebals, Füle, Georgieva) has been constructive, e.g. in monitoring the situation in the Arab World. To this end, and in an effort to keep his VP in check, Barroso published an Information Note from the President, *Commissioners Groups*, SEC (2010) 475 final, Brussels, 22 April 2010. For further analysis on this the latter, see Erkelens and Blockmans, loc. cit. See, more generally, Brok 2011.

[53] Article 3(4) EEAS Council Decision.

'appropriate' support remains unclear, but going by previous practice, it is not expected to amount to much more than sharing information, most notably with the Foreign Affairs (AFET) Committee of the Parliament.

In return for all this assistance, the EEAS, too, may benefit from the support and cooperation of the above-mentioned actors, albeit not with the same generosity with which the Service itself is expected to deliver. The High Representative and the EEAS shall be assisted 'where necessary' by the GSC and the relevant departments of the Commission,[54] and 'as appropriate' by the European Parliament, other institutions and bodies, including agencies.[55] Arguably, the words 'where necessary' and 'as appropriate' leave a margin of discretion to the GSC and the Commission that even the service-level arrangements, which may be drawn up to that end by the said parties,[56] or between the EEAS and other offices or inter-institutional bodies of the Union,[57] could—in all likelihood—not close. The relationship between the EEAS, on the one hand, and the Commission services and GSC, on the other, is inherently asymmetrical with the EEAS performing the role of an assistant to multiple political masters *and* their services.

In short, the EEAS has been endowed with the task to support the Council and the Commission (directly) and the HR (in his/her task to assist the two institutions) in fulfilling their Treaty obligation to ensure coherence between the different areas of the Union's external action and between those areas and the EU's other policies. Moreover, the EEAS has been tasked to serve the President of the European Council and the President of the European Commission in the exercise of their respective functions in the area of external relations. The European Parliament and other institutions and bodies are supported whenever appropriate. The fact that—conversely—the EEAS and its political headmaster/mistress, the HR, *may* receive the support from the GSC and the relevant departments of the Commission should provide further ground for enhancing coherence in all fields of EU external action. Yet, as Avery has pointed out, there is a grave risk of friction and rivalry between EEAS and the services of the Commission.[58] The threat is significant because much of the EU's action in international affairs is related to common policies, such as environment, energy, trade and agriculture. We will now turn to an analysis of the Action Service's responsibilities with respect to strategic policy planning and programming.

---

[54] Article 4(5) EEAS Council Decision.

[55] Article 3(4) EEAS Council Decision.

[56] Article 4(5) EEAS Council Decision.

[57] Article 3(3) EEAS Council Decision. The terms 'offices' and 'inter-institutional bodies' leave room for coordination and cooperation between the EEAS and the office (cabinet) of the President of the European Council, the Publications Office, the European Personnel Selection Office, the European Administrative School and others.

[58] Avery 2011, 2.

7.3.2 *Strategic Planning and Programming*

It is a self-proclaimed objective of the European Union to increase its strategic approach to tackling global challenges.[59] In fact, there is no shortage of strategic aims that guide the Union's external action. The problem is that they are scattered over so many policy documents and strategic partnerships that the EU 'begins to look rather rudderless'.[60] The ESS,[61] the European Consensus for Development,[62] the EU Strategy for Sustainable Development,[63] and 'Trade, Growth and World Affairs'[64] are just a few examples. Their contents are often closely connected, as the challenges posed by the security-development nexus have taught us.[65] Tackling the coordination issue therefore calls not only for better institutional coordination (see the previous Section), but also for more strategic decision-making.[66]

Since the entry into force of the Lisbon Treaty, the onus has been on the European Council, which, according to Article 22(1) TEU, 'shall identify the strategic interests and objectives of the Union' that relate to the CFSP and to other areas of EU external action and take decisions which 'may concern the relations with a specific country or region or may be thematic in approach.' Whereas the President of the European Council, Herman van Rompuy, has started off a long-overdue and necessary debate on the EU's strategic priorities, the first European Council Summit to that effect was unfortunately not a great success as it amounted to not much more than a general brainstorming exercise in which not even the term

[59] See ESS 2008.

[60] Duke 2010, 35.

[61] *European Security Strategy: A Secure Europe in a Better World*, Brussels, 12 December 2003.

[62] See Joint statement by the Council and the representatives of the governments of the Member States meeting within the Council, the European Parliament and the Commission on European Union Development Policy: 'The European Consensus', *OJ* 2006 C 46/1. The relationship between coherency and development policy is explored in more detail by Broberg (this volume).

[63] See the European Commission's 2009 review of the 2001 EU Strategy for Sustainable Development, available at <http://eur-lex.europa.eu/LexUriServ/LexUriServ.do?uri=COM:2009:0400:FIN:EN:PDF>.

[64] DG TRADE's 'Trade Policy as a Core Component of the EU's 2020 Strategy', available at <http://trade.ec.europa.eu/doclib/docs/2010/november/tradoc_146955.pdf>. The strategy aims to enhance the position of EU economy by getting new opportunities for trade and investment, deepening the existing trade and investment links, helping EU businesses access global markets, gaining foreign investment, implementing enforcement measures, and enhancing the 'spirit of multilateralism and partnership' in trade. These aims, no doubt, entail political consequences.

[65] Ashton 2010), V. See also ESS 2008, 8–9; and ECJ, Case C-91/05 *Commission* v. *Council* (Small Arms and Light Weapons/ECOWAS), ECR 2008, I-03651.

[66] As recognised in the ESS 2008, at 8–9.

'strategic partner' was defined.[67] The analyses prepared by HR Ashton's team at the time (September 2010) have been described as 'rather disappointing'.[68] It is here that a fully fledged European External Action Service could prove instrumental in supporting the HR and the President of the European Council with a well-thought-out medium and long-term analytical approach for the Union's foreign and security policy.

Under the terms of Article 22(2) TEU, the HR—for the area of CFSP—and the Commission—for other areas of external action—may submit joint proposals to the Council. A recent example has been provided by the Commission with its report 'Towards a new Energy Strategy for Europe 2011–2020', adopted by the Council in 2010.[69] Elements thereof made it on to the strategic agenda of the European Council and were then bounced back to both Commission and the HR:

> There is a need for better coordination of EU and Member States' activities with a view to ensuring consistency and coherence in the EU's external relations with key producer, transit, and consumer countries. The Commission is invited to submit by June 2011 a communication on security of supply and international cooperation aimed at further improving the consistency and coherence of the EU's external action in the field of energy. The Member States are invited to inform from 1 January 2012 the Commission on all their new and existing bilateral energy agreements with third countries; the Commission will make this information available to all other Member States in an appropriate form, having regard to the need for protection of commercially sensitive information. The High Representative is invited to take fully account of the energy security dimension in her work. Energy security should also be fully reflected in the EU's neighbourhood policy.[70]

The organisational chart of the EEAS includes 'strategic planning' and 'training', but—at the time of writing—adequate resources had not yet been allocated to these important functions.[71] As for strategic planning, one of the successes of Javier Solana's team was the development of the ESS as an overarching concept. One of the weaknesses of the Commission in external relations was its lack of overall planning capacity.[72] This is where the hybrid HR/VP position, supported by the EEAS composed of Commission and Council staff, plus seconded national experts from the Member States, is expected to make a difference. However, we have still to see the first proposal coming from the HR in the

---

[67] European Council Conclusions of 16 September 2010, Press Release EUCO 21/10, CO EUR 16, CONCL 3.

[68] See A. Rettmann, 'Ashton designates six new 'strategic partners'', *EUObserver*, 16 September 2010.

[69] Conclusions of the 3017th Transport, Telecommunications and Energy Council meeting, Brussels, 31 May 2010.

[70] European Council, Conclusions on Energy, Press Release PCE 026-11, 4 February 2011, pt. 11.

[71] For an analysis of how training can contribute towards fulfilling the EEAS objectives and in nurturing a new EU diplomacy, see Lloveras Soler 2011.

[72] See Avery 2011.

field of CFSP.[73] In the wake of the historical changes in parts of the Arab World, and against the wider background of the rise of the BRIC's, the ESS is an obvious candidate for a thorough revision.[74]

A crucial task when establishing the function of the EEAS in achieving overall consistency in EU external action is to identify the policy areas where coordination is necessary. Virtually every EU policy has to it an external dimension that fits into the grander scheme of EU presence in the world and could therefore also fall within the ambit of the EEAS' activities. These policy areas include those with a clear, chiefly external character—CFSP, CSDP, Common Commercial Policy (CCP), development cooperation, humanitarian aid, enlargement, and the ENP—as well as those usually classified as internal Union policies—the Area of Freedom Security and Justice, agriculture and fisheries, public health, environment, energy, tourism. The added value of the EEAS' involvement in strategic planning certainly lies at the crossroads of EU external policies, as has been shown by the nexus between development cooperation and security policy.[75] The overarching development goal in the Lisbon Treaty is the eradication of poverty. The coordination on the level of ensuring consistency of aims between the overall foreign and security policy goals in general and those of development policy in particular—a task specifically entrusted to the EEAS[76]—entails a degree of strategic planning, in addition to the task of eventually coordinating the activities between the institutions implementing the cooperation programmes in the end.

In terms of programming, planning and implementation, the tasks of the EEAS are more or less clear. According to Article 9(2) of the EEAS Council Decision, the HR 'shall ensure overall political coordination of the Union's external action, ensuring the unity, consistency and effectiveness of the Union's external action, in particular through [a number of thematic and geographic] external assistance

[73] Ashton has been criticised—so far most vocally by the Belgian Minister of Foreign Affairs—for not proposing a well-thought-out medium and long-term analytical approach for the Union's foreign and security policy. See L. Maroun, 'Steven Vanackere dit ses quatre vérités à Cathy Ashton', *Le Soir*, 4 May 2011, at 14 : 'Bien sûr, pour beaucoup de pays, la politique extérieure est au cœur de la souveraineté nationale. Nous, nous avons toujours voulu que le Service d'action extérieure soit l'axe central autour duquel les Etats membres peuvent s'organiser. Mais en l'absence d'un axe central qui répond, fait des analyses et tire des conclusions rapidement, les Allemands aujourd'hui, les Français demain, ou les Anglais, prennent une partie de ce rôle d'axe central, et c'est alors autour d'eux que les autres doivent s'organiser ! Le résultat est centrifuge, pas centripète. (…) Il est normal qu'Ashton ne soit pas partout en même temps. Il faut faire des choix, se concentrer sur les vrais enjeux, éviter de se perdre dans les détails, et une bonne gestion d'agenda. (…)Mais aujourd'hui, je n'ai pas l'impression qu'avec le Service d'action extérieure, on en soit déjà là. On peut accepter que certains réagissent plus vite qu'Ashton, mais à condition qu'elle puisse prouver qu'elle travaille sur le moyen et le long termes—et sur des thèmes hyper-importants, comme l'énergie par exemple. Mais ça, je n'ai pas encore vu non plus.'

[74] The ENP review of May 2011, which goes far beyond the limits of the CFSP proper, was published by both the European Commission and the HR. See COM(2011) 303, 25 May 2011.

[75] See Van Vooren 2001b, forthcoming.

[76] See the fourth recital of the preamble of the EEAS Council Decision; Article 21(2)d TEU and Article 208 TFEU.

instruments'. These instruments include the Development and Cooperation Initiative (DCI), European Development Fund (EDF), the new European Neighbourhood Instrument (ENI), the European Instrument for Democracy and Human Rights (EIDHR), the Instrument for Cooperation with Industrialised Countries, the Instrument for Nuclear Safety Cooperation (INS), and part of the Instrument for Stability (IfS). The relevant article in the EEAS Council Decision states that,

> (…) throughout the whole cycle of programming, planning and implementation of the instruments referred to in para 2, the High Representative and the EEAS shall work with the relevant members and services of the Commission without prejudice to Article 1(3). All proposals for decision will be prepared by following the Commission's procedures and will be submitted to the Commission for adoption.[77]

Thus, the EEAS Council Decision entrusts the Action Service with co-responsibility for preparing the Commission decisions on the strategic, multi-annual steps within the programming cycle.[78] More specifically, this covers the first three multi-annual steps within the programming cycle: country and regional allocations; country and regional strategic papers; and national and regional indicative programmes.[79] The objection that the EDF and DCI, which in budget terms represent the largest portion of the overall external action budget, imply a different and essentially long-term approach to programming while much of the programming in other aspects of EU external action is annual or shorter-term appears to have been accommodated by the EEAS Council Decision. In both cases, any proposals 'shall be prepared jointly by the relevant services in the EEAS and in the Commission *under the direct supervision and guidance of the Commissioner responsible for Development Policy* and shall be submitted jointly with the High Representative for adoption by the Commission'.[80] Similar stipulations apply in the ENI context with reference to the Commissioner for Enlargement and Neighbourhood Policy.[81]

In short, the EEAS Council Decision does not *prima facie* remove either the Commission's 'management functions' its rights of initiative or those of implementation (Article 17(1) TEU). Article 210(2) of the TFEU, which permits the Commission 'to take any useful initiative' to promote coordination between

---

77 Article 9(3) EEAS Council Decision.

78 To be sure, actions undertaken under: the CFSP budget; the Instrument for Stability (other than the part referred to in Article 9(2) EEAS Council Decision); the Instrument for Cooperation with Industrialised Countries; communication and public Diplomacy actions, and election observation missions, are under the responsibility of the HR/EEAS. The Commission is responsible for their financial implementation under the authority of the HR in his/her capacity as Vice-President of the Commission. The Commission department responsible for this implementation shall be co-located with the EEAS. See Article 9(6) EEAS Council Decision.

79 Article 9(3) EEAS Council Decision.

80 Article 9(4) EEAS Council Decision (emphasis added).

81 Article 9(5) EEAS Council Decision.

the Union and the Member States on development cooperation is seen as further proof that the Commission should continue as the implementer of development policy. However, there is nothing in the *travaux préparatoires* of the EEAS Council Decision to suggest that any such transferral of implementation of development cooperation instruments to the EEAS has been seriously entertained.[82]

Based upon the EEAS Council Decision, substantial management and implementation tasks are retained by the Commission with the EEAS playing a role in the programming aspects. Programming can be conceived of as relating to the political level where strategic goals are connected with more specific policy-making towards a country or region (cf the competence of the European Council ex Article 22 TEU), while the actual management of projects (especially their financial aspects) and their execution will be tasks retained by the Commission.

It is only when the President of the European Council, who is backed by the HR/VP's recommendations (prepared by the EEAS), presents the broad priorities of the EU on the international stage—who the key strategic partners are, and how the often difficult dialogue between values and interests should be conducted—that the Action Service's general tasks will become much more clear. In the absence of any such strategy at the macro level it is difficult to see how the EEAS will make critical decisions on programming priorities related to financial instruments.[83] In a way, as long as its organisational structure does not allow for the proper development of medium- and long-term strategies, the EEAS is trapped in a sort of circular logic.

7.4 The Organisational Structure of the EEAS

7.4.1 Putting Flesh on the Bones

In view of the fact that the most recent organisational structure from 1 April 2011 is still being fleshed out and thus liable to change,[84] it is too early to give a hard and fast answer to the question whether the envisaged structure of the Service

---

[82] See further Duke and Blockmans 2010.

[83] It is important to once more make a distinction between the EEAS political role and its legal position. On the first point, the EEAS is potentially vested with significant influence on EU external relations policy-making but so far the Commission has 'gone solo' on several issues with a significant external dimension, e.g. trade, energy security and climate change. As for its legal position, the EEAS has not been formally conferred with competences to adopt legally binding instruments.

[84] The organisational chart of 1 April 2011 was available online as late as on 1 July 2011. For updates, see <http://eeas.europa.eu/background/organisation/index_en.htm>.

corresponds to its mandate and whether this match will enable the EEAS to enhance institutional coherence in EU external action.[85] Nevertheless, one can draw some initial conclusions on the semi-crystallised structure, especially when one observes that certain parts of the architecture have remained constant in the series of organisational charts that have been published after the first of its kind was leaked in March 2010.[86] For instance, the crisis management (i.e. former Second Pillar) bodies have remained apart from the former First Pillar units, thereby structurally engraining the dichotomy in the Treaties between the 'specific' CSDP and the other external action policies of the Union.[87] Other examples concern the position of the managing director in charge of 'crisis response and operational coordination' and that of the EU Special Representatives, which remain completely unattached, but to the HR/VP him/herself.[88]

The central foundations of the Union's new functionally autonomous structure were created by the EEAS Council Decision. Article 4(3)(a) foresees the establishment of a number of directorates-general comprising geographic desks covering all countries and regions of the world, as well as several multilateral and thematic tasks. Also, a directorate-general for administrative, staffing, budgetary, security and communication and information system matters is foreseen, managed

[85] For the purpose of this essay, we will restrict our analysis to reviewing the functionality of the Action Service's central administration in promoting institutional coherence in the EU. On the role of the Union Delegations (provided for in Article 5 of the EEAS Council Decision), see Emerson et al. 2011, 5: 'The EU Delegations are now in principle well placed institutionally to represent the EU in the main centres of multilateral diplomacy (New York, Geneva, Vienna, etc.) precisely because of their capacity to represent the entire EU—and not just the Commission, as in the pre-Lisbon era—in international organisations (…).' At 52: 'For representation abroad, the Heads of the 136 EU Delegations, substituting those of the Commission, are accountable to the HR, and take over the coordinating role on the ground, which had so far been carried out by the embassy of the member state holding the rotating Presidency—potentially a far-reaching change. In principle the Delegations should develop a key role in articulating EU policies towards third countries, linking not only to the EEAS in Brussels but also to Commission directorates general responsible for sectoral policies with important external aspects (e.g. agriculture, aid, trade, transport, energy migration).'

[86] This first draft chart accompanied the High Representative's proposal of 25 March 2010 and is on file with the authors.

[87] Article 4(3)(a) of the EEAS Council Decision states: 'the crisis management and planning directorate, the civilian planning and conduct capability, the European Union Military Staff and the European Union Situation Centre, placed under the direct authority and responsibility of the High Representative, (…) shall assist him/her in the task of conducting the Union's CFSP in accordance with the provisions of the Treaty while respecting, in accordance with Article 40 TEU, the other competences of the Union.' Moreover, '[t]he specificities of these structures, as well as the particularities of their functions, recruitment and the status of the staff shall be respected.' Crisis management post-Lisbon is analysed in more detail by Schmidt (this volume).

[88] They are seen as being in direct competition with the directors of the thematic and geographical desks. As reported by H. Mahony, 'Diplomatic Service Blues', *EUObserver*, 29 June 2011.

by an Executive Secretary-General.[89] Finally, the central administration of the EEAS also includes a strategic policy planning department, a legal department, and departments for inter-institutional relations, information and public diplomacy, internal audit and inspections, and personal data protection.

Bureaucratic realities and inter-service rivalries have forced the architects of the organisational structure of the EEAS to draw the Service's organigramme somewhat differently though. A so-called 'Foreign Policy Instruments Service' incorporates desks devoted to budget, finance and inter-institutional relations, Stability Instrument operations, CFSP operations and public diplomacy and election observation. Being a service of the European Commission, it reports directly to the VP. This is surprising when one considers that any serious effort in this regard should be reflected within the EEAS at the level of (what was previously called) the 'Policy Board',[90] i.e. involving strategic communication (which also reports directly to the HR/VP) and strategic planning (which—like the desks responsible for policy coordination, legal affairs and relations with the EP and national parliaments—falls under the command of the Corporate Board).

Fleshing out the EEAS Council Decision, the draft organigramme also spells out the titles of the Policy Board's main directorates. Flanking five geographical directorates[91] is a directorate called 'Global and Multilateral Issues'. The latter comprises four thematic/multilateral desks: (1) multilateral relations and global governance, (2) human rights and democracy, (3) conflict prevention and security policy and (4) non-proliferation and disarmament. In terms of scope, the division between the geographic and thematic desks is to be reviewed each year before the general review of the service, which is due in 2013. As stated above, the crisis management bodies are bureaucratically separate from the Policy Board. The same applies to the FPI desk on public diplomacy and election observation. This is a pity, as these topics will be essential for longer-term visibility and acceptance of the EU in the world.

7.4.2 Internal Coherence

Internally, i.e. within the limits of the organisational chart of the EEAS, full coordination between all the structures of the EEAS shall be ensured.[92] How this

---

[89] Pierre Vimont, on a par with the Chief Operating Officer (David O'Sullivan), and assisted by the Deputy Secretary General for Inter-institutional Affairs (Maciej Popowski) and the Deputy Secretary General for Political Affairs (Helga Schmid). Together, they form the 'Corporate Board' of the EEAS, headed by the HR. The Managing Director Crisis Response and Operational Coordination may also be invited to attend the Corporate Board as necessary.

[90] The term was dropped with the adoption of the provisional organisational chart of 21 December 2010.

[91] Asia & Pacific; Africa; Europe & Central Asia; North Africa, Middle East, Arabian Peninsula, Iran & Iraq; Americas.

[92] Article 4 (3) EEAS Council Decision.

principle of internal coherence will be operationalised, however, is not entirely clear. It does not help that, in its first year of activities, the Service is not yet in a single headquarters. Its people are scattered over different buildings.[93] But aside from the logistics, there is a more fundamental problem of disconnect between a top heavy management and the expert desk officers down the chain. On paper, the EEAS is there to provide expert analysis to the HR. On-the-ground presence and knowledge should beef up the Union's foreign policy aims. This is supposed to provide bottom-up coherence to EU external action, even if coherence at the very top (i.e. the Corporate Board and the cabinet) is currently missing. By several accounts on the early days of the EEAS, the Service is suffering from a 'lack of morale, damaging infighting and a hazy chain of command'.[94]

These problems are partly structural, i.e. due to how the European External Action Service is set up: as noted in the previous section, it contains officials from the European Commission and the Council General Secretariat, as well as diplomats from the Member States. In an annex, the EEAS Council Decision lists those departments and functions to be transferred to the Service. In numerical terms this means that on 1 January 2011 585 administrator (AD) posts were transferred from the European Commission's DG Relex (i.e. staff previously serving the geographical desks), 93 from DG Development (i.e. from the geographical directorates-general D and E) and 436 from the delegations. In addition, 411 posts were transferred to the EEAS from the Council Secretariat. Hundred and eighteen new posts will be created in the period 2011–2013. The total number of AD level positions created in the EEAS is therefore 1,643. By the time the EEAS reaches its full capacity, staff coming from the Member States, Council Secretariat and Commission will each compose one-third of the EEAS' staff,[95] both at headquarters and in the delegations.[96] Although it will take a while before the EEAS is fully staffed, the configuration of the initial transfer of 3,645 civil servants (1,611 in headquarters and 2,034 in delegations) suggests that the organisational *ethos* will be predominantly based on the administrative routines inherited from the European Commission.[97] This will require an adaptation in working methods from the experts transferred from the Council General Secretariat's DG-E (i.e. the

93 A move is expected at the end of 2011.

94 See H. Mahony, 'Diplomatic Service Blues', *EUObserver*, 29 June 2011.

95 See European Commission, Draft amending Budget No. 6, COM (2010) 315 final, Brussels, 17.6.2010, at 5. This new configuration is expected to create synergies and efficiency gains. According to Ashton, on the fringes of the Gymnich of 10 September 2010, one could expect financial efficiency gains of at least 10%.

96 According to Article 5(2–3) of the EEAS Council Decision, the Head of Delegation shall receive instructions from the HR and the EEAS, and from the European Commission in areas where the Commission exercises the powers conferred upon it by the Treaties (cf. Article 221(2) TFEU) and shall be responsible for their execution. S/he shall also be accountable to the HR for the overall management of the work of the delegation and for ensuring the coordination of all actions of the Union.

97 See D. O'Sullivan, 'Setting up the EEAS', Speech at the IIEA, Dublin, 14 January 2011, 3, available at <http://www.iiea.com>. See also Lefebvre and Hillion 2010.

geographical and global and multilateral elements). However, the prevalence of Council Secretariat routines can be anticipated in some areas, most notably crisis management.[98] Also, it will be interesting to see how the diversity in national diplomatic cultures among temporarily seconded national experts will impact on the development of an *esprit de corps* within the EEAS.[99] The early practice within the EEAS is sobering. In the words of one observer:

> Taking experts from one bureaucracy and simply lumping them together with those from another in the name of a fuzzy greater good was always going to be difficult. Habits are ingrained. Loyalties are divided. And if there is no one specifically keeping an eye on such things—and there isn't—resentments grow. While the top layer is busy fighting with one other (…) the rest is looking for some political guidance and some sense of backup. (…) Poor human resources management is compounding the bad feeling. (…) [T]he human resources department is too small and staffed by Commission officials.[100]

Arguably, these problems could be compounded by the unclear relationship between the geographical and the thematic directorates. It is the Policy Board's task to ensure internal coherence and coordination and to make sure that the global and multilateral issues are reflected in the geographical and regional concerns and vice versa.[101] The idea is thus to 'mainstream' thematic—usually very technical—issues on a systematic basis to the geographical directorates, and that the geographical directorates treat the thematic directorates as resource bases. The extent to which this will work in practice is questionable. However, the intention to be borne in mind is that the Policy Board aims for an integrated policy approach. To this end, the Corporate Board—most notably the Deputy Secretary-General for Political Affairs (Schmid)—offers 'guidance' to the Policy Board.

Externally, that is beyond the borders of the organisational chart but still within the Union's institutional realm, the different parts of the External Action Service's

---

[98] See Duke 2011, 77–78.

[99] The EEAS Council decision stipulates that seconded national experts shall constitute no more than one-third of the positions at senior level, i.e. approximately 350 diplomats in total. The EEAS Council Decision stipulates that the members of the staff of the EEAS are subject to a high degree of mobility, in particular between the central administration and the delegations. Because of this, all EEAS staff will in principle serve periodically in EU delegations. This rotation is essential for staff to acquire experience on the ground and also to avoid an excessive identification with the interests of the states in which they are posted. Likewise, it is stated that civil servants serving in the EEAS will have the right to apply for posts in their institution of origin under the same conditions as internal candidates. It is by no means impossible that in the long term the existing links between the Action Service and the staff's institutions of origin should be weakened, thus reinforcing the institutional autonomy of the EEAS.

[100] Ibid.

[101] Incidentally, it should be observed that while the organisational chart of 23 July 2010 still bore the tag line 'The EEAS: a service for conflict prevention, security + stability', this motto has been dropped from the organigramme floated on 21 December 2010 and has not returned in the chart of 1 April 2011. Arguably, these themes do therefore no longer represent the overriding goals to which all activities of the EEAS should be geared, but thematic issues which like all other global and multilateral issues covered by the directorate, which should be mainstreamed in the policy-making and decision-shaping of the geographical directorates of the EEAS.

central administration are expected to provide inter-institutional coherence and coordinate decision-shaping to support the HR/VP, the President of the European Council, the President of the European Commission and the Commission as a whole. In addition to what has already been mentioned about inter-institutional cooperation at the highest level,[102] one can point to some lower-level linkages. Whereas the legal department of the EEAS is obliged to 'work closely' with the Legal Services of the Council and of the Commission, Article 4(3)(a) of the EEAS Council Decision prescribes that the directorates comprising geographical, multilateral and thematic desks shall coordinate 'as necessary' with the General Secretariat of the Council and with the relevant services of the Commission. The Policy Board is likely to become the 'essential bridge' between the EEAS and the Foreign Affairs Council, the General Affairs Council and the Council General Secretariat.[103] At the senior level, the office of Deputy SG Popowski should link up with the relevant DGs of the European Commission, the EP and national parliaments. As a policy recommendation, Duke has pointed out that '[i]f the Policy Board is to be pro-active, and not merely reactive, [Popowski's office] is also the point at which the Joint Situation Centre, the Special Representatives and the PSC chair could inform the Corporate Board's secretariat of potential agenda items'.[104] But like so many other aspects pertaining to the organisational structure and the operationalisation thereof, the coordination mechanisms have yet to be fully worked out.

7.5 Conclusion

In 2002, Javier Solana famously said: 'Europe can choose to speak with a single voice, or Europe can decide not to be heard.'[105] Coordinated action on the international scene would enable the European Union to finally speak with this single voice. This advancement, however, presupposes the existence of a set of common objectives and an understanding on how they should be attained through coordination between the many actors endowed with the competences to operate externally—the European Council, the President of the European Council, the Council, the HR/VP, the Commission and its Commissioners. While the Lisbon Treaty has merged the Union's foreign policy objectives in Article 21 TEU so as to

[102] See supra, Section 3.

[103] See Duke 2011, at 77.

[104] Ibid. Also, '[t]he linkage between the Managing Director Crisis Response and Operational Coordination, Agostino Miozzo, and the Corporate Board (on request) and the Policy Board is of particular importance since, aside from the HR/VP herself, this is the only obvious link with the CSDP bodies.'

[105] Speech delivered on 19 February 2002 in Brussels on the occasion of the launch of CER publication by Steven Everts, 'Shaping an effective EU foreign policy', www.consilium.europa.eu/uedocs/cms_data/docs/pressdata/en/discours/69508.pdf. Accessed 25 July 2011.

create greater coherence at the overarching policy level, these objectives need to be specified and turned into concrete policies within different institutional quarters, sometimes (like in the case of trade) falling outside of the European External Action Service's reach. The tension between competence delimitation within the Treaties and the need to speak with one voice to the world seems to have been structurally engrained into the structures of the EEAS.

Of course, it is important to make a distinction between the Action Service's legal position and its political role. On the first point, the EEAS has not been formally conferred with competences to adopt legally binding instruments. In fact, the EEAS' hands are tied to the competences attributed to the political masters it is supposed to serve. But however important the structures and competence allocation are, they are never an end in themselves but merely instruments. The key question underlying our chapter has been whether the new body is fit for its intended purpose. Will it be able to provide the essential support to and coordinate the policies and actions of the senior EU posts in external relations? While it is still early days to draw definitive conclusions, the analysis in this chapter does provide enough grounds for some initial findings on the impact the EEAS may have on the efforts to enhance coherence in EU external action. In its political role, as a bridge-builder between the institutions, sharing information and acting as a common source of expertise, to a certain extent even representing several institutions, the EEAS is potentially vested with significant influence on EU external relations policy-making, at least as long as the Commission's services and the Council General Secretariat—the bodies that pack the biggest punch in terms of implementation—cooperate on issues with a significant external dimension, e.g. development cooperation, humanitarian aid, enlargement, ENP, energy security and climate change.[106] But the fields of activity of the EEAS are significantly wider than those of national diplomatic services (diplomacy, military security and parts of development cooperation) and the number of foreign policy actors far bigger. Composing a common hymn sheet from which the Lisbon Treaty's many external action heroes can sign with a single voice is a task far more perplexing than one would encounter at a national foreign ministry. Still, going by the mandate and organisational structure—and looking beyond its teething problems, the External Action Service's potential lies in becoming a true inter-institutional 'decision-shaping' body, working towards achieving greater coherence in EU external action. Still, as the successes of its coordination efforts rely to a great extent on the executive deeds of its political masters, it would perhaps have been better to avoid the term 'action' in naming the EEAS and call it the 'European External Coordination Service' instead.

106 Dragneva and Wolczuk point to the fact that will have more underlying policy durability than any Member States and will potentially be better positioned to develop stronger 'local knowledge' but also to feed this knowledge into decision-making processes within the EU, this volume, Sect. 3.

References

Ashton C (2010) Foreword. In: Blockmans S, Wouters J, Ruys T (eds) The European Union and peacebuilding policy and legal aspects. T.M.C. Asser Press, The Hague

Avery G (2011) The EU's External Action Service: new actor on the scene. European Policy Centre—EPC commentary. www.epc.eu/documents/uploads/pub_1223_the_european_external_action_service_-_new_actor_on_the_scene.pdf. Accessed 25 June 2011

Brok E (2011) Préjugés, défis et potentiels: une analyse sans idées préconçues du Service européen pour l'action extérieure, Fondation Robert Schuman Policy Paper, Question d'Europe n°199

Craig P (2010) The Lisbon Treaty: law, politics and treaty reform. Oxford University Press, Oxford

Cremona M (2011) Coherence in European Union foreign relations law. In: Koutrakos (ed) European foreign policy: legal and political perspectives. Edward Elgar, Cheltenham, pp 55–92

Devuyst Y (2008) The European Union's institutional balance after the Treaty of Lisbon: "community method" and "democratic deficit" reassessed. Georgetown Journal of International Law 39:247–325

Drieskens E, Van Schaik L (eds) (2010) The European External Action Service: preparing for success. Clingendael Paper No 1, The Hague

Duke S (2010) Parameters for success. In: Drieskens E, Van Schaik L (eds) The European External Action Service: preparing for success. Clingendael Paper No 1, The Hague

Duke S (2011) A difficult birth: the early days of the European External Action Service. In: Koutrakos P (ed) The European Union's external relations a year after Lisbon, CLEER Working Papers 2011-3, pp 69–81

Duke S, Blockmans S (2010) The Lisbon Treaty stipulations on development cooperation and the council decision of 25 March 2010 (Draft) establishing the organisation and functioning of the European External Action Service. CLEER Legal Brief, 4 May 2010

Emerson M et al (2011) Upgrading the EU's role as global actor: institutions, law and the restructuring of European diplomacy. The Centre for European Policy Studies (CEPS), Brussels

Hillion C (2008) Tous pour un, un pour tous! Coherence in the external relations of the European Union. In: Cremona M (ed) Developments in EU external relations law. Oxford University Press, Oxford, pp 10–36

Koutrakos P (2001) Trade, foreign policy and defence in EU constitutional law. Hart, Oxford

Lefebvre M, Hillion C (2010) The European External Action Service: towards a common diplomacy? SIEPS European analysis 6. www.sieps.se/sites/default/files/642-2010_6epa.pdf, Accessed 25 June 2011

Lloveras Soler JM (2011) The new EU diplomacy: learning to add value. European University Institute—EUI Working Papers, RSCAS 2011/05, Florence

Piris J-C (2010) The Lisbon Treaty: a legal and political analysis. Cambridge University Press, Cambridge

Skytte Christoffersen P (2010) A guinness record for speed. In: Drieskens E, Van Schaik L (eds) The European External Action Service: preparing for success. Clingendael Paper No 1, The Hague

Tietje C (1997) The concept of coherence in the Treaty on European Union and the common foreign and security policy. European Foreign Affairs Review 2:211–234

Vaisse J, Kundnani H (eds) (2011) European foreign policy scorecard 2010. ECFR, London

Van Vooren B (2001a) A legal-institutional perspective on the European External Action Service. Common Market Law Review 48:475–502

Van Vooren B (2001b) The European External Action Service: avoiding past disputes in the security-development nexus? In: Larik J, Moraru M (eds) Ever-closer in Brussels, ever-closer in the world? EU external action after the Lisbon Treaty. European University Institute—EUI LAW Working Papers 2011/2010, Florence, pp 19–28

Vanhoonacker S, Duke S (2010) Chairs' conclusions. In: Drieskens E, Van Schaik L (eds) The European External Action Service: preparing for success. Clingendael Paper No 1, The Hague

Chapter 8
The High Representative, the President and the Commission—Competing Players in the EU's External Relations: The Case of Crisis Management

Julia Schmidt

Abstract In its aim to become a global security actor, the European Union (EU) is increasingly engaged in civilian and military crisis management missions all over the world. According to its comprehensive approach to crisis management, these missions are not the only means by which conflicts can be addressed. The EU has a long-standing tradition of using instruments such as trade agreements, development aid and economic sanctions to promote its values to the outside world. However, this comprehensive approach to crisis management can only be successful if the EU is able to provide coherent international action. This chapter will assess whether the new institutions of the High Representative for Foreign Affairs and Security Policy that will be assisted by the European External Action Service, and the permanent President of the Council will be able to provide the EU with more effective and coherent external relations. It will be argued that although the High Representative from now on links the Council with the Commission which appears to be the key to a more efficient policy, some serious problems still lie ahead. These problems are likely to arise due to the continuing difficulties in the delimitation of competences between different policy fields of the European Union that have foreign policy implications.

Julia Schmidt—Ph.D. candidate, The University of Edinburgh.

J. Schmidt (✉)
The University of Edinburgh, Edinburgh, UK
e-mail: j.r.schmidt@sms.ed.ac.uk

P. J. Cardwell (ed.), *EU External Relations Law and Policy in the Post-Lisbon Era*,
DOI: 10.1007/978-90-6704-823-1_8, © T.M.C. ASSER PRESS, The Hague,
The Netherlands, and the authors 2012

Contents

8.1 Introduction

Since the Common Security and Defence Policy (CSDP) became operational in 2003, the European Union (EU) has been engaged in more than 22 crisis management operations. So far, these operations have included police missions,[1] rule of law missions,[2] border assistance missions,[3] missions in support of security sector reforms,[4] monitoring missions[5] and military missions.[6] These examples demonstrate the EU's ambition to become a global security actor whose international role mirrors its economic influence. However, these crisis management missions are not the only means by which the EU tries to solve pressing international issues. European development and humanitarian aid for example can be regarded as a measure to prevent the outbreak of new conflicts and to consolidate peace. Economic sanctions may be imposed to encourage the targeted state to change its behaviour to prevent a crisis from worsening. 'Positive' measures, including (for example) the granting of unilateral trade preferences, can be used to exercise diplomatic and political pressure.

---

[1] See for example Council Joint Action 2008/229/CFSP of 17 March 2008 on EU Police Mission in Afghanistan, EUPOL AFGHANISTAN.

[2] See for example Council Joint Action 2008/124/CFSP of 4 February 2008 on EU rule of law mission in Kosovo, *EULEX KOSOVO*.

[3] See for example Council Joint Action 2007/359/CFSP of 23 May 2007 on EU Border Assistance Mission at Rafah Crossing Point in the Palestinian Territories *EU BAM Rafah*.

[4] See for example Council Joint Action 2008/112/CFSP of 12 February 2008 on EU mission in support of security sector reform in Guinea-Bissau, *EU SSR Guinea-Bissau*.

[5] See for example Council Joint Action 2005/643/CFSP of 9 September 2005 on the Aceh Monitoring Mission (AMM).

[6] See for example Council Joint Action 2007/677/CFSP of 15 October 2007 on EUFOR in Chad.

The variety of different tools at the disposal of the EU to either prevent or help resolve a conflict are scattered over different policy fields and involve different institutional settings and procedures. European crisis management can therefore only be successful if the varieties of different tools are coordinated with each other. In addition, a more coherent European external action will save European resources and can help to avoid duplication of work.[7] The link between the EU's comprehensive concept of crisis management and the need for greater coherence in order to make the EU's crisis management more effective has already been expressed in the European Security Strategy and continues to shape the EU's external policies.[8] One of the aims behind the drafting of the Constitutional Treaty, and retained in the Treaty of Lisbon, was to enhance the coherence of the EU's external action.[9] In this respect, the Treaty introduced a new title on the EU's external action and also created the role of the High Representative for Foreign Affairs and Security Policy that links the Council with the Commission.

This chapter will look at whether the High Representative can enhance the coherence of the EU's external action. The chapter will start with a description of the EU's comprehensive concept of crisis management in order to show that the varieties of different instruments are scattered over different policy areas and therefore involve different institutional settings. As crisis management measures are not used in isolation from each other but in combination, only their coherent usage can guarantee effective European crisis management. Following the assessment of the principle of coherence and its different aspects, Sect. 8.4 will discuss whether the new post of the High Representative for Foreign Affairs and Security, linking the Council with the Commission, can be seen as the answer to the current problems. It will be argued that due to continuing difficulties in the delimitation of competences between different policy fields of the EU that have foreign policy implications, the High Representative is less likely to enhance institutional coherence.

8.2 A Comprehensive Concept of Crisis Management

Although no internationally agreed definition on crisis management exists, the statements of the EU (most importantly the European Security Strategy) which presents the first strategic concept for the Union and its actual practice support the

---

7 Koutrakos 2007, 250.

8 European Council (2003) A Secure Europe For A Better World: European Security Strategy, 12 December 2003 Brussels, www.consilium.europa.eu/uedocs/cmsUpload/78367.pdf, 11 [hereinafter *European Security Strategy*]. Last accessed 3 June 2011.

9 Council of the European Union (2007) Brussels European Council, Presidency Conclusions, 21/22 June 2007, 11177/1/07 REV 1, ANNEX I, IGC Mandate, Brussels, para 1 [hereinafter *Brussels European Council*].

view of a comprehensive concept of crisis management.[10] The European approach to crisis management is comprehensive in two ways. First, the EU is prepared and willing to act in the whole life cycle of a conflict, including conflict prevention, peace-making, peace-enforcement, peace-keeping as well as post conflict stabilisation. Second, it is willing to use a variety of tools that are at its disposal to fulfil these different aims.[11]

In response to the identified key threats to the EU, including terrorism, the proliferation of Weapons of Mass Destruction (WMD), regional conflicts, state failure and organised crime, the European Security Strategy recommends the use of a mixture of instruments and considers the EU to be 'particularly well equipped to respond to such multi-faceted situations'[12]:

> Proliferation may be contained through export controls and attacked through political, economic and other pressures while the underlying political causes are also tackled. Dealing with terrorism may require a mixture of intelligence, political, judicial, military and other means. In failed states, military instruments may be needed to restore order, humanitarian means to tackle the immediate crisis. Regional conflicts need political solutions but military assets and effective policing may be needed in the post conflict phase. Economic instruments serve reconstruction, and civilian crisis management helps restore civil government.

In scholarly debate, economic sanctions are usually not incorporated into the concept of European crisis management.[13] However, to address the whole lifecycle of a conflict, the use of a variety of tools available to the EU is necessary and used in practice. The European Security Strategy itself mentions trade measures, including economic sanctions, alongside other tools requiring the EU to be more active in pursuing its strategic objectives, which,

> applies to the full spectrum of instruments for crisis management and conflict prevention at our disposal, including political, diplomatic, military and civilian, trade and development activities. Active policies are needed to counter the new dynamic threats. We need to develop a strategic culture that fosters early, rapid, and when necessary, robust intervention.[14]

---

[10] Blockmans 2008, 10; On the comprehensive approach to crisis management that asks for the right mixture of different elements see also Simón 2010, 16–17.

[11] European Council (2003) A Secure Europe For A Better World: European Security Strategy, 12 December 2003 Brussels, www.consilium.europa.eu/uedocs/cmsUpload/78367.pdf, 11 [hereinafter *European Security Strategy*]. Last accessed 3 June 2011.

[12] European Council (2003) A Secure Europe For A Better World: European Security Strategy, 12 December 2003 Brussels, www.consilium.europa.eu/uedocs/cmsUpload/78367.pdf, 7 [hereinafter *European Security Strategy*]. Last accessed 3 June 2011.

[13] In favour of the inclusion of sanctions into the EU's comprehensive approach to crisis management: Anthony 2002, 203.

[14] European Council (2003) A Secure Europe For A Better World: European Security Strategy, 12 December 2003 Brussels, www.consilium.europa.eu/uedocs/cmsUpload/78367.pdf, 11 [hereinafter *European Security Strategy*]. Last accessed 3 June 2011.

In addition, the Council document *Basic Principles on the Use of Restrictive Measures (Sanctions)* perceives 'the effective use of sanctions as an important way to maintain and restore international peace and security' and states that the 'Council is committed to using sanctions as part of an integrated, comprehensive policy approach which should include political dialogue, incentives, conditionality and could even involve, as a last resort, the use of coercive measures in accordance with the UN Charter'.[15] Furthermore, economic sanctions are not only used independently but they often accompany civilian and military EU crisis management operations. They are an available tool to be used in practice to help end a conflict. As such, they should therefore be included in the overall concept of crisis management.

The experience of the EU with the Democratic Republic of Congo (DRC) as well as with Sudan can serve as an example to illustrate the EU's above described comprehensive approach to crisis management. The EU has been supporting a peaceful settlement of the conflict in the DRC since the 1990s, in particular through its Special Representative for the Great Lakes Region.[16] From June to September 2003, the EU led a military operation in the DRC. Operation ARTEMIS, mandated by UN Security Council Resolution 1484 (2003) was tailored to stabilise the security environment as well as to improve the humanitarian situation in Bunia in the Ituri region of the Orientale Province in the northeast of the DRC.[17] In June 2005, the EU started to deploy EUSEC DR Congo, an EU mission to provide advice and assistance for security sector reform in the DRC, and which aimed to help Congolese authorities to build modern, efficient administrative structures within the Armed Forces. The mandate expired on 30 September 2010.[18] During the period of the presidential elections in 2006, the EU deployed military operation EUFOR RD CONGO in support of the United Nations Organisation Mission in the Democratic Republic of Congo (MONUC).[19] In the aftermath of the election, the EU continued its commitment in the DRC with a view to consolidating the rule of law, security and stability and sent the EUPOL RD Congo mission from July 2007 until June 2010, in order to support the reform

---

[15] Council of the European Union (2004) Basic Principles on the Use of Restrictive Measures (Sanctions), 7 June 2004, 10198/1/04 REV 1, PESC 450, Annex 1, Brussels, 7 June 2004, paras 1 and 5.

[16] Council of the European Union, CONSILIUM-ARTEMIS/DRC, available at www.consilium.europa.eu/showPage.aspx?id=605&lang=en. Last accessed 3 June 2011; Council Joint Action (2000/792/CFSP) of 14 December 2000 appointing the Special Representative of the European Union for the African Great Lakes Region and repealing Joint Action 96/250/CFSP.

[17] Council Joint Action 2003/423/CFSP of June 2003 on the European Union military operation in the Democratic Republic of Congo.

[18] Consilium Fact Sheet (2010) EU Mission to provide advice and assistance for security sector reform in the Democratic Republic of Congo (EUSE DR CONGO), EUSEC RDC/08, available at www.consilium.europa.eu/uedocs/cms_data/docs/missionPress/files/100426%20Factsheet%20EUSEC%20RD%20Congo%20-%20version%208_EN.pdf. Last accessed 3 June 2011.

[19] Consilium Fact Sheet, *EUFOR RD Congo: THE MISSION*, available at www.consilium.europa.eu/uedocs/cmsUpload/The_mission.pdf. Last accessed 3 June 2011.

of the security sector in the area of the police and its interactions with the criminal justice system.[20] EUPOL RD Congo worked closely EUSEC DR Congo and MONUC. In parallel to these military and civilian crisis management missions, the EU also imposed economic and financial sanctions[21] against the DRC, including for example, a ban on provision of certain services, including brokering services and other services related to military activities, the freezing of funds of listed individuals and entities, travel bans and an arms embargo.[22]

With a wide range of measures, the EU has also supported activities by the African Union (AU) since 2004 in an attempt to stabilise the Darfur region in Sudan. Financial, political and personnel support to the Abuja peace talks process and the Ceasefire Commission followed European assistance with planning, equipment, technical and financial support to the AU's mission in the region (AMIS). Following a request from the AU, the EU launched its first combined civilian and military mission between 2005 and 2007, assisting and supporting the AU's political, police and military efforts in an attempt to end the crisis. Amongst other tasks, the EU assisted and trained the police and made military observers and experts available to the AU. The EU also imposed a number of sanctions, including a travel ban, the freezing of funds and economic resources, an arms embargo and the ban on provision of certain services, including brokering services and other services related to military activities.[23] At the end of 2007, AMIS handed over to a joint UN/AU peacekeeping operation named UNAMID, as authorised by UN Security Council Resolution 1769 (2007).[24]

To conclude, European crisis management includes all types of military and civilian CSDP operations, covering the whole lifecycle of a conflict reaching from conflict prevention to post conflict rehabilitation and covering the whole external dimension of security, across the different policy areas of the EU,[25] as well as a variety of economic, diplomatic and political tools. However, different crisis management instruments can only be applied in an efficient manner if the policy frameworks they are adopted in are coherent with each other.

---

[20] Consilium Fact Sheet (2010) EU Police Mission for the DRC (EUPOL RD CONGO), EUPOL RDC/08, June 2010, available at www.consilium.europa.eu/uedocs/cms_data/docs/missionPress/files/100616%20Factsheet%20EUPOL%20RD%20Congo%20-%20version%208_EN.pdf. Last accessed 3 June 2011.

[21] An updated list of negative measures applied by the EU against third countries can be viewed at European Commission—Restrictive measures (sanctions) in force (measures adopted in the framework of the Common Foreign and Security Policy), ec.europa.eu/external_relations/cfsp/sanctions/docs/measures_en.pdf. Last accessed 3 June 2011.

[22] Council Common Position 2008/369/CFSP of 14 May 2008 concerning restrictive measures against the Democratic Republic of the Congo and repealing Common Position 2005/440/CFSP.

[23] Council Common Position 2005/411/CFSP of 30 May 2005 concerning restrictive measures against Sudan and repealing Common Position 2004/31/CFSP.

[24] Consilium Fact sheet (2008) EU support to the African Union Mission in Darfur—AMIS, AMIS II/08, January 2008, www.consilium.europa.eu/uedocs/cmsUpload/080109-Factsheet8-AMISII.pdf. Last accessed 3 June 2011.

[25] Blockmans 2008, 11.

8.3 The Treaty of Lisbon and the Need for Greater Coherence in the EU's External Action

Before the entry into force of the Treaty of Lisbon, the instruments used for crisis management have been scattered over the different pillars of the EU and have been influenced by different institutional settings and procedures. For example, civilian and military crisis management missions have been organised under the intergovernmental Common Foreign and Security Policy (CFSP). Trade measures as well as matters related to development cooperation were part of the supranational European Community pillar. Within the CFSP, the Foreign Affairs Council could be considered as the key player whilst the involvement of the Commission has been only marginal. Within the European Community pillar on the other hand, the Commission played a strong role in putting in place trade-related measures including the Common Commercial Policy. In respect to development cooperation, the power has been traditionally shared between the Council and the Commission. Assigning instruments of crisis management to different institutions however bears with it the potential of inconsistent action.

The combination of different tools of crisis management can only lead to a successful outcome if the different elements are coordinated with each other and are used in a coherent way. The Laeken Declaration on the future of the EU defined the need to enhance the coherence of European foreign policy as one of the key questions to be addressed in the context of the failed process of creating a Constitution for Europe.[26] The awareness of the need to enhance the coherence of the EU's external action carried on into the mandate of the Intergovernmental Conference that was designed with the task to draw up the Reform Treaty in 2007.[27] The Treaty of Lisbon responds to that request by putting more emphasis on the principle of consistency. The task to ensure consistency of the EU's external action is assigned to the newly founded post of the High Representative of the Union for Foreign Affairs and Security Policy.[28] The Treaty on European Union (TEU) also explicitly recognises the need for consistency between the EU's external action and other policy areas.[29] In this respect the task to ensure consistency is shared by the Council and the Commission, assisted by the High Representative.[30] Chairing the Foreign Affairs Council and serving as one of the

---

[26] European Council (2001) Laeken Declaration On the Future Of The European Union, European Council Meeting in Laeken, 14 and 15 December 2001, Presidency Conclusions, Annex I, 23 www.consilium.europa.eu/ueDocs/cms_Data/docs/pressData/en/ec/68827.pdf. Last accessed 3 June 2011.

[27] Council of the European Union (2007) Brussels European Council, Presidency Conclusions, 21/22 June 2007, 11177/1/07 REV 1, ANNEX I, IGC Mandate, Brussels, para 1 [hereinafter *Brussels European Council*].

[28] Treaty on European Union, Article 18 (4).

[29] Treaty on European Union, Article 21 (3).

[30] Treaty on European Union, Article 21 (3).

Vice Presidents of the Commission, the High Representative appears to be especially suited to fulfil this task.[31]

Whether this 'double-hatting' will enhance the coherence of the EU's actions on the international scene will be discussed in more detail in Sect. 8.5. But this is not only for those plain references to consistency in the TEU that appear to be beneficial for achieving greater coherence in the EU's external action but also for innovations such as the abolishment of the pillar structure of the Union, its single international legal personality and the reorganisation of the Union's external relations into a separate title. 'Title V on General provisions on the Union's external action and specific provisions on the CFSP' connects the Union's external competences under the Treaty on the Functioning of the European Union (TFEU) with the CFSP and the CSDP. Thereby the Treaty not only formally recognises that the EU's action on the international scene is linked to a variety of different Union policies that are spread over different parts of the EU Treaties but also bases them on common objectives.[32]

Before the assessment of whether the role of the High Representative is the key to more coherent action of the EU on the international scene, the principle of coherence will have to be examined in more detail. The different language versions of the Treaty of Lisbon use either the term coherence[33] or the term consistency.[34] Although the terms are often used interchangeably in academic discussions,[35] this contribution will argue that the principle of consistency is not equivalent to the principle of coherence. More important than their formal designation is the definition of their substance.[36]

Consistency demands a lack of contradictions, whereas coherence describes a dynamic concept referring to positive connections.[37] Legal concepts can be coherent to differing degrees but they are either consistent with each other or they are not.[38] Coherence therefore is 'a broader and more flexible concept than consistency'.[39] For coherence to be meaningful in the context of the EU's external relations, not any level of synergy however is sufficient.[40] If different policy sectors are only coherent to a small extent, the EU's contribution to international

---

31 See also Missiroli 2010, 432.

32 Treaty on European Union, Article 21.

33 See for example the German language version of Article 18 (4) Treaty on European Union: Der Hohe Vertreter der Union für Außen- und Sicherheitspolitik "sorgt für die Kohärenz des auswärtigen Handelns der Union".

34 See for example the English language version.

35 See for example Nuttall 2005, 96–98.

36 The differences between coherence and consistency have been thoroughly examined by Christophe Hillion who also indicates that some authors that refer to "consistency" in fact address issues of the concept of coherence, Hillion 2008, 14.

37 Wessel 2000, 1150; Blockmans and Wessel 2009, 288.

38 Hillion 2008, 14; Vanhoonacker 2008, 146.

39 Cremona 2008, 14.

40 Hillion 2008, 17.

crisis management is not going to become more effective. To be meaningful, different EU policy sectors are not only in need to be free from contradictions but they also have to add value to the EU's system of external relations.[41]

The principle of coherence can be studied from three different angles.[42] A horizontal approach to coherence examines to which extent different EU policies that are set out to achieve different objectives are in line with each other.[43] The second category, institutional coherence, takes place predominantly on a horizontal level too, but puts its emphasis on the problem of how different sets of actors that are bound to follow different procedures pursue the same policy objective of external relations.[44] In this respect, it is important to assess how the actions of the Commission, the Foreign Affairs Council, and the President of the European Council as well as of the High Representative for Foreign Affairs and Security Policy fit into each other. In contrast to horizontal coherence, vertical coherence studies to what degree domestic policies of the Member States are in line with EU policies.[45] Vertical coherence can also be studied from an external perspective and then intends to identify to what degree the EU's crisis management efforts fit in with the work of other international actors.[46] Aspects of vertical coherence will not be the subject of this chapter.[47]

In the light of the above described concepts of horizontal and institutional coherence, the following part will assess in more detail whether the institution of the High Representative for Foreign Affairs and Security Policy that will be assisted by the European External Action Service (EEAS) can be the key to a more effective European crisis management structure.

Therefore the following section will look at the powers of the High Representative and the special role she plays within the CSDP. Essential for the understanding of the practical significance of the work of the High Representative in respect of the coordination of CSDP initiatives with other Union activities of external relevance is not only its double-hatting, but also the powers she and the EEAS have taken over from different actors. In order to assess whether the High Representative together with the EEAS can provide the EU with more coherent and therefore more effective crisis management, the chapter will then look at the

---

[41] Hillion 2008, 14–17.

[42] Nuttall 2005, 96–98; Neuwahl distinguishes between material and organizational consistency: Neuwahl 1994, 235–236. Cremona analyses coherences as multi-layered concept and distinguishes between rules of hierarchy; rules of delimitation and principles of cooperation and complementarity; and applies all three levels or elements of coherence with regards to vertical, horizontal and institutional coherence; see Cremona 2008, 11–36.

[43] Nuttall 2005, 97.

[44] Nuttall 2005, 97; Cremona 2008, 25.

[45] Nuttall 2005, 98. As Broberg notes, in this volume, vertical coherence is primarily achieved through the principle of sincere cooperation (Articles 4(3) and 24(3) TEU).

[46] De Vasconcelos 2009, 11.

[47] On the topic of vertical internal coherence between the EU and its Member States, see for example Hillion 2010, 87–115.

interplay between different aspects of crisis management. Elements of the EU's external action are still scattered over different Union policy sectors. Although the European Community has been succeeded by the EU and the pillar structure as established by the Treaty of Maastricht no longer exists, the CFSP is still subject to specific rules and procedures.[48] It will be argued that the High Representative might be able to enhance horizontal coherence between the CFSP and policy fields that have been part of the former European Community to some extent, but she will not be capable of solving all problems. These problems are linked to the scope of the CFSP that is only vaguely defined by the Treaties itself. EU policy areas that are included in Part Five on External Action By The Union in the TFEU[49] and other policy areas that can have foreign policy implications need to be distinguished from the CFSP due to differing procedures and institutional settings. Section 8.6 will briefly outline whether there are problems of coherence between the CFSP on the one hand and the CSDP on the other hand. In this respect, the respective roles played by the High Representative for Foreign Affairs and Security Policy and the President of the European Council will be scrutinised. It will be argued that the Treaty of Lisbon does not offer sufficient guidelines on how both bodies are supposed to divide the workload of representing the Union in the international arena.

8.4 The High Representative and the European External Action Service

The new position of the High Representative for Foreign Affairs and Security led to the abolishment of the position of the Secretary General of the Council that exercised the function of High Representative for the CFSP[50] and also made the position of the Commissioner for External Relations redundant. Chairing the Foreign Affairs Council[51] and serving as one of the Vice Presidents of the Commission she now links the Council with the Commission.[52] The High Representative's main task is to conduct the Union's CFSP as well as its CSDP.[53] Through her proposals she contributes towards the preparation of CFSP measures and ensures implementation of the decisions adopted by the European Council and the Council.[54] She represents the Union for matters relating to the CFSP; conducts political dialogue with third parties on the Union's behalf and expresses the

---

48 Treaty on European Union, Article 24 (2).

49 "Part Five on External Action By The Union", includes amongst others a title on restrictive measures, a title on the common commercial policy and a title on cooperation with third countries which is subdivided into provisions on development cooperation, on economic, financial and technical cooperation with third countries, as well as on humanitarian aid.

50 Treaty on European Union (pre-Lisbon), Article 18 (3).

51 Treaty on European Union, Article 18 (3).

52 Treaty on European Union, Article 18 (4).

53 Treaty on European Union, Article 18 (2).

54 Treaty on European Union, Article 27 (1).

Union's position in international organisations and at international conferences.[55] Within the CSDP the High Representative enjoys her strongest role. Decisions relating to the CSDP initiating a crisis management mission are to be adopted by the Council on either her proposal or on the initiative from a member state.[56] Council decisions that form part of the CFSP however do not have to be proposed by the High Representative.

In her work, the High Representative will be assisted by the EEAS.[57] The EEAS is a functionally autonomous body that works under the authority of the High Representative.[58] Several departments and functions that have been previously exercised by the General Secretariat of the Council as well as by the Commission and Commission Delegations have been transferred to the EEAS. Apart from now being in charge of the Policy Unit, the CSDP and crisis management structures that contain the Crisis Management and Planning Directorate, the Civilian and Conduct Capabilities and the EU Military Staff; the EEAS will also take over the Directorate-General E as well as the officials of the General Secretariat of the Council on secondment to EU Special Representatives and CSDP missions.[59] In relation to the departments and functions previously exercised by the Commission, the EEAS will take over the Directorate-General for External Relations, including Directorate A (Crisis Platform and policy coordination in CFSP), Directorate B (Multilateral Relations and Human Rights) and Directorate D (European Neighbourhood Policy Coordination). Additionally, the Directorate-General for Development as well as the Commission's External Service will be transferred to the EEAS.

The expectations for the EEAS are high and Catherine Ashton, the first EU High Representative for Foreign Affairs and Security Policy has held that the establishment of the EEAS:

> will mark a new beginning for European foreign and security policy as we bring together and streamline all of the Union's existing resources, staff and instruments.[…] This combination of staff and resources will be more than the sum of its parts: we will be able to find synergies and develop new ideas, which will enhance our ability to act more creatively and decisively in an increasingly challenging world.[60]

---

55 Treaty on European Union, Article 27 (2).

56 Treaty on European Union, Article 42 (4).

57 Treaty on European Union, Article 27 (3).

58 Council of the European Union Council Decision 11665/1/10/REV1establishing the organisation and functioning of the European External Action Service, 20 July 2010, Brussels, para 1. On the role and organisation of the EEAS, see Blockmans and Laatsit (this volume).

59 A detailed list can be found in Council of the European Union Council Decision 11665/1/10/REV1 establishing the organisation and functioning of the European External Action Service, 20 July 2010, Brussels, Annex.

60 EUROPA Press Release IP/10/1769 (2010) A new step in the setting-up of the EEAS: Transfer of staff on 1 January 2011, 21 December 2010, Brussels, europa.eu/rapid/pressReleasesAction.do?reference=IP/10/1769&format=HTML&aged=0&language=EN&guiLanguage=en. Last accessed 3 June 2011.

8.5 The Scattering of the EU's External Relations Across Different Union Competences

The distribution of the Union's external relations across different Union policies is one of the main obstacles in achieving greater coherence and effectiveness in the EU's crisis management activities. From a horizontal perspective, the introduction of a new part in the Treaty on the EU's external relations, basing them on general objectives, appear to enhance the coordination between different elements of the EU's external action, even if they are still scattered over different Union sectors. This effect is underlined by the role of the High Representative that is chairing the Foreign Affairs Council and is sitting as one of the vice Presidents of the Commission. The 'double-hatting' has the potential of optimising the flow of information between the CFSP and other EU policy sectors and therefore appears capable of improving the coordination of the EU's external action.

From an institutional perspective, the situation is not as good as it appears to be on a first glimpse. Leaving aside the CFSP for now, even within EU policies that have formally been recognised as being part of the EU's external action, the institutional involvement differs. The Commission plays a strong role in all trade-related matters as part of the EU's Common Commercial Policy. With regard to development cooperation, the Commission however has to share its duties with the Council. Although the High Representative fulfils functions in both institutions, she might find it difficult to reconcile power struggles between both institutions that are used to having different institutional identities, agendas and priorities.[61] The fact that both institutions have lost some of their functions to the EEAS might also not be very likely to increase their cooperation with the High Representative. As a consequence, institutional coherence might not improve significantly with the first few years of the post-Lisbon era.

When focusing on the CFSP and EU policy sectors that form part of the EU's external action, institutional coherence appears to be as difficult to obtain now as it has been before the entry into force of the Treaty of Lisbon. Although the Treaty of Lisbon abolished the pillar structure that has been introduced by the Treaty of Maastricht, the CFSP is still subject to specific rules and procedures as pointed out above.[62] The involvement of the Commission and the European Parliament is limited and the Court of Justice has no jurisdiction.[63] In the majority of cases, the Council will have to decide on measures by unanimity voting, although qualified majority can be sufficient in very rare cases.[64] Within other EU policies, the Commission is usually much stronger involved and decisions are predominantly adopted by qualified majority. With regard to institutional involvement and

---

[61] Wouters et al. 2008, 155.

[62] See the contributions in this volume by Sari and Puetter.

[63] Treaty on European Union, Article 24 (1).

[64] Treaty on European Union, Article 31.

procedures it therefore still matters significantly whether action is taken under the auspices of the CFSP or another EU policy field.

The delimitation of competences between the CFSP on the one hand and other EU policy sectors has not been made easier by the Treaty of Lisbon and hence cannot be counterbalanced by the double-hatting of the High Representative. Part of the problem of the delimitation of competences is the open language used by the Treaties and the lack of Court jurisdiction in respect of the CFSP that make it difficult to define its scope. Article 24 (1) TEU provides for a broad role for the CFSP by stating that

> [t]he Union's competence in matters of CFSP shall cover all areas of foreign policy and all questions relating to the Union's security, including the progressive framing of a common defence policy that might lead to a common defence.

It has been suggested that since the beginning of European cooperation in foreign policy, the lack of clear guidelines for the delimitation between areas of intergovernmental cooperation and supranational Union matters represent a compromise in favour of member states' worries how the Union should be structured.[65]

Although the TFEU introduced a separate part on 'The Union's External Action', including amongst others a title on the common commercial policy and a title on cooperation with third countries, the demarcation of these policy areas from the CFSP is not clearer than before. Any form of external action can still be brought within the terms of 'foreign and security policy' creating the problem of overlapping competences.[66]

Examples of Union policies that have not been formally characterised by the Treaty of Lisbon as forming part of the Union's external action but that nonetheless can have foreign policy implications include[67]:

- title XII of the TFEU, focusing on education, vocational training, youth and sport, stating that the 'The Union and the Member States shall foster cooperation with third countries and the competent international organizations in the field of education and sport, in particular the Council of Europe'[68];
- title XIX TFEU on research and technological development and space[69];

---

[65] Baratta 2002, 64; Dashwood on the other hand argues that in principle a clear demarcation would have been intended by the treaties. Dashwood 2008, 83.

[66] The ECJ faced the difficult task of drawing the line between the CFSP and development cooperation in Case C-91/05 *Commission v. Council*, [2008] ECR I-3651. For a detailed discussion of the judgment see Van Vooren 2009a, b, 7–24 and 231–248 as well as Kronenberger 2008, 199–211.

[67] See also Wessel 2000, 1152.

[68] Treaty on the European Union, Article 165 (3).

[69] See in particular Treaty on the European Union, Article 186.

- title XX TFEU on the environment, providing that the EU shall contribute to 'promoting measures at international level to deal with regional or worldwide environmental problems, and in particular combating climate change'[70];
- title XVI TFEU on trans-European networks in the areas of transport, telecommunications and energy infrastructures, stating that '[t]he Union may decide to cooperate with third countries to promote projects of mutual interest and to ensure the interoperability of networks'[71];
- title XIII TFEU on culture[72];
- title XIV TFEU on public health[73];

Not only do the above-mentioned Treaty articles ask for a delimitation of competences between the former first and the second pillar, but also some doubtful external practices of the Union itself, using instruments of the CFSP when instruments of other policy sectors could have been used instead.[74] It has been argued that some of the EU's civilian crisis management missions, for example its rule of law mission EUJUST THEMIS in Georgia[75] could have been undertaken outside the framework of the CSDP.[76] The promotion of the rule of law and democracy is an objective that is pursued not only within the CSDP but also within other external Union policies, including the Union's economic, financial and technical cooperation with third countries.[77] It has been suggested that when a rule of law missions is predominantly concerned with the reformation of the public sector by offering political and legal advice in the aftermath of a crisis, it could be adopted outside the CSDP.[78] If expert advice is however provided during an acute crisis to consolidate the judiciary or the criminal justice system it should be based on the CSDP.[79] The decision to undertake a rule of law mission in Georgia was adopted several months after the peak of the revolution in the country. As Georgia had already received technical assistance under a Community programme,[80]

---

70 Treaty on the European Union, Article 191 (1).

71 Treaty on the European Union, Article 171 (3).

72 See in particular Treaty on the European Union, Article 167 (3) LTFEU.

73 See in particular Treaty on the European Union, Article 168 (3) LTFEU.

74 Wessel 2000, 1154.

75 Council Joint Action 2004/523/CFSP of 28 June 2004 on EU rule of law mission in Georgia, *EUJUST THEMIS*.

76 Wessel 2000, 1154; Hoffmeister 2008, 164–167.

77 Treaty on the European Union, Article 212 (1), 205 in conjunction with Treaty on the Functioning of the European Union, Article 21 (2) b.

78 Hoffmeister 2008, 165.

79 Hoffmeister 2008, 165.

80 Council Regulation (EC, EURATOM) No 99/2000 of 29 December 1999 concerning the provision of assistance to the partner States in Easterb Europe and Central Asia. The Tacis programme was aimed amongst other things to consolidate democracy and the rule of law and ran between 2000 and 2006.

the reinforcement of the rule of law could have been pursued outside a CSDP mission instead.[81]

Although the High Representative from now on links the Council with the Commission, she cannot compensate for the unclear division between different Union competences under which crisis management activities can take place. Power struggles between the Union institutions might influence under which competence the same objective is going to be pursued. When it is unclear under which provisions crisis management action should take place, the EU's response to a crisis is more likely to be delayed, incoherent and ineffective.

8.6 Coherence Between the CFSP and the CSDP: Who Represents the Union on the International Stage?

Problems of coherence not only arise in respect of the CFSP and other EU policies that can have foreign policy implications but they also arise between the common CFSP on the one hand and the CSDP on the other, under which civilian and military crisis management missions take place.

The CSDP forms an integral part of the EU's CSFP.[82] Therefore horizontal coherence again does not appear to be the main problem. Nevertheless, the institutional setting and procedures slightly differ from each other which raises concerns from an institutional perspective.[83] Under the CSDP, the High Representative enjoys a greater role. Decisions relating to the CSDP initiating a crisis management mission shall be adopted by the Council on either its proposal or on the initiative from a Member State.[84] Council decisions that only form part of the CFSP however do not have to be proposed by the High Representative. From a procedural point of view, decisions relating to the CSDP need to be adopted by unanimity.[85] Decisions relating to the CFSP on the other hand in general ask for unanimity but may be adopted by qualified majority.[86] A qualified majority for example can be sufficient when the Council is adopting a 'decision implementing a decision defining a Union action or position' that has been previously adopted by a unanimous vote or when the Council is "adopting a decision defining a Union action or position, on a proposal which the High Representative of the Union for Foreign Affairs and Security Policy has presented following a specific request

[81] Hoffmeister 2008, 165 and 166.

[82] Treaty on the European Union, Article 42 (1).

[83] Wessel 2007, 225–226.

[84] Treaty on European Union, Article 42 (4).

[85] Treaty on European Union, Article 42 (4).

[86] Treaty on European Union, Article 31.

from the European Council, made on its own initiative or that of the High Representative. Nevertheless, Member States can oppose the adoption of a decision by qualified majority out of vital and stated domestic reasons.[87] Thus, it can make a difference whether a Council decision falls within the ambit of the CSDP or not. As both CFSP and CSDP share an element of policy relating to 'security', it can be difficult to determine under which policy a measure should be adopted.

The achievement of greater institutional coherence additionally will not be facilitated by the new position of the President of the European Council. According to Article 15 (6) TEU:

> The President of the European Council shall, at his level and in that capacity, ensure the external representation of the Union on issues concerning its CFSP, without prejudice to the powers of the High Representative of the Union for Foreign Affairs and Security Policy.

However, the High Representative, too 'shall represent the Union for matters relating to the CFSP. He shall conduct political dialogue with third parties on the Union's behalf and shall express the Union's position in international organisations and at international conferences'.[88]

The TEU does not offer much guidance on the question of how the President of the European Council and the High Representative for Foreign Affairs and Security Policy should divide the task of representing the Union between each other in respect of the CFSP. The wording of Article 15 (6) TEU seems to suggest that the High Representative has the power of first choice and can choose when to represent the EU in the international arena. The President might have to take care of the remaining tasks. The Commission will continue to represent the EU in other aspects of its external relations which will add to the confusion behind the delimitation of functions between the High Representative, the President and the Commission.[89] At the moment it seems most likely that the first office holders will shape their respective portfolios through practice. Their actions in the Libyan crisis have the potential of setting the guidelines for future tasks and represents the first real 'test' of the High Representative and the President.

8.7 Conclusion

The ongoing crisis in Libya of 2011 demonstrates the High Representative's strong impact on all aspects related to European crisis management missions. The complex decision-making process behind the launch of a European crisis

---

87 Treaty on European Union, Article 31 (2).

88 Treaty on European Union, Article 27 (2).

89 Van Elsuwege 2010, 992; Juncos and Whitman 2009, 33.

management operation starts with the monitoring of the situation and is usually accompanied by a fact finding missions. Catherine Ashton organised an extraordinary, informal Foreign Affairs Council meeting at the beginning of March 2011 in order to assess the ongoing developments in Libya[90] and sent a technical fact-finding mission to the country in order to examine humanitarian needs.[91] In the aftermath of the adoption of UN Security Council resolution 1973, Ashton reminded Colonel Khadafi of his choice to follow the respective UN resolution but also indicated future actions in case he did not correspond to the demands of the Libyan people and international actors such as the EU.[92] At the meeting of the Foreign Affairs Council on 21 March 2011, and after having spoken with the NATO Secretary General in order to ensure that a European crisis management contribution would be complementary to NATO action, she indicated the ongoing planning of a European humanitarian mission and the evaluation of the existing economic sanction programme.[93] On 1 April, the Council finally decided on a European military operation in support of humanitarian assistance operations in response to the crisis in Libya.[94] In contrast, Hermann Van Rompuy as the President of the European Council appears to concentrate more on the human rights dimension of the crisis by creating awareness for the developing humanitarian problems in Libya and its borders but also by raising awareness for the need of some member states for assistance with the resulting flows of migrants.[95] Nevertheless, the importance of his role in the overall context of crisis management has been highlighted by the fact that the UN Security Council resolution

[90] European Union (2011) High Representative Catherine Ashton convenes an extraordinary Foreign Affairs Council, Press Release A 083/11, 3 March 2011, Brussels, www.consilium.europa.eu/uedocs/cms_data/docs/pressdata/EN/foraff/119567.pdf. Last accessed?

[91] European Union (2011) EU High Representative Catherine Ashton sends fact-finding team to Libya ahead of European Council, Press Release A 092/11, 6 March 2011, Brussels, www.consilium.europa.eu/uedocs/cms_data/docs/pressdata/EN/foraff/119614.pdf. Last accessed 3 June 2011.

[92] European Union (2011) Statement by the High Representative Catherine Ashton, on Libya, Press Release A 116/11, 19 March 2011, Brussels, www.consilium.europa.eu/uedocs/cms_data/docs/pressdata/EN/foraff/120045.pdf. Last accessed 3 June 2011.

[93] European Union (2011) Remarks by High Representative Catherine Ashton ahead of the Foreign Affairs Council, 21/03/11, Press Release A 116/11, 21 March 2011, Brussels, www.consilium.europa.eu/uedocs/cms_data/docs/pressdata/EN/foraff/120061.pdf. Last accessed 3 June 2011.

[94] Council of the European Union (2011) Council decides on EU military operation in support of humanitarian assistance operations in Libya, Press Release, 8589/11 PRESSE 91, 1 April 2011, Brussels, www.consilium.europa.eu/uedocs/cms_Data/docs/pressdata/EN/foraff/121237.pdf. Last accessed 3 June 2011.

[95] European Council (2011) The President, Remarks by President Herman Van Rompuy at the press conference following the extraordinary European Council on EU Southern Neighbourhood and Libya, Press Release PCE 065/11, 11 March 2011, Brussels, www.consilium.europa.eu/uedocs/cms_data/docs/pressdata/en/ec/119779.pdf. Last accessed 3 June 2011.

1973 on Libya,[96] authorising the use of force, has been welcomed by him and Catherine Ashton in a joint statement.[97]

Overall, the Libyan crisis indicates that European crisis management has the potential of turning into a testing ground for the principle of coherence. From the start of the deterioration of the situation in Libya, the EU has responded with the adoption of additional economic sanctions and subsequently decided to launch a military operation if the UN Office for the Coordination of Humanitarian Affairs would request it.[98] The European efforts in the Libyan crisis appeared to be successful in the early stages of the conflict. The overall success of the EU's contribution to the settlement of the Libya crisis will depend to a large extent on how the different elements of its comprehensive concept of crisis management that are still scattered over different policy sectors are going to be coordinated with each other. Although the High Representative from now on links the Council with the Commission which is likely to improve the flow of information between both actors, she cannot counterbalance the unclear delimitation of Union competences. The improvement of institutional coherence therefore will depend on the will of the institutions involved in crisis management to cooperate with each other in order to achieve timely decisions and to avoid the duplication of resources. The different crisis management actors need to be encouraged to develop clear guidelines on what legal basis crisis management measures should be adopted if several Union competences seem suitable.

References

Anthony I (2002) Sanctions applied by the European Union and the United Nations, SIPRI (Stockholm International Peace Research Institute) Yearbook 2002: Armament, Disarmaments and International Security. Oxford University Press, Oxford, pp 203–228

Baratta R (2002) Overlaps between European Community Competence and European Union Foreign Policy Activity. In: Cannizzaro E (ed) The European Union as an actor in international relations. Kluwer Law International, The Hague, pp 52–75

Blockmans S (2008) An introduction to the role of the EU in crisis management. In: Blockmans S (ed) The European Union and crisis management: policy and legal aspects. T.M.C. Asser Press, The Hague, pp 1–13

Blockmans S, Wessel RA (2009) The European Union and crisis management: will the Lisbon Treaty make the EU more effective? Journal of Conflict and Security Law 14:265–308

[96] UN Security Council Resolution 1973 (2011), 17 March 2011.

[97] Joint statement by President of the European Council Herman Van Rompuy, and EU High Representative Catherine Ashton (March 2011) on UN Security Council resolution on Libya, Press Release PCE 02/11, A 110/1, 17 March 2011, Brussels, www.consilium.europa.eu/uedocs/cms_Data/docs/pressdata/en/ec/120012.pdf. Last accessed 3 June 2011.

[98] Council Decision 2011/210/CFSP of 1 April 2011 on a European Union military operation in support of humanitarian assiatnace operations in response to the crisis situation in Libya (EUFOR Libya).

Cremona M (2008) Coherence through law: what difference will the Treaty of Lisbon make? 3 Hamburg Rev Soc Sci 3:11–36. www.hamburg-review.com/fileadmin/pdf/03_01/B_Cremona_03.pdf. Last accessed 3 June 2011

Dashwood A (2008) Article 47 TEU and the relationship between first and second pillar competences. In: Dashwood A, Maresceau M (eds) Law and Practice of EU external relations: salient features of a changing landscape. Cambridge University Press, Cambridge, pp 70–103

De Vasconcelos Á (ed) (2009) The European Security Strategy 2003–2008: building on common interests, 5 ISS Report, EU Institute for Security Studies, pp 1–79. www.iss.europa.eu/uploads/media/ISS_Report_05.pdf. Accessed 3 June 2011

Hillion C (2008) Tous pour un, un pour tous! Coherence in the external relations of the European Union. In: Cremona M (ed) Developments in EU external relations law. Oxford University Press, Oxford, pp 10–36

Hillion C (2010) Mixity and coherence in EU external relations: the significance of the duty of cooperation. In: Hillion C, Koutrakos P (eds) Mixed agreements revisited: the EU and its member states in the world. Hart publishing, Oxford, pp 87–115

Hoffmeister F (2008) Inter-pillar coherence in the European Union's civilian crisis management. In: Blockmans S (ed) The European Union and crisis management: policy and legal aspects. T.M.C. Asser Press, The Hague, pp 157–180

Juncos A, Whitman R (2009) The Lisbon Treaty and the foreign, security and defence policy: reforms, implementation and the consequence of (non-) ratification. European Foreign Affairs Review 14:25–46

Koutrakos P (2007) Security and Defence Policy within the context of EU external relations: issues of coherence, consistency, and effectiveness. In: Trybus M, White N (eds) European security law. Oxford University Press, Oxford, pp 249–269

Kronenberger V (2008) Coherence and consistency of the EU's action in international crisis management: the role of the European Court of Justice. In: Blockmans S (ed) The European Union and crisis management: policy and legal aspects. T.M.C. Asser Press, The Hague, pp 199–211

Missiroli A (2010) The new EU "foreign policy" system after Lisbon: A work in progress. European Foreign Affairs Review 15:427–452

Neuwahl N (1994) Foreign and Security Policy and the implementation of the requirement of "consistency" under the Treaty on European Union. In: O'Keeffe D, Towney PM (eds) Legal issues of the Maastricht Treaty. Chancery Law Publishing, London, pp 227–246

Nuttall S (2005) Coherence and consistency. In: Hill C, Smith M (eds) International relations and the European Union. Oxford University Press, Oxford, pp 91–111

Simón L (2010) Command and control? Planning for EU military operations. 81 Occasional Paper, European Union Institute for Security Studies, pp 1–48. www.iss.europa.eu/uploads/media/Planning_for_EU_military_operations.pdf. Last accessed 3 June 2011

Van Elsuwege P (2010) EU external action after the collapse of the pillar structure: in search of a new balance between delimitation and consistency. Common Market Law Review 47:987–1019

Vanhoonacker V (2008) The European Security and Defence Policy and Coherence Challenges in the Council. In: Blockmans S (ed) The European Union and crisis management: policy and legal aspects. T.M.C. Asser Press, The Hague, pp 145–156

Van Vooren B (2009a) EU-EC external competences after the small arms judgment. European Foreign Affairs Review 14:7–24

Van Vooren B (2009b) The small arms judgment in an age of constitutional turmoil. European Foreign Affairs Review 14:231–248

Wessel RA (2000) The inside looking out: consistency and delimitation in EU external relations. Common Market Law Review 37:1135–1171

Wessel RA (2007) Differentiation in EU Foreign, Security, and Defence Policy: between coherence and flexibility. In: Trybus M, White ND (eds) European security law. Oxford University Press, Oxford, pp 225–248

Wouters J et al (2008) The European Union's external relations after the Lisbon Treaty. In: Griller S, Ziller J (eds) The Lisbon Treaty: EU constitutionalism without a constitutional Treaty? European Community Studies Association of Austria (ECSA Austria) Publication Series 11. Springer, Wien, pp 144–203

Chapter 9
Don't Mess with the Missionary Man! On the Principle of Coherence, the Missionary Principle and the European Union's Development Policy

Morten P. Broberg

Abstract With the entry into force of the Lisbon Treaty, the focus upon coherence between the different Union policies has increased considerably, as reflected in a number of provisions in the Treaty on European Union and the Treaty on the Functioning of the European Union. The Lisbon Treaty has also introduced, as a general obligation, that the European Union shall further so-called European values beyond its borders. An important consequence of these two changes is that, read in conjunction, they will obligate the European Union to further European values through its development cooperation policy to a higher degree than it does today. This chapter first outlines the changes brought about by the Lisbon Treaty with regard to the coherence obligation and the obligation to further European values (sometimes referred to as the Principle of Coherence and the Missionary Principle). Thereupon the chapter identifies the likely effects which the combination of these two principles will have on the European Union's development cooperation policy. Finally, the chapter takes a broader perspective to the matter in order to point to some problems that are likely to arise from these presumed effects.

Professor Morten P. Broberg—Faculty of Law, University of Copenhagen, Copenhagen, Denmark. This chapter was first presented as a paper at the conference *EU External Relations Law and Policy in the post-Lisbon Era* held at the University of Sheffield in January 2011. The author gratefully acknowledges the extensive suggestions for changes he received from Paul James Cardwell as well as the comments he received from Simon Bulmer, who acted as discussant, and the other participants at the conference.

M. P. Broberg (✉)
Faculty of Law, University of Copenhagen, Copenhagen, Denmark
e-mail: morten.broberg@jur.ku.dk

P. J. Cardwell (ed.), *EU External Relations Law and Policy in the Post-Lisbon Era*,
DOI: 10.1007/978-90-6704-823-1_9, © T.M.C. Asser press, The Hague,
The Netherlands, and the authors 2012

Contents

9.1 Introduction

With the entry into force of the Lisbon Treaty on 1 December 2009 a number of both major and minor changes to the European Union's Treaty foundation were introduced. As is well known, some of these changes were intended to significantly strengthen the European Union's manoeuvrability on the international stage, *inter alia* through the creation of the combined post of 'High Representative of the Union for Foreign Affairs and Security Policy' and Vice-President of the European Commission. It is less well known that with the Lisbon Treaty it has also been explicitly laid down that the European Union is obligated to further its values beyond its borders (the missionary principle) and that it has been made a generally applicable requirement that the Union must assure coherence between its different policies—external as well as internal (the principle of coherence).

This chapter sets out to identify the likely effects which the combination of the two aforementioned principles will have on the European Union's development cooperation policy. I first outline the changes brought about by the Lisbon Treaty with regard to the principle of coherence and the missionary principle (Sect. 9.2). Thereupon, I identify the likely effects which the combination of these two principles will have on the European Union's development cooperation policy (Sect. 9.3). Finally, I take a broader perspective to the matter in order to point to possible causes why the European Union is promoting its values in the wider world and to consider the criticism that has been levelled against the Union for doing so (Sect. 9.4).

9.2 The Missionary Principle and the Principle of Coherence Following the Lisbon Treaty

9.2.1 The Missionary Principle

In particular over the last two decades, as part of its external relations policies, the European Union has actively tried to promote what are sometimes referred to as

'European values'. With the entry into force of the Lisbon Treaty this has become an explicit obligation weighing on the Union in its external actions. Hence, Article 3(5) of the Treaty on European Union now provides that:

> In its relations with the wider world, the Union shall *uphold and promote* its values and interests and contribute to the protection of its citizens. It shall contribute to peace, security, the sustainable development of the Earth, solidarity and mutual respect among peoples, free and fair trade, eradication of poverty and the protection of human rights, in particular the rights of the child, as well as to the strict observance and the development of international law, including respect for the principles of the United Nations Charter.[1]

This missionary principle is also reflected in Article 21(1) of the Treaty on European Union[2] which provides that:

> The Union's action on the international scene shall be guided by the principles which have inspired its own creation, development and enlargement, *and which it seeks to advance in the wider world*: democracy, the rule of law, the universality and indivisibility of human rights and fundamental freedoms, respect for human dignity, the principles of equality and solidarity, and respect for the principles of the United Nations Charter and international law.[3]

Moreover, in Article 21(2)(a–c) of the Treaty on European Union it is laid down that:

> The Union shall define and pursue common policies and actions, and shall work for a high degree of cooperation in all fields of international relations, in order to:
> (a) safeguard its values, fundamental interests, security, independence and integrity;
> (b) consolidate and support democracy, the rule of law, human rights and the principles of international law;
> (c) preserve peace, prevent conflicts and strengthen international security, in accordance with the purposes and principles of the United Nations Charter, with the principles of the Helsinki Final Act and with the aims of the Charter of Paris, including those relating to external borders; ....

The duty to further 'European values' in the wider world, as set out above, applies with respect to all third countries, not merely with regard to the developing ones. With particular regard to the latter, Article 208(1) of the Treaty on the Functioning of the European Union merely provides that:

> Union policy in the field of development cooperation shall be conducted within the framework of the principles and objectives of the Union's external action. ...[4]

---

[1] Emphasis added.

[2] See also Treaty on the Functioning of the European Union, Article 205 which provides that '[t]he Union's action on the international scene, pursuant to this Part, shall be guided by the principles, pursue the objectives and be conducted in accordance with the general provisions laid down in [Articles 21 and 22] of the Treaty on European Union.'

[3] Emphasis added.

[4] The provision's phrase' the framework of the principles and objectives of the Union's external action' presumably is a reference to Treaty on the Functioning of the European Union, Article 205 which in turn refers to Treaty on European Union, Articles 21 and 22 TEU, cf. note 2 above.

This, somewhat bland, formulation does not fully reflect that in practice the role played by European values is particularly important in the Union's development policy (as well as in the neighbourhood policy).[5] On occasion, as Khaliq has noted, the standards required from third countries in terms of the respect for the 'rule of law' and 'good governance' have been relatively high.[6]

9.2.2 'European Values'

The early articles of the revised Treaty on European Union contain several references to values (generally) and the European Union's values, though without full definition or comprehensive identification. Article 3 of the Treaty on European Union provides that the Union's aim 'is to promote peace, its values and the well-being of its peoples'. Thus, even before considering the external dimension, the Treaty can be read in terms of its being a value-laden approach to European integration.

The obligation that, in its relations with the wider world, the Union must promote 'its values' necessarily evokes the question: what are those values that must be furthered? Article 3(5) not only lays down the missionary principle, but also sets out the objectives that shall guide the Union's behaviour on the international stage.[7] These objectives are (or at least should be) a reflection of the Union's values—but are not values as such. In contrast, Article 21(1) of the Treaty on European Union provides the following (non-exhaustive) list of values:

> The Union's action on the international scene shall be guided by the principles which have inspired its own creation, development and enlargement, and which it seeks to advance in the wider world: *democracy*, the *rule of law*, the *universality and indivisibility of human rights and fundamental freedoms*, *respect for human dignity*, the *principles of equality and solidarity*, and *respect for the principles of the United Nations Charter and international law*.[8]

Further specification of several of the Union's values may be found in its Charter of Fundamental Rights,[9] in the case-law of the Court of Justice and in secondary legislation such as the European Consensus on Development.[10]

---

[5] The emphasis on the promotion of values within the context of the European Neighbourhood Policy is discussed in further detail by Ghazaryan (this volume).

[6] Khaliq 2008, 156.

[7] The relevant part of Article 3(5) TEU provides that the Union shall contribute to: 'peace, security, the sustainable development of the Earth, solidarity and mutual respect among peoples, free and fair trade, eradication of poverty and the protection of human rights, in particular the rights of the child, as well as to the strict observance and the development of international law, including respect for the principles of the United Nations Charter.'.

[8] Emphasis added.

[9] Charter of Fundamental Rights of the European Union (2000) OJ C364/1.

[10] Joint statement by the Council and the representatives of the governments of the Member States meeting within the Council, the European Parliament and the Commission on European Union Development Policy: 'The European Consensus' (2006) OJ C46/1.

This joint statement by the European Parliament, Council and Commission in 2005 included a set of so-called 'common values' to be promoted with third countries; human rights, good governance, gender equality, the rule of law, solidarity and justice.

Whereas, therefore, it is possible to encircle the European Union's values, it seems rather difficult to establish an unequivocal, detailed list thereof: democracy, rule of law and human rights arguably constitute the 'core' of those values which the European Union must promote in the wider world, but other values must also be taken into account. This is for example the case with regard to 'free and fair trade' which is mentioned in Article 3(5) TEU, but given the objectives which are defined for the EU's external action in Article 21 TEU, the protection of the environment (including fighting climate change) and eradication of poverty are two additional examples.

9.2.3 *Promoting European Values*

From the early 1990s the European Union has included what is normally referred to as human rights clauses in virtually all trade and cooperation agreements between the Union and a third-country.[11] These clauses require the European Union on the one hand and the other contracting party or parties on the other hand to pay due respect to human rights and democracy based on the rule of law.

Today these human rights clauses are as a rule made 'an essential element' of the agreement which means that where one of the parties fails to respect the clause, the other party may terminate or suspend the operation of the agreement in whole or in part.[12] It is difficult to estimate what impact the inclusion of human rights clauses has made, but it is clear that in particular towards a number of developing countries the European Union has actively used the possibility of sanctioning serious infringements by, for example, cutting down on its development assistance to the developing country in question.[13] On the other hand, full suspension of the agreements due to breaches of the human rights clause is a rare occurrence, though the clauses today make clear that full suspension is a measure of last resort.

---

[11] See in particular Communication from the Commission on the inclusion of respect for democratic principles and human rights in agreements between the Community and third countries, COM(95)216 final and the Council Conclusions of 29 May 1995 (reported in EU Bulletin No 5 1995 at point 1.2.3).

[12] This follows from Article 60 of the Vienna Convention on the Law of Treaties, Done at Vienna on 23 May 1969. Entered into force on 27 January 1980. United Nations, *Treaty Series*, vol. 1155, p. 331.

[13] See for instance Council decision of 27 September 2010 concerning the conclusion of consultations with the Republic of Niger under Article 96 of the ACP-EU Partnership Agreement (2010) OJ L260/6.

Furthermore, the relationship with third countries has, in most cases, reflected a multi-faceted approach and has not been limited to, for example, trade-related issues. For instance, the Commission's most recent Annual Report on the Union's development and external assistance policies point to the importance of tying human rights/democracy considerations to other areas for discussion:

> The Commission strives to mainstream human rights into its political dialogue with third countries. They are raised, as appropriate, at all levels of political dialogue with partner countries,…. Discussing these issues is not only a way for the EU to state its own position and enquire about that of its partners, but also to pave the way for cooperation activities. Human rights and democracy issues are not necessarily firmly anchored in partner country government priorities. This has an important implication for Commission support strategies: the pursuance of these objectives through political dialogue should be an attempt to contribute positively and achieve pro-poor policy agenda in partner countries, presupposing a proactive/advocacy approach. By promoting these values universally, the Union has set itself the challenge to achieve legitimacy for these fundamental values and to promote substantial change in the direction of the values.[14]

Trade preferences, i.e., the provision of favourable customs duties which are only awarded to some selected countries, is another way whereby the European Union seeks to further its values. On the face of it this would seem to conflict with the WTO's requirement that where a member of the WTO offers a third-country preferential treatment, this treatment must be extended to all WTO members; the so-called Most-Favoured Nation (MFN) principle. It is, however, possible to divert from this principle where the preferential treatment is offered only to developing countries and where the criteria which the developing countries must meet do not discriminate between the different developing countries.

The European Union has therefore established a preferential customs system[15] which includes what is referred to as a 'special incentive arrangement'; or the GSP+ as it is normally called. Under this arrangement, a group of 'vulnerable' developing countries are offered attractive customs duties on condition that they ratify and effectively implement 27 specified international conventions and that they accept regular monitoring and review of their implementation record with regard to these conventions. These 27 conventions include Convention on the Elimination of All Forms of Discrimination Against Women (CEDAW), Convention on the Rights of the Child, the Montreal Protocol on Substances that Deplete the Ozone Layer, and Convention on International Trade in Endangered Species of Wild Fauna and Flora (CITES). If a developing country benefitting from the GSP+ scheme fails to comply with one or more of these conventions the European Union may fully or partly

---

[14] European Commission (2010), Annual Report on the European Union's Development and External Assistance Policies in 2009, 141. ec.europa.eu/europeaid/multimedia/publications/documents/annual-reports/europeaid_annual_report_2010_en.pdf. Accessed 25 July 2011.

[15] Regulation 732/2008 applying a scheme of generalised tariff preferences, OJ (2008) L211/1.

withdraw the beneficial treatment.[16] Put differently, the GSP+ arrangement means that those developing countries which implement the European Union's values are rewarded with reduced customs duties when exporting to the Union.

A further means whereby the Union seeks to further its values is a European Parliament and Council Regulation providing the European Union with financing for the promotion of democracy and human rights worldwide, as the measure's title explains.[17] More than €1 billion has been allocated towards the financing activities under the instrument.[18] In practice, the financing instrument is closely related to the Union's development assistance, although it may equally be used for financial and technical cooperation with other (i.e., non-developing) third countries. A remarkable aspect of the instrument is that it may also be used for the financing of non-State actors. For instance, the European Union may use it to support Non-Governmental Organisations (NGOs) whose aim it is to watch over human rights breaches in a dictatorship.[19]

Lastly, the fundamental principles of the European Union together with the objectives that are laid down in the Treaties regarding the Union's action on the international scene form the framework for the Union's external policies. As will be shown in the following section, this framework applies to external policies falling under the Common Foreign and Security Policy (CFSP) as well as to such policies falling outside the CFSP. The Union's external action policies must therefore comply with these principles and pursue those objectives.

9.2.4 Coherence

Somewhat surprisingly perhaps, legislators are, as a general rule, not obliged to create a coherent body of legislation. Intentionally or unintentionally they may adopt pieces of legislation that are mutually incoherent—or even incompatible. In this regard the European Union appears to be the exception to prove the rule since some Treaty provisions require the Union's legislation to comply with a formal

---

16 Cf. Regulation 732/2008 applying a scheme of generalised tariff preferences, Article 15(2). For an example, see Implementing Regulation 143/2010 of the Council of 15 February 2010 temporarily withdrawing the special incentive arrangement for sustainable development and good governance provided for under Regulation 732/2008 with respect to the Democratic Socialist Republic of Sri Lanka (2010) OJ L45/1.

17 Regulation 1889/2006 on establishing a financing instrument for the promotion of democracy and human rights worldwide, OJ (2006) L386/1. Sometimes merely called the 'Financing Instrument'.

18 See further, Commission (2011) A financing instrument for the promotion of democracy and human rights in the world (2007–2013). europa.eu/legislation_summaries/external_relations/relations_with_third_countries/latin_america/l14172_en.htm. Accessed 25 July 2011.

19 Cardwell 2011, 33.

coherence requirement.[20] On the other hand, the actual impact of these provisions appears questionable—at least with regard to new legislation that affects developing countries.

Before the entry into force of the Lisbon Treaty, Article 178 of the EC Treaty provided that:

> The Community shall take account of the objectives referred to in [the Article laying down the EU's policy in the sphere of development cooperation] in the policies that it implements which are likely to affect developing countries.

In practice this provision appears not to have played any material role.[21] Equally, before the Lisbon Treaty Article 3 of the (then) EU Treaty provided:

> The Union shall be served by a single institutional framework which shall ensure the consistency and the continuity of the activities carried out in order to attain its objectives while respecting and building upon the *acquis communautaire*.
> The Union shall in particular ensure the consistency of its external activities as a whole in the context of its external relations, security, economic and development policies. The Council and the Commission shall be responsible for ensuring such consistency and shall cooperate to this end. They shall ensure the implementation of these policies, each in accordance with its respective powers.[22]

As concerns the European Union's policies towards the developing countries, the role played by Article 3(2) of the EU Treaty (prior to Lisbon) requiring there to be 'consistency' between the development policy and the CFSP policies (external relations and security) is not clear. On the face of it, it required there to be 'consistency' between the external activities under the first and second pillars, but it appears that in reality such 'consistency' has only been introduced on an *ad hoc* basis.

Arguably, the primary obstacle to ensuring cross-pillar consistency was the Union's inconsistent organisational structure. So, it is for good reasons that the drafters of the Lisbon Treaty first of all have set out to ensure a higher degree of coherence in the European Union's external policies through a new organisational structure.

However, if we exclude the institutional changes and instead focus exclusively on the formal requirements on attaining consistency and coherence, it appears that the Lisbon Treaty has merely carried over the two pre-existing provisions cited above into the new treaties. Thus, Article 208(1) of the Treaty on the Functioning of the European Union provides as follows:

---

[20] For a careful examination of the notion of coherence, see Hillion 2008, 10. It may be noted that the present chapter is only concerned with Union legislation as such, i.e. horizontal coherence. It therefore does not cover coherence requirements regarding the relationship between Union legislation and Member State legislation, i.e. vertical coherence, which is achieved *inter alia* through the fulfilment of the principle of sincere cooperation (Treaty on European Union, Articles 4(3) and 24(3)).

[21] Broberg 2010, 7.

[22] See also Treaty on European Union (pre-Lisbon version), Article 27 (a)(1).

> … The Union shall take account of the objectives of development cooperation in the policies that it implements which are likely to affect developing countries.

And Article 21(3)(2) of the Treaty on European Union provides:

> The Union shall ensure consistency between the different areas of its external action and between these and its other policies. The Council and the Commission, assisted by the High Representative of the Union for Foreign Affairs and Security Policy, shall ensure that consistency and shall cooperate to that effect.

In one respect the Lisbon Treaty has, however, brought about a change which may prove to be important. Hence, Article 7 of the Treaty on the Functioning of the European Union lays down that:

> The Union shall ensure consistency between its policies and activities, taking all of its objectives into account and in accordance with the principle of conferral of powers.

Whereas this provision is not concerned with consistency regarding the Union's external activities as it does not cover the CFSP,[23] it must be recalled that Part V of the Treaty on the Functioning of the European Union covers the 'External Action of the Union' which, amongst others, includes the common commercial policy, economic, financial and technical cooperation with third countries, and humanitarian aid. It therefore clearly enforces the obligation of consistency weighing on the European Union. What impact this new provision as well as the others set out above, may have on Union legislation affecting developing countries is discussed in Sect. 9.3.

9.2.5 Anything New Under the Sun?

With the entry into force of the Lisbon Treaty, the missionary principle was unequivocally introduced into Union law. At first glance, the introduction of a new principle may appear to constitute an important change. However, as has been shown above, for years the European Union has already been very active in promoting its values in the wider world. It nevertheless remains that with the entry into force of the Lisbon Treaty, the Union has come under a much clearer legal obligation to actively further its own values in all international relations than was the case prior to 1 December 2009. When it comes to the coherence principle, the main change introduced by the Lisbon Treaty appears to be the new provision in Article 7 of the Treaty on the Functioning of the European Union laying down a generally applicable obligation to ensure consistency between the various Union policies.

Viewed independently, the changes regarding the missionary principle and the principle of coherence do not seem to be so very far-reaching. If, however, the two

[23] Provisions on the CFSP are covered in a set of 'specific provisions'—Treaty on European Union, Articles 23–46.

are viewed together the introduction of the missionary principle together with the strengthening of the coherence principle (in both the Treaty on European Union and the Treaty on the Functioning of the European Union) arguably means that in its development policy the European Union has been placed under an unambiguous legal duty to further European values such as human rights, democracy and the rule of law. In other words, this author argues that the Lisbon Treaty has led to an appreciable strengthening of the obligation weighing on the European Union to promote its own values *vis-à-vis* (amongst others) the developing countries.

9.3 The Effects on EU Development Policy

Over the last two decades the European Union has undergone a procedure where increasingly it has strived to promote its values—first of all in the developing world. The centrality of development policy within the process of European integration has long since been stressed: pre-dating the formation of European Political Cooperation (EPC), which led to the CFSP. Indeed, the development of the African continent was described as one of Europe's 'essential tasks' in the Schuman Declaration. The introduction of the missionary principle in the Treaty on European Union and the strengthening of the coherence principle may therefore simply be viewed as a 'codification' and—possibly also as a climax—of this long process.

However, I believe that the changes are much more than a 'codification'. In my opinion they have consequences for the Union's development policy in at least the three following respects.

First, the very fact that the Treaties now explicitly oblige the European Union to promote its values in the wider world together with the strengthening of the coherence principle arguable entails that the Union is given less leeway when framing its external policies—including its development policy. It simply means that today the Union is under a formal obligation of framing these policies in such a way that they will further its values. This does not mean that the Union cannot abandon some of those measures that it applies today in order to further its values. For instance, it must be possible for the Union to give up its GSP+ scheme without being obliged to replace it by some other value promoting arrangement—provided that the Union's development policy viewed as a whole continues to actively further these values to an appreciable extent.

Second, prior to the entry into force of the Lisbon Treaty not all of the EC Treaty's legal bases for entering into international agreements with developing countries necessarily also allowed the European Union to actively further its own values by, for instance, introducing human rights clauses into these agreements.[24]

[24] See in this respect ECJ, Case C-268/94 *Portugal* v. *Council (India Agreement)* [1996] *ECR* I-6177.

In contrast, today the missionary principle and the coherence principle in combination means that the Union now is obliged to further the pursuit of democracy (etc) whenever it enters into international agreements.

In this respect it may be observed that the majority of all agreements between the European Union and developing countries which are in force today (i.e., 2011) have been entered into prior to the entry into force of the Lisbon Treaty. With regard to these pre-Lisbon agreements it is much less obvious that those which have been founded on legal bases that did not refer to the objectives of furthering democracy and the rule of law must—or may—pursue these objectives. In this regard it may be observed, on the one hand, that Articles 177 and 178 of the then applicable EC Treaty in combination obliged the European Union to take account of democracy and the rule of law in the policies that it implemented and which were likely to affect developing countries. On the other hand, not all international agreements with developing countries were based on the EC Treaty's development provision (*in casu* Article 181 of the EC Treaty).[25] Therefore, where prior to the entry into force of the Lisbon Treaty the European Union intended to include a human rights clause in an agreement with one or more developing countries, it ought to give due consideration to whether, in addition to the agreement's primary legal basis, also Article 181 of the EC Treaty should be included as the legal basis.[26]

Third, arguably the explicit introduction of the missionary principle and the strengthening of the coherence principle will increase awareness of the European values in the Union institutions and in the Member State administrations and thereby lead these values to a more prominent position on the agenda whenever new policies and new measures are negotiated. Of the three points listed above, the last one may well turn out to be the most important in practice. EU institutions consistently point to the position of the EU as a whole as the world's leading donor of development assistance. Therefore, any moves on this front are likely to have demonstrable practical effects—moving these considerations beyond the purely academic level.

---

25 For example, the European Union's arguably most important international agreement in the field of development cooperation, the Cotonou Agreement, is based exclusively on Article 310 of the EC Treaty, which concerned association agreements.

26 This seems to have been particularly relevant with regard to trade agreements founded on the EC Treaty's Article 133 on the European Community's Common Commercial Policy (now Treaty on the Functioning of the European Union, Article 207). See, for example, Proposal for a Council Decision concluding the Interim Economic Partnership Agreement between the European Community and its Member States, on the one part, and the [Southern African Development Community] SADC EPA States, on the other part, COM(2008)565 final. It may be noted, however, that international agreements exclusively based on Article 133 of the EC Treaty are rather unusual.

9.4 The Broader Perspective

The above examination gives rise to at least two fundamental questions. First, why has the European Union vested so much effort in the exporting of its own values to the wider world? Second, some apparently take the view that promotion of European values in reality is a manifestation of neo-colonialism; but is that really true?

9.4.1 Why Does the European Union Promote Its Own Values Abroad?

With regard to the first question, it is certainly true that, on the face of it, the promotion of human rights, democracy, free trade etc. in the wider world may seem to be a purely altruistic endeavour, producing tangible benefits only outside the Union. Nonetheless, whilst there is no reason to doubt that there is an idealistic side to the promotion of European values, there may also be some more tangible benefits for the Union weighing in favour of such promotion.

First, the most tangible benefit may well be in the economic field. Increased prosperity in developing countries in combination with improved market access for European exporters, through the promotion of free trade, presumably will benefit the European Union.[27] This has been particularly acute in the EU's relations with neighbouring countries: documentation on the European Neighbourhood Policy stresses the importance of the economic benefits for 'stability'.[28] However, it may be questioned as to whether the EU's support for the (former) governments in countries such as Tunisia and Egypt demonstrate a preference for stability ensured by regimes which would fall short on the democratic values the EU expounds.

Second, the increased reciprocity in a broad sense between the developing countries and the European Union may also make it easier to generate the necessary support within the Union to accord preferential treatment to these countries. From the European Union's early days preferential treatment (trade and aid) has been focussed on former European colonies; primarily in Africa, but also in the Caribbean and the Pacific (the so-called ACP countries). To a considerable extent the historical ties between these developing countries and certain Member States have been maintained through the various agreements which the European Union has entered into with the ACP countries. Arguably, the Union's increased

---

[27] This is also a consideration within the EU's drive for investment-related agreements with states—both developed and developing—the world over. For further discussion, see the contributions to this volume by Wu and Dimopoulos.

[28] Batt et al. 2003; Gould 2004. See also the discussion in Sect. 9.2 of the chapter in this volume by Dragneva and Wolczuk.

use of conditionality in its relations with these countries makes the preferential treatment more acceptable to Member States without strong ties to the ACP countries, to the European Parliament and other institutions, and to the public at large.

Third, if the promotion of European values proves to be effective, arguably the increased sharing of common values will tie the developing countries (primarily ACP countries) more closely to the West, rather than to 'competing powers' such as China.[29]

Finally, the promotion of European values forms an integral part of some of the European Union's strategies *vis-à-vis* the wider world. For instance, the European Union's Security Strategy lays down that part of the Union's strategic objectives shall be to promote the Union's values, *inter alia* based on the argument that '[t]he best protection for our security is a world of well-governed democratic States'.[30] Likewise, the European Union's promotion of its values in the economic sphere also corresponds well with its policy objectives regarding external trade.[31] There has been an increase in development aid to countries where security related concerns are at stake, in particular Iraq and Afghanistan.

To sum up, whilst it is true that those who presumptively will benefit the most from the European Union's endeavours to improve the human rights situation etc. in developing countries are the inhabitants of these countries, this does not mean that the Union does not also have a self interest in promoting its values in the wider world. By consolidating the missionary principle and coherence/consistency obligation within the Treaty, the EU institutions can sell its role as human rights and democracy promoter as part of its *raison d'être*. Of course, alongside other grand statements within the treaties, such as the provisions on the Union forging a strong common foreign and security policy, this potential argument may seem rather hollow if there is no discernable impact stemming from the missionary principle.

9.4.2 Is the Promotion of European Values Good or Bad?

It is difficult not to view the combined introduction of the missionary principle together with the re-enforcement of the principle of coherence as a reflection of the European Union intending to be a normative power on the international scene.

[29] Trueb (this volume) makes a similar point with regard to the EU's relationships with states in Latin America.

[30] Council (2003) 'A secure Europe in a better world—European security strategy', Brussels, 12 December 2003. www.consilium.europa.eu/uedocs/cmsUpload/78367.pdf. Accessed 25 July 2011.

[31] European Commission (2006), 'Global Europe: competing in the world'. http://trade.ec.europa.eu/doclib/docs/2006/october/tradoc_130376.pdf. Accessed 25 July 2011. For critical comments on this policy paper, see for example Resolution of 7–8 December 2006 adopted by the European Trade Union Confederation (ETUC) Executive Committee. www.etuc.org/a/3390. Accessed 25 July 2011.

As Bickerton has remarked, discussions about the EU as a normative power have moved beyond scholarly circles and into the policy-making realm of official rhetoric.[32] Some have however gone much further and have characterised the European Union's promotion of its values in the developing countries as a modern type of imperialism or empire.[33] The terms 'imperialism' and 'empire' carry with them a rather negative ring of ascendancy and where the terms are used to characterise the relations between the European Union and developing countries they easily evoke the picture of re-colonisation. The question is, however, whether the European Union really has engaged upon re-colonising developing countries (primarily ACP countries)? In my opinion three aspects must be taken into account when considering this question.

First, the European Union's promotion of its values is not merely aimed at former colonies in Africa and elsewhere but at the outside world in general. Indeed, the countries that arguably have been under the strongest pressure to comply with the European values are not former colonies, but rather Eastern European neighbours that have been required to meet the Copenhagen criteria when applying for accession.[34] I therefore argue that it is inaccurate to qualify the furthering of European values as simply being a kind of re-colonisation.

Second, the introduction of conditionality in the legal measures governing the relations between the European Union and the developing countries has been met with strong criticism, in particular from the ACP countries and from a number of NGOs.[35] This criticism to a large extent appears to be founded on the view that as colonial powers the European countries exploited the colonies and therefore Europe is now under a moral obligation to make good her sins of the past. As a matter of principle this must give rise to the fundamental question of for how long the iniquity of the fathers must be visited upon the children. Even if we accept that the European Union continues to be under such moral obligation, it does not seem obvious that it completely excludes any kind of reciprocity.

Third, the European Union's focus upon its values is a relatively new phenomenon. Amongst those factors that presumably have influenced its appearance, the end of the Cold War stands out as particularly important. During the Cold War confrontations between the two superpowers—United States and Soviet Union—left the European Union with only little room for manoeuvre. This situation materially changed with the demise of the Soviet Union. First because the so-called European values to a considerable extent are shared by the United States,

---

32 Bickerton 2011, 77.

33 See, for example, Sepos 2010.

34 The criteria setting the political, economic and administrative standards for EU membership applicants.

35 See for example Oxfam, Unequal Partners: How EU–ACP Economic Partnership Agreements (EPAs) could harm the development prospects of many of the world's poorest countries, Oxfam Briefing Note. www.oxfam.org/sites/www.oxfam.org/files/unequal%20partners.pdf. Accessed 25 July 2011.

the sole remaining superpower. And second because a third-country could no longer turn, or at least threaten that it would turn, to the Soviet Union if it were dissatisfied with the European Union's insistence that compliance with European values should be part of any agreement between the parties. This naturally increased the European Union's power to impose its values through its external policies. Arguably, the end of the Cold War and the consequent lack of competing foreign powers *vis-à-vis* the developing countries is a condition *sine qua non* for the salient position of the European values in the Union's policy towards the developing countries today. In addition, the speed with which countries in Central and Eastern Europe expressed their desire to join the European Union after overthrowing communism strengthened the credentials of the EU as a proponent of democratic values. Through the successful implementation of the Copenhagen Criteria in the ten former communist countries which joined the EU in 2004 and 2007, the EU arguably gained in confidence to be more open about adopting a value-led approach and did not seek to hide this with a discourse about the benefits of the EU relating only to trade.

9.5 Conclusion

The question remains whether the power vacuum which ensued from the end of the Cold War is sustainable. As long as the United States is the only superpower, it can afford to let the European Union act as a normative power. However, with China emerging as a new world power and with countries like India and Brazil also taking on new, strengthened positions—not just regionally but also on the world stage—it seems reasonable to expect that in the future the European Union's room to act as a normative power will become increasingly tighter. This is likely to be particularly felt in countries with strong, ex-colonial ties to Europe, particularly in Africa. In other words, whilst the European Union's constitutional foundation (the Treaties) increasingly requires the Union to act as a normative power in the world, it seems likely that in practice the Union will have to take on an increasingly *realpolitisch* approach in the coming years. In other words, the 'missionary man' may take a primarily supporting role to the 'trade missionary man' in the years to come.

Finally, the criticism directed at the European Union's promotion of its values should evoke two fundamental questions. First, whether human rights, democracy, good governance and free trade are merely European values, or whether they are not much more widely shared? And second whether it is really wrong to promote these values? Of course it may be that *the way* in which the European Union seeks to further its values should be subject to criticism; for example, there may be differences of opinion with regard to the validity of certain specific values. Nevertheless, if we focus solely upon the values as such, at a more general level it is not obvious why the promotion thereof should be considered unacceptable.

References

Batt J et al (2003) Partners and neighbours: a CFSP for a Wider Europe. Chaillot Paper, No 64

Bickerton C (2011) European Union Foreign Policy: from effectiveness to functionality. Palgrave Macmillan, Basingstoke

Broberg M (2010) Furthering democracy through the European Community's Development Policy: legal limitations and possibilities. International IDEA, Stockholm

Cardwell PJ (2011) Mapping out democracy promotion in the EU's external relations. European Foreign Affairs Review 16:21–40

Gould T (2004) The European economic area: A model for the EU's Neighbourhood Policy? Ukraine's place in the Wider Europe. Perspectives on European Politics and Societies 5(2):171–202

Hillion C (2008) Tous pour un, un pour tous! Coherence in the external relations of the European Union. In: Cremona (ed) Developments in EU external relations law. Oxford University Press, Oxford, pp 10–36

Khaliq U (2008) Ethical dimensions of the foreign policy of the European Union. Cambridge University Press, Cambridge

Sepos A (2010) Imperial power Europe? The EU's relations with the ACP countries. Paper presented at workshop—imperial power Europe? The EU's quest for supremacy. Manchester Jean Monnet Centre of Excellence, Manchester University, 27 May 2010

Part III
The EU in the Wider World

Chapter 10
Pre and Post-Lisbon Institutional Trends in the EU's Neighbourhood

Nariné Ghazaryan

Abstract The agenda of the EU institutions and its Member States has not been always coherent when it comes to the European Neighbourhood Policy (ENP). The development of the European Neighbourhood Policy has been significantly affected by the changing Presidency of the Council, where at times the policy has not been paid sufficient attention, or the Southern or Eastern neighbourhood was prioritised due to specific Member State interests. Moreover, the various EU institutions lacked a unified vision of the EU's role in its neighbourhood. As a result, the objectives and the substance of the policy changed from document to document causing many concerns as to its ultimate success. Against this background this chapter analyses the prospects of new institutional dynamics with reference to the Treaty of Lisbon. Landmark developments, such as the establishment of the position of the Presidency of the European Council and of the High Representative for Foreign Affairs and Security Policy will serve as a reference point for evaluating their possible impact on inter-institutional dynamics as regards the neighbourhood policies. Other developments, more specific to the European Neighbourhood Policy, in particular the introduction of a new Article 8 TEU which requires the Union to develop a special relationship with neighbouring countries, will be analysed to reveal the implications it might have for the EU institutions and Member States. Most importantly, the rationale behind the introduction of the article will be discussed with a view of evaluating the possibility of

Dr. Nariné Ghazaryan—Lecturer at the Brunel Law School, Brunel University. The author would like to express her gratitude to Professor Marise Cremona for inviting attention to one of the issues discussed in this chapter. The author is most grateful to Paul James Cardwell for many valuable comments.

N. Ghazaryan (✉)
Brunel University, Uxbridge, UK
e-mail: narine.ghazaryan@brunel.ac.uk

P. J. Cardwell (ed.), *EU External Relations Law and Policy in the Post-Lisbon Era*, DOI: 10.1007/978-90-6704-823-1_10, © T.M.C. Asser press, The Hague, The Netherlands, and the authors 2012

overcoming the Member States' fears of neighbours' aspirations to join the EU and thus creating a more united front in the relations with the neighbours of the EU.

Contents

10.1 Introduction

Among the major flaws of conducting European Union (EU) external action before the entry into force of the Treaty of Lisbon were the absence of its legal personality and the multi-pillar structure of its constitutional order. These have been emphasised by numerous authors, including contributors to this volume. The European Neighbourhood Policy (ENP) was no exception in this respect. It was initiated in 2003 in order to solve the 'inclusion–exclusion' dilemma the EU faced after the 2004 round of enlargement. The ENP promises a level of integration with the EU—without membership—to sixteen neighbouring countries in the East and South.[1] The main policy documents envisaged cooperation in wide ranging areas from all so called 'pillars' of EU constitutional order based on fulfilment of Copenhagen–like criteria formulated in the language of 'shared values'.[2] In addition to this conditionality element the policy is based on the principles of joint ownership and differentiation. As a result, various neighbouring states included in the policy have developed a different pace of relations with the EU.[3] Ukraine, for instance, advanced its relations with the EU to the stage of signing a new bilateral agreement. Some others, including Algeria, Libya, Syria and Belarus have opted out from signing the main policy document envisaged under the ENP, the Action Plans.

---

1 Countries envisaged for participation in the ENP are Algeria, Egypt, Israel, Jordan, Lebanon, Libya, Morocco, Palestinian Authority, Syria, and Tunisia in the Mediterranean region. The countries in Eastern Europe are Ukraine, Belarus, Moldova, and the South Caucasian states of Armenia, Georgia and Azerbaijan.

2 Communication from the Commission to the Council and the European Parliament (2003) Wider Europe-Neighbourhood: a New Framework for Relations with our Eastern and Southern Neighbours, 11.04.2003 COM (2003) 104 final; Commission Communication (2004) ENP Strategy Paper, Brussels, 12.5.2004 COM (2004) 373 final; Communication from the Commission to the Council and the European Parliament (2006) on Strengthening the ENP, 4 December 2006 COM (2006) 726 final.

3 ENP Strategy Paper, at p. 8, 14.

The agenda of official EU institutions and its Member States has not been always coherent when it comes to the ENP. The focus on the policy has depended on the rotating presidency of the Council, where at times the policy was not paid sufficient attention or the Southern or Eastern neighbourhood was prioritised due to special links existing with certain Member States. Moreover, various institutions at the supranational level have not had a united vision of the EU's role in its neighbourhood: the goals and substance of the policy has changed from document to document leaving many doubts as to the prospects for its ultimate success. Although the official objectives of the policy were initially articulated around the idea of avoiding new dividing lines in Europe and spreading stability to the neighbourhood, gradually the focus has shifted to security-oriented cooperation areas allowed positioning of security concerns as central to the ENP's objectives. Other articulated objectives, such as the stability and prosperity of the neighbourhood are, therefore, contributing to the EU's objective of 'internal' security.

Against this background the Treaty of Lisbon amended the Treaty on European Union (TEU) and the Treaty establishing the European Community by introducing a number of amendments concerning the conduct of EU external action. Although the new Article 47 of the TEU ensures legal personality for the EU, it preserves the intergovernmental nature of decision-making in the area of Common Foreign and Security Policy (CFSP).[4] Most importantly, a new Article 8 TEU on neighbourhood policy is provided in Title I on Common Provisions.

Within this context, this chapter analyses the emerging institutional outlook of the ENP stemming from the Lisbon Treaty. First, the role of the institutions prior to the ratification of Lisbon Treaty will be discussed in order to identify the major actors that influenced the formation and the implementation of the policy. In the second part, the chapter will address the amendments introduced in the Lisbon Treaty in order to evaluate their possible impact on inter-institutional dynamics as regards the neighbourhood policies. The chapter will conclude by emphasising the main advantages of the new legal framework for the purposes of the efficient implementation of the ENP and the possible shifts in the role the EU institutions play in this process.

10.2 EU Institutions and Member States: The ENP Prior to the Ratification of the Treaty of Lisbon

Although this chapter does not aim at analysing integration theories, which are covered by other contributors to this collection,[5] they are useful as a reference point for the discussion of the role of institutions in the development and

---

[4] On the legal and political consequences of this, see the contributions by Sari and Puetter in this volume.

[5] See, in particular, Puetter's discussion of deliberative intergovernmentalism and Bendiek's application of 'European realism' to external relations.

implementation of the ENP. At first sight, the activities of the EU institutions within the ENP can be generally assessed as fitting into the theory of liberal intergovernmentalism. The first initiative of the activity appears on the intergovernmental meeting agenda and is subsequently passed to the Commission which follows the issue up and then the Council, as an agent of the Member States, makes a decision to adopt a particular instrument.[6] The Member States acted as the principals, where the Commission and then the Council's High Representative for the Common Foreign and Security Policy were the agents.[7]

However, this integrationist theory does not solely explain the evolution of the ENP, since the Commission is an actor which has active participation in elaborating on the scope and content of the policy. The Commission's role must therefore be taken seriously. As was noted by one of the Brussels officials 'with its plethora of rhetorical devices, the Council of Ministers may have appeared as the most influential arbitrator of EU foreign policy, however when we are talking about 'real' foreign policy impact of the Union in the last decade, the power vests with the Commission'.[8] Such a salient role of the Commission can be generally explained with the institutional set up for the elaboration of the ENP drawn from the enlarge-ment experience. The latter was noted to be 'characterised by a high level of integration,' which involves a special arrangement between the institutions and the Member States, with a central role for the Commission in the policy formation and its subsequent implementation.[9] As Dragneva and Wolczuk argue in this volume, the place of law export as part of the ENP, in a manner inspired by the legislative approximation undertaken by candidate countries in the enlargement process, has been central.

The Commission acted on the December 2002 Copenhagen European Council's initiative to enhance relations with Union's neighbours. It brought forward the Wider Europe Communication setting out the main ideas for future policy.[10] In June 2003, the Thessaloniki European Council welcomed this Communication as a basis for developing a new range of policies towards the neighbours and defined the overall goals and principles. A certain level of confusion was caused by the fact that the ENP was envisaged to include also the Southern neighbours which previously had a multilateral framework of cooperation with the EU, namely the Barcelona Process.[11] The Council's conclusions looked forward to the work to be undertaken by the Council and Commission in elaborating the essential

6 Moravcsik 1993, 480.

7 Emerson et al. 2005, 32.

8 Kelley 2006, 31.

9 Cremona and Hillion 2006, 28.

10 Communication from the Commission to the Council and the European Parliament (2003) Wider Europe-Neighbourhood: a New Framework for Relations with our Eastern and Southern Neighbours, 11.04.2003 COM (2003) 104 final.

11 The Barcelona Process or Euro-Mediterranean Partnership was launched in 1995 and was aimed at creating a large free trade area with the North African and Middle Eastern countries. Association Agreements have been signed within the Barcelona Process with countries concerned. See Cardwell 2011.

features of these policies.[12] Since the launch of the ENP initiative the decision-making was undertaken by the Council. At the beginning of the process the Commission prepared Country Reports assessing the political and economic situation of relevant countries. The reports were submitted to the Council which decided whether to proceed with the next stage of relations. The next stage included the elaboration and signing of the ENP Action Plans with the partner countries. As a 'watchdog' of the implementation of all EU policies, also here the Commission is responsible for monitoring the process of the implementation of the Action Plans by the partner states. The Action Plans have come to be seen as the main policy documents of the ENP.[13]

The formation of the ENP on the basis of successful experience with the enlargement policy of the EU has been widely discussed.[14] Since the Commission played a major role in the transformation of acceding countries, subsequently it continued to play the same role in relation to the ENP. Also, the Commission itself was eager to retain its leading role in the foreign policy of the Union, and therefore by adapting the pre-accession process to the ENP, it has extended the significant foreign policy role it acquired previously.[15] Consequently, the reliance on the pre-accession strategy in developing the ENP by the Commission is considered to be an important institutional 'mission creep'.[16] Since the Commission is traditionally considered to be a strong internal actor as opposed to its place in foreign relations domain, the role played by the Commission within the ENP is not happily accepted by the Member States, who conceded their leading role in foreign policy since the initiation of the policy.[17] Such a leading role for the Commission in the policy elaboration and monitoring process has been evaluated by commentators with positive connotations: it will pursue the Union's interests impartially therefore, avoiding different interests of the Member States.[18] Nevertheless, despite the Commission's central role, one cannot dismiss the significant roles of the Council and the Member States in the ENP.

The Council is the ultimate decision-making body.[19] It seemed that the Council wished to limit the role of the Commission and to ensure its presence in the process of policy formation, in particular via the participation of the then High Representative for the CFSP. For instance, after approval from the Council, the ENP Strategy Paper prescribed participation of the High Representative on the issues of political cooperation and CFSP matters during the Action Plans'

---

[12] Commission Communication (2004) ENP Strategy Paper, Brussels, 12.5.2004 COM (2004) 373 final.

[13] ENP Strategy Paper, at p. 10.

[14] Kelley 2006, Magen 2006, Meloni 2007, Cremona and Hillion 2006 etc.

[15] Magen 2006, 396.

[16] Emerson et al. 2005, 5.

[17] Emerson et al. 2005, 5.

[18] Ott and Wessel 2006, 51.

[19] Balfour and Missiroli 2007, 21.

preparation.[20] Accordingly, while drafting national reports, the Commission worked in close cooperation with the CFSP High Representative. In particular, for the Action Plans with South Caucasian Republics, the Council instructed the Commission to undertake joint discussions in close cooperation, for questions connected with political cooperation and the CFSP, with the Presidency and the High Representative and, where appropriate with the Special Representative for the South Caucasus.[21] Close cooperation with the High Representative for CFSP was to be required for drafting periodic reports on the implementation of the Action Plans on the issues related to political dialogue and cooperation, as well as CFSP.[22] This cooperation between the Commission and the High Representative for the CFSP was considered to be the contrasting point with the institutional practice of the enlargement policy demonstrating the first steps towards the 'double-hatting' system endorsed by the Lisbon Treaty.[23]

Second, the Council significantly influenced the pragmatic and rationalist turn the policy took after the Commission's Wider Europe Communication as noted earlier. The promise of 'everything but institutions' in the initial speeches[24] and Wider Europe Communication was substantially abandoned since the ENP Strategy Paper. Not only the Council 'shuffled priorities' shifting the focus to the security challenges of the neighbourhood, but it also limited the incentives, where the freedom of movement of persons was noted to be 'the first victim of the Council's intervention'.[25]

As to the role of the European Parliament, parliaments are traditionally considered to be weak foreign policy actors. The European Parliament in its turn was excluded from being an actor in the foreign policy of the Union at all, and the general feature of the EU's policy action assumed a weak role for the European Parliament.[26] However, the Parliament has gained considerable weight through its partial powers over the budget, where together with the Court of Auditors it established certain presence over matters of financial control.[27]

---

20 ENP Strategy Paper, at p. 4.

21 Council Conclusions, 25 April 2005.

22 On 13 December 2004, the GAER Council recalled its intention to undertake a first review of the implementation of the action plans at the latest two years from their adoption, on the basis of assessment reports to be prepared by the Commission, in close co-operation with the Presidency and the SG/HR on issues related to political cooperation and the CFSP, and with the contribution of ENP partners. At its meeting on 16/17 December 2004, the European Council also invited the Commission and the High Representative to report regularly on progress accomplished.

23 New Article 17 TEU provides that the High Representative of the Union for Foreign Affairs and Security Policy shall at the same time occupy a position of a Vice-President of the Commission; Copsey and Mayhew 2006, 33.

24 Prodi 'A Wider Europe-A Proximity Policy as the Key to Stability', Speech to the Sixth ECSA-World Conference, 2002, Brussels 5–6 December, Speech/02/619.

25 Balfour and Rotta 2005, 12–13.

26 Stetter 2004, 733.

27 Emerson et al. 2005, 34.

In the case of the ENP, the Parliament has adopted certain soft law instruments, such as its resolution on the European Neighbourhood Policy.[28] It expressed its solidarity with other EU institutions in elaboration and further promotion of the ENP, and invited Commission's attention to certain aspects of the process of developing the ENP,[29] as well as to demand greater focus on particular neighbouring regions.[30]

Parliament's role is particularly important in relation to the issues of democracy and human rights on the external agenda of the EU. An early example of the Parliament upholding these values took place before the conclusion of the Partnership and Cooperation Agreements with South Caucasian states. The Parliament threatened to block the agreements if the Council did not include Title VIII on the Democratic clauses.[31] The European Parliament remained loyal to its stance also in relation to the ENP. In its 2006 Resolution, the Parliament emphasised the need to establish an effective monitoring mechanism and demonstrated readiness to restrict or suspend aid and even to cancel agreements with countries violating European and international standards of democracy.[32] Although the ENPI Regulation entitles the Council to suspend aid to a misbehaving state based on a proposal from the Commission,[33] a certain role is preserved for the European Parliament. A dialogue should be maintained between the Commission and the Parliament and annual report on the implementation of the assistance allocation should be presented to the Parliament and the Council.[34]

Such institutional interactions support the standpoint that the role of the EU institutions within the ENP stepped over the ordinary constitutional set up envisaged by the EC Treaty replicating institutional arrangements of the

[28] European Parliament Resolution on the European Neighbourhood Policy, P6_TA (2006) 0028.

[29] Other documents by Parliament include European Parliament Resolution of 15 November 2007 on Strengthening the European Neighbourhood Policy (2007/2088(INI)); European Parliament Report on the Review of the European Neighbourhood and Partnership Instrument (2008/2236(INI)).

[30] European Parliament Resolution on the Communication from the Commission to the Council and the European Parliament on The European Union's Relations with the South Caucasus under the Partnership and Cooperation Agreements, P5_TA (2002) 0085, *OJ* C 293 E/96, 28.11.2002; Bosse 2007, 43.

[31] European Parliament (2006) The European Parliament and the Defence of Human Rights, Sanctions, EP Report, Brussels.

[32] European Parliament Resolution on the European Neighbourhood Policy, 19.01.2006, 2004/2166(INI).

[33] Article 28 of the Regulation No 1638/2006 of the European Parliament and of the Council laying down general provisions establishing a European Neighbourhood and Partnership Instrument, *OJ* L 310/1, 09.11.2006 (ENPI Regulation).

[34] ENPI Regulation, Articles 25 and 26.

pre-accession experience.[35] The Commission's activity is more than a mere guardian of the Treaty *vis-à-vis* the Member States.

However, a more sceptical view has been expressed by Kochenov as to the precise role of all the institutions together with 27 Member States in the implementation of the ENP, according to which the institutional rivalry affects the direction of the ENP.[36] Although it is possible to disagree on qualifying the relations between the institutions as 'rivalry,' one can agree with the rationale that the sensitivities of the Member States will likely affect the progress of the ENP.[37] These remind us that the intergovernmentalist aspects of the EU foreign policy cannot be abandoned.

Most importantly, the concerns of the Member States are reflected through the Council's participation in the policy. An example is noted above: the ENP objectives received a more 'securitarian outlook' with the Council's push. In addition, the European Council, heads of governments or states, serves as an alternative arena for Member States to influence the elaboration and subsequent development of the policy. Most importantly, the 2002 Copenhagen Summit acknowledged the opportunity brought by the enlargement 'to take forward relations with neighbouring countries based on shared political and economic values' setting the ground for the subsequent policy development.[38] Consequently, the role of the European Council seemed to be marginal leaving the tasks of policy formation to the Commission and the Council.[39] However, it is without a doubt that where a serious political decision is to be made, the European Council will be the platform for such decision-making. The inability to implement a coherent policy towards all neighbours in the East and South led to the necessary split in the policy according to its regional dimension, as predicted by Missiroli.[40]

The historical links of Southern European Member States with the Mediterranean region influenced their initiative of launching a Mediterranean Union within the ENP during the French Presidency in July 2008. On the other hand, Sweden together with Poland brought up an initiative of Eastern Partnership endorsed at the European Council in June 2008. The Eastern Partnership will include Ukraine, Moldova, Armenia, Azerbaijan, Georgia and possibly Belarus. Most importantly, the dissenting opinions of the Member States will be apparent in the instances of

35 Hillion 2008, 317, Cremona and Hillion 2006, 28.

36 Kochenov 2008, 12.

37 Kochenov 2008, 12.

38 Copenhagen European Council (2002) 12 and 13 December 2002, Presidency Conclusions, 6.

39 Thessaloniki European Council (2003) 19 and 20 June 2003, Presidency Conclusions, 13; Brussels European Council (2003) Presidency Conclusions 16 and 17 October 2003, 13.

40 Missiroli 2007.

reacting to international developments, which was evident in the EU's reaction to Russia after the Georgian-Russian war in 2008.[41]

10.3 New Inter-Institutional Dynamics?

At the Intergovernmental Conference leading to the adoption of the Lisbon Treaty, the European Council stated that '[i]n order to secure our future as an active player in a rapidly changing world and in the face of ever-growing challenges, we have to maintain and develop the European Union's capacity to act'.[42] It is the capacity of the EU to act which is crucial in its relations with the neighbouring states.

10.3.1 General Provisions on Institutional Reform

There are a number of provisions in the Lisbon Treaty which are relevant for the representation of the EU in the neighbourhood and the conduct of its policies therein. One such development is the introduction of legal personality of the EU in Article 47 TEU, which is presumed to contribute to the strengthening of its international identity.[43] It is also, as Sari notes in this volume, a product of the simplification process of the EU's treaty arrangements. Endowing the EU as a whole—as opposed to the previous European Communities 'pillar' only—with legal personality will enhance the clarity in the international representation of the latter. Nevertheless, the Lisbon Treaty did not abolish the intergovernmental nature of the CFSP/CSDP. In its specific provisions on the CFSP the modified EU Treaty requires unanimity vote for adopting decisions related to CFSP/CSDP in both the European Council and the Council[44] suggesting that mixity in the representation of the EU will be a continuous feature in the ENP, at the same time compelling the EU institutions to rely on soft law in order to avoid competence complications. Senden defines soft law as 'rules of conduct that are laid down in

[41] The Member States were divided, with the Baltic and Eastern European states calling for a tough response to Russia and most of the old Member States calling for a more careful approach. The EU's ultimate response was the suspension of a new agreement with Russia until the complete withdrawal of Russian troops from Georgian territory; 'EU shies away from strong action against Russia', *EU Observer*, 01.09.2008, available at http://euobserver.com/?aid=26667; 'EU diplomats keen to avoid Russia controversy', *EU Observer*, 13.08.2008, available at http://euobserver.com/?aid=26605; 'EU suspends talks on Russia pact', 1 September 2008, available at http://news.bbc.co.uk/1/hi/word/europe/7592541.stm'EU secures deal on Russia withdrawal', *EU Observer*, 09.09.2008, http://euobserver.com/?aid=26708.

[42] Presidency Conclusions, June 2007, para 2.

[43] Craig and de Búrca 2007, 225.

[44] Title V of the Treaty of the European Union, Article 31.

instruments which have not been attributed legally binding force as such, but nevertheless may have certain (indirect) legal effects, and that are aimed at and may produce practical effects'.[45] It is the absence of binding legal force that places soft law acts on a level below legal acts, which required a formal adoption by the relevant EU institutions or Member States and which create legal obligations for the latter.

New Article 21 TEU provides a single framework for the conduct of EU external action binding the EU institutions to act based on the principles of 'democracy, the rule of law, the universality and indivisibility of human rights and fundamental freedoms, respect for human dignity, the principles of equality and solidarity, and respect for the principles of the United Nations Charter and international law'. For the first time, there is a common list of objectives for Union's external action in Article 21 TEU, including the so called 'normative' objectives. Despite the fact that the provisions on external relations are still scattered over the TEU and TFEU, providing common objectives of action for all areas of foreign relations is a significant development. It suggests that there is a common framework of action for all EU institutions. There is an obligation in para 3 of the same article to ensure consistency between the different areas of external action, and it is the Council and the Commission, assisted by the High Representative of the Union for Foreign Affairs and Security Policy, that are required to ensure this consistency.[46]

Translated to the context of the neighbourhood such consistency has various dimensions. Consistency between the approaches of different institutions is required, as well as vertical consistency between the Union and the Member States.[47] In relation to the ENP, consistency shall also be preserved between various elements of the policy, as well as loyalty to its methodology. Substantive elements of the policy should not be undermined by *realpolitik* considerations. In this sense, consistency might be synonymous with continuity. For instance, the conditionality element of the ENP loses credibility when the relations between the EU and one of the neighbouring partners progress despite the conditionality element, but rather in response to the EU's urge of establishing a presence in its vicinity. Such an example was the swift turn to negotiating of a visa facilitation agreement with Georgia in 2008.[48] The talks on the agreement were initiated immediately after the 2008 August war with Russia within the general approach of the EU's support to the country.

The presence of common objectives binding all institutions and the Member States will not automatically ensure a unified vision of EU's identity in the

---

[45] Senden 2005, 112.

[46] On this point, see further the contributions by Schmidt and Broberg to this volume.

[47] Chalmers et al. 2010, 637.

[48] The Extraordinary European Council of 1 September 2008 decided 'to step up relations with Georgia, including visa facilitation measures'. The agreement was signed in June 2010; 'European Union signs visa facilitation agreement with Georgia', Press Release IP/10/737, 17 June 2010.

neighbourhood. There are other institutional developments that might contribute to this. First of all, the position of the European Council has been clarified in this respect. Article 13 TEU recognises the European Council among other institutions and provides for a separate article on the role of the European Council.[49] According to Article 15 TEU the European Council 'shall provide the Union with the necessary impetus for its development and shall define the general political directions and priorities'. Decisions of the European Council will relate not only to the CFSP action, but all areas of foreign policy.[50] The European Council consisting primarily of the heads of state or government of the Member States will preserve its main role as the platform for the Member States to bring in their own visions of what the action of EU should be in its neighbourhood. One could suggest that the presence of the European Council will allow for the disagreements between the Member States to continue, a problem which followed the ENP from its commencement resulting in its split into Eastern Partnership and the Union for Mediterranean.[51]

It is the rotating presidency of the Council which was particularly detrimental in influencing the foreign policy agenda and promoting particular interests of the presiding state. In this sense the new permanent position of the President of the European Council shall contribute to continuity of established policies. Indeed, under Article 15 TEU the President of the European Council *inter alia* shall ensure the continuity of the work of the European Council, as well as shall aim at facilitating cohesion and consensus within the European Council. Moreover, the President will 'ensure the external representation of the Union on issues concerning its common foreign and security policy'.

This is not without complications. A further development was envisaged in the Lisbon Treaty establishing the position of High Representative for Foreign Affairs and Security Policy as the Vice-President of the Commission. As others in this volume have noted, the High Representative has a number of roles. Under Article 15 TEU the High Representative shall take part in the work of the European Council. In addition, the High Representative chairs Foreign Affairs Council and is responsible for the conduct of external relations as the Vice-President of the European Commission.[52] A number of issues should be raised in relation to the role of this institution as regards the conduct of the ENP and the representation of the EU in the neighbourhood. First, it is not possible to determine the clear mandate of the High Representative based solely on the language of Article 18 TEU. According to the latter, the High Representative 'shall be responsible within the Commission for responsibilities incumbent on it in external relations and for coordinating other aspects of the Union's external action'. It has been noted that

[49] Previously European Council was only mentioned in the Treaty on the European Union, Article 4.

[50] Cremona 2003, 1349.

[51] Hillion and Mayhew 2009, 20.

[52] Treaty on the European Union, Article 18.

the article left doubts as to the role of the High Representative, in particular whether it extends beyond CFSP to other areas of foreign action, including the ENP.[53] An important role in this respect belongs to the EU institutions together with the Member States, and importantly to the President of the Commission,[54] whose right-hand the High Representative should be. The mandate of the High Representative, Baroness Ashton, does not include the ENP as decided by the Commission President in the end of 2009.[55]

This will be problematic in terms of external representation. The confusion for the neighbouring countries as to who represents the EU in which matters will continue to exist, as both the President of the European Council and the High Representative will represent the EU in addition to President of the Commission and respective Commissioner for Enlargement and the ENP 2010–2014, Štefan Füle. Therefore, the 'opaque nature' as well as the significant overlap in the mandate of the positions of the President of the European Council and the High Representative has been emphasised as a potential pitfall.[56] For instance, one the most recent documents on the ENP that is the Medium Term Programme for a renewed European Neighbourhood Policy for the period of 2011–2012, derived from the Office of the High Representative, despite the Commission's presence and its established role in the issues of the ENP.[57] Depending on the context and on the personalities the substance of this position might alter over time. Ultimately, even after the Lisbon Treaty 'the international representation of the European Union would still not be the responsibility of just one actor'[58]: personalities will matter again in terms of allocating roles between these various institutions, as well as competition between all actors whose portfolio will include the external representation of the EU in relation to various policy areas.

Creation of the position of the High Representative as the necessary link between the Council and the Commission, the so called 'double-hatting,' has been long viewed as a significant achievement in constitutional development of the EU. Nevertheless, the operation of this institution will largely depend on the personality and the institutional loyalty of the person occupying this position, as one would expect opposing or differing approaches to the same question in the Council and the Commission.[59] In addition, it is considered that the position will add strength to the powers of the Commission in relation to the CFSP matters: it will connect the CFSP with other areas of external relations.[60] Prior to Lisbon Treaty, the role of the Commission in the area of CFSP was confined to right of initiative

[53] Koutrakos 2008, 672.

[54] Koutrakos 2008, 672.

[55] Koutrakos 2010, 1.

[56] Koutrakos 2010, 1.

[57] Joint Staff Working Paper, SEC (2011) 650, Brussels, 25.05.2011.

[58] Koutrakos 2008, 672.

[59] Craig and de Búrca 2007, 226.

[60] Cremona 2003, 1355.

provided under Article 22 TEU.[61] The new arrangement allows the Commission to play a more prominent role in relation to the CFSP issues within the ENP general framework. In addition, it can potentially contribute to the idea of consistency referred to in Article 21 TEU, in particular by ensuring that the CFSP and other elements of the ENP do not undermine, but rather complement one another.

Much will depend on the smooth operation of the European External Action Service (EEAS). Article 27 TEU envisaged the establishment of a new institution with a role of assisting the High Representative in fulfilling his/her mandate. A Council decision is required after consultation with the Parliament and obtaining the consent of the Commission in order to establish the regulatory framework for the functioning of the EEAS. A proposal for Council decision was presented by Baroness Ashton in 2010 and adopted by the Council in July 2010. The decision envisages a prominent role for the EEAS in certain areas of Commission's expertise, in particular the management of EU external cooperation programmes.[62] Most importantly, with regard to the ENPI the proposal requires all the documents relating to changes in basic regulations and programming to be prepared both in the EEAS and the Commission under the direct supervision of the responsible Commissioner, that is, the Commissioner for the Enlargement and ENP. Not only will this require a united vision of the neighbourhood, but also a highly coordinated action on behalf of relevant units in the EEAS and the Commission. In addition, the involvement of the EEAS in this area can lead to unnecessary institutional rivalry due to the staffing of EEAS by both Commission and national officials.

On the other hand, the possible tandem of the Commission and the Council is capable of strengthening the executive branch.[63] This is detrimental to the role of the European Parliament which is not major in formation and implementation of the ENP or other areas of EU external action, despite growing willingness to participate and widening of its powers. Although as noted above parliaments traditionally are weak foreign policy actors, in relation to the EU's external action it would be regrettable to accord the Parliament with a secondary role as often it is the only institution eager to observe the adherence to EU's values, including democracy and human rights. In this respect, the High Representative shall regularly consult the Parliament and make sure that its views are taken into account under Article 36 TEU. Nevertheless, the article refers to CFSP/CSDP without referring to other areas of EU external relations including ENP.

---

[61] Wessel 1999, 90.

[62] Council Decision (2010) Establishing the organisation and functioning of the European External Action Service, OJ L 201/30, Article 8.

[63] Craig and de Búrca 2007, 226.

10.3.2 Neighbourhood-Specific Provisions

While considering the developments in the Lisbon Treaty capable of influencing the relationship between the EU and its neighbours, one cannot avoid mentioning new Article 8 TEU

> The Union shall develop a special relationship with neighbouring countries, aiming to establish an area of prosperity and good neighbourliness, founded on the values of the Union and characterised by close and peaceful relations based on cooperation.

The article is remarkable in a number of aspects. First of all, it is provided separately from the Title V on External Action of the EU and CFSP and is included in the Common Provisions in Title I of the TEU. On the one hand, such separation might suggestion special significance that the EU attributes to its neighbourhood and that the relations with neighbours can no longer be overlooked. However, on the other hand, the exclusion of this article from the other section related to external action has deeper motives. Thus, it has been noted that providing an article expressly referring to the neighbours of the EU in the first part of the TEU is aimed at accentuating its alternative character to the accession process.[64] Others potentially view this provision as capable in certain context of functioning as 'pre-pre-accession' stage.[65] The last view might prove true at some time in the distant future given the necessary political context. However, the former opinion is in more accord with the present reality: establishing the obligation for cooperation with the neighbours in a separate provision, without any reference to Copenhagen criteria as in Article 49 TEU, sends a signal that the ENP is a distinct and alternative policy to the enlargement.

Although the text of the article does not seem to lead to major institutional changes, it can be noted that for the first time the Treaty establishes the framework for relations with the neighbours binding all institutions to act on the basis of 'the values' of the Union. Although the main documents of the ENP were previously drafted using the language of the EU 'values', the soft law nature of those documents did not oblige the EU institutions to promote those values. In addition, no specification for the EU values was provided in previous treaties. For the first time, the Lisbon Treaty stipulated the values of the EU in Article 2 TEU, including respect for human dignity, freedom, democracy, respect for human right etc. Most importantly, promotion of its values is envisaged as an aim for the EU both internally and externally.[66]

It should be also mentioned that Article 8 TEU provides for a prospect of concluding new agreements containing reciprocal rights and obligations. Even before the ratification of the Lisbon Treaty various ENP policy documents

---

[64] Cremona 2003, 1365.

[65] Bechev and Nicolaidis 2010, 494.

[66] Treaty on the European Union, Articles 3 and 21.

provided for a prospect of concluding new agreements with the neighbours.[67] As the Lisbon Treaty did not abolish the separate legal characteristic of the CFSP, mixity will be the acceptable form for such an agreement, implying joint conclusion on behalf of the EU and its Member States. This is due to the fact that the ENP potentially covers cooperation under various areas of EU policy-making, which are by no means limited to the CFSP. Mixity is the panacea allowing 'to negotiate, conclude and implement an international agreement whose subject-matter falls within the competence of both' the EU and Member States.[68] The mixed nature of the ENP content also suggests that the institutions will continue relying on soft law instruments in order to avoid possible competence complications.

It is clear from the most recent ENP documents that association agreements are the new forms of agreement to be concluded with the Eastern neighbours.[69] In fact, negotiations on association agreements with Ukraine, Moldova, Georgia, Armenia, and Azerbaijan have been already under way prior to making references to this form of agreement in the latest documents. Signing an agreement falling short of 'privileged links'[70] will not prove a major development as it is no longer necessary to make political distinction, as in the case of the Europe Agreements and the Partnership and Cooperation Agreements, and as it will undermine the importance of the cooperation as opposed to the Southern neighbours.[71]

According to Article 218 of TFEU the Council shall authorise the opening of negotiations, adopt negotiating directives, authorise the signing of agreements and conclude them. In contrast with Article 300 of EC Treaty, Article 218 TFEU does not directly prescribe it to the Commission the conduct of negotiations, leaving it to the Council to appoint a negotiator. However, as this will take place based on a recommendation submitted by the Commission or the High Representative, it can be assumed that the Commission will not be deprived of its role as the negotiator. The role of the European Parliament has been preserved in relation to association treaties: the Council should obtain the consent of the Parliament to adopt a decision concluding an agreement.

---

[67] Communication from the Commission to the Council and the European Parliament (2003) Wider Europe-Neighbourhood: A New Framework for Relations with our Eastern and Southern Neighbours, 11.04.2003 COM (2003) 104 final, 17; Communication from the Commission to the Council and the European Parliament on Strengthening the ENP (2006) 4 December 2006 COM (2006) 726 final (hereinafter Communication on Strengthening the ENP), 4–5.

[68] Koutrakos 2006, 150.

[69] A Medium Term Programme for a renewed European Neighbourhood Policy (2011–2014), Joint Staff Working Paper, SEC (2011) 650, Brussels, 25.05.2011.

[70] Cases C-12/86 *Demirel* [1987] ECR 3719, para 9.

[71] Europe Agreements were Association Agreements concluded in the beginning of the 1990s with the Eastern European states which were not members of the Soviet Union and the Baltic states among the members of the USSR; Hillion 2007, 175–176.

10.4 Conclusion

The institutional trends in the formation and implementation of the ENP prior to the ratification of the Lisbon Treaty represented an amalgam of previous enlargement practice and the special nature of the ENP with its political element, where the Member States through the Council and the European Council were able to exert influence over the direction of the policy.

The Lisbon Treaty provides for a new framework which should ensure consistency between different institutions as they are bound by the same foundations of conducting external action provided in Article 21 TEU. The new positions of the President of the European Council and the High Representative for Foreign Affairs and Security Policy are intended to guarantee institutional cooperation and continuity in the policy. In this respect one would agree with the view that the Treaty creates 'a framework within which the institutions and the Member States could choose to carry out the European Union's international affairs in an effective and coherent manner'.[72] Whether this framework will be used in order to ensure such effectiveness and coherence is a different matter.

As regards the ENP, the European Council will continue playing its role as the suitable arena for Member States to influence the direction of the policy. Council in its turn will continue playing important role over decision-making process. The position of the High Representative can hardly be seen as guaranteeing a common stance between the Commission and the Council, as currently the ENP is not included in the portfolio of Baroness Ashton. In addition, the neighbours will still be confused as to the representation of the EU: there will be no single representation, and possibly mixed signals will be sent out to the neighbours.

It has been noted that after the ratification of the Lisbon Treaty, there will not be other occasions in the near future for treaty amendments, and therefore in this respect it might have been a missed opportunity for 'genuine constitutional simplification in the field of external relations'.[73] Despite this failure to solve all the complications inherent in the area of EU external action, the Lisbon Treaty has far more reaching effects in relation to the EU neighbourhood than any other previous treaty revisions. However, the legal framework currently in force has its own weaknesses. The past and present threats emerging from the wider neighbourhood, including *inter alia* the unresolved conflicts in the South Caucasus and Transnistria, and the expanding instability in the Middle East following the so called 'Arab Spring' revolutions, will serve as a testing ground for the efficiency of the new institutional arrangements. The ever changing political dynamics will either necessitate further developments to create a unified front for the EU or in the worst case scenario it will significantly discredit the EU as a serious political actor on the international scene.

---

72 Koutrakos 2008, 674.

73 De Witte 2008, 15.

References

Balfour R, Missiroli A (2007) Reassessing the European Neighbourhood Policy. European Policy Issue Paper No 54, 21
Balfour R, Rotta A (2005) Beyond enlargement. The European neighbourhood policy and its tools. Int Spect 40:7,9,12,13
Bechev D, Nicolaidis K (2010) From policy to polity: can the EU's special relations with its 'neighbourhood' be decentred? Journal of Common Market Studies 48:475, 494
Bosse G (2007) Values in the EU's neighbourhood policy: political rhetoric or reflection of a coherent policy? European Political Economy Review 7:38
Cardwell PJ (2011) EuroMed, ENP and the union for the mediterranean: overlapping policy frames in the EU's governance of the mediterranean. Journal of Common Market Studies 49:219–241
Chalmers D, Davies G, Monti G (2010) European Union law: cases and materials. Cambridge University Press, Cambridge
Craig P, de Búrca G (2007) EU law: text, cases and materials. Oxford University Press, Oxford, p 225
Cremona M (2003) The draft constitutional treaty: external relations and external action. Common Market Law Review 40:1347
Cremona M, Hillion C (2006) L'Union fait la force? Potential and limitations of the ENP as an integrated EU foreign and security policy. In: Copsey N, Mayhew A (eds) European neighbourhood policy: the case of Europe. Sussex European Institute. SEI Seminar Papers Series Number 1, pp 20–44
De Witte B (2008) Too much constitutional law in the European Union's foreign relations? In: Cremona M, De Witte B (eds) EU foreign relations law: constitutional fundamentals. Hart, Oxford, pp 3–15
Emerson M, Aydin S, Noutcheva G, Tocci N, Vahl M, Youngs R (2005) The reluctant debutante: the European Union as promoter of democracy in its neighbourhood. Centre for European Policy Studies, Working Document No 223,32
Hillion C (2007) Mapping-out the new contractual relations between the European Union and its neighbours: learning from the EU–Ukraine, 'enhanced agreement'. European Foreign Affairs Review 12:169
Hillion C (2008) The EU's neighbourhood policy towards Eastern Europe. In: Dashwood A, Maresceau M (eds) Law and practice of EU external relations. Cambridge University Press, Cambridge, pp 309–333
Hillion C, Mayhew A (2009)The Eastern Partnership–something new or window-dressing. Sussex European Institute, Working Paper No 109, 20
Kelley J (2006) New wine in old wineskins: policy learning and adaptation in the new European neighbourhood policy. Journal of Common Market Studies 44:29
Kochenov D (2008) The ENP conditionality: pre-accession mistakes repeated. In: Delcour L, Tulmets E (eds) Pioneer Europe? Testing EU foreign policy in the neighbourhood. Nomos, Baden Baden 12
Koutrakos P (2006) EU external relations law. Hart, Oxford, p 150
Koutrakos P (2008) Primary law and policy in EU external relations: moving away from the big picture. European Law Review 33:666
Koutrakos P (2010) New links in the Union's institutional chain. European Law Review 35 (1–2):1
Magen A (2006) The shadow of enlargement: Can the European neighbourhood policy achieve compliance? Centre on Democracy, Development and the Rule of Law, Stanford Institute for International Studies, Working Papers, No 68
Meloni G (2007) Is the same toolkit used during enlargement still applicable to the countries of the new neighbourhood? A problem of mismatching between objectives and instruments. In:

Cremona M, Meloni G (eds) The European Neighbourhood Policy: A New Framework for Modernisation? EUI Working Papers, LAW 2007/21, pp 97–111

Missiroli A (2007) The ENP three years on: Where from-and where next? European Policy Centre, Policy Brief

Moravcsik A (1993) Preferences and power in the European community: a liberal intergovernmentalist approach. Journal of Common Market Studies 473:31

Ott A, Wessel R (2006) The EU's external relations regime: multilevel complexity in an expanding union. In: Blockmans S, Lazowski A (eds) The European Union and its neighbours: a legal appraisal of the EU's policies of stabilisation, partnership and integration. T.M.C Asser Press, The Hague, pp 19–59

Senden A (2005) Soft law in European community law. Hart, Oxford

Stetter S (2004) Cross-pillar politics: functional unity and institutional fragmentation of EU foreign policies. Journal of European Public Policy 11:720

Wessel R (1999) The European Union's foreign and security policy: a legal institutional perspective. Kluwer Law International, The Hague

Chapter 11
EU Law Export to the Eastern Neighbourhood

Rilka Dragneva and Kataryna Wolczuk

Abstract This chapter examines the export of law in the EU's external policy and the impact that the Lisbon Treaty may have on the existing formula for law export. It focuses on the European Neighbourhood Policy (ENP), which has centred on the intensive and extensive expansion of EU rules outside its borders. In this chapter we broaden the analysis of the EU's external policy looking at the ENP against the global context for exporting law. We argue that, outside the accession context, the role of the EU in its neighbourhood is not dissimilar from that of other global actors—states or international organisations, which have promoted rules and norms to third countries for the purpose of development. We discuss the ENP law export formula against some key features of international experience, especially the factors behind effective legal transplantation. No doubt, the EU has sought to incorporate many of the lessons of exporting legal reform in the 1990s. Nevertheless, the question remains as to whether in its policy towards the neighbours the EU has moved from a paradigm based on compliance with EU law to one where 'demand for law' and political economy of legal reforms are sufficiently factored in. We argue that the Lisbon Treaty will not obliterate the essential contradictions and tensions underlying the EU's policy towards its neighbours. However, it may

Versions of this paper were presented at the BASEES Annual Conference, Cambridge, Fitzwilliam College, 2–4 April 2011 and the 41st Annual Conference of UACES, Cambridge, Robinson College, 5–7 September 2011. Preparation of this chapter was facilitated by the ESRC research grant (No. RES-360-25-0096).

R. Dragneva (✉)
School of Law, University of Manchester, Manchester, UK
e-mail: rilka.dragneva-lewers@manchester.ac.uk

K. Wolczuk
Centre for Russian and East European Studies,
University of Birmingham, Birmingham, UK
e-mail: k.wolczuk@bham.ac.uk

P. J. Cardwell (ed.), *EU External Relations Law and Policy in the Post-Lisbon Era*,
DOI: 10.1007/978-90-6704-823-1_11, © T.M.C. Asser Press, The Hague,
The Netherlands, and the authors 2012

still help to foster demand-driven, pragmatic law export formula more closely tailored to partners' capacities and needs, in line with international experience of legal transplants.

Contents

11.1 Introduction

The coming into force of the Lisbon Treaty re-invigorated the debates on the EU as a foreign policy actor in terms of procedural basis and institutional configuration. This chapter turns its attention to the export of law in the EU's external policy and the impact that the Lisbon Treaty may have on the existing formula for law export. The expansion of EU rules beyond its borders, including to the Eastern neighbourhood, is one of the most important dimensions of EU external policy. Yet the neighbourhood context for export of rules is new territory for the EU: there is no precedent for promoting the *acquis* as a template for development and modernisation without a concurrent offer of a membership perspective. The key vehicle through which EU's normative projection to the Eastern post-Soviet countries has taken place is the European Neighbourhood Policy (ENP) and its recent extension, the Eastern Partnership initiative.[1] There has been a great deal of scepticism, however, with regard to the ability of the ENP to contribute to effective domestic reform. The bulk of the critique of the ENP has focused on its macro-framework. Inspired by a rationalist, incentives-based model,[2] it has pointed out the inferior incentives structure or 'compliance-pull'[3] of the ENP relative to EU's enlargement policy.[4] Reliance on the enlargement toolbox, while lacking the membership perspective, in particular, has been seen as the key design flow of the ENP, amplified by the relatively inferior starting conditions of the Eastern neighbours compared to those of the new Member States of Central and Eastern

---

[1] Ghazaryan, in the previous chapter in this volume, examines the institutional development of the ENP and Eastern Partnership and its workings in the post-Lisbon era.

[2] Schimmelfennig and Sedelmeier 2005.

[3] Magen 2006.

[4] Noutcheva and Emerson 2005; Kelley 2006; Cremona and Hillion 2006.

Europe. However, so far discussions have been predominantly EU-centred,[5] even where a different framework for conceptualising the ENP as a vehicle for projecting EU's influence has been proposed.[6]

In this chapter we seek to broaden the analysis of the EU's external policy looking at the ENP against the global context for exporting law.[7] We argue that, outside the accession context,[8] the role of the EU in its neighbourhood is not dissimilar from that of other global actors—states or international organisations, which have promoted rules and norms to third countries for the purpose of development. While a full appreciation of the place of the EU in this global 'market for law' is beyond the scope of this chapter, we seek to discuss the ENP law export formula against some key features of international experience, especially the factors behind effective legal transplantation. We note that given the historical record of countries 'queuing at its doors', and especially the perceived success of its latest enlargement, the EU has often taken its magnetism for granted and has viewed itself as naturally ahead of other actors in the field.[9]

Yet, we argue that despite the theoretical projection of the *acquis* as the 'right' legal template for development, the EU may in fact be in a position that is more difficult than that of other international actors acting as law donors. In justifying this we draw on the lessons of the law and development literature in emphasising the critical role of the way in which exports takes place rather than the right supply *per se*.

In many respects, the EU's neighbourhood policy has shown significant learning from its history of external engagement particularly with the new Member States.[10] It has also learned from some of the lessons of global legal reform in the 1990s.[11] Nevertheless, the experience in legal assistance shows that the demand for law generally, but especially in post-Soviet countries, is a complex phenomenon that does not respond well to top-down approaches and requires flexible strategies for adaptation of foreign legal templates to local conditions. Thus, the EU regulatory model as exported through the ENP and the Eastern Partnership exhibits important deficiencies in its potential for becoming a 'living law' in the neighbouring countries. As a result, so far the EU has remained limited in its ability to export its corpus of law in a way that would sufficiently maximise its receptivity. Despite some expected gains in coherence in EU's external action resulting from the Lisbon Treaty, the essential contradictions and tensions

---

[5] Barbé et al. 2009.

[6] Sasse 2008; Lavenex 2009.

[7] See also the examination of the export of the EU's values by Broberg (this volume).

[8] In the accession context, 'EU demands for pre-accession legal and institutional alignment—however onerous, one-sided and asymmetrical they may be—are legitimized by the prospect of full inclusion and the promise of future equality of participation.' Magen 2006, 422.

[9] Dodini and Fantini 2006, 507; Herdina 2007; Magen 2006, 398.

[10] Kelley 2006; Magen 2006; Sasse 2008.

[11] Escribano 2006.

underlying the EU's macro-policy towards its Eastern neighbours will persist. However, bearing in mind the existing mismatch between the EU law export formula and the demand for law in the Eastern neighbourhood, the institutional 'streamlining' resulting from the Lisbon Treaty, especially through the European External Action Service (EEAS), could help deliver some context-specific solutions, thereby facilitating the import of EU law.

11.2 Law Export in a Comparative Perspective

There is a long tradition of global promotion of legal reform and legal transplantation for the purposes of economic development.[12] This process includes a boom in legal assistance by various international actors in supporting large-scale political and economic reform in Eastern Europe as of the 1990s.[13] In this section we summarise some of the main findings of the critical law and development literature developed in analysing this experience with the aim to provide a background against which the EU law export to the Eastern neighbourhood can be discussed.

One of the *first* lessons identified in the literature relates to what with a hindsight is a plain realisation that 'law is not a kitchen appliance that we can unplug in the United States or Germany and simply plug in again in Russia'[14] and that introducing the 'right' laws as such will be sufficient to create incentives for the 'right' behaviour in developing and transition countries. In essence, the process of borrowing the 'right laws' is not a new phenomenon. As it has been pointed out, home-grown legal innovation is the rarity, with most legal change taking place on the basis of legal borrowing.[15] Yet, Western templates have often been used as a non-negotiable recipe book with insufficient adaptation to local conditions or needs. The 'old' law and development movement assumed the wide applicability of the Western model of 'legal liberalism' and its validity as a path to modernity, the possibility to introduce it through top-down approaches and the very use of formal law as a tool for social engineering.[16] More recent efforts have been in the

[12] A strong impetus to this phenomenon was given by the so called 'old' law and development movement in the 1960–1970s, where USAID and private US-based foundations and academics advocated the export Western legal templates in an effort to induce economic development. The early 1990s witnessed the revival of the efforts to promote development through law, primarily through the efforts of international organisations, like the World Bank and the IMF, as well as individual country's development agencies. The 'new' law and development took place in a very different historical context and with very different theoretical underpinnings. See Tamanaha 1995; Trubek 2006.

[13] Ajani 1995; deLisle 1999; Smits 2003.

[14] Holmes 1999, 71.

[15] Sacco 1991.

[16] Trubek and Galanter 1974.

direction of promoting general rule of law and quality of governance as concepts of formal rather than substantive legality. Nevertheless, key law and development entrepreneurs also promoted substantive notions about what are the 'right' laws to be adopted to stimulate development.[17]

At the same time, legal reforms were predominantly donor-driven. The inclusion of the legal reform requirement into an existing policy framework centred around the traditional instruments used by international financial institutions, such as lending conditionality, boosted the image of legal reform as a donor-driven, top-down process, where 'compliance' with donor norms has become virtually synonymous with 'success' in legal reform. Accordingly, a range of ratings and monitoring mechanisms were developed to reflect progress in compliance with internationally formulated norms and best practice. As it has been argued elsewhere, this 'compliance' paradigm was particularly strong with respect to post-communist countries that embarked on large-scale legal reform in the early 1990s.[18] Far from avoiding the problems associated with the 'old' law and development movement, the 1990s saw the spread of the 'hasty transplant-syndrome' synonymous within top-down transplantation and donor-driven legislative agendas.[19] These problems were exacerbated by the context of 'campaign reform' where the timing of output matched project and financial facility constraints, rather than local needs or conditions.

This links closely to the *second* key lesson that we want to emphasise—the pivotal role of adaptation and demand. This lesson relates to the problem of insufficient adaptation to local conditions and appreciation of the differences in, or indeed the lack of, demand for law.[20] As Wade Channell put it,

> [T]he crux of the problem is not the origin of the law per se. [...] Rather it lies in the pursuit of law reform processes that generally do not permit users to participate in adapting the draft—whatever its origin—to local conditions. [...] Lack of local input, not transplantation, is the problem.[21]

The critique of this 'new' law and development particularly in Central and Eastern Europe was abundant in pointing out the technical deficiencies in carrying out legal reform abroad as well as the importance of the social context of legal institutions in view of their deep embeddedness. The need to engage with 'deep' institutions was pointed out referring not just to the 'structural' elements of law but also 'the patterns of repetitive behaviours that law can help change and create'.[22] There was also the realisation of the bigger problem of mismatch between the domestic demand for law, and attitudes to law and formal legality more generally, and the supply of foreign models.[23] This problem relates not only to the legal

[17] Santos 2006.

[18] Hendley 1999; Dragneva 2007.

[19] Hendley 1999; Holmes 1999, 71; Channell 2006.

[20] Hendley 1999.

[21] Channell 2006, 140.

[22] Seidman and Seidman 1996; Dahan and Dine 2003.

[23] Hendley 1999.

nihilism characterising Soviet societies, but also to the preference of business elites for personal-based rather than rule-based approaches to protecting their rights.[24] As the study of company law reform in Ukraine shows, for example, vested interests which were successful in capturing the state saw no particular benefit in formal legal reform and reception of international norms while they were able to protect their interests successfully through extra-legal means.[25] This aspect of the problematic demand for law links to the deeper scepticism expressed by some about the usefulness of formal law as an instrument for social change more generally.[26] Certainly, in Eastern Europe there have been many examples where informal social norms operate not just in parallel but also instead of and contrary to formal laws.[27]

In this sense, the challenges to legal assistance are many and pose difficult questions. Responding to some of those, scholars sought to redefine the role of foreign legal consultants in terms of identifying needs, understanding the function of legal reform in the context of the policy and economic aim which is to be achieved, and examining the legal problem in its institutional context in order to make sure that the regulations proposed are workable.[28]

The experience of the 'new' law and development movement served also to reawaken an old discussion about the preconditions for transplant effectiveness more generally. Most scholars tend to associate 'success' with some form of adaptation and internalisation of the legal transplant that results in it 'taking hold' in the recipient country. Berkowitz et al., in particular, argued that how a law is transplanted is a more reliable predictor of its viability than whether it is the 'right' law in terms of its legal origin. What matters for law to be effective, the authors argued, was

> [F]irst, …it must be meaningful in the context in which it is applied so citizens have the incentive to use the law and to demand institutions that work to enforce and develop the law. Second, the judges, lawyers, politicians, and other legal intermediaries that are responsible for developing the law must be able to increase the quality of law in a way that is responsive to demand for legality.[29]

Based on a study of 49 countries, they conclude that transplants can be described as receptive transplants when they are adapted to local conditions or that the population already had familiarity with basic legal principles of the transplanted law. Thus, for them, adaptation and previous familiarity are key determinants for legality.

---

24 Aslund 1999.

25 Dragneva and Dimitrova 2010.

26 Davis and Trebilcock 2009.

27 Pistor 1999.

28 Markovits 2004.

29 Berkowitz et al. 2003, 167.

Kahn-Freund, a leading comparativist, made a similar emphasis on the importance of 'adaptation' rather than 'adoption' arguing that without it 'any attempt to use a pattern of law outside the environment of its origin continues to entail risk of rejection'.[30] For him, this risk materialises when the 'legalistic spirit' ignores the social and above all, the political context of the law. The key 'organic' element in law relates precisely to that political context and to '... all that concerns the organisation of law-making and decision-making power and the relation between self-governing social groups and the official apparatus of the state'.[31]

Related to the above is the *third* lesson we point to, namely that legal reform has a complex political economy behind it both on the demand and supply side, something that is often ignored when 'compliance' is presented as a technical issue. The importance of the political context as an obstacle or a channel to rule of law reform, in particular, is underlined by Daniels and Trebilcock.[32] For them, political economy-based considerations, synonymous with either the lack of effective demand for reform or vested supply-side interests, become more important impediments to transplants than other obstacles, such as technical and resource-oriented difficulties, or social, cultural and historical factors that create an inhospitable environment. The policy lesson, for the authors, is that 'despite understandable efforts especially by external donors to depoliticize rule of law reform' what is required is a 'central engagement with the politics of rule of law reform in these contexts and the development of strategies to change the political dynamics surrounding particular rule of law initiatives'.[33] This is particularly relevant to the ENP policy framework, with its focus on low-politics, developmental agenda, without altering political dynamics, stakes and time-horizons in the partner countries.[34]

A *fourth* lesson relates to the simplification of the expected outcome of law transplants in terms of 'compliance'.[35] Donors have often relied on binary terms, referring to 'compliance' or 'non-compliance'. At best, they provide intermediary categories, such as 'low' or 'medium'. Yet, these categories represent little more than nominal simplifications which remain short of capturing the reality of resulting legal change. Legal reform in practice is manifested in infinite degrees of rule changes, some of which are examples of fine-tuning or 'pro-transplant adaptation', yet others cross-over into distortion of the original rule.[36] As Peerenboom has pointed out,

30 Kahn-Freund 1974, 27.

31 Kahn-Freund 1974, 4.

32 Daniels and Trebilcock 2004–2005.

33 Daniels and Trebilcock 2004–2005, 109–110.

34 Jacoby 2006; Wolczuk 2009; Langbein and Wolczuk 2011.

35 Peerenboom 2006.

36 Cohn 2010.

> rather than being passive recipients, legal actors in the targeted state actively choose elements and reject others, interpret terms consistent with local perceptions and understandings, and modify or rework institutions, rules or practices in light of domestic circumstances.[37]

International policy practice, including that of the EU, however, rarely offers a clear picture of the degree of change that leads to convergence or uses such a picture consistently in measuring the effects of legal reform.[38]

The critique of the 'new' law and development movement is not theoretically coherent or, indeed, united by common motives. Yet, there is a growing consensus that there is a need for a more nuanced analysis of the process, redefined in terms of 'transposition', 'transformation', 'tuning' or 'adaptation' rather than a linear, unidirectional, top-down 'transplantation'.[39] It is possible to observe that this has led to important policy changes in the activities of global actors, such as the World Bank in incorporating some lessons. One of the key themes has been about the recognition of the key importance of demand and ownership of legal reform and the rejection of uniform approaches. In the preface to the report of the World Bank, 'Economic Growth in the 1990s: Learning from a Decade of Reform', the vice-president Gobind Nankani who oversaw the project defined one of the key lessons as '... there is no unique universal set of rules.... [W]e need to get away from formulae and the search for elusive "best practices"...'.[40] Another vice-president, Roberto Dañino, elaborated that,

> The Bank recognises the importance of each country's own initiative and leadership in the area of legal reform, not only as a matter of sovereign prerogative but also to support a deliberative legislative process which involves the reasoned balancing of competing interests and sometimes of legal traditions. ... We certainly do not propose the "transplant" theory of legal and judicial reform, in which the developed world arrives at the doorstep of the Ministry of Justice of a developing country with a "one-size fits all model" and a pre-wrapped set of laws and institutions for the national Parliament to rubber stamp and enact. ... Efforts in the area of law reform must be led by the countries themselves, and must have broad societal consensus to be sustained.[41]

Despite these signs of rethinking dominant paradigms in the direction of emphasising demand, certainly there remains the sceptic warning that the World Bank is a complex bureaucratic organisation that does not necessarily speak with one voice,[42] but also that not all international institutions have been equally open to those messages.[43] While there are clear signs that the EU has sought to

[37] Peerenboom 2006, 827.
[38] Taylor 2007.
[39] Orucu 2002.
[40] World Bank 2005, xiii.
[41] Dañino 2004.
[42] Santos 2006.
[43] Rodrik 2006.

incorporate many of the lessons of exporting legal reform in the 1990s,[44] the question remains as to whether in its policy towards the neighbours the EU has moved from a paradigm based on compliance with EU law to one where 'demand for law' and political economy of legal reforms are sufficiently factored in.

11.3 The ENP Law Export Formula

After a rather inconspicuous start to the EU's engagement in legal reforms in the post-Soviet region, the launch of the European Neighbourhood Policy (ENP) in 2004 offered a marked step up in engagement. However, EU's law export as promoted within the framework of the neighbourhood policy has been characterised by a number of particular features that are difficult to reconcile with the need for sufficient adaptation to foster receptivity.

As with other international actors, in the early 1990s, in reaction to political changes in the former Soviet Union, the EU sought ways to engage in legal and developmental assistance. An early report, in fact, sought to provide a comprehensive blueprint for systemic legal reform to aid the transition to a market economy, yet it was not taken forward at the level of the EU.[45] The main instrument through which the EU engaged in the area was the Partnership and Cooperation Agreements (PCA) offering progressive trade liberalisation and political and economic cooperation.[46] Importantly, the PCAs include legislative approximation to EU law as an important precondition for achieving the objectives of the agreement. The normative standard for approximation was defined very generally, referring to:

> laws and regulations governing investments by companies, customs law, company law, banking law, company accounts and taxes, intellectual property, protection of workers at the workplace, financial services, rules on competition, public procurement, protection of health and life of humans, animals and plants, the environment, consumer protection, indirect taxation, technical rules and standards, nuclear laws and regulations and transport.[47]

Despite being described as 'priority areas', which appears to narrow the scope of the task, this remains a very broad legislative agenda by any standards. Nonetheless, the justification for this was functional to the purposes of the agreement and its undertaking was left to the voluntary actions and discretion of the partners. The legislative approximation clause was largely identical to that contained in the Association Agreements with the Central and East European

---

[44] Escribano 2006.

[45] EC/IS (Independent States) 1993.

[46] Hillion 2005.

[47] See, for example the EU-Ukraine PCA, Article 51.2, Official Journal L 049, 19/02/1998, p. 0001–0002.

countries but was embedded in a 'softer' framework of institutions and disciplines. It contained elements of political and economic conditionality, yet ones virtually impractical to activate,[48] and lacked the promise of EU membership. The EU set up facilities to help countries undertake this legislative approximation through TACIS and other technical assistance vehicles, and relied primarily on socialisation mechanisms in stimulating partner governments to adopt EU rules.

The context, however, changed significantly for the EU in the aftermath of the eastern enlargement. As has been widely analysed, the EU initiated the European Neighbourhood Policy (ENP), driven by the desire to ensure 'prosperity, security and stability' in its new neighbourhood, build on its successful experience of projecting its 'transformative power' through exporting its regulatory model, yet abstain from extending its borders and key institutions.[49] The policy seeks to respond to the membership aspirations of some neighbouring states by deflecting them by offering 'access to the internal market' and thereby minimising the internal adjustment effects for the EU. Hence, the Action Plans with the individual ENP partner countries concluded in the period 2004–2007 refer to a 'new partnership perspective', characterised by a 'stake in the EU's internal market', the possibility 'to participate progressively in key aspects of EU's policies and programmes' and an upgraded political dialogue and enhanced people-to-people contacts.

In this sense, the main justification for the extension of EU law, especially in the area of the internal market, is a *functional* one related to the level of economic relations proposed with the ENP partners. Despite its 'fuzzy' content, it has been clear that 'a stake in the internal market' (and, indeed, anything more ambitious than a preferential trade agreement), 'would require progressive convergence with internal market rules, coupled with stepped-up consultation and co-operation, as well as adaptation of institutional practices to EU standards'.[50] The ENP relies on the appeal of economic benefits, which accrue from access to the EU market, which pre-supposes adopting relevant parts of the *acquis*. This includes institutional harmonisation in the economic sphere, which is wide in scope and encompasses all major horizontal policy areas, although the degree of harmonisation differs across different policy areas, being the highest for industrial products, sanitary and phyto-sanitary standards and competition policy.[51]

However, it is clear that while flying on the 'wings' of its enlargement success, the EU goes beyond this immediate functional justification in emphasising the broad developmental benefits in transferring EU rules. The beneficial effects of rule transfer are not limited to increased trade but include further investment, enhanced competition and reduced corruption, which lead to better governance, higher economic efficiency, growth and welfare in partner countries. The process

[48] Hillion 2005.

[49] Batt et al. 2003; Gould 2004.

[50] Dodini and Fantini 2006, 511.

[51] ENEPO (EU Eastern Neighbourhood: Economic Potential and Future Development) 2007.

of alignment with the regulatory mechanisms as developed in the EU are expected to transform the public policies of the neighbouring states, resulting in growth, stability and prosperity. Alignment will lead to increased credibility of reforms and certainty in the economy owing to the improved domestic institutions and the system of economic governance.[52] According to Commission officials, the EU model is superior to that of other international actors in terms of the quality and density of its regulation, the comprehensiveness of reform it entails and the degree to which it avoids controversies surrounding the activities of some international institutions.[53] In their view, the EU regulatory environment is superior to those of the neighbourhood countries and 'adopting the EU acquis, irrespective of any imperfections, would still represent and improvement over the *status quo*'.[54] Indeed, one of the main 'selling points' has been the fact the EU *acquis* represents a ready-made corpus of rules which will be difficult to develop in the absence of effective domestic policy-making and legislative process.[55] From the EU perspective, the neighbours face a choice of either adopting EU *acquis* or developing a regulatory framework from scratch.[56] In that respect, the EU has often viewed the countries of the former Soviet countries as 'empty vessels' for the export of the *acquis* without sufficient attention to existing legal frameworks and/or political economy considerations behind *the status quo*.[57] This view is shared by many European Studies scholars. For example, the external governance approach with its focus on the projection of EU's 'systems of rule' in external relations, implies that the more precise, binding and enforceable EU rules are, the more likely it is that they will be transplanted by bringing about a more hierarchical mode of interaction.[58] Thus, the EU law is seen within the Union as offering an appropriate and modern template for socio-economic modernisation of third countries, regardless of the pre-existing conditions and related costs of alignment.

While the ENP aims to boost the implementation objectives of the PCAs, particularly in relation to legislative approximation, it also modifies the context for it. Firstly, the EU is keen to be seen as departing from the top-down approach to adopting the *acquis* followed in the Eastern enlargement. It seeks to strengthen the voluntary aspect of legal borrowing and move towards the 'partnership' paradigm, where the centre stage is given to countries' own preferences and priorities in defining rule transfer rather than the EU imposing them. As the ENP Strategy Paper puts it:

---

52 Kolesnichenko 2009.

53 Dodini and Fantini 2006, 517.

54 Dodini and Fantini 2006, 513.

55 Herdina 2007.

56 Dodini and Fantini 2006, 517.

57 Popescu and Wilson 2009, 98.

58 Lavenex and Schimmelfennig 2009, 794, 802.

> Joint ownership of the process, based on the awareness of shared values and common interests, is essential. The EU does not seek to impose priorities or conditions on its partners. The Action Plans depend, for their success, on the clear recognition of mutual interests in addressing a set of priority issues. There can be no question of asking partners to accept a pre-determined set of priorities.[59]

In that sense, the ENP documents, including Action Plans, emphasise *selectivity* in the introduction of EU rules. As the Commission official Andreas Herdina put it, 'the ENP does not seek to 'export' the *acquis* wholesale. This would be unwise, unrealistic and—in some aspects—unaffordable'.[60] He notes further that the outcome expected is close to full compliance only in some sectors, such as those related to market access, whereas for most sectors it is a matter of 'realistic levels (often much) below alignment with the *acquis*'.[61]

At the same time, however, selectivity is promoted without specificity. The EU eschews providing specific legal templates in its key documents governing bilateral relations. Given the emphasis on reform rather than on legal approximation as such, the language of the Action Plans changes: it departs from the usage of the term *acquis* altogether (which featured prominently in early ENP strategy documents) and refers to 'EU norms and standards'.[62] Yet, one consequence of this is that the Action Plans provide a very sketchy and vague legal template.[63] Even in internal market-related areas, the language is rarely specific: sometimes a reference is made to 'EU norms', or 'international and EU standards', and sometimes to a broad area of law. Thus, the ENP legal template incorporates broad international norms, which may be viewed as conducive to a wider choice for recipient countries. This, however, adds to the fuzziness of the agenda for legal reform. Some of what is termed 'international norms' can indeed be defined clearly and is a matter of 'hard' law (e.g., WTO legislation or Anti-corruption conventions). Other norms, such as the OECD Principles of Corporate Governance, are 'soft' law representing best practice. Given their wide acceptance, their promotion by the EU can be viewed positively. Yet, important concerns have been raised with regard to suitability of international standards and codes to be a template for development-oriented legal reform.[64] Moreover, 'international norms' are sometimes a proxy for the strong views of academics involved in legal reform consultancy or rules promoted by country's agencies, and which are not necessarily free from con-

[59] Commission Communication 2004 ENP Strategy Paper, Brussels, 12.5.2004 COM (2004) 373 final.

[60] Herdina 2007, 502.

[61] Herdina 2007, 502.

[62] Magen 2006, 422.

[63] Noutcheva and Emerson loc. cit. no. 3.

[64] Pistor 2000.

troversy or self-interest.[65] Finally, 'international' and EU norms are not necessarily in agreement with each other. In this sense, Eastern neighbours are presented with an often misleading picture of unproblematic law export and convergence higher that is possible or, in fact, desirable.[66]

Despite the positive view one can take on this low specificity and high selectivity of the legal template,[67] it carries important disadvantages.[68] These disadvantages are not just in terms of the low 'compliance-pull' it leads to, but also wider problems of lack of clarity in the rules supplied, resulting in, first, the need for institutions for its subsequent specification, second, the danger of discretionary interpretation—both by the EU and the partners, and, third, lack of clear benchmark for evaluating the progress in implementing a task. In fact, one may ask whether the flexibility of the approach actually conceals the 'problem of knowledge' experienced by global actors in legal reform promotion. As Carothers argues,

> understanding how law functions in a society, the roles it plays, and how it can change is extremely difficult, especially in societies that are not well understood by aid providers from many points of view (…). Grasping the problem of the shortcomings of law throughout the developing and post-communist worlds is an enormous intellectual and practical challenge.[69]

In the case of the ENP, the 'problem of knowledge' is combined with the uncertainty about the implications of access to the internal market for the eastern neighbours and the Union itself. As Dodini and Fantini acknowledge, 'there is as yet no 'theory' prescribing firmly what elements of internal market legislation are essential in its functioning, both from the perspective of new participants and existing ones … The decision on what parts of the *acquis* should be taken on board by the neighbour countries will be the result of negotiations'.[70] There has been no ENP/neighbourhood equivalent of the 1995 'White Paper on the Preparation of the Associated Countries of Central and Eastern Europe for Integration into the Internal Market of the Union', which would spell out the scope and sequence of

---

[65] A good example of such a controversy is provided by cumulative voting for company directors, which was strongly recommended by influential legal reform advisors, such as Professor Bernard Black, in an effort to improve corporate governance (minority shareholder protection, in particular). Yet, its effectiveness has been challenged both as a matter of policy and academic analysis, see Maassen and Dragneva 2007.

[66] The area of company law and corporate governance provides a good example of an area where there has been an active debate on global convergence, with strong views taken in extremes. Furthermore, the necessary level of company law harmonisation within the EU itself has also been subject to extensive debate.

[67] For example, as Noutcheva and Emerson argue: 'Partners are not in a position to determined the EU regulatory rules but they have more freedom to negotiate the import of a sub-set of those rules only. In this sense they are better placed than the accession candidates to define the limits of external influence on their domestic governance structures'. Noutcheva and Emerson 2005, 93.

[68] Magen 2006, 422.

[69] Carothers 2006, 23.

[70] Dodini and Fantini 2006, 511.

integrating the ENP partners into the single market. Thus Dodini and Fantini point to the two risks in getting it wrong—over-regulation or 'hollowing out the internal market'—for partner countries and the EU, respectively.[71]

The risk of over-regulation is particularly important for the Eastern neighbours not just because of the general concerns expressed already, but also because despite its numerous advantages EU law has not been developed as a template for modernisation of non-members as such. The suitability of the common market *acquis* as a template for post-communist reforms was already questioned during enlargement.[72] As Grabbe has pointed out, the EU rules were never designed as a development agenda for poorer countries; instead they are the incremental results of negotiations, agreements and compromises between Member States on common rules for themselves over decades of European integration.[73]

The 'problem of knowledge', as shown in the discussion of the global law and development efforts, is certainly not unique to the EU. It has affected many other law donors such as the World Bank, the IMF and the United States, amongst others. However, the EU seems to have put itself in a more disadvantageous position by reliance on many of the institutional templates of the enlargement policy. Certainly, in the practical realisation of the ENP, the wholesale version of the *acquis,* rather than a bilaterally negotiated or a partner-defined list, remains a reference point in technical assistance and in the evaluation of the progress made. This is not least because of the absence of explicit benchmarks against which progress in the ENP countries can be evaluated by those implementing the ENP 'on the ground'. It can be seen, for example, that the Ukrainian-European Policy and Legal Advice Centre (UEPLAC) report on draft Ukrainian company legislation[74] continues interpreting the scope of EU law in the terms of the 1995 White Paper on the Preparation of the Associated Countries of Central and Eastern Europe for Integration into the Internal Market of the Union, and refers to a maximal list of the company law *acquis* ignoring sometimes the differences in bindingness of actual provisions of the Directives for the Member States. Furthermore, the report clearly speaks a language of 'compliance' rather than acceptance of a voluntary definition of priorities and 'appropriateness' of reception. It chastises the drafters for not taking seriously the *acquis*, not taking advantage of EU's 'considerable experience' and more importantly, arrives at a strangely confident and disproportionately far-reaching conclusion regarding the established lack of compliance with EU law: '… the draft law does not seem in position to ensure mutual trust between Ukrainian enterprises and trading or investment partners. […] it cannot be considered therefore as a core building block

[71] Dodini and Fantini 2006, 511.

[72] Grabbe 2003.

[73] Grabbe 2003.

[74] Report prepared for UEPLAC on 'Making the draft Law on Joint Stock Companies more workable for enterprises and better aligned to international benchmark and EU legislation', J. Tallineau, June 2007.

of the market economy in Ukraine.' In that instance, strong views of experts substitute for the shared understanding between the EU and the partner countries about the underlying rationale of the law transposition.

As noted below, the ENP defines the goals of co-operation in the elusive terms of 'new partnership' and a 'stake in the internal market'. Despite the adjustments of the policy approach discussed above, however, the ENP continues to rely on many of the enlargement disciplines linked to a conditionality paradigm.[75] The reliance on the enlargement templates is evident in the explicit use of multiple and wide-ranging conditions as well as the use of policy instruments, such as Progress Reports, Technical Assistance and Information Exchange (TAIEX) instruments and Twinning.[76] Importantly for this chapter, progress in legal reform is to be a benchmark for evaluating the fulfilment of the Action Plans and ultimately, for the upgrade of the relationship. As the EU-Georgia Action Plan explicitly states, for example, '[T]he level of ambition of the relationship will depend on the degree of Georgia's commitment to common values as well as its capacity to implement jointly agreed priorities, in compliance with international and European norms and principles'. As been pointed out by various authors, the very principle of partnership sits uncomfortably with the use of top-down mechanism, such as monitoring, and in the context of profound asymmetry between the EU and its Eastern partners.[77] For example, during the 'negotiations' of the Action Plans, the European Commission endeavoured the 'non-negotiation strategy' with the neighbours, not least because of concern for safeguarding the fragile consensus within the Council and to ensure normative consistency.[78]

Notwithstanding the prevailing trust in the 'right supply', the emphasis on flexibility and selectivity is 'safer' for the EU as it absolves the Union from clear responsibility for 'getting it right', thereby lowering the costs and risks of EU external governance. Ultimately, however, this approach reflects two types of tensions: first, between the ENP as a macro-policy in external relations and sectoral policy-making (e.g., agriculture and labour movement) and, second, the continuous disagreement amongst the Member States on the ENP.[79] A combination of these tensions prevents the effective use of benefits of access to the internal market as an incentive for compliance.[80] Initially analysts of the ENP pointed to a lack of clarity on rewards offered partner countries and hence the preliminary nature of their analyses.[81] Almost a decade since the launch of the ENP,

---

[75] Kelley 2006; Cremona and Hillion 2006; Magen 2006, 422.

[76] Modelling of the ENP on enlargement was conditioned by the available human resources within the Commission, especially a need to re-deploy Commission officials who worked in eastern enlargement and time pressure under which the policy was devised, Kelley 2006.

[77] Sedelmeier 2007; Vachudova 2007.

[78] Wolczuk 2009, 189.

[79] The diverging aims behind the ENP for the EU Member States—as well as the EU institutions themselves—are explored in the contribution by Ghazaryan to this volume.

[80] Sedelmeier 2007, 203.

[81] Weber et al. 2007.

this persistent lack of clarity becomes its ubiquitous design feature, underscoring challenges of EU foreign policy-making when it spills into other aspect of policy-making within the Union. The very way in which the ENP straddles different paradigms ultimately reflects the fact that relations with the post-Soviet neighbours are affected by differentiation, regionalisation and competing interests of particular EU Member States to an extent much greater than within relations with other regions.[82] Nevertheless, the flipside of the resulting 'low-risk and low-cost' nature of the ENP is the weakened credibility and effectiveness of the EU as a law exporter.[83]

In the ENP, voluntary aspects of legal reception in the ENP are compromised by the asymmetry of the relations between EU and the neighbours and intertwining of conditionality and partnership paradigms. There remain top-down elements particularly regarding the internal market *acquis*, but the lack of bright lines in delineating its scope and necessary depth, allow for the practical application of wide, enlargement-like interpretations, as argued above. More importantly, the ENP law export approach may be viewed as difficult to reconcile with the need for adaptation to foster demand for law. Ultimately, as Magen points out, the *acquis* is an instrument whose scope, trajectory and interpretation remain exclusively in … [EU's] hands'.[84] Given the presence of conditionality and unclear standards for evaluation of convergence, adaptation may be regarded as 'lack of compliance'.

At the same time, watering down of conditionality relative to the eastern enlargement is evident in the very few details provided in the Action Plans on benchmarks, timings and follow-up arrangements.[85] The problem of the clarity of the standard for evaluation or the 'margin of deviation' from it has been mentioned already. There is also lack of clarity of the *finalité* of this 'relationship', which has proved to be something of a 'moving target'. It evolved from the 'extension of the four freedoms' in 2003 to a 'stake in the internal market' in 2004 via 'improved access to goods and services among ENP partners' in 2006. The Eastern Partnership, in turn, offers 'further economic integration centred on the creation of a deep and comprehensive Free Trade Area'.[86] As of 2011 the relationship is defined in terms of 'closer economic integration and stronger political co-operation'.[87] The lack of clarity on the *finalité* reflects a continuous disagreement amongst the Member States as to the extent to which the EU could and should become a driver

---

[82] Cichocki 2010.

[83] See, for example, on Ukraine's disillusionment with the EU in general and the ENP in particular see Granovsky and Nanivska 2010.

[84] Magen 2007, 387.

[85] Sasse 2008; Wolczuk 2009.

[86] European Council (2009) Declaration on the Eastern Partnership (Annex to the EU Presidency Conclusions), European Council summit, 19–20 March.

[87] Joint Communication from the High Representative of the Union for Foreign Affairs and Security Policy and the European Commission to the European Parliament, the Council, the European Economic and Social Committee and the Committee of the Regions: A New Response to a Changing Neighbourhood, 25.05.2011, Com (2011) 303.

for reforms in general and offer attractive (and thus potentially costly for the Union and its Member States) incentives in particular. The *finalité,* however, ultimately dictates the functional rationale for the export of EU law. This is because the nature and scope of the *acquis* to be transposed into the countries' legal systems is dependent on the intended level of integration between the EU and non-Member States.

11.4 The ENP Law Export Formula and the Lisbon Treaty

The impact of the Lisbon Treaty on the conduct of EU external relations has been analysed extensively in this volume and elsewhere. Therefore, this penultimate section will focus only on the three selected but interrelated aspects, which merit attention in the light of the preceding discussion: the *finalité* of the ENP, the institutional configuration in external relations and the role of the European External Action Service (EEAS).

As noted above, while in its design the ENP relies on the enlargement templates; its fuzzy *finalité* reflects divergent preferences of EU actors since the inception of the ENP. Relations with the post-Soviet states, including Russia, are affected by differentiation, regionalisation and competing interests of particular EU Member States to an extent much greater than within relations with other regions.[88] The very way in which the ENP straddles different paradigms reflects the endeavours to compensate for a clear *finalité* but remain something, which EU institutions, especially the Commission, have been unable to mitigate for. The overarching aim of the ENP vis-à-vis the Eastern neighbours—whether a temporary 'holding position' or a permanent alternative—remains a matter of contestation between the Member States. The way that the ENP is anchored in the Lisbon Treaty—both with regard to the content of a relevant article and its place in TEU—codifies and institutionalises this ambiguity. Article 7a of TEU refers to 'special relationship' between the EU and its neighbours, thereby feeding diverse interpretations as to the meaning of the special or privileged relations, stopping short of candidate status.[89] Equally intriguing is the place of the article on the ENP in the system of TEU: it is located in 'General Provisions' rather than listed with other provisions on external action (e.g., 'General Provisions on the Union's External Action and Specific Provisions on the Common Foreign and Security Policy'). While the Union is under obligation to develop a 'special relationship' with neighbouring states, the article is vague on the instruments, while its position generates diverse interpretations on the overarching objectives of the neighbourhood policy, especially when compared to enlargement.

In institutional terms, the Lisbon Treaty does not clarify where leadership of the ENP resides. This is because the institutional configuration for delivering the ENP

---

88 Cichocki 2010.

89 Bechev and Nicolaïdis 2010.

shares the same characteristics as other external action, such as double-hatting and shared competences, which other contributors to this volume have explored. Moreover, like the CFSP, the ENP appears ring-fenced from other areas of European integration process. In that respect, external action remains more subservient to the will of the Member States than the 'supranational' institutions.[90] With the Member States retaining their control over the policy objectives and design, a lack of consensus on the *finalité* results in adaptation rather than innovation (as evidenced by the 2011 review of the ENP[91]). Adaptation of the ENP (through extensive use of 'soft law') means that the widely noted design inconsistencies of the macro-policy are unlikely to be addressed. In particular, the existing institutional set up does not provide effective mechanisms to eradicate persistent gaps between macro-level of external policies and (intra-EU) sectoral policy-making, notwithstanding the requirement of increased coherence of policy outputs stipulated in Article 21 TEU.

However, in our view, the potentially most significant reform to the conduct of the ENP is the creation of the EEAS. Combining the weight of the Council with the international experience and technical expertise of the Commission through personnel and competencies, the formation of the EEAS carries a promise of a greater coherence and enhanced coordination within the constraints of the existing consensus amongst the Member States. This is because the delegations in partner countries could be more visible and foster a stronger political and dip-lomatic role than prior to the Lisbon Treaty. At the same time, the EEAS in general and the delegations in particular will have more underlying policy durability than any Member States. They will be better positioned not only to develop stronger 'local knowledge' but also to feed this knowledge into decision-making processes within the EU (e.g. financial programming).

Through greater visibility and the combination of a political role with technical expertise, the delegations could be more effective in engaging with domestic actors and responding to domestic demands. As noted above, the precondition for successful transplants is a deep understanding of the essence of the imported rules in their living context beyond what technical assistance can do in representing them. The EEAS will help to foster 'local knowledge' by overcoming the high turnover among delegations' contract staff. This high turn-over of staff made it difficult to build up the required expertise, caused a loss of institutional memory and reduced the efficiency of operations.

Overcoming these limitations would enable the EEAS to tailor supply of reform templates and assistance to domestic demand, and indeed generate and diversify this demand.[92] In practice this means working out selective and pragmatic

[90] Ghazaryan, in this volume, reaches the same conclusion in view of the Council's attempt to dominate the agenda of the ENP. But see also Blockmans and Laaksit (this volume) who investigate the future impact on external policies, including the ENP, of the composition of the EEAS by staff drawn from the EU institutions and national diplomatic services.

[91] Joint Communication (2011).

[92] See Langbein and Wolczuk 2011.

solutions reflecting domestic demand and capacity in the context of bilateral relations. At present, domestic actors in eastern neighbourhood often lack an understanding of what needs to be transferred and how and why. In the case of Ukraine, for example, the implementation of the Action Plan was hampered by the lack of clarity as to the ultimate aims of the rule transfer into national legislation.[93] The EEAS could pursue more effectively 'managerialist concepts of collaborative, technocratic problem-solving, transfer of know-how, thereby creating reform-oriented epistemic communities in partner countries',[94] partially compensating for inconsistencies and tensions at the macro-level of the ENP.

The need to engage with wide-ranging domestic actors is especially pertinent in the post-Soviet context in view of the elusive demand of law emanating from the governmental level. It is often presumed that the EU is already demand-driven in its Eastern policy in the sense of its application of the partnership principle, the enhanced selectivity of its normative template and the mitigation of conditionality. Indeed, at present the very formal, government-led participation in the ENP tends to be equated with the demand for law.[95] While engaging the governments in partner countries, the Commission has often been submerged in details relating to particular policies and what has been lacking so far is the comprehensive re-evaluation of the implementation ENP in light of the receptivity problems in the Eastern neighbourhood.

While the creation of the EEAS may help to develop pragmatic policy guidance on the direction of bilateral relations between the EU and Eastern partners,[96] there are clear limits to the EEAS's ability to deal with persistent gaps between macro-external and (intra-EU) sectoral policy. Issues of agriculture, trade and freedom, security and justice (AFSJ)—of vital interest for Eastern neighbours—are not within the EEEA's remit but that of the Commission. Thus there is a high risk of friction and rivalry between the EEAS and the Commission becoming a permanent feature of inter-institutional interactions. This would have a particularly damaging effect on the implementation of the ENP, given that the policy is closely related to policies such as trade, energy, agriculture and environment. Nevertheless, the organisational structure and policy objectives of the EEAS offer a chance to promote the coordination of Union and Member States actors engaged in the Eastern neighbourhood though, as Blockmans and Laatsit (in this volume) state, 'it would perhaps have been better to avoid the term "action" in naming the EEAS and call it the "European External Coordination Service" instead'. Some key relations already developed in an informal and efficient manner, namely between the High Representative and the Commissioner for Enlargement/Neighbourhood, something which will be essential in programming for the financial instruments. With informal relations imbued with flexibility, the EU would be better positioned

[93] Razumkov Centre 2008; Wolczuk 2009.

[94] Magen 2006, 424.

[95] Leigh 2007.

[96] Hillion 2010.

to move faster in changing circumstances. Therefore, while leaving many questions unanswered, the Lisbon Treaty can provide a framework for building up institutional commitment from the EU to bolster effectiveness of its law export formula within the framework of the ENP.

11.5 Conclusion

In engaging in this discussion, we do not seek to pretend that other international actors have succeeded in delivering effective responses to the lessons of years of law and development promotion. If anything, the review of the efforts in this direction reveal a pattern of repeated mistakes and ignorance of the findings of comparative law scholarship regarding the viability of legal transplants or, indeed, the critique of the Soviet system in relation to the societal role of law.

The EU has endeavoured, as noted, to incorporate third countries' preferences as one of the key determinants to receptivity to a much greater extent than it used to when exporting the *acquis* to the EFTA/EEA or accession countries. Nonetheless, the EU exhibits important disadvantages in its institutional ability to respond more fully to this challenge. According to Kelley, 'much as the EU has to offer its neighbouring states, the absence of the membership incentives for most countries should require significant adjustment, not just adaptation, of the enlargement strategy'.[97] While exporting law through the ENP, the EU faces a challenge of adapting its complex and dynamic corpus of rules to the needs of third countries, while being constrained by a lack of consensus on the *finalité* of relations and limited human and financial resources allocated to External Relations in general and the ENP in particular.

The ENP has been aptly described as 'a bureaucratic response to a political question'.[98] The political question is where the final borders of the EU should be drawn. Thus, from the very beginning ambiguities and tensions were built into the most wide-ranging, ambitious and sophisticated foreign policy ever launched by the EU. As Missiroli asserts, the ENP seems to suffer from being neither enlargement nor foreign policy proper: 'it cannot exercise conditionality as effectively as the former, nor does it bring to bear all the political tools and levers of the latter'.[99] This undermines EU law export in the Eastern neighbourhood, resulting in a paradox: the EU developed an extensive corpus of rules, the projection of which is an integral aspect of its external policy but has had limited ability to export its law in its vicinity unless operating in the context of enlargement.

---

97 Kelley 2006, 50.

98 Author's interview with the European Council official, March 2006.

99 Missiroli 2008, 5.

At the time of writing, a re-evaluation of the ENP is mediated by the evolving institutional configuration resulting from the adoption of the Lisbon Treaty. Given the intra-EU implications of devising a system of rewards for partner countries, the neighbourhood policy sits uneasily at the crossroads of internal and external policy-making. Even though the Lisbon Treaty laid institutional foundations for the EU's evolution into a more coherent foreign policy actor, the ENP exemplifies the *sui generis* nature of the EU external action. Even a greater degree of coherence in foreign policy decision-making resulting from the Lisbon Treaty will not obliterate the essential contradictions and tensions underlying the EU's policy towards its non-members. However, it may help to foster demand-driven, pragmatic law export formula more closely tailored to partners' capacities and needs, in line with international experience of legal transplants.

References

Ajani G (1995) By chance and prestige: legal transplants in Russia and Eastern Europe. American Journal of Comparative Law 43:93

Aslund A (1999) Law in Russia. East European Constitutional Review 8:96

Barbé E et al (2009) Drawing the neighbours closer … to what? explaining emerging patterns of policy convergence between the EU and its neighbours. Cooperation and Conflict 44:378–399

Batt J et al (2003) Partners and neighbours: a CFSP for a wider Europe. Chaillot Paper, No 64

Bechev D, Nicola K (2010) From policy to polity: can the EU's special relations with its 'neighbourhood' be decentred? Journal of Common Market Studies 48(3):475–500

Berkowitz D et al (2003) Economic development, legality and the transplant effect. European Economic Review 47:165

Carothers T (2006) The rule of law revival. In: Carothers T (ed) Promoting the rule of law abroad: in search of knowledge. Carnegie Endowment for International Peace, Washington

Channell W (2006) Lessons not learned about legal reform. In: Carothers T (ed) Promoting the rule of law abroad: in search of knowledge. Washington, Carnegie Endowment for International Peace

Cichocki M (2010) European Neighbourhood Policy or Neighbourhood Policie. In: Henderson K, Weaver C (eds) The Black Sea Region and EU policy: the challenge of divergent agendas. Ashgate, Aldershot, pp 9–27

Cohn M (2010) Legal transplant chronicles: the evolution of unreasonableness and proportionality review of the administration in the United Kingdom. American Journal of Comparative Law 58:583

Cremona M, Hillion C (2006) L'Union Fait la Force? potential and limitations of the European Neighbourhood Policy as an integrated EU foreign and security policy. EUI Working Papers, Law, 2006/39, European University Institute, Florence

Dahan F, Dine J (2003) Transplantation for transition—discussion on a concept around Russian reform of the law on reorganisation. Legal Studies 23:284

Daniels R, Trebilcock M (2004–2005) The political economy of rule of law reform in developing countries. Michigan Journal of International Law 26:99

Dañino R (2004) Speech, available at: siteresources.worldbank.org/INTLAWJUSTICE/214576-1139604306966/20818449/LJRWBParisBarAssociationConference111104.pdf. Last accessed 3 June 2011

Davis K, Trebilcock M (2009) The relationship between law and development: optimists versus sceptics. American Journal of Comparative Law 57:765

deLisle J (1999) Lex Americana?: United States' legal assistance, American legal models, and legal change in the post-communist world and beyond. University of Pennsylvania Journal of International Economic Law 20(2):179

Dodini M, Fantini M (2006) The EU Neighbourhood Policy: implications for economic growth and stability. Journal of Common Market Studies 44(3):507–532

Dragneva R (2007) CIS model legislation and its contributions to company law reform and harmonization. In: Dragneva R (ed) Investor protection in the CIS: legal reform and voluntary harmonization. Martinus Nijhoff, Leiden

Dragneva R, Dimitrova A (2010) The politics of demand for law: the case of Ukraine's company law reform. European Journal of Law Reform 12(3–4):147–168

EC/IS (Independent States) (1993) Joint task force on legal reform in the independent states, shaping a market-economy legal system. European Economy 2:29

ENEPO (EU Eastern Neighbourhood: Economic Potential and Future Development) (2007) Working Paper on concepts and definitions of institutional development (harmonisation) and methodology of measuring them, June

Escribano G (2006) Europeanisation without Europe? the Mediterranean and the Neighbourhood Policy. Robert Schuman Centre for Advanced Studies, European University Institute, EUI RSCAS Working Papers, No 2006/19

Gould T (2004) The European economic area: a model for the EU's Neighbourhood Policy? Ukraine's place in the wider Europe. Perspectives on European Politics and Societies 5(2):171–202

Grabbe H (2003) Europeanisation goes East: power and uncertainty in the EU accession process. In: Featherstone K, Radaelli C (eds) The politics of Europeanisation. Oxford University Press, Oxford, pp 303–323

Granovsky V, Nanivska V (2010) Eurointegration: resets, inside Ukraine, #11, Sept 2010

Gray C (1997) Reforming legal systems in developing and transition countries. Finance and Development 34:14–16

Hendley K (1999) Rewriting the rules of the game in Russia: the neglected issue of the demand for law. East European Constitutional Review 8:89

Herdina A (2007) Approximation of laws in the context of the European Neighbourhood Policy—a view from Brussels. European Journal of Law Reform 9(3):501

Hillion Ch (2005) The evolving system of the EU external relations as evidenced in the EU partnerships with Russia and Ukraine, PhD thesis, University of Leiden, Leiden

Hillion Ch (2010) The Post-Lisbon EU system of external relations: implications for EU-Ukraine relations. Wider Europe Working Papers 5/2010

Holmes S (1999) Can foreign aid promote the rule of law? East European Constitutional Review 8:68

Kahn-Freund O (1974) On uses and misuses of comparative law. Modern Law Review 37:1

Kelley J (2006) New wine in old wineskins: promoting political reforms through the new European Neighborhood Policy. Journal of Common Market Studies 44:29

Kolesnichenko A (2009) Institutional harmonization and its costs and benefits in the context of EU cooperation with its neighbours. An overview, CASE Network Studies and Analyses, Issue No 387

Langbein J, Wolczuk K (2011) Convergence without membership? the impact of the European Union in the neighbourhood: evidence from Ukraine. Journal of European Public Policy 1–19

Lavenex S (2009) A governance perspective on the European neighbourhood policy: integration beyond conditionality? Journal of European Public Policy 15(6):938–955

Lavenex S, Schimmelfennig F (2009) EU rules beyond EU borders: theorizing external governance in European politics. Journal of European Public Policy 16(6):791–812

Leigh M (2007) Making a success of the ENP: challenge and response. In: Weber K, Smith ME, Baun M (eds) Governing Europe's new neighbourhood: partners or periphery? Manchester University Press, Manchester, pp 209–217

Maassen G, Dragneva R (2007) Cumulative voting and Protection of minority Shareholders in the CIS. In: Dragneva R (ed) Investor protection in the CIS: legal reform and voluntary harmonization. Martinus Nijhoff, Leiden

Magen A (2005–2006) The shadow of enlargement: Can the European Neighbourhood Policy achieve compliance? (European Legal Studies Center, Columbia University, 2006) 12:383

Magen A (2007) Transformative engagement through law: the Acquis Communitaire as an instrument of EU external influence. The European Journal Law and Religion Reform 9(3): 361–392

Markovits I (2004) Exporting law reform——but will it travel? Cornell International Law Journal 37:95

Missiroli A (2008) The ENP five years on: looking backward——and forward, central.radiopod.gr/en/wp-content/uploads/2008/10/missiroli-the-enp-five-years-on.pdf. Last accessed 3 June 2011

Noutcheva G, Emerson M (2005) Extending the EU's norms of economic governance into the neighbourhood. CEPS Working Document No 233/December 2005

Orucu E (2002) Law as transposition. International and Comparative Law Quarterly 51:205

Peerenboom R (2006) What have we learned about law and development? Describing, predicting and assessing legal reforms in China. Michigan Journal of International Law 27:823

Pistor K (1999) Supply and demand for law in Russia. East European Constitutional Review 8:105

Pistor K (2000) The standardization of law and its effect on developing economies. G-24 Discussion Paper (June)

Popescu N, Wilson A (2009) The limits of enlargement-lite: European and Russian power in the troubled neighbourhood. European Council on Foreign Relations, London

Razumkov Centre (2008) Ukraina-EU: Vid Planu Diy Do Posylenoi Uhody [Ukraine-EU: From Action Plan to a New Agreement] Kyiv: Razumkov Centre

Rodrik D (2006) Goodbye Washington consensus, hallo Washington confusion? www.hks.harvard.edu/fs/drodrik/Research%20papers/Lessons%20of%20the%201990%20review%20_JEL_.pdf. Last accessed 3 June 2011

Sacco R (1991) Legal formants. American Journal of Comparative Law 39:397

Santos A (2006) The World Bank uses of the 'rule of law' in development assistance: past, present and future. In: Trubek D, Santos A (eds) The new law and economic development: a critical appraisal. Cambridge University Press, New York, p 74

Sasse G (2008) The European Neighbourhood Policy: conditionality revisited for the EU's Eastern neighbours. Europe-Asia Studies 60(2):295–316

Schimmelfennig F, Sedelmeier U (eds) (2005) The Europeanisation of Central and Eastern Europe. Cornell University Press, Ithaca

Sedelmeier U (2007) The European Neighbourhood Policy: a comment on theory and policy. In: Weber K, Smith ME, Baun M (eds) Governing Europe's new neighbourhood: partners or periphery? Manchester University Press, Manchester, pp 195–208

Seidman A, Seidman RB (1996) Drafting legislation for development: lessons from a Chinese project. American Journal of Comparative Law 44:1

Smits J (2003) Import and export of legal models: the Dutch experience. Transnational Law and Contemporary Problems 13:551

Tamanaha B (1995) The lessons of law and development studies. American Journal of International Law 89:470

Taylor V (2007) The law reform olympics: measuring the effects of law reform in transition economies. In: Lindsey T (ed) Law reform in developing and transitional states. Routledge, New York

Trubek D (2006) The rule of law in development assistance: past, present and future. In: Trubek D, Santos A (eds) The new law and economic development: a critical appraisal. Cambridge University Press, New York, p 74

Trubek D, Galanter M (1974) Scholars in self-estrangement: some reflections on the crisis in law and development studies in the United States. Wisconsin Law Review 4:1062

Vachudova M (2007) Trade and the internal market. In: Weber K, Smith ME, Baun M (eds) Governing Europe's new neighbourhood: partners or periphery? Manchester University Press, Manchester, pp 97–113

Weber K, Smith ME, Baun M (eds) (2007) Governing Europe's new neighbourhood: partners or periphery? Manchester University Press, Manchester

Wolczuk K (2009) Implementation without coordination: the impact of EU conditionality on Ukraine under the European Neighbourhood Policy. Europe-Asia Studies 61(2):187–211

World Bank (2005) Economic growth in the 1990s: learning from a decade of reform. Washington

Chapter 12
Eu-North Africa Relations in Cross-Border Law Enforcement: New Legal Challenges for the EU in the Post-Lisbon and Post-Stockholm Era

Maria O'Neill

Abstract The Stockholm Programme, allied to the Lisbon Treaty, heralds a new era of development of the EU provisions on cross-border law enforcement. The focus is shifting from the ongoing internal EU developments to the external relations of the EU. Many North African countries have had long legal relationships with the EU through the Euro-Mediterranean Partnerships. A number of these partnership agreements make express references, at the political level, to the development of cross-border law enforcement provision, as is the case of Morocco and Algeria with regard to drug trafficking and manufacture, or the lengthy references by Egypt to many of the crimes of interest to the EU's own law enforcement legal framework. Algeria is currently focusing on modernising their own police forces, with both Algeria and Tunisia, reforming their criminal judicial frameworks. Another key player, Libya, currently has no legal agreements with the EU, and at least until the recent conflict, maintained an observer status in the Euro-Mediterranean process. At a practitioner level, the European Police College (CEPOL) is currently involved in the Euromed Police II programme. Clearly momentum is developing, both within the EU and from a number of Euro-Med North African countries to develop closer law enforcement co-operation. This may well develop further with the recent changes in governments of a number of North African countries. The EU approach in the Police and Judicial Cooperation in Criminal Matters (PJCCM) policy area is to develop a legal framework upon which EU cross-border law enforcement will be based. The current EU cross-border law enforcement framework is the product of many years of multi-level negotiations. Challenges will arise as new countries from different legal and policing traditions will attempt to engage with already highly detailed legal and practice frameworks. The shared European legal traditions will not necessarily be

M. O'Neill (✉)
Dundee Business School, University of Abertay Dundee, Scotland, UK
e-mail: m.oneill@abertay.ac.uk

P. J. Cardwell (ed.), *EU External Relations Law and Policy in the Post-Lisbon Era*,
DOI: 10.1007/978-90-6704-823-1_12, © T.M.C. Asser press, The Hague,
The Netherlands, and the authors 2012

reflected in the North African countries. This chapter critically analyses, from an EU legal perspective the problems and issues that will be encountered as the EU's North African partner countries attempt to articulate into the existing, and still developing EU cross-border law enforcement framework.

Contents

12.1 Introduction

At the time of writing this chapter, early in 2011, North Africa was undergoing some major transformations. As a region it remains on the external border of the EU. Fears of instability in the region, and their consequent knock on effects on the EU, through large-scale illegal immigration into the EU remain, together with the allied threats of organised crime and terrorism. The EU is, through both the focus of the Stockholm Programme and the changed legal structure of the Lisbon Treaty, now both willing and able to further develop its external law enforcement provisions. The Euro-Mediterranean agreements remain the EU's legal forum for engagement with North African states. The EU's relations with the North African states, post their current period of rapid internal changes, and new or refocused North African administrations that have had a chance to settle into their new roles, will come quickly back to the top of the EU's external relations agenda.

The EU's relations with North Africa seem to suffer from a serious case of variable geometry, much to the dislike of the Arab League, which considers the whole effort to be a 'balkanisation' of the Arab world.[1] Further 'balkanisation' is also likely to arise in the area of cross-border policing, depending on the extent to which the new or refocused North African administrations are prepared to engage with the democracy and human rights agendas. Some members of the Arab world, namely Somalia and Sudan, are dealt with only on the basis of the much looser Cotonou Agreement, which governs EU relations with the African, Caribbean and

[1] Lannon 2008, 360.

Pacific (ACP) countries, most of whom are former colonies of one or other of the EU member states. Mauritania for its part is now part of the Euro-Mediterranean (EuroMed) process and is still a Cotonou member.[2] The Arab Gulf states, which form the membership of the Gulf Cooperation Council (GCC),[3] have their own direct relationship with the EU, separate from all other legal relationships. Some Arab states are members of the more formal and legally based Union for the Mediterranean (EuroMed),[4] along with a number of non-Arab countries. Some are also members of the European Neighbourhood Policy (ENP), which 'more closely resembles a traditional (as far as this is possible within the context of the EU) instrument of foreign policy'.[5] In addition to the above, there has been a further initiative called *Strengthening the EU's partnership with the Arab World,* which was launched in 2003,[6] which, as pointed out by Lannon, did not include all the Arab countries, but rather only 16 out of the 22 members of the Arab League, and also included, despite its title, the non-Arab countries of Israel, Iran and Turkey.[7] The Arab League continues 'to criticise the EU for not developing a comprehensive Euro–Arab strategy'.[8]

The ongoing conflict between the two EuroMed partners of Israel and the Palestinian Territories have coloured the east Mediterranean partnership, with the highly controversial invasion of Iraq, and its subsequent reconstruction also having an effect on EU–Arab relations.[9] However, and pointed out by Cardwell, the EuroMed process 'has demonstrated a remarkable level of resilience to events in the region'.[10] In an effort to keep a focus on legal frameworks, and in particular on law enforcement issues, rather than the consequences of war, or the aftermath of war, a number of North African EuroMed countries have been chosen for the purposes of the discussion in this chapter, without the intention of the writer to further add to the 'balkanisation' of the Arab world. Internal divisions within the Arab world must however also be taken into account. An example of this is the Arab Maghreb Union,[11] which was launched in 1989, having been 'modelled on the EU with joint decision making bodies (with) an agenda for functional cooperation on a wide range of issues'.[12] The Arab Maghreb Union has one of its members, Mauritania, recognised both under the EuroMed agreements, and under the Cotonou Agreement, one, Libya,

---

[2] Cardwell 2009, 126.

[3] Namely Bahrain, Kuwait, Oman, Qatar, Saudi Arabia and the United Arab Emirates.

[4] The 'Arab Mediterranean countries' are Algeria, Egypt, Libya, Jordan, Lebanon, Morocco, Syria and Tunisia.

[5] Cardwell 2009, 111.

[6] Lannon 2008, 360.

[7] Lannon 2008, 361.

[8] Lannon 2008, 360.

[9] See, generally, Bicchi 2011.

[10] Cardwell 2011, 235.

[11] Whose membership comprises Tunisia, Algeria, Morocco, Libya and Mauritania.

[12] Gomez 2003, 50.

maintaining an observer status under the Euro-Mediterranean policy, despite, at least until recently, operating joint anti-illegal immigration patrols with the Italians in the Mediterranean. The three other members of the Arab Maghreb Union have long been actively involved in the EuroMed process. The Arab countries themselves find these varying EU–Arab strategies problematic, with Algeria, for example, opting out of the ENP provisions but remaining in the EuroMed agreement framework,[13] claiming that 'there was a lack of consistency' between the objectives of the two processes.[14] This can perhaps be explained by Gillespie who states that the EU's Mediterranean initiatives where 'suffering from excessive European direction', especially since 2004, with the ENP in particular 'treating the Mediterranean as just one part of the wider European periphery'.[15]

Relations between the EuroMed countries and the EU in the area of illegal immigration are well developed, are discussed elsewhere,[16] and are not the subject matter of this chapter. Rather the focus of this chapter is on traditional law enforcement activities of the pre-Lisbon's EU Police and Judicial Co-operation in Criminal Matters (PJCCM) policing provisions. In addition, while the 'ENP places much more weight on counter-terrorism issues than had been the case in EuroMed',[17] it is the more legally based EuroMed which provides the greatest potential for development of cross-border law enforcement capacity in the EuroMed area, to include cross-border counter terrorism policy measures.

With both the Lisbon Treaty providing the legal framework for the EU, and the Stockholm programme focusing on the need to develop the external law enforcement provisions of the EU, the post-Lisbon era of the EU is going to throw up new challenges for the further development of the EU's police and judicial cooperation in criminal matters (PJCCM) provisions. Worth noting are that the EU, in Article 8 TEU (post-Lisbon) intends to develop 'a special relationship with neighbouring countries', which will be founded 'on the values of the Union'.[18] The issue of the extent, or otherwise, that a particular North African state has embraced issues such as democracy and human rights, and due process in criminal procedure, is therefore highly relevant in this context. The EU needs a stable and established government to be in place in a partner third state in order to be able to effectively negotiate, and to enter into treaty contracts. These are currently absent in a number of North Africa states. As matters stabilise and the new North African governments overcome their pressing internal issues, their external relations with the EU, and their new neighbours in other North African countries, will come to the fore.

[13] Lannon 2008, 368.

[14] Lannon 2008, 368.

[15] Gillespie 2008, 279.

[16] Cardwell 2009.

[17] Cardwell 2009, 176.

[18] The nature of this provision is discussed further in this volume by Broberg and, in the context of neighbouring states, by Ghazaryan.

12.2 The EuroMed Agreements with North Africa

Unlike Eastern European initiatives within the EU, the relationship with the Mediterranean 'was chiefly concerned with improving the management of existing relationships..... over the longer term'[19] rather than aiming to achieve a rapid transformation of an existing situation. The basic document of the EuroMed relationship is the Barcelona Declaration 1995,[20] which is not a legal document, but a statement of policy intent, with the Union intending that the EuroMed Partnership be based on bilateral agreements with the intention of developing from them a multi-lateral framework covering all the countries of the Mediterranean Basin. The Euro-Mediterranean Partnership originally recognised three separate partnership areas; a political and security partnership,[21] an economic and financial partnership,[22] which it is envisaged, will lead to a Euro-Mediterranean Economic Area (EMEA), and a partnership in social, cultural and human affairs.[23] The balance between these three partnership areas has been at issue in a number of the individual relationships, with concern having been 'expressed about the EU's over-emphasis of the politico-security dimension' and 'its lack of attention to a range of socio-cultural issues'.[24] In addition, the traditional strength of the EU, that of trade, suffered from the protectionist attitude of a number of mainly southern EU member states with respect to Mediterranean agricultural products, with the 'collective interest' of the EU in developing better relations with its Mediterranean neighbours being 'routinely overridden by strong (internal to the EU) national interest'.[25] Further, the collapse of the Berlin wall, and the refocusing of EU interests, and finance, to the integration of the central and eastern European countries into the EU has diverted attention from the Mediterranean region.

The definition of the 'security' aspect of the Mediterranean partnership has also been problematic, with a military definition of security not being appropriate in this region, despite the fact that 'perceptions of a security "threat" from the Mediterranean' are 'a key factor in propelling the region up the EU's agenda and in stimulating the search for a strategy'.[26] Concerns about 'cultural imperialism', and 'western attitudes towards Islam' did not assist in the development of

[19] Gomez 2003, 114. For discussion of the aims of the EU's policies towards the Eastern partners in the ENP, see the chapter in this volume by Dragneva and Wolczuk.

[20] Barcelona Declaration, adopted at the Euro-Mediterranean Conference, 27th and 28th November 1995.

[21] To include the establishment of a common area of peace and stability.

[22] With a view to creating an area of shared prosperity.

[23] The aim here being to develop human resources, prompting understanding between cultures and exchanges between civil societies.

[24] Gomez 2003, 73.

[25] Gomez 2003, 116.

[26] Gomez 2003, 10.

security-related policies in this region.[27] One Mediterranean partner country official called for 'a greater balance between the three pillars' stating that 'of course, there are problems which occupy Southern Europe, including terrorism and drugs, but the security aspect should not dominate'.[28] Security within the EU has since been defined, not only to cover military issues, but also the increasingly important (for the EU) issues of cross-border law enforcement, to include counter terrorism, as well as illegal immigration.

After much rhetoric, the political and security partnership was downgraded from its original objective to the level of 'the development of a network of security experts comprising academics, diplomats and some military personnel'.[29] Nevertheless the Barcelona Declaration has contained references, from the beginning, to combating both terrorism and organised crime in both its first and third chapters.[30] While some partner countries were calling for less emphasis on the security aspects, Algeria was insisting in 1997, on a stronger justice and home affairs component,[31] which appeared to be an effort to combat the hosting of Algerian opposition leaders by EU member states.[32] A divergence on the definition of 'terrorism' was clearly at work here. Separately of concern in the early years of the EuroMed process was the 'capture of a policy issue', the 1990s Algerian crisis, by 'a single member state' on the behalf of the EU, namely France.[33] France had, as the former colonial power in Algeria, its own views as to how matters should be conducted in that country. The issue of post-colonial bilateral ties could add its own dynamic to sensitive issues such as counter-terrorism, something which would be less obvious in a multi-lateral setting.

Of direct relevance to the subject matter of this chapter, on the tenth anniversary of the Barcelona Declaration a fourth pillar, or 'basket' was added to the Barcelona process, that of 'migration, social interaction, justice and security'.[34] This was pursuant to the 'Euro-Mediterranean Ministerial Conference Five Year work programme', which at point (f) provided for the 'ratification and further implementation of the relevant UN conventions on combating organised crime and drugs, and [to] improve co-operation by law enforcement agencies'. Much of the focus in 2005 was on migration, however other cross-border law enforcement was already envisaged at that stage. For his part the then JHA Commissioner, Vitorino, was of the view that 'the JHA mandate [was] to cover 'the entire field of Justice and Home Affairs'', and not just the issue of migration.[35]

---

[27] Gomez 2003, 73.

[28] Gomez 2003, 79.

[29] Gomez 2003, 79.

[30] Gomez 2003, 171.

[31] Gomez 2003, 161.

[32] Gomez 2003, 161.

[33] Gomez 2003, 162.

[34] Cardwell 2009, 101.

[35] Cardwell 2009, 181.

12.3 Law Enforcement Within the EU

Within the EU some would argue that the post-Lisbon Area of Freedom Security and Justice has imbalances in its provisions, with much more development being seen under security, rather than in freedom and justice, leading to an incomplete, and therefore unfair EU legal framework in the area of cross-border law enforcement. It is clearly the intention of the Commission, being supported by the European Parliament, to address these imbalances between a relatively well developed security policy, in the absence of similarly well developed freedom and justice provisions within the post-Lisbon EU legal framework.[36] Nevertheless, substantial provisions have been developed in the area of cross-border EU law enforcement, despite differences in legal systems and police practices across the EU. In chronological order these involve the provisions of the Schengen Convention 1990, the development of Europol,[37] originally by way of international treaty in 1995, the provisions of the EU Convention on Mutual Assistance in Criminal Matters 2000, and more recently in the Prüm Council Decision[38] which built on the provisions of the earlier Treaty of Prüm 2005, which is only in force in some member states of the EU.[39] Cross-border investigations and prosecutions are being facilitated, to include the issue of bridging diverse criminal and evidentiary legal frameworks by the development of Eurojust[40] and the European Judicial Network in Criminal Matters.[41] This entire framework, to include European Arrest

[36] In particular, Commission (2010) Strategy for the effective implementation of the Charter of Fundamental Rights by the European Union, COM (2010) 573. These developments are also evidenced in the recent Directive 2010/64/EU of the European Parliament and of the Council of 20 October 2010 on the right to interpretation and translation in criminal proceedings, OJ L 280, 1.

[37] Currently operating under Council Decision 2009/371/JHA establishing the European Police Office, OJ L 121/37.

[38] Council Decision 2008/615/JHA on the stepping up of cross-border cooperation, particularly in combating terrorism and organised crime, OJ L 210/1, as implemented by Council Decision 2008/616/JHA, OJ L 210/1.

[39] Belgium, Germany, Spain, France, Luxembourg, the Netherlands and Austria.

[40] Eurojust is currently operating on the basis of Council Decision 2002/187/JHA of 28 February 2002 setting up Eurojust with a view to reinforcing the fight against serious crime, OJ L 63, 06/03/2002, 1. However in 2011 this legal framework will be updated by Council Decision 2009/426/JHA of 16 December 2008 on the strengthening of Eurojust and amending Decision 2002/187/JHA setting up Eurojust with a view to reinforcing the fight against serious crime, OJ L 138, 04/06/2009, 14.

[41] Council Decision 2008/976/JHA on the European Judicial Network, OJ L 348/130, repealing and replacing Joint Action 98/428/JHA, OJ L 191, 07/07/1998, 4.

Warrants[42] and European Evidence Warrants[43] are protected by detailed data protection,[44] data security[45] and security classification[46] provisions.

What makes the whole system work, at least to a greater level of efficiency than might otherwise be the case, is the development of shared definitions, and minimum sanctions for a number of key crimes having a cross-border dimension within the EU. Shared definitions have been developed in the areas of drug trafficking and manufacture,[47] organised crime,[48] terrorism,[49] trafficking in human beings[50] and, subject to a UK and Republic of Ireland opt out, illegal immigration.[51] In addition, for the crimes of terrorism and illegal immigration further organisations and frameworks are provided in order the make the EU legal system work in these areas.

The facilities that are available for the law enforcement practitioner operating in a cross-border context within the EU range from, subject to a UK and Ireland opt out, traditional hot pursuit activity,[52] and, subject to an Ireland opt out, cross-border covert surveillance,[53] to provisions for much more complicated and detailed

---

[42] Council Framework Decision 2002/584/JHA on the European Arrest Warrant, OJ L 190, 18/07/2002 P. 0001–0020.

[43] Council Framework Decision 2008/978/JHA of 18 December 2008 on the European evidence warrant for the purpose of obtaining objects, documents and data for use in proceedings in criminal matters, OJ L 350, 30/12/2008, 72.

[44] *Inter alia*, Regulation (EC) No. 45/2001 of the European Parliament and of the council on the protection of individuals with regard to the processing of personal data by the Community institutions and bodies and on the free movement of such data, OJ L 8/1, and Council Framework Decision 2008/977/JHA on the protection of personal data processed in the framework of police and judicial cooperation in criminal matters, OJ L 350/60.

[45] *Inter alia*, Council Act of 3 November 1998 adopting rules on the confidentiality of Europol information (1999) OJ C 316, 27/11/1995, 1.

[46] Council Decision 2001/264/EC of 19 March 2001 adopting the Council's security regulations, OJ L 101/1, and Council Act of 3 November 1998 adopting rules on the confidentiality of Europol information (1999) OJ C 316, 27/11/1995, 1.

[47] Council Framework Decision 2004/757/JHA of 25 October 2004 laying down minimum provisions on the constituent elements of criminal acts and penalties in the field of illicit drug trafficking, OJ L 335.and, inter alia, Council Decision 2005/387/JHA of 10 May 2005 on the information exchange, risk-assessment and control of new psychoactive substances, OJ L 127, 20/05/2005, 32.

[48] Council Framework Decision 2008/841/JHA of 24 October 2008 on the fight against organised crime, OJ L 300, 11/11/2008, 42.

[49] Council Framework Decision 2002/475/JHA of 13 June 2002 on combating terrorism, OJ L 164, 22/06/2002 p. 3, as updated by Council Framework Decision 2008/919/JHA of 28 November 2008 amending Framework Decision 2002/475/JHA on combating terrorism, OJ L 330, 09/12/2008 21.

[50] Council Framework Decision 2002/629/JHA of 19 July 2002 concerning trafficking in human beings, OJ 2002 L203/1, which should be updated soon.

[51] *Inter alia*, Council Directive 2002/90/EC of 28 November 2002 defining the facilitation of unauthorised entry, transit and residence, OJ L 328 of 05/12/2002.

[52] Schengen Convention 1990, Article 41.

[53] Schengen Convention 1990, Article 40.

operations and investigations. For lengthy and in depth investigations involving criminal activity in a number of EU countries, such as drug trafficking, Joint Investigation Teams[54] are facilitated as are Europol Analysis Work Files,[55] with the necessary translation and interpretation support in a security classified environment. For less complicated cases the Schengen Information System, also known as SIRENE,[56] is used, with Europol providing both an Information System[57] and an Indexing system[58] for more complicated criminal investigations, to include counter terrorism operations.[59] Joint Investigation Teams may or may not involve or be led by either Europol or Eurojust, depending on the level of complexity involved. However, outwith the formal EU organisational structures, controlled deliveries[60] and provisions for the placing of an undercover officer across borders are also provided for.[61] Telecommunication intercepts across borders within the EU have been legislated for,[62] as has direct access to DNA,[63] fingerprint[64] and vehicle registration number plate databases,[65] without having to make a prior request for information. All of this is in addition to the traditional levels of information transfer and bilateral cooperation which would exist between friendly neighbouring states. A very high level of trust has therefore been established across the EU, with the combating of crime, to the benefit of all countries, overriding any differences in approach of the criminal and policing systems and practices, which exist across the EU. The EU has even gone so far as to facilitate joint patrols and joint operations,[66] with officers crossing borders, not only being able to continue to use their service weapons

---

[54] Council Act of 29 May 2000 establishing in accordance with Article 34 of the Treaty on European Union the Convention on Mutual Assistance in Criminal Matters between the Member States of the European Union, OJ C 197, Article 13.

[55] Council Decision 2009/371/JHA, Article 14.

[56] Schengen Convention 1990, Articles 92–119.

[57] Council Decision 2009/371/JHA, Article 11.

[58] Council Decision 2009/371/JHA, Article 15.

[59] Council Decision of 3 December 1998 instructing Europol to deal with crimes committed or likely to be committed in the course of terrorist activities against life, limb, personal freedom or property, OJ C 26, 22.

[60] Council Act of 29 May 2000 establishing in accordance with Article 34 of the Treaty on European Union the Convention on Mutual Assistance in Criminal Matters between the Member States of the European Union, OJ C 197, Article 12.

[61] Council Act of 29 May 2000 establishing in accordance with Article 34 of the Treaty on European Union the Convention on Mutual Assistance in Criminal Matters between the Member States of the European Union, OJ C 197, Article 14.

[62] Council Act of 29 May 2000 establishing in accordance with Article 34 of the Treaty on European Union the Convention on Mutual Assistance in Criminal Matters between the Member States of the European Union, OJ C 197, Articles 17–22.

[63] Council Decision 2008/615/JHA on the stepping up of cross-border cooperation, particularly in combating terrorism and organised crime, OJ L 210/1 Articles 2–7.

[64] Council Decision 2008/615/JHA, Articles 8–11.

[65] Council Decision 2008/615/JHA, Articles 12–15.

[66] Council Decision 2008/615/JHA, Article 17.

(all be it in restricted circumstances)[67] but also now to take 'executive action', in other words, to effect an arrest.[68]

Much of the EU cross-border law enforcement provisions were developed by a small group of drugs enforcement officers,[69] who traditionally would take an international view of the challenges that they faced, and were built on the very high levels of trust that had developed between different forces across Western Europe. These negotiations and developments were then adopted by the respective home office ministries, and enacted at the (Home Office) Council of the European Union. This is in contrast to most EU legislative developments which are originally drafted in-house by the relevant directorate of the Commission or by the civil servants based in the relevant ministries of individual member states. It is only after most of the drugs enforcement framework had been put in place that counter-terrorism provisions came to the top of the EU law enforcement agenda, in particular post 9/11. The pre-existing EU drugs law enforcement framework was then adopted to meet the requirements of what had traditionally been a more internally focused counter-terrorism law enforcement community, who would traditionally be more interested in protecting their own particular country, rather than operating in a more systematic transnational framework. The current EU law enforcement framework on counter-terrorism involves only the police, with the national intelligence services, where they exist, remaining outside the formal EU legal framework.[70] There are however provisions within the Common Foreign and Security Policy (CFSP) for the exchange of counter-terrorism intelligence by the military intelligence services, via the CFSP's Joint Situation Centre, SitCen.[71] Given that the EU itself did not ask its counter-terrorism operatives to develop the EU law enforcement framework, it is perhaps problematic that the driver for the EU-North African relationship is counter-terrorism, rather than the more internationally focused drugs trafficking concerns. In addition the bottom up approach of the EU, with the law enforcement practitioners designing the necessary frameworks, which were then endorsed at the government/ministerial level, has led to the development of a workable framework. The traditional top down, diplomatic/ministerial design, if adopted within the EuroMed legal framework for cross-border law enforcement provisions may well prove to be unworkable in practice.

12.4 Internal EU Structural Issues

The developments of external EU provisions to complement internal provisions is proving problematic for the EU's legal structure, as evidenced by the pre-Lisbon

---

[67] Council Decision 2008/615/JHA, Article 19.

[68] Council Decision 2008/615/JHA, Article 17.2.

[69] See *inter alia*, Fijnaut 1993.

[70] Treaty on the Functioning of the European Union, Article 73.

[71] See in particular the Cooperation arrangement between Europol and the General Secretariat of the Council 27/09/2005, doc. 12332/1/05.

Passenger Name Recognition (PNR) case,[72] which involved the first PNR agreement between the EU–US. This involved the transfer to the US of personal data of persons flying into US air space on board EU based aeroplanes, part of the EU–US counter-terrorism legal framework. Despite the great similarity in legal systems, at least in comparison to the differences between the EU and North African legal systems, problems arose as the US was found not to have a data protection legal framework comparable to that insisted upon by the EU.[73] The consequence of this legal disagreement with the US was the voiding of the original EU–US PNR agreement, with 'the USA having to sign an identical agreement, based this time on the correct legal basis'.[74]

The post-Lisbon EU constitutional framework continues to pose problems for the development of the EU's external relations within the area of law enforcement generally, and counter-terrorism law enforcement in particular. The coming into force of the Lisbon Treaty has brought with it a fundamental re-structuring of the EU's external relations institutional framework. The intention was to bring greater coherence, clarity and transparency to the EU's foreign policy. However, academic writers who have started to grapple with the post-Lisbon framework have been pointing out that this will not necessarily be the case.[75] With PJCCM provisions moving from the pre-Lisbon 'third pillar' to the new unitary structure, having its own place with the TFEU, radical changes will arise in the external relations of PJCCM. This however does not give a clear and straight forward answer to the EU's external relations in the area of law enforcement generally, or counter-terrorism in particular, with EU provisions relevant to both law enforcement and counter-terrorism being scattered across the EU policy areas. In addition the EU's post-Lisbon CFSP counter-terrorism provisions, in particular the military response to terrorism, remain in the Treaty on European Union (TEU), and outside the unitary structure of the post-Lisbon EU. In the context of external agreements, while it 'is possible to conclude agreements that cover more than one pillar of the Union (so-called 'inter pillar mixity')', this has not been much used by the EU, as evidenced in the two separate Schengen provisions between the EU and Switzerland, dealing with the Schengen provisions in the then first[76] and third pillar[77] of the EU.[78] Law enforcement generally, and counter-terrorism in particular, is not in a similar position to, for example, the Common Commercial Policy, where a

[72] Cases C-317/04 & C-318/04, *Parliament* v. *Council* [2006] *ECR* I-4721.

[73] Papakonstantinou and De Hert 2009, 900. For further discussion, see also the chapter in this volume by Quesada and Mincheva, who note that the US has generally been the driving force behind cooperation in data exchange, with the EU playing a more reactive role, largely because of the more burdensome decision-making processes.

[74] De Witte 2008, 11.

[75] De Witte 2008, 11. See also the contributions in this volume by Broberg, Schmidt and Puetter.

[76] Council Decision 2004/860/EC, OJ 2004 L 37/78.

[77] Council Decision 2004/849/EC, OJ 2004 L 368/26.

[78] Cremona 2008, 38.

specific 'external' legal base exists for the conclusion of an agreement. The choice of EU treaty legal basis in external relations is of 'constitutional significance',[79] as dealt with by the ECJ in *Opinion 2/2000*,[80] and will not be an issue that can be easily ignored.

The hierarchy of legal bases within the EU has also changed with the coming into force of the Lisbon Treaty, with the pre-Lisbon case law being in a position only to guide us as to the likely outcome of any post-Lisbon Court of Justice litigation on the matter. Those external relations which are exclusively justice and home affairs in focus will be expected to be 'designed to achieve the objectives established by the relevant (internal) provision',[81] while still complying with Article 21 TEU, which deals with the general provisions in the Union's external action. However, a reading of Article 21 TEU itself will not assist in deciding the legal base for an external action, leading 'to a greater emphasis on the content of a measure'.[82] Post-Lisbon if a provision was to be exclusively in the area of JHA it is worth noting that a different, 'special' legislative procedure is to be used for cross-border law enforcement operations,[83] while the 'ordinary' legislative procedure is to be used for other aspects of the JHA policy area. The significance of this is that the 'ordinary' legislative procedure, which is the re-branded co-decision procedure, has a high level of involvement by the European Parliament. The 'special' legislative procedure involves the Council acting unanimously, after having consulted the European Parliament. More sovereignty therefore rests with the individual EU Member States under the special legislative procedure, with the Home Office ministers very much in control of developments in this area. Counter-terrorism in particular is not an exclusively JHA policy area, with substantial parts, including the counter-terrorism strategy and the counter-terrorism coordinator, located in the CFSP pillar, both pre- and post-Lisbon. In addition, much of the counter-terrorism financing provisions, are located with the money laundering provisions, upon which they are based. These money laundering provisions, are highly relevant to effective law enforcement, and are to be found with the EU free movement of capital legal provisions, which were part of the pre-Lisbon EC legal framework.

Pre-Lisbon there was no real hierarchy between EC policy areas, but there was a clear hierarchy between the EC and EU Treaties. Both PJCCM and the CFSP were located in the latter. The EU was then 'to be seen as supplementary' to the EC, with reliance being made on Article 47 EU which stated that 'nothing in (the EU treaty) shall affect' the EC treaty, with the meaning of the word 'affect' being considered to be 'ambiguous'.[84] This was evidenced in the pre-Lisbon

---

79 Cremona 2008, 39.

80 *Opinion 2/2000 (re Cartegena Protocol)*, [2001] *ECR* I-9713, para 5.

81 Cremona 2008, 42.

82 Cremona 2008, 42.

83 Treaty on the Functioning of the European Union, Article 89.

84 Cremona 2008, 42/43.

Environmental Penalties[85] case, where a first pillar legal tool should have been used, based on the Environmental policy, to impose criminal sanctions for an environmental crime, rather than a third pillar PJCCM legal tool, which was more focused on crime generally.[86] In cases involving the EC and the CFSP, the then ECJ highlighted the 'aim and content' of a particular measure, in order to determine whether the matter should have been deal with under one pillar or the other.[87]

Post-Lisbon this balance between the TEU and the TFEU has changed, with the treaty framework seeking keep the CFSP competence separate from the other foreign policy competences which were derived from the pre-Lisbon EC Treaty. The post-Lisbon Article 40 TEU provides that the CFSP and the other policy areas 'shall not affect' each other. This has led to Cremona discussing the 'Chinese wall' which has now been erected between the CFSP and the other Union policies, both 'internal and external', with the intention of protecting 'both sides'.[88] This talk about a Chinese wall between the CFSP and the policy areas now enshrined in the TFEU is not going to be helpful in discussing the external relations of the EU in the area of counter-terrorism, when the EU's Counter-Terrorism strategy, and its coordinator are located in the CFSP pillar, but the active law enforcement provisions are located on the other side of this new 'Chinese wall' of the EU.

The issue of negotiating this new post-Lisbon Chinese wall is being analysed by academics as requiring the establishment of the 'centre of gravity of a given (cross-pillar/cross-policy) measure'.[89] Cremona has pointed out that the lack of an explicit reference in the post-Lisbon treaty framework to 'external action in relation to the Area of Freedom, Security and Justice' is 'surprising', and 'might have been expected given its importance'.[90] While there is clearly an external capacity to act, where that capacity ranks with cross-policy and cross-pillar issues has yet to be established. If this matter is to be left to the Court of Justice this will add complexity and expense to an already highly sensitive field of activity. The matter has already been addressed by way of an Advocate General's opinion in Case 91/05 *Commission* v *Council* (*re SALW*)[91] when AG Mengozzi stated that 'even if the preservation of peace and the strengthening of international security must inspire action by the Community' that this is not an EC matter, but a CFSP matter.[92] The then ECJ, in Grand Chamber, held that the CFSP could not be

---

85 Case C-176/03 *Commission* v *Council* [2005] *ECR* I-7879.

86 Cremona 2008, 43/44.

87 *Commission* v *Council* [2005] and Case C-91/05; *Commission* v *Council* (*re SALW*), [2008] *ECR* I-03651.

88 Cremona 2008, 45.

89 Dashwood 2008, 101.

90 Cremona 2008, 49.

91 Opinion of AG Mengozzi in Case C-91/05; *Commission* v *Council* (*re SALW*), [2008] *ECR* I-03651.

92 Opinion of AG Mengozzi in Case C-91/05; *Commission* v *Council* (*re SALW*), [2008] *ECR* I-03651 at para 159.

allowed to encroach 'upon Community competence',[93] 'otherwise Article 47 (EU) would be deprived of a large part of its useful effect'.[94]

In this writer's view a similar point could be made with regard to any potential development within the CFSP of EuroMed law enforcement provisions, under the heading 'security'. It is to be presumed, therefore that post-Lisbon this ruling will continue to hold relevance in managing the Chinese wall between the CFSP and any law enforcement issue arising from the now mainstream Area of Freedom, Security and Justice legal and practice framework. Care will nevertheless have to be taken that the interior ministers, and the EU law enforcement community, to include the law enforcement practitioners based in the relevant EU agencies, are fully on board with any external relations developments in this area. In addition it remains unclear how CFSP competence affects Member States' powers.[95] A number of issues of relevance to the EU's external relations in the area of counter-terrorism clearly still have to be established. In the mean time any developments in this area will have to be progressed carefully, in order to avoid a repeat of the EU–US *PRN* issues,[96] of considerable embarrassment at an international relations level, and potentially very serious from a law enforcement perspective, if either a suspected terrorist cannot be traced, or if the file prepared in his or her prosecution is compromised by breach of national data protection provisions.

In addition to the above, there is the added complication of the geographic location of a particular partner country. Academics have found that the EU's substantive external relations 'are often difficult to place in precise and accurate legal frameworks', in particular those 'relations that have been developed with countries in the EU's proximity'.[97] Pre-Lisbon a 'fragmentary approach' was being adopted by the EU in its relations 'with different groups of third countries'.[98] This approach in defining 'legal bases for different categories of relationship' has been perpetuated in the post-Lisbon treaty structure.[99] For example, the EU trade and development policies, upon which the EU-ACP agreements are based, were mainstream EC law pre-Lisbon, and are now found in the TFEU post-Lisbon. However, the external relations with 'neighbouring countries', which would include both the ENP, and the EuroMed Policy, are dealt with separately from other CFSP matters in the post-Lisbon TEU.[100]

---

[93] Case C-91/05; *Commission* v *Council* (*re SALW*), [2008] *ECR* I-03651 para 29 of the ruling of the ECJ.

[94] Case C-91/05; *Commission* v *Council* (*re SALW*), [2008] *ECR* I-03651 para 23 of the ruling of the ECJ.

[95] Cremona 2008, 65.

[96] Cases C-317/04 & C-318/04, *Parliament* v *Council* [2006] *ECR* I-4721.

[97] Dashwood and Maresceau 2008, 6.

[98] Cremona 2008, 50.

[99] Cremona 2008, 50.

[100] Treaty on European Union, Article 8.

These changes imply 'a separate kind of status for neighbouring States, rather than merely a field of external action'.[101] Academics are asking whether these 'agreements with the neighbours' are to be 'seen as part of Union foreign policy or as something different'.[102] Equally, it could be asked whether the concept of 'neighbours' only applies to participants in the ENP, or whether it also extends to our neighbours when they participate in the EuroMed policy. Equally, questions could be asked, in the context of the EU's external counter-terrorism provisions, whether there would be a requirement to have a differentiated, and preferential relationship with our 'neighbours' based on Article 8 TEU, rather than on the general CFSP provisions, which may well have to be used to form the legal basis for (e.g.) the more highly developed relationship with the USA. One argument being made for this level of differentiation is that it enhances 'the ability of the Union to fine-tune its relationships with key groups of third countries'.[103] However, as Cremona points out, 'this is outweighed by the lack of clarity as to what exactly the differences entail' which is added to by the increasing variety of potential legal bases for enactment of EU laws and negotiation of external agreements, which can now 'be found in different places in the Treaties'.[104] The potential for legal and institutional 'boundary disputes' within the EU for the development of its external relations can only be seen to be increasing.

12.5 Current Work on this Area

At a political level, there is a readiness to engage with the issues of counter-terrorism and law enforcement generally within the framework of the EuroMed partnership, building on a 'spill-over of a "permissive consensus," prevalent amongst European and North African elites' as reported by Wolff.[105] This is particularly in light of 'the changing composition of the security landscape, particularly in North Africa and the Sahel region',[106] and the perception of 'a security "threat" from the Mediterranean'.[107] These developing relationships between the EU and North Africa are not however 'completely novel',[108] with many North African states maintaining close historical ties with individual EU Member States. In particular 'France has historically maintained close relations with the intelligence services of

[101] Cremona 2008, 50.
[102] Cremona 2008, 50.
[103] Cremona 2008, 50.
[104] Cremona 2008, 50.
[105] Wolff 2010, 136.
[106] Wolff 2010, 150.
[107] Gomez 2003, 10.
[108] Wolff 2010, 149.

North African countries',[109] and the Madrid bombing in 2004 has led to an increase in Spanish—Moroccan cooperation.[110] From a legal point of view it is completely understandable that 'most cooperation' in this area is at a bilateral level, with former colonies having modelled both their legal systems and police practice on those of their former coloniser. The variety of legal systems and police practice which is engaged in across the EU is problematic enough for the EU-based lawyer or law enforcement practitioner, who often requires the support of either Eurojust[111] or Europol[112] in order to assist in the variety of cross-border law enforcement activities discussed earlier. A third country which is still in a developmental phase would find having to negotiate these differences extremely difficult. Nevertheless the emphasis of the EuroMed legal framework is to move from its initially bilateral EU—individual North African state commercial relations onto the multilateral stage. It is to be anticipated that similar developments will be encouraged in the EU–North African law enforcement sphere, particularly as 'EU counter-terrorism policy increasingly affects the relationship of the EU and its member states with the Mediterranean region'.[113]

In addition to the Arab League becoming a member of the Union for the Mediterranean, the Arab countries have themselves developed multi-lateral provisions in the area of counter-terrorism, with the adoption by the Council of Ministers of Justice of the Arab League of a Convention on Terrorism in 1998, which due to the vagueness of its definition of terrorism lead to international condemnation. This was subsequently followed by a 'Euro-Mediterranean Code of Conduct on Countering Terrorism of 2005', which was drafted by British diplomats. This document presents terrorism as a common threat for EuroMed citizens.[114] While the EU has for its own purposes developed a definition of terrorism, in the Framework Decision on Terrorism,[115] in order to facilitate cross-border law enforcement within the EU in this crime area, the lack of a global definition of terrorism continues to bedevil global action, and will be a continuing issue for EuroMed development. In addition, the EU

[109] Wolff 2010, 148.

[110] Wolff 2010, 149.

[111] Currently operating on the basis of Council Decision 2002/187/JHA of 28 February 2002 setting up Eurojust with a view to reinforcing the fight against serious crime, OJ L 63, 06/03/2002, 1, but about to be replaced by Council Decision 2009/426/JHA of 16 December 2008 on the strengthening of Eurojust and amending Decision 2002/187/JHA setting up Eurojust with a view to reinforcing the fight against serious crime, OJ L 138, 04/06/2009, 14.

[112] Now operating on the basis of Council Decision 2009/371/JHA establishing the European Police Office, OJ L121/37.

[113] Wolff 2010, 149.

[114] Wolff 2010, 145.

[115] Council Framework Decision 2002/475/JHA of 13 June 2002 on combating terrorism, OJ L 164, 22/06/2002, 3, as amended by Council Framework Decision 2008/919/JHA of 28 November 2008 amending Framework Decision 2002/475/JHA on combating terrorism, OJ L 330, 09/12/2008, 21.

and the North African states 'differ on the analysis of terrorism',[116] despite the fact that the 2002 Valencia conference requested 'the Euro-Mediterranean partners to commit themselves to the fight against terrorism'.[117]

At a practical level the EU has already provided 'technical assistance through a 2004 counter-terrorism capacity-building project with Algeria', and Morocco, having a 'network of national contact points' which were 'created to facilitate co-operation'.[118] Technical assistance has been provided for dealing with 'radicalization in particular in key environments', and the development of 'border, airport and maritime security'. Training has also been provided in the area of crisis management to Morocco and Algeria.[119] All these form part of the EU's own internal security provisions under the headings of protect, prevent and respond, within the EU counter-terrorism strategy. This strategy builds on the European Council's 'Declaration on Combating Terrorism',[120] and the Council Common Position 2001/930/CFSP of 27 December 2001 on combating terrorism,[121] which sets out the agreed methods of combating terrorism within the EU, many of which are taken up by other EU policy areas. The EU's counter-terrorism strategy[122] for internal EU cooperation in this area maintains a 'four-pronged approach'[123] entitled protect, prevent, pursue and respond. Clearly what is missing from the Euro-Med provisions is a matching provision in the area of 'pursue'. The development of a 'pursue' capability is certainly envisaged in the Instrument for Stability[124] which is aimed at developing the capacity of both 'judicial and civil authorities' which are engaged in the 'fight against terrorism and organised crime', with assistance to be provided by the EU to include, inter alia, 'the development of international procedures for law enforcement'.[125]

External developments in this area, in particular with the EuroMed countries, may well run a risk in engaging with countries which do not share the basic underlying principles of the EU Member States, which underpin all of the EU legal and law enforcement structures, namely a shared understanding of the tripartite division of power, the rule of law, an independent judiciary, and a basic

---

[116] Wolff 2010, 144/5.

[117] Wolff 2010, 144/5.

[118] Wolff 2010, 146.

[119] Wolff 2010, 147.

[120] Brussels, 25 March 2004.

[121] Council Common Position 2001/930/CFSP of 27 December 2001 on combating terrorism, OJ L 344/90.

[122] The European Union Counter—Terrorism Strategy, Brussels, 30 November 2005, 14469/4/05, Rev 4.

[123] Report on the Implementation of the European Security Strategy—Providing Security in a Changing World—Brussels, 11 December 2008, S407/08, at I. Global Challenges and Key Threats, Terrorism and Organised Crime, 4.

[124] Regulation (EC) No 1717/2006 of the European Parliament and of the Council of 15 November 2006 establishing an Instrument for Stability, OJ L 327, 24/11/2006, 1, Article 4.1.a.

[125] Regulation (EC) No 1717/2006, Article 4.1.a.

understanding of human rights. This has been pointed out by Cardwell, who refers to the 'double-edged nature of the EU's engagement with the Mediterranean partners, especially post 9/11', with the drive to 'secure cooperation on crime and terrorism' despite the Barcelona Process' emphasis on 'encouraging reform'.[126] It does have to be pointed out that the Barcelona signatories undertook, under the heading of 'political and security partnership' to 'refrain from interference in a partner's internal affairs' while at the same time to 'strengthen co-operation in combating terrorism'.[127] The EU's Counter-Terrorism Strategy, for its part, 'is based on respect for human rights and international law'.[128] As Wolff reports, there is a lack of 'independent judiciaries' and 'police forces that respect human rights' in many of the Mediterranean countries,[129] leading to a dilemma for the EU which wishes to pursue a strategy 'in which it seeks cooperation in the fight against terrorism with law enforcement agencies that do not enjoy full independent from executive power, and do not apply basic principles of justice'.[130]

A number of the EuroMed association agreements make express reference, at the political level, to the development of cross-border law enforcement provision, as is the case of Morocco[131] and Algeria[132] with regard to drug trafficking and manufacture, or the lengthy references by Egypt to many of the crimes of interest to the EU's own law enforcement legal framework.[133] Algeria[134] is currently focusing on modernising their own police forces, with both Algeria[135] and Tunisia,[136] reforming their criminal judicial frameworks. At a practitioner level CEPOL is currently involved in the Euromed Police II programme.[137]

[126] Cardwell 2009, 137.

[127] Hakura 1997, 343/4.

[128] Report on the Implementation of the European Security Strategy—Providing Security in a Changing World—Brussels, 11 December 2008, S407/08, at I. Global Challenges and Key Threats, Terrorism and Organised Crime, 4.

[129] Wolff 2010, 150.

[130] Wolff 2010, 150.

[131] Mid-Term Review of the Country Strategy Paper Morocco 2007–2013 and National Indicative Program 2011–2013, 2.2. Changes in Horizontal External EU Policies or unforeseen events, para 6, 5.

[132] Instrument Européen de voisinage et de Partenariat Algerie Programme Indicatif National 2011–2013, 2. Changements dans les politiques externs horizontals de l'UE, 4, para 6.

[133] EU/Egypt Action Plan, 2. Actions, 2.4. Migration, social integration, justice and security, *b) Law enforcement cooperation,* 28.

[134] Instrument Européen de voisinage et de Partenariat Algerie Programme Indicatif National 2011–2013, III. Cooperation Financiere, 1. Enseignements de la Cooperation Passee, at p. 6, para 3.

[135] Instrument Européen de voisinage et de Partenariat Algerie Programme Indicatif National 2011–2013, IV. Programme Indicatif National 2011–2013, 1. Priorites et Objectifs Principaux, at p. 7.

[136] Tunisie: Programme Indicatif National, 2011–2013, 2. Relations avec l'UE et situations du Pays, 2.2. Changements des politiques horizontales extérieures de l'UE et événements Imprévus, 3.4. Programme d'appui au secteur de la justice, *3.4.1. Contexte,* at p. 24.

[137] Which involves EU relations with Algeria, Egypt, Israel, Lebanon, Jordan, Morocco, the Palestinian Authority, Syria and Tunisia.

The Stockholm Programme, which was signed off by the European Union in December 2009, sets out the plans for development of the post-Lisbon Area of Freedom, Security and Justice. Chapter 7 focuses on the external relations of the EU in this policy area. It is clear that in the forthcoming years the EU, and its Member States 'will cooperate closely with their neighbours',[138] in the 'key thematic priorities' such as 'the fight against terrorism, organised crime, corruption, drugs, the exchange of personal data in a secure environment and managing migration flows', with work in the area of the 'trafficking in human beings and smuggling of persons' to be 'stepped up'.[139] Better coherence has to be developed between 'traditional external policy instruments and internal instruments with significant external dimensions, such as freedom, security and justice'.[140] It is this writer's opinion that an external dimension to the 'pursue' aspect of the EU Counter-terrorism policy, and law enforcement provisions more generally, are envisaged for development in this regard. New tools will be required in order to engage with third countries, both under the security heading, to cover the combating of 'serious and organised crime, terrorism, drugs, trafficking in human beings and smuggling of persons', with 'internal and external security (being seen to be) inseparable',[141] and in the area of justice, with a focus to be made on the promotion of 'the rule of law and human rights, good governance, (and the) fight against corruption'.[142]

Regular references are made in the Stockholm Programme to the need to 'promote European and international standards',[143] and the promotion of 'the values of the Union' in the area of human rights, with the 'development of international law' being 'respected'.[144] The issue of compliance with EU standards of human rights or data protection and security may still be problematic for these external developments. Despite the fact that the Stockholm Programme states that 'Interpol is an important partner for the Union'.. 'for law enforcement cooperation',[145] this would not appear to be the sole method of law enforcement cooperation of the EU in its anticipated developments. The development of law enforcement capacity is expressly referred to in the context of the EU agencies, *inter alia*, of Europol and Eurojust and the need for 'external relations [to]... inform and guide the prioritisations of [their] work'.[146] Equally, with the 'threat of terrorism and organised crime [remaining] high', there is a recognised need for

---

[138] Stockholm Programme—An open and secure Europe serving and protecting the citizens, Brussels, 2 December 2009, 17024/09, 7.1, para 1.

[139] Stockholm Programme 2009, 17024/09 7.3, para 1.

[140] Stockholm Programme 2009, 17024/09 7.1, para 2.

[141] Stockholm Programme 2009, 17024/09 7.3, para 2.

[142] Stockholm Programme 2009, 17024/09 7.3, para 2.

[143] Stockholm Programme 2009, 17024/09 7.1, para 1.

[144] Stockholm Programme 2009, 17024/09 7.2.

[145] Stockholm Programme 2009, 17024/09 7.6, para 5.

[146] Stockholm Programme 2009, 17024/09 7, para 4.

'operational agreements by Eurojust, Europol, as well as working arrangements with Frontex, [to] be strengthened'.[147]

In the context of the external relations of the EU in the AFSJ policy area with the Mediterranean, a plan was expected in 2010 to deal with the upgrading of the relationship in the context of maritime migration, 'border surveillance, preventing and fighting drug trafficking, civil protection, law enforcement and judicial cooperation'.[148] This document does not appear to have surfaced at the time of writing, although its importance has been emphasized in a May 2010 European Parliament resolution, which has stated 'recalling the important of what is known and the fourth chapter of Euro-Mediterranean cooperation (on migration, social integration, justice and security) and highlights the need for the UFM to drive forward cooperation on this chapter'.[149] By March 2011 the EU was talking about 'more effective law enforcement cooperation',[150] and 'mobility partnerships', which 'should be launched with partner countries'.[151] These would, inter alia, cover initiatives which would enhance 'the capacity and abilities of law enforcement authorities to effectively fight trans-border organised crime and corruption'.[152] Recognising the complexity of what is being proposed in the short term, 'legal migration legislation and visa policy in support of the goal of enhanced mobility, in particular for students, researchers and business persons' was to be prioritised.[153] In light of the call in the Stockholm Programme for 'Rapid action to face the challenges' of cross-border control and measures to combat organised crime, with the Mediterranean area 'is a priority',[154] it can be assumed that work has commenced in developing this area, but that it may be some time before effective structures and provisions at a multi-lateral level can be put in place. In the context of the ENP, 'and other key partners' the Stockholm Programme states that 'the EU should cooperate on all issues in the area of freedom, security and justice'.[155]

---

[147] Stockholm Programme 2009, 17024/09, 7.3, para 4.

[148] Stockholm Programme 2009, 17024/09, 7.5, para 7.

[149] Union for the Mediterranean—European Parliament resolution of 20 May 2010 on the Union for the Mediterranean (2009/2215(INI)), OJ C 161E, 31/05/2011, p. 126.

[150] Joint Communication to the European Council, the European Parliament, the Council, the European Economic and Social Committee and the Committee of the Regions—A Partnership for Democracy and Shared Prosperity with the Southern Mediterranean, COM (2011) 200.

[151] Joint Communication to the European Council, the European Parliament, the Council, the European Economic and Social Committee and the Committee of the Regions—A Partnership for Democracy and Shared Prosperity with the Southern Mediterranean, COM (2011) 200.

[152] Joint Communication to the European Council, the European Parliament, the Council, the European Economic and Social Committee and the Committee of the Regions—A Partnership for Democracy and Shared Prosperity with the Southern Mediterranean, COM (2011) 200.

[153] Joint Communication to the European Council, the European Parliament, the Council, the European Economic and Social Committee and the Committee of the Regions—A Partnership for Democracy and Shared Prosperity with the Southern Mediterranean, COM (2011) 200.

[154] Stockholm Programme 2009, 17024/09, 7.5, para 8.

[155] Stockholm Programme 2009, 17024/09, 7.5, para 1.

12.6 Conclusion

The issue remains as to what approach is going to be developed for cross-border law enforcement and counter-terrorism with the North African countries, under the Stockholm Programme. Will these plans be as ambitious as the provisions already in place for within the EU, or will they be less concerned, perhaps with placing law enforcement officers across borders, and more focused on intelligence and data exchange? Either option will pose challenges for both the EU and its partner countries. Choices will also be determined by the internal governance of each of the potential North African countries after they have recovered from the period of instability in early 2011. From an EU perspective the developments will pose substantial constitutional challenges, not least in establishing whether these developments are to be within the CFSP policy area, or are to be an extension of the PJCCM policy area. Equally, the willingness of the EuroMed partners countries to engage with these developments will be an issue, although it is clear, from the above discussion, that at least some of these countries are interested in progressing with this agenda. Whether this interest persists after the changes of a number of relevant North African governments still has to be established. This area will need to be further researched, both from the political and legal perspective of each of the EuroMed partner states, as 'imposing (a) notional unity on the Mediterranean region' could lead to any developments being seen as 'merely as another convenient vehicle for westernisation rather than the basis for (putting) relations between the Union and the partners on a new footing'[156] The complexities which may arise in negotiating with the EU in this matter may prove to be highly challenging for EuroMed partner states, particularly given the complexity of achieving any developments in this area within the EU. The traditional view of the EuroMed partners of viewing 'internal divisions over competences' within the Union as being 'a sign of weakness'[157] will have to be overcome, recognising that these differences, and the consequent compromises, often give rise to a more robust and workable framework. High levels of complexity have, however, never prevented the EU from progressing with any particular policy area, once the will of all partners has been shown for a particular development. 'History making' decisions are often accompanied by 'infighting among the EU's institutions and Member States'.[158]

By 'making the links between … both internal and external security more clear' in the EuroMed context, 'non-Mediterranean EU members have begun to perceive [the] EuroMed as a more useful framework for action'.[159] The 'general tendency to favour soft law operational instruments'[160] will not however work in this

---

[156] Gomez 2003, 73.

[157] Gomez 2003, 175.

[158] Gomez 2003, 114.

[159] Cardwell 2009, 118.

[160] Lannon 2008, 367.

policy area, with cross-border law enforcement, whatever its tools, requiring the full engagement of the legal systems of all partner countries for it to be acceptable by the criminal judiciary of the relevant partner state. While the Union for the Mediterranean has been launched with much publicity, it is at the practical day-to-day operational level that its success will be measured. The law enforcement security framework within the EU has however, to a large extent, been built by the law enforcement community, and initially, by the drugs trafficking officers. Given the lack of clarity on whether EuroMed provisions will be classified as CFSP or PJCCM provisions, the emphasis of this chapter is that the framework, however legally conceived, should have the EU's law enforcement community on board from the beginning. It is necessary to ensure that whatever systems are developed they will in fact work, and be properly integrated into pre-existing practices and procedures. They must also be legally acceptable within the criminal courts of the EU member states, as well as being acceptable within the criminal courts of the EuroMed partner states.

The EuroMed was always seen as being 'wide-ranging (in) nature', and 'has generally been characterised as a 'cross-pillar' project'.[161] The development of any cross-border law enforcement capacity requires the EuroMed to be even more wide ranging, bringing in more layers of traditional state structure, to include the criminal law practitioner and judiciary, and the law enforcement community. It is likely that the rapidly changing situation in North Africa in 2011 will have an impact on the potential to develop external EU relations in the area of law enforcement. After a period of stabilisation, it would be reasonable to assume that countries which encompass more of the 'values of the Union'[162] will be able to develop a deeper and more constructive relationships, than was originally anticipated at the time of the initial drafting of either the Lisbon Treaty, the Stockholm Programme or any of the other EU policy and legal documentation of relevance to the subject matter of this chapter.

References

Bicchi F (2011) The Union for the Mediterranean, or the changing context of Euro-Mediterranean relations. Mediterr Politics 16(1):3–19

Cardwell PJ (2009) EU external relations and systems of governance, the CFSP, Euro-Mediterranean partnership and migration. Routledge, Oxford

Cardwell PJ (2011) EuroMed, European Neighbourhood Policy and the union for the Mediterranean: overlapping policy frames in the EU's governance of the Mediterranean. Journal of Common Market Studies 49(2):219–241

Cremona M (2008) Defining competence in EU external relations: lessons from the Treaty reform process. In: Dashwood A, Maresceau M (eds) Law and practice of EU external relations; salient features of a changing landscape. Cambridge University Press, Cambridge, pp 34–69

[161] Cardwell 2009, 207.

[162] Treaty on European Union, Article 8.1.

Dashwood A (2008) Article 47 TEU and the relationship between first and second pillar competences. In: Dashwood A, Maresceau M (eds) Law and practice of EU external relations; salient features of a changing landscape. Cambridge University Press, Cambridge, pp 70–103
Dashwood A, Maresceau M (eds) (2008) Law and practice of EU external relations; salient features of a changing landscape. Cambridge University Press, Cambridge
De Witte B (2008) Too much constitutional law in the European Union's foreign relations. In: Cremona M, De Witte B (eds) EU foreign relations law; constitutional fundamentals, essays in European law. Hart Publishing, Oxford, pp 3–15
Fijnaut C (ed) (1993) The internationalization of police cooperation in western Europe. Kluwer Law and Taxation Publishers, Leiden
Gillespie R (2008) A 'Union for the Mediterranean'… or for the EU? Mediterranean Politics 13(2):277–286
Gomez R (2003) Negotiating the Euro-Mediterranean partnership; strategic action in EU foreign policy? Ashgate Publishing, Aldershot
Hakura FS (1997) The Euro-Mediterranean policy: the implications of the Barcelona declaration. Common Market Law Review 34:337–366
Lannon E (2008) The EU's strategic partnership with the Mediterranean and the middle east: a new geopolitical dimension of the EU's proximity strategies. In: Dashwood A, Maresceau M (eds) Law and practice of EU external relations; salient features of a changing landscape. Cambridge University Press, Cambridge, pp 360–375
Papakonstantinou V, De Hert P (2009) The PRN agreement and transatlantic anti-terrorism co-operation: no firm human rights framework on either side of the Atlantic. Common Market Law Review 46:885–919
Wolff S (2010) The Mediterranean dimension of EU Counter-terrorism. In: Wolff S et al (eds) The external dimension of justice and home affairs: a different security agenda for the European Union? Routledge, Abingdon, pp 135–154

Chapter 13
Boost or Backlash? EU Member States and the EU's Latin America Policy in the Post-Lisbon Era

Bettina Trueb

Abstract This chapter assesses the impact of the Lisbon Treaty on the EU's relations with Latin America. In particular, it focuses on the interaction between the EU and three important Member States: Germany, Spain, and the UK. Given the importance of these three Member States within the EU in general and, especially in the case of Spain, in relations with Latin America in particular, they should be particularly instructive. This chapter assesses three dimensions of policy-making towards Latin America upon which the Lisbon Treaty might have an effect. The first is the 'home' dimension and concerns policy-making in the respective Foreign Ministries. Are Member States more constrained than previously in their relations with Latin America? Does the Lisbon Treaty provide an opportunity to 'outsource' aspects of policy to the EU? Or does it cause a 'backlash' effect, leading to greater national assertiveness? This should be particularly relevant for countries with weaker direct interests in Latin America. The 'Brussels' dimension refers to the interaction between domestic and EU policy. Does the Lisbon Treaty diminish the Member States' opportunities to influence the EU's policy towards the region? Are there substantial changes in the policy itself? This aspect should be especially relevant for Spain: can it maintain its traditionally strong influence at the EU level? Finally, the 'Latin American' dimension concerns European representation on the ground. What does the establishment of the EU's External Action Service (EEAS) mean for Member States' activities in Latin America itself? Does the EU take a more active role, and are the Member States concerned about this? Or do they rather see it

This research was carried out with generous support of the Mannheim Centre for European Social Research (*MZES*)

B. Trueb (✉)
Center for Doctoral Studies in Social and Behavioral Sciences (CDSS),
University of Mannheim, Mannheim, Germany
e-mail: btrueb@mail.uni-mannheim.de

P. J. Cardwell (ed.), *EU External Relations Law and Policy in the Post-Lisbon Era*,
DOI: 10.1007/978-90-6704-823-1_13, © T.M.C. Asser Press, The Hague,
The Netherlands, and the authors 2012

as an opportunity to 'outsource' representation, especially in times of budgetary constraints? This might be particularly relevant to the UK, which has a relatively weak policy towards Latin America and might be able to use the EEAS to strengthen its profile or delegate responsibilities. By triangulating interview data with government and EU documents, I assess the push and pull factors the Lisbon Treaty exerts on Member States' relations with the EU's Latin American policy and on Member States' own relations with the region. While relations with Latin America are just one example, they should also be instructive for links with other regions.

Contents

13.1 Introduction

One of the Lisbon Treaty's intentions was to give greater coherence and consistency to European external action. While analysts tend to agree on the Treaty's potential to achieve this, the extent to which it is realised is seen as depending on the Member States.[1] It is thus worth assessing how Member States have so far reacted to changes in EU external relations brought about by the Treaty.

This contribution considers the effect of the Treaty upon relations with Latin America.[2] It focuses on the foreign policies of three important EU Member States: Germany, Spain, and the UK. This focus is instructive since all three have varying levels of interaction with Latin America both at national level and within the EU framework. Germany is one of the EU's 'great powers', but has traditionally promoted external action at the EU level, including in policy towards Latin America. Has it continued to do so? Spain, on the other hand, has a special relationship with Latin America and is known for its attempts to promote closer EU relations with the region. It also held the rotating EU Presidency during the first half of 2010, when the latest EU-Latin America and Caribbean (EU-LAC) Summit took place. How has Spain used this opportunity and how is its Latin American policy affected by the new framework? Finally, the UK's policy towards Latin America has mainly been characterised by its low-key approach. Does Lisbon provide an opportunity for Britain to 'delegate' relations with Latin America to the EU, or does traditional British Euroscepticism prevent this?

---

[1] Allen and Smith 2010, 209; Duke 2008, 13; Gardner and Eizenstat 2010. See also, in this volume, the contributions by Bendiek and Puetter.

[2] The Caribbean is also considered in the context of the EU-Latin America and Caribbean (EU-LAC) process, and in the context of relations with Cuba.

Policy towards Latin America serves, for the purposes of this chapter, as an example of EU relations with third countries and regions. While LAC has certainly not been a priority region for the EU, the EU-LAC relationship nevertheless covers just about any topic relevant to external relations. Additionally, the relationship's low priority gives it an 'everyday' character that makes it an interesting subject for the study of relations with third countries and regions as they occur on a routine basis. Additionally, it could be seen as a testing ground for longer-term external policies, as it is not subject to the same periodic attention given to other third regions such as the neighbourhood or North Africa.

The chapter focuses on political as well as economic relations. The EU-LAC relationship is characterised by a focus on the economic dimension. This is not free of tensions, as the negotiation of Association Agreements with regional associations (such as Mercosur) or individual countries is complicated because of disputes over the liberalisation of the agricultural market, for example. However, in recent years the political relationship has also become more tense as Latin American concerns about the EU's migration policy have arisen,[3] and Latin American countries begin to assert themselves more strongly on the international stage. Additionally, the EU's region-to-region strategy has encountered some difficulties as Latin America has become more politically diverse and some regional integration schemes, in particular the Andean Community, have become much less relevant.

I assess EU external relations and their interaction with the national level on three dimensions. The first is the 'home' dimension and covers the impact of the Treaty on foreign policy-making in the national foreign ministries. How will Member States conduct national policy towards Latin America in the future, under the new opportunities offered and limitations imposed by the Treaty? The second dimension is the 'Brussels' dimension and concerns the direct interaction of Member States with the European level in external relations. How is this affected by the creation of new posts, institutions, and rules? The third dimension concerns the new interaction between EU Member States' diplomatic missions and the former EC-turned-EU Delegations 'on the ground' in Latin America. How do the Member States envision the interaction between their own missions and those of the EU, and what does it mean for their visibility on the ground?

The chapter is based on interviews carried out during the course of 2010 at the national foreign ministries of Germany, the UK, and Spain. I interviewed government officials concerned both with the LAC region and EU external relations. Additionally, I assess government and EU documents to complement the interviews. In line with the evolving nature of the EU's external relations, this chapter is of a rather explorative nature. As interviewees from all three countries pointed out, only time will tell how things will develop, especially as the Treaty provisions frequently do not go into detail on how exactly the EU's foreign policy institutions are going to work. However, the reconfiguration process is currently at a particularly dynamic stage of development, as the EEAS becomes operational

3 Acosta 2009.

and institutions and their interaction with the Member State level develop. Current events are an exciting opportunity to observe a highly dynamic process of foreign policy configuration and institution-building.[4]

I find that in all three Member States the necessity to adapt to the Treaty's configurations is acutely perceived. In all three states under scrutiny, this takes both positive—the Treaty as an opportunity—and negative—the Treaty as a constraint—forms. Overall, it is clear that the Treaty's provisions for external relations have made Member States more aware of having to safeguard their own foreign policy distinctiveness, albeit to varying degrees. At the same time, there is also awareness that Lisbon provides an opportunity for a more coherent EU foreign policy position vis-à-vis Latin America and the Caribbean, and for more concerted efforts 'on the ground'. Officials regard it as certain that the Treaty will increase the EU's competences and profile in external relations. However, there is a surprising degree of uncertainty surrounding the Treaty and its consequences for foreign policy-making. Frequently, interviewees made statements like 'nobody knows today how this will work' (a German official),[5] 'the path will be made while walking it' (a Spanish official), or pointed out 'a lack of clarity' in the Treaty's provisions (a British official).

The chapter proceeds by assessing the three aforementioned dimensions of Latin America policy: I begin with the 'home' dimension, then analyse the 'Brussels' dimension, and third the 'Latin America' dimension. Finally, I draw conclusions and outline possible scenarios that may await EU-LAC relations under the Treaty.

13.2 Member States, the EU, and Latin America: What Changes With Lisbon?

In this section, I analyse the changes resulting from the Treaty of Lisbon that concern the relationship with Latin America in national foreign policies, at the EU level, and 'on the ground'.

13.2.1 The 'Home' Dimension: Policy-Making in the Foreign Ministries

With the entry into force of the Treaty, national policies are subject to change as some competences migrate to the European level and national foreign ministries have to adapt to new rules and institutions. To what extent does the Treaty

[4] The definition of 'institutions' here is a rather broad one of institutions as the rules of the game shaping human interaction, as is the case in most institutionalist literature dealing with the EU. Jupille and Caporaso 1999, 429.

[5] Interviews in Germany and Spain were conducted in German and Spanish, respectively. All translations are by the author.

introduce new constraints for policy-making towards Latin America at home? What opportunities does it present?

One of the most important changes affecting policies towards LAC concerns the Common Commercial Policy (CCP), as trade-related Foreign Direct Investment (FDI) migrates to the Union.[6] All three Member States under scrutiny have substantial investments in Latin America, which they wish to protect. Many interviewees responded 'investment and economic promotion' when asked about aspects of policy towards Latin America that should be kept bilateral. In this area, states are in competition with the other EU Members and therefore prefer to keep it under their own control. Concerns about this issue are clearly echoed in the German Government's 2010 Strategy Paper on Latin America:

> The German Government strives to ensure that the high level of protection provided by existing bilateral investment protection and promotion agreements is maintained and, if possible, enhanced, even after the transfer to the EU of competence for the treaty-based protection and promotion of investments.[7]

Additionally, according to Wouters et al., the Treaty is unclear on what this will mean for the Member States' capability to conclude bilateral investment treaties, a problem that would probably only be resolved by the European Court of Justice (ECJ).[8] Policy autonomy towards Latin America will therefore be restricted in an area traditionally considered vital in pursuing national economic interests. Additionally, competences for trade in services and trade-related aspects of intellectual property are also moved to the CCP.[9] This carries implications for the further negotiation of trade and association agreements with Latin American countries and regions, where the Member States will have less to say. Especially for those with important trade and investment interests in the region, this may be difficult to accept. There is already a feeling among some that the EU is not negotiating good trade agreements in Latin America in the interest of all Member States. This, according to one official, is due to some states' very strong interest 'which clouds the rest of the EU's judgement'. Even one Spanish official conceded that there is a sentiment that the EU attends to the interests of the country with the biggest interest. By removing further aspects of trade from the Member States' competence, the Treaty might actually improve this, as all Members' needs have to be considered. However, Spain as the EU Member State with the most important commercial interests in Latin America is likely to defend them wherever it can

---

[6] Treaty on the Functioning of the European Union, Article 207 (1). The CCP and Investment provisions in the post-Lisbon era are discussed extensively in this volume in chapters by Wu and Dimopoulos.

[7] Auswärtiges Amt (2010) Germany, Latin America and the Caribbean: A Strategy Paper by the German Government, Auswärtiges Amt, Berlin, 37.

[8] Wouters et al. 2008, 170 et seq. It might be noted here that the Commission's view is that the provisions on investment as included within the CCP mean that the EU now has exclusive competence. For further discussion, see Dimopoulos (this volume).

[9] Treaty on the Functioning of the European Union, Article 207 (1).

even under the Treaty. Likewise, Germany and the UK will also continue defending theirs—perhaps harder than previously, as Latin America becomes a more interesting economic partner given its current economic growth rates.

Interviews show that the Treaty generates a host of expectations and attitudes within the foreign ministries on how European Latin America policy will be conducted in the future and what the individual countries' role is within that policy. Additionally, policy documents are assessed to analyse how policy-makers in the capitals intend to use the opportunities offered by the Treaty and deal with the constraints it imposes.

13.2.1.1 Germany

In the German context, it is important to compare the Strategy Paper on Latin America published by the Federal Government in August 2010[10] with its predecessor, the Guidelines on Latin America Policy published in 2004.[11] These Guidelines stated the need that 'German LAC policy be constantly evaluated regarding whether it can better reach its goals through bilateral or European action', and that '[e]ssentially, European action is preferable wherever it is possible'.[12] The new paper takes a somewhat different approach. In fact, Günther Maihold notes the shift in emphasis towards bringing a stronger national voice to the EU level as one of few changes in German policy vis-à-vis Latin America.[13] The desire for further Europeanisation that permeated the 2004/2007 Guidelines is indeed no longer as striking. Instead, the Government postulates that in order 'to fully represent our values and interests in Latin America, we have to use our influence in a targeted manner to help shape European policy on Latin America and the Caribbean'.[14] In comparison with earlier documents, this is a rather strong expression of interests.

It seems that Europeanization has reached a level where Germany feels the need to steer relations with Latin America in a direction congruent with its own preferences. This is in no small part due to the Treaty, a view also expressed by German interviewees. As several officials stated, the 2004/2007 Guidelines were written under different circumstances, when Germany's entire foreign policy was influenced by the idea of strengthening the EU's external dimension. But, as one official said, 'today, we are at a level, with the decisions of Lisbon that still have to be put into practice, where you do not have this perspective so much any more. Where you say [...] we should actually be a bit careful and see where there are

---

[10] Auswärtiges Amt (2010) Germany, Latin America and the Caribbean: A Strategy Paper by the German Government, Auswärtiges Amt, Berlin.

[11] The guidelines were slightly amended in 2007, but not in the EU section.

[12] Auswärtiges Amt (2007) Leitlinien für die deutsche Außenpolitik gegenüber Lateinamerika und der Karibik, Auswärtiges Amt, Berlin.

[13] Maihold 2010.

[14] Auswärtiges Amt (2010) Germany, Latin America and the Caribbean: A Strategy Paper by the German Government, Auswärtiges Amt, Berlin.

certain national interests that have to be protected.' However, interviews also show that it is not Lisbon alone that has brought about this shift in attitudes. Enlargement also played a role, with the new search for national identities and the increased reluctance to Europeanise policy perhaps connected to the size the EU has now reached. This is in line with recent papers studying the relationship between Germany and the EU and finding a new willingness to assert a national position at the EU level.[15]

What is remarkable is that in a country which used to be a prime example of Europeanism, this attitude has trickled down into areas of policy that are by no means vital to the German national interest, such as policy towards Latin America. The impact of the Treaty combines with enlargement and the more immediate impact of the economic crisis that has seen Germany reluctantly agree to bail-out deals of other Member States. Together, they create an environment in which policy-makers feel the need to more strongly assert themselves at the European level. In the case of Latin America, the feeling that the region has been 'left to Spain' for too long at the European level also contributes to this attitude. This issue will be further discussed below.

Thus, in the German case the Treaty has indeed caused a backlash—not for national policy, but for the European dimension. Combined with the abovementioned other factors, this leads to Germany wanting to make its voice heard more strongly in the EU's policy towards Latin America in the future, and to actually wanting to develop a stronger bilateral policy.

13.2.1.2 Spain

The Spanish case is that of another 'Europeanist' Member State forced to reconsider its role in the EU. While previously Spain saw itself as the problem and Europe as the solution, the EU's global disorientation leaves Spain in a difficult position where perhaps 'more Europe' is no longer the way forward.[16] Within policy towards Latin America, Spain has long seen itself as a 'bridge' between the EU and LAC countries.[17] At the same time, the EU level has been just one among several channels of conducting policy vis-à-vis the region. As one official stated, whenever Spain considers how to approach a country or an issue in Latin America, both the bilateral and the European paths are put to work together. Other officials

---

[15] Bulmer and Paterson 2010, 1071.

[16] Torreblanca 2010.

[17] In fact, a protocol laying out the importance of Spain's special relationship with Latin America had been annexed to the country's accession treaty to the European Communities. See: Treaty between the Member States of the European Communities concerning the Accession of the Kingdom of Spain and the Portuguese Republic to the European Economic Community and to the European Atomic Energy Agency Community: Joint Declaration of Intent on the Development and Intensification of Relations with the Countries of Latin America, L 302, Official Journal of the European Communities (1985), 479.

pointed out that during the 2010 rotating Presidency, Spain used bilateral channels—for example visits by high-ranking policy-makers—in order to achieve goals at the EU level. The decreased role of the rotating Presidency in external action will to some extent deprive Spain of the possibility to use its bilateral ties in order to influence EU-LAC relations. Simultaneously, interviewees confirmed the rising importance of the EU in Spanish Latin America policy, especially as a result of Lisbon—thus creating a double effect of removing EU policy towards Latin America further from Spain's control, while at the same time increasing its influence on Spanish national policy.[18]

Perhaps as a result of this, one official came up with an interesting way in which Spain might be able to use the European level in the future. If—as the interviewee suspected—the EU-LAC process were to be come more focused on global issues, then Member States and Spain in particular could actually build up a more powerful bilateral policy towards the region by delegating global issues to the EU. Similarly, another interviewee mentioned that the Treaty created the possibility for Spain to 'free up capacities' for bilateral affairs.[19] However, interviewees recognised that the ability to use the EU in this way depends on how consolidated the bilateral policy is. Delegating to the EU in order to be able to put a greater effort into bilateral policy was seen as an option only for those with an already well-established national Latin America policy. For Member States who have not yet developed such a policy, it would be difficult to do so due to the competences of the High Representative of the Union for Foreign Affairs and Security Policy and the European Council President under the Treaty. For Spain, one interviewee pointed out, this might mean that in the future, access points to EU external relations might become more thematic than geopolitical, focusing on issues such as technology cooperation.

Spanish interviewees in general had a hard time estimating the effects of the Treaty, as it has so far been eclipsed by the rotating Presidency and the flurry of Latin America-related activity that came with it. The real impact of the Treaty will only be felt with time. However, Spanish national policy towards Latin America is not only affected by the Treaty's entry into force, but also by other factors. The economic crisis has hit Spain severely and led to the Foreign Ministry's Secretariat of State for Iberoamerica being merged with the Secretariat of State for External Affairs in order to cut costs. The effects of this change for Spain's national policy towards Latin America also remain to be seen. Furthermore, Torreblanca points to the fact that both Spain itself and Europe as a whole are becoming less relevant for Latin America: the region no longer requires them to achieve its global goals, and it does not seek their political or economic inspiration.[20] Thus, Spain may at some point see itself in a position where its relationship with Latin America becomes

[18] The workings of the Spanish Presidency and the immediate impact of the Treaty of Lisbon on the rotating Presidency are discussed in more detail by Morillas (this volume).

[19] This idea will be further discussed in Sect. 13.2.3 on the 'Latin American' dimension.

[20] Torreblanca 2010.

much less special, not so much due to the effects of the Treaty, but rather due to a decreasing interest on behalf of Latin America. However, at least for the moment, Spanish diplomats remain convinced of the important role they have to play in the EU's Latin American policy.

13.2.1.3 United Kingdom

In the UK, so far there has been little in the way of direct repercussions of the Treaty on policy towards Latin America. However, this is probably mostly due to the overall low profile of Latin America in British foreign policy. Nevertheless, the last few months have seen some interesting developments. On 9 November 2010, the new Conservative Foreign Secretary William Hague gave the annual Canning House lecture on Latin America—the first time a British Foreign Secretary has given this lecture.[21] The speech, entitled 'Britain and Latin America—Historic Friends, Future Partners', highlighted the importance of the relationship and promised to put a greater emphasis on Latin America in the future. However, the EU is scarcely treated in the speech. It is only mentioned in connection with UK and EU action vis-à-vis the coup attempt in Ecuador in autumn 2010, and the UK's support for 'ambitious trade agreements' with Mercosur, the Andean region, and Central America, in the UK's 'role as undoubtedly the strongest and most persistent advocate of free trade in the European Union'.[22] An earlier, pre-Lisbon, Strategy Paper published by the Foreign and Commonwealth Office (FCO) under the Labour Government in 2007, reveals little more about how the UK then saw its role in the EU-LAC relationship and how EU membership affected bilateral relations aside from a focus on trade and drugs combat within the EU and 'a leading role' in all areas of EU-LAC relations.[23]

Given the low profile of UK-Latin American relations—this remains low despite promises to give the region more attention, according to one interviewee—it is thus likely that not much will change, either as a result of the Treaty or of the change in Government. Certainly, and similarly to the German case, the UK's national policy towards Latin America—even if it does grow stronger under the new government—will not require the same degree of reorientation as the Spanish national policy. Changes will occur within a wider EU-related reorientation of the UK. According to Gardner and Eizenstat, the notion that the Treaty represents a high-water mark of European integration is particularly strong in the UK.[24] This is confirmed by the Government's actions so far: it has introduced the European

[21] Hague 2010b.

[22] Hague 2010b.

[23] Foreign and Commonwealth Office (FCO) (2007) Latin America to 2020: a UK Public Strategy Paper, Foreign and Commonwealth Office, London, 19.

[24] Gardner and Eizenstat 2010.

Union Act 2011 to subject future treaty changes to greater control by Parliament and the people, including through referenda.[25] Additionally, in particular regarding external relations, the UK pushed for attaching two declarations to the Treaty on the separation of the CFSP from 'Communitarised' policies, reaffirming that the Treaty would not have a negative impact on national foreign policies.[26] According to former EU High Representative for the Common Foreign and Security Policy, Javier Solana, this distinction was 'important conceptually' for the UK.[27] Similarly to the German government though, the new British government has affirmed that it will make its voice heard within the EU and will remain an active player within the Union committed to achieving the UK's interest.[28] Interviews confirm that it intends to do so also in policy towards Latin America, but that the primary line of UK engagement in Latin America remains bilateral, more so because some Latin American countries such as Brazil—with whom the UK has relatively intense relations compared to the rest of the region—are reluctant to engage with the EU as a whole and prefer bilateral action.[29] As in the case of Spain, which seems to be losing some relevance to Latin America, this is not directed by the EU or the UK, but rather by the Latin American side.

Overall, therefore, we are likely to see some adjustments to national Latin America policies as a result of the entry into force of the Treaty. These are likely to be felt most harshly in Spain, which has the most active policy towards Latin America and thus has to make the biggest adjustments. In Germany, the Treaty—along with other factors—has caused a change in the overall attitude towards the EU, with Germany wanting to pursue a stronger national agenda at the EU level and to intensify its bilateral relations with Latin America. Interestingly, both Spain and Germany see Lisbon as an opportunity to develop a more powerful national policy. In the UK, finally, the impact of the Treaty is felt at an even more general level, but mingles also with the effects of the change of Government after 13 years of Labour rule. For the UK's Latin America policy, changes are thus most likely to be felt within this more general context. It is therefore important, as all three cases have shown, not to overstate the impact of the Treaty on national Latin America policy. Changes at the global and national levels, as well as within Latin America itself, also play an important role.

---

[25] The European Union Act 2011 received Royal Assent—and therefore entered into effect—on 19 July 2011.

[26] Treaty on the Functioning of the European Union, Declarations 13 and 14 concerning the Common Foreign and Security Policy.

[27] House of Commons Foreign Affairs Committee (2008) Foreign Policy Aspects of the Lisbon Treaty: Third Report of Session 2007–2008. Report, together with formal minutes, oral and written evidence, The Stationary Office, London.

[28] Hague 2010a.

[29] This may give an indication of how seriously Brazil takes its 'strategic partnership' with the EU, but this discussion is beyond the scope of this paper.

13.2.2 The 'Brussels' Dimension: Interaction Between National Policies and the EU Level

How does the Treaty of Lisbon affect the Member States' interaction with the European level and their ability to influence the EU's policy vis-à-vis Latin America? This section addresses this question by analysing how the newly created posts and their responsibilities play out, assessing developments during the first year of EU-Latin America policy-making under the Treaty, and the impact this has on the Member States.

13.2.2.1 New Rules, New Posts, New Policy?

Although not technically the creation of a new post, one of the Treaty's most important innovations was recasting the High Representative's post, currently occupied by Baroness Catherine Ashton from the UK. In theory, the High Representative has the possibility to bring greater coherence to the EU's external policy with her double hat of Commission Vice-President and Chair of the Foreign Affairs Council (FAC). That way, she should be able to bridge the tension between Community external policies and the CFSP. This potential is in line with the Treaty bringing all aspects of external action under the same principles laid out in Article 21(1) of the Treaty on European Union.[30]

Many interviewees are currently dissatisfied with the lack of coherence of EU action in relations with Latin America. One official described the CFSP agenda regarding the region as 'extremely bizarre', with Brazil—Latin America's most important country—almost never coming up at the Council Working Group for Latin America (COLAT), while Cuba—of interest only to a few—appeared almost every month. Other issues that are central to relations with Latin America, such as drugs and counternarcotics, as well as development, are dealt with through other mechanisms and never appear on COLAT's agenda. According to the interviewee, the EU's approach to Latin America—as to any other third region—is uncoordinated at best. Ironically, the UK's insistence on keeping the CFSP separate from the Community areas of cooperation under the Treaty will have prolonged this situation.

Given that many interviewees would like to see greater coherence of EU relations with Latin America, the new arrangements might be an opportunity. However, this may be problematic, as in addition to the Member States and the High Representative, a team of four Commissioners is still involved in external relations (Neighbourhood and Enlargement, Trade, Development, and International Co-operation, Humanitarian aid and Crisis Response). All of these, except for Neighbourhood and Enlargement, are relevant for EU-LAC relations.[31] To what

[30] Treaty on the European Union, Article 21 (1); Treaty on the Functioning of the European Union, Articles 205, 207(1), and 208(1); see also Hillman and Kleimann 2010, 2.

[31] Allen and Smith 2010, 207.

extent this rearrangement can lead to greater coherence is questionable.[32] As Gardner and Eizenstat point out, this might not be a big problem if the High Representative were an experienced, well-respected figure able to impose herself on the Commissioners and the Member States. But by choosing relatively low profile Catherine Ashton, the Member States made clear that they want 'the High Representative to be their servant, not their rival.'[33]

Another post created by the Treaty with competences in the EU's external dimension is the European Council President. He 'shall, at his level and in that capacity, ensure the external representation of the Union on issues concerning its common foreign and security policy, without prejudice to the powers of the High Representative'.[34] The Treaty leaves open how exactly this will be done. That way, the European Council President is unlikely to contribute to greater consistency and easier communication between the EU and its external partners, especially as the President of the Commission, Barroso, also continues to see a role for himself in external relations, an area in which he had previously been very active already.[35]

These multiple posts lead to what Gardner and Eizenstat term 'overrepresentation',[36] a problem that is currently particularly pronounced as the EU makes the transition from the pre-Lisbon system of external representation to the post-Lisbon era. This became clearly evident at the EU-LAC Summit in Madrid in May 2010, which saw the Spanish Presidency, the High Representative, the European Council President, and the Commission President all giving speeches, issuing statements, and evaluating the process—of course, alongside representatives of some 60 European and Latin American states who were also trying to make their voices heard. One press release evaluating the Summit, for example, included statements by the Spanish Prime Minister, the European Council President, and the Commission President.[37]

Yet, while the High Representative faces competition in her external representation of the EU, on the whole this is perhaps not the worst that could happen in relations with Latin America and the Caribbean. Due to Ashton's vast portfolio, there is a distinct possibility for her external relations team to become overworked and torn between duties in Brussels and abroad.[38] Regions like Latin America that do not push themselves to the forefront through major political, economic, or security significance, might slip further into insignificance. Latin America has always struggled with the fact that it is neither rich, nor poor, nor mired in conflict

---

32 A similar point is made in relation to the EU's neighbourhood by Dragneva and Wolczuk (this volume).

33 Gardner and Eizenstat 2010.

34 Treaty on the European Union, Article 15 (6); see also Wouters et al. 2008, 153.

35 Allen and Smith 2010, 207.

36 Gardner and Eizenstat 2010.

37 Spanish Presidency of the EU (2010) The Madrid Summit has been "a success" according to EU and Latin American leaders, Spanish Presidency of the EU, Madrid. www.eu2010.es/en/cumbre_ue-alc/noticias/may18_ue-alc_clausura.html. Last accessed 3 June 2011.

38 Duke 2008, 15.

and therefore not particularly high on the list of European external priorities. The problem of an overstretched external relations team may, however, present a possibility for particularly interested countries to retain more importance in external relations than they would otherwise. Thus, there may be an opportunity for Spain to take Latin America off the High Representative's shoulders. However, if this route is not taken, it is very likely that the window of opportunity for constructing a special EU relationship with Latin America that opened with Spain's accession and began closing with successive enlargements has closed completely with the Treaty.

A further factor is the diminishing importance of the rotating Presidency, which has already been alluded to. I focus on the Spanish Presidency during the first half of 2010, since it intended to emphasise EU-LAC relations and hosted the 6th EU-LAC Summit in Madrid. Overall, the Spanish Presidency tried to remain very active in EU external relations.[39] However, Spanish interviewees did see the reconfigurations resulting from the Treaty as a limitation on their ability to carry out a 'Presidency as usual'. As Torreblanca puts it, Spain 'has been the first country to swallow the bitter medicine of accepting the secondary role the treaty gave national capitals',[40] as the arrival of Ashton and van Rompuy meant Spain had to hand over the reins on important issues. Spanish interviewees were highly conscious of the provisional character of external representation as the Treaty's provisions slowly began to take effect during the Spanish Presidency. Therefore, as one interviewee mentioned, there seems to have been a sentiment of getting some things done either 'now or never' in relations with Latin America. Read in this light, the fact that for the first time ever an Action Plan setting out goals for the strategic partners was approved at the Madrid Summit could be seen as a means to codify some action items before the new external relations team took over control. As one official put it, 'in the context of the Lisbon Treaty, it would be impossible under a Belgian or a Hungarian future presidency to achieve these objectives.' I return to this point below.

In terms of output, Spanish interviewees are very pleased with the output of the Madrid Summit. Indeed, in comparison to earlier EU-LAC Summits, this edition and the surrounding sub-regional summits (EU-Central America, EU-Mercosur, etc.) have achieved a number of things[41]:

- The Madrid Declaration and corresponding Action Plan.
- The Latin America Investment Facility (LAIF), supposed to mobilise funding for investment projects.

---

[39] Allen and Smith 2010, 208.

[40] Torreblanca 2010.

[41] Council of the European Union, Madrid Declaration: Towards a new stage in the bi-regional partnership—innovation and technology for sustainable development and social inclusion; Council of the European Union (2010b) Madrid Action Plan 2010–2012.

- The creation of an EU-LAC Foundation to foster ties.
- The conclusion of negotiations on an Association Agreement with the states of Central America.[42]
- The conclusion of negotiations on multi-party trade agreements with Peru and Colombia.
- The re-opening of negotiations on an Association Agreement with Mercosur.

Spanish officials were keen to point out that their political will to make progress was essential in achieving these outcomes. This squares with other interviewees pointing to the high importance of rotating Presidencies in advancing the EU-LAC relationship. The extent to which the new external relations team can uphold the political will developed by the Spanish Presidency is rather questionable. Additionally, one Spanish official points out that neither Baroness Ashton nor van Rompuy have had a chance to build up a sensitivity towards Latin America and are therefore unlikely to give the relationship a strong boost.[43] Hence, Spanish policymakers feel that their country has to maintain a strong presence in the EU's institutions to keep the process invigorated.

However, some difficulties remain with the achievements of the Madrid summit. First, the extent to which the steps laid out in the Action Plan are binding is doubtful. Given the abovementioned difficulties the new external relations team may have in keeping up the relationship, it is possible for the Action Plan not to be followed up. Second, both the Association Agreement with Central America and the multi-party agreements with Peru and Colombia still have to be finalised and ratified. Under the Treaty's rules, the European Parliament gets to approve or reject them, an issue that may complicate ratification. Additionally, there appears to be some confusion over the precise nature of the agreements with Peru and Colombia. I return to this point below. Third and finally, it is doubtful whether the differences that brought EU-Mercosur negotiations to a halt five years ago can actually be resolved today. Some Member States, including France and Ireland, were unhappy with the re-opening of the negotiations due to their strong stance on agricultural issues, which makes completion of the process even harder. None of these issues will disappear with the passing of external relations from the rotating Presidency to the High Representative. The headquarters question has been resolved.

[42] This agreement is particularly important as it is the EU's first region-to-region agreement, thus giving its approach to foster regional integration through negotiating agreements with regional blocs a much-needed boost, especially after the breakdown of negotiations with the Andean Community (from which the bilateral agreements with Colombia and Peru emerged) and the difficult negotiations with Mercosur that stalled from 2004 to 2010.

[43] However, it is worth mentioning that the previous High Representative, Javier Solana, did not develop a particularly high profile in the EU-LAC relationship either, despite his Spanish nationality.

The diminishing importance of the rotating Presidency is also felt at the 'everyday level' of policy-making. Until the end of 2010, the COLAT Working Group was still being chaired by the rotating Presidency. Similarly, at recent meetings of the EU-Chile Association Committee and the EU-Mexico Joint Committee,[44] the head of the Commission Directorate responsible for Latin America, and the COLAT Chair from the Belgian rotating Presidency jointly chaired the EU side.[45] However, on 22 December 2010 the High Representative appointed Rafael Gelabert—a Spaniard—as the permanent Chair of COLAT, thus taking over responsibility for agenda-setting and preparation of the Working Group.[46] Thus, an important instrument for setting the EU-LAC agenda disappears from the powers of the rotating Presidency. However, the rotating Presidency will continue to have an importance, also seeing as it continues to chair meetings concerned with what used to be the 'Community' areas of external relations,[47] with development and trade being of considerable importance to the EU-LAC relationship.

Overall, while the disappearance of the rotating Presidency from external relations has important implications for the ability of individual Member States to influence the agenda, it must not be overstated, as enlargement already considerably increased the gaps between each individual country's successive Presidencies. Combined with the effects of the Treaty, however, these two factors substantively reduce the importance of the rotating Presidency in external relations.

13.2.2.2 Agreements With Latin America and the Caribbean: An Increased Role for the European Parliament

The conclusion of agreements with third countries and regions, crucial for EU-LAC relations, will also be affected by the Treaty, as it gives the European Parliament increased competences in the conclusion of trade agreements. The CCP passes under the ordinary legislative procedure.[48] Any trade agreement is thus now subject to the Parliament's co-decision,[49] effectively giving it veto power. 'Pure' trade agreements have to be approved by the Parliament only, while mixed agreements including areas where the Member States retain competences have to be ratified also by Member

[44] These committees exist in connection with the cooperation agreements of the EU with these countries.

[45] European Union (EU), 10th Joint Committee Mexico—European Union, 29 October 2010, Delegation of the European Union to Mexico, Mexico City; European Union (EU), VIII Comité de Asociación Chile-Unión Europea-Comunicado Conjunto, 25 de noviembre de 2010, Delegation of the European Union to Chile, Santiago de Chile. ec.europa.eu/delegations/chile/documents/press_corner/20101126_es.pdf. Last accessed 3 June 2011.

[46] European External Action Service (EEAS), EU Delegations, European External Action Service, Brussels. eeas.europa.eu/delegations/index_en.htm. Last accessed 3 June 2011.

[47] Duke 2008, 14.

[48] Hillman and Kleimann 2010, 3.

[49] Treaty on the Functioning of the European Union, Article 218(6) (a); see also Hillman and Kleimann 2010, 3.

States. In the case of the multi-party agreements with the Andean countries, this has already given rise to some confusion. One interviewee complained that nobody knew for certain whether the agreements were mixed or not, and that ratification by the European Parliament alone would not be easy—let alone the ratification by 27 Member States if they did turn out to be mixed.[50] Although the Parliament cannot directly influence the negotiation process, it can signal its red lines to the negotiating team. The question is what stance the Parliament will take on trade agreements and to what extent it will become a protectionist force. The negotiations with Mercosur, which are already very complex—especially concerning agricultural issues—are unlikely to be facilitated. It is also possible that the Parliament position itself as a guardian of the principles of EU external action, meaning that issues such as sustainable development or human rights may now impact more strongly upon trade than previously.[51] Such issues should be of considerable importance in agreements with Latin America, where for example the question of human rights continues to trouble many Europeans. As one interviewee pointed out, the issue of human rights is particularly important in the context of the multi-party trade agreement with Colombia. It may therefore resurface as the Parliament considers the agreement. If we add Latin America's increasing ability (and willingness) to 'shop around' the world for the best agreements and thus for alternatives to the EU to this increased complexity on the EU side,[52] this will likely make the conclusion of new agreements even more difficult.

13.2.2.3 Member State Interaction on the 'Brussels' Dimension

A number of changes results from the new rules slowly beginning to take hold on the 'Brussels dimension'. For the Member States, this means trying to maintain a national influence in the face of increased competition from the High Representative and the European Council President in particular. However, while Spain tries especially hard to keep up its influence on European Latin America policy, other Member States might see the changes caused by the Treaty as chance for diminishing precisely this influence. Several Spanish interviewees expressed the view that there is essentially little or no difference between Spanish and EU interests in Latin America, and that other Member States trust Spain in dealing with the region. However, it seems that this is not seen entirely the same way in other Member States. While officials in Germany and the UK highly appreciate Spain's concern for Latin America and the effort put into the relationship during the 2010 Presidency, they are cautious regarding Spain's overall influence. There

[50] On the ratification process of agreements involving trade and agricultural matters under the Treaty of Lisbon, see also Wouters et al. 2008, 180.

[51] Hillman and Kleimann 2010.

[52] Agreements with China have proliferated in recent years, and are generally free of political conditionality. They have thus become an attractive alternative for Latin American countries as trade with China has increased substantially.

thus seems to be a cleavage between how Spain believes other Member States see its role on Latin America and how it is in fact perceived. At the same time, several Spanish officials also stated that Spain would like to see other EU members to be more involved in the EU-LAC relationship, but that it has been difficult to get them interested.[53] It is therefore difficult to blame Spain for the impression that the other Member States seem to be fine with its leading role, since nobody—perhaps aside from Portugal—ever seems to have tried very hard to match their engagement. Lisbon may solve this problem to some extent by diminishing the overall role of individual states. How good this is for EU-LAC relations as a whole remains to be seen. Additionally, even in the departments responsible for Latin America at European institutions, Spanish nationals dominate. As many staff will continue in their posts after the reshuffle, this is not likely to change in the near future, if ever. If Spain continues to successfully place its nationals in these positions—the recent nomination of a Spaniard as chair of COLAT points in this direction—it is likely to retain its significant influence, unless the other Member States begin making a greater effort. The 2010 German Strategy Paper, as we have seen, may lead to a more active German role in EU-LAC policy.

Another important area of interaction between Member States in relations with Latin America is the issue of Cuba. One of the Spanish Presidency's goals had been an overhaul of the EU's Common Position on Cuba,[54] whose creation had been strongly supported by the previous conservative Spanish government in 1996. Since the Cuban question quite politicised in Spain,[55] the current socialist government has rather a different idea of what the Common Position should look like, wanting to open up the possibility for further dialogue and even an agreement. However, the Spanish Presidency did not succeed in changing the Common Position.[56] Its yearly revision was first delayed to the autumn to give new events in Cuba a chance to develop.[57] However, the Member States again did not reach agreement in October 2010, as for example Germany and the UK remain firmly opposed to the revision. The High Representative was thus tasked with exploring the possibilities for relations with Cuba and report back to the Council.[58] This example shows how the making of policy towards Latin America at the EU level is slipping from the Presidency's task list onto that of the High Representative. Pre-Lisbon, drafting a paper on the future of relations would probably have been

[53] Such difficulties were already perceived by del Arenal 2006, 311.

[54] Common Position 96/697/CFSP of 2 December 1996 defined by the Council on the basis of Article J.2 of the Treaty on European Union, on Cuba.

[55] Gratius 2010.

[56] Although the first ever Country Strategy Paper for Cuba was adopted by the Commission in May 2010: European Commission (2010) Republic of Cuba–European Union Country Strategy Paper and National Indicative Programme for the period 2011–2013.

[57] Then Spanish Foreign Minister Moratinos helped broker a deal on the release of 52 political prisoners.

[58] Council of the European Union (2010) Press Release, 3041st Council meeting–Foreign Affairs, Luxembourg, 25 October 2010.

entrusted to the current Presidency, thus representing a significant possibility for individual Member States to influence EU foreign policy. While any new policy will still have to meet Member State approval before translating into practice, the initial direction can now be set by the High Representative and her team.

13.2.3 *The 'Latin American' Dimension: Interaction 'on the Ground'*

With Commission Delegations in third countries turning into EU Delegations and the creation of the EEAS, the way in which Member States interact with the new EU diplomats 'on the ground' will also change. In fact, the 'Latin American' dimension is where one British interviewee suggests the Treaty's impact on British policy towards the region will be the strongest, as the ways of working with the other Member States and the EU Delegations change. Interaction with the EEAS on the ground has several dimensions.

First, the diminished role of the rotating Presidency also makes itself felt here. Heads of diplomatic missions of EU Member States hold regular meetings in which they discuss current affairs affecting them and their host country. These meetings are no longer chaired by the rotating Presidency, but by a representative of the local EU Delegation. This takes away one important tool of the Presidency to steer its fellow Member States into a certain direction during its six-month term. Within Latin America policy, this impact should be especially harshly felt by any future Spanish (or Portuguese) Presidencies. The 2010 Spanish Presidency, next to the work put in through the EU, also made a strong bilateral effort to facilitate the achievements of the Madrid Summit, including through embassies and consulates. If in the future, representation of the Union as a whole is largely taken over by the EU Delegations, this is quite likely to further reduce the role of the Presidency and the visibility of individual Member States.

On the other hand, this new arrangement also represents a chance for more consistent EU representation. So far, this was hugely dependent on the manpower and dedication of the rotating Presidency to activities in a certain country or region during their term. While Spain focused a lot of its energy on Latin America, other countries did so to a much lesser extent—beginning with the problem that not all EU Member States, especially the smaller and newer ones, have embassies in all Latin American countries. Even the UK has reduced its presence in Central America considerably. Therefore, with its fairly tight web of representations—15 Delegations in the LAC region, plus six further local offices staffed by chargés d'affaires[59]—the EU can provide better coverage of the region than some of the

[59] European External Action Service (EEAS), EU Delegations, European External Action Service, Brussels. eeas.europa.eu/delegations/index_en.htm. Last accessed 3 June 2011; Formuszewicz and Kumoch 2010, 30 et seq.

Member States. Additionally, a shift away from the six-month rotation system might bring greater continuity to EU representation on the ground, as intensity and emphases shift less.

In addition to the representational role the Delegations will take on, the EEAS staff at EU missions will assume responsibility for the implementation of EU aid policies and expenditure. This leads to worries that EU development aid in general may be in danger of becoming more a tool of European foreign policy than focused on eradicating poverty and hunger.[60] For Latin America, however, it may be a chance for improvement, as interviewees from all three Member States complain about the low degree of EU aid coordination. However, especially British interviewees were also concerned about a current lack of transparency in the way EU aid is spent and a lack of information on this on behalf of the Commission. This is especially relevant for UK aid to Latin America, where the British government closed its bilateral programme in 2008 and now only delivers aid through NGOs and multilaterally—among others through the EU.[61] The UK is therefore likely to want to keep a close eye on the EU Delegations' delivery of aid in Latin America to ensure it gets administered in the way the British government wants this to happen. Aid delivery under the auspices of the EEAS is thus only likely to be successful in the eyes of the Member States if it is accompanied by a transparent information policy.

Furthermore, as previously mentioned, not all Member States have or can afford to build up a strong diplomatic network around the world. The tightening and increased competence of EU external representation may thus offer an opportunity for states with limited capacities to be represented in locations where they would not normally have an embassy. The example of the UK in Central America, where cost-cutting exercises have led to the closure of diplomatic missions, however, shows that not only small or new Member States may benefit. One British official toyed with the idea of closer collaboration with EU delegations in these countries as one potential possibility to capitalise on the Treaty's changes. Similarly, Spanish officials are thinking about how the delegations might be used. One official stated that collaboration in consular affairs through the delegations might liberate some capacities to concentrate on other issues. On the whole, Spanish officials seemed the most enthusiastic about 'outsourcing' some policy areas to the EU Delegations. However, interviews confirm that some states might have an interest in delegating competences to the EU Delegations 'for less noble reasons' such as financial constraints.[62] Especially as Spain battles the current economic

---

[60] Allen and Smith 2010, 211.

[61] Aside from a residual bilateral programme in Nicaragua and an 'emerging markets' programme in Brazil. See Department for International Development (2008) Working Partnership in Latin America, Department for International Development, London. www.dfid.gov.uk/pubs/files/english-latin-america-civil-society-launch.pdf. and Department for International Development (2009) Latin America Region, Department for International Development, London/Glasgow. www.dfid.gov.uk/Where-we-work/Latin-America–Caribbean/. Last accessed 3 June 2011.

[62] Duke 2008, 17.

crisis, and Spanish enterprises pressure the government for better support in the Asian growth markets, Spain appears to see itself confronted with some diplomatic overstretch and might welcome the EU Delegations taking some work off their shoulders. Other Member States, including Germany, however, are sceptical. 'This is not likely to happen,' one German interviewee commented on the idea of consular cooperation through the Delegations.

In all three Member States under scrutiny, there is a high degree of consciousness that EU Delegations have to be staffed with officials from their respective diplomatic services or at least their nationals. With respect to Latin America, this seems to have worked to some degree for Spain under the 2010 rotation, where a Spaniard—Alfonso Díez Torres—became head of the EU delegation to Argentina.[63] In designing the EEAS, Germany was heavily in favour of having German diplomats rotate in and out of the EEAS, 'in order to maintain national influence,' as one interviewee stated, while the UK was also keen on getting 'proper representation' of its nationals.[64] The Council decision of 26 July 2010 stipulates that members of the EEAS recruited from national diplomatic services—who will eventually represent one-third of the overall EEAS staff[65]—will indeed be 'temporary agents'.[66] Recruitment of EEAS staff itself should 'be based on merit [...]. The staff of the EEAS should comprise a meaningful presence of nationals from all the Member States.'[67] The recruitment of nationals from the Member States to positions in Latin America is thus an important factor in ensuring influence 'on the ground', even more so if these officials are members of the national diplomatic service whose loyalties to the national level are ensured by regular rotation. Overall, in the LAC region, Spaniards currently dominate among the Heads of Delegations.[68]

---

[63] European External Action Service (EEAS) (2010b) High Representative Catherine Ashton appoints new Heads and Deputy Heads of EU Delegations under the 2010 rotation, European External Action Service, Brussels. www.consilium.europa.eu/uedocs/cms_data/docs/pressdata/EN/foraff/116509.pdf. Last accessed 3 June 2011.

[64] House of Commons Foreign Affairs Committee (2008) Foreign Policy Aspects of the Lisbon Treaty: Third Report of Session 2007–2008. Report, together with formal minutes, oral and written evidence, The Stationary Office, London, 67.

[65] Council of the European Union, Council Decision of 26 July 2010 establishing the organisation and functioning of the European External Action Service, Official Journal of the European Union, Preamble (12).

[66] Council of the European Union, Council Decision of 26 July 2010 establishing the organisation and functioning of the European External Action Service, Official Journal of the European Union, Article 6 (2).

[67] Council of the European Union (2010e) Council Decision of 26 July 2010 establishing the organisation and functioning of the European External Action Service, Official Journal of the European Union, Preamble 10.

[68] European External Action Service (EEAS) (2010a) EU Delegations, European External Action Service, Brussels. http://eeas.europa.eu/delegations/index_en.htm. Last accessed 3 June 2011; Formuszewicz and Kumoch 2010, 33 et seq.

However, all officials interviewed were keen to point out that any ideas mentioned in connection with the EEAS were mainly based on speculation. Only time will tell how the interaction between Member States and the EU 'on the ground' will look like. The extent to which the new delegations will be subject to agency drift and begin developing their own remit depends not only on how tightly Member States manage to wrap them in a well-defined margin of competences, but also on the extent to which Member State delegations on the ground can put them to work at their service rather than letting them set the tune. Either way, Member States are unlikely to give up control over the EEAS and the EU delegations willingly and will do everything in their power to make them work in their favour by keeping them tightly controlled.

13.3 Conclusion

EU and Member State relations with Latin America will change in a number of ways as a result of the Treaty. Member States will have to adapt their national foreign policies. Spain, as the country with the most active national policy, will have to adapt the most. Germany and the UK's Latin America policies will be affected more indirectly. In Germany, the Treaty, combined with enlargement and the current Euro crisis, has provoked greater Euroscepticism, while in Britain, the Treaty combines with the 2010 Government change to take the already extant Euroscepticism up one further notch. On the other hand, at least in Spain and Germany, policy-makers see the shift of competences towards the EU level also as a chance to focus more on some aspects of national policy towards Latin America.

Moreover, Member States will have fewer possibilities to influence EU-Latin America policy directly through the rotating Presidency, as the High Representative and her team take over responsibility for large areas of EU external relations—although the Treaty does not necessarily make EU external representation less complex. The beginnings of this takeover process have become evident in relations with Latin America during the Spanish EU Presidency, both at the 6th EU-LAC Summit, and in relations with Cuba. Although Member States remain in the driver's seat of the Union's foreign policy, the High Representative clearly has the possibility to influence its course. The question is the extent to which she can realise this potential in relations with Latin America, as her portfolio and that of her team are vast. This might be a possibility for interested Member States to retain control of policy areas the High Representative cannot prioritise.

Finally, Member States have to rethink their interaction with EU Delegations on the ground. As in bilateral policy, there is a possibility of the Delegations taking some aspects of policy off their shoulders, thus freeing up capacities for bilateral policy matters, a possibility considered interesting especially by Spain and, to some extent, the UK, while Germany is more sceptical. In Spain, the possibility to actually intensify bilateral policy without having to step up costs predominates, while in the UK, the possibility to get representation with little national presence seems more predominant.

Overall, the Treaty of Lisbon presents both possibilities for boosts and backlashes regarding European policy towards Latin America. Only time will tell which paths are chosen, but several things are certain. First, Latin America will not become a priority region for the EU. Second, as Latin America becomes more powerful politically and economically, Europe has to make a greater effort to remain an attractive partner. Third and finally, the Member States will not willingly give up their competences, unless they can gain something from it.

References

Acosta D (2009) Latin American reactions to the adoption of the returns directive. Centre for European Policy Studies, Brussels

Allen D, Smith M (2010) Relations with the rest of the world. Journal of Common Market Studies 48:205–223

Bulmer S, Paterson WE (2010) Germany and the European Union: From 'tamed' to normalized power? International Affairs 86:1051–1072

del Arenal C (2006) Una relación singular: España y las relaciones UE-América Latina. In: Freres C, Sanahuja JA (eds) América Latina y la Unión Europea: Estrategias para una relación necesaria. Icaria, Barcelona

Duke S (2008) The Lisbon Treaty and external relations. Eipascope 1:13–18

Formuszewicz R, Kumoch J (2010) The practice of appointing the heads of EU delegations in the wake of the council decision on external action service. Polish Institute of International Affairs, Warsaw

Gardner AL, Eizenstat SE (2010) New Treaty, new influence? Foreign Affairs 89:104–119

Gratius S (2010) Why does Spain not have a policy for Latin America? FRIDE, Madrid

Hague W (2010a) Britain's Foreign Policy in a networked world: speech outlining the Government's vision for UK foreign policy, 1 July 2010, Foreign and Commonwealth Office (FCO), London. www.fco.gov.uk/en/news/latest-news/?view=Speech&id=22472881. Last accessed 3 June 2011

Hague W (2010b) Britain and Latin America: historic friends, future partners. 2010 Canning Lecture, 9 Nov 2010, Foreign and Commonwealth Office, London. www.fco.gov.uk/en/news/latest-news/?view=Speech&id=25092682. Last accessed 3 June 2011

Hillman J, Kleimann D (2010) Trading places: the new dynamics of EU trade policy under the Treaty of Lisbon. German Marshall Fund of the United States, Washington

Jupille J, Caporaso JA (1999) Institutionalism and the European union: beyond international relations and comparative politics. Annual Review of Political Science 2:429–444

Maihold G (2010) Das neue Lateinamerikakonzept der Bundesregierung: Politikinnovation durch Konzeptentwicklung? Iberoamerikanisches Institut, Berlin

Torreblanca JI (2010) Foreign policy needs a rethink above and beyond Europe, Financial Times Online. www.ft.com/cms/s/0d38ed5c-71d2-11df-8eec-00144feabdc0. Last accessed 3 June 2011

Wouters J, Coppens D, De Meester B (2008) The European union's external relations after the Lisbon Treaty. In: Griller S, Ziller J (eds) The Lisbon Treaty: EU constitutionalism without a constitutional treaty. Springer, Wien, pp 144–203

Chapter 14
No Data Without Protection? Re-Thinking Transatlantic Information Exchange for Law Enforcement Purposes After Lisbon

María Quesada Gámez and Elitsa Mincheva

Abstract In the area of Justice and Home Affairs, the issue of data protection has generated significant controversy in the framework of the EU's external relations. More specifically, the USA and the EU have developed particularly close ties in counter-terrorism cooperation under the umbrella of the New Transatlantic Agenda and the sharing and protection of information holds a central place in the transatlantic security relationship. The challenge posed to the Passenger Name Record (PNR) agreement before the European Court of Justice and the European Parliament's rejection of the interim SWIFT agreement provide a good example of the concerns which arise with regard to data privacy on one side of the Atlantic and of the way this tension affects transatlantic cooperation in the area of counter-terrorism action. The Treaty of Lisbon came into force at a time when the EU–US PNR and SWIFT agreements were pending ratification, and shortly after the adoption of the Stockholm Programme by the Council. Against this background, this contribution explores the extent to which the entry into force of the Treaty of Lisbon is likely to affect current and future transatlantic agreements in the area of information exchange for law enforcement purposes, namely the EU–US PNR,

María Quesada Gámez—Academic Assistant, Department of EU International Relations and Diplomacy Studies, College of Europe, Bruges, Belgium.
Elitsa Mincheva—Academic Assistant, Department of EU General Studies, College of Europe, Bruges, Belgium.

M. Quesada Gámez (✉)
Department of EU International Relations and Diplomacy Studies,
College of Europe, Bruges, Belgium
e-mail: maria.quesada-gamez@coleurope.eu

E. Mincheva
Department of EU General Studies, College of Europe, Bruges, Belgium
e-mail: elitsa.mincheva@coleurope.eu

P. J. Cardwell (ed.), *EU External Relations Law and Policy in the Post-Lisbon Era*,
DOI: 10.1007/978-90-6704-823-1_14, © T.M.C. ASSER PRESS, The Hague,
The Netherlands, and the authors 2012

SWIFT and data protection agreements. It also explores the ways in which this impact translates in the transatlantic security agenda.

Contents

14.1 Introduction

Transatlantic cooperation in security matters is traditionally characterised as a strong partnership founded on shared interests and common values. However, particularly in the context of the fight against terrorism, the partners have had to face divergences on important matters, one of which is information exchange for law enforcement and security purposes.

EU–US cooperation in the area of Justice and Home Affairs (JHA) took off in the mid-1990s under the umbrella of the New Transatlantic Agenda, in the form of bi-annual 'informal' JHA 'Troika' meetings.[1] The terrorist attacks in the US and Europe provided impetus not only for the adoption of internal measures to combat terrorist activity in both the EU and the US, but also gave momentum to transatlantic cooperation on matters of police, judicial and border-control policy. In the EU, this included the adoption of a common definition of terrorism and a list of terrorist groups, a Europe-wide arrest warrant, enhanced tools to stem terrorist financing and new measures to strengthen EU border controls and improve aviation security, as well as the appointment of an EU Counter-Terrorism Coordinator. Europol and Eurojust's powers were strengthened.[2]

The US administration, on the other hand, adopted in 2002 a strategy of 'smart borders' which required that goods and persons be screened prior to their arrival in the US.[3] The instruments for implementation of this policy included, among

[1] Faull and Soreca 2008.

[2] Maria O'Neill, in this volume, discusses the legal and institutional nature of these developments within the context of EU–North Africa relations.

[3] The White House, Smart Borders for the twenty-first century, Office of the Press Secretary, Washington, DC, 25 November 2002.

others, the expansion of the US-VISIT Programme[4] to new areas, the creation of the Electronic System of Travel Authorisation[5] and the Passenger Name Record (PNR).[6] Besides, the US Treasury set up secretly in 2001 the Terrorist Finance Tracking Programme (TFTP). The programme allows to request the global leader of financial messaging services, SWIFT, to transfer financial transaction data to the US authorities for counter-terrorism purposes. The contents of the programme breached European data protection rules. These unilateral American policies and the related measures were seen as resulting in the emergence of large zones of virtual, transnational border-control practices.[7] It is the extraterritorial nature of the US regulations that provoked disagreements between the EU and the US. The European Parliament was particularly vocal in opposing this type of 'creeping extra-territoriality'.[8] It has been argued that 'the transnational nature of the US homeland security regulations and their coercive mechanisms compelled the EU to adjust its policies in line with those of the US'.[9]

In the context of the fight against terrorism, the exchange of personal data quickly developed as one of the most important—and most difficult—issues in the transatlantic security dialogue. Arrangements for data sharing and resulting provisions on data protection were made in a number of agreements, in a piecemeal fashion.[10] In all cases, EU concerns about data protection made negotiations difficult. The two most controversial agreements, PNR and SWIFT, revealed significant divergences between the two partners—in terms of both process and substance. The Treaty of Lisbon came into force at a time when both agreements were pending ratification, and shortly after the adoption of the Stockholm Programme by the Council. Against this background, the present contribution makes a brief overview of the main factors shaping EU–US cooperation in the area of information exchange for law enforcement and security purposes pre-Lisbon and subsequently explores the extent to which the entry into force of the Treaty of Lisbon is likely to affect current and future transatlantic agreements—the EU–US PNR, TFTP and data protection agreements.

We argue that the entry into force of the Lisbon Treaty brings a new dimension in EU–US cooperation in data sharing for counter-terrorism purposes. In effect, the

---

[4] The programme was created in order to help identify visa-overstayers and since 9/11 includes biometric information on travellers.

[5] ESTA is a recent pre-travel authorisation programme for travellers from visa-waiver countries.

[6] It requires air carriers operating passenger flights to or from the US, to make PNR information available to the Customs Service, with non-compliance leading to the imposition of fines or even refusal of landing rights.

[7] Pawlak 2009a, 2.

[8] Pawlak 2009a, 3.

[9] Pawlak 2009a, 2.

[10] These include the agreements between the US and Europol of 2001 and 2002, an agreement between the US Department of Justice and Eurojust of 2006. In 2010 two new EU–US agreements on extradition and mutual legal assistance entered into force, providing for the exchange of information in the framework of criminal investigations.

new legal and institutional framework established by the Treaty has given the EU the tools to shape a traditionally unbalanced relationship, mainly—but not exclusively—through a shift in the institutional balance in the negotiation and conclusion of these agreements. Furthermore, we argue that the Lisbon Treaty may contribute to inducing changes in policy thinking on both sides of the Atlantic.

14.2 The United States as the Motor of Transatlantic Cooperation in the Area of Information Exchange Pre-Lisbon

The factors shaping transatlantic cooperation are both endogenous and exogenous to the EU. One factor which has led to tension in the transatlantic relationship in the area of data exchange is the difference in data protection culture across the Atlantic. In the EU, the right to privacy and the right to data protection are recognised as fundamental human rights. As the European Court of Human Rights (ECtHR) has held, the scope of the right to private life provided for Article 8 ECHR covers the systematic collection and storage of information concerning an individual's private life by public authorities.[11] The EU Charter on Fundamental Rights (CFR), in Article 8, provides that personal data must be processed fairly for specified purposes, with the consent of the person concerned or another legitimate basis laid down by law and that everyone has the right of access to data collected concerning him or her as well as the right to have it rectified. In the US, on the other hand, personal information is treated as a commodity and the right to privacy is protected by common law mechanisms and the Privacy Act of 1975. It is telling that, within the US, concerns have been expressed that personal data is used for inappropriate purposes, without transparency.[12] The Electronic Privacy Information Centre, an independent research organisation in the area of privacy and civil liberties based in Washington, has called for amendments to US data protection law. From a transatlantic perspective, there are three main deficiencies of the US system.[13] First, the present definitions in the Privacy Act, coupled with the use of a data mining instrument could result in the exclusion of a significant number of databases from its scope.[14] Second, the Privacy Act only allows judicial redress for

[11] European Court of Human Rights, *Amann* v. *Switzerland*, [2000], 27798/95, ECHR 2000-II.

[12] European Parliament (2010) Hearing Data Protection in a Transatlantic Perspective, Brussels, 7, www.statewatch.org/news/2010/nov/ep-report-on-eu-usa-data-transfer-hearing-25-10-10.pdf. Last accessed 3 June 2011.

[13] De Hert and Bellanova 2008, 17.

[14] This refers to the definition of the notion of 'system of records' in the Act: 'a group of any records under the control of any agency from which information is retrieved by the name of the individual or by some identifying number, symbol, or other identifying particular assigned to the individual'. It has been argued that this definition could lead to the exclusion of an enormous database from the Privacy Act, since it could be taken not to cover databases not directly associated to names but retrieved by proxies such as country codes, De Hert and Bellanova 2008, 17.

US citizens or residents. Transferring individuals' personal information to the US, which could not be challenged by EU citizens, constitutes a prima facie violation of Article 8 of the Charter of Fundamental Rights. Third, while the US has been open to establishing an administrative procedure for redress, the EU insists on the judicial character of such a procedure.

Another factor shaping transatlantic cooperation in information exchange is the rapid development of US counter-terrorism structures and the formulation of policies aiming to foster international cooperation with the US post-9/11.[15] The EU, on the other hand, due to its non-state nature, was much slower to develop anti-terrorism instruments and adopt the necessary measures. Experts such as Den Boer, Monar and Dubois[16] have argued that the adoption of a common definition of terrorism and the European Arrest Warrant was partly driven by the EU's desire to prove itself as a credible partner in the field.[17] It is due to these differences along with the US' unilateral and extraterritorial approach that Argomaniz defines the transatlantic relationship in border security as an 'asymmetric framework of cooperation'.[18]

In terms of endogenous factors, the institutional structure of the EU also played a role in shaping EU–US cooperation. Under the Nice Treaty rules, information exchange for law enforcement purposes fell in the scope of the former third pillar. Therefore, decision-making followed an intergovernmental logic, with the Council in charge of the adoption of common positions, framework decisions and decisions by unanimity. The European Parliament was to be consulted in the adoption of any of these measures but was only to be kept informed of the other developments in the third pillar. Under Article 38 TEU, the procedure followed for the conclusion of international agreements in the third pillar gave the Presidency the power to conduct negotiations on the basis of a mandate granted by the Council. The Commission was called to assist the Presidency and the European Parliament was merely to be kept informed. The jurisdiction of the Court of Justice did not cover international agreements in the third pillar.

The EU's margin for manoeuvre in negotiations with the US has also been affected by the difficulties related to the borderline between first and third pillar issues concerning information exchange. This is well demonstrated in the case of the PNR agreement where the legal basis chosen by the Council fell under the Community pillar: Article 95 EC and Article 25 of the Data Protection Directive, while the ECJ ruled that the agreement fell in the scope of the third pillar. The legal basis for the adoption of the second PNR agreement was Articles 24 and 38 TEU.[19] However, this did not do away with the uncertainty in the determination of legal basis. For instance, as the European Data Protection Supervisor (EDPS)

---

15 Argomaniz 2009, 121.

16 Den Boer 2007; Den Boer and Monar 2002; Dubois 2002.

17 Argomaniz 2009, 127.

18 Argomaniz 2009, 126.

19 Council of the European Union, Decision 2006/729/CFSP/JHA, 27.10.2006, OJ, L 298/27.

mentions, while the transfer of personal reservation data to the US was a matter falling in the scope of the third pillar, the ECJ has held that the storage of traffic data by telecoms for the purpose of combating serious crime could be regulated under the first pillar.

Aside from these formal legal-institutional factors, informal cooperation and personal relationships between security officials on the two sides of the Atlantic have gradually developed, facilitating US influence on EU JHA policies. The development of new structures and the emergence of new actors meant that formal channels for cooperation became ineffective and EU and US officials sought to establish informal bodies. Pawlak has argued that this led to the emergence of networks 'with more organisations and cultural homogeneity' between the EU and the US.[20] Argomaniz also emphasises the privileged access of US officials to Council working groups.[21]

Focusing on specific examples, one of the most controversial EU–US agreements concerning data exchange is the PNR agreement, which was prompted by one of the unilateral counter-terrorism measures adopted by US authorities. While the agreement raised serious concerns about undermining the data privacy rights of European citizens, the Commission pressed on to negotiate a temporary agreement despite the vocal criticisms of the EU's data protection authorities and the European Parliament.[22] The Parliament challenged the agreement before the ECJ on the basis that the US did not offer an adequate level of data protection.[23] While the Court annulled the Council decision concluding the agreement, its reasoning was not based on the data protection standards, but on the lack of appropriate legal basis. Indeed, the treaty had been concluded on a legal basis under the first pillar, whereas the Court ruled that, since it fell under the Member States' criminal law legislation, it had to be negotiated according to the rules specific to the former third pillar. In consequence, the Parliament had no say in the negotiations and the Presidency signed a final agreement in 2007, which was not ratified by all Member States at the date of the entry into force of the Lisbon Treaty, although applied on a provisional basis since 2007.

The PNR agreement serves as a clear example of the EU acting as receptor or 'norm-taker', while the US is in the role of agenda-setter driving EU policy.[24] This 'internalisation' of US-advocated security norms[25] has both an international and a domestic dimension. Externally, the EU–US PNR agreement formed the basis for

[20] Pawlak 2009b.

[21] Argomaniz 2009, 121.

[22] Pawlak 2009b.

[23] ECJ, Joined Cases C-317/04 and C-318/04 *European Parliament* v. *Council of the European Union and European Parliament v. Commission of the European Communities* [2006] *ECR* I-4721.

[24] Argomaniz 2009, 130; Pawlak 2009b.

[25] Argomaniz 2009, 121.

the PNR agreements with Canada and Australia.[26] The EU–US agreement had been strongly criticised by the Parliament, in contrast to the PNR agreements with Canada and Australia, which were considered more data protection-friendly. The Parliament had opposed fiercely the EU–US agreement on the grounds, *inter alia,* that it did not offer sufficient safeguards for the protection of personal data of EU citizens when processed by US authorities. On the EU level, the EU–US PNR agreement prompted the adoption of a Commission proposal for an EU-wide PNR system, aiming to harmonise the use of PNR data throughout the EU.[27] While the formal rationale for the Commission's proposal did not refer to the US PNR initiative, it has been argued that the proposal for an EU PNR was 'in a number of areas almost the exact mirror of the transatlantic PNR system'.[28] The Parliament had, at the time, fiercely questioned the necessity of such a system and its usefulness in the fight against terrorism.[29] Within the EU, there are substantial differences from one Member State to another: while the UK has a PNR system in place, other Member States have either enacted the relevant legislation or are testing using PNR data. Therefore, the examination of the proposal in the Council during the French Presidency did not lead to any agreement.[30]

More recently, the restructuring of SWIFT, the global leader of financial messaging services, led to the transfer of some of its servers from the US to the EU. Since this would deprive the US of transaction data originating in Europe in the framework of its TFTP as of 1 January 2010, the Council agreed in July 2009 to negotiate an interim agreement.[31] The decision to conclude the 'SWIFT I

[26] The agreement with Australia was also pending ratification at the date of the entry into force of the Lisbon Treaty whereas the agreement with Canada had already expired as a result of the expiry of the Adequacy Decision in September 2009. See European Commission, 'Decision on the adequate protection of personal data contained in the Passenger Name Record of air passengers transferred to the Canada Border Services Agency', OJ L 91, 23 March 2006.

[27] European Commission, Proposal for a Council framework decision on the use of Passenger Name Record for law enforcement purposes, Brussels, 6.11.2007, COM(2007) 654 final. The European Parliament refused to vote on the proposal and it has now been included in the Stockholm Programme.

[28] Argomaniz 2009, 130. See also, Pawlak 2009b. The criteria for comparison used by the author focus on the purpose of the arrangements for data exchange, the use of sensitive data, the data retention periods authorised, the number of data items, access to data by data subjects and means of redress, as well as the reciprocity of data transfers.

[29] European Parliament, Resolution on the proposal for a Council framework decision on the use of Passenger Name Record (PNR) for law enforcement purposes, Strasbourg, 20 November 2008.

[30] For a brief overview of the questions surrounding the setting-up of an EU PNR system, see Hustinx P (2010) European Data Protection Supervisor, Data Protection for Law Enforcement after Lisbon, speech at the ERA Conference on 'Data Protection in the Age of SWIFT, PNR, Prüm and E-Justice', Trier, 31 May 2010. www.edps.europa.eu/EDPSWEB/webdav/site/mySite/shared/Documents/EDPS/Publications/Speeches/2010/10-05-31_Speech_ERA_EN.pdf. Last Accessed 3 June 2011.

[31] The agreement was only transitional and valid for 9 months. Since it was initiated under the pre-Lisbon Treaty framework, it was to be replaced by a long-term agreement fully negotiated under the new rules.

agreement'[32] with provisional application as of 1 February was taken by the Council one day before the entry into force of the Lisbon Treaty accompanied by strong concerns expressed by the Parliament.

Finally, since 2006 a EU–US High-Level Contact Group on data protection (HLCG) has been working on establishing a set of core principles on privacy and personal data protection, which would serve as minimum standards in transatlantic cooperation, and would form the basis of a specific EU–US agreement on data protection.[33]

The brief overview of the main factors shaping EU–US cooperation in data exchange has demonstrated that the US has been more proactive and has significantly shaped EU policy in the area of data exchange. The unclear boundaries between the pillars and the lack of a comprehensive legal framework for data protection in the EU created obstacles to transatlantic cooperation. The predominant decision-making role of the Council and the development of informal networks for transatlantic cooperation facilitated US influence. This left EU officials and the European Parliament with the impression that they were merely implementing US unilateral policies without necessarily safeguarding the rights of their citizens. We will now move on to consider to what extent the Treaty of Lisbon may change this.

14.3 The New Lisbon Architecture

In addition to its effects on the CFSP, which several contributors to this volume have explored in detail,[34] the abolition of the three-pillar structure by the Treaty of Lisbon has strongly affected the EU legal framework and institutional decision-making set-up in the area of police and judicial cooperation in criminal matters. The Treaty has introduced the ordinary legislative procedure and what was formerly known as the 'Community method' in an area previously characterised by the opacity of the decision-making process within the walls of the Justus Lipsius (Council) building. This institutional shift has also changed the set of the game in transatlantic cooperation. This section will explore the impact of the Lisbon Treaty on the EU legal framework and on the main EU institutions directly or indirectly involved in policy-making in transatlantic information exchange, namely the

[32] In this contribution, both the terms 'SWIFT agreement' and 'TFTP agreement' refer to the EU–US agreement to make available to the United States Treasury Department financial payment messaging data to prevent and combat terrorism and terrorist financing. Both terms are commonly used in reference to this agreement.

[33] EU–US High-Level Contact Group (2009) Final Report on information sharing and privacy and personal data protection. http://register.consilium.europa.eu/pdf/en/09/st15/st15851.en09.pdf. Last accessed 3 June 2011.

[34] See inter alia, the chapters by Brkan, Morillas and Sari.

European Parliament, the European Commission, the Council and the Court of Justice.

14.3.1 A New Legal Framework for Data Exchange

The abolition of the pillar structure under the Lisbon Treaty means that difficult discussions about the boundaries between the different pillars will no longer be as relevant. This was problematic not only in the PNR case, but also concerning the interim SWIFT agreement. In its resolution of 17 September 2009, the Parliament expressed concern as to the divergences between the legal services of the institutions.[35] In particular the Council legal service considered a Community legal basis more appropriate.[36] Now challenges to the validity of international agreements have become less likely because similar procedural rules will apply across former first and third-pillar areas. This will serve to enhance legal certainty. The Treaty of Lisbon introduces a single procedure for the negotiation and conclusion of international treaties in Article 218 TFEU. According to this provision, the consent of the European Parliament is required in a significant number of cases. For instance, the TFTP agreement had as substantive legal basis Articles 87(2)(a) and 88(2), in conjunction with Article 218 (6)(a) TFEU and required the consent of the Parliament.[37]

In addition, the Treaty of Lisbon introduces a comprehensive legal framework on data protection. By virtue of Article 16(1) TFEU, everyone has a subjective right to the protection of their personal data. It applies to acts falling under both the former first and third pillars.[38] These provisions enhance the visibility of the right to data protection and provide a legal basis for a future EU–US agreement of minimum standards of data protection. Moreover, in its resolution of 11 November 2010, the Parliament emphasises that, since the purpose of PNR agreements is to ensure that

---

[35] European Parliament (2009) Resolution on the envisaged international agreement to make available to the United States Treasury Department financial payment messaging data to prevent and combat terrorism and terrorist financing, P7_TA(2009)0016, 17 September 2009. www.europarl.europa.eu/sides/getDoc.do?type=TA&reference=P7-TA-2009-0016&language=EN&ring=B7-2009-0038. Last accessed 3 June 2011.

[36] The European Parliament has repeatedly asked the Council unsuccessfully to forward the Opinion of the Council Legal Service: European Parliament (2009) Resolution on the envisaged international agreement to make available to the United States Treasury Department financial payment messaging data to prevent and combat terrorism and terrorist financing, P7_TA(2009)0016, 17 September 2009, para 6.

[37] Council of the European Union (2010) Decision on the conclusion of the Agreement between the European Union and the United States of America on the processing and transfer of Financial Messaging Data from the European Union to the United States for the purposes of the Terrorist Finance Tracking Program, 2010/0178 (NLE), Brussels, 24 June 2010, http://register.consilium.europa.eu/pdf/en/10/st11/st11222-re01.en10.pdf. Last accessed 3 June 2011.

[38] By way of derogation to TFEU Article 16(2), the TEU, Article 39 lays out a specific procedural legal basis for the adoption of data protection measures in the CFSP.

the transfer of data is in line with European data protection standards, the legal base must include Article 16 TFEU.[39] The significant importance accorded to the right to data protection under the revised treaty framework seems to support its reasoning.

14.3.2 A Dramatic Increase in the European Parliament's Powers

The most visible new paradigm that the Lisbon Treaty has created in the EU's institutional framework is the increased powers acquired by the European Parliament. The adoption of internal legislation, including measures to facilitate the collection, storage, processing, analysis and exchange of information in police cooperation is now governed by the ordinary legislative procedure[40] and, by virtue of Article 218(6)(a) (v) TFEU, international agreements require its consent. In order for the Parliament to effectively exercise its power of consent, Article 218(10) TFEU states that it will be 'immediately and fully informed at all stages of the procedure'. In the year following the entry into force of the Lisbon Treaty, the Parliament has been eager to exercise its long awaited new powers. But what specific role is it seeking to play in the negotiation and conclusion of agreements after Lisbon? The Parliament is showing no shyness in its demands and is seeking to shape or even determine the content of measures intended to facilitate transatlantic data sharing for law enforcement and security purposes. In fact, the institution attempts to position itself both as an agenda-setter and as the advocate for fundamental rights, making specifically data protection the centrepiece of its approach to transatlantic cooperation in this field, as shown by the role it has adopted in the agreements under consideration.

The Parliament has tried to shape both the internal and the external policy agendas with relative success. As regards the transatlantic exchange of information in the framework of the TFTP, the Parliament hampered a smooth cooperation. In the SWIFT I agreement the failure of the Council to meet Parliament's demands for the postponement of the conclusion of the interim agreement and for the inclusion of stronger data protection provisions triggered its rejection on 11 February 2010.[41] Despite calls from the Council Presidency to delay the vote until

[39] European Parliament (2010) Resolution of 11 November 2010 on the global approach to transfers of passenger name record (PNR) data to third countries, and on the recommendations from the Commission to the Council to authorise the opening of negotiations between the European Union and Australia, Canada and the United States, P7_TA-PROV(2010)0397, point 5. www.europarl.europa.eu/sides/getDoc.do?pubRef=-//EP//TEXT+TA+P7-TA-2010-0397+0+DOC+XML+V0//EN. Last accessed 3 June 2011.

[40] Treaty on the Functioning of the European Union, Article 87(2).

[41] The two demands were expressed in the letters sent by the President of the European Parliament Jerzy Buzek to Mr. Fredrik Reinfeldt and Jose Luis Rodriguez Zapatero as well as to the President of the Commission, José Manuel Durão Barroso. President Buzek mentions the letters in the Parliament Plenary Session of 10 February 2010. These demands had been previously expressed in the Resolution of 17 September 2009.

the expiry of the application of the interim SWIFT agreement the negative vote proved to the Council and the Commission that the Parliament was serious when criticising both the content and the procedure followed for its conclusion, and that it would not hesitate to use its new power of consent to reject an international agreement that did not meet its demands.[42]

As a result of this negative vote, the Parliament gained bargaining power vis-à-vis the Council and the Commission for the permanent SWIFT—SWIFT II-agreement. It made them as well as US authorities aware that for a permanent agreement to be struck its views would need to be properly taken into account not only at the final stage of negotiations but already at the early stage of the adoption of the mandate. Yet this is a troubled issue, since both the content and the formalities for the adoption of a negotiating mandate are formally a prerogative of the Council. Thus, the Council at least has to show to the Parliament that it considers its views when granting the mandate to the Commission if it does not want to trigger an adverse predisposition to the agreement. Probably to prevent the Parliament from seeing another demonstration of the Council's lack of consideration to its views, it adopted the mandate for negotiating the SWIFT II-agreement after the vote in plenary of the Parliament's Resolution, although agreement had been reached within the Council well before. In fact, the Council was expected to adopt the mandate on 22 April 2010 but it only did so formally on 11 May 2010.[43] Thus less than a week after the Parliament finally passed a Resolution containing its demands on 5 May 2010.[44] The demands included, *inter alia*, the designation of an EU judicial authority 'to receive requests from the US Treasury Department', a solution for the bulk data transfers, and the appointment of EU personnel to 'join SWIFT officials in the oversight of the extraction process in the US'.[45] Although the delay probably did not bring any substantial changes to the negotiating mandate, it was a sign to the Parliament that the Council was taking its views seriously,

[42] In the plenary session of 10 February 2010, the President-in-office tried to convince the Parliament to postpone the vote on security concerns grounds. The Council was worried that, if subject to vote, the agreement would face the rejection of the Parliament, as eventually happened.

[43] European Parliament (2010) Resolution on the Recommendation from the Commission to the Council to authorise the opening of negotiations for an agreement between the European Union and the United States of America to make available to the United States Treasury Department financial messaging data to prevent and combat terrorism and terrorist financing, 5 May 2010, Recital J.

[44] European Parliament (2010) Resolution on the Recommendation from the Commission to the Council to authorise the opening of negotiations for an agreement between the European Union and the United States of America to make available to the United States Treasury Department financial messaging data to prevent and combat terrorism and terrorist financing, 5 May 2010.

[45] European Parliament (2010) Committee on Civil Liberties, Justice and Home Affairs, Recommendation on the draft Council decision on the conclusion of the Agreement between the European Union and the United States of America on the processing and transfer of Financial Messaging Data from the European Union to the United States for the purposes of the Terrorist Finance Tracking Program, 5 July 2010. See the Explanatory Statement by the Rapporteur Alexander Alvaro.

consequently increasing the likelihood of a positive vote in Parliament of the negotiating outcome. Some of its requests were eventually reflected in the final agreement, particularly the appointment of a public authority to verify compliance of US requests with the agreement, and the designation of a person appointed by the Commission to monitor data processing by US Treasury Department.[46] The Parliament considered these improvements sufficient and approved the agreement accordingly, despite resistance from some MEPs.[47]

Yet the Parliament did not only shape the external policy agenda, but it also managed to determine the mirroring internal policy in the form of a joint commitment from the Commission and the Council to explore the feasibility of establishing an EU system, equivalent to the US TFTP, that would enable data to be extracted in EU soil.[48] Such an EU system would put an end to bulk data transfers to the US in the future, and thus addressed the main demand from the Parliament.[49] The European Council had previously called the Commission in the Stockholm Programme to 'examine the possibilities to track terrorist financing within the Union'.[50] This call was consequently included in the Action Plan elaborated by the Commission, which has recently presented a communication on the options available for a European terrorist finance tracking system.[51] Yet the novelty in the Council decision to conclude the SWIFT II-agreement is that it includes a provision stating that if an equivalent EU system is not established

46 Agreement between the European Union and the United States of America on the processing and transfer of Financial Messaging Data from the European Union to the United States for the purposes of the Terrorist Finance Tracking Program, OJ L195, vol. 53, 27 July 2010. Article 4 of the Agreement designates Europol as the authority to verify compliance of US requests with the agreement. Article 12 does not specify who will be the person appointed by the Commission to monitor and oversee data processing in the US.

47 European Parliament (2010) Committee on Civil Liberties, Justice and Home Affairs, Recommendation on the draft Council decision on the conclusion of the Agreement between the European Union and the United States of America on the processing and transfer of Financial Messaging Data from the European Union to the United States for the purposes of the Terrorist Finance Tracking Program, 5 July 2010. See the Minority Opinions attached to the European Parliament Recommendation.

48 Agreement between the European Union and the United States of America on the processing and transfer of Financial Messaging Data from the European Union to the United States for the purposes of the Terrorist Finance Tracking Program, OJ L195, vol. 53, 27 July 2010, Article 11.

49 For further information on the demands from the Parliament, see European Parliament (2009) Resolution on the envisaged international agreement to make available to the United States Treasury Department financial payment messaging data to prevent and combat terrorism and terrorist financing, Strasbourg, 17 September 2009.

50 Council of the European Union (2010) The Stockholm Programme—An open and secure Europe serving and protecting the citizens, Brussels, 2 December 2010, 52.

51 European Commission (2010) Communication from the Commission to the European Parliament, the Council, the Economic and Social Committee and the Committee of the Regions, Delivering an area of freedom, security and justice for Europe's citizens, Action Plan Implementing the Stockholm Programme, Brussels, 20.4.2010, COM(2010) 171 final, 41. European Commission (2011) Communication from the Commission to the European Parliament and the Council on a European terrorist finance tracking system, COM(2011) 429 final, Brussels, 13.7.2011.

within five years after the date of the entry into force of the agreement, the EU may not renew the agreement.[52] The Parliament will likely use its power as co-legislator to define this EU system and, if it faces reluctance from the Council as to its adoption or if it does not agree with the Member States on its content, it may exercise political pressure to terminate the agreement on the grounds that the EU was unable to act internally. Therefore, the Parliament has reserved itself a prominent role in the definition of both the external and the internal EU policy in the fight against terrorism financing.

Attempts to influence the external and the internal EU policy agendas through the new powers conferred by the Treaty of Lisbon are also visible in the PNR case, where the Parliament linked both in its Resolution of 5 May 2010 on the launch of negotiations for PNR agreements with the US, Australia and Canada.[53] Doubts as to the necessity and proportionality of the use of PNR data in the fight against terrorism have not vanished, yet the EU's policy is conditioned by the unilateral policy of the US. Acknowledging that the absence of a transatlantic agreement would be harmful for European air carriers, the Parliament decided in May 2010 to postpone the vote on the request for consent for the agreements with Australia and the US.[54] Submitting them instead to vote would have likely led to the rejection of the agreements. Yet the Parliament conditioned the postponement of the vote to the adoption of a new approach to PNR, a horizontal approach that would cover all the cases where PNR is used, be it internally or externally.

In its external dimension, the Parliament called for the establishment of a set of principles on the sharing of PNR data which would be applied equally in every international agreement that the EU would conclude with third countries and set a deadline for the Commission to present new negotiating mandates for agreements with the US, Canada and Australia.[55] As a result of these demands, the Commission presented a 'PNR package', reaffirming the key objective of standardising the external dimension of the exchange of PNR data.[56] In addition, it submitted to the JHA Council of October 2010 the draft negotiating directives for PNR

---

[52] Council of the European Union (2010) Council Decision on the conclusion of the Agreement between the European Union and the United States of America on the processing and transfer of Financial Messaging Data from the European Union to the United States for the purposes of the Terrorist Finance Tracking Program, Official Journal of the European Union, L195, 27 July 2010, Article 2.

[53] European Parliament (2010) Resolution on the launch of negotiations for Passenger Name Record (PNR) agreements with the United States, Australia and Canada, Brussels, 5 May 2010.

[54] European Parliament (2010) Resolution on the launch of negotiations for Passenger Name Record (PNR) agreements with the United States, Australia and Canada, Brussels, 5 May 2010, para 4.

[55] European Parliament (2010) Resolution on the launch of negotiations for Passenger Name Record (PNR) agreements with the United States, Australia and Canada, Brussels, 5 May 2010, para 7.

[56] European Commission (2010) Communication from the Commission On the global approach to transfers of Passenger Name Record (PNR) data to third countries, Brussels, COM 492 final, 21 September 2010.

agreements with the USA, Canada and Australia with identical content as requested by the Parliament. The three mandates eventually identical were adopted by the JHA Council of December. Therefore the Parliament is succeeding in shaping the external dimension of PNR.

Besides, the Parliament has also shaped the internal PNR policy. The Commission proposal for a Directive on an EU PNR was finally presented in February 2011.[57] It is being discussed jointly by the Council and the Parliament as co-legislators in the ordinary legislative procedure. It has recently been criticised by the Article 29 Working Party[58] which questions the necessity of the suggested measures, their proportionality and draws attention to the insufficient level of data protection.[59] Similar criticisms have been raised by the EDPS and the EU Fundamental Rights Agency, and have been well received by the Parliament.[60] With all of these concerns, even the predicted timeframe for the adoption of the proposal—2 years—appears overly optimistic.[61]

14.3.3 A Stronger Role for the European Commission

The enshrinement of data protection as a fundamental right and the abolition of the pillars in the EU's legal framework have affected the role of the European Commission in the transatlantic exchange of information. On the one hand, data protection is currently a political priority for the Commission even though the existence of two different Commissioners responsible for transatlantic cooperation in this field may sometimes lead to inconsistent public discourses. On the other

---

57 European Commission (2011) Proposal for a Directive of the European Parliament and of the Council on the use of Passenger Name Record data for the prevention, detection, investigation and prosecution of terrorist offences and serious crime', Brussels, 2.2.2011, COM, 32 final.

58 The Article 29 Working Party is the independent EU Advisory Body on Data Protection and Privacy, which was established by Article 29 of the Directive 95/46/EC on the protection of individuals with regard to the processing of personal data and on the free movement of such data. It is made up of representatives of the data protection authorities of the Member States, the Commission and the European Data Protection Supervisor.

59 European Commission (2011) Article 29 Working Party Press Release, Brussels, 11 April 2011, http://ec.europa.eu/justice/policies/privacy/news/docs/pr_11_04_11_en.pdf. Last accessed 3 June 2011.

60 European Data Protection Supervisor, Opinion on the proposal for a Council Decision on the conclusion of the Agreement between the European Union and the United States of America on the processing and transfer of Financial Messaging Data from the European Union to the United States for purposes of the Terrorist Finance Tracking Program, http://www.edps.europa.eu/EDPSWEB/webdav/site/mySite/shared/Documents/Consultation/Opinions/2010/10-06-22_Opinion_TFTP_EN.pdf. Last accessed 3 June 2011.

61 European Commission (2011) Press release, EU Proposal for passenger data to fight serious crime and terrorism, Brussels, 2.02.2011, IP/11/120, http://europa.eu/rapid/pressReleasesAction.do?reference=IP/11/120&format=HTML&aged=0&language=frEN&guiLanguage=. Last accessed 3 June 2011.

hand, the Commission's role in the internal and external dimension of information exchange for law enforcement purposes has shifted.

The Barroso II Commission has accorded political emphasis to the AFSJ reflecting its almost complete 'communitarisation' through the appointment of two different Commissioners, Viviane Reding, responsible for Justice, Fundamental Rights and Citizenship, and Cecilia Malmström, in charge of Home Affairs, both taking up the duties previously carried out by the Commissioner for Freedom, Security and Justice. The administrative structures have changed accordingly. Since July 2010 the Directorate-General for Justice, Freedom and Security has been divided into two separate Commission services: a Directorate-General for Justice and a Directorate-General for Home Affairs. Whereas previously a single Commissioner supported by a single Commission service was responsible for international cooperation in information exchange for law enforcement and security purposes, the current duality entails splitting up the responsibility for bilateral agreements between two Commissioners and two administrative services. Transatlantic agreements like the PNR, SWIFT and data protection agreements are cross-cutting since they may touch upon both police cooperation in criminal matters, under the responsibility of Cecilia Malmström, and data protection and judicial cooperation, under the responsibility of Viviane Reding. The stance of the Barroso I Commission on such agreements was unitary since any potential internal difference was quietened by the voice of a single Commissioner. On the contrary, in the first year since the appointment of the Barroso II Commission differences have emerged between the current two Commissioners, conveying contradictory messages.

Differences appeared already in the SWIFT I Agreement. On her very first day as Commissioner for Home Affairs, Cecilia Malmström strongly defended it before the Parliament, following previous informal contacts with the heads of the political groups. While acknowledging that the agreement could have included stronger data protection provisions, she emphasised that it was necessary in order to avoid a security gap and that it was not only beneficial to the US but also to the EU, as the Bruguière report had shown.[62] Conversely, Viviane Reding moved from expressing slight concerns regarding the agreement during her public hearing as Commissioner designate to publicly criticising the agreement and welcoming its

[62] In the debate in the European Parliament's plenary session of 10 February 2010 she stated: 'the interim agreement is not only a favour to the US; it is in our own common interest.' European Parliament Debate Plenary Session (2010) Agreement between the EU and the USA on the processing and transfer of Financial Messaging Data from the European Union to the United States for the purposes of the Terrorist Finance Tracking Programme www.europarl.europa.eu/sides/getDoc.do?pubRef=-//EP//TEXT+CRE+20100210+ITEM-013+DOC+XML+V0//EN. Last accessed 3 June 2011.

rejection by the Parliament.[63] This inconsistency was regarded with concern by the Spanish Presidency, who expressed to the US that Reding was not 'entitled to speak against the position of the Commission' and that her position responded to her populist politics.[64]

Notwithstanding the scattering public inconsistencies, it is clear that data protection is a political priority for the Commission, including in the area of Home Affairs, as the announcement of a proposal to modify the data retention directive demonstrates. Besides, the Stockholm Programme calls on the Commission to present a proposal for a comprehensive data protection legal framework.[65] Consequently, the Commission is currently working on a comprehensive approach to personal data protection in the EU, which would apply to former third-pillar policies.[66] Moreover, the timing of the launch of negotiations of the EU–US PNR agreement, under the responsibility of Malmström, and the data protection agreement, under the responsibility of Reding, might strengthen a common Commission stance in transatlantic information exchange. In fact, both agreements are being negotiated at the same time and the US–EU agreement on data protection is expected to apply to any sector-specific agreement.

The Commission's role in the framing of former third-pillar policies has shifted. The Commission does not have yet an exclusive right of initiative in the area of police and judicial cooperation in criminal matters, which is shared with the Member States.[67] However, with the abolition of the pillar structure it has gained political weight and consideration as the natural initiator of legislation, building on its traditional role in the former 'community' pillar. It is thus the task of the Commission to propose legislation, *inter alia,* in the field of data protection in the former third pillar. In this context, the Commission has just presented a proposal for a European PNR, is examining the possibility of establishing a European TFTP and has included

[63] In an interview published in Le Soir, on 20 April 2010, 45, Commissioner Reding stated: 'Les responsables américains ont comme devoir de protéger leurs citoyens. Pour ce faire, ils ont mis en place un éventail de mesures. C'est leur affaire. Nous, nous avons nos règles de protection des individus et de protection des données personnelles. C'est les valeurs européennes. Jusqu'ici, ni le Parlement européen ni la Commission véritablement n'avait été un joueur dans ce dossier. Tout avait été réglé par les ministres de l'Intérieur avec les américains. Il était temps que le Parlement européen dise 'stop' et demande de réexaminer la chose. C'est ce que nous avons commencé à faire.'.

[64] A cable reporting a phone call from the US Ambassador to the EU to the Spanish Permanent Representative to the EU on 1 February 2010 was revealed by Wikileaks. The Guardian (2010) US Embassy Cables: Obama says no to EU–US climate summit in Madrid, 13 December 2010, www.guardian.co.uk/world/us-embassy-cables-documents/246940. Last accessed 3 June 2011.

[65] Council of the European Union (2010) The Stockholm Programme- An open and secure Europe serving and protecting the citizens, Brussels, 2 December 2010, 19.

[66] European Commission (2010) Communication from the Commission to the European Parliament, the Council, the Economic and Social Committee and the Committee of the Regions, A comprehensive approach on personal data protection in the European Union, COM 609/3 draft, Brussels, 4.11.2010.

[67] See Treaty on the Functioning of the European Union, Article 76.

both measures in its Communication on the EU Internal Security Strategy, given the new competences the EU has acquired in the field of home affairs.[68]

The Commission has also acquired greater powers in the negotiation of transatlantic agreements in this field. The practise established post-Lisbon is that the Commission will be designated as single negotiator on behalf of the Union, as it has been the case in the negotiations of the SWIFT II, PNR and data protection agreements. This shift entails a growing prominence of the Commission at the expense of the Council Secretariat and may increase its autonomy when dealing with US authorities. Yet the Commission will be closely monitored by the preparatory bodies of the Council, given the sensitivity of the dossiers. Besides, its accountability towards the Parliament has surely also increased given the duty of the negotiator to keep the Parliament informed.

14.3.4 A Loss of Prominence for the Council

The previous two sections have analysed the power increase experienced by the institution democratically elected by EU citizens as well as by the institution promoting the general interest of the Union. This section will subsequently explore the extent to which this shift has taken place at the expense of the institution representing Member States' governments. It will be argued that the Council has lost exclusivity in decision-making power, which entails the necessity for a new working culture that reflects the new EU institutional balance of power.

The Council has lost the prominent decision-making power it traditionally held in JHA, including in its external dimension. First of all, it has lost power at the advantage of the Commission. Most internal measures in the framework of police and judicial cooperation in criminal matters will be proposed by the Commission instead of by the Member States. Although the Treaty of Lisbon has not abolished the right of initiative of the Member States in this field, it has surely rendered its exercise more difficult.[69] Initiatives of Member States are facing informal opposition from the Commission, who sees itself as the only institution legitimately entitled to initiate Union legislation.[70] The responsibility for elaborating the

---

[68] See European Commission (2010) Communication from the Commission to the European Parliament and the Council—The EU Internal Security Strategy in Action: Five Steps towards a more secure Europe, COM673 final, Brussels 22.11.2010.

[69] Whereas under the Treaty on the European Union, former Article 34(2), any Member State could initiate legislation; now Treaty on the Functioning of the European Union, Article 76 gives the right of initiative to a quarter of Member States.

[70] It has been the case for instance with the proposal from 12 Member States for a directive on the European Protection Order which the Commission opposes because it is planning to present in early 2011 a broader package on the rights of victims. See www.europeanvoice.com/article/imported/commission-and-spain-in-row-over-protection-order/67808.aspx. Last accessed 3 June 2011.

Action Plan of the Stockholm Programme will certainly officialise the Commission's prominent role as agenda-setter, decreasing the amount of Member States initiatives put forward in each Council Presidency.

Yet the effects of the Treaty of Lisbon on the role of the Council Presidency and the Council Secretariat are not perfectly clear.[71] Whereas the Presidency is no longer taking part directly in the negotiation of transatlantic agreements and may therefore lose some room for manoeuvre to shape the final outcome of negotiations, its role as consensus builder among EU Member States and as defender of the agreement before the Parliament will likely not change. On the one hand, QMV has been introduced in the Council in a field where unanimity was previously required. Although decisions will still probably be taken by consensus, the rule of QMV allows for more flexibility when building consensus given the formal possibility to overpass the position of a Member State who disagrees. On the other hand, the duty of the Presidency to keep the Parliament informed has not necessarily been softened since Article 218(10) TFEU does not impose it solely on the negotiator. It is thus likely that the Lisbon Treaty will get the Council Presidency and the Council Secretariat closer to the Commission during the negotiations.

Reflecting this new environment, the Council working structures have changed or discussions are going on to accommodate its working methods to a new reality where former specificities are no longer justified.[72] Yet Member States' officials dealing with former third-pillar policies have not necessarily changed. But they had to adapt their working methods and mentalities to reflect the new institutional balance. The introduction of the ordinary legislative procedure for the adoption of internal legislation triggered a new relationship with the Parliament.

Most illustrative of the new working culture is the way the Council dealt with the Parliament in the SWIFT case, because it demonstrated how it intended to engage with the Parliament in post-Lisbon transatlantic agreements. In a vivid debate in the Parliament plenary of February 2010, where the Council and the Commission tried desperately to convince the Parliament not to reject the SWIFT I agreement, the President-in-office stated: 'in case some people [MEPs] do not trust the Council's word, and it would be their right not to, they should remember that the Treaty forces us to do things differently'.[73] What needed to be done differently was to take into account the views and concerns of the Parliament. Consequently, the Council issued a commitment to negotiate an inter-institutional agreement that would enable easier access to classified documents relating to international

---

[71] Wolff et al. 2009, 20.

[72] A restructuring of the Council preparatory bodies is being discussed. Novelties include the creation of COSI (Committee on Internal Security), the re-evaluation of the role of CATS, the creation of a Working Party on Terrorism and the permanent character of the JAI-RELEX Working Party, previously the JAI-RELEX Ad Hoc Support Group.

[73] The transcript of the intervention is available at www.europarl.europa.eu/sides/getDoc.do?pubRef=-//EP//TEXT+CRE+20100210+ITEM-013+DOC+XML+V0//EN. Last accessed 3 June 2011.

agreements.[74] This commitment addressed a demand from the Parliament, who was asked in the past to give its opinion about agreements without having access to related documents. Therefore, the apparent post-Lisbon aim in inter-institutional relations is to place all institutions, including the Parliament, in the same position regarding transatlantic agreements. This will require informal contacts between Member States' officials and MEPs, specially the rapporteurs and the shadow rapporteurs. Whereas previously these contacts did not necessarily occur systematically, they will now need to be further institutionalised, particularly contacts between Presidency officials and the Parliament. Moreover, participation and attendance of Council officials in the debates in the Civil Liberties, Justice and Home Affairs (LIBE) Committee has been more systematic after Lisbon. Through these informal contacts in the premises of the Parliament, Council officials may be able to engage more effectively with the MEPs, putting an end to a previous relationship based on mistrust.

The Treaty of Lisbon has therefore induced a shift in the institutional balance of power requiring a new working mentality in the Council on how to engage with the other EU institutions. For internal measures and transatlantic agreements to be adopted, it needs to work closely with the Commission and the Parliament. The Council is no longer the agenda-setter and will now see how some initiatives for which consensus was not previously found, like the creation of a European PNR or a European TFTP, will need to be re-examined as demanded by the Parliament.

14.3.5 The European Court of Justice

The Lisbon Treaty also introduces judicial control over treaty-making in JHA by the ECJ according to Article 218(11) TFEU and by the ECtHR, as a result of the EU's accession to the ECHR, provided for in Article 6(2)TEU. Article 218(11) allows a Member State, the European Parliament, the Council or the Commission to ask the Court to deliver an opinion on the compatibility of an envisaged agreement with the Treaties. In case the opinion is negative, the agreement may not enter into force unless it is amended or the Treaties are revised. Under the previous framework, Articles 24 and 38 TEU did not foresee any role for the ECJ in relation to agreements concluded under the second and third pillar. Despite its limitations due to the restrictions in the number of applicants and the a priori nature of review, introducing this form of judicial oversight certainly constitutes an improvement.[75] In addition, the question of compatibility of EU data exchange agreements with human rights standards imposed by the ECHR could come before the Strasbourg court once the

---

[74] A statement including this commitment was sent by the Council to the European Parliament on 9 February 2010.

[75] Cf. the position of the ECJ in relation to the CFSP, explored more fully by Brkan (this volume).

EU accedes to the Convention. While the accession modalities are still under discussion,[76] there is no reason to imagine that international agreements concluded by the EU would be excluded from the scope of ECtHR jurisdiction.

14.4 Introducing Policy Shifts in Transatlantic Exchange of Information

As Argomaniz notes, the transatlantic security relationship is asymmetrical and characterised by 'US pro-activeness as a producer and catalyst of initiatives in contrast to the more reactive role that the EU has adopted'.[77] Yet the new EU legal and institutional framework resulting from the Treaty of Lisbon may somewhat change the set of the game and induce policy shifts on both sides of the Atlantic.

The European perception of the transatlantic security relationship has changed. The Treaty of Lisbon has given it the tools to shape a relationship previously based on the almost automatic adoption of American policies that did not necessarily fit in the European context. The main factor inducing this change has been the inclusion of the European Parliament in policy-making. Its new institutional powers are thus being reflected in policy content. Calls for the respect of the principles of reciprocity, proportionality and necessity in transatlantic exchange of information are being taken into account by other EU institutions. This policy change is to materialise in the EU–US data protection agreement as well as in the PNR agreement currently under negotiation.

The launch of negotiations for a transatlantic data protection agreement covering exchange of information in the framework of police and judicial cooperation in criminal matters reflects this change. This 'umbrella' agreement was proposed by the US and advocated by the Parliament since 2003, but initially faced scepticism from EU Member States. The understanding from the US side was that such an agreement would put an end to European concerns as to the level of data protection offered by the US when processing EU data and to critics pointing out that the US data protection legal framework was not adequate, as required by EU legislation. On the basis of the final report from the HLCG and Parliament calls to start negotiations as soon as possible, the EU mandate was adopted in December 2010—at the same time as the mandate for the PNR agreement—and negotiations started in March 2011.[78] It reflects the two main demands from the Parliament:

---

[76] Official talks on EU accession began on 7 July 2010 and are still underway.

[77] Argomaniz 2009, 125.

[78] The mandate for a EU–US agreement that will cover personal data when transferred and processed for the purpose of preventing, investigating, detecting or prosecuting criminal offenses, including terrorism, in the framework of police and judicial cooperation in criminal matters, was adopted by the JHA Council of 2–3 December 2010. The press release is available at www.consilium.europa.eu/uedocs/cms_data/docs/pressdata/en/jha/118183.pdf. Last accessed 3 June 2011.

that the bilateral instrument resulting from the work of the HLCG would be a binding international agreement and that it would apply to existing and future transatlantic agreements providing for sector-specific data sharing, such as the SWIFT and PNR agreements. The agreement will have to be legally sound in terms of the substantive data protection content if it is not to face the veto from the European Parliament. On the one hand, the rapporteur, Jan Philippe Albrecht, has been one of the main opponents to previous transatlantic agreements. On the other hand, the opinions of the EDPS and the Article 29 Working Party, which have been critical to previous transatlantic agreements are likely to gain prominence through their reception by the Parliament. The Parliament is also inducing policy change in sector-specific transatlantic agreements such as the PNR. Its demands include a ban of bilateral cooperation between individual Member States and the US, the rejection of the use of data for data mining or profiling or the inclusion of Article 16 TFEU as the legal basis.[79] Internally, the Parliament is demanding the introduction of a Privacy Impact Assessment for new legal measures and a proportionality test.[80]

Although negotiations of both the EU–US data protection agreement and the EU–US PNR agreement are not formally linked, there seems to be a certain concern on the EU side that if negotiations on the latter come to an end before agreement is reached on the former, the US will lose interest in the negotiations of the 'umbrella' agreement. Both EU mandates were adopted at the same time but negotiations on the 'umbrella' agreement were launched three months after the negotiations on the PNR started because the US was lagging behind with the appointment of its negotiator. This delay triggered suspicions in the EU as to the real interests of the US.[81] Thus, it is likely that the conclusion of both agreements will be linked, at least by the European Parliament, who considers the umbrella agreement as a precondition for new data sharing deals.

Furthermore, policy shifts are also being induced by other actors. The adoption of the EU TFTP and EU PNR has even been advocated by the EU Counter-Terrorism Coordinator, Gilles de Kerchove, who argues that their development would lead to a 'more equal partnership with the US'.[82] Individual Member States

---

79 European Parliament (2010) Resolution of 11 November 2010 on the global approach to transfers of passenger name record (PNR) data to third countries, and on the recommendations from the Commission to the Council to authorise the opening of negotiations between the European Union and Australia, Canada and the United States, P7_TA-PROV(2010)0397, see para 5, www.europarl.europa.eu/sides/getDoc.do?pubRef=-//EP//TEXT+TA+P7-TA-2010-0397+0+DOC+XML+V0//EN. Last accessed 3 June 2011.

80 European Parliament (2010) Resolution on the launch of negotiations for Passenger Name Record (PNR) agreements with the United States, Australia and Canada, Brussels, 5 May 2010, para 5.

81 Pop V (2010) 'Reding slams US over data privacy', EU Observer, 21 December 2010, http://euobserver.com/891/31555. Last accessed 3 June 2011.

82 EU Counter-Terrorism Coordinator, EU Counter-Terrorism Strategy- discussion paper, Brussels, 26 November 2009, 7, http://register.consilium.europa.eu/pdf/en/09/st15/st15359-re01.en09.pdf. Last accessed 3 June 2011.

may also find in the Treaty of Lisbon a new framework whereby they can express more freely their concerns regarding transatlantic exchange of information. Whereas the prominence of the Council in decision-making before Lisbon led individual Member States that were sceptical about the content of the agreements with little room of manoeuvre to openly show opposition under the risk of undermining their bilateral relationship with the US, they can now harmlessly use their MEPs to shape or oppose the content of the agreements.

On the side of the US, it appears that the break between the Bush and Obama administration in counterterrorism policy is not as clear-cut as initially expected. In effect, as scholars and commentators note, the difference between the two administrations is less one of policy substance than one of rhetoric or 'packaging'.[83] The most plausible explanation for this appears to be the large agreement of the American political elite that the country is in an 'unprecedented era of peril' post-9/11 requiring the adoption of extraordinary measures.[84] On the other side of the Atlantic, the danger of terrorism has not triggered the same anxiety. Moreover, the need for the US to negotiate, on the one hand, with the EU as a bloc and overcome the hostile reaction of the Parliament, and with individual Member States on the other hand, exacerbates the feeling that the two partners are not singing from the same song sheet. Although the Department of Homeland Security under the Obama Administration seems to be more flexible than under the Bush Administration, the challenge for the US in the context of transatlantic cooperation still is to be less unilateral in its approach. To make transatlantic cooperation run smoothly, the US will have to make way for the demands of the Parliament and give serious consideration to EU concerns over the respect of data protection standards set by the Charter of Fundamental Rights and the ECHR.

The American experience of working with the EU on data sharing has so far been facilitated by the prominent role of the Council in the area under the Treaty of Nice rules. The lack of parliamentary oversight and judicial control over the third-pillar agreements pre-Lisbon meant that the US administration faced little difficulty in securing approval of its policies across the Atlantic. With the Treaty of Lisbon, the American administration will have to take into account the new powers of Parliament as well as the possibility for legal challenge to information sharing treaties. As Hamilton notes, 'the Treaty of Lisbon [...] does not necessarily make life easier [...]. The US continues to need strong bilateral relationships with EU Member States' but it also brings the need for both the Administration and the Congress to 'adjust their relationship with the EU'.[85] The US administration put significant effort in lobbying the Parliament to approve the interim SWIFT agreement. However, too little was done too late and the frantic last-minute involvement of high-level US officials did

---

[83] Desch 2010, 425–429.

[84] Desch 2010, 427.

[85] Hamilton D S (2009) The Lisbon Treaty: Implications for Future Relations between the European Union and the United States', Testimony to the House Committee on Foreign Affairs, Subcommittee on Europe, 15 December 2009, 7, http://transatlantic.sais-jhu.edu/bin/q/z/dh_Lisbon_Treaty_testimony_dec_15_2009.pdf. Last accessed 3 June 2011.

not help. This has led the US Government to recognise the need to forge closer relations with the Parliament.[86] In his address to the House of Representatives, Hamilton emphasised the need to assess whether the US is adequately equipped to deal with the EU post-Lisbon, in particular with a stronger Parliament.[87] He stresses the need to boost cooperation between the Parliament and Congress in the framework of the Transatlantic Legislators Dialogue (TLD). Hamilton recommends the establishment of an office of the US Congress in Brussels—which had already been suggested by the Parliament, whereas the latter already has an office in Washington. In addition, the creation of a joint consultative committee on the extraterritorial effects of US legislation could temper the adverse effects of US unilateral policies with cross-border implications. Strengthening institutional cooperation at the level of legislatures could indeed help address the 'lack of understanding and tact' demonstrated by the US administration in the case of SWIFT.[88] Steps have been taken in this regard as in April 2011 a delegation from the Civil Liberties Committee of the Parliament visited Washington to hold bilateral meetings with Congress members on data protection and security matters.[89]

In terms of transatlantic relations, much remains to be done. Concerning SWIFT, the US has undertaken to offer support for an EU decision to develop its own TFTP.[90] In relation to PNR, the US will need to deal with Parliamentary concerns with the issues of data retention period, onward transfers of data and reciprocity since a lot of the data transferred in the PNR agreement flows from the EU to the US but not vice versa. Finally, concerning the adoption of a framework agreement on data protection, the US had favoured the conclusion of such an umbrella treaty as it would facilitate transfers of personal data across the Atlantic. However, views on this point differ: to US officials it constitutes a way to avoid 'painstaking and time-consuming negotiations'[91] with the EU on every individual

---

[86] Kennard W (2010) US Ambassador to the EU, 'Data protection in a transatlantic perspective', Remarks before the Committee on Civil Liberties, Justice, and Home Affairs, 25.10.2010, www.europarl.europa.eu/document/activities/cont/201010/20101027ATT90670/20101027ATT90670EN.pdf. Last accessed 3 June 2011.

[87] Hamilton D S (2009) The Lisbon Treaty: Implications for Future Relations between the European Union and the United States', Testimony to the House Committee on Foreign Affairs, Subcommittee on Europe, 15 December 2009, 10. http://transatlantic.sais-jhu.edu/bin/q/z/dh_Lisbon_Treaty_testimony_dec_15_2009.pdf. Last accessed 3 June 2011.

[88] Monar 2010, 151.

[89] European Parliament (2011) Civil Liberties Delegation to Washington-Data Protection and Security', Press Release, www.europarl.europa.eu/nl/pressroom/content/20110412IPR17600/html/Civil-Liberties-Delegation-to-Washington-Data-Protection-and-Security. Last accessed 3 June 2011.

[90] Archick K (2010) US–EU Cooperation Against Terrorism, CRS Report for Congress 7-5700, 9.07.2010, 9; www.crs.gov. Last accessed 3 June 2011.

[91] Hamilton D S (2009) The Lisbon Treaty: Implications for Future Relations between the European Union and the United States', Testimony to the House Committee on Foreign Affairs, Subcommittee on Europe, 15 December 2009, 7. http://transatlantic.sais-jhu.edu/bin/q/z/dh_Lisbon_Treaty_testimony_dec_15_2009.pdf. Last accessed 3 June 2011.

agreement on information exchange; to the EU, it would provide minimum standards for data protection in transatlantic data exchange but would not constitute a legal basis for data transfers and, consequently, would not oust the need for specific agreements. More recently, the Belgian Presidency recognised that a general transatlantic agreement would never be able to cover all cases.[92] The negotiating mandate has raised concerns in the US due to the retroactive effect proposed by the EU as it could jeopardise information sharing under the existing arrangements.[93] The US also seeks a clear statement of mutual recognition of data protection regimes which the EU will be reluctant to agree to since it would result in automatic data transfers. Negotiations are thus proving to be difficult. On the one hand, it seems that after the entry into force of other instruments such as the Mutual Legal Assistance agreement, the US does not seem to be convinced of the necessity of such an umbrella treaty. On the other hand, it is an Executive Agreement in the US, which is being negotiated solely by the Executive without the involvement of Congress. Therefore, expectations created in the EU as to the level of concessions from the US will not easily be fulfilled.

14.5 Conclusion

Despite the difficulties and divergences, cooperation in information exchange holds benefits for both the EU and the US. The joint review of the implementation of the PNR agreement demonstrates that the agreement does serve the purpose of supporting the fight against terrorism and crime.[94] The EU team concluded that the DHS generally implements its commitments towards the EU, in terms of filtering data, passenger rights or handling of data. Improvement appears necessary with respect to the better keeping of records by DHS of its activities, ad hoc pulls and redress requests. Enhanced monitoring of the use of PNR data by the DHS has also been recommended.

There is no doubt that the US will continue to be the driving force behind EU–US cooperation in data exchange and that the EU will continue to adopt a reactive role—at the very least for structural reasons, since EU decision-making is more

[92] European Parliament (2010) Report on EU–USA data transfer hearing, Brussels, 25/10/2010, 3, www.statewatch.org/news/2010/nov/ep-report-on-eu-usa-data-transfer-hearing-25-10-10.pdf. Last accessed 3 June 2011.

[93] Kennard W (2010) US Ambassador to the EU, 'Data protection in a transatlantic perspective', Remarks before the Committee on Civil Liberties, Justice, and Home Affairs, 25.10.2010, www.europarl.europa.eu/document/activities/cont/201010/20101027ATT90670/20101027ATT90670EN.pdf. Last accessed 3 June 2011.

[94] Report on the joint review of the implementation of the Agreement between the European Union and the United States of America (2010) on the processing and transfer of Passenger Name Record (PNR) data by air carriers to the United States Department of Homeland Security (DHS), Brussels, 7.4.2010, www.statewatch.org/news/2010/apr/eu-usa-pnr-joint-review-com.pdf. Last accessed 3 June 2011.

burdensome and time-consuming. Yet transatlantic information exchange post-Lisbon has entered into a new dynamic. The introduction of the Parliament in policy-making, the political weight accorded to the fundamental right to data protection in the Commission, the decision-making power decrease in the Council and the introduction of judicial control over the former third pillar, have triggered a new attitude in the EU towards transatlantic cooperation. All these factors have contributed to strengthening the EU's negotiating position. It appears that greater flexibility, better knowledge of the EU decision-making machinery post-Lisbon and greater consideration for European standards of human rights protection on the US side, is an important factor for the success of EU–US cooperation in data exchange. Since the Obama administration is less unilateral in its approach and more open to considering internationally negotiated measures, it is well placed to operate this shift.

On the other hand, the EU has also made progress in the field of information exchange and is more united in working on internal data sharing measures, a field in which the US has made commitments to provide assistance. The adoption of the EU PNR and the EU TFTP will face challenges. The establishment of these measures is costly and, above all, many Member States are still reluctant to share intelligence, as evidenced by the recent reservations to the accession of Bulgaria and Romania to the Schengen area. Besides, the Parliament will closely monitor the necessity and proportionality of such measures. The mistrust created by the SWIFT experience is having repercussions on these internal measures and, above all, on other transatlantic agreements, particularly on the PNR. Given that negotiations on the PNR and the umbrella agreements are still on-going, it is difficult to fully assess at this stage the extent to which the EU will take advantage of the tools it has been given by Lisbon to shape a transatlantic relationship traditionally driven by the US. New relationships of trust need to be built both among EU institutions as well as between the US and the EU—mainly, but not solely, with the Parliament. The outcome of the current negotiations, the level of US concessions on stronger data protection demands, and how the Parliament receives the three PNR agreements with the US, Australia and Canada, will all together determine whether the shift which appeared in the first year of Lisbon's existence—both in substance and procedure—will be sustained in the long term.

References

Argomaniz J (2009) When the EU is the "norm-taker": the passenger name records agreement and the EU's internalisation of US border security norms. Journal of European Integration 31(1):121

De Hert P, Bellanova R (2008) Data protection from a transatlantic perspective: the EU and US move towards an international data protection agreement? Study for the European Parliament, Brussels, 17. www.europarl.europa.eu/studies. Accessed 3 June 2011

Den Boer M (2007) A diagnosis of the Area of Freedom, Security and Justice: remedies and reforms in the domains of immigration, terrorism and security. In: Blockmans S, Prechal S (eds) Reconciling the deepening and widening of the European Union. TMC Asser Press, The Hague, pp 13–28

Den Boer M, Monar J (2002) 11 September and the challenge of global terrorism to the EU as a security actor. Journal of Common Market Studies Annual Review 40:11–28

Desch M (2010) The more things change, the more they stay the same: the liberal tradition and Obama's counterterrorism policy. Political Science and Politics 43:425–429

Dubois D (2002) The attacks of 11 September: EU–US cooperation in the field of justice and home affairs. European Foreign Affairs Review 7:317–335

Faull J, Soreca L (2008) EU–US relations in justice and home affairs. In: Martenczuk B, van Thiel S (eds) Justice, liberty, security: new challenges for EU external relations. VUBPRESS, Brussels

Monar J (2010) The rejection of the EU–US SWIFT interim agreement by the European parliament: a historic vote and its implications. European Foreign Affairs Review 15:151

Pawlak P (2009a) Made in the USA? the influence of the US on the EU's data protection regime, CEPS Working Paper, 2 Nov 2009. www.ceps.eu. Last accessed 3 June 2011

Pawlak P (2009b) Network politics and transatlantic homeland security cooperation. Perspectives on European Politics and Society 10(4): 560–581

Wolff S et al (2009) The external dimension of justice and home affairs: a different security agenda for the EU? Journal of European Integration 31(1):20

Part IV
Principles, Policies and Practices of EU External Relations

Chapter 15
Challenges in EU External Climate Change Policy-Making in the Early Post-Lisbon Era: The UNFCCC Copenhagen Negotiations

Lisanne Groen and Arne Niemann

Abstract The 15th United Nations Framework Convention on Climate Change (UNFCCC) Conference of the Parties (COP) meeting held in Copenhagen from 7 to 18 December 2009, which took place one week after the entry into force of the Treaty of Lisbon on 1 December 2009, has brought about rather disappointing outcomes from the perspective of the European Union (EU), which had previously displayed substantial leadership within the UN climate regime. Contrary to the EU's objectives for the COP15 meeting, no legally binding agreement was reached to succeed the Kyoto Protocol after 2012 and the final Copenhagen Accord contained disappointingly few ambitious targets. This chapter tries to explain how this result came about and what the main challenges have been for the EU in this context. In the first place, we argue that the EU's internal decision-making process was far from optimal. The unanimity rule, in combination with the heterogeneity of preferences of the 27 different EU Member States on many agenda items, negatively affected the EU's ability to play a leadership role at the negotiations in Copenhagen. Secondly, the EU's outreach strategy towards third parties seems to have missed its effect because it was not sufficiently adapted to the highly challenging external context of the negotiations, namely the positions that major third parties like the United States and China had adopted concerning a post-2012 climate regime. The entry into force of the Treaty of Lisbon on 1 December 2009

Lisanne Groen—Ph.D. candidate, Vrije Universiteit Brussel.
Arne Niemann—Professor of International Relations, University of Mainz.

L. Groen (✉)
Department of Political Science, Institute for European Studies (IES),
Vrije Universiteit Brussel, Brussels, Belgium
e-mail: lisannegroen@hotmail.com

A. Niemann
Department of Political Science, University of Mainz, Mainz, Germany
e-mail: arne.niemann@uni-mainz.de

P. J. Cardwell (ed.), *EU External Relations Law and Policy in the Post-Lisbon Era*,
DOI: 10.1007/978-90-6704-823-1_15, © T.M.C. Asser press, The Hague,
The Netherlands, and the authors 2012

does not seem to have had much effect on the EU during the Copenhagen negotiations held one week later. Overall, it seems that the Lisbon provisions point into the right direction and could help to overcome some of the challenges that the EU currently faces in the conduct of its external climate policy. An analysis of the EU's performance at future UNFCCC COP meetings, which are held once a year in December, should facilitate finding an answer to the question of how the Lisbon provisions will be implemented in this particular field.

Contents

15.1 Introduction

According to the European Union (EU), climate change, a global common good problem, needs to be tackled by means of multilateral cooperation.[1] The EU has been characterised as a leader in the multilateral negotiations of the United Nations Framework Convention on Climate Change (UNFCCC) already since the very beginning of this global convention.[2] A few years ago, when the people in France and the Netherlands rejected the Treaty establishing a Constitution for Europe by referendum, climate change has become the saviour issue for the EU's integration project, since the EU is able to add significant value to the actions of its Member States on this transboundary problem, given the experience and record it has in achieving cooperation between sovereign states. At the same time, by aiming to be a leader in this global climate regime the EU tries to increase its power on the global stage and to export its own standards to the rest of the world. The solutions to the global problem of climate change that the EU provides correspond with the solutions that it has provided earlier on to secure peace and prosperity within the EU itself, namely to advance through international treaties and to establish institutions, thereby relying on the principles of cooperation, solidarity and the rule of law.[3]

---

[1] European Commission (2010), 'Working with international partners', Official website, Section Climate Action, Policies, International Partners, Climate Negotiations, available at http://ec.europa.eu/clima/policies/international/negotiations_en.htm. Accessed on 8 January 2011.

[2] Zito 2005; Groenleer and Van Schaik 2007; Oberthür 2009b.

[3] Curtin 2010; Van Schaik 2010.

Given the importance of external climate change policy for EU external relations (and European integration more generally), the main question of this chapter—what are the EU's principal challenges for asserting itself at international climate change negotiations in the early post-Lisbon era?—is a particularly salient one. Contrary to previous negotiations, the UNFCCC 15th Conference of the Parties (COP) meeting in Copenhagen from 7 to 18 December 2009 brought about disappointing outcomes from the perspective of the EU. This disappointment was particularly acute given that the meeting took place 1 week after the entry into force of the Lisbon Treaty, which did not seem to have had much effect on the EU's ability to act at Copenhagen. Contrary to the EU's objectives, no legally binding agreement was reached to succeed the Kyoto Protocol after 2012 and the final Copenhagen Accord regrettably contained few ambitious targets. This result asks for an examination of the EU's internal decision-making process and its outreach towards third parties (insofar as its dealings with the external context are concerned) both in the run up to the Copenhagen conference and at the conference itself. Part of this examination will focus on the question concerning the extent to which the entry into force of the Treaty of Lisbon affected the way in which the EU acted at the Copenhagen negotiations. The question regarding the degree to which the Lisbon Treaty will impact on the EU in future UN climate change negotiations will be addressed at the end of this chapter.

'The EU' here denotes the legal entity which has been accepted as a party within the UNFCCC and which has been represented at the negotiator level, the lowest negotiation level at the COP15 meeting in Copenhagen, by the Swedish EU Council Presidency and by two EU negotiation teams, consisting of lead negotiators and issue leaders from both the EU Member States and the European Commission. At the higher negotiation levels the EU has been represented by the Swedish Council Presidency and the 'EU troika'. Since the Amsterdam Treaty, the EU troika has consisted of the current EU Council Presidency (here Sweden), the upcoming Presidency (Spain) and the European Commission.[4] In the most important bilateral negotiations and smaller negotiating sessions the EU is (also) represented by the EU troika. In addition to the EU, its Member States are present separately as parties to the negotiations.[5]

We proceed as follows: first, we will sketch the context of the EU's leadership in the UNFCCC climate change negotiations before the negotiations at the COP15 meeting in Copenhagen. Second, we will outline the course of affairs at the Copenhagen meeting and clarify the role that the EU played during these negotiations. Third, we will explain why the EU failed to play a leading role in Copenhagen and to what extent the Lisbon Treaty influenced the way in which the EU acted at Copenhagen. Fourth and finally we will analyse the likely impact of the Lisbon Treaty on the EU's external climate change policy more generally.

---

4 Oberthür 2009a, 13. Morillas (this volume) discusses the Spanish Presidency as it dealt with the immediate consequences of the entry into force of Lisbon.

5 Lacasta et al. 2002, 361.

15.2 The EU's Leadership at the UNFCCC Negotiations Before Copenhagen

The United Nations Framework Convention on Climate Change, created in response to the growing scientific evidence about the dangers posed by greenhouse gas emissions to life on earth, was adopted on 9 May 1992[6] and entered into force on 21 March 1994.[7] The Conference of the Parties (COP), the highest decision-making body of the UNFCCC in which all parties to the convention are represented, holds an annual meeting, the first of which took place in 1995. During the negotiating process before the adoption of the convention in 1992 the EU already provided leadership by pushing for stringent international measures to tackle climate change in the form of binding greenhouse gas emissions reduction targets for industrialised countries.[8] At the first COP meeting in Berlin in 1995, parties agreed that industrialised states (the 'Annex-I' group of countries including both the EU (the 'European Community' in 1995), and all of its Member States, except for Cyprus, which joined the EU in 2004) would negotiate real cuts in their greenhouse gas emissions and that these negotiations were to be concluded in 1997 at the COP3 meeting in Kyoto.[9] In Kyoto legally binding greenhouse gas emissions targets, stating that Annex-I countries shall reduce emissions of six different greenhouse gases by at least 5% from 1990 levels in the period 2008–2012, were adopted. The EU agreed to the highest percentage of emissions reduction of all participants (8%). At the COP3 meeting in Kyoto detailed rules for the operation of the system were not provided. Negotiations about these rules continued at later COP meetings.

At the COP6 meeting in 2000 in The Hague negotiations broke down because of disagreements between the EU and the US about rules for the operation of the Kyoto mechanisms. In March 2001 the new US government, led by George W. Bush, announced its withdrawal from the negotiations.[10] From that moment onwards the EU played a vital role in the implementation process of the Kyoto Protocol.[11] Later on in 2001, at the COP7 meeting in Marrakech, the EU made sure that the Marrakech Accords were agreed upon by persuading Annex-I countries to give their approval. The Accords contained detailed implementing rules for the Kyoto Protocol and were of high importance in the process culminating in the entry into force of the Protocol in 2005.[12] The ratification process was another stumbling block on the way towards the entry into force of the Protocol

---

6 Sands 1992, 270.

7 CAN Europe 2009.

8 Groenleer and Van Schaik 2007, 983; Oberthür and Roche Kelly 2008, 36.

9 Damro 2006, 185.

10 Damro 2006, 187.

11 Zito 2005; Oberthür 2009b.

12 Damro 2006, 187; Oberthür and Roche Kelly 2008, 36.

that the EU tried to overcome by urging all parties to ratify the Protocol as soon as possible and by persuading Russia in particular to support the Protocol.[13] As a result of these efforts, the Kyoto Protocol entered into force in February 2005.

The first commitment period of the Kyoto Protocol will come to an end in 2012. In order to start up the process of designing a follow-up agreement for the Protocol after 2012, the EU was the first party to provide concrete emissions reduction commitments for 2020.[14] In March 2007 the EU committed to the goal of a 20% greenhouse gas emissions reduction by 1990 levels, offering to scale this commitment up to a 30% emissions reduction if the other convention parties would make comparable efforts, thereby launching the negotiations on a global post-2012 climate agreement. At the COP13 meeting in Bali in 2007 the Bali Road Map was agreed upon, in which parties expressed their willingness to finalise the negotiations on a global post-2012 agreement at the COP15 meeting in Copenhagen in December 2009. With various diplomatic instruments, such as diplomatic missions and bilateral meetings, the EU tried to convince other UNFCCC parties to aim for a maximum global temperature increase of 2°C in line with the advice provided in the Fourth Assessment Report of the Intergovernmental Panel on Climate Change (IPCC) from 2007. As a result, the Bali Road Map explicitly mentions that climate change policies need to be guided by the IPCC's findings and makes reference to the Fourth Assessment Report of the IPCC.[15]

However, the leadership role of the EU within the UN climate change regime cannot be taken for granted. Both problems inside the EU itself and difficult external circumstances may challenge the EU's leading position. This became clear at the COP15 meeting in Copenhagen in December 2009.

15.3 The EU at the UNFCCC COP15 Meeting Negotiations in Copenhagen

In this section we present the course of affairs at the Copenhagen climate change negotiations and clarify the role that the EU played at these particular negotiations. The Treaty of Lisbon, which had entered into force only several days before the start of the COP15 meeting on 7 December 2009, brought about one change that was already visible at Copenhagen: the EU, by acquiring legal personality in Article 47 of the Treaty on European Union (TEU), inserted by the Treaty of Lisbon, replaced the European Community (EC) as a party at the UNFCCC Copenhagen negotiations.[16] This legal personality was envisaged to give the EU a clearer representation and a stronger voice in international negotiations. It might

[13] Damro 2006, 187.

[14] Oberthür and Roche Kelly 2008, 36; Van Schaik and Schunz (2012).

[15] Van Schaik and Schunz (2012).

[16] For a detailed analysis on the EU and the legal personality it has acquired under the Treaty of Lisbon, see Sari (this volume).

have indeed increased the EU's visibility as a negotiating party and thereby its recognition as such at the Copenhagen negotiations. However, the fact that the EU acquired legal personality did not seem to have strengthened the EU's influence on other negotiating parties in terms of moving them to follow its lead.[17]

The negotiations in Copenhagen took place at different levels. They began at the negotiator level where the negotiations were held on two separate tracks. The first negotiation track concerned the Ad Hoc Working Group on Long-term Cooperative Action under the Convention, in which all UNFCCC parties took part, with the goal of enabling full and effective implementation of the framework convention on climate change. This Working Group exists since the adoption of the Bali Road Map at the COP13 meeting in Bali in 2007 and it should have reached an agreed outcome at the COP15 meeting (which was not the case). The second negotiation track concerned the Ad Hoc Working Group on further commitments for Annex-I parties under the Kyoto Protocol, in which the countries that are parties to the Kyoto Protocol took part. This Working Group exists since the COP meeting in 2005 and aims at initiating a process to consider further commitments by Annex-I parties for the period beyond 2012. Two EU negotiation teams, one on the Convention track and one on the Kyoto Protocol track, both consisting of a group of lead negotiators and issue leaders, negotiated the text of the Copenhagen Accord together with negotiation teams from third parties in the first week of the Copenhagen meeting.

In 2004 the EU system of 'issue leaders' and 'lead negotiators' was introduced.[18] On behalf of the EU Council Presidency lead negotiators from EU Member States (other than the Member State which holds the Presidency) and from the European Commission are appointed to take over the lead from the Presidency in the international negotiations in various negotiating groups at the negotiator level in order to reduce the workload of the Presidency[19] and in cooperation with the issue leaders the lead negotiators prepare the common EU negotiating position for the international negotiations.[20]

The second stage of the negotiations in Copenhagen, which started in the second week, was the ministerial level during which the environment ministers from the UNFCCC parties met. However, the ministers did not have a clear role at the Copenhagen meeting. Normally, the environment ministers are present at a COP meeting to take the final decisions, but at Copenhagen heads of state and government were invited to conclude the follow-up agreement of the Kyoto Protocol, because this new agreement would concern many different issue areas linked to climate change, such as finance and development, and would be of very

[17] Other changes to the EU's external climate policy that occurred as a result of the entry into force of the Treaty of Lisbon but were not relevant for the EU's performance at the Copenhagen negotiations, and changes that may occur in the future as a result of the Treaty, will be discussed in Sect. 15.5.

[18] Oberthür and Roche Kelly 2008, 38.

[19] Oberthür 2009a, 14.

[20] Oberthür and Roche Kelly 2008, 38.

high importance compared to the final agreements at earlier COP meetings. Thus, at Copenhagen the ministers more or less assisted the heads of state and government. The final stage of the negotiations at Copenhagen was the head of state and government level, during which the leaders of the parties took the decisions regarding the final outcome, the Copenhagen Accord. From 16 to 18 December 2009 the heads of state and government were present at the 'high-level segment' of the negotiations.

It could be argued that before the start of the COP15 meeting the EU generally tried to display 'directional leadership'.[21] The EU realised domestic innovation in policies and technology in the area of climate change, for example by developing its own Emission Trading System, and encouraged others to copy it.[22] Furthermore, the ambitious EU goals for the COP15 meeting that it had set early on, such as its aim to keep the global temperature rise below 2°C and to adopt emission reduction targets and measures in line with this objective, in combination with the foreign policy actions that it performed to realise these goals—guided by normative aspirations to tackle climate change[23]—indicate that the EU has tried to lead by example at the Copenhagen negotiations. The EU was the first party to bring concrete proposals to the Copenhagen negotiation table. In March 2007 the EU presented a concrete emissions reduction target for 2020: a 20% CO_2-emissions reduction by 2020 compared to 1990 levels, scaling it up to a 30% reduction should others make comparable efforts.[24] After having presented this EU proposal, other major parties such as Australia, Japan, Russia and the United States moved closer to the ambitious position of the EU. The EU built up political momentum before the conference and set the ambition level for the negotiations.[25]

In the beginning of the COP15 meeting, at the first stage of the negotiations, the technical negotiator level or 'preparatory' level, at which experts on various subjects such as mitigation, finance and technology operate, the EU acted as an important negotiating party, representing the joint vision of the 27 EU Member States. As one delegate subsequently said:

> [At this senior civil servant level] it was really clear that the others saw the EU as a player with important knowledge and expertise that had to be taken into consideration. At this technical level there was clearly respect for the EU. You could feel that people perked up their ears when the EU was talking.[26]

---

21 Gupta and Grubb 2000, xiv.

22 European Commission (2010), 'Emission Trading System (EU ETS)', Official website, Section Environment, Climate Change, Emission Trading System, available at http://ec.europa.eu/environment/climat/emission/index_en.htm, accessed on 7 July 2010.

23 Van Schaik and Schunz (2012).

24 Council of the European Union (2007), Presidency Conclusions of the Brussels European Council, Brussels, 9 March 2007, 7224/07.

25 Interview with Council Secretariat representative, Brussels, 3 May 2010; Interview by telephone with Swedish EU Council Presidency delegate, 3 May 2010.

26 Interview by telephone with UK delegate, 10 May 2010.

Non-EU UNFCCC parties negotiated actively and vibrantly with the Commission and the team of the Swedish EU Council Presidency. This has not only been confirmed through interviews, but can also be substantiated by the webcasts from the preparatory plenary negotiation sessions in the first week of the conference.[27] NGOs likewise interacted with representatives from the Commission and the Swedish EU Presidency during the preparatory negotiations[28] and EU Member States cooperated smoothly with the EU negotiation teams and the Swedish Council Presidency both at internal EU meetings, including the daily EU coordination meetings that were held, and during the plenary negotiating sessions.[29]

However, the negotiations at this preparatory level did not progress as well as they should have and the EU was not able to change this situation.[30] There were too many disagreements that persisted on sub-issues of the envisaged Copenhagen agreement between the EU, developing countries, the United States and the group of advanced developing countries, the 'BASIC countries' (Brazil, South Africa, India and China). These disagreements centred especially on mitigation of climate change by means of the reduction of greenhouse gas emissions and certain aspects of climate finance.[31] As a result of these struggles, much of the effort to conclude a final agreement in Copenhagen was left to the heads of state and government. A text proposal from the Danish COP Presidency for a Copenhagen agreement, which was brought about as a compromise text, could have been a way out of these problems. However, this compromise text, based on earlier discussions in 2009 on both the Working Group and the Kyoto Protocol negotiation track, was not accepted by the largest part of the delegates in Copenhagen, who stated that this proposal had not come about in a transparent and democratic way. This meant that the heads of state had to adjust (simplify) and complete the text of the final agreement themselves that resulted from the negotiations at the preparatory level full of brackets, a situation that was not planned beforehand.

At the final decision-making stage of the negotiations in Copenhagen, the high-level segment among the heads of state and government, no party followed the ambitious EU proposals, namely to agree with a binding greenhouse gas emissions reduction goal in line with the 20% reduction goal that the EU had set itself and to aim for a universal, legally binding agreement in Copenhagen. This proposal of the

---

[27] UNFCCC Webcast (2009), United Nations Climate Change Conference, 7–18 December 2009, Copenhagen, available at http://cop15.meta-fusion.com/kongresse/cop15/templ/ovw.php?id_kongressmain=1&theme=unfccc, accessed on 7 August 2010; Interview with Council Secretariat representative, Brussels, 3 May 2010; Interview with UK delegate by telephone, 10 May 2010; Interview with participant-observer by telephone, 11 May 2010; Interview with Dutch delegate, The Hague, 12 May 2010; Interview with Japanese delegate by e-mail, 25 June 2010.

[28] Interview with CAN Europe representative, Brussels, 4 May 2010.

[29] Interview with Dutch delegate, The Hague, 12 May 2010; Interview with Swedish Council Presidency delegate by telephone, 3 May 2010.

[30] International Institute for Sustainable Development (IISD) 2009.

[31] International Institute for Sustainable Development (IISD) 2009.

EU was not reconcilable with the interests of the United States and the BASIC countries, who did not want to compromise on their economic growth by agreeing with drastic emission cuts unless all of them would do so. The latter were not convinced by the normative arguments of the EU, but sought to protect their diverse interests.[32] This resulted in the marginalisation of the EU during the bargaining process, further depriving it from playing a leadership role at the negotiations, with the final result that the United States and the BASIC countries mainly concluded the Copenhagen Accord together.

At the final high-level segment of the negotiations the EU lost its grip on the negotiating process. Third parties no longer negotiated with the Swedish EU Presidency, being the main EU representative at this final stage of the negotiations when the decisions had to be taken, and even the leaders of the big EU Member States such as Angela Merkel from Germany, Nicolas Sarkozy from France and Gordon Brown from the United Kingdom most of the time seem to have been unable to influence the course of the final negotiations. Thus, the EU was unable to change the outcome of the COP15 meeting, which turned out to be (very) disappointing when measured against the ambitious goals that the EU had set. The United States and the BASIC countries mainly concluded the Copenhagen Accord together at a decisive informal non-plenary meeting on the last day of the conference without the EU being present.[33] It has been suggested that German Chancellor Merkel, French President Sarkozy and Spanish Prime Minister Zapatero had to wait until head of state and government leaders Wen (China), Singh (India), Lula (Brazil) and Zuma (South Africa) had finished their conversation before being allowed to contribute at the final decisive negotiations.[34] As has been reported, 'the Swedish [Presidency] leader [Reinfeldt] hinted that the Europeans had been caught badly off guard. Mr. Reinfeldt said he had gotten his first signals that a deal had been struck while still engrossed in meetings. "We had very tough negotiations two and a half hours after I read on my mobile telephone that we were already done" he said.'[35]

15.4 Why the EU Did Not Play a Leadership Role at the COP15 Meeting

In this section we analyse both the shortcomings in the EU's internal decision-making process and in its outreach towards third parties in the run up to and at the Copenhagen conference itself that led to the EU's marginalisation at the COP15 meeting negotiations. As part of this examination attention will be paid to the

32 Van Schaik and Schunz (2012).

33 Curtin 2010; Van Schaik and Schunz (2012).

34 Luttikhuis (2009).

35 Kanter (2009).

question of the extent to which the entry into force of the Lisbon Treaty changed the way in which the EU operated at the Copenhagen negotiations.

15.4.1 The EU's Internal Decision-Making Process

The Swedish EU Council Presidency, the EU troika and the EU lead negotiators and issue leaders had the competence to act on behalf of the EU during the Copenhagen negotiations, but were obliged to operate within the constraints of the EU negotiation mandate. Hence, the delegation of decision-making power to these EU representatives during the negotiations could only extend as far as the limits of what the EU Member States had agreed upon in the mandate. In order for the EU to demonstrate leadership at the negotiations this EU negotiating mandate must be flexible. It needs to be quickly adaptable according to the changing circumstances of the negotiations and it needs to include fall-back positions, especially in the decisive phases, in order to allow the EU negotiators to take the right decisions at the right time to substantially influence the negotiation process.[36] As for the flexibility of the mandate at the COP15 negotiations, EU negotiators were not permitted to deviate from the mandate before the 27 EU Member States had unanimously approved of changes. As one insider said, 'after a mandate has been fixed it is difficult to alter it because of the unanimity rule.'[37] Every single Member State has to agree with a change of the mandate before this change can be carried through. This unanimity requirement substantially constrained the flexibility of the EU mandate at the COP15 meeting. The low degree of flexibility of the mandate in turn negatively affected the EU's ability to play a leadership role at the negotiations in Copenhagen. As the EU mandate, which suffered from insecure positions on many negotiating items, could not be significantly altered during the negotiations, EU negotiators did not get the possibility to close strategic deals with important third parties like the United States or China in order to make them agree with (or move closer towards) EU goals like the inclusion of binding CO_2 reduction commitments in the final Copenhagen Accord.

Another detrimental effect of the unanimity rule is that, 'given the frequent differences between the Member States, you only get the lowest common denominator in the EU negotiation mandate'.[38] For some issues on the COP15 negotiation agenda no concrete common EU position could be formulated because the 27 EU Member States were unable to reach sufficient agreement; 'the EU negotiation mandate is often formulated in words that mask the underlying differences of opinion [between the EU Member States]. This is why you don't have

[36] Lacasta et al. 2002, 414.

[37] Interview with Council Secretariat representative, Brussels, 3 May 2010.

[38] Interview by telephone with UK delegate, 10 May 2010.

a position in the EU mandate at some points at all.'[39] For example, the issue of providing climate finance to developing countries was fraught with difficulty for EU negotiators in Copenhagen because the EU Member States had not reached proper agreement on this issue before the start of the COP15 meeting and therefore the EU mandate contained no concrete proposals with which the EU negotiators could negotiate in order to steer the negotiations in the direction that the EU would have wanted to. This reduced the ability of the EU negotiators to take on a leadership role at the Copenhagen negotiations. The EU was similarly paralysed in its dealings with third parties at Copenhagen on the issue of 'hot air'[40] where the EU Member States had remained divided.[41]

From the above it can be concluded that the unanimity rule seriously hampered the EU's efforts to play a leadership role at Copenhagen. However, it should be noted that there is a factor behind the unanimity rule that makes it difficult for the EU to deal with this rule, namely the fact that the EU consists of (27 different) Member States with diverging preferences (that can often not be brought into agreement with each other). This heterogeneity of preferences formed the basis of the EU's inability to perform a leading role at the Copenhagen negotiations. Because of the heterogeneity of preferences among the EU Member States several important issues on the Copenhagen agenda remained on which no concrete positions were included in the EU negotiation mandate, the 27 EU Member States being unable to reach agreement on them. These issues will be outlined below.

To start with, there was underlying disagreement among the EU Member States on the question of whether the EU should commit itself to a CO_2-emissions reduction goal of 30% compared to 1990 levels by 2020 and under which conditions it should do so.[42] The mandate specifies that the EU should do so when 'other developed countries commit themselves to comparable emission reductions and [...] developing countries contribute adequately according to their responsibilities and respective capabilities.'[43] The decision to set a conditional reduction goal of 30% had already been taken in 2007,[44] but this goal nevertheless remained controversial among the EU Member States, with Italy and Poland openly speaking out against the decision and many other Member States quietly

---

39 Interview with Council Secretariat representative, Brussels, 3 May 2010.

40 'Hot air' refers here to the question of whether the Eastern European countries, which have a surplus of CO2-emission rights left under the Kyoto Protocol because of the collapse of their industries after 1990, should be allowed to carry over these rights into the second period of the Kyoto Protocol or not.

41 Interview with Council Secretariat representative, Brussels, 3 May 2010; Interview with UK delegate by telephone, 10 May 2010.

42 Interview with Dutch delegate, The Hague, 12 May 2010; Bloemen (2009).

43 Council of the European Union (2009), Environment Council of Ministers Conclusions, Brussels, 21 October 2009, 14790/09, 5.

44 Council of the European Union (2007), Presidency Conclusions of the Brussels European Council, Brussels, 9 March 2007, 7224/07, 12.

supporting their protest.[45] With almost every European Council meeting the issue was again put on the table. Poland and Italy pushed for the deletion of the 30% conditional reduction goal while the UK and France, on the other hand, sought to defend it.[46] The mandate failed to specify exact conditions to be fulfilled in order for the EU to commit to a 30% CO_2 reduction. In the absence of prior agreement between the EU Member States this question had to be sorted out during the COP15 meeting, as a result of which the EU was paralysed on the issue during the Copenhagen negotiations. Even after the negotiations this debate continued.

Second, the EU negotiation mandate laid out no concrete position on land use, land use change and forestry (LULUCF).[47] LULUCF is the agreement that covers forestry for the developed countries that have pledged to reduce their emissions under the Kyoto Protocol.[48] Since a few EU Member States, namely Finland, Austria and Sweden, have a large timber industry and wanted to protect it, the Environment Council of Ministers was unable to adopt a specific position on accounting rules for forestry in developed countries.[49] Third, the EU Member States disagreed as to what should be done with the unused Assigned Amount Units (AAUs), also known as 'hot air', in the second period of the Kyoto Protocol after 2012. The unused AAUs are one of the 'environmental loopholes' in the Kyoto Protocol. Because of the collapse of their heavy industries in the 1990s precipitated by the fall of communism, the CO_2-emissions of the Eastern European EU Member States had fallen significantly. As a result, these Member States retained surplus AAUs. The question of debate in the EU was whether the Eastern European Member States should be allowed to carry over these units into the second period of the Kyoto Protocol. As no agreement could be reached on this issue, the mandate stated only that 'the EU will further consider options in view of discussions with other Parties'.[50] During the summit a group of seven Eastern European countries were fighting for the AAUs to be retained, releasing a statement that any deal 'should keep the door open for allowing the full transfer of the surplus represented by the AAUs to the post-2012 framework'.[51] 'Progressive' EU Member States like the UK, the Netherlands, Denmark and Sweden were against such a transfer of unused AAUs to a second period of the Kyoto Protocol after 2012.

Fourth, at the start of the Copenhagen conference the EU Member States had not yet agreed on a quantified financial contribution payable to developing

---

[45] Interview by telephone with UK delegate, 10 May 2010.

[46] Interview with Dutch delegate, The Hague, 12 May 2010; van der Kris (2009).

[47] Council of the European Union (2009), Environment Council of Ministers Conclusions, Brussels, 21 October 2009, 14790/09, 13–14.

[48] Rosenthal (2009a).

[49] Interview with CAN Europe representative, Brussels, 4 May 2010; Greenpeace 2009; Rosenthal (2009b).

[50] Council of the European Union (2009), Environment Council of Ministers Conclusions, Brussels, 21 October 2009, 14790/09, 15.

[51] Murray (2009).

countries for adaptation and mitigation measures. Because of the financial crisis many EU Member States, most notably the Eastern European Member States, were reluctant to donate.[52] On the other hand, 'progressive' Member States like the Netherlands, the UK, Germany, France, Denmark and Sweden were ready to put concrete amounts of money on the table.[53] The mandate stated that 'the EU is prepared to take on its fair share, in the framework of a global and comprehensive Copenhagen agreement which entails appropriate and adequate contributions by Parties',[54] but no concrete amounts of money were mentioned. An agreement on finance for developing countries was closed only at the very last moment, when the COP15 negotiations had already started.[55] The above findings are indicative of a significant number of issues in the EU mandate before the Copenhagen negotiations on which no concrete agreement was reached within the EU. Many EU Member States appeared unwilling to sacrifice their own interests in order to agree with the ambitious EU proposals for the Copenhagen negotiations. It seems that only a few EU Member States, such as France, the UK and perhaps the Netherlands and Denmark, firmly supported a progressive EU position until the very end of the negotiations.[56] This seriously affected the EU's ability to act as a leader at Copenhagen.

15.4.2 The EU's Outreach Towards Third Parties and Handling of the External Context

In order for the EU to steer the outcome of the negotiations in the preferred direction (and take on a leadership role) it would have been necessary to make offers to other negotiating parties to close 'deals' with them. Based on the results of various interviews held with participants at the COP15 meeting negotiations it seems that not many deals could be closed at the Copenhagen negotiations between the EU and third parties. The EU's outreach strategy towards third parties seems to have missed its effect because it was not sufficiently adapted to the highly challenging external context of the negotiations, namely the positions that major third parties like the United States and China had adopted concerning a post-2012 climate regime. Both the United States and China, the leader of the group of BASIC countries, entered the debate on a post-2012 climate regime with strong interests and positions that they would not easily give up. These were most of the time rather opposed to the EU's interests and positions. The strategy chosen by the

[52] Carrington (2009).
[53] Interview with Dutch delegate, The Hague, 12 May 2010.
[54] Council of the European Union (2009), Environment Council of Ministers Conclusions, Brussels, 21 October 2009, 14790/09, 19.
[55] van der Kris (2009).
[56] Interview by telephone with UK delegate, 10 May 2010; van der Kris (2009).

EU, specified in its mandate, was a fairly ambitious and normative one: the EU tried to convince third parties to make efforts comparable to the EU's own greenhouse gas emissions reduction targets in order to save the planet.[57]

At the end of November 2009, before the start of the COP15 meeting negotiations in Copenhagen in December, it turned out that the CO_2 emissions reduction targets of the United States and China were considerably less ambitious than those of the EU.[58] The sheer distance between the positions of the United States and China and that of the EU made it an unrealistic aim to convince third parties to adopt the same ambitious goals as the EU had done. At this point in time the EU Member States could have agreed to adjust their negotiating strategy to ensure that the EU would be taken seriously by the United States and China as a negotiating partner and would preserve influence over the outcome of the negotiating process. However, the EU Member States could not reach unanimous agreement on the adjustment of the mandate. As a result the United States, China and others increasingly sidelined the EU during the negotiations as any compromise close to EU objectives was unrealistic.

15.5 The Impact of the Treaty of Lisbon on EU External Climate Policy

Besides the EU acquiring legal personality, four other changes regarding the EU's external climate policy have taken place with the entry into force of the Treaty of Lisbon. In the first place, the Treaty of Lisbon made official and legally binding the decision to have the Council Presidency held by groups of three Member States for a period of eighteen months and to let each of these three Member States chair the Council for a 6-month period, by mentioning this in a special 'Draft decision of the European Council on the exercise of the Presidency of the Council'. Based on a Council decision from September 2006 this so called 'triple Presidency' has already been in operation since 2007.[59] Thus, it did not change much about the EU's external representation at Copenhagen. The system has been introduced to improve the efficiency of the rotating Presidency. The other three changes that will be mentioned below were not in operation before the Treaty of Lisbon entered into force.

A second change in the EU's external climate policy introduced by the Treaty of Lisbon concerns the role of the European Parliament (EP). Before the entry into

[57] Van Schaik and Schunz (2012).

[58] The US target was to cut greenhouse gas emissions by 17% by 2020 from 2005 levels and the Chinese target was to reduce the amount of carbon dioxide emitted per unit of economic output by 40–45% by 2020 compared to 2005 levels, which would not even decrease the total amount of emissions in 2020 compared to 2005, while the EU aimed for a cut of greenhouse gas emissions by 20–30% by 2020 from 1990 levels (New York Times, 26 November 2009).

[59] Afionis 2009, 45–46.

force of the Treaty the European Parliament only played an advisory role in the process of ratifying international agreements, but with the coming into effect of Article 218 of the Treaty on the Functioning of the European Union (TFEU) in the Treaty of Lisbon, which replaces Article 300 EC, the European Parliament has obtained the power to veto future international agreements, including climate agreements. The European Parliament may use this power to demand a more prominent position in the EU's external climate policy. Given Parliament's generally strong pro-environmental stance this change is likely to strengthen the 'progressive' stance within EU climate change policy. Another important question is what impact this enhanced role of the EP will have on the influence that the EU will have on external climate change policy in international negotiations. On the one hand, the involvement of the EP could further contribute to a politicisation of EU climate change policy and (thus) threaten to hamper policy-making processes within the EU. On the other hand, the European Parliament could be conveniently used as a bargaining chip in two- or three-level games.[60] The EU could strengthen its bargaining position in international negotiations by referring to the requirement of EP consent, as practised by US negotiators with regard to Congress.

Third, changes have been made to the legal basis for EU activities in international environmental agreements. The former Article 174 EC has been amended with the entry into force of the Treaty of Lisbon. Article 191 TFEU now states that EU policy on the environment shall contribute to, among others, 'promoting measures at international level to deal with regional or worldwide environmental problems, *and in particular climate change*.'[61] This means that the Treaty, for the first time ever, has created a specific formal EU competence for the adoption of legislative acts in the area of climate change. This formal legal competence is accompanied by qualified majority voting (QMV) in the Council of Ministers, which will enter into force in November 2014 and will still be subject, until 2017, to being blocked by recourse to the voting rules introduced by the Treaty of Nice.[62] The future will have to show what this change will bring about in practice. More elements of QMV may enhance the EU's flexibility at international negotiations, which has been found wanting at the Copenhagen conference, and reduce the chance of lowest common denominator positions. Since climate change negotiations usually constitute 'reformist' cases for the EU—i.e., cases where the EU Member States median preferences are further away from the status quo than those of its negotiating partners[63]—the possibility to go beyond lowest common denominator positions will increase the likelihood that negotiation outcomes develop into a more favourable direction for the European Union.

[60] Cf. Putnam 1988.

[61] Emphasis added.

[62] See Article 16 (4) TEU, Article 238 (2) TFEU and Declaration 7 attached to the Treaty. The transitional measures were set out in Council Decision of 13 December 2007 (2009/857/EC).

[63] Cf. Meunier 2000.

Fourth, the Treaty of Lisbon has created the new post of a High Representative of the Union for Foreign Affairs and Security Policy, in which the roles of High Representative for Foreign and Security Policy, chair of the Foreign Affairs Council and Vice-President of the European Commission have been merged.[64] In addition to this change, another institutional innovation was carried through, namely the introduction of the post of the President of the European Council, who is appointed for a renewable term of two and a half years.[65] Until the time of writing (July 2011), the Treaty of Lisbon has not yet resulted in changes in the EU's representation at the UNFCCC COP meetings in practice. More than ten years ago, the EU Member States decided not to allow the Commission to negotiate at the UNFCCC, preferring to give the rotating EU Council Presidency the power to represent and coordinate the EU position at the UNFCCC COP meeting negotiations.[66] At the COP15 meeting in Copenhagen the Swedish EU Council Presidency was still the main spokesperson for the EU and at the COP16 meeting in Cancún in December 2010 it was the Belgian EU Council Presidency. It may be the case that the EU's representation at the UNFCCC COP meetings will change in the future to strengthen the EU's performance at international climate negotiations. One possible scenario is that the High Representative, assisted by her own European External Action Service (EEAS),[67] will take over the position of the rotating Council Presidency as the main EU representative in external climate policy in order to strengthen the EU's performance as a strategic and diplomatic negotiator by providing a more permanent structure (and coherent approach) for EU coordination and external representation.[68] It is expected that the High Representative will create a strong linkage between external environmental issues and other external affairs issues. However, as others in this volume have noted, thus far the role of the High Representative is still unclear, and this includes her role in international climate policy. That the European Commission becomes the main EU representative at international climate negotiations is another possible scenario. During the COP16 meeting in Cancún in December 2010 the Commission, in the form of Climate Action Commissioner Connie Hedegaard, took care of representing the Union during certain parts of the negotiations, instead of the Belgian EU Presidency. However, most EU Member States fiercely oppose handing over the overall EU representation at the UNFCCC COP negotiations to the Commission, which makes such a scenario rather unlikely.

[64] For further analysis of the role of the High Representative, see Schmidt (this volume).

[65] Treaty on European Union, Article 15 (5).

[66] Lacasta et al. 2002, 369.

[67] On the creation and workings of the EEAS and problems encountered therein so far, see Blockmans and Laatsit (this volume).

[68] Van Schaik 2010, 272.

15.6 Conclusion

The UNFCCC COP15 meeting held in Copenhagen from 7 to 18 December 2009, which took place one week after the entry into force on 1 December 2009 of the Treaty of Lisbon, has brought about rather disappointing outcomes from the perspective of the EU, which had previously displayed substantial leadership within the UN climate regime. Contrary to the EU's objectives for the COP15 meeting no legally binding agreement was reached to succeed the Kyoto Protocol after 2012 and the final Copenhagen Accord contained disappointingly few ambitious targets. In this chapter we have tried to explain how this result came about and what the main challenges are for the EU in this context.

In the first place, the EU's internal decision-making process was far from optimal. As for the flexibility of the mandate at the COP15 meeting negotiations, EU negotiators were not permitted to deviate from the mandate before the 27 EU Member States had unanimously approved of changes. This negatively affected the EU's ability to play a leadership role at the negotiations in Copenhagen. Another detrimental effect of the unanimity rule was that it was quite difficult to formulate clear EU negotiating positions. The crucial factor that made it difficult for the EU to deal with this rule was the heterogeneity of preferences of the 27 different EU Member States on many issues on the COP15 agenda like the EU's CO_2 reduction goal and climate finance.

Secondly, the EU's outreach strategy towards third parties seems to have missed its effect because it was not sufficiently adapted to the highly challenging external context of the negotiations, namely the positions that major third parties like the United States and China had adopted concerning a post-2012 climate regime. Both the United States and China entered the debate on a post-2012 climate regime with strong positions and interests, which considerably differed from the EU stance. The ambitious and normative approach chosen by the EU, namely to convince third parties to make efforts comparable to the EU's own greenhouse gas emissions reduction targets, was not effective in this context.

The entry into force of the Treaty of Lisbon on 1 December 2009 does not seem to have had much effect on the EU during the Copenhagen negotiations held one week later. A clearly visible change was the fact that the EU acquired legal personality and replaced the European Community as a party at the UNFCCC Copenhagen negotiations. However, this legal personality does not seem to have increased the EU's ability to play a leadership role at the Copenhagen negotiations.

One of the other changes that occurred with the entry into force of the Treaty of Lisbon is the creation of the post of the High Representative of the Union for Foreign Affairs and Security Policy. This High Representative (Baroness Catherine Ashton) is expected to create a strong linkage between external environmental issues and other issues relating to external affairs. If the High Representative will take over the role of the rotating Presidency at the UNFCCC negotiations this should contribute to an improved coordination and representation of the EU at these negotiations, enabling the EU to speak with a stronger voice.

In order for the EU to regain its leadership position at the UNFCCC negotiations in the current challenging circumstances it needs to invest a lot of time in the preparation of possible issue linkages and package deals that can be closed with third parties at future negotiations. Thus, the EU should invest more time in climate diplomacy: by reaching out towards third countries on a regular basis before COP meetings to get a detailed view of third parties' positions so that a clever strategy, for both the short and the long term, can be designed in order for the EU to lead the negotiations.

The shift from unanimity to qualified majority voting in the Council as a result of the Lisbon Treaty may enable the EU to change its mandate more easily during the negotiations so that it can keep up with the negotiating pace set by its negotiating partners. EU representatives at future COP negotiations need to be enabled to behave more flexibly at the negotiations, by not having to wait for the unanimous consent of the 27 Member States, especially in the decisive phases of the negotiations. Another option—not mentioned by the Treaty of Lisbon—is the creation of a system of lead countries, so that the heterogeneity of preferences of its Member States will have a less detrimental effect on the EU's performance at future UNFCCC COP meetings.

Overall, it thus seems that the Lisbon provisions point into the right direction and could help to overcome some of the challenges that the EU currently faces in the conduct of its external climate policy. An analysis of the EU's performance at future UNFCCC COP meetings, which are held once a year in December, should facilitate finding an answer to the question of how the Lisbon provisions will be implemented in this particular field. Only if the High Representative will attain more central coordination and representation functions, if the European Parliament can be used as a bargaining chip and enable the EU to play more credible two/three-level games and, most importantly, when substantially more elements of QMV will be introduced to increase the EU's flexibility at climate change negotiations, will the EU be able to effectively assert itself and thus perhaps be in a position to reclaim a leadership role in this field.

References

Afionis S (2009) European Union coherence in UNFCCC negotiations under the new Treaty of Lisbon (Reform Treaty). Sustainable Development Law and Policy 9:43–47

Bloemen R (2009) Klimaattop Verdeelt Europa, Algemeen Nederlands Persbureau, 9 December 2009

Carrington D (2009) EU set to double climate aid for developing countries to EUR2bn, Guardian, 11 December 2009

CAN Europe (2009) History of the UNFCCC process, 9 October 2009. hwww.climnet.org/index.php?option=com_content&view=article&id=144%3Ahistoryh&catid=272%3Aun-climate-negotiations&Itemid=284. Accessed 28 Dec 2010

Curtin J (2010) The Copenhagen conference: How should the EU respond? Institute of International and European Affairs, Dublin

Damro C (2006) EU–UN environmental relations: shared competence and effective multilateralism. In: Verlin Laatikainen K, Smith KE (eds) The European Union at the United Nations: intersecting multilateralisms. Palgrave, London, pp 175–192

Greenpeace (2009) Evaluation: the Swedish Presidency gets a red card for environmental failure, 22 December 2009

Groenleer MLP, van Schaik LG (2007) United we stand? The European Union's international actorness in the cases of the International Criminal Court and the Kyoto Protocol. Journal of Common Market Studies 45:969–998

Gupta J, Grubb M (2000) Climate change and European leadership: A sustainable role for Europe? Kluwer, Dordrecht

International Institute for Sustainable Development (IISD) (2009) 112 Earth Negotiations Bulletin, COP15 final. www.iisd.ca/climate/cop15/. Accessed 24 Feb 2010

Kanter J (2009) Europeans, their hopes dashed, grimly accept final deal, International Herald Tribune, 21 December 2009

Lacasta NS, Dessai S, Powroslo E (2002) Consensus among many voices: articulating the European Union's position on climate change. Golden Gate University Law Review 32: 351–414

Luttikhuis P (2009) 'Kopenhagen' verdeelt wereld; Europa stond aan de zijlijn', NRC Handelsblad, 21 December 2009

Meunier S (2000) What single voice? European institutions and EU–US trade negotiations. International Organization 54:103–135

Murray J (2009) Draft Copenhagen agreements still feature large gaps, Guardian Unlimited, 16 December 2009

Oberthür S (2009a) The performance of the EU in international institutions: negotiating on climate change. Paper presented at International Studies Association Annual Convention New York, 15–18 February 2009, 1–23

Oberthür S (2009b) The role of the EU in global environmental and climate governance. In: Telò (ed) The European Union and global governance. Routledge, London, pp 192–209

Oberthür S, Roche Kelly C (2008) EU leadership in international climate policy: achievements and challenges. The International Spectator 43:35–50

Putnam R (1988) Diplomacy and domestic politics: the logic of two-level games. International Organization 42:427–460

Rosenthal E (2009a) A gathering noted for many nuances; From a 'logging loophole' to the ouster of N.G.O.s, a look at an odd 2 weeks, International Herald Tribune, 19 December 2009

Rosenthal E (2009b) In a busy conference center, an alphabet soup of causes and clauses, New York Times, 19 December 2009

Sands P (1992) The United Nations framework convention on climate change. Review of European Community and International Environmental Law 1:270–277

van der Kris J (2009) EU: 7,2 miljard voor klimaat; Europa blijf verdeeld over doelen na 2012—Afspraken lopen tot en met 2012, NRC Handelsblad, 11 December 2009

Van Schaik LG (2010) The sustainability of the EU's model for climate diplomacy. In: Oberthür S, Pallemaerts M (eds) The new climate policies of the European Union: internal legislation and climate diplomacy. VUB Press, Brussels, pp 251–280

Van Schaik LG, Schunz S (2012) Explaining EU activism and impact in global climate politics: Is the Union a norm- or interest-driven actor? Journal of Common Market Studies, 1–24 (forthcoming)

Zito AR (2005) The European Union as an environmental leader in a global environment. Globalizations 2:363–375

Chapter 16
The EU, NATO and the Treaty of Lisbon: Still Divided Within a Common City

Simon Duke

Abstract Both the European Union (EU) and the North Atlantic Treaty Organization (NATO) speak of their mutual importance to each other, yet their relationship is both ill-defined and sensitive. The EU insists that the continuing development of the Common Security and Defence Policy (CSDP) is essential to the Union's aspirations to be a global actor and key strategic partner. Meanwhile, NATO's recent and well-publicised New Strategic Concept (NSC) underlined its ability to assume new challenges and thus enhance its relevance. This chapter considers the extent to which the Treaty assists the EU to form a strategic vision for itself what this means for its relationship with NATO. Special attention is given to the place of Permanent Structured Cooperation (PESCO) and the role of the European Defence Agency (EDA) in the Treaty. The conclusions argue that the Lisbon Treaty does little to actually change CSDP, or to fundamentally realign EU-NATO relations. The changes introduced by the Treaty either codify existing practices or serve as tools to encourage development of the policy area by the EU Member States. The development of what may appear to be overlapping mandates by both the EU and NATO is generally exaggerated but, even where there is overlap, they remain unlikely to lead to zero-sum competition between the organisations in the short to medium-term. As a whole, the findings of this chapter

---

Dr. Simon Duke—Professor at the European Institute of Public Administration (EIPA), Maastricht. An earlier version of this chapter was presented at the European Union Studies Association conference in Boston in March 2010. My thanks are due to the participants who made critical but constructive comments. The earlier and shorter version was first published as an article in Studia Diplomatica (2011, volume 64 (2)) and parts are reproduced here with kind permission of the editor, Prof Sven Biscop.

S. Duke (✉)
European Institute of Public Administration (EIPA), Maastricht, The Netherlands
e-mail: s.duke@eipu.eu

P. J. Cardwell (ed.), *EU External Relations Law and Policy in the Post-Lisbon Era*,
DOI: 10.1007/978-90-6704-823-1_16, © T.M.C. ASSER PRESS, The Hague,
The Netherlands, and the authors 2012

point to co-existence as the remaining norm for the indefinite future of EU-NATO relations in the post-Lisbon era.

Contents

16.1 Introduction

There is a gap between image and reality when it comes to European Union-North Atlantic Treaty Organization (EU-NATO) relations. Both organisations talk, sometimes surreally, of their mutual importance to one another yet this often belies the reality of their relations. The EU insists that the continuing development of the Common Security and Defence Policy (CSDP) is essential to the Union's aspirations to be a global actor and key strategic partner. Meanwhile, NATO's recent and well-publicised New Strategic Concept (NSC) underlined not only the virility of the Alliance in its middle age, but also its ability to assume new challenges and thus enhance its relevance.

The definition of relations between the two organisations is an ongoing and sensitive issue. This chapter will consider the extent to which the EU's Lisbon Treaty promotes partnership between the EU and NATO, or whether it merely highlights existing incongruence. Three specific treaty-based aspects are seen as of core importance to the future of mutual relations.

The first is the extent to which the Lisbon Treaty contributes to the formation of a compelling strategic direction for the EU and, by implication, what type of partner (or competitor) the EU may become. The recent unveiling of NATO's NSC is also analysed alongside the relevant EU treaty text in order to establish the extent to which there is strategic complementarity.

The second broad theme goes beyond the general security heading to consider three inter-related terms—collective defence, mutual aid and assistance and the solidarity clause. Together the terms have been portrayed, correctly or incorrectly, as constituting a reorientation of the EU's security role. This section will consider the three clauses, their meanings and linkages and whether or not they should be construed as an emerging competitive element between (and possibly within) the organisations.

The third area to be examined considers the perennial resource issue, which features heavily in the CSDP provisions of the Lisbon Treaty. Two related aspects, outlined in the treaty, are of special relevance—Permanent Structured Cooperation (PESCO) and the role of the European Defence Agency (EDA). The former is often portrayed as one of the significant developments of the Lisbon Treaty and, if the aspirations behind PESCO develop into reality, this will indeed have important positive knock-on effects for the EU and NATO. There are though, as argued below, many hurdles along PESCO's course. The Lisbon Treaty reinforces the EDA's role as well as the political importance attached to the Agency's mission. The wisdom of doing so, especially when the fundamental powers of the agency remain limited, will be assessed.

The conclusions argue that the Lisbon Treaty does little to actually change CSDP, or to fundamentally realign EU-NATO relations. The changes introduced by the treaty either codify existing practices (such as the expanded Petersberg tasks) or serve as tools to encourage development of the policy area by the EU members (like PESCO). The development of what may appear to be overlapping mandates by both the EU and NATO is generally exaggerated but, even where overlap is, they remain unlikely to lead to zero-sum competition between the organisations in the short to medium-term. Co-existence will remain the norm for the indefinite future. This also suggests that there is unlikely to be any dramatic improvements in mutual relations, not only because of the Cyprus problem, but aso because of underlying concerns about NATO's relevance and American hegemony and equally strong reservations about the political and military fundamentals of CSDP. In short, the two organisations are likely to remain divided within a common city.

16.2 The Vision Thing: Ships Passing in the Night

It has become fashionable, with justification, to lament the lack of a compelling strategic vision for the EU in its external action. The lack of strategic vision is reflected in the debates in the literature about the nature of the EU's actorness, especially when it comes to security matters.[1] As a consequence, this lack of vision hampers the development of EU external action and, in the specific context of EU-NATO relations, stymies the development and pursuit of common goals.[2] The development of institutionalised relations between the EU and the NATO is a relatively recent phenomenon, commencing in 2001. The adoption of a framework for permanent relations and Berlin Plus in 2003 promised greater coordination on crisis-management consultation and planning, the exchange of classified information and EU access to NATO planning, NATO European command options and use of NATO assets and capabilities.[3] In spite of the undoubted good intentions

[1] Sjursen 2006.

[2] Biscop 2009; Howorth 2010; Vennesson 2010; de Vasconcelos 2010.

[3] Council (2003), EU-NATO: The Framework for Permanent Relations and Berlin Plus.

behind the framework document, high-level civilian and military meetings have produced little of substance. The agendas at these meetings are highly restricted and normally limited to Bosnia–Herzegovina where there is a clear shared interest due to NATO's hand-over of its mission to the EU. This, however, belies the practical and quiet cooperation on the ground, in Afghanistan, Bosnia or Kosovo, which strongly suggests that the main logjams are at the highest political levels. In this context the Cyprus problem is often cited, but the reality is more complex since there are also reservations about American global strategy and leadership on the Alliance side, and by acute national sensitivities towards security and defence issues and any hint of *communautarisation* on the EU side.

The formulation of the European Security Strategy and the Lisbon Treaty on the EU side, and the NSC on the NATO one, marked the first instance where strategic convergence could have been consciously promoted. For the most part, it was not. Although it is not the job of a treaty to lay out strategy, the Lisbon Treaty nevertheless provides a useful context for any current or future strategies. The treaty makes it clear that the Union's external action should be based upon *both* values and interests. It reminds the EU members what they should stand for (respect for human dignity, freedom, democracy, equality, the rule of law and respect for human rights) but goes further than the old version of the treaties by significantly expanding the objectives of the Union. To quote the relevant part of the treaty:

> In its relations with the wider world, the Union shall uphold and promote its *values and interests* and contribute to the protection of its citizens. It shall contribute to peace, security, the sustainable development of the Earth, solidarity and mutual respect among peoples, free and fair trade, eradication of poverty and the protection of human rights, in particular the rights of the child, as well as to the strict observance and the development of international law, including respect for the principles of the United Nations Charter.[4]

The values and interests of the Union in its external action are certainly not unique to the EU since the preamble to the North Atlantic Treaty, signed on 4 April 1949, contains rather similar wording. Article 2 of the North Atlantic Treaty reads as follows:

> The Parties will contribute toward the further development of peaceful and friendly international relations by strengthening their free institutions, by bringing about a better understanding of the principles upon which these institutions are founded, and by promoting conditions of stability and well-being. They will seek to eliminate conflict in their international economic policies and will encourage economic collaboration between any or all of them.[5]

This article occupied the back seat for much of the Cold War due to the prominence of NATO's Article 5 mission whereby in the event of an armed attack against any Alliance member they shall individually or in concert use 'such action as it deems necessary, including the use of armed force, to restore and maintain the

[4] Treaty on European Union, Article 3 (5). The value-led approach to EU external relations within the context of development policy is explored by Broberg (this volume).

[5] North Atlantic Treaty (1949), Article 2.

security of the North Atlantic area'.[6] It was the core Article 5 commitment that prompted Karl Deutsch to describe NATO as a 'security community' in 1957, whose sense of community rested upon the extreme unlikelihood of violence or aggression between the Alliance members and a sense of common purpose.[7]

With the fading of the Cold War and the collapse of the Soviet Union the far broader wording of Article 2 came to the fore as the underpinning justification for the assertion of broad range of military and civilian roles. Article 4, which provides for consultation 'whenever, in the opinion of any of them, the territorial integrity, political independence or security of any of the Parties is threatened', was also invoked in order to underpin NATO's claim that it was never just a collective defence alliance. The political dimensions of NATO's mission were further strengthened by the post-Cold War enlargement of NATO which, while resting on less arduous conditions than those applying in the EU context, nevertheless emphasised good neighbourly relations. The emphasis on the non-Article 5 aspects of the treaty paved the way for the Alliance to go 'out of area' and to thus attempt to reinforce its continued vitality and relevance, most notably in Afghanistan and the Western Balkans. The events surrounding 9/11 reinforced the perceived need for NATO to be able to operate beyond the formal geographical delimitations of the treaty and were used to justify an even broader mandate.

Logically, the assumption of new tasks that go beyond the transatlantic community and that aim to respond to a far greater range of threats, risks loosening the threads binding the 'security community' together and, arguably, contributing to a sense of strategic drift. This is why NATO's November 2010 NSC had to reassure all NATO members that the Alliance's 'greatest responsibility' is to 'protect and defend our territory and our populations against attack'.[8] Paradoxically, as Article 5 appears more and more otiose in light of the lack of any credible territorial threat to the Alliance area, its relevance as the political bedrock for the Alliance has increased. The importance of an increasingly irrelevant guarantee has been reinforced by open disagreements between the United States and its allies over a number of fundamental questions of international politics and security (Iraq, Afghanistan, multilateralism, Guantanamo, renditions etc.). The assumption of new missions by NATO, alongside the lack of any obvious alternative to the Alliance, led to increasingly expansive versions of the Alliance's future including that of 'global NATO'.[9] According to this concept the renewed Alliance would expand its protection to all democracies, including Australia, India, Japan, New Zealand and South Korea, transforming it into a quasi-league of democracies. The concept was primarily promulgated by American think tanks as a way of tying

---

[6] North Atlantic Treaty (1949), Article 5.

[7] Deutsch et al. 1957.

[8] NATO (2010), 'Strategic Concept For the Defence and Security of The Members of the North Atlantic Treaty Organisation'. Adopted by Heads of State and Government in Lisbon. 19 November 2010 (NATO Strategic Concept), para 16.

[9] Daalder and Goldgeier 2006.

a virtuous link between the search for a new *raison d'être* for the Alliance and American global strategy. Such ideas found limited traction among the allies, especially since any such league of democracies would be built around American strategy and leadership.

As NATO tries to move from collective defence to collective security and crisis management, the EU is doing more or less the opposite. The EU has approached its security mandate from a 'comprehensive approach' perspective and has yet to develop any credible defence policy or common defence—the 'D' in ESDP was always silent, and will probably remain so for reasons explored below. The 2004 Barcelona Report of the Study Group on European Security strongly advocated a 'human security' which is broadly compatible with the emphasis upon development issues, the Millennium Development Goals, good governance, the rule of law and human rights.[10]

Historically, discussions on defence have tended to exhibit the opposite effect in the EU than in NATO and are more likely to divide than unite (the history of the European Defence Community being a case in point). The Western European Union (WEU) played the symbolically important role of framing the 'defence related implications' of the Union's work (at least for the ten full members who are also EU members) and in the practically important matter of providing 'access to an operational capability'.[11] The latter applied notably, but not exclusively, in the context of the Petersberg Tasks, as defined by the WEU in 1992. These tasks were subsequently assumed by the EU in Article J.7 of the Amsterdam Treaty. The current Article 43 TEU includes a modified list of these tasks (new ones are italicised):

> … *joint disarmament operations*, humanitarian and rescue tasks, military advice and assistance tasks, *conflict prevention* and peace-keeping tasks, tasks of combat forces in crisis management, including peace-making and *post-conflict stabilisation*.

The EU does not enjoy a monopoly when it comes to any of these tasks but they call to the particular strengths of the Union which is its ability (some may argue potential) to link together the various facets of peace and stability ranging from classical tools (diplomacy, political dialogue) to economic leverage (either positive, as in development aid and assistance, or negative in the case of economic sanctions). The events in the Western Balkans in the 1990s illustrated that the exercise of 'soft' forms of power and influence were insufficient and this provided the rationale for the development of ESDP towards the end of the decade. This latter part remains very much a work in progress and the Lisbon Treaty used every opportunity to emphasise the importance of CSDP, the updated acronym for ESDP, to the overall security efforts of the Union.

The evolution of both the EU and NATO in recent years underlines the fallacy that NATO is solely a military alliance or that the EU is purely a soft or civilian

---

[10] Barcelona Report (2004). 'A Human Security Doctrine for Europe: presentation of the Barcelona Report of the Study Group on European Security'.

[11] Treaty of Amsterdam, Article J.7(2).

power *par excellence*. The post-Cold War changes in the international system have tended to play to the EU's strengths by emphasising the breadth of the Union's programmes and instruments that can be focussed on crisis prone countries or regions, whereas they have demanded greater efforts at reinvention and self-justification from NATO as the Alliance moves ever further from its original mandate and mission. Military power is, of course, still relevant but this does not necessarily play to the advantage of NATO for three reasons.

First, it is not only the ability to operationalise military force that is in question but the application of *appropriate* military resources and expertise to crisis scenarios. More often than not these are not combat-related missions, but demand the ability to execute the delicate tasks associated with crisis management, protection of humanitarian operations, securing vital assets for follow-on activities and protection of borders and civilians. These are the kind of missions where a number of EU members have considerable expertise and credibility (and some, like Sweden, are not NATO members). Since many military missions have to be seen in the context of a broader range of security-related tasks related to conflict prevention or post-conflict stabilisation, the issue of how to link up the military role with civilian missions and different instruments is critical. This is an area where the EU has the potential to be an inherently broader security actor than NATO.

The second factor is that NATO remains very reliant upon the United States. In the Cold War context the umbrage provided by the United States was welcome and largely uncontested (with the important exception of the placement of nuclear weapons on European soil in a number of countries). The role of the United States in the post-Cold War context has become a double-edged sword. On the one hand overwhelming American military force and technology gives NATO's deterrence and defence roles credibility that they would otherwise lack. Yet, very few allies can actually work alongside the American military owing to technological incompatibilities and thus lack of interoperability. This puts the allies in the awkward position of providing primarily political support to often predominant U.S. operations. The difficulties of working with its allies, both political and material, reinforced the tendencies of successive post-Cold War American administrations, notably the first term in office of George W. Bush, to work with coalitions of the willing. The frequent use of such coalitions, even if sometimes subsequently dubbed with a NATO hat, has had the overall effect of weakening the Alliance. Hence, the initially American-led International Security Assistance Force (ISAF) only became a nominally NATO-led operation in 2003, but is now commonly portrayed as the Alliance's 'litmus test'. It is, just as much if not more so, a litmus test for American leadership.

The third factor is shaped by economic considerations. The United States is unable to afford its current defence expenditure, not only due to the ongoing financial crisis but also at a more political level. The allies are generally preoccupied with their own financial woes and any serious efforts to increase military expenditure have been off the cards for a while. In all cases it is apparent that more will have to be done with the same, or even less. This implies clear choices about what is affordable and feasible economically and politically. The dilemma for many of the European allies is that the temptation to free ride on American backs is clearly present, but this also implies tacit consent to Washington's policies. The alternative is to accept primarily Anglo-French leadership when it comes to the harder elements of the EU's external action.

Given the tendency for the EU and NATO's missions to converge around a number of conflict prevention, crisis management and more general security concerns, it will not really come as a surprise that there is relatively little to differentiate the EU and NATO at the strategic level. Both have framed their security 'concepts' in similar ways. The rather inappropriately named European Security Strategy (ESS) of December 2003 is not so much a strategy but more of a *tour d'horizon*, reflecting the international system of that year and with the political objective of mending fences between the EU members after their bitter divisions over Iraq and, more importantly, to send reassuring messages across the Atlantic. With the latter objective in mind, the ESS bears more than a passing resemblance to the United States National Security Strategy of September 2002. The list of principal challenges is the same and includes terrorism, proliferation of Weapons of Mass Destruction (WMD), regional conflicts, state failure and organised crime.[12] Beyond this, the ESS offers no clear priorities or specific responses to the challenges outlined and is thus less of a 'strategy' and more of a concept.

The ESS does, *in passim*, note the important role of transatlantic relations to global peace and security. One of the core elements of the international system is seen as 'the transatlantic relationship' which is 'not only in our bilateral interest but strengthens the international community as a whole. NATO is an important expression of this relationship'. The importance of the Berlin Plus arrangements are also seen as increasing the 'operational capability' of the EU.[13]

NATO adopted its much trumpeted NSC on 19 November 2010 at a summit meeting in Lisbon, updating the earlier versions of 1991 and 1999. The NSC is described as a 'roadmap' for the next decade. The brief (and thus readable) 2010 NSC confirms the centrality of NATO's collective defence role (Article 5); it presents NATO as an Alliance capable of employing an 'appropriate mix' of political and military tools to help manage developing crises before they escalate into conflicts, to stop ongoing conflicts where they affect Alliance security and to consolidate Alliance security in post-conflict situations. Finally, the NSC asserts its willingness to engage in international security through partnerships with relevant countries and international organisations, under the rubric 'cooperative security'.[14]

The NSC refers to the 'strategic partnership' between the EU and NATO and notes that both 'should play complementary and mutually reinforcing roles in

---

[12] European Council (2003), 'A Secure Europe in a better world', Brussels. 12 December 2003 (European Security Strategy).

[13] European Security Strategy, 1.

[14] NATO Strategic Concept, para 4 (c).

supporting international peace and security', although both parties are equally conscious of the realities of the political *impasse* between the two organisations over the Cyprus problem. The NSC also refers to the need to respect 'the autonomy and institutional integrity' of the two organisations, which may have knock-on effects for the likelihood for any *ad hoc* institutional opening up of the EU to Turkey on CSDP issues which has been demanded on numerous occasions and is supported by the United States.

In those areas where there is convergence on the respective 'concepts', such as the civilian aspects of crisis management, conflict prevention, counter-terrorism and the non-proliferation of WMDs, there is no clear understanding of who should take the lead, how they will be integrated or coordinated. Even on the broadest of security-related aspect, such as climate change or environmental issues, human trafficking or cyber-attacks, the EU and NATO are both claiming competences. Most of these are issues where the EU is, arguably, an inherently deeper actor. The ability of the EU to use its considerable financial leverage for various forms of conditionality, which can be applied to a wide range of security-related challenges, stands in marked contrast to NATO whose main leverage lies in the membership of the United States—leverage that is often positive but can, as noted, may also be perceived as a double-edged sword.

The first general conclusion at the strategic level is that the EU and NATO are developing not only in potentially complementary but also in potentially competitive directions. The convergence of both organisations around a basket of 'soft' security challenges should, in theory, offer synergies and efficiency. The practice may be quite different especially given the political difficulties that hamper the development of any meaningful inter-institutional dialogue. As noted, the overarching political log jam, in the form of the Cyprus problem, is the most visible manifestation of the difficulties faced by the organisations. It is not, however, an overarching explanation since it does not explain why in those instances where there could have been greater cooperation, such as piracy operations off the coast of Somalia or the training of police officers in Afghanistan, parallel virility competitions have emerged between the two organisations.

The second general conclusion is that much of NATO's credibility as an actor depends upon the willingness and ability of the United States to underwrite the organisation. The Alliance has always been Washington's preferred vehicle for projecting American influence. But, this is changing. Doubts about the direction of the United States' external relations and how important Europe is to their global interests, as well as differences in understanding over effective multilateralism and the role of the rule of law in the international system, have raised question marks over the role of the Alliance in a number of allied capitals. NATO will remain important, if only because it is Washington's preferred forum for security dialogue with the allies, but it may be undermined gradually by the EU's growing relevance to a wider number of security issues.

Third, both organisations suffer from a lack of strategic vision. The apparent lack of a compelling strategic vision for the EU in its external action explains, at least in part, the accompanying crisis of confidence in CSDP which has seen no new operations launched for almost 2 years—in notable contract to 7 years of rapid growth and activity. The focus within NATO on expeditionary forces, crisis-management teams and intelligence cooperation, fails to address the realities of the problems of resources, political preferences, leadership and intelligence sharing. Communication at the strategic level suggests the desire for more EU-NATO complementarity and cooperation but the politics of the respective members, who are for the most part one and the same, suggests a studied ambivalence about the extent to which either should cooperate.

16.3 The EU Plays With Words: Common Defence, Mutual Assistance and Solidarity

An example of the studied ambivalence from the EU side can be seen in three related, but imprecise, concepts. The first is what has often confusingly been termed common defence, which is often related to the idea of mutual assistance (the 'mutual aid and assistance clause') and, finally, the so-called solidarity clause. The three concepts represent the outcomes of compromises between the EU members during the Convention on the Future of Europe (notably in the Working Group on defence chaired by Michel Barnier), with the result that the exact intentions of the resultant treaty are confusing. The three concepts will be examined in turn.

The first notion, 'common defence' appears to transgress on NATO's main responsibility by moving the EU towards a quasi-Article 5 commitment, as opposed to the emphasis on the Petersberg tasks which are the current focus of CSDP. The move towards some type of defence commitment in the EU context was not entirely unwarranted, especially since the 'D' in ESDP (now CSDP) has been essentially silent. At first glance the attempt to put some substance to the 'D' is therefore welcome. The treaty states that:

> The common security and defence policy shall include the progressive framing of a common Union defence policy. This will lead to a common defence, when the European Council, acting unanimously, so decides. It shall in that case recommend to the Member States the adoption of such a decision in accordance with their respective constitutional requirements.[15]

The use of the imperative 'will' is a change from the previous TEU which contented itself with the framing of a common defence policy that '*might* lead to a common defence, should the European Council so decide'.[16] Part of the reason for the vaguer language may stem from the legacy of the WEU who had promoted as their objectives to 'build up the WEU in stages as the defence component of the European Union' and to 'develop WEU as a means to strengthen the European

[15] Treaty on European Union, Article 42 (2). Emphasis added.

[16] Treaty on European Union (pre-Lisbon version), Article 17 (1). Emphasis added.

pillar of the Atlantic Alliance'.[17] The essential ambiguity about where defence belonged in the grander scheme of European integration was not of essential concern, so long as the WEU existed. With the disappearance of the WEU's dual role as the European pillar of NATO and the EU's defence component, via Article V of the Modified Brussels Treaty, the resolution of the issue became unavoidable.

The Lisbon Treaty attempted to solve this dilemma by the use of the imperative, but also noting that it remains for the European Council to decide. Even with the emphatic 'will', the possibility of any mutual defence commitment remains highly qualified. Not only would it be subject to a referendum in Ireland's case, it would also have to respect the constitutional specificities of Austria (whose post-war state treaty prohibits membership of a military alliance, or foreign bases on her territory, and commits Austria to perpetual neutrality). The unresolved Cyprus problem would be an additional, and potent, reason for caution. Denmark also continues to exercise three opt-outs, one of which relates to all 'defence related' aspects of the treaties. Then there are the likely objections of the Atlanticists (Denmark, Italy, Portugal, the Netherlands, Poland and the United Kingdom, to name but a few obvious examples), who see their primary defence commitments as being provided through NATO.

The Irish 'no' campaign, who were successful in derailing the first referendum on the Lisbon Treaty, distorted the rationale of the Convention's Working Group on Defence who clearly had in mind not so much NATO but the WEU when it came to common defence and mutual aid and assistance. They argued, with the WEU's demise in mind, that 'Member States who so wished could share between themselves the obligations laid down in the Brussels Treaty relating to mutual assistance, thus bringing to an end the Western European Union'.[18] This was not an entirely new idea since it reflected the pre-Amsterdam Treaty debates about creating a 'fourth' defence-related pillar advanced by the United Kingdom. The rationale behind this idea was to abolish the WEU and create a new defence pillar to which the decision-making aspects of the WEU's role would be transferred, while the military functions would be subsumed into NATO.[19]

In the interim between the 'fourth pillar' proposals in 1998–1999 and the implementation of the Lisbon Treaty, the political ground in European security has shifted, making the idea of a specifically European defence posture, backed by assistance guarantees, less relevant. At the time of the Convention, EU and NATO relations were far more polarised over issues of whether or not the EU should have an independent planning and operational capability. The French *rapprochement* with NATO was also unfinished. The conclusion of the *rapprochement* in April 2009 essentially put to rest the *canard* of a distinct and independent European

[17] Western European Union (1991). 'Declaration on Western European Union', Maastricht, 10 December 1991.

[18] European Convention (2002). 'Final report of Working Group VIII—Defence'. Report from the Chairman of Working Group VIII. CONV 461/02. 16 December 2002, para 61.

[19] Whitman 1999; Grant 1998.

defence stance and allowed France to play its full role in the Alliance as a way of redressing the 'flaccid atlanticism that so often prevails in NATO circles'.[20]

It was of little surprise that the appearance of a 'mutual aid and assistance' clause, especially when read in conjunction with the collective defence aspects, re-ignited debate about whether the EU was adopting a *quasi* Article 5/V commitment. It also served as a reminder that the disappearance of the WEU has occurred without a resolution of the divisive question of who, or what, should assume its political role. This clause shares a number of similar misapprehensions with its 'common defence' counterpart. It reads as follows:

> If a Member State is the victim of armed aggression on its territory, the other Member States shall have towards it an obligation of aid and assistance by all the means in their power, in accordance with Article 51 of the United Nations Charter. This shall not prejudice the specific character of the security and defence policy of certain Member States. Commitments and cooperation in this area shall be consistent with commitments under the North Atlantic Treaty Organisation, which, for those States which are members of it, remains the foundation of their collective defence and the forum for its implementation.[21]

The latter stipulations were then reinforced by two declarations attached to the Final Act of the Lisbon Treaty, both concerning CFSP, where it was again recalled that the CSDP provisions 'do not prejudice the specific character of the security and defence policy of the Member States'.[22]

The Convention's Working Group on defence saw 'broad support' for such a clause but one that would enable 'all of the instruments of the Union to be mobilised'.[23] The Working Group was emphatic that 'such a clause would *not* be a clause on collective defence entailing an obligation to provide military assistance, but would apply to threats from non-state entities'. Nor was the idea to establish any type of associated European army since it was well-understood that the management of an attack would be provided 'only at the request of the civilian authorities of the country concerned'.[24] The Working Group was not specific about what threats emanating from non-state entities it had in mind. Terrorism is the obvious one that comes to mind, but this is not only addressed in the 'Solidarity Clause' (see below) but also appears in the revised Petersberg tasks, all of which 'may contribute to the fight against terrorism'.[25]

In this context the debates in and around NATO are instructive since a series of parallel debates were held about whether acts of aggression could be extended beyond their traditional and understood context, as an act of armed aggression

---

[20] d'Aboville 2008.

[21] Treaty on European Union, Article 42 (7).

[22] Treaty on European Union, Declarations 13 and 14.

[23] European Convention (2002). 'Final report of Working Group VIII—Defence'. Report from the Chairman of Working Group VIII. CONV 461/02. 16 December 2002, para 57.

[24] European Convention (2002). 'Final report of Working Group VIII—Defence'. Report from the Chairman of Working Group VIII. CONV 461/02. 16 December 2002, para 58.

[25] Treaty on European Union, Article 43 (1).

against the territory of a member by a hostile state, to one that could include cyber-attacks, attacks on critical infrastructure or essential lines of communication or trade routes perpetrated by non-state actors. The Group of Experts, chaired by former U.S. Secretary of State Madeleine Albright, noted that although such activities 'may or may not reach the level of an Article 5 attack, NATO must update its approach to the defence of Alliance territory'.[26]

In the EU context the core agency dealing with cyber-attacks is the European Network and Information Security Agency, founded in 2004. In the same year the European Council requested the development of a European Programme for Critical Infrastructure Protection and the resultant Commission directive adopts an 'all hazard' approach and not one that stems only from acts of terrorism. Given existing EU awareness and actions in these areas, the added value of extending the definition of an act of 'armed aggression' to cover cyber-attacks, or attacks against critical infrastructure, would only seem warranted in the case of a lack of awareness or action.

The third related clause is the 'solidarity clause' which has its origins in a Declaration included in the European Council conclusions of 25–26 March 2004 following the Atocha, Madrid, bombings. The relevant part of the clause, as incorporated into the Lisbon Treaty reads:

> The Union and its Member States shall act jointly in a spirit of solidarity if a Member State is the object of a terrorist attack or the victim of a natural or man-made disaster. The Union shall mobilise all the instruments at its disposal, including the military resources made available by the Member States….[27]

The important addition to the original clause was the extension beyond terrorist attacks to include natural or man-made disasters—most notably due to the lessons learned from the 2005 Indian Ocean tsunami. Unlike the 'mutual aid and assistance' clause, which does not specify what kind of assistance might be provided but merely 'all means in (the Member States') power', the solidarity clause specifically mentions military resources.

The 'Solidarity Clause' reflects a broader post 9/11 struggle within CFSP to define the second pillar role with regard to terrorism. The role is largely limited to the provision of military support in the event of a terrorist attack and, in the case of the Joint Situation Centre (SitCen), intelligence support for counter-terrorism efforts. The mention of a civil protection-related role under the CFSP title of the TEU raises a broader problem of how the clause relates to wider EU mechanisms such as the Civil Protection Mechanism (CPM), the Monitoring and Information Centre (MIC), the Argus Network and so forth. This is likely to result in short-term

---

[26] NATO (2010), Analysis and Recommendations of the Group of Experts on a New Strategic Concept for NATO, 'NATO 2020: Assured Security; Dynamic Engagement'. Brussels: NATO Public Diplomacy Division. 17 May 2010, 9.

[27] Treaty on European Union, Article 222 (1).

confusion since the civil protection aspects of the Union's work are not particularly well joined up, notwithstanding the existence of the EEAS.[28]

What are we to make of this confusing jumble of words and clauses? Three points arise from this analysis. First, the Lisbon Treaty poses no fundamental challenge to NATO's *defence* role, since it is evident from the above discussion that any defence component to the EU's activities remains highly sensitive and premature.[29]

Second, it is relatively clear that the EU has a *mutual assistance* task in mind, whereas NATO (and the WEU) was designed with a *mutual defence* task to the fore. The general use of the term 'defence' (with notions of deterrence and protection against armed aggression against territory in mind) when in fact 'security' (the response to a far broader range of security challenges including assistance to third parties) is what is meant has created a confusing picture which the Lisbon Treaty did little to clarify.

Third, mutual assistance has more to do with the solidarity clause than it does with defence since we have established that the original intention was for it to apply to acts emanating from non-state entities and not those of state-driven acts of territorial aggression. The solidarity clause draws attention to the fact that civil protection remains pillarised within the EU and lacks any obvious connection between the EU and NATO, although it is an obvious candidate for confidence building measures between the respective organisations.

16.4 The Default 'Soft Power': Resources and Manpower

The third broad area that the Lisbon Treaty calls our attention to is the collective military shortcomings of the EU's members. These were well-understood prior to ESDP, having been previously identified in the WEU context. The result of this was a series of military, and shortly thereafter civilian, 'headline goals', exhorting the Union's members to do more individually and collectively. Although the detail varies from one individual EU member to another, the overall picture was one where, as Nick Witney observed, 'a significant minority of Member States demonstrate, by their reluctance to make an serious investment in defence, or by their tendency to sit on their hands when the call goes out for contributions to crisis-management operations, that they really do not want to be involved'.[30] This has

---

[28] von Ondarza and Parkes 2010. The challenges facing the EEAS are explored in detail by Blockmans and Laatsit (this volume).

[29] European defence and the Lisbon Treaty—reply to the annual report of the Council (2010), European Security and Defence Assembly of the Western European Union. Doc. A/2067.

[30] Witney 2008, 3.

led some, like Robert Kagan, to imply that the EU is not entirely Venus-like by choice, given its 'military incapacity and political disarray'.[31]

The shortcomings of the EU apply to NATO as well, given the heavy overlap in membership. Accordingly, there are parallel EU and NATO attempts to address the identified shortcomings—on the EU side with the 2001 European Capability Action Plan (ECAP) and the 2008 European Capability Action Plan (CAP), and on the NATO side the 1999 Defence Capabilities Initiative (DCI) process and the 2002 Prague Capabilities Commitment.[32] The founding of the EDA and its subsequent 2006 Long-Term Vision (LTV) report formed the basis for the CAP. This was adopted by the EU members in July 2008 and is described as 'an attempt to address the well-documented fragmentation in demand for European military capabilities, caused in part by a lack of coordinated military requirements and comprehensive priorities'.[33] Twelve priority areas were identified in the CAP, based upon the LTV.

The shortcomings are therefore well-known, but the issue of how to persuade the Member States to address them, especially in the throes of a financial crisis, remains on ongoing challenge. A detailed analysis of the improvement in the EU's capabilities is beyond the remit of this chapter but, suffice it to say that at the official level the EU claims the 'capacity to conduct the full spectrum of ESDP operations within the parameters of the Strategic Planning Assumptions, with different levels of operational risk arising from identified shortfalls'.[34]

The Treaty's mechanism to promote the EU's security and defence role and the related personnel and resource issues is PESCO. The effective implementation of PESCO would have profound and positive implications for the ability of the EU members to generate relevant and effective force contributions for a range of missions that could also be NATO or UN-related. The relevant provision of the treaty states:

> Those Member States whose military capabilities fulfil higher criteria and which have made more binding commitments to one another in this area with a view to the most demanding missions shall establish PESCO within the Union framework.[35]

The details of PESCO are addressed in an accompanying Protocol attached to the Treaty.[36] Article 1 of the Protocol states, ambitiously, that it is open to any Member State to 'proceed more intensively to develop its defence capacities' and to increase contributions to EU battlegroups by 2010. Those Member States who wish to participate in PESCO will have to commit to:

---

[31] Kagan 2003, 22.

[32] Boland 1999.

[33] European Defence Agency (2008). 'EU Governments endorse capability plan for future military needs, pledges joint efforts'. Brussels. 8 July 2008, 1.

[34] European Council (2010), 'Background note on the Development of European Military Capabilities', 1.

[35] Treaty on European Union, Article 42 (6).

[36] Treaty on the Functioning of the European Union, Protocol 10.

i. Achieving 'approved objectives' of investment expenditure on defence equipment;
ii. Bring their defence apparatus into line with each other 'as far as possible', through harmonisation, pooling and, where appropriate, specialising defence means and capabilities, and cooperation in training and logistics;
iii. To take 'concrete measures' to enhance the availability, interoperability, flexibility and deployability of their forces and, in 'in particular by identifying common objectives regarding the commitment of forces, including possibly reviewing their national decision-making procedures';
iv. To 'make good' the shortfalls perceived in the framework of the 'Capability Development Mechanism' without prejudice to the undertakings in this regard within NATO;
v. To take part 'where appropriate' in the 'development of major joint or European equipment programmes' in the framework of the EDA.

The general aims of PESCO are bolstered by two additional parts of the treaty. First, Article 42(3) of the TEU states that the 'Member States *shall* make civilian and military capabilities available to the Union for the implementation of the CSDP' and that those Member States which together establish multinational forces '*shall* make them available to the CSDP'.[37] The use of the imperative (again) is forceful but is, ultimately, a political statement since CSDP is heavily reliant upon seconded personnel to work within the CSDP structures and positive national decisions to release resources and personnel for military or civilian missions.

The second aspect that appears to bolster PESCO is Article 45 of the TEU relating to the EDA. The EDA has been involved in work on pooling and sharing and this is a priority of the current Steering Board, chaired by Catherine Ashton. To date, over 70 pooling and sharing activities are underway in the EDA framework. The European Defence Ministers agreed in December 2010 that the Agency's activities on pooling and sharing should 'be enhanced'. Thus, in addition to existing projects such as those pertaining to helicopter availability, air transport, third party logistics support and airworthiness, more opportunities exist in areas such as 'satellite communication, medical support and naval logistics'.[38]

Its general role, laid out in the treaty, is central to the avoidance of duplication, waste and competition, especially in times of financial stringency. It is also clear from the Protocol on PESCO that the EDA is intended to play a central role through its contribution 'to the regular assessment of the participating Member States' contributions with regard to capabilities… and shall report thereon at least once a year'.[39] Whether this level of supervision will be welcomed by the Member States, since it would demand high degrees of transparency, is open to question.

---

[37] Emphasis added.
[38] European Defence Agency (2010), 'Seeking Savings Through Pooling and Sharing'. Press Release, Brussels, December.
[39] Treaty on the Functioning of the European Union, Protocol 10.

The current staffing levels and budget of the EDA would also have to be reviewed given this important function.

Several questions arise when reviewing PESCO. The first is that it is a voluntary scheme and, as such, some may choose not to reach the 'higher criteria' necessary for PESCO, especially if looming public sector cuts pose tough choices. The precise methodology for measuring 'higher criteria' are vague and it is also unclear whether they are to be attained prior to entry, or whether as a result of PESCO over a specified period of time. The establishment of total defence expenditure targets, or total armed force capabilities, risks putting too much emphasis upon the 'input' aspects such as overall defence expenditure, personnel and so forth and not enough emphasis upon 'output' aspects, which stress the deployability and interoperability of forces and material. PESCO also faces an obvious need to balance inclusivity with effectiveness and, as Sven Biscop has observed, the optimal PESCO is 27 while 'a more exclusive *avant-garde* of just a few like-minded Member States could probably yield deeper integration and would thus yield more immediate results'.[40]

The second main concern with PESCO lies in the various national responses to the initiative. The idea of greater cooperation, more efficient procurement, pooling of resources, joint research and development are not new; they have been an integral part of the EDA's mandate since 2004 and, more generally, the Commission's efforts to encourage more efficient procurement (through the application of European procurement rules to the greatest extent possible) to the defence industrial sector. These worthy efforts have been complicated by a deep psychological attachment to notions of sovereignty, national security and defence, manifest in this context by: the conduct of national strategic reviews with little or no coordination; the assertion of national defence priorities over any collective security efforts; the procurement of duplicative and non-compatible platforms and systems; the protection of national defence industrial champions; the financing of excessive armed force personnel in the EU Member States (around 1.8 million); redundant assets and capabilities; and, finally, low deployability rates throughout the EU.

In the face of these challenges, the EDA has little formal power to cajole the EU members into different patterns of behaviour, other than through persuasion and informal practices (such as the voluntary placement of tenders worth more than €1 million on the EDA's website). A number of instruments have been applied in order to change the picture painted above including regular Capability Improvement Conferences that have been held since 2001, subsequent Capability Improvement Plans, Headline Goals and numerous declarations on military (and civilian) capabilities. In spite of the fact that it is easy to be sceptical about the real outcome of these various initiatives, the picture is not entirely negative. The European Air Transport Command (EATC), launched in September 2010 at Eindhoven, the Netherlands, is one such example of a positive development.

[40] Biscop 2008, 6.

There are also examples of existing multinational force structures, either created through NATO or through the (former) Forces Answerable to the WEU (FAWEU), that provide platforms which in many cases can usefully be adapted for CSDP missions.

The success, or otherwise, of PESCO will be determined most critically by two developments. The first is the ongoing financial crisis which may have both centripetal and centrifugal elements. The Council of the EU has chosen to emphasise the former by arguing that:

> …the financial crisis and its impact on national defence budgets into an opportunity, to give a new impetus to European military capability development in order to meet its level of ambition, to address remaining shortfalls and to safeguard the defence capabilities required to support the EU's CSDP as well as to achieve national capability targets, while avoiding unnecessary duplication between Member States.[41]

According to the Council's vision cooperation would be a 'force multiplier' with particular emphasis on pooling and sharing options. The EATC is often forwarded as example of this (notwithstanding the fact that the successive delays in the entry into service of the A400M transport aircraft continue to hamper the EU's heavy air-lift capabilities). The idea of establishing a 'Wise Pen Team' who would identify more specifically those areas for further pooling and sharing is also positive. It should, however, be borne in mind that the rationalisation of personnel functions and costs is achievable in the short-term whereas the procurement cycles for larger-ticket items is typically made a decade or more before entry into service.

The second development of note was the signing of an Anglo-French Defence Cooperation Treaty in 2010. The treaty did not come out of the blue but was designed to build upon a history of cooperation, while apparently turning a blind eye to the differences that have also punctuated their defence relations. Many of the initiatives unveiled in the treaty were, in effect, merely repackaging of existing initiatives that had been agreed to a previous summits. Nevertheless, the treaty's potential lies in the simple fact that the two countries account for half of the defence budgets of the EU members and two-thirds of the research and technology spending. The Anglo-French treaty noted the desire to:

> ….enable our forces to operate together, to maximise our capabilities and to obtain greater value for money from our investment in defence. We plan to increase the range and ambition of our joint defence equipment programmes, and to foster closer industrial cooperation.[42]

A number of specific plans within the treaty, such as the 10 year strategic plan for the Complex Weapons sector, aim to produce efficiency savings of up to 30%. An annual budget of around €50 million will be devoted to shared research and development focussing on ten priority areas. A brigade-size Combined Joint

---

[41] Council Conclusions on Military Capability Development. 3055th Foreign Affairs (Defence) Council meeting, Brussels, 9 December 2010, 1.

[42] 'Declaration on Defence and Security Cooperation', 2 November 2010, para 5.

Expeditionary Force (CJEF) will be developed as a 'non-standing bilateral capability' which could act bilaterally, or through EU, NATO or other coalition arrangements. The CJEF will be supported by a Joint Integrated Carrier Strike Group which will include both British and French assets by 2020. A separate treaty addresses nuclear cooperation but did not go as far as warhead testing, although it does include hydrodynamic and other forms of testing using British and French scientific facilities. A Senior Level Group, operating under the terms of the treaty, will report back to the respective governments on these and other initiatives on a regular basis.

The treaty has elicited mixed responses, some being cautiously positive, while others were quick to point to the differing Anglo-French positions on the Falklands, Bosnia, military intervention in Iraq in 2003 and the use of the French veto on military targets during 'Operation Allied Force' in Kosovo in 1999.[43] Many viewed the treaty as the result of a rather pragmatic understanding of the prevailing international economic and security currents and the resultant realisation that neither could afford their independent aspirations to regional or even global roles. It was, as the Financial Times pithily put it, an 'entente frugale'.[44]

By way of contrast to the political vagaries of the Anglo-French treaty, a German-Swedish 'Food for Thought' paper entitled 'Intensifying Military Cooperation in Europe' advocated enhanced cooperation, 'with a view to spending resources in Europe more efficiently and to maintain a broad array of military capabilities to ensure national objectives as well as Europe's ability act credibly in crises'.[45] The paper identified the harmonisation of military requirements, research and development, acquisition, training and exercises, command structures and procedures and operating costs, as the principle headings for cooperation in the EU context.

The implications of PESCO, the Anglo-French Treaty, the German-Swedish 'Food for Thought' paper and the work of the EDA are unclear, given the time spans involved in defence procurement and expenditure cycles. PESCO may well have come at a propitious moment in the midst of a financial crisis in terms of efforts to identify economies of scale and efficiencies. It is also apparent that PESCO is not only about the EU since its success, or otherwise, will have a profound effect on the ability to contribute to NATO, UN and other coalition missions. PESCO's influence is likely to depend upon the extent to which 'higher criteria' and 'binding commitments' are exclusive or inclusive. By stipulating more rigorous criteria PESCO may create a group of *avant-garde* and those who are excluded may then feel compelled to make further efforts, given the supposed discomfort of exclusion. Alternatively, a lower bar is likely to discourage free-

---

[43] Taylor 2010, 14–15.

[44] Financial Times (2010). 'Entente frugal in defence contracting', 3 November 2010. http://search.ft.com/search?queryText=entente+frugale&ftsearchType=type_news. Accessed 20 July 2011.

[45] European Council, 'Background note for Foreign Affairs Council', 2010. Defence Ministers and Development Ministers, Brussels, 9 December 2010, 3.

rider behaviour and, in particular, dependence upon the political and resource whims of a few key players.

16.5 Conclusion

It is unlikely that EU-NATO relations will be further developed or complicated in the immediate future by the stipulations of the Lisbon Treaty. In the longer-term, as indicated above, the Lisbon Treaty may open the doors to an important debate about the EU's role on the world stage and to a more capable and effective CSDP. The advent of the defence, mutual aid and assistance and solidarity clauses in the EU context is unlikely to fundamentally intrude on NATO's core mandate. The development of non-military roles that veer more to the realm of foreign (rather than security) policy by NATO is likely to overlap with the EU and risks becoming a progressive source of antagonism.

The types of security challenges facing the EU and NATO are likely to demand comprehensive approaches that may have a military element, but which are also likely to demand civilian skills and those associated more typically with foreign policy. Even where military power is necessary, the overall effectiveness of any operation is likely to be judged by the ability to secure longer-term stability in a country or region. The ongoing operations in Afghanistan have illustrated the shortcomings of over-reliance on military assets, especially when it comes to longer-term national building.

In spite of the ESS, the Lisbon Treaty and NATO's most recent NSC, relations between the EU and NATO remain ill-defined and lack much meaningful substance. But, neither is in imminent danger of going out of business. NATO remains the preferred security partner for Washington DC which remains generally sceptical about CSDP. The promise of a more effective and capable CSDP held out by the Lisbon Treaty would be of obvious benefit to the EU and, if the treaty-based aspirations are realised, the EU will have the potential to address a far wider range of foreign policy and security challenges than NATO. The attainment of any such vision will require not only harmony but also the combined efforts of 27.

The future of EU-NATO relations will of course be influenced by developments *hors* the Lisbon Treaty. The ongoing Cyprus problem is often cited as the key impediment to not only the future development of EU-NATO relations but also to the implementation of the Berlin Plus arrangements. The Cyprus problem risks becoming an excuse, even a convenient one, to avoid any serious attempt to address the strategic drift besetting both the EU and NATO and the potential for 'hollow security' that may come about as the result of austerity programmes on both sides of the Atlantic. In a similar vein, it is essential that virtue is made of necessity with regard to the global financial crisis, the emphasis must be placed squarely on how to do more with the same, or even less, capitalising on the tactic realisation that the old, essentially national, models of strategic planning, procurement and operation are rapidly becoming *passé*.

The strategic overlap between the two organisations and the presence of well-known political impediments to advancing mutual relations, suggests either that the EU and NATO relations will not advance until the high-level logjam is resolved, or until the practical cooperation that exists on the ground is built upon in the form of a confidence building exercise, in a bottom-up approach. A number of possible areas for collaboration, such as conflict prevention, cyber crime or the protection of critical infrastructure, have been suggested as suitable candidates.

References

Biscop S (2008) Permanent structured cooperation and the future of ESDP. Egmont Paper 20. www.egmontinstitute.be/paperegm/ep20.pdf. Accessed 20 July 2011

Biscop S (2009) Odd couple or dynamic duo? The EU and strategy in times of crisis. European Foreign Affairs Review 14:367–384

Boland F (1999) NATO's defence capabilities initiative: preparing for future challenges. NATO Review 47:26–28

d'Aboville B (2008) The thinking behind France's NATO rapprochement. In: Europe's World, Autumn. www.europesworld.org/NewEnglish/Home_old/Article/tabid/191/ArticleType/articleview/ArticleID/21274/language/en-US/Default.aspx. Accessed 20 July 2011

Daalder I, Goldgeier J (2006) Global NATO. Foreign Affairs 85:105–113

de Vasconcelos A (ed) (2010) A strategy for EU Foreign Policy. EU Institute for Security Studies Report, Paris

Deutsch K et al (1957) Political community and the North Atlantic area: international organization in the light of historical experience. Princeton University Press, Princeton

Grant C (1998) Can Britain lead in Europe? Centre for European Reform, London, pp 44–50

Howorth J (2010) Strategy and the importance of defence cooperation among EU member states. Egmont Security Policy Brief 12. www.egmontinstitute.be/papers/10/sec-gov/SPB-12_Howorth-defence-cooperation.pdf. Accessed 20 July 2011

Kagan R (2003) Of paradise and power: America and Europe in the new world order. Knopf, New York

Sjursen H (2006) What kind of power? Journal of European Public Policy 13:169–181

Taylor C (2010) Franco-British Defence Cooperation, House of Commons, International Affairs and Defence Section, SN/IA/5750

Vennesson P (2010) Competing visions for the European Union grand strategy. European Foreign Affairs Review 15:57–75

von Ondarza N, Parkes R (2010) The EU in the face of disaster. Stiftung Wissenschaft und Politik Comments 9

Whitman RG (1999) Amsterdam's unfinished business? The Blair Government's initiative and the future of the Western European Union. EU Institute for Security Studies Occasional Papers 7, pp 1–10

Witney N (2008) Re-energising Europe's security and defence policy. European Council on Foreign Relations Policy Paper. ecfr.eu/page/-/documents/ESDP-report.pdf. Accessed 20 July 2011

Chapter 17
The External Dimension of the EU's Non-proliferation Policy: Overcoming Inter-institutional Competition

Kamil Zwolski

Abstract For many years, the EU's policy on non-proliferation of Weapons of Mass Destruction (WMDs) has been a victim of institutional fragmentation, imbedded in the post-Maastricht formal separation of the European Community from the CFSP. On the one hand, since the beginning of the 1990s, the European Commission was developing capacity-building projects on non-proliferation and nuclear safety, utilising its geographical and thematic financial instruments. On the other hand, more recently, permanent bureaucratic structures entrusted with implementing the EU's WMD Strategy were established in the Council General Secretariat. This posed a challenge to consistency of the EU's non-proliferation efforts and even triggered inter-institutional competition over limited resources. The European External Action Service offers an opportunity to solve these problems by bringing selected bureaucracies from the Commission and Council General Secretariat together. Will it be sufficient to develop a consistent policy on the non-proliferation of WMDs for the EU? This chapter analyses structural problems which have been negatively affecting the EU's profile as an actor in non-proliferation policy. Further, it evaluates prospects for enhancing this profile following the institutional reforms introduced by the Lisbon Treaty.

Dr. Kamil Zwolski—Department of History, Politics and Philosophy, Manchester Metropolitan University. This chapter was first published as an article in *European Foreign Affairs Review* [2011] volume 16 (3), pp. 325–40. The editor of this volume is extremely grateful to the *EFA Rev.* editors for allowing it to be reproduced here.

K. Zwolski (✉)
Department of History, Politics and Philosophy, Manchester Metropolitan University, Manchester, UK
e-mail: k.zwolski@mmu.ac.uk

P. J. Cardwell (ed.), *EU External Relations Law and Policy in the Post-Lisbon Era*, DOI: 10.1007/978-90-6704-823-1_17, © T.M.C. Asser press, The Hague, The Netherlands, and the authors 2012

Contents

17.1 Introduction

> It is a disaster that the EU does not have a unified representation when conducting its policy on the non-proliferation of WMDs. Countries such as the US and Russia are fed up with this situation, it is annoying to them.

A high-level EU official working on non-proliferation[1]

Undeniably, the EU has been struggling to develop a unified representation in the area of non-proliferation policy. In fact, two different types of the EU's non-proliferation policy could easily be identified, the one conducted by the Council General Secretariat within the Common Foreign and Security Policy (CFSP) framework, and another one conducted by the European Commission within the former Community framework. This institutional dualism has undermined the effectiveness and recognition of the EU as an international actor in non-proliferation of weapons of mass destruction (WMDs).[2] Furthermore, two different types of policy can still be identified in the newly-established European External Action Service (EEAS),[3] because bringing selected bureaucracies from the aforementioned institutions together does not automatically lead to the integration of their policies and competences. This chapter examines the duality of competences and resources in the non-proliferation policy of the EU; in particular, it argues that this division led to competition between the Commission and the Council General Secretariat over limited resources, thus undermining the overall performance and profile of the EU as an actor in this policy field.

Untangling the challenge of this duality requires distinguishing between the concepts of institutional consistency and inter-institutional competition. With regard to consistency of the EU's international policy, Nuttall offers

[1] This interview was a part of a series of interviews conducted mainly in Brussels between March and June 2009.

[2] This has been confirmed during research interviews by officials who used to work on non-proliferation policy in the European Commission and the Council General Secretariat.

[3] On the EEAS, see, e.g., Vanhoonacker and Reslow 2010; Missiroli 2010; Weiss 2009; Duke 2009 and Blockmans and Laatsit (this volume).

a comprehensive categorisation.[4] Notably, he recognises horizontal consistency (consistency between different types of EU policy), vertical consistency (consistency between the policies of member states and the outcomes that they have agreed upon within the CFSP) and institutional consistency (consistency between two different bureaucratic apparatuses, the one of the Council and the one of the Commission[5]).

Although all three types of consistency are relevant when analysing the non-proliferation policy of the EU, this chapter focuses on institutional consistency, arguing that the formal separation of foreign policies of the Council General Secretariat and those of the European Commission has created structural conditions for institutional consistency to be constantly under strain in non-proliferation policy. Of particular significance were two distinctive institutional cultures and sets of competences, with Council General Secretariat performing more diplomatic roles, whilst the European Commission entrusted with lower-profile capacity-building activities, through a number of geographic and thematic instruments at its disposal.[6] The EEAS offers an opportunity to create structural conditions for a unified non-proliferation policy of the EU. Yet, this will depend on a number of factors, such as the degree of trust and understanding between different entities working on the same policy in this EU's diplomatic service.

Whilst the constant challenge of ensuring institutional consistency was inherent in the post-Maastricht 'pillarisation' of the EU's international security policy, inter-institutional competition in the EU's non-proliferation policy was grounded in the discrepancy between resources available for the Council General Secretariat and the Commission.[7] More specifically, the European Commission has traditionally had more financial resources at its disposal to develop non-proliferation and nuclear-safety projects as compared to the Council General Secretariat, operating within the CFSP framework. Partially as a result of this discrepancy, the Personal Representative on non-proliferation of WMD has been questioning the legitimacy of the Commission to develop non-proliferation policies, arguing that this competence belongs to member states.[8] Again, the EEAS offers an opportunity to overcome this inter-institutional competition, allowing former Council General

[4] Nuttall 2005.

[5] On institutional consistency in the foreign and security policy of the EU please see also: Stetter 2004; Missiroli 2001; Bendiek 2006; Schmalz 1998; Van Elsuwege 2010; Dijkstra 2009; Duke 2006; Tietje 1997.

[6] These include: Technical Aid to the Commonwealth of Independent States (TACIS), which expired in 2006; Instrument for Stability, which has taken over the non-proliferation component of TACIS; and the Instrument for Nuclear Safety Cooperation, which has taken over the nuclear-safety element of TACIS.

[7] On inter-institutional competition in the EU's foreign and security policy please see, e.g., Smith 2005; Howorth 2007.

[8] House of Lords (2005) 'Preventing Proliferation of Weapons of Mass Destruction: The EU Contribution', HL Paper 96, 13th Report of Session 2004–2005, Stationery Office Limited, London.

Secretariat officials to participate in developing strategies and multi-year planning for the Instrument for Stability (IfS) and the Instrument for Nuclear Safety Cooperation (INSC).[9]

In order to capture the dynamics outlined above and examine the potential of the EEAS to alleviate them, the argument in this chapter will unfold in the following manner. The first section will discuss EU's early attempts at developing common European non-proliferation policy; in particular, it will examine original conditions which eventually led to competition over competences and resources. Building on this background, the two subsequent sections will focus on the nature of inter-institutional competition in the EU's non-proliferation policy, by examining two distinctive sets of bureaucracies, with two separate institutional cultures, competences and resources at their disposal: the Council General Secretariat and the Commission. In the final section, this chapter will explore the possibility for the EU to increase its profile as a non-proliferation actor through developing a more unified policy, following institutional reforms introduced by the Lisbon Treaty.

17.2 EU Non-Proliferation Policy: Institutions and Processes

Most of the recent debates on the non-proliferation policy of the EU have been focusing on the EU's role in negotiations with Iran over its nuclear programme.[10] At the same time, the EU's involvement in preventing the proliferation of WMDs from Russia and the former Soviet Union (in the 1990 s but also after 9/11 attacks) has been slightly overlooked in research terms.[11] It is important to briefly examine these earlier efforts of the EU in establishing the common non-proliferation policy, in order to identify the structural conditions which later led to the challenge of ensuring consistency and overcoming inter-institutional competition between two sets of bureaucracies. Paradoxically, the dual (intergovernmental and supranational) structure which enabled to establish the EU's profile as a non-proliferation actor, later contributed to affecting the effectiveness and consequently the recognition of the EU in this policy field.

Within the Cold-War context, the institutional instruments of European states to conduct a common foreign and security policy were mainly confined to the European Political Cooperation (EPC)—an informal framework established in 1970 with the so-called 'Luxemburg Report'.[12] In this report, six member states of the European Economic Community (EEC) undertook a very cautious attempt to

[9] Research interview in the European Commission, November 2010.

[10] Denza 2005; Harnish 2007; Kile 2005; Leonard 2005.

[11] Denza 2005; see also Anthony 2004; Höhl et al. 2003.

[12] European Communities (1970) 'Davignon Report, Luxembourg, 27 October 1970', Bulletin of the European Communities 11, 9–14.

coordinate their international policies. The framework was informal and non-binding, because the report was not ratified by national legislation. Yet, this document 'marked the first successful attempt at foreign policy cooperation by the member states of the European Community'.[13]

The work for ministers was prepared by the Political Committee, further divided into working groups. One of these working groups, established in 1981 at the British–Dutch initiative, concerned the policy on the non-proliferation of WMDs.[14] The purpose of this working group was defined as follows: 'Anxious to ensure that the civil use of nuclear energy does not contribute to the proliferation of nuclear arms and explosives, the Ten sought it necessary to have discussions, consultations and exchanges of information on questions involving aspects of non-proliferation which could be discussed in political co-operation'.[15] Its establishment resulted in adopting a number of common declarations within the framework of international non-proliferation regimes, but these efforts were of purely intergovernmental character, not embedded in any formal institutional framework.[16]

In this context, the Treaty of Maastricht introduced important reforms, integrating the informal EPC into the structure of the Council of the European Union, thus establishing the CFSP. Nuttall[17] notes that this rearrangement offered an opportunity for greater institutional consistency in the area of foreign and security policy, because it limited the number of bureaucratic machineries to just two: the Commission and the Council.[18]

These intergovernmental efforts to develop common non-proliferation policy for the EPC, and subsequently the EU, have enabled to establish the EU's limited profile as an international actor in this policy area. As such, they did not challenge the consistency of the EU's non-proliferation policy or trigger inter-institutional competition. Nonetheless, they led to the development of one of the 'pillars' of the EU's non-proliferation policy, later strengthened by establishing permanent bureaucratic structures in the Council General Secretariat.

Initially, this intergovernmental cooperation was the only pillar of the European non-proliferation policy, because the Commission did not play any substantial role in this policy area. This has changed in the 1990s. Following the disintegration of the Soviet Union, Russia was left with the largest chemical, biological, radiological and nuclear (CBRN) stockpile, located in the largest number of buildings, with insufficient security and safety measures.[19] In response to this threat of the proliferation of CBRN materials, the Commission got involved in providing

[13] Smith 2002, 68.

[14] Sauer 2003.

[15] Quoted in Goens 1987, 44.

[16] Sauer 2003.

[17] Nuttall 2005.

[18] Anthony 2009; Portela 2003; Grand 2000.

[19] Turpen and Finlay 2009; Alibek 2000.

technical and financial assistance to the Commonwealth of Independent States, most notably Russia.[20]

Consequently, through its non-proliferation and nuclear-safety assistance, the European Commission emerged as the second pillar in the EU's non-proliferation policy, adding to already existing intergovernmental efforts. Importantly, the involvement of the Community in this policy area did not become the source of inter-institutional tension for over a decade. This is because the activities of the Commission were considered of purely financial and technical character, but mainly because the Council General Secretariat did not have a permanent non-proliferation bureaucratic structure until 2003.

Nonetheless, the experience of non-proliferation activities in Russia and Ukraine throughout the 1990s has helped the Commission to further develop its non-proliferation expertise. This has become problematic from the Council General Secretariat's point of view, when the High Representative (HR) for the CFSP Javier Solana appointed his Personal Representative on non-proliferation of WMD in 2003. The office of Ms Annalisa Giannella was located in the Justus Lipsius building, almost opposite Directorate-General (DG) External Relations (Relex) (hereinafter 'DG Relex')—the directorate responsible for programming non-proliferation projects of the European Commission. These institutional developments have subsequently led to the fragmentation of the EU's non-proliferation policy, undermining the recognition of the EU as a non-proliferation international security actor.

17.3 The Council: Legitimacy with Modest Resources

One of the first areas defined by member states as a possible object of joint actions, agreed upon even before the Maastricht Treaty came into force, was policy on the non-proliferation of WMDs.[21] Since 1993, the Council has adopted a number of joint actions on non-proliferation; most notably, in 1994, member states utilised their newly-acquired CFSP instrument in order to collectively support the indefinite extension of the Non Proliferation Treaty (NPT), in preparation for the 1995 NPT Review Conference.[22] This and other joint actions have enhanced the EU's

[20] Anthony 2009.

[21] European Council (1992), 'Annex I to the Presidency Conclusions of the Lisbon European Council, 26 and 27 June 1992: Report to the European Council in Lisbon on the likely development of the Common Foreign and Security Policy (CFSP) with a view to identifying areas open to joint action vis-à-vis particular countries or group of countries', European Council, SN 3321/1/92, Lisbon.

[22] Council (1994) 'Decision 94/509/CFSP concerning the Joint Action regarding preparation for the 1995 Conference of the States Parties to the Treaty on the Non-proliferation of Nuclear Weapons', Council of the European Union, OJ L 205, Brussels; see also Grand 2000.

profile and recognition in non-proliferation policy, particularly after France acceded to the NPT in 1992.[23]

However, it was in 2003, when non-proliferation took a much higher political profile within the EU; this was a result of a few important political and institutional developments, which resulted in establishing the second pillar of the EU's bureaucratic structure concerned with non-proliferation policy. Politically, three important documents were adopted by the European Council in 2003, i.e.: (a) the Action Plan for the Implementation of the Basic Principles of an EU Strategy against the Proliferation of Weapons of Mass Destruction[24]; (b) the European Security Strategy, identifying the proliferation of WMDs as one of the key threats[25]; and (c) the EU Strategy against Proliferation of WMDs (WMD Strategy).[26]

Institutionally, the Council General Secretariat has become home for EU member states to develop more permanent bureaucratic structures in the area of non-proliferation policy. Of particular importance in this context has been the appointment of Ms Giannella as the Personal Representative on non-proliferation of WMD in October 2003. Hierarchically, prior to the establishment of the EEAS, the Directorate for Non-Proliferation of Weapons of Mass Destruction was located within DG E of the Secretariat, dealing with External and Political-Military Affairs. Upon the appointment and over time, the Personal Representative was entrusted with the following tasks: (a) contributing to the further development of the WMD Strategy; (b) further enhancing the profile of non-proliferation policy in EU's relations with third countries; (c) contributing to the implementation of the EU SALW (Small Arms and Light Weapons) Strategy[27]; (d) assisting EU member states in their efforts to coordinate policies in the area of conventional arms exports controls; and (e) assisting E3 (Germany, France and the UK) and the HR for the CFSP in negotiations with Iran over its nuclear programme.

Consequently, since 2003, the EU's non-proliferation policy has been developed in two separate institutions, with different cultures, instruments and resources. On the one hand, the European Commission has been involved in long-term capacity-building activities of a relatively low political profile, but with significant resources at its disposal. On the other hand, the Council General Secretariat has

---

23 See Sauer 2003.

24 Council (2003) 'Action Plan for the Implementation of the Basic Principles of an EU Strategy against the Proliferation of Weapons of Mass Destruction', Council of the European Union, 10354/1/03 REV 1, Brussels.

25 Council (2003) 'A Secure Europe in a Better World: European Security Strategy', Council of the European Union, 15895/03, Brussels.

26 Council (2003) 'Fight against the proliferation of weapons of mass destruction—EU Strategy against Proliferation of Weapons of Mass Destruction', Council of the European Union, 15708/03, Brussels; see also Àlvarez-Verdugo 2006; Müller 2007.

27 Council (2003) 'EU Strategy to combat illicit accumulation and trafficking of SALW and their Ammunition', Council of the European Union, 5319/06, Brussels.

become the main focal point for the EU to implement the WMD Strategy, mainly through international negotiations and agreements.

The EEAS, discussed further in this chapter, constitutes the most robust effort to ensure institutional consistency in the EU's foreign and security policy. Nonetheless, it is important to recognise that in the area of non-proliferation policy, there have been other efforts, undertaken within the existing institutional structure. Most notably, in 2006, the WMD Monitoring Centre was established and located within the Council General Secretariat.[28] This initiative aimed particularly at 'enhancing effectiveness and consistency without any modification of institutional settings and prerogatives, by establishing a cooperative working method which allows the Council Secretariat/HR, the Commission services and Member States to work together, and ensure better synergy'.[29]

This indicates that member states recognised the challenge of ensuring institutional consistency in non-proliferation policy long before establishing the EEAS. In fact, the idea of creating the WMD Monitoring Centre was already expressed in the WMD Strategy, which called for '[s]etting up, as agreed in Thessaloniki, a unit which would function as a monitoring centre, entrusted with the monitoring of the consistent implementation of the EU Strategy and the collection of information and intelligence, in liaison with the Situation Centre. This monitoring centre would be set up at the Council Secretariat and fully associate the Commission'.[30] Yet, it was only in 2006, when the concept paper, providing for the establishment of this informal body, was drafted and adopted by the Council.[31] The Centre proved to be a valuable forum for various parties (including the Council General Secretariat and the Commission) to discuss more specific thematic issues, but also to have a more general exchange of information.[32]

Another outcome of the WMD Strategy, the organisation of a six-monthly debate on the implementation of the WMD Strategy, has also contributed to bringing Council General Secretariat and the Commission closer together.[33] To this end, the Personal Representative on non-proliferation of WMD, together with the Commission, drafted reports on the EU's non-proliferation activities every six

---

[28] Council (2006) 'EU Strategy against the proliferation of WMD: Monitoring and enhancing consistent implementation', Council of the European Union, 16694/06, Brussels.

[29] Council (2006) 'EU Strategy against the proliferation of WMD: Monitoring and enhancing consistent implementation', 3.

[30] Council (2003) 'Fight against the proliferation of weapons of mass destruction—EU Strategy against Proliferation of Weapons of Mass Destruction', Council of the European Union, 15708/03, Brussels, 13.

[31] According Ms Giannella, the main reason for the delay was that her office was awaiting more details concerning the EU's Joint Diplomatic Service; see House of Lords (2005) 'Preventing Proliferation of Weapons of Mass Destruction: The EU Contribution', HL Paper 96, 13th Report of Session 2004–2005, Stationery Office Limited, London, 39.

[32] De Jong 2010.

[33] Council (2003) 'Fight against the proliferation of weapons of mass destruction—EU Strategy against Proliferation of Weapons of Mass Destruction', Council of the European Union, 15708/03, Brussels, 13.

months. These drafts then go through the usual procedure in the Council, where they are discussed by working groups, the Political and Security Committee, COREPER and ministers.[34]

These efforts to increase institutional consistency in the EU's non-proliferation policy are important, but they did not overcome two structural obstacles to a better synergy between the policies developed in the Council and the Commission. These obstacles include, on the one hand, the problem of different institutional cultures, competences and sensitivities, and, on the other hand, the discrepancy in funding for non-proliferation and nuclear safety policies available for the Council General Secretariat (within the CFSP framework) and the Commission (within the former Community pillar). The following section addresses these two obstacles in greater detail.

17.4 The Commission: Resources with Contested Legitimacy

The institutionalisation of the intergovernmental dimension of the EU's non-proliferation policy, in the form of establishing permanent bureaucratic structures in the Council General Secretariat in 2003, has certainly increased the political profile of non-proliferation policy on the EU's security agenda. Yet, this 'CFSP' pillar, as already indicated, did not represent the whole spectrum of EU's activities in this policy field. Already at the beginning of the 1990s, the European Community initiated technical assistance (known as the Technical Aid to the Commonwealth of Independent States (TACIS)[35]) to the former Soviet Union, with the security and safety of nuclear installations constituting an important component of this assistance.[36] With regard to preventing the proliferation of WMDs as such, redirection of former Soviet scientists became the most prominent area of involvement for the European Community.[37]

As already mentioned, one of the key threats to international security, directly following the collapse of the Soviet Union, was the lack of employment for thousands of former Soviet scientists, whose knowledge was valuable for actors

[34] House of Lords (2005) 'Preventing Proliferation of Weapons of Mass Destruction: The EU Contribution', HL Paper 96, 13th Report of Session 2004–2005, Stationery Office Limited, London, 39.

[35] On the origins of TACIS, please see Sodupe and Benito 1998, 51–68.

[36] Commission (1993) 'TACIS: Annual Report from the Commission, 1991 and 1992', Commission of the European Communities, COM(93) 362 final, Brussels; Anthony 2004; Höhl et al. 2003.

[37] Commission (2001) 'TACIS Regional Cooperation: Strategic Considerations 2002–2006 and Indicative Programme 2002–2003. Annex C: The ICTC/STCU Indicative Programmes for 2002–2003', European Commission, 27 December 2001, Brussels.

wishing to develop CBRN weapons.[38] In order to prevent this threat, two scientific centres were established: the International Science and Technology Centre (ISTC) in Russia and the Science and Technology Centre in Ukraine (STCU). The main goal of these centres was to redirect scientists, in order to enable them to use their expertise for peaceful purposes. During the period between 1994 and 2003, more than 60.000 scientists were supported through the centres in Russia and Ukraine. More than $500 million was invested in their activities, including the Commission's contribution of almost €90 million.[39] According to Höhl,[40] the Commission was an ideal partner for developing this initiative, due to its 'technical expertise, financial flexibility and back-up from nuclear research centres (which can help evaluate incoming research proposals).'

The relatively low profile of the Community's activities channelled through TACIS, combined with the lack of permanent Council bureaucracy dealing with non-proliferation, allowed the Commission to develop its assistance relatively uncontested, apart from the criticism directed at the actual effectiveness of TACIS.[41] This has changed following the Commission's 2004 proposal for a regulation establishing the IfS.[42] In its original proposal, the Commission suggested that this new instrument of the European Community should enable providing assistance for the following purposes: (a) responding to conflicts and threats to human rights, democracy and the rule of law (building on the Rapid Reaction Mechanism[43]); (b) furthering cooperation between the EU and third countries with regard to trans-border security challenges; and (c) preventing the proliferation of WMDs.

In contrast to the low-key activities of the Community under TACIS, the IfS was about to become the EU's main instrument for delivering security-oriented financial assistance. Furthermore, in 2004, institutional circumstances were also different, compared to the situation from the 1990s. Most notably, permanent bureaucratic structures were already set in the Council General Secretariat, entrusted with implementing the WMD Strategy and coordinating the EU's non-proliferation policy in general. Consequently, the Commission's proposal sparked controversy, leading to concerns that the Community pillar would effectively become an alarmingly powerful actor in non-proliferation policy, considering its

---

38 In an unprecedented survey concluded in 2003 by D.Y. Bal & T.P. Gerber, 20% out of 602 Russian physicists, biologists and chemists responded that they would consider working in Iran, North Korea, Syria or Iraq.

39 Commission, 'TACIS ISTC/STCU Action Programme 2003', European Commission. http://ec.europa.eu/europeaid/where/neighbourhood/regional-cooperation/enpi-east/documents/annual_programmes/istc_stcu_2003_en.pdf. Accessed 25 June 2011.

40 Höhl et al. 2003, 13.

41 Sodupe and Benito 1998; Holden 2009.

42 Commission (2004) 'Proposal for a Regulation of the Council establishing an Instrument for Stability', European Commission, COM(2004) 630 final, Brussels.

43 Council (2001) 'Council Regulation (EC) No 381/2001 of 26 February 2001 creating a rapid-reaction mechanism', Council of the European Union, OJEC L57.

much larger budget compared to very limited resources within the CFSP framework. These concerns were fully expressed in 2005 by Ms Giannella, the Personal Representative on non-proliferation of WMD, and are quoted in length:

> As I have said, there are procedures which are different; there are prerogatives which are different in the two pillars; and there are financial resources which are very different. Despite the fact that I believe non-proliferation is mainly a foreign and security policy area, I think there is a tendency to try, through the budgetary procedures and instruments, putting it in a simplistic way, to "communiterise" non-proliferation. If you look at the financial perspectives and at the stability instruments put forward by the Commission, stability instruments basically would work as a Community programme. There would be a sort of framework decision by the Council and then the programme would be managed and all the projects would be prepared and decided by the Commission with very little power in the hands of Member State.[44]

Partially as a result of these controversies, the negotiations on the IfS were long and difficult, and the instrument was finally established in 2006.[45] In the final version of the regulation, almost all references to non-proliferation policy were removed. Instead, the IfS is primarily intended (under Article 3) to allow a prompt response to situations of crisis or emerging crisis. Around 75% of the budget allocated for the IfS for the years 2007–2013 is designated for this purpose.[46] The remaining 25% is intended for providing assistance in the context of stable conditions for cooperation, including 'risk mitigation and preparedness relating to chemical, biological, radiological and nuclear materials or agents.'[47]

Even though the 'non-proliferation' element was played down in the final regulation as compared to the original Commission's proposal, the IfS, following the expiration of TACIS in 2006, emerged as 'the sole Community instrument that can directly address issues relating to the risks presented by the weaponisation of chemical, biological, radiological and nuclear agents.'[48] Furthermore, the Commission still had more significant resources at its disposal for non-proliferation and nuclear safety projects as compared to the resources of the Council within the framework of the CFSP. For example, in 2010, the CFSP budget for non-proliferation and nuclear safety was over €22 million,[49] whilst average annual IfS and INSC budget for non-proliferation is around €112 million for the period

---

[44] House of Lords (2005) 'Preventing Proliferation of Weapons of Mass Destruction: The EU Contribution', HL Paper 96, 13th Report of Session 2004-2005, Stationery Office Limited, London, 38.

[45] Regulation (EC) no 1717/2006 of the European Parliament and the Council of 15 November 2006 establishing an Instrument for Stability', OJEU L 327 (Instrument for Stability Regulation).

[46] Instrument for Stability Regulation, 10.

[47] Instrument for Stability Regulation, 4.

[48] Commission, 'The Instrument for Stability: Strategy Paper 2007–2011', European Commission. http://ec.europa.eu/europeaid/how/finance/documents/eidhr/ifs_strategy_2007-2011_en.pdf. Accessed 11 August 2010.

[49] Council (2011) '2010 CFSP Budget—Final update of the 2010 CFSP Budget', Council of the European Union, 5230/11, Brussels.

2007–2013.[50] The Commission's funding included both the IfS as well as the INSC, which took over the 'nuclear safety' component of TACIS.[51]

This financial discrepancy unveils the structural causes of inter-institutional competition between the Commission and the Council General Secretariat in the area of non-proliferation policy. This competition added to an already difficult challenge of ensuring institutional consistency between policies developed by two non-proliferation 'pillars' of the EU. Consequently, the effectiveness of the EU as an actor in non-proliferation policy has been negatively affected. These and other problems stemming from the fragmentation of the EU's international security policy were recognised by member states. Consequently, the Lisbon Treaty opens an opportunity to overcome them, but in the area of non-proliferation policy this will not happen automatically.

17.5 The EEAS: from Inter- to Intra-Institutional Competition?

The quest for consistency in European external policy-making has a long history.[52] For example, the Single European Act states that 'The external policies of the European Community and the policies agreed in European Political Co-operation must be consistent'.[53] The Treaty of Maastricht further emphasises the need for consistency in the EU's external relations, security, economic and development policies. In this context, 'Council and the Commission shall be responsible for ensuring such consistency'.[54]

Yet, following the formal 'pillarisation', ensuring institutional consistency in the EU's foreign and security policy was easier said than done, considering the duality of institutional cultures, competences and resources available within the Community and CFSP pillars. This duality, as this chapter has demonstrated, turned into inter-institutional competition between the Council General Secretariat and the Commission in the area of policy on non-proliferation of WMDs, undermining the EU's performance on the world stage. The Lisbon Treaty aims to

---

[50] Commission, 'The Instrument for Stability: Strategy Paper 2007–2011', European Commission. http://ec.europa.eu/europeaid/how/finance/documents/eidhr/ifs_strategy_2007–2011_en.pdf. Accessed 11 August 2010; Council (2007) 'Council Regulation (EURATOM) No 300/2007 of 19 February 2007 establishing an Instrument for Nuclear Safety Cooperation', Council of the European Union, OJEU L 81.

[51] Council (2007) 'Council Regulation (EURATOM) No 300/2007 of 19 February 2007 establishing an Instrument for Nuclear Safety Cooperation', Council of the European Union, OJEU L 81.

[52] Nuttall 2005; see also Stetter 2004; Missiroli 2001; Bendiek 2006; Schmalz 1998; Van Elsuwege 2010; Dijkstra 2009; Duke 2006; Tietje 1997.

[53] Single European Act, Article 30 (5).

[54] Treaty on European Union, Article C; see also Tietje 1997, 211–233.

overcome this duality by bringing relevant bureaucracies and processes from the Council Secretariat and the Commission together, into the EEAS.[55]

Following prolonged discussions, in 2010 the Council decided that the following administrative entities from the Council Secretariat would be transferred into the EEAS: Policy Unit; CSDP and crisis management structures (e.g. EU Military Staff, EU Situation Centre); Directorate-General E (External and Political-Military Affairs). Further, the Council decided to also move into the EEAS almost entire DG Relex of the European Commission.[56] This means that the entire bureaucratic apparatus involved in conducting the non-proliferation policy of the EU has been moved into the EEAS. This rearrangement offers an opportunity to bring a higher degree of cooperation and consistency across different EU non-proliferation policies and instruments, but this convergence is unlikely to happen automatically.

Some scholars even suggest that inter-institutional cooperation within the EU tends to be better than intra-institutional cooperation—within a single institution. For example, Christiansen[57] argues that structurally determined tensions between the Council General Secretariat and the Commission have led to the low level of expectations for close cooperation between them. Yet, against this low level of expectations, officials from both institutions have developed collegial approaches in the areas of shared responsibility. On the other hand, significant tensions could be identified within the Commission and the Council General Secretariat: 'the differing organizational logics of distinct administrative tasks constitute internal tensions which then require substantive institutional resources for their resolution.'[58] This argument would call for a degree of caution when assuming that bringing officials, instruments and resources into one institution will in itself assure consistency and close cooperation on non-proliferation policy.

At the time of writing, it has been established that roughly one-third of the unit dealing with non-proliferation in the EEAS will consist of officials formerly working in DG Relex of the European Commission; another one-third will be composed of officials who used to work in Ms Giannella's office in the Council General Secretariat (Ms Giannella was appointed in charge of the non-proliferation unit of EEAS); the remaining one-third will consist of the representatives of member states.[59] This means that three bodies with distinctive diplomatic cultures and experiences will be working together. They will be involved in developing two dimensions of the EU's non-proliferation policy, formerly developed by separate bureaucracies.

---

[55] Council (2010) 'Council Decision of 26 July 2010 establishing the organisation and functioning of the European External Action Service (2010/427/EU)', Council of the European Union L 201, Brussels.

[56] Council Decision of 26 July 2010 establishing the organisation and functioning of the European External Action Service, Annex.

[57] Christiansen 2001.

[58] Christiansen 2001, 766.

[59] Based on a research interview conducted in the European Commission in November 2010.

First, the diplomatic dimension of non-proliferation policy, including international negotiations, will be conducted mainly by officials previously working in the Council General Secretariat. Second, the capacity-building dimension, including the development of strategies and multi-year planning for the IfS and the INSC, will be carried mainly by officials previously working in DG Relex of the European Commission.[60] One of the indicators determining the degree of consistency achieved as a result of these institutional reforms will be the extent to which officials previously working in one institution will now be involved in developing policies which are historically the competence of another institution.

Consequently, the EU has now an opportunity to overcome the duality in its non-proliferation policy, and thus to enhance its profile as a security actor in international relations. However, to achieve this result, a high degree of mutual trust and understanding will be necessary among three aforementioned bodies working together in the newly-established EU's diplomatic service. In particular, it will be crucial for all parties to recognise their mutual added value.

On the one hand, officials who used to work in the Council General Secretariat must recognise the value of activities formerly developed in the Commission; most importantly, these include capacity-building through utilising flagship thematic instruments, i.e. the IfS and the INSC. One of the most important projects in this respect is the creation of the regional centres of excellence on CBRN, envisaged in the IfS Indicative Programme for the years 2009–2011.[61] The centres will aim to bring regional actors together in order to pursue the objectives defined in Article 4(2) of the regulation establishing the IfS, such as the promotion of civilian research activities, enhancing the safety of CBRN facilities, establishing and enforcing frameworks for controlling the export of dual-use items.[62] Seven regional centres are envisaged: three in Africa, one in the Middle East, one in South-East Asia, one in Central Asia and one in Caucuses.

On the other hand, officials formerly working in the Commission must recognise the value of diplomatic efforts aiming to develop new and manage existing multilateral non-proliferation agreements and regimes.[63] However, in a long term, in order to best utilise different types of non-proliferation resources at the EU's disposal (diplomatic, political and financial), it will be critical to merge not just institutions and processes, but also competences and policies. This means that: (a) capacity-building instruments must be developed in a way that fully supports the political and diplomatic non-proliferation goals of the EU; and (b) political goals and agreements at the international level must support building long-term capacities in regions of proliferation concern.

---

[60] Based on a research interview conducted in the European Commission in November 2010.

[61] Commission (2009) 'The Instrument for Stability—Multi-annual Indicative Programme 2009-2011', European Commission, (2009) 2641, Brussels.

[62] Regulation (EC) no 1717/2006 of the European Parliament and the Council of 15 November 2006 establishing an Instrument for Stability', OJEU L 327.

[63] In this context, of particular importance is the non-proliferation clause inserted into agreements with third parties.

17.6 Conclusion

The aims of ensuring institutional consistency and overcoming inter-institutional competition in the EU's international security policy are at the core of creating the EEAS. The EU's policy on non-proliferation of WMDs has been in dire need of such a reform, considering that two different bureaucracies were entrusted with developing non-proliferation policies and projects for the EU.

As this chapter has demonstrated, on the one hand, the European Commission was involved in non-proliferation and nuclear safety capacity-building projects in Russia and former Soviet Union countries, through a number of geographical (TACIS) and thematic (IfS, INSC) instruments. More recently, the Commission recognised the importance of moving beyond this geographical region, thus programming projects in places such as the Middle East, Africa and Asia. The most prominent amongst these new initiatives are the regional centres of excellence on CBRN, aiming to bring regional actors together, in order to further advance the culture of non-proliferation and nuclear safety.[64]

On the other hand, following the adoption by the EU of the WMD Strategy in 2003, former HR for the CFSP Javier Solana appointed his Personal Representative on WMDs. Consequently, a permanent bureaucratic structure was established in the Council General Secretariat, entrusted with implementing the WMD Strategy. Yet, rather paradoxically considering the solid legitimacy of this new body, the Council's Directorate for Non-Proliferation of Weapons of Mass Destruction was chronically underfunded, receiving only a small portion of already limited CFSP budget.

This situation quickly led to a degree of resentment towards the European Commission, which was entrusted with managing proportionally much larger resources in the area of non-proliferation and nuclear safety policy. This problem of inter-institutional competition amongst two bureaucracies added to the broader challenge of ensuring institutional consistency—the problem imbedded in the EU's three-pillar structure and long recognised in literature.[65]

Further research is necessary to assess the extent to which the EEAS will indeed bring synergy into the EU's non-proliferation policy, thus enhancing the effectiveness and recognition of the EU as an actor in this field. This in turn will greatly depend on mutual trust and understanding among different entities working together in the newly-established diplomatic service of the EU. However, it has also been suggested that, in a longer term, the merging of bureaucracies will have to be followed by developing a truly-coherent policy, in which relatively low-key capacity-building projects in regions of proliferation concern are supported by

---

[64] Commission (2009) 'The Instrument for Stability—Multi-annual Indicative Programme 2009–2011', European Commission, C(2009)2641, Brussels.

[65] See Nuttall 2005, Stetter 2004; Missiroli 2001; Bendiek 2006; Schmalz 1998; Van Elsuwege 2010; Dijkstra 2009; Duke 2006; Tietje 1997.

high-level diplomatic efforts, and vice versa. Catherine Ashton's leadership role will be crucial in this respect.[66]

The EEAS, under the leading role of the HR of the Union for Foreign Affairs and Security Policy, may potentially help to overcome competition between the Council Secretariat and the Commission. However, further research will also be necessary to examine potential tensions over competences at the higher level, between the HR and the President of the European Council. The latter was entrusted by the Lisbon Treaty with ensuring 'the external representation of the Union on issues concerning its common foreign and security policy (…)'.[67] To be sure, Herman Van Rompuy already started exercising this competence in the area of non-proliferation, for example by representing the EU at the April 2010 Nuclear Security Summit in Washington.[68] In addition, the European Parliament is increasingly asserting its role on matters of foreign and security policy, 'trying to have an ever bigger say on expenditure, appointments, and policy guidelines'.[69] Its ambitions in matters such as non-proliferation policy deserve close attention.

References

Alibek K (2000) Biohazard. Arrow Books, London

Àlvarez-Verdugo M (2006) Mixing tools against proliferation: the EU's strategy for dealing with weapons of mass destruction. European Foreign Affairs Review 11:417–438

Anthony I (2004) Reducing threats at the source: a European perspective on cooperative threat reduction, SIPRI research report 19. Oxford University Press, Oxford

Anthony I (2009) The role of the EU in WMD nonproliferation. In: Busch NE, Joyner DH (eds) Combating weapons of mass destruction: the future of international nonproliferation policy. The University of Georgia Press, Athens, pp 197–221

Bendiek A (2006) Cross-Pillar security regime building in the European Union: effects of the European security strategy of December 2003. European integration, online papers 10

Bergenäs J (2010) What role for WMD nonproliferation under the EU's new foreign policy chief: a six month review and analysis of Lady Ashton's Tenure, issue brief. Nuclear Threat Initiative

Christiansen T (2001) Intra-institutional politics and inter-institutional relations in the EU: Towards coherent governance? Journal of European Public Policy 8:747–769

De Jong S, Sterkx S, Wouters J (2010) The EU as a regional actor: weapons of mass destruction. Working Paper 10, EU-GRASP

Denza E (2005) Non-proliferation of nuclear weapons: the European Union and Iran. European Foreign Affairs Review 10:289–311

---

66 Bergenäs 2010.

67 Nugent, 2010, 166.

68 European Council (2010) 'Statement by President Herman Van Rompuy, on behalf of the European Union at the Nuclear Security Summit in Washington', European Council the President, PCE 68/10 Washington.

69 Missiroli 2010, 444.

Dijkstra H (2009) Commission versus Council Secretariat: an analysis of bureaucratic rivalry in European foreign policy. European Foreign Affairs Review 14:431–450

Duke S (2006) Areas of grey: tensions in EU external relations competences. EIPASCOPE 1:21–27

Duke S (2009) Providing for European-level diplomacy after Lisbon: the case of the European External Action Service. The Hague Journal of Diplomacy 4:211–233

Goens J (1987) The opportunities and limits of European co-operation in the area of non-proliferation. In: Müller H (ed) A European nonproliferation policy. Clarendon Press, Oxford

Grand C (2000) The European Union and the non-proliferation of nuclear weapons. Chaillot Papers 37, Institute for Security Studies, Paris

Harnish S (2007) Minilateral cooperation and transatlantic coalition-building: the E3/EU-3 Iran initiative. European Security 16:1–27

Höhl K, Müller H, Schaper A, Schmitt B (2003) EU cooperative threat reduction activities in Russia. Chaillot Papers 61, Institute for Security Studies, Paris

Holden (2009) In search of structural power: EU aid policy as a global political instrument. Ashgate, Burlington

Howorth J (2007) Security and defence policy in the European Union. Palgrave Macmillan, Basingstoke

Kile S (2005) Europe and Iran: perspectives on non-proliferation, SIPRI research report 21. Oxford University Press, Oxford

Leonard M (2005) Can EU diplomacy stop Iran's nuclear programme? Centre for European Reform, London

Missiroli A (2001) European security policy: the challenge of coherence. European Foreign Affairs Review 6:177–196

Missiroli A (2010) The new EU "foreign policy" system after Lisbon: a work in progress. European Foreign Affairs Review 15:427–452

Müller H (2007) Europe and the proliferation of weapons of mass destruction. In: Foradori P, Rosa P, Scartezzini R (eds) Managing multilevel foreign policy. Lexington Books, Lanhan, pp 181–200

Nugent N (2010) The government and politics of the European Union. Palgrave Macmillan, Basingstoke

Nuttall S (2005) Coherence and consistency. In: Hill C, Smith M (eds) International relations and the European Union. Oxford University Press, Oxford, pp 91–112

Portela C (2003) The role of the EU in the non-proliferation of nuclear weapons: the way to Thessaloniki and beyond, PRIF report 65. Peace Research Institute, Frankfurt

Sauer T (2003) How "common" is European nuclear non-proliferation policy. Joint Session of Workshops of the European Consortium for Political Research, Edinburgh

Schmalz U (1998) The Amsterdam Provisions on external coherence: Bridging the Union's foreign policy dualism? European Foreign Affairs Review 3:421–442

Smith (2002) European Union foreign policy: what it is and what it does. Pluto Press, London

Smith ME (2005) Implementation: making the EU's international relations work. In: Hill C, Smith M (eds) International relations and the European Union. Oxford University Press, Oxford, pp 154–175

Sodupe K, Benito E (1998) The evolution of the European Union's TACIS programme, 1991–96. Journal of Communist Studies and Transition Politics 14:51–68

Stetter S (2004) Cross-pillar politics: functional unity and institutional fragmentation of EU. Journal of European Public Policy 11:720–739

Tietje C (1997) The concept of coherence in the Treaty on European Union and the Common Foreign and Security Policy. European Foreign Affairs Review 2:211–233

Turpen E, Finlay B (2009) US–Russia cooperative nonproliferation. In: Busch NE, Joyner DH (eds) Combating weapons of mass destruction: the future of international nonproliferation policy. The University of Georgia Press, Athens, pp 302–324

Van Elsuwege P (2010) EU external action after the collapse of the pillar structure: in search of a new balance between delimitation and consistency. Common Market Law Review 47:987–1019

Vanhoonacker S, Reslow N (2010) The European External Action Service. European Foreign Affairs Review 15:1–18

Weiss S (2009) External action service. Much ado about nothing. Spotlight Europe 5, pp 1–8

Chapter 18
Foreign Direct Investment as Common Commercial Policy: EU External Economic Competence After Lisbon

Chien-Huei Wu

Abstract The Treaty of Lisbon added a new impetus to the Common Commercial Policy (CCP) with the inclusion of Foreign Direct Investment (FDI) within its scope. The latter thus falls within exclusive competence of the European Union (EU). The redistribution of competences between the Union and its Member States as well as the enlargements of the Union do however create legal uncertainties and poses challenges to pre-existing agreements signed between the Member States and third countries. This chapter examines the various efforts that the Commission has made in lessening the potential difficulties. It firstly looks to the EU-US understanding and services agreements with interested World Trade Organisation (WTO) members which gave rise to the competence issues. It also examines relevant recent case-law, *Commission v. Austria*, *Commission v. Sweden*, and *Commission v. Finland*, which again complicate the situation. This chapter investigates a proposed Regulation on transitional arrangements for Member State Bilateral Investment Treaties (BITs) and finds the authorisation mechanism insufficient to ensure the smooth transition for the Union taking over this new competence on FDI. This chapter also examines external economic policy changes from the Lisbon Strategy to the Europe 2020 Strategy and reflects whether this new competence on FDI, situated in the context of CCP, contributes to the strengths of EU within the WTO and with its trading partners in Free Trade Agreement (FTA) talks. I thus examine the position of the EU within the WTO and relevant investment provisions in the EU-Chile Association Agreement, EU-Indonesia Partnership and Cooperation Agreement (PCA) and EU-Korea Free Trade Agreement. The EU-Korea FTA,

---

Dr Chien-Huei Wu—Assistant Research Fellow at the Institute of European and American Studies. The research leading to this chapter is funded by National Research Council of Taiwan (99-2410-H-001-110-MY2) which the author gratefully acknowledges.

C.-H. Wu (✉)
Institute of European and American Studies, Academia Sinica, Taipei, Taiwan
e-mail: wch@gate.sinica.edu.tw

P. J. Cardwell (ed.), *EU External Relations Law and Policy in the Post-Lisbon Era*,
DOI: 10.1007/978-90-6704-823-1_18,

being the first in the post-Lisbon era with ambitious market access commitments and substantive national treatment and MFN treatment obligations, offers a good model for integrating FDI into CCP and investments issues into trade agreements in the field of EU external economic relations.

Contents

18.1 Introduction

The Common Commercial Policy (CCP), as an exclusive competence of the European Union (EU), has been one of the major elements of the EU external relations. The exercising of this competence can be dated back to the General Agreement of Tariffs and Trade (GATT) era, when the EU (formerly the EEC) was not a formal Contracting Party thereto, but *de facto* the EU spoke on behalf of its Member States. The establishment of the World Trade Organisation (WTO) marked a new stage for the EU's CCP in that the EU (under the designation 'European Communities') could acquire its own membership alongside its Member States. This wider scope covered by the WTO went beyond the traditional trade in goods and shifted towards trade in services and trade-related intellectual property rights that brought about competence issues that were eventually resolved by the Opinion 1/94[1] of the European Court of Justice (ECJ). Similarly, controversies arose when the ten Central and Eastern European (CEE) Member States joined the Union in 2004. In order to rearrange the commitments of these acceding Member States and to bring their services schedules in line with that of the Union, negotiations were carried out between the Union and other interested WTO Members such as the United States. This again gave rise to competence issues, particularly in who was eligible to sign the services agreements, and this was finally resolved by the ECJ's Opinion 1/08.[2]

The complexity that resulted from the 2004 (CEE countries) and 2007 (Romania and Bulgaria) enlargements went beyond the scope of trade. Given that

[1] ECJ, Opinion 1/94 of Court on 15 November 1994 on Competence of the Community to conclude international agreements concerning services and the protection of intellectual property—Article 228(6) of the EC Treaty [1994] ECR I-05267.

[2] ECJ, Opinion 1/08 of Court of 30 November 2009 [2009] ECR I-11129.

these CEE Member States had signed and maintained a number of Bilateral Investment Treaties (BITs) with the existing EU Member States (intra-EU BITs) and with third countries (extra-EU BITs), the legal status of both became highly contentious, especially when the provisions thereof are incompatible with EU law. Investor-state disputes arising from intra-EU BITs have been heard in the Arbitral Institute of the Stockholm Chamber of Commerce[3] and in the International Centre for Settlement of Investment Disputes (ISCID).[4] Concerns thus arise as to whether these arbitral tribunals have the position to interpret the EU law and as to whether their interpretation undermines the uniformity of EU legal order. In recognition of the threat posed by these BITs to the EU legal order in the previous enlargement, the European Commission commenced infringement proceedings against Austria, Sweden[5] and later Finland[6] on the ground that they failed to take appropriate measures to eliminate incompatibilities with EU law that were contained in their BITs with third countries before their accession to the Union and thus violated their obligation as set out in by Article 307(2) EC.[7] In *Commission* v. *Austria* and *Commission* v. *Sweden*, the ECJ subsequently held that, by not taking the appropriate steps to eliminate the incompatibilities contained within the BITs, Sweden and Austria failed to fulfil their obligations under Article 307(2) EC. In delivering his opinion, Advocate General Maduro also relied heavily on the duty of loyal cooperation as enshrined in Article 10 EC.[8] In *Commission* v. *Finland*, Advocate General Sharpston's reasoning is strongly conditioned by the former two joined cases where the Court essentially repeats itself.

The story does not end here. The coming into force of Lisbon Treaty adds new impetus to CCP, with the inclusion of FDI and thus falling into the exclusive competence of the Union. The Treaty on the Functioning of the European Union (TFEU) instructs the Union to contribute, in the name of common interest, to the harmonising development of world trade, to progressively abolish restrictions on international trade and FDI, and to lower customs and other barriers.[9] It also directs the Union to pursue CCP in the context of the principles and objectives of

---

[3] Stockholm Chamber of Commerce Arbitral Institute, *Easter Sugar B. V. (Netherlands)* v. *Czech Republic*, Partial Award of 27 March 2007, SCC No. 088/2004. Also see, Burgstaller 2009, 181.

[4] Several cases have been reported at the ISCID arbitral tribunals. See e.g., ISCID, award of 2 October 2006, *ADC Affiliate Limited and ADC & ADMC Management Limited* v *The Republic of Hungary*, ICSID Case No. ARB/03/16.

[5] ECJ, Case C-205/06 *Commission* v. *Austria* [2009] ECR I-01301; ECJ, Case C-249/06 *Commission* v. *Sweden* [2009] ECR I-01335.

[6] ECJ, Case C-118/07 *Commission* v. *Finland* [2009] ECR I-10889.

[7] Article 307(2) EC, now incorporated into the Treaty on the Functioning of the European Union ('TFEU') under Article 351(2). As the case-law discussed in this chapter dates from before the Lisbon Treaty entered into force, the previous treaty references have been retained.

[8] Article 10 EC, now incorporated into the Treaty on European Union (TEU), Article 4(3).

[9] Article 206 TFEU.

the Union's external action,[10] thus creating a synergy with the general principles of consistency in the EU's external relations explored extensively in other contributions to this volume. The redistribution of competences between the Union and its Member States creates legal uncertainties and poses challenges to the pre-existing BITs, especially those signed between Member States and third countries. In response, the Commission has published a Communication entitled '*Towards a comprehensive European international investment policy*',[11] proposing a new Regulation that establishes transitional arrangements for BITs concluded between Member States and third countries.[12]

In this context, this chapter thus aims to explore how FDI integrated into the trade-centric CCP and to assess FDI's impact on CCP. This chapter will examine the phasing integration of FDI into CCP, as an analysis of the EU's internal development, and how this newly expanded CCP operate within the Union's existing policies with the WTO and its bilateral Free Trade Agreements (FTA) negotiations. In other words, the main objective of this chapter is to examine the incorporation of FDI into the existing trade-based CCP and to reflect on how FDI adds to strength of the Union's CCP and thus enhances its competitiveness. I will limit myself to trade-based regimes and will not venture into the unchartered field of Union's potential participation in the ICSID system or its envisaged stand-alone EU BITs negotiations.

This chapter is organised as followed: Sect. 18.2 examines the negotiations with third countries both on the trade and investment issues resulting from the Union's enlargement and explores the relationship between trade and investment. It will also look at the case-laws of the ECJ in *Commission* v. *Sweden*, *Commission* v. *Austria* and *Commission* v. *Finland* and then deal with the proposed Regulation. The aim of this section is to answer whether the proposed Regulation can help to eliminate the incompatibilities noted in the relevant case laws and whether the proposed Regulation's transitional mechanism can create legal certainty and meet the expectations of third countries as well as their investors, especially on the predictability of this transitional regime. Section 18.3 will examine whether having exclusive competence on FDI adds any strengths to the Union's participation within the WTO and to its bilateral FTA talks. A conclusion will be provided in Sect. 18.4 pointing to the insufficiency of the regulatory framework set out in the proposed Regulation and the lessons drawn from EU-Korea FTA to other trade agreement negotiations in the post-Lisbon era.

---

[10] Article 207(1) TFEU.

[11] Communication from the Commission to the Council, the European Parliament, the European Economic and Social Committee and the Committee of Regions: Towards a Comprehensive European International Investment Policy, COM (2010) 343 final.

[12] Proposal for a Regulation of the European Parliament and of the Council Establishing Transitional Arrangements for Bilateral Investment Agreements between Member States and third Countries, COM (2010) 344 final (hereafter as 'Proposed Transitional Arrangements Regulation').

18.2 The Phasing-In of FDI as CCP

In approaching FDI within the context of CCP, two independent issues need to be indentified: the legal status of prior-accession BITs and the resultant obligation to eliminate any incompatibilities contained therein with EU law; and the adjustment and rearrangement of these BITs as a result of the Union taking over this competence. The former has been partly dealt with through negotiations between new CEE Member States and third countries (notably the US) prior to their accession. Similar practices are also set in place in regard to their services commitments which are incorporated into the Union's services schedules leading to the ECJ's Opinion 1/08.

In addition to the negotiation approach, the Commission has also launched infringement proceedings against certain Member States for failing to eliminate incompatibilities and violating their obligations under Article 351(2) of the TFEU. With the entry into force of Lisbon Treaty, FDI has been merged into CCP and thus become an exclusive competence of the Union. Although FDI is not precisely defined and its scope remains unclear, its exclusivity prevents Member States from taking any related measures, even for the purpose of removing the contested incompatibilities.[13] This thus necessitates an empowering mechanism for Union to grant Member States the power to renegotiate with third countries or to denounce the BITs. Regarding those BITs where no incompatibilities were found, its legal certainty may still be endangered in that, while their legal validity remains intact under public international law, the Union may decide to terminate these BITs on the ground that they undermine the development and implementation of CCP. This causes a surging demand for a regulatory regime to deal with those transitional issues before the Union 'fills in the gap'. In response to the necessity for an empowerment mechanism and transitional regime, the Commission addressed this issue by proposing a draft Regulation to satisfy this regulatory demand.

This section examines the legal status of prior-accession agreements and subsequent adjustment and rearrangement, covering all relating political efforts, judicial proceedings and legislative attempts. I will draw particular attention to two of the most important prior-accession agreements: services trade commitments under the WTO, and BITs with the US.

18.2.1 Political Efforts Through Negotiation Along with Newly Acceded Member States

With ten CEE countries joining the Union in 2004, the Commission took great caution over the potential impact of their accession upon the EU legal order, in particular the Union's international obligations. In regards to investment related

[13] Dimopoulos (this volume) examines in more detail the types of FDI envisaged as part of the EU's new competence in Sect. 2.

issues, the Commission paid great attention to the BITs concluded by the CEE Member States with third countries, notably with the US which prompted the Commission to put forward an Understanding,[14] with the US on the one side, and the Commission and the acceding and candidate states on the other. As for trade related matters, the EU was concerned with the CEE Member States' commitments under the WTO, especially in relation to services trade. Compensation negotiations with interested WTO members to modify or withdraw the CEE Member States' services schedules were thus initiated and successfully concluded.

The understanding, in the preamble, firstly points to the contribution of the US BITs to investor confidence in these eight acceding and candidate states and the potential benefits that US investors may reap from the EU enlargement.[15] The understanding then underlines the need to balance the protection of investors' rights and the implementation of obligations resulting from the accession to the EU.[16] The understanding also stresses upon the full acceptance of *acquis communautaire* by the acceding states and the obligation to eliminate incompatibilities between *acquis* and their agreements with third countries.[17] The understanding highlights seven major issues and proposes appropriate interpretations or amendments to the US BITs. The seven issues are as followed: capital movements; performance requirements; measures in sensitive sectors or matters; obligations with respect to third countries arising from the EU membership; incompatibilities arising from future development of the EU law; the scope and operation of Article 48 EC[18]; and the protection of existing investments.[19] The understanding finally makes it clear that it constitutes only as a political arrangement reflecting the participants' intentions and that it is not a legal binding agreement under international law.[20] It also directs the acceding states to interpret and amend their BITs with the US no later than 30 April 2004, the date prior to their accession to Union.[21]

Regarding the services trade under the WTO framework, the Commission, under Article V:5 of the General Agreement on Trade in Services (GATS), filed on 28 May 2004 a list of envisaged commitments modifications and withdrawals to the WTO, with the aim to merge the services schedule of the 13 countries that had joined the Union in 1995 and 2004 into the existing schedules of the EC and of its

---

14 Understanding Concerning Certain US Bilateral Investment Treaties, signed by the US, the European Commission, and the acceding and candidate countries for their accession to the European Union, 22 September 2003, available at http://www.state.gov/s/l/2003/44366.htm (last accessed 04/01/2011). Those eight acceding and candidates states are Czech Republic, Estonia, Latvia, Lithuania, Poland, Slovak Republic, Bulgaria, and Romania.

15 US-EU Understanding, second and third preambular.

16 US-EU Understanding, fourth preambular.

17 US-EU Understanding, fifth preambular.

18 Article 48 EC, now Article 53 TFEU.

19 US-EU Understanding, Section I–VII.

20 US-EU Understanding, Concluding Provisions, para 1.

21 US-EU Understanding, Concluding Provisions, para 3.

Member States.[22] On 4 April 2005, the Commission further notified the WTO of its intension to withdraw from those commitments contained within the services schedules of Malta and Cyprus.[23]

When negotiations with interested WTO members under Article XXI of the GATS were successfully concluded, the Commission, the Council of the EU and the Member States had divergent views on the legal bases of the conclusions reached for these services agreements. The Commission claimed that, since the compensation adjustment contained in the services agreements did not go beyond the Community's internal powers and did not lead to harmonisation of the laws and regulations of the Member States in any area where the treaty excludes such harmonisation, the second subparagraph of Article 133(6) EC[24] is thus inapplicable, making that services agreements falling within the exclusive competence of the Community.[25] Nonetheless, this view was not shared by the Council or the Member States who asserted that Article 133(6) EC[26] should also be relied upon for the conclusion of these services agreements. When these services agreements relate to transport services, the Council and Member States argued that Article 71 and 80(2) EC[27] are also relevant.[28] While the debates continued, Member State's ratification processes had been taking place.[29]

The main issue before the Court was whether the Community, by virtue of Article 133(5) EC[30] that was inserted into the EC Treaty by the Treaty of Nice, has acquired exclusive competence in concluding the contested services trade agreements covering all four modes of services supply. A relevant issue is the correct interpretation of the relationship between Article 133(5) and 133(6) EC. The Court firstly clarified that, in interpreting the concept of 'trade in services' within the scope of the Community legal order, the GATS plays a particular importance function, owing both to its general nature and global level coverage. This is particular true in light of the term 'trade in services' which had been employed both within Article 133(6) EC and the GATS documents.[31] The Court therefore rejected the idea advanced by the United Kingdom that 'trade in services' should be limited solely to mode 2 (consumption abroad). Instead, the Court declares that

---

22 ECJ, Opinion 1/08, para 16.

23 ECJ, Opinion 1/08, para 16.

24 Art. 133(6) EC, now Art. 207(4) TFEU.

25 ECJ, Opinion 1/08, para 24.

26 Article 133(6) EC, second paragraph, now 207 (4) TEEU, third paragraph, indent (b).

27 Article 71 & 80(2) EC, now 91 & 100(2) TFEU.

28 ECJ, Opinion 1/08, para 69.

29 ECJ, Opinion 1/08, paras 25–26.

30 The regulation of 'trade in services' originally contained in Article 113 (5) EC is now merged into Article 207 (1) TFEU.

31 ECJ, Opinion 1/08, para 121.

it should also cover mode 3 (commercial presence)[32] and mode 4 (presence of natural persons).[33]

The Court then reaffirmed its decision in Opinion 1/94 where it held that mode 1 (cross-broader supply of services trade) shares the same features as trade in goods and falls within the scope of CCP under Article 133(1) EC,[34] consequently belonging to the exclusive competence of the Community.[35] The competence transferred to the Community by virtue of treaty revision at the Nice Treaty thus relates only to the other three modes of services supply.[36] The Court further emphasised that the scope of trade in services, being part of CCP and thus one of the exclusive competences of the Community by virtue of Article 133(5) EC, should be defined in accordance with Article 133(6) EC where cultural and audiovisual services, educational services, social and human health services are explicitly identified. In the view of the Court, it is evident through usage of words such as 'without prejudice to' as employed in Article 133(5) EC and 'by way of derogation' as employed in second subparagraph of Article 133(6) EC that the contested competences are to be shared by the Community and the Member States.[37] This nature of shared competence remains unaffected no matter how the contested services agreements regulate these areas (i.e., through horizontal or sectoral approaches). The court then assessed the balance between the need to establishing a coherent and efficient external commercial policy and a right of the Member States to defend their special interests in sensitive areas.[38] The unanimity requirement set out in Article 133(6) EC and the nature of shared competence are set in place to help with the maintaining of this balance. In regard to the contested services agreements covering these sensitive areas that by nature are shared competence, the court thus held that they should be jointly concluded by the Community and the Member States.

As far as CCP is concerned, even before the coming into force of the Lisbon Treaty, it is not true that the Community has had no role to play in investment policy. Among the four modes of services supply, the provision of services

[32] In delivering services trade under the GATS, there are four modes of services supply: mode 1 (cross-border supply); mode 2 (consumption abroad); mode 3 (commercial presence); and mode 4 (natural person presence). Mode 1 means the services are supplied from the territory of one member into that of another. A typical example of mode 1 may be the digital recording services done in one country and subsequently transmitted to another country. Mode 1 greatly resembles the conventional trade in goods. Mode 2 means the services are supplied in the territory of one member to the consumers of another member. A typical mode 2 service supply is to go abroad for receiving education or health services. Mode 4 is supplied by nationals of a member in the territory of another member, which necessitates the physical presence of the services provider in the host country. A typical example would be English teachers teaching abroad.

[33] ECJ, Opinion 1/08, para 122.

[34] Article 133(1) EC, now Article 207 (1) TFEU.

[35] ECJ, Opinion 1/08, para 118.

[36] ECJ, Opinion 1/08, para 122.

[37] ECJ, Opinion 1/08, paras. 132–133.

[38] ECJ, Opinion 1/08, paras. 134–135.

through mode 3 (commercial presence) by establishing an office, branch or subsidiary in a foreign country is in fact one of typical activities of FDI. Services trade proves to be one of the competences of the Community that is most closely related to FDI. According to the Opinion 1/94, mode 1 (cross-border supply) draws its legal basis from Article 133(1) EC while the other three modes of services supply are based on Article 133(5) EC. This in fact is an awkward position which the Lisbon Treaty aimed to remedy. The Lisbon Treaty thus merges these two paragraphs into one paragraph and deals with these subject matters under the framework of CCP.[39] With regard to these sensitive sectors (namely cultural and audiovisual services, social, education and human health services), they are also integrated into CCP though unanimity may be required during the decision-making processes wherever 'prejudice[ing] linguistic and cultural identity' or 'risk[ing] seriously disturbing the national organisation of such services and prejudicing the responsibility of Member States to deliver them'.[40] Nonetheless, it should be made clear that this does not change their exclusivity nature and Member States do not have an unconditional power.[41]

18.2.2 Judicial Litigation Through Infringement Proceedings

The efforts to eliminate the incompatibilities contained within the international agreements concluded by Member States prior to their accession to the Union are three-dimensional: in addition to the political approach through negotiations, the Commission also pursues this objective via infringement proceedings and legislative proposals. There are three cases on this subject matter that should be further examined. Before their accession to the Union in 1995, Austria, Sweden and Finland had entered into several BITs with third countries all of which contain a standard provision to ensure 'without undue delay, the free transfer, in free convertible currency, of payments connected with an investment'.[42]

Potential conflicts could have arisen given that certain EU Treaty provisions, notably Article 57(2), 59 and 60(1) EC,[43] allowed some conditions where the Commission could restrict the free movement of capital, for the purpose of taking safeguard measures or interrupting or reducing economic relations with third countries. Article 57(2) EC provided that 'the Council may, acting by a qualified majority on a proposal from the Commission, adopt measures on the movement of capital to or from third countries involving direct investment—including investment in real estate—establishment, the provision of financial services or the

---

[39] Article 207(1) TFEU.

[40] Article 207(4) TFEU, third subparagraph.

[41] Woolcock 2008, 4.

[42] ECJ, *Commission* v. *Austria*, para 3; *Commission* v. *Sweden*, para 3.

[43] These provisions are now found in Articles 64(2)&(3), 66, 75(1) TFEU respectively.

admission of securities to capital markets'. It further added that in the case of restrictive measures constituting as a step back for the Community on the issue of liberalising capital to/from third countries, unanimity would be required.[44] Article 59 EC was then an opportunity for the Union to take safeguard measures in exceptional circumstances where serious difficulties in the operation of Economic and Monetary Union (EMU) arose and these safeguard measures were strictly necessary. In these cases, safeguard measures may be adopted by the Council by qualified majority on a proposal from the Commission. In adopting these measures, the Council shall also consult the European Central Bank.[45] Article 60 EC then authorised the Community to take necessary urgent measures relating to the free movement of capital or to payments when the Member States have adopted a common position or a joint action under the Common Foreign and Security Policy (CFSP) and thus taken a Community action to interrupt or to reduce economic relations with third countries.

According to Article 307(1) EC, rights and obligations arising from an international agreement signed by an acceding Member State before its accession will remain unaffected. Yet, the next paragraph obliges the acceding Member to take all appropriate measures to eliminate incompatibilities with the EU law that have been agreed upon within international agreements concluded prior its accession. The pertinent provisions, namely Article 57(2), 59 and 60(1) EC, basically offered an opportunity for the Community to restrict free movement of capital for different reasons: to restrict free movement of capital to or from third countries involving direct investment, establishment, the provision of financial services, or the admission of securities to capital markets; to adopt safeguard measures for the operation of EMU; and to take Community actions in accordance with common positions or common attitude under the CFSP. Nonetheless, the standard provisions to ensure free movement of capital as contained within the BITs concluded by Austria, Sweden and Finland did not provide any space for these safeguards and restrictive measures. The Commission thus claimed that incompatibilities existed between those prior-accession international agreements concluded by the three countries and EU law. The Commission was also worried by the development of the arbitral proceedings taking place at the Arbitration Institute of the Stockholm Chamber of Commerce and the ISCID. After delivering a reasoned opinion to the three Member States, and after the parties failed to reach a satisfactory resolution, the Commission referred these disputes to the ECJ under Article 226 EC.[46]

The Advocate General Maduro and the Court approached this dispute differently. The former relied heavily on the duty of the loyal cooperation while the latter underlined the importance of the effectiveness of pertinent provisions in the EC Treaty. The Advocate General stated that three relevant issues need to be dealt with in this dispute: Whether there is a treaty obligation under the EC law; whether

[44] Article 57(2) EC, now Article 64(3) TFEU.

[45] Article 59 EC, now Article 66 TFEU.

[46] Article 226 EC, now Article 258 TFEU.

there is a conflicting international obligation stemming from investment agreements; and in case that the incompatibilities exist, is there any mechanism for Austria and Sweden to employ to adequately address them?[47]

According to Advocate General Maduro, the pertinent provisions are meant to empower the Community to act, giving rise to treaty obligations only when these provisions are part of the exclusive competence of the Community, which was not the case in this dispute.[48] Nonetheless, the Advocate General found the treaty obligations stemming from the duty of loyal cooperation as enshrined in Article 10 EC. And, in view of Advocate General Maduro, Article 307 EC is an explicit expression of this duty.[49] By drawing a parallel with the obligations of the Member States during the period for implementing directives, the Advocate General argued that Member States are under an obligation not to 'jeopardise a Community objective'.[50] The Advocate General then clarified that it is unnecessary to avoid all possibilities which may jeopardise the Community objective because in effect it would turn shared competence into exclusive competence. The obligation arises only 'where the national measures or the international obligations of member states are liable to jeopardise the effectiveness of possible future Community legislation and, in doing so, *de facto* restrict the freedom which the Treaty confers on the Community to act in those areas'.[51] This in turn will depend on the nature of the national measures or the international obligations in question and the Community competences affected.[52] In examining the urgent nature of safeguard measures and the potential undermining of the Community legislation's effectiveness in prior-accession international agreements, the Advocate General found these agreements liable to seriously compromise the exercise of Community competence. He then emphasised the obligation for Member States to 'take all appropriate steps to prevent their pre-existing international obligations from jeopardising the exercise of Community competence'.[53]

Based on this reasoning, the Advocate General further found incompatibilities between Austria's and Sweden's treaty obligations under EU law and their obligations under international agreements before they joined the Union. He also concluded that the arguments put forward by Sweden and Austria, by applying principles of international law, notably *rebus sic stantibus* or *clausularebus sic stantibus*, were not sufficient to resolve those incompatibilities.[54]

---

47 Opinion of Advocate General Poiares Maduro delivered on 10 July 2008, ECJ, *Commission* v *Austria & Commission* v. *Sweden*, [2009] *ECR I-01301,* para 19.

48 Opinion of Advocate General Maduro, para 28.

49 Opinion of Advocate General Maduro, para 33.

50 Opinion of Advocate General Maduro, para 39.

51 Opinion of Advocate General Maduro, para 40.

52 Opinion of Advocate General Maduro, para 40.

53 Opinion of Advocate General Maduro, para 42.

54 Opinion of Advocate General Maduro, paras 57–62.

In contrast, the Court's reasoning mainly relied on the basis of the effectiveness of Community measures taken under the said provisions. According to the Court, in order to ensure the effectiveness of those provisions, measures restricting free movement of capital must be capable of being applied immediately.[55] These measures may impact those third countries that have BITs with these three Member States. Since the Council can unilaterally adopts restrictive measures in certain subject-matters which may be identical or connected to those contained within the prior-accession agreements, incompatibilities exist because 'first, the agreement does not contain a provision allowing the Member State concerned to exercise its rights and to fulfil its obligations as a member of the Community and, second, there is also no international-law mechanism which makes that possible'.[56] The Court then concluded that by not taking the appropriate steps to eliminate incompatibilities concerning the provisions on the transfer of capital contained in the investment agreements signed by Austria and Sweden before it joined the Union, they have failed to fulfil their obligations under Article 307(2) of the EC Treaty.[57]

In commenting on the cases, Koutrakos argued that the Advocate General's emphasis on the nature of shared competence does not help to resolve the dispute since the issue before the Court is not one relating to the Member States' exercising of power reserved by the Community. Rather, the pertinent issue is whether the conduct of Member States before their accession to the Union would undermine the effectiveness of the exceptional measures that the Community may take. Therefore, in view of Koutrakos, the starting point of analysis is to ascertain the nature of the relevant Community rules and their implications to Community actions.[58] However, Koutrakos does not find the Court's reasoning based on effectiveness persuasive. Interestingly, citing Maduro's words that the loss of effectiveness is less clear, Koutrakos argues that the Court's decision may lends the Commission too wide discretion in forcing the Member States to renegotiate or denounce their prior-accession BITs based on a criterion too uncertain and indeterminate, whereas the effects resulting therefrom are too onerous and drastic.[59]

Similarly, Denza also cautions against the potential loss instead of gains of the Union's interests as a result of the Court's decision. She firstly points to the entry into force of the Lisbon Treaty, shortly after the handing down of the Court's decision and highlights the huge amount of BITs currently maintained by Member States of which Austria, Sweden and Finland only take a tiny share. Even though the Member States are enabled to renegotiate with third countries or to denounce the BITs with the aim of eliminating incompatibilities contained therein with EU

[55] *Commission* v. *Austria*, para 36.

[56] *Commission* v. *Austria*, para 37.

[57] *Commission* v. *Austria*, para 45; *Commission* v. *Sweden*, para 45.

[58] Koutrakos 2009, 2067.

[59] Koutrakos 2009, 2067.

law, it would never be an easy task.[60] These challenges identified by Denza thus calls for a great demand of a regulatory regime leading to the Commission's legislative proposals.

18.2.3 A Regulatory Framework as a Solution?

With the Lisbon Treaty entering into force, FDI has become part of CCP and thus fallen within the scope of Union's exclusive competence. The redistribution of competences gives rise to some legal problems. On the one hand, the ECJ in *Commission* v. *Austria* and *Commission* v. *Sweden* makes it clear that Member States are under an obligation to eliminate the incompatibilities as contained in their BITs concluded before their accession to the Union. On the other hand, given the nature of exclusivity, Member States are prevented from legislating or acting of their own accord. This necessitates a mechanism for the Union to empower Member States to enter into negotiations with third countries with the aim to modifying existent agreements. Further, Member States may find it desirable to negotiate or conclude new BITs with third countries. In response to this demand, the Commission proposes a Regulation to regulate the legal status of the BITs signed by Member States before FDI became a part of CCP and to formulate a framework to empower Member States to legislate or adopt legally binding acts in that regard.

The proposed Regulation, in its third recital, firstly makes it clear that the BITs concluded by Member States before FDI become exclusive competence of the Union, remain binding on Member States under public international law, but at the same time, it also stresses that these BITs will be progressively replaced by future Union agreements relating to the same subject-matter. The proposed Regulation then points to the need to regulate the conditions for the continual existence of these BITs and their relationship with other Union's policies having a bearing on FDI, particularly CCP.[61] The same spirit is reflected in Article 1 of the proposed Regulation that spells out its subject matter and scope: the proposed Regulation is to 'establish the terms, conditions, and the procedure under which Member States are authorised to maintain in force, amend or conclude bilateral agreements with third countries relating to investment'.[62] The proposed Regulation subsequently regulates topics such as 'maintain in force' (Chapter II) and 'amend or conclude bilateral agreements' (Chapter III).

It would be interesting to note that while recognising the legal binding effects of the BITs under public international law, the proposed Regulation designates an authorisation mechanism for these BITs to maintain in force. In other words, if the

---

[60] Denza 2010, 269–271.

[61] Proposed Transitional Arrangements Regulation, 4th recital.

[62] Proposed Transitional Arrangements Regulation, Article 1.

BITs are still binding, nothing has to be done for them to maintain in force. The rationale put forward by the Commission in the explanatory note lies mainly on legal certainty. In this line, the Commission prefers to spell out the legal binding nature of these pre-existing BITs through a legal instrument, instead of a soft law instrument such as a declaration or statement by the Commission.[63] By virtue of authorisation, the proposed Regulation aims to reduce the legal uncertainty which might undermine investment confidence. Nonetheless, this authorisation is subject to withdrawal under the conditions set out in Article 6.

In cases where an agreement conflicts with the law of the Union, other than the incompatibilities arising from the re-allocation of competence, overlaps with an agreement of the Union, or constitutes an obstacle to the development and implementation of the Union's policies relating to investment, including in particular CCP,[64] such authorisation may be withdrawn by the Commission. Article 6(1)(d) then deals with a particular condition for the withdrawal of authorisation: an agreement signed by the Member States and notified to the Commission under Article 2(1) of which the scope overlaps with the envisaged agreement to be negotiated under the CFSP.[65] When the Commission decides to withdraw this authorisation, it shall deliver a reasoned opinion and enter into a consultation with the Member State concerned.[66] The Commission may nevertheless unilaterally withdraw the authorisation when the consultation cannot reach any mutually-satisfactory results.[67] In this decision-making process, the Commission is to be assisted by an Advisory Committee.[68]

Chapter III of the proposed Regulation further regulates the procedures and conditions for the Commission to authorise Member States to open and conclude the BITs. Member States that wish to amend or to conclude an agreement, or to enter into a new agreement with third countries on investment related matters needs to notify the Commission with relevant information, including the objectives of the negotiations and the specific provisions to be addressed.[69] The requested authorisation is usually granted unless the opening negotiations will be interpreted as 'be[ing] in conflict with the law of the Union', 'undermin[ing] the objectives of negotiations underway or imminent between the Union and the third country concerned' or 'constitut[ing] an obstacle to the development and the implementation of Union's policies relating to investment, including in particular the common commercial policy',[70] and thus do not satisfy the conditions as set out for in Article 9(1) of the proposed Regulation.

---

63 Commission Proposal, 2.

64 Proposed Transitional Arrangements Regulation, Article 6(1)(a–c).

65 Proposed Transitional Arrangements Regulation, Article 6(1)(d).

66 Proposed Transitional Arrangements Regulation, Article 6(2).

67 Proposed Transitional Arrangements Regulation, Article 6(3).

68 Proposed Transitional Arrangements Regulation, Article 15(1).

69 Proposed Transitional Arrangements Regulation, Article 8(2).

70 Proposed Transitional Arrangements Regulation, Article 9(1).

Even if the authorisation has been granted, in the course of the negotiations, the Commission needs to be informed of the progress and the result of the negotiation; if needed, the Commission should be allowed to participate in the negotiations.[71] When the negotiations come to an end, the Member State concerned should notify the Commission of the result of the negotiations and transmit a copy of the documents.[72] The Commission should authorise the Member State concerned to sign and conclude the agreement unless it finds that the four conditions set out in Article 11(3) have not been fulfilled. The first three conditions are identical to the aforementioned three conditions as contained in Article 9(1); the forth condition relates to special requirements, if any, laid down by the Commission when giving its authorisation for the Member State to open the negotiations.

If one looks closer into the conditions to authorise to 'maintain in force, amend or conclude' BITs with a third country relating to investment, one may find that the main concern is not to frustrate the objectives of Union policies. The existence of conflicts between those BITs concluded by Member States and the EU law would compromise the Union policies; the same applies when a Member State's BIT discourages the third country concerned from negotiating or concluding a BIT with the Union. All these circumstances would jeopardise the Union's objectives. In a word, the maintaining, amending or concluding of the BITs with third countries should never constitute an obstacle to the development and implementation of the Union's policies relating to investment. Among those Union's policies, CCP is pertinent. As the proposed Regulation makes it clear, those BITs concluded by Member States have a great impact on the formulation and functioning of CCP. The potential adverse effects thereon should thus be carefully assessed and closely monitored.

In view of the third countries, the Commission's decision on whether or not to authorise the Member States to 'maintain in force, amend or conclude' BITs with third countries brings about concerns on legal certainty. In commenting the proposed Regulation, Woolcock points to the potential impact of rejecting or endorsing the Commission proposal. On the one hand, the rejection of this proposal risks of the legal certainty of these BITs concluded by Member States during the transitional period. On the other hand, endorsing the proposal would lead to granting an extremely wide discretionary power to the Commission which may also undermine legal certainty. He thus proposes that the regulatory procedure take a comitological approach, a good vehicle to balance Member States' interest in ensuring a smooth transition and the European general public's interests in ensuring the transparent and democratic nature of the decision-making process.[73]

In addition to the individual option, namely through the Union's authorisation to individual Member States to maintain, amend or denounce the BITs they concluded, the collective option through the joint efforts of the Union initiatives

---

[71] Proposed Transitional Arrangements Regulation, Article 10.

[72] Proposed Transitional Arrangements Regulation, Article 11(1).

[73] Woolcock 2010, 68–70.

has also proposed by Ghouri.[74] In view of the treaty revision that assigns FDI to be an exclusive competence of the Union, there seems to be a strong case for this collective option. However, given the number of BITs concluded by the Member States and complexities involved, it would not be so easy for the Union to take its first step.

18.3 FDI as an New Impetus for the EU to Compete n the World

In this section, I will explore whether FDI can add new impetus to CCP for the Union to compete in the world. I will firstly review major policy shifts from the 'Lisbon Strategy' to the 'Europe 2020 Strategy', including the Global Europe Communication[75] which plays an important factor in defining the role of CCP. I will then proceed to examine whether the designation of FDI as part of CCP can enhance the Union's strengthen in multilateral negotiations under the WTO framework and in the Union's bilateral FTA talks.

18.3.1 From the Lisbon Strategy to Europe 2020 Strategy

At the Lisbon European Council held in 2000 three strategic goals, namely strengthened employment, economic reform and social cohesion, were identified as major themes of the Lisbon Strategy. The strategy sets the Union's strategic goals from 2000 to 2010: to 'become the most competitive and dynamic knowledge-based economy in the world, capable of sustainable economic growth with more and better jobs and greater social cohesion'.[76] One of the major objectives of the Lisbon Strategy was thus to enhance the Union's competitiveness in the global world. In the context of renewed Lisbon Strategy from 2005 onwards, 'Global Europe Communication' aimed to contribute to the Union's growth and jobs opportunities and to help the Union to complete in the world. Global Europe Communication stressed the intertwining relationship between internal market policy and external market opening.[77] One the major features of the Global Europe Communication was the Union's lift of the *de facto* moratorium on FTA negotiations.[78] Global Europe Communication then sets out two criteria for the priority

---

74 Ghouri 2010, 8/26–829.

75 Global Europe: Competing in the World: A Contribution to the EU's Growth and Jobs Strategy.

76 Presidency Conclusions 2000, para 5 (emphasis original).

77 Global Europe, 4–8.

78 Bungenberg 2010, 129.

to commencing FTA talks: the market potential and level of protection. Based on these two criteria, the Republic of Korea, the Association of Southeast Asian Nations (ASEAN) and the South Common Market (Mercosur) have been identified as the priorities, while India and Russia and Gulf Cooperation Council should also be considered.[79] As for China, given the combined complexities stemming from the opportunities and risks presented, the Commission has opted for a sectoral approach, focusing on intellectual property rights enforcement, market access strategy and investment opportunities.[80]

One decade since the Lisbon Strategy, the Commission then proposed its 'Europe 2020' Strategy[81] as its main policy blueprint for the following decade where smart, sustainable and inclusive growth is prioritised. According to the Europe 2020 Strategy, the Union's growth should be smart by 'developing an economy based on knowledge and innovation'[82]; the growth would be sustainable by 'prompting a more resource efficient, greener and more competitive economy'[83]; the growth must be inclusive by 'fostering a high-employment economy delivering social and territorial cohesion'.[84] Similar to the Lisbon Strategy, the Commission's major concerns lie in creating sustainable economic growth via knowledge innovation and thus contributing to employment opportunities.[85] In the Europe 2020 Strategy, enhancing the Union's competitiveness remains to be one of the major objectives.[86] At the same time, the Commission also makes it clear that trade policy is a core component of the Europe 2020 Strategy and its scope must be broadened to keep its competitive edge. This includes, inter alia, trade and investment policies.[87] In addition to developing a comprehensive investment policy, the Commission also 'seek[s] to integrate investment protection together with investment liberalisation into ongoing trade negotiations'.[88] The Commission then adds that it will soon propose updating the relevant negotiating directives, starting with Singapore, Canada and India, to include a wider scope of investment issues. Stand-alone investment agreements with third countries, such as China, will also be taken into consideration.[89]

In the Commission's Communication entitled 'Towards a Comprehensive European International Investment Policy', the Commission views investment as a

[79] Global Europe, 11.
[80] Global Europe, 13.
[81] Commission, Europe 2020: A Strategy for Smart, Sustainable and Inclusive Growth, Communication from the Commission, COM (2010) 2020 final.
[82] Europe 2020 Strategy, 10.
[83] Europe 2020 Strategy, 10.
[84] Europe 2020 Strategy, 10.
[85] Europe 2020 Strategy, 10.
[86] Europe 2020 Strategy, 14.
[87] Trade, Growth, and World Affairs, 6.
[88] Trade, Growth, and World Affairs, 6.
[89] Trade, Growth, and World Affairs, 6.

new frontier for CCP. Reflecting the inclusion of investment with the CCP, the Commission's Communication clearly places investment policy at its heart. According to the Commission, this would increase EU competitiveness and contribute to the objectives of smart, sustainable and inclusive growth as set out in the Europe 2020 Strategy.[90] The Commission also points to its efforts on investments both at the multilateral and bilateral level. At the multilateral level, the commitments on the supply of services through mode 3 have been brought under the GATS. At the bilateral level, the newly concluded EU-Korea FTA also covers provisions relating to market access for investors and establishments.[91] The major message signalled in this Communication is that, for the Commission, the criteria for prioritising Union's BIT negotiations depend highly on the actual trade and investment flows.[92] According to the Commission, in the short term, investment can be integrated into CCP through the inclusion of investment into ongoing trade negotiations. Currently, market access is limited to investors. Widening the scope of investment issues can help the Union to unleash the market potential in both trade and investment. The Commission then targets Canada, Singapore, India and Mercosur for competitiveness-driven FTA or trade and investment talks.[93] The Commission further adds that, in the short to medium term, stand-alone investment agreements may be desirable for China. Investment negotiations in the context of a compressive agreement replacing the existent Partnership and Cooperation Agreement with Russia may also be pursued.[94]

18.3.2 Investment in the Multilateral Trading System

Even before the Union obtains its exclusive competence in FDI, it is not unprecedented for the Union to approach subject-matter pertaining to investment within the WTO framework. As noted earlier in this chapter, mode 3 services supply (commercial presence), is an interconnected area between services trade and investment. The WTO's Agreement on Trade-related Investment Measures (TRIMs) also deals with investment measures related to trade in goods.[95] It also includes an illustrative list of measures which are considered inconsistent with the national treatment requirement as set out in Article III: 4 of the GATT 1994. During the 1996 Singapore Ministerial Conference, a set of issues on investment, competition, government procurement and trade facilitation, which are commonly called the Singapore issues, were set out in the negotiation agenda. The Union was

90 Trade, Growth, and World Affairs, 1.

91 Towards a Comprehensive European International Investment Policy, 5.

92 Towards a Comprehensive European International Investment Policy, 6.

93 Towards a Comprehensive European International Investment Policy, 7.

94 Towards a Comprehensive European International Investment Policy, 7.

95 Agreement on Trade-related Investment Measures, Article 1.

one of the proponents for the inclusion of investment policy into the WTO framework. Nonetheless, these Singapore issues, except trade facilitation, were dropped off from the Doha Development Agenda (DDA) on 1 August 2004.[96] It would thus be interesting to ask whether the Union's acquisition of FDI competence will add anything to the multilateral trading system. The answer would be a very pessimistic one. Given that the current DDA has already had enough troubles, it is hard to imagine making the situation even more complex by bringing investment issue back onto the table. Therefore, the game in the multilateral trading system seems to remain more or less unchanged, no matter whether the EU has exclusive competence on FDI or not.[97] This should be nevertheless attributed to mostly, if not all, to the current WTO negotiation scheme and has less to do with the EU.

18.3.3 Investment Elements in EU External Agreements

Compared to the limited role played in the multilateral trading system, the inclusion of FDI into CCP offers a greater potential to exploit in the Union's external trade agreements. In fact, before the Union obtains its exclusive competence in FDI, the Union had already inserted investment policy into its FTA and Economic Partnership Agreements (EPAs) talks. Provisions contained in these FTAs and EPAs are closely related to the notion of establishment, generally understood as the setting up of a permanent presence in another country with the aim to engaging in economic activities other than of a salaried character, covering 'both the constitution of a legal persons and the setting-up of an undertaking, a branch or a representative office for the purposes of performing an economic activity'.[98]

In addition, the Council adopted the 'Minimum Platforms on Investments for EU Free Trade Agreements (hereafter as 'MPoI') on 27 November 2006.[99] The MPoI serves as a basis for negotiations on trade in services and establishment (investment) in EU bilateral trade negotiations; it is a standardised negotiation proposal for ongoing and future FTA negotiation with third countries pertaining to

---

[96] Understanding the WTO: Cross-Cutting and New Issues: Investment, competition, procurement, simpler procedures. www.wto.org/english/thewto_e/whatis_e/tif_e/bey3_e.htm. Accessed 20 July 2011. See also Cardwell and French 2011, 213.

[97] Another interesting question to ask is whether the Member States are obliged to withdraw from the WTO given that the Union has acquired exclusive competence on trade in services and commercial aspects of intellectual property rights. This question needs to be dealt with on two levels. In addition to the EU law level, it is also important to examine the possibility and, subsequently, feasibility for the Member States to withdraw from the WTO. See also, Bungenberg 2010, 133–135.

[98] Ceyssens 2005, 275.

[99] Council of the European Union, 15376/06, 27 November 2006.

services trade and investment. The coming into being of the MPoI demonstrates the Union's ambition to play a more proactive role in investment issues and suggests a far-reaching investment chapter to be included in the EU external economic agreements. It may go well beyond investment liberalisation and cover ambitious investment protection provisions.[100]

Prior the coming into force of the Lisbon Treaty, the EC-Chile Association Agreement[101] is an illustrative example since it contains the most number of investment issues, ranging from investment liberalisation to investment protection. In the post-Lisbon era, it is worthy to follow the EC-Indonesia PCA[102] and EU-Korea FTA[103] developments, given that ASEAN and Korea are among the priorities set out in 'Global Europe Communication'. I will thus examine provisions relating to investment as contained in these agreements.

The EC-Chile Association Agreement includes a whole list of titles that regulate trade in services and establishment,[104] aiming at liberalising trade in services in accordance with Article V of the GATS[105] and improving the investment environments, particularly the conditions for establishment on the basis of non-discrimination principle.[106] Establishment is defined as: '(i) the constitution, acquisition or maintenance of a legal person, or (ii) the creation or maintenance of a branch or a representative office, within the territory of a Party for the purpose of performing an economic activity'.[107] The Agreement then clarifies that establishment, insofar as natural persons are concerned, should not 'extend to seeking or taking employment in the labour market' or 'confer a right of access to the labour market' of a contracting party.[108] Establishment, as part of trade and trade-related matters, is subject to the dispute settlement mechanism which has jurisdiction on the interpretation and application of these subject-matters, unless expressed otherwise.[109] The dispute settlement mechanism provided therein is mainly state-to-state nature; investor-state arbitral procedures are not covered. Admittedly, the scope of the establishment as covered within the EU-Chile Association Agreement is rather limited and the procedural protection to investors is not as comprehensive

[100] Eilmansberger 2009, 393.

[101] Agreement Establishing an Association between the European Community and its Member States, of the one part, and the Republic of Chile, of the other part, OJ L 352/1, 30 November 2002.

[102] Proposal for a Council Decision on the signing of the Framework Agreement on comprehensive and Cooperation between the European Community and its Member States, of the one part, and the Republic of Indonesia, of the other part, COM (2009) 492 final.

[103] Free Trade Agreement between the European Union and its Member States, of the one part, and the Republic of Korea, of the other part, OJ L 124/6, 14 May 2011.

[104] EC-Chile Association Agreement, title III.

[105] EC-Chile Association Agreement, Article 94(1).

[106] EC-Chile Association Agreement, Article 94(2).

[107] EC-Chile Association Agreement, Article 131(1)(d).

[108] EC-Chile Association Agreement, Article 131(2).

[109] EC-Chile Association Agreement, Article 182.

as those typically found in BITs (investor-state arbitrations). Nonetheless, it is clear that even before the Union obtained its exclusive competence in FDI, investment policy was not completely absent from the Union's external agreements, regardless of the mixed characteristic of the agreements.

In the EC-Indonesia PCA, investment policy also played a role. However, the investment provision covered therein is more economic cooperation like in nature than in the form of legally binding commitments. Article 14 of the EC-Indonesia PCA provides that 'the Parties shall encourage a greater flow of investment through the development of an attractive and stable environment for reciprocal investment through a consistent dialogue aimed at enhancing understanding and cooperation on investment issues, exploring administrative mechanisms to facilitate flows, and promoting a stable, transparent, open and non-discriminatory investment regime'.[110] The EU-Indonesia PCA underlines the encouragement of greater investment flow, facilitation of administrative mechanism and establishment of a sound investment regime. The primitiveness of these investment provisions may be explained by the fact that the EC-Indonesia PCA is an agreement setting out the framework for cooperation between the EU and Indonesia. Substantive liberalisation commitments will be covered in the envisaged EU-Indonesia FTA.

The EU-Korea FTA includes, as it currently stands, the most comprehensive investment provisions when compared to the other EU external trade agreements. It follows the same definition of 'establishment' as contained in the EC-Chile Association Agreement, but the footnote 9 within clarifies that the 'constitution' and 'acquisition' of a juridical person should include 'capital participation in a juridical person with a view to establishing or maintaining lasting economic links'.[111] The EU-Korea FTA also defines the meaning of 'investor' and 'economic activity'.[112] Article 7.10 then defines the scope of the economic activities by excluding the application to five sensitive sectors: mining, manufacturing and processing of nuclear materials; production of, or trade in, arms, munitions and war material; audio–visual services; national maritime cabotage; and domestic and international air transport services and services directly related to the exercise of traffic rights.[113]

---

[110] EC-Indonesian PCA, Article 14. Similar arrangement can be found in Article 16 of EU-Philippines PCA. Proposal for a Council Decision on the signing of the Framework Agreement on Partnership and Cooperation between the European Union and its Member States, of the one part and the Republic of the Philippines, COM 460 final, Brussels 6 September 2010. The EU-Vietnam PCA, in Article 17, provides similar regulation. Proposal for a Council Decision on the signing of the Framework Agreement on Comprehensive Partnership and Cooperation between the European Union and its Member States, on the one part, and the Socialist Republic of Vietnam, of the other part, COM (2010) 699 final, 29 November 2010.

[111] EU-Korea FTA, footnote 9 to chap. 7.

[112] EU-Korea FTA, Article 7.9 (b), (c).

[113] EU-Korea FTA, Article 7.10.

Article 7.11 of the EU-Korea FTA then addresses market access of establishment. A schedule containing the commitments is annexed to the agreement with the specified terms, limitations and conditions agreed upon by both Parties; investors and establishments should be accorded treatment no less than that provided for therein. In those sectors where specific commitments have been undertaken, six categories of measures are explicitly prohibited: limitation of the number of establishments, total value of transaction or assets, total number of operations or total quantity of output, participation of foreign capital in terms of maximum percentage or total value, total number of natural persons, or restriction or requirement on specific types of legal entity or joint venture.[114]

In addition to market access aspect, the EU-Korea FTA, in Articles 7.12 and 7.14 prescribes national treatment and MFN treatment to be accorded to establishments and investors of the other Party. According to Article 7.12(1), in those sectors where the Parties have undertaken commitments, the Parties are obliged to provide treatment no less favourable than that accorded to its own like establishments and investors with regard to all measures affecting establishment.[115] The subsequent paragraphs then clarifies that to meet with the requirement of 'no less favourable than' may take the form of formally identical or formally different treatment[116] on the condition that the treatment concerned does not modify the 'condition of competition' between the establishments or investors of one Party and like establishments or investors of the other Party.[117] However, if a competitive disadvantage is inherently resulted from the foreign character of the relevant establishments or investors, a Party is not required to compensate it.[118] In a word, the key to determine whether a treatment is 'less than favourable' lies not in the formality of the treatments, being identical or different but in the substantive 'condition of competition'. Given that the Parties are not liable to the disadvantage resulting inherently from the foreign character of an establishment or investor, this disadvantage should not be factored for the consideration of the 'condition of competition'. Regarding MFN treatment, each Party should grant treatment to establishments and investors no less favourable than that granted to like establishments and investors of any third country in the context of an economic integration agreement signed after the coming into force of this EU-Korea FTA.[119] The following paragraph then provides exception in three areas and a general exception for economic integration agreements with 'a significantly higher level of obligations'. These three areas of exception to MFN treatment relates to: recognition of qualifications, licenses, or prudential measures; taxation; and the MFN exemption list as set out in Annex 7-C. Treatments granted to establishments and

[114] EU-Korea FTA, Article 7.11.2.

[115] EU-Korea FTA, Article 7.12.1.

[116] EU-Korea FTA, Article 7.12.2.

[117] EU-Korea FTA, Article 7.12.3.

[118] EU-Korea FTA, Article 7.12.4.

[119] EU-Korea FTA, Article 7.14.1.

investors of third countries on the basis of sectoral or horizontal commitments of the economic integration agreements with 'a significantly higher level of obligations' than those provided in the establishment section as set out in Annex 7-B (MFN Exemption Annex) also constitutes an exception to the MFN treatment.

As clarified by the MFN Exemption Annex, to satisfy the threshold of 'a significantly higher level', obligations prescribed by a regional integration agreement should either 'create an internal market on services and establishment'[120] or 'encompass both the right of establishment and the approximation of legislation'.[121] The evaluation of the level of obligations should be conducted on either sectoral or horizontal basis.[122] The footnote to this provision then defines 'an internal market on services and establishments' to be 'an area without internal frontiers in which the free movement of services, capital and persons is ensured'[123] and specifies that the only internal market on services and establishment with third countries that the EU maintains at the time of signature is the European Economic Area.[124]

The MFN Exemption Annex then, in Article 1(a) and 1(b), provides further guidance on 'right of establishment' and 'approximation of legislation'. The right of establishment means that, when coming into force of an economic integration agreement, all Parties are obliged to 'abolish in substance all barriers to establishment' among them. Such right of establishment should include the rights of nationals of the Parties to the said integration agreement to 'set up and manage undertakings' under the conditions laid down for nationals of the host countries.[125] The approximation of legislation may take the form of alignment of legislation among the Parties or incorporation of common legislation into the legal order of the Parties to the said integration agreement.[126]

Finally, According to Article 14.2, unless otherwise provided, such as the Protocol on Cultural Cooperation, the dispute settlement chapter applies in any dispute arising from the interpretation and application of the EU-Korea FTA. Therefore, a dispute arising from the interpretation and applications of this establishment section may be referred to this dispute settlement mechanism. Unsurprisingly, it contains only state-to-state dispute settlement mechanism; investor-state arbitration is not available.

Compared to the investment provisions as contained in the EU-Chile Association Agreement and EU-Indonesia PCA, the EU-Korea FTA sets out more ambitious investment liberalisation package and substantive investment rules.

---

[120] EU-Korea FTA, Annex 7-B (MFN Exemption Annex), Article 1, first sentence.

[121] EU-Korea FTA, Annex 7-B (MFN Exemption Annex), Article 1, first sentence.

[122] EU-Korea FTA, Annex 7-B (MFN Exemption Annex), Article 1, second sentence.

[123] EU-Korea FTA, Annex 7-B (MFN Exemption Annex), footnote to Article 1.

[124] EU-Korea FTA, Annex 7-B (MFN Exemption Annex), footnote to Article 1.

[125] EU-Korea FTA, Annex 7-B (MFN Exemption Annex), Article 1(a).

[126] EU-Korea FTA, Annex 7-B (MFN Exemption Annex), Article 1(b).

Three categories of measures in those areas where market access commitments are made are explicitly prohibited, including economic needs test. A well tailored criterion is set out for in ascertaining whether national treatment obligation is infringed. While stretching the MFN treatment to other integration agreements, the EU also provides a safeguard for the EEA agreement. In view of the expectation put forward in the Commission's investment communication, the state-to-state dispute settlement mechanism does not appear as satisfactory. However, it would difficult to imagine how the EU can include an investor-state dispute settlement mechanism when the EU internally has not been able to agree upon the content of the new obtained competence on FDI. Being the first FTA signed in the post-Lisbon era, the EU-Korea FTA demonstrates the EU's ambition to exploit its new competence on FDI as leverage to pursue the competitiveness driven FTA. This model may be followed by the ongoing EU-Singapore and EU-India FTA talks. The EU-Singapore FTA will merit particular attention given its highly-developed services industry. Nonetheless, the constraints on the EU-Korea FTA in relation to the dispute settlement mechanism may persist unless the EU and its Member States can work out a clear definition of the FDI and the way to exercise this competence.

18.4 Conclusion

This chapter has investigated the potential strength of CCP with its expansion to encompass FDI. It examines the course of integrating of FDI into CCP through political negotiations, judicial proceeding and legislative proposal. While the successful conclusion of the Understanding and Services Agreement helped to reduce the complexities relating to Investment issue and Services trade resulting from the enlargement of the Union, the Commission was not completely comfortable with the uniformity of EU legal order. This threat prompted the Commission to commence infringement proceedings against those three Members joining the Union in the 1990s, namely, Austria, Sweden and Finland. Sharing the same sense of insecurity of the EU legal order, the Court relied upon the effectiveness of pertinent provisions and found against the three Member States on the ground that they failed to eliminate the incompatibilities of their prior-accession agreements with EU law and thus violated their obligations as set out in Article 302(2) EC or 351(2) TFEU. Whereas the Court's decisions have merit in pressing the Member States to amend or renegotiate their BITs with third countries, it has also jeopardised the Member States since they are no longer in a position to act as the Lisbon Treaty assigns FDI, being part of CCP, to an element of the Union's exclusive competence. This thus necessitates a regulatory regime to facilitate the transitional process and the Commission thus proposed a regulation to meet with this regulatory demand.

While this regulatory regime might contribute to the legal certainty of the BITs concluded by the Member States with third countries, it would not be able to achieve the objectives set out in the Commission's Investment Communication since substantive elements pertaining to investment, such as the scope and coverage of FDI, are missing. Even the authorisation mechanism, a core element of the Proposed Transitional Arrangement Regulation, lacks in clear-defined criteria and procedures which would undermine not only the interests of third countries and their investors but also those of the Union. In view of third countries and their investors, the complicated EU structure, including its decision-making and functioning has already made it extremely difficult to comprehend. The loosely-defined authorisation criteria and the procedural imprecision and inaccuracy pose great challenges to investor confidence. From the perspective of the Union, it would take a long time to fill the gap by positioning and supplementing BITs concluded by Member State with Union-level BITs. If the Union is too eager to exercise its long awaited competence, the risk is that this would damage rather than enhance the interests of the Union.

After analysing the processing of integration FDI into CCP, this chapter also explored whether the expansion of CCP can enhance the Union's negotiation power in the multilateral WTO framework and in its bilateral FTA talks. I argue that the relevance of investment issues within the WTO landscape seems to be limited; however, this is mostly due to the constraints of this multilateral trading framework and has little to do with the EU. In contrast, there is an aggressive expansion of investment issues in EU's bilateral trade agreements. The inclusion of the investment issues in the trade negotiations contributes to the smooth transition of the Union's taking over the FDI as the Union has long exercised its exclusive competence on CCP. Building upon its experiences of CCP, the EU may pave its way to stand-alone Union-BITs through FTAs with ambitious investment chapters. As FDI is situated in the broader context of CCP, the Commission may also make sure that it would continue to lead in the key issues.

Compared to the EU-Chile Association Agreement and EU-Indonesia PCA, the EU-Korea FTA includes more ambitious market access commitments and substantive obligations on national treatment and MFN treatment. With the conclusion of the EU-Korea FTA, one of the priorities set out in the Global Europe strategy has been achieved. Being the first FTA in the post-Lisbon era, the EU-Korea FTA has also fulfilled with the short-term objective of the Commission Investment Communication and Europe 2020 Strategy by integrating FDI into trade negotiations. The EU-Korea FTA is also an evidence on how this integration approach facilitates the transition of the EU's taking over of FDI competence and the Commission's identification of investment issues as a core agenda in trade negotiations. This practice may be a good model for other ongoing FTAs identified in Global Europe Strategy and Europe 2020 Strategy. Locating FDI within CCP and integrating FDI into trade agreements would thus strengthen the EU's leverage in external economic relations and contribute to its EU's competitiveness in the post-Lisbon era.

References

Bungenberg M (2010) Going global? The EU common commercial policy after Lisbon. European Yearbook of International Economic Law 1:123–151

Burgstaller M (2009) European law and investment treaties. Journal of International Arbitration 26:181–216

Cardwell PJ, French D (2011) The European Union as a global investment partner: law, policy and rhetoric in the attainment of development assistance and market liberalization? In: Brown C, Miles K (eds) Evolution in investment treaty law and arbitration. Cambridge University Press, Cambridge, pp 201–222

Ceyssens J (2005) Towards a common foreign investment policy?—Foreign investment in the European constitution. Legal Issues of Economic Integration 32:259–291

Denza E (2010) Bilateral investment treaties and EU rules on free transfer: comment on Commission v Austria, Commission v Sweden and Commission v Finland. European Law Review 35:263–274

Eilmansberger T (2009) Bilateral investment treaties and EU law. Common Market Law Review 46:383–429

Ghouri A (2010) Resolving incompatibilities of bilateral investment treaties of the EU Member States with the EC treaty: individual and collective options. European Law Review 16:806–830

Koutrakos P (2009) Case C-205/06, Commission v. Austria, judgment of the Court (Grand Chamber) of 3 March 2009; Case C-249/06, Commission v. Sweden, judgment of the Court (Grand Chamber) of 3 March 2009. Common Market Law Review 46:2059–2076

Woolcock S (2008) The potential impact of the Lisbon Treaty on European Union external trade policy, European policy analysis. Swedish Institute for European Policy Analysis

Woolcock S (2010) The EU Approach to International Investment Policy after the Lisbon Treaty, Study Commissioned by Directorate-General for External Policies, 21 Oct 2010, Brussels. www.lse.ac.uk/collections/law/news/2010-11-03%20EU.pdf. Accessed 7 Jan 2011

Chapter 19
Creating an EU Investment Policy: Challenges for the Post-Lisbon Era of External Relations

Angelos Dimopoulos

Abstract The introduction of EU competence over foreign direct investment (FDI) in Article 207 TFEU after the Lisbon Treaty has generated broad discussions regarding the scope of the 'new' EU competence and how it will affect Member States' foreign investment policies and in particular their Bilateral Investment Treaties (BITs). Recently, the European Commission announced its intentions to create a new EU investment policy, indicating its aim to transform the EU into a major player in the field of foreign investment. Within this framework, the purpose of this chapter is to examine the challenges that the creation of an EU investment policy presents which the involved political actors will have to tackle within the following years. In that regard, this chapter looks firstly at the scope and content of EU competence, arguing that neither EU institutions nor Member States have fully grasped the broad scope of foreign investment regulation and how different areas of EU law besides the Common Commercial Policy can impact on it. Secondly, the chapter looks at the specific objectives and content of future EU investment agreements. It is argued that although the Commission intends to cover matters that exist under Member State BITs, such as protection against expropriation and investor-state arbitration, it does not have a clear vision of how to integrate them within the framework of the new 'constitutional' objectives of EU external relations. Thirdly, the chapter explores the institutional implications that the creation of an EU investment policy raises, focusing on the effects of concluding investment agreements as mixed agreements. Finally, the chapter examines the practical problems that emerge during the transition from national to EU investment policies. As the smooth transition from Member State BITs to EU investment

---

Dr. Angelos Dimopoulos—Assistant Professor, Tilburg Law School, The Netherlands.

A. Dimopoulos (✉)
Tilburg Law School, Tilburg, The Netherlands
e-mail: A.Dimopoulos@uvt.nl

P. J. Cardwell (ed.), *EU External Relations Law and Policy in the Post-Lisbon Era*,
DOI: 10.1007/978-90-6704-823-1_19, © T.M.C. Asser press, The Hague,
The Netherlands, and the authors 2012

agreements is necessary to preserve European investors' interests and rights and to sooth the concerns of third countries, the Commission's planned action focuses only on short-term measures, which merely postpone the uncertainty that EU investment policy will raise.

Contents

19.1 Introduction

Regulation of foreign investment presents one of the most topical and controversial subjects in EU external relations. The adoption of the Lisbon Treaty and the introduction of EU competence over Foreign Direct Investment (FDI) in Article 207 TFEU has generated broad discussions regarding the scope of the 'new' EU competence and how it affects Member States' foreign investment policies and in particular their Bilateral Investment Treaties (BITs). However, the foundations for an active EU role in the field of foreign investment were already laid by the Court of Justice. In 2009 the Court declared that certain provisions of Member State BITs are incompatible with EU law, indicating that the existing legal framework has to be amended.[1] Following these developments, the European Commission announced in July 2010 its intention to establish a new EU investment policy.[2] This has sparked a broad debate within EU institutions and Member States

[1] ECJ, Case C-205/06, *Commission* v. *Austria* [2009] *ECR* I-1301; ECJ, Case C-249/06 *Commission* v. *Sweden* [2009] *ECR* I-1335; ECJ, Case C-118/07 *Commission* v. *Finland*, [2009] *ECR* I-10889.

[2] Communication from the Commission to the Council, the European Parliament, the European Economic and Social Committee and the Committee of the Regions 'Towards a comprehensive European international investment policy', Brussels 7.7.2010, COM (2010) 343 (hereinafter Communication on Investment Policy); Proposal for a regulation of the European Parliament and of the Council establishing transitional arrangements for bilateral investment agreements between Member States and third countries, Brussels 7.7.2010, COM (2010) 344 (hereinafter Proposed Bilateral Investment Agreements Regulation).

regarding the future orientation of EU investment policy.[3] Although all EU institutions have rendered clear their aim to transform the EU into the main player in the field of foreign investment, the emergence of EU investment policy faces a number of legal, political and practical challenges, which the involved political actors will have to tackle in the following years. Considering that Member States have been the primary international actors in the field of foreign investment, having concluded so far more than 1,200 BITs with third countries, the determination of the proper role of EU investment policy within the existing framework raises significant questions.

Firstly, the very existence of an EU investment policy depends on the specific delineation of the scope of EU competence over foreign investment, not only under Article 207 TFEU but also under other provisions of the EU Treaties. The demarcation of EU and Member States' powers over the different forms of foreign investment, such as FDI and portfolio investment, as well as over the different aspects of foreign investment regulation, is necessary in order to materialise a comprehensive EU investment policy based on solid foundations.

Secondly, the successful materialisation of a common EU investment policy rests on the careful determination of the specific objectives and content of future investment agreements. Whether the EU will promote the insertion of more traditional BIT-oriented provisions, which focus on the protection of foreign investment against expropriation and investor-state arbitration and how it will attempt to integrate them within the framework of the new 'constitutional' objectives of EU external relations, which incorporate, among others, liberalisation and development goals, are fundamental questions, which will also influence the orientation of international regulation of foreign investment.

Intertwined with these questions is, thirdly, the determination of the roles of the EU and its Member States in policy-making in the field of foreign investment. EU institutions and Member States have to set up an investment policy that in the long-term guarantees the integration and interaction of Member States' national investment policies with EU policy both in substantive and in institutional terms. Assuming that Member States retain certain (shared) powers in the field of foreign investment, close cooperation between Member States and EU institutions is necessary in order to achieve complete and complementary regulation of foreign investment at a European level.

Fourthly, practical problems emerge during the transition from national to EU investment policies. The smooth transition from Member States' investment policies to EU investment policy is necessary to preserve European investors'

---

[3] Council of the European Union, *Conclusions on a comprehensive European international investment policy,* Luxembourg 25.10.2010; European Parliament Resolution of 6 April 2011 on the future European international investment policy (2010/2203IINI)), (hereinafter Parliament Investment Resolution); Report on the proposal for a regulation of the European Parliament and of the Council establishing transitional arrangements for bilateral investment agreements between Member States and third countries (COM(2010)0344—C7-0172/2010—2010/0197(COD), A7, 0148/2011, 14.4.2011 (Parliament Report on Investment Regulation).

interests and rights and to sooth the concerns of third countries. Legal certainty is a key concern of EU investment policy, so as to ensure the rights of third country investors, which arise from existing agreements, and to avoid multiple and conflicting obligations towards the EU, its Member States and their nationals.

19.2 Determining the Scope of EU and Member State Competence in the Field of Foreign Investment

The entry into force of the Lisbon Treaty presented the key factor that triggered the renewed interest in EU investment policy, as it established for the first time an express exclusive competence over FDI by including it in the scope of the Common Commercial Policy (CCP). Even though the debate over the inclusion of FDI generated great controversy and criticism,[4] the Lisbon Treaty, following the text of the Constitutional Treaty, extended the scope of the CCP to cover FDI.

Recognising the key role of the Lisbon Treaty in the field, EU institutions aim to build an EU investment policy on the foundations provided in Article 207 TFEU. As the Commission points out, 'an international investment policy geared towards supporting the competitiveness of European enterprises will be best served by cooperation and by negotiations at the level of the Union'.[5]

However, the inclusion of FDI as part of the CCP does not mean that the EU can take action under the new provision with regard to all matters concerning foreign investment regulation. In order to delimitate the EU from Member States competence on foreign investment as well as to clarify and identify the scope of the specific legal bases on foreign investment, it is necessary to examine the different forms of foreign investment separately, examining whether and to what extent the different regulatory aspects of each form of foreign investment fall under EU competence.

19.2.1 The Different Forms and the Definition of Foreign (Direct) Investment

As the new competence under Article 207 TFEU is limited only to FDI, the first difficulty concerns the definition of FDI. Even though there is no further clarification of the term in the TFEU, the concept of FDI should be interpreted with regard to EU rules that refer to direct investment and most importantly in

[4] There were many suggestions at the European Convention which advocated that foreign investment should not be included within the scope of the Common Commercial Policy. See Krajewski 2005, 104.

[5] Communication on Investment Policy, 5.

accordance with the notion of FDI in international law.[6] Similar to the concept of trade in services, which in the framework of the CCP should be interpreted by reference to international trade practice and not to the identically worded Treaty chapter on provision of services,[7] the international law definition of FDI is more important for defining FDI within the scope of the CCP. However, the concept of direct investment under EU law internal market provisions is also important,[8] not only because it can inform the interpretation of the relevant term under the CCP, but also because it assists in the distinction between direct and non-direct foreign investment, given that under EU law non-direct foreign investment is defined and regulated under the internal market provisions. In that respect, although the concept of direct investment in both EU and international law emphasises duration and managerial control as the main elements of FDI,[9] it is necessary to identify further the elements of duration and managerial control and when they constitute a direct investment.[10]

The demarcation of the concept of FDI leads to the next question on what other forms of foreign investment fall under EU competence. Of course, portfolio investment constitutes the next important category of foreign investment, which covers, in contrast with FDI, short-term investments.[11] Unlike FDI, primary EU law does not confer express powers on the EU with regard to portfolio investment. However, as the main regulatory aspects of portfolio investment concern the movement of capital and the participation of foreign investors in the capital market of the host state, the EU's competence to regulate portfolio investment is based on the provisions on capital movements.[12] As the EU shares competence with the Member States in the field of capital movements, Member States are not precluded, as a matter of principle, from taking external action affecting capital movements related to portfolio investment.

More importantly, the concept of foreign investment, as defined in international investment agreements goes beyond FDI and portfolio investment. While in EU law an investment appears to be conceived as an activity, namely as a transfer of

---

[6] For an analysis of the definition of investment in international investment law see Rubins 2004, 284; Yala 2005.

[7] ECJ, Opinion 1/2008 [2009] ECR I-11129, paras 119–121.

[8] In EU law, the term direct investment is used in Article 64(2) TFEU and it is associated with establishment or participation in new or existing undertakings via equity or security holdings which are characterised by the existence of a lasting link and managerial control of their activity. See Council Directive [EEC] 88/361 of 24 June 1988 for the implementation of Article 67 of the Treaty (1988) OJ L 178/5; *Commission v. Spain* [2003] ECR I-4581, para 53; Handoll 2006, 27–28.

[9] Communication on Investment Policy, p. 2–3; Ceyssens 2005, 274; Krajewski 2005, 112; Karl 2003, 420; Tietje 2009, 15–16; Johannsen 2009, 15.

[10] For a discussion of the concept of direct investment under capital rules, see Hindelang 2009, 47–52.

[11] Communication on Investment Policy, 3; Parliament Investment Resolution, para 11.

[12] Woolcock and Kleinheisterkamp 2010, 10–11; Ceyssens 2005, 275; Communication on Investment Policy, 8.

assets or as the establishment of an undertaking, this definition is contrary to the international law asset-based perception of investment.[13] The economic assets that qualify as investments under international law are broadly defined in most BITs. BITs include under the definition of investment traditional or new forms of property rights, such as shares, real estate and rights related to them, securities and other portfolio investments, which in fact are assets 'that accompany an investment and make it possible in practice'.[14] However, BITs also include in the definition of investment contractual rights that have similar characteristics to FDI, which under EU law are treated as provision of services rather than as capital movements.[15] In that respect, it becomes apparent that a complete EU investment policy, which reflects and fits within international investment law, cannot only rely on the simplistic distinction between FDI and portfolio investment. Bearing in mind the broad definition of foreign investment under BITs, a number of other TFEU provisions may be relevant for determining EU and Member State powers over the different forms of foreign investment.

In that respect, EU institutions have not yet formulated a clear position whether a broad asset-based definition of foreign investment or a specific, detailed description of the different forms of foreign investment will be used in future EU International Investment Agreements (EU IIAs). Although this choice may not impact on the breadth of activities covered under future EU IIAs, the choice of the definition of foreign investment will impact on the scope of protection given to the different forms of foreign investment. Although the Parliament seems to favour a distinction between the different forms of foreign investment,[16] it is exactly the ambiguity of the concept of FDI and the different nature of EU competence that may result in a broad asset-based definition. Avoiding questions of competence and guaranteeing broad protection of foreign investors, EU institutions may ultimately opt for a broad asset-based definition of foreign investment, which would also be easier to negotiate with third countries.

---

[13] Rubins 2004, 292.

[14] Communication on Investment Policy, 8.

[15] At first glance, the notion of services, as 'any kind of economic activities which are only temporarily provided for remuneration' (Article 57 TFEU) appears to exclude investments, since risk assumption and duration do not seem to be characteristics of services. However, the broad interpretation of the requirements of remuneration, which includes any form of economic consideration, and of temporariness, which is used only for contradistinction with the permanent link that characterises establishment, entails that services contracts of a longer duration which are not offered for predetermined remuneration fall under the scope of the Treaty provisions on provision of services. See ECJ, Case C-263/86 *Humbel* [1988] ECR 5365, paras 16–20; ECJ, Case C-231/03 *Coname* [2005] ECR-I 7287; ECJ, Case C-358/00 *Die Deutsche Bibliothek* [2002] ECR-I 4685.

[16] Parliament Investment Resolution, para 11.

19.2.2 The Different Aspects of Foreign Investment Regulation

In a nutshell, foreign investment regulation touches upon diverse regulatory interests, as it focuses mainly on the admission of foreign investment, its treatment and its protection against expropriation or political risks.[17] The inclusion of FDI within the scope of the CCP provides an important legal basis, solidifying Union competence with regard to certain aspects of foreign investment regulation. Indeed, EU institutions seem to rely almost exclusively on Article 207 TFEU as the essential power conferring provision. However, it is unclear whether Article 207 TFEU confers power on the Union to take action concerning all aspects of FDI regulation, let alone other forms of foreign investment.

Indeed, issues of admission of foreign investment fall within the scope of FDI competence.[18] Its placement under the CCP, which is based on principles of uniformity and liberalisation, reveals that FDI competence is primarily concerned with market access, hence allowing the EU to take action with regard to the initial establishment of foreign investors. However, it is less clear whether and to what extent the provisions on capital movements, establishment and services confer implied powers to the EU with regard to the admission and treatment of non-FDI forms.[19] In any case, the existence of shared competence entails that Member States still hold powers in the area of foreign investment.

Even with regard to FDI, it is unclear whether Article 207 TFEU presents the only appropriate provision to cover all aspects of FDI regulation. For example, it requires further examination whether capital movements relating to FDI fall under Article 63 or 207 TFEU. It can be argued that the mere fact that measures adopted under the CCP have repercussions on certain economic sectors falling under other Treaty chapters does not constitute a reason to exclude them from the scope of the CCP.[20] However, this is not necessarily the case for investment-related capital movements. International investment agreements not only have effects on capital movements, but also aim, among other things, to provide a framework for their liberalisation. On the other hand, Article 63 TFEU does not provide explicitly for the conclusion of international agreements, while Article 207 TFEU concerns predominantly EU action in the international sphere. The same concerns arise also with regard to the post-establishment treatment of FDI, as Article 49 TFEU

---

[17] Originally the main subject of foreign investment regulation concerned the protection of foreign investors' property from expropriation and the guarantee of a minimum standard of treatment. Over time, international foreign investment regulation has been expanded to standards of treatment of foreign investors and specific issues important for foreign investors such as performance requirements. Admission of foreign investment has been traditionally kept under national control but it has been incorporated gradually into international investment agreements.

[18] Woolcock and Kleinheisterkamp 2010, 9–10; Ceyssens 2005, 276–277; Krajewski 2005, 114.

[19] For a detailed description, see Dimopoulos 2011, Sects. 2.3 and 2.4.

[20] ECJ, Opinion 1/78 [1979] ECR 2871, para 49.

remains the basic provision concerning treatment of EU companies regardless of corporate ownership or control.[21]

Moreover, even if Article 207 TFEU could be used as a legal basis for regulating post-establishment treatment of FDI, it is uncertain whether it could be used to provide in future EU IIAs standards such as Fair and Equitable Treatment (FET), which is a core provision of most Member State BITs.[22] Answering this difficulty, para 6 of Article 207 TFEU plays a crucial role. This provision preserves Member States' powers in fields which are excluded entirely from Union interference or from harmonisation by means of Union legislation. For example, the EU cannot use its FDI competence to regulate issues falling outside the scope of its powers nor can it use its competence to harmonise areas of law where harmonisation is ruled out, such as public health, cultural or social services.[23] Thus, the scope of EU competence would ultimately depend on whether the EU can internally provide for treatment of investors, which amounts to what is referenced under international investment law as Fair and Equitable Treatment.

More controversial is whether Article 207 TFEU brings protection of foreign investors against expropriation and other political risks within EU competence. The Commission intends to include provisions on the protection of foreign investment against expropriation and other political risks in future EU IIAs, thus indicating its preparedness to assert EU competence over this aspect of foreign investment regulation.[24] However, significant reservations have been voiced concerning mainly whether Article 345 TFEU, which preserves the property ownership system of the Member States, excludes investment protection from the scope of EU competence.[25] On the other hand, it is strongly argued that Article 345 TFEU should be narrowly construed, which, together with the broad pronouncement of FDI competence under Article 207 TFEU indicates that Article 207 TFEU covers also protection of FDI against expropriation.[26]

Finally, EU institutions seem to neglect to determine whether primary EU law allows the inclusion of investor-state dispute settlement provisions in future Union agreements and the conclusion of international agreements concerning investor-

---

[21] Article 54 TFEU grants EU nationality to all firms having their registered office, central administration or principal place of business in the EU, regardless of whether they are owned or controlled by foreign nationals. Hence, Article 54 TFEU obliges the EU to treat foreign investors established in the territory of EU Member States as EU nationals.

[22] Woolcock and Kleinheisterkamp 2010, 10–11; Communication on Investment Policy, 8. Ceyssens 2005, 281 argues that FET is excluded from the scope of new FDI competence. Basing his argument on parallelism, he asserts that FET is not regulated in the internal market, and therefore it cannot be regulated in external relations. However, this argument does not take into account the fact that the lack of exercise of internal powers does not preclude in the framework of the Common Commercial Policy the exercise of external competence.

[23] For the precise scope of the limitation set out in Article 207(6) TFEU see Dimopoulos 2008, 117–119.

[24] Communication on Investment Policy, 8–9.

[25] See indicatively Tietje 2009, 14–15; Johannsen 2009, 16; Ceyssens 2005, 281.

[26] Bungenberg 2011, 36–37; Hermann 2010, 211; Shan and Zhang 2010, 1060–1061.

state dispute settlement, such as the International Centre for Settlement of Investment Disputes (ICSID) Convention.[27] As a general rule, EU competence to enter into an international agreement containing provisions for the settlement of disputes arising out of its application is a self-evident implication of its legal personality. However, dispute settlement mechanisms adopted in Union agreements must conform to the jurisdictional limits set by Opinion 1/91,[28] which was further clarified in Opinions 1/00 and 1/09,[29] emphasising the link between dispute settlement and the autonomy of the EU legal order. Thus, EU institutions need to be very careful when designing future EU IIAs, so as to ensure that investor-state arbitration respects the jurisdiction of the Court of Justice over matters of EU law.

As a result, the mere enunciation of the fact that Article 207 TFEU covers all aspects of FDI regulation is not sufficient to justify EU action that covers the entire spectrum of foreign investment regulation. The limitations that are intrinsic in Article 207 TFEU as well as in other provisions of the TFEU require a more elaborate analysis of the exact scope of Union powers, based on the totality of relevant provisions.

19.3 Setting Out the Substantive Content of EU Investment Policy

The creation of a broad common investment policy raises a number of questions regarding its substance. So far, the EU has concluded a considerable number of international agreements including provisions related to foreign investment,[30] which indicate the main characteristics of EU investment policy orientation so far. Building on them, the creation of a comprehensive EU investment policy raises a number of challenges regarding the content of future EU IIAs.

---

[27] The question of EU competence to accede to the ICSID Convention is different from the question concerning the eligibility of the EU as a supranational organisation to accede to it as a matter of international law. As Article 67 of the ICSID Convention allows only states to accede to it, the Convention should be amended in order for the EU to become a contracting party.

[28] ECJ, *Opinion 1/91* [1991] ECR I-6079.

[29] ECJ, *Opinion 1/00* (*Common Aviation Area*) [2002] ECR I-3493; *Opinion 1/09* (*European Patent Court*) [2011] nyr. For an analysis of these criteria see Govaere 2010, 192–199.

[30] Foreign investment provisions are found in the agreements with countries aiming at future accession to the EU, such as the Stabilisation and Association Agreements (SAAs) with Balkan countries, in agreements with neighbouring countries aiming at enhanced economic and political cooperation, such as the Euro-Mediterranean Agreements and the Partnership and Cooperation Agreements, and in 'pure' economic and free trade agreements that the EC has concluded with other countries, such as those with South Africa, Mexico, Chile, Korea and CARIFORUM States. For a detailed description of these agreements see the chapter in this volume by Chien Huei Wu.

19.3.1 The Objectives of Liberalisation and Competitiveness

Existing EU agreements differentiate substantially in terms of content from the standards provided in IIAs. The overwhelming majority of EU IIAs deal with admission and post-admission operation and treatment of foreign investment. Unlike BITs, EU IIAs exclude property protection against expropriation and investor-state dispute settlement from their scope. But even with regard to admission and operation of foreign investment, EU IIAs differentiate significantly from BITs, since FDI is regulated separately from other forms of foreign investment. More importantly, EU IIAs provide only for relevant standards of treatment, namely for Most-Favoured-Nation and National Treatment of foreign investment, while they lack absolute standards of treatment, such as Fair and Equitable Treatment.[31] The different content of EU IIAs illustrates the different regulatory aims that the EU investment policy was pursuing so far. The emphasis was placed on admission and operation of foreign investment, which is linked with the pursuance of the goals of liberalisation, market access and competitiveness.[32] These objectives remain at the heart of EU investment policy.[33] Adhering to these objectives, the EU seems to prioritise the demand for increasing investment flows, addressing the role of regulation of admission of foreign investment, in particular in the field of services, as a major economic determinant of foreign investment.[34] In addition to liberalisation and competitiveness, the EU investment policy intends to focus also on the more 'neglected' goals of international regulation of foreign investment. EU institutions and in particular the Parliament attempt to link foreign investment with development and broader public policy considerations. Building on provisions found under existing Union agreements with third countries, such as those on investors' behaviour, maintenance of standards and investment promotion, EU institutions aim to draw away from the obscurity that characterises development and public policy concerns in most BITs.[35]

19.3.2 The New Objective of Investment Protection

Until 2010 investment protection, accompanied by a rigorous dispute settlement system, was excluded from the objectives of EU action in the field of foreign investment. However, the Communication on Investment Policy identifies for the first time the importance of investment protection norms and investor-state arbitration for guaranteeing an environment favourable to

[31] Dimopoulos 2010, 9–13, 19–20.

[32] Dimopoulos 2010, 17–18.

[33] Woolcock and Kleinheisterkamp 2010, 9; Communication on Investment Policy, 9.

[34] Ibid.

[35] Woolcock and Kleinheisterkamp 2010, 39–40; Parliament Investment Resolution, paras 6, 23–26.

foreign investment.[36] Aiming to establish a comprehensive investment policy, EU institutions identify the 'gaps' of existing Member State BITs, which do not focus on admission of foreign investment. The Commission and the Parliament indicate that future EU IIAs will address both liberalisation and protection of foreign investment, which will not only increase EU leverage as an international actor, but can lead to overall better competitive conditions for all EU investors abroad.[37] Complementing the existing regime, the Commission intends to broaden the scope of treatment offered to foreign investments by providing absolute standards of treatment.[38] Building upon existing Member State BITs, EU agreements will incorporate this additional standard of treatment in future EU IIAs.

However, it remains uncertain how the EU will attempt to define absolute standards of treatment and in particular the standard of Fair and Equitable Treatment. Considering that there is no consensus on the customary international law content of the term,[39] it is unclear whether the EU institutions will attempt to bind the treatment offered in its agreements to the international minimum standard or whether they will attempt to provide a more specific definition of the term.[40]

Similar questions arise also with regard to the inclusion in future EU IIAs of provisions on protection of foreign investors against expropriation. Although the Commission recognises the importance of expropriation provisions for a complete regulatory framework on foreign investment,[41] the controversial and ambiguous content of investment protection provisions found in BITs[42] requires further consideration from the EU as to the existing formulation of investment protection provisions. In that respect, the Commission already highlights that the robustness of the investment protection provisions included in future EU IIAs will also depend on the 'political, institutional and economic climate of partner countries'.[43]

---

[36] Communication on Investment Policy, 4, 6.

[37] Woolcock and Kleinheisterkamp 2010, 19.

[38] Communication on Investment Policy, 8.

[39] On the history of the international minimum standard and the FET standard see Tudor 2008, 1–4.

[40] Woolcock and Kleinheisterkamp 2010, 35–36.

[41] Communication on Investment Policy, 8.

[42] Customary international law and BITs have formed a substantial body of law regulating outright takings of foreign property, determining their legality and providing for compensation, however without always using the same criteria and offering the same solutions. Even though nationalisations and outright takings of foreign investments have become less frequent in international practice, the emergence of new forms of takings, broadly defined as 'indirect', 'regulatory', 'creeping' and de facto expropriation, have expanded the regulatory scope of expropriation norms, which are in most BITs so broadly defined as to include anything 'tantamount or equivalent' to a taking. In addition, divergent criteria are used for determining compensation, ranging from 'just' to 'prompt, adequate and effective' compensation, while the same standards have been contradictory interpreted and applied in different fora. For a general overview of expropriation regulation in international investment law see Dolzer and Schreuer 2008, 89–119.

[43] Communication on Investment Policy, p. 9.

Hence, the Commission retains its flexibility to adjust the degree of investment protection with regard to different countries and more importantly to increase its negotiating leverage. Secondly, the determination of the scope of expropriation provisions will need to be compatible with primary EU law and in particular the provisions of the Charter on Fundamental Rights, so as to avoid conflicts between the Charter and the interpretation of expropriation provisions by investment tribunals. Hence, drafting the provisions on expropriation in light of the wording of the charter would actually require a careful determination of the right to regulate, which is particularly emphasised by the Parliament.[44]

Indeed, the question on the proper balance between investment objectives and public policy considerations is particularly delicate, as the adoption of a traditional model of investment regulation can minimise even further the existing potential for public policy exceptions, the determination of which falls largely within the discretion of arbitral tribunals. In that respect, the scope and content of public policy exceptions to future EU IIAs provisions on FET and protection against (indirect) expropriation will indicate the degree of adherence of the EU to a balance between investment objectives and public policy considerations. The reference in EU policy documents to specific public policy goals, such as the protection of the environment, decent work, consumer protection and cultural diversity,[45] indicate the willingness of EU institutions to curve exceptions from investment protection for the pursuance of public policy objectives. But even if the Commission is successful in promoting public policy exceptions to investment protection provisions in future EU IIAs, it would not address the criticism raised against existing EU IIAs, that they exclude affected stakeholders from dispute settlement and that they limit excessively the discretion enjoyed by (supra)national governments to determine and pursue their public policy interests.

In contrast, EU institutions provide clearer guidelines as regards the inclusion of provisions on settlement of investment disputes. The incorporation in future EU IIAs of provisions for the settlement of investment disputes between private investors and host countries indicates that the EU recognises that investor-state arbitration is a key characteristic of investment regulation.[46] What is more important though is that the EU indicates already the basic principles that will guide the negotiation of future investment agreements. Aiming to enhance transparency and legal certainty, the Commission states that it will attempt to increase the openness of arbitral proceedings and insert provisions that will enhance consistency and predictability in arbitral proceedings.[47] In addition, EU institutions are aware of the difficulties that arise from the fact the EU is not a party to the

44 Parliament Investment Resolution, paras 23–26.

45 Communication on Investment Policy, p. 9; Parliament Investment Resolution, para 25.

46 Communication on Investment Policy, p. 9; Parliament Investment Resolution, para 32.

47 Communication on Investment Policy, 10; Parliament Investment Resolution, para 31. For a detailed analysis of ways to enhance transparency and avoid forum-shopping see Woolcock and Kleinheisterkamp 2010, 45–49.

ICSID Convention, which is open only to states, and have expressed the willingness of the EU to accede to the ICSID Convention after amending it so as to allow for Regional Economic Integration Organisations (REIO) to be parties.[48]

19.3.3 Investment and Development Objectives

The development objectives of EU action in the field of foreign investment are recognised by the Commission and more prominently by the Parliament. Although the Commission is primarily concerned with guaranteeing benefits for the EU and its investors, it also underlines the importance of market openness and competitiveness for the development of third countries. Nevertheless, despite the importance of development considerations for EU external relations, the specific policy objectives of EU foreign investment policy, as set by the Commission, seem to grant only a secondary role to development objectives. On the other hand, the European Parliament stresses out the development aspects of the future EU investment policy proposing many audacious solutions.[49]

Other contributors to this volume have noted the emphasis placed by the Treaty of Lisbon on promoting European values in external relations. One of the areas where this is prominent is in development cooperation.[50] However, according to the Commission, development considerations seem to be relevant only when the relevant measures promote EU competitiveness and the interests of European investors. For example, in the field of regulatory cooperation, the Commission underlines the need for technical assistance of developing countries in order to advance structural reforms and the creation of an institutional environment favourable for foreign investment, encouraging for example the training of foreign regulators.[51] More importantly, the EU emphasises the need for linkages between foreign investment and international standards, fostering the global convergence of minimum regulatory standards, such as health or labour standards, which can promote economic and social development in third countries.[52] However, these efforts aim primarily to ensure better treatment of EU investors and maintain high internal standards, rather than contribute to sustainable development goals. On the contrary, the Parliament stresses adequate and appropriate tools for materialising the development aspects of foreign investment activity. The Parliament emphasises the need to provide support to developing countries to strengthen their

---

48 Communication on Investment Policy, 10; Parliament Investment Resolution, para 33.

49 On the role of development objectives in EU investment policy until the entry into force of the Lisbon Treaty see Cardwell and French 2010, 433–451.

50 See the contribution to this volume by Broberg.

51 Communication on Investment Policy, 9.

52 Woolcock and Kleinheisterkamp 2010, 50–51.

productivity, encourage transfer of technology and promote FDI in areas other than natural resources, thus boosting local economic development.[53]

Another example would be the different attitude towards the social, environmental and human rights aspects of foreign investment regulation. Focusing on the OECD Guidelines for Multinational Enterprises, as 'an important instrument to help balance the rights and responsibilities of investors', the Communication on Investment Policy seems to prioritise the development of non-binding standards of corporate social responsibility rather than the insertion of legally binding provisions in EU IIAs. On the contrary, the Parliament emphasises the importance of creating legally binding obligations so that foreign investors respect at least human rights and anti-corruption standards.[54]

The difference stance taken by EU institutions on the linkages between investment and development casts doubts and entails dangers for the coherence of the future EU investment policy, in particular in light of the common values, principles and objectives of EU external relations that were adopted after Lisbon. Although the Commission recognises the importance of consistency and the role of common principles and objectives,[55] the substantive elements of the emergent EU investment policy seem to undermine non-economic objectives, considering them only secondarily and to the extent that they are compatible with the objective of promoting EU competitiveness. Bearing in mind the different approach taken by the Parliament, this tension can seriously affect the efficient development of EU investment policy, as internal controversies impact also on the EU's negotiating leverage.

19.4 Promoting Cooperation Between EU Institutions and Member States

The success of EU foreign investment policy relies heavily on the cooperation between EU institutions and Member States. Successful cooperation between the EU and its Member States would enhance the EU negotiating leverage. It allows the EU to negotiate together with the Member States as a single bloc more effectively, thus enhancing EU competitiveness. Indeed, the Commission identifies the criteria for the selection of its future negotiating partners, indicating the importance of those markets for EU investment policy.[56]

However, the conclusion of future investment agreements is bound to meet a series of procedural hurdles, which may impede its successful implementation. First of all, the diversity of the procedural requirements in the various power

[53] Parliament Investment Resolution, paras 38–39.

[54] Parliament Investment Resolution, para 37.

[55] Communication on Investment Policy, 9.

[56] Communication on Investment Policy, 6–7.

conferring provisions indicates that the choice of legal basis has significant implications for the conclusion of an EU IIA. The choice of legal basis affects the institutional balance by determining the role of each institution 'in the institutional structure of the [Union] and the accomplishment of the tasks entrusted to the [Union]'.[57] In addition, it serves as an indicator of the scope and nature of EU competence, determining the international posture of the EU and the degree of involvement of Member States in the formation of an EU foreign investment policy.[58]

Recognising these concerns, the Court has insisted that the choice of a legal basis must rest on objective factors, amenable to judicial review.[59] Ensuring the application of a correct institutional balance and demarcating the scope and (exclusive) nature of EU competence, the Court adopted an 'aim and content' test in order to define the proper legal basis.[60] Applying the criteria of aim and content to EU IIAs, it is difficult to determine *in abstracto* the appropriate legal basis for their conclusion, as EU IIAs will regulate different aspects of foreign investment that may fall under different legal bases. However, the use of multiple legal bases has significant implications on the procedural requirements for the conclusion of EU agreements. Recourse to more than one legal basis is possible only if the decision-making procedures laid down in the various provisions are compatible with each other, in particular if they do not undermine the role of the Parliament.[61] As a result, the conclusion of comprehensive EU IIAs would require in most instances unanimity in the Council as well as the assent of the Parliament.

Alongside the choice of legal basis, an important concern for the conclusion of EU IIAs is the degree of direct involvement of Member States. As was already discussed, foreign investment remains a field of shared competence, so that Member States can autonomously conclude IIAs with third countries. Although the exclusive nature of FDI competence under the CCP indicates that Member States will have a minor role in the conclusion of EU IIAs, the existence of shared competence over the other forms of foreign investment will enable Member States to preserve mixity for the conclusion of future EU IIAs. Exercising their powers, Member States may be eager to participate directly alongside the EU in the conclusion of international agreements with third countries, which will take the

57 ECJ, Case C-70/88 *European Parliament* v. *Council* [1990] ECR I-2041, para 21.

58 Cremona 2008, 39–40.

59 ECJ, Case C-54/86 *Commission* v. *Council GSP* [1987] ECR I-01493; ECJ, Case C-300/89 *Commission* v. *Council* (*Titanium dioxide*) [1991] ECR I-1689.

60 See ECJ, *Opinion 2/00*(*Cartagena Protocol on Biodiversity*)[2001] ECR I–9713; ECJ, Case C–281/01 *Commission* v. *Council* (the Energy Star Agreement)[2002] ECR I–12049; ECJ, Case C–94/03 *Commission* v. *Council* (Rotterdam Convention)[2006] ECR I–1; ECJ, Joined Cases C–317/04 and C–318/*04 European Parliament* v. *Council (PNR)* [2006] ECR I–4721. For an analysis of these cases and the importance of the choice of legal basis see Koutrakos 2009, 176–185; and in the context of the ECJ and the interface between the CFSP and other aspects of external relations, contributions in this volume by Brkan and Sari.

61 ECJ, Case C–94/03 *Commission* v. *Council* (Rotterdam Convention)[2006] ECR I–1, para 52.

form of mixed agreements. Of course, mixity is not a unique characteristic of EU IIAs, as it follows a long-established practice in EU external relations.[62] Nevertheless, the conclusion of EU IIAs as mixed agreements has significant implications not only for their negotiation and conclusion, but more importantly for their application and implementation. The inclusion of foreign investment provisions in mixed agreements generates a number of international and EU law questions that stem from the inability of precise determination of the actor exercising its competence.

Without entering into the implications of the mixed procedure on the negotiation and conclusion of EU IIAs, it is worth pointing out one major difficulty that arises from the need for coherence and coordination. The conclusion of EU IIAs as mixed agreements raises concerns as regards the international responsibility of the EU and its Member States under future EU IIAs. On the one hand, in areas of EU *a priori* exclusive competence only the EU should be internationally responsible for any violation resulting from EU or Member State conduct. This rule is particularly important for the FDI provisions of future EU IIAs, the violation of which will result only in EU international responsibility. Of course, the recognition of EU exclusive responsibility in cases of violations of FDI obligations poses questions, in particular as regards international responsibility for expropriations resulting from Member State measures. As the EU can regulate only the conditions under which nationalisation or privatisation occurs and not the right of Member States to nationalise private property, either directly or indirectly, a Member State will still be able to expropriate foreign investments. Given that investment obligations will be assumed only by the EU because of its exclusive competence, it is questionable whether the EU bears responsibility for acts of expropriation of Member States, which it cannot hinder. On the other hand, in areas of shared competence, even if EU competence is rendered subsequently exclusive by virtue of implied powers,[63] the question of international responsibility is much more complicated. Not only does international responsibility relies on apportionment of the international law obligations, namely whether the EU or the Member States undertook a specific obligation under an EU IIA, but also on the attribution of the conduct of Member States organs to the EU and vice versa.[64]

---

[62] On the origins and development of mixed agreements see Heliskoski 2001, 27–69; Rosas 2000, 200–220.

[63] Based on a long standing jurisprudence of the Court of Justice, the EU is not only endowed with express powers to conclude international agreements, but it may also conclude international agreements where the conclusion of an agreement is necessary in order to achieve, within the framework of the Union's policies, one of the objectives referred to in the Treaties, or is provided for in a legally binding Union act or is likely to affect common rules or alter their scope (Article 216 TFEU). On the definition of implied powers see Cremona 2011, 219–268.

[64] For an overview of the *problématique* concerning EU international responsibility under mixed agreements see Kuijper 2010; Hoffmeister 2010.

19.5 Ensuring the Smooth Transition from a Member State to an EU Investment Policy

The existence of more than 1,200 BITs concluded by Member States with third countries indicates the significant body of international norms on foreign investment which future EU agreements have to replace. In light of the ambiguity of the scope and content of future EU investment policy, the smooth transition from Member States' investment policies to EU investment policy presents a key challenge for the success of future EU agreements in the post-Lisbon era of external (economic) relations.

Although foreign investment presents a new field for EU external action, it is not the first time that the EU is faced with such challenges. The introduction of express EU competences to act externally, such as in the areas of development policy, environment and monetary policy, as well the expansion of the scope of EU implied powers, such as in the areas of air transport and freedom, security and justice, raised concerns in the past regarding the transition from a national to an EU policy framework.[65] Drawing from past experiences, the EU and its Member States can use similar methods in order to replace existing Member States agreements by new agreements, promoting legal certainty and guaranteeing the advantages accrued to EU and third country investors under the existing network of BITs.

Within this framework, the Commission has proposed a Regulation aiming to provide the general framework regarding existing and future Member State BITs, in order to ensure legal certainty until their replacement by EU agreements. Indeed, a comprehensive EU investment policy would be unattainable, were Member State BITs kept intact beyond a transitional period. This long-term objective, which presents the main rationale behind the proposed regulation on transitional arrangements for Member State BITs, is explicitly recognised by EU institutions.[66] Indeed, the Parliament emphasises the 'transitional validity of bilateral investment agreements concluded by Member States', as the 'Commission shall take the necessary steps towards a progressive replacement of all existing agreements'.[67]

Regarding existing Member State BITs, the Regulation acknowledges their international legal validity, while arguing that these BITs should be terminated if the Commission finds them to be in conflict with the Union *acquis*. For this purpose the Commission proposes a 'conditional authorisation' system. More specifically, the notification mechanism established in Article 2 of the proposed Regulation enables the screening of existing Member State BITs. Moreover, the

---

[65] For an overview on the transition from national to EU policy in the fields of air transport and freedom, security and justice see Lykotrafiti 2011, 13–25; Cremona 2009, 16–18. See also the chapters in this volume by O'Neill and Broberg.

[66] Proposed Bilateral Investment Agreements Regulation, recital 4.

[67] Parliament Report on Investment Regulation, recitals 4 and 5.

proposed regulation allows the amendment and renegotiation of Member State BITs.[68] Subjecting the amendment of existing Member State BITs to authorisation and close scrutiny by the Commission, this mechanism enables Member States to adapt their BITs in cases where their authorisation is withdrawn because of incompatibilities with EU law.[69] Hence, this additional mechanism addresses the need for continuity of Member State BITs, as their duration can be prolonged until their replacement by EU agreements, without leaving a gap in case they have to be terminated.

The mechanism established in Chapter II of the Proposed Regulation on authorisation of Member State BITs provides a useful model for the renewal of existing BITs, preserving the autonomy and supremacy of EU law, while preserving Member States agreements. Based on the previous experiences and in particular on the mechanism established in Articles 1–3 of Decision 69/464/EEC, which concerned the transition from Member States to EU trade agreements,[70] the Proposed Regulation aims to achieve continuity in Member States action, preserving investors' interests. Of course, the authorisation of existing Member States' BITs and the potential for their amendment need not result in a lengthy transitional period as in the field of trade.[71] In that respect, the granting of review and authorisation powers to the Commission instead of the Council, as well as the recognition of the delay in the Council to authorise the opening of EU negotiations on investment with a specific third country as a valid ground for withdrawal of authorisation of Member State BITs are innovative elements that can contribute to the speedier and more efficient implementation of EU investment policy.[72] Addressing the main handicap of the authorisation mechanism provided in Decision 69/464/EEC, the EU can also draw insights from other tools used during the transition from national to Community policies in the past. The Commission could insist, for example on the inclusion of a clause that would provide that any future renegotiation of the BIT would be undertaken by the EU (in addition to the

[68] For a detailed analysis of the Regulation proposal see the chapter in this book by Chien-Hui Wu.

[69] 'In recognition of the fact that Member States may be required or may find necessary to amend or modify investment agreements, in particular to bring them in compliance with Treaty obligations, this proposal also establishes a framework and conditions to empower Member States to enter into negotiations with a third country with a view to modifying an existing bilateral agreement relating to investment'. Proposed Bilateral Investment Agreements Regulation, Explanatory Memorandum, p. 1.

[70] Council Decision 69/494/EEC of 16 December 1969 on the progressive standardisation of agreements concerning commercial relations between Member States and third countries and on the negotiation of Community agreements, OJ L326, 29.12.1969, p. 39–42.

[71] Until 2001 the Council issued regulations that authorised Member States to renew certain bilateral trade agreements with third countries. Recognising the benefits arising from the substantive scope of such agreements, the Commission was eager to propose their renewal as long as there were not similar or conflicting rules established at the EU or at the international level.

[72] See Woolcock and Kleinheisterkamp, *op. cit.*, at 64–65.

contracting Member State), which could assist in the faster recognition of the EU as an international actor in the field of foreign investment.

Nevertheless, this proposed transitional regime can be perceived as undermining legal certainty. As the proposed Regulation empowers the Commission to request from Member States to terminate their BITs whenever it finds a conflict with the law of the Union, the future of Member State BITs is vague, which in turn will cause doubts to investors who rely on the BITs when planning and executing their investments. Resolving the problem, the 'authorisation system' proposed by the Commission, could be complemented by a 'replacement system', whereby Member State BITs need only to be terminated once the EU has concluded and ratified an EU IIA or an FTA with an investment chapter with a particular country.

In addition to the authorisation of existing Member State BITs, the proposed Regulation grants the authority to the Commission to authorise the conclusion of new BITs by Member States, under close supervision by the Commission and based on common guidelines. However, this mechanism should be viewed with scepticism. The authorisation of Member States to conclude new international agreements in areas of EU exclusive competence on behalf of the EU has been used very scarcely, mainly in order to substitute for the lack of international stand of the EU under specific international legal frameworks. Member States were authorised to conclude trade agreements for example only where it was impossible for the EU to participate.[73] However, there is no legal or external political impediment for the conclusion of investment agreements by the EU. On the contrary, the conclusion of new BITs by Member States could impact negatively on the establishment of EU investment policy, as it deprives a major incentive for Member States to cooperate with the Commission and conclude jointly new agreements. More importantly, the conclusion of new investment agreements, would not add to legal certainty as proposed,[74] but it would rather prolong uncertainty, given that Member State BITs would constantly be under revision by the Commission, which could withdraw authorisation, if it found incompatibilities with EU law or that the BIT obstructs the development of EU investment policy.[75]

Last but not least, it is important to take into account that the substitution of Member State BITs by EU investment agreements would necessarily imply a tremendous coordination and resources in order to be completed. Besides, it may

---

[73] For example agreements concluded under the aegis of the UN, such as the International Labour Organisation or the International Maritime Organisation, where only States are entitled to participate in agreements. See Cremona 2009, 1–3.

[74] Proposed Bilateral Investment Agreements Regulation, 2.

[75] See Woolcock and Kleinheisterkamp 2010, 67, who argue that the mechanism proposed 'does not really contribute to enhancing legal certainty but could be seen as an instrument to give the Commission more leverage in its relation with Member States that are reluctant to change or give up their BITs'. Although this mechanism is probably the most efficient solution so as to eliminate incompatibilities and maintain legal protection arising from existing BITs, it is questionable whether additional uncertainty should be created regarding new Member States' BITs.

be politically difficult, as it would require Member States to convince third states to renegotiate their agreements with the EU, thus losing their negotiating leverage. Nevertheless, the recording and grouping of Member States investment agreements as well as the prioritisation of their renegotiation could be well planned and executed by the EU and its Member States. In that respect, the prioritisation of EU negotiating partners which the Commission proposes[76] can boost the proper implementation of EU investment policy, as it is based on clear criteria that reflect the objectives of EU investment policy.[77]

19.6 Conclusion

The development of an EU common investment policy creates a new era in EU external economic relations. However, the centralisation of policy-making in the field of foreign investment does not guarantee as such that it will be beneficial for home and host states and foreign investors. It is the specific scope and content of the common investment policy that will determine its positive or negative effects. EU institutions and Member States will have to tackle successfully with a number of challenges in order to set up a common investment policy, in particular establishing the formula for future EU IIAs that will take into account the requirements of primary EU law and the peculiarities regarding the international law position of the EU and its Member States, as well as securing the smooth transition from Member State BITs to EU-wide IIAs. But more importantly, policy makers will have to set out the specific objectives of an EU common investment policy, incorporating them in future EU IIAs. It rests in the hands of the EU and Member States' political institutions whether the EU will be a pioneer in international investment law, proposing a regulatory framework that on the one hand preserves the protection of foreign investors and enhances their investment opportunities and on the other addresses the host states' public policy concerns, or whether the EU will merely replicate existing EU IIAs and Member State BITs, adding to the current dichotomy and the proliferation of norms of international investment law.

From this angle, the Commission proposals set the basic foundations for the establishment of a complete and successful EU investment policy. Affirming the main competences of the Union in the field and sketching the main elements of EU future investment policy, EU institutions have already set the general framework for the development of the future EU investment policy. Nevertheless, the different approaches to EU foreign investment policy put forward by EU institutions threaten the coherent and efficient development of EU investment policy. More

---

[76] Communication on Investment Policy, 6–7.

[77] For an analysis of the relevant criteria for prioritising negotiating partners see Woolcock and Kleinheisterkamp 2010, 20–30.

importantly, the proposals do not seem to have taken into consideration all complications that arise from the substitution of national investment policies. Touching only upon selective problems, they fail to recognise delicate matters that can complicate the development of EU investment policy.

References

Bungenberg M (2011) The division of competences between the EU and its Member states in the area of investment policies. In: Bungeberg M, Griebel J, Hindelang S (eds) International investment law and EU law. Nomos, Heidelberg, pp 29–42

Cardwell PJ, French D (2010) Liberalizing investment in the CARIFORUM-EU economic partnership agreement: EU priorities, regional agendas and developmental hegemony. In: Cordonier-Segger MC, Gehring M, Newcombe A (eds) Sustainable development in World Investment Law. Kluwer, Alphen aan den Rijn, pp 429–450

Ceyssens J (2005) Towards a Common Foreign Investment Policy?—foreign investment in the European Constitution. Legal Issues of Economic Integration 32:259–291

Cremona M (2008) Defining competence in EU external relations: lessons from the Treaty reform process. In: Dashwood A, Maresceau M (eds) Law and practice of EU external relations. Hart, Oxford, pp 34–69

Cremona M (2009) Member States as Trustees of the Community Interest: participating in International Agreements on behalf of the European Community. EUI Working Paper LAW 2009/17

Cremona M (2011) External relations and external competence of the European Union: the emergence of an integrated policy. In: Craig P, De Búrca G (eds) The evolution of EU law. Oxford University Press, Oxford, pp 217–268

Dimopoulos A (2008) The Common Commercial Policy after Lisbon: establishing parallelism between Internal and External Economic Policy. Croatian Yearbook of European Law and Policy 4:76–101

Dimopoulos A (2010) Shifting the emphasis from investment protection to liberalization and development: the EU as a new global actor in the field of Foreign Investment Policy. Journal of World Investment and Trade 11:3–26

Dimopoulos A (2011) EU foreign investment law. Oxford University Press, Oxford (forthcoming)

Dolzer R, Schreuer C (2008) Principles of international investment law. Oxford University Press, Oxford

Govaere I (2010) Beware the Trojan Horse: dispute settlement in (mixed) agreements and the autonomy of the EU legal order. In: Hillion C, Koutrakos P (eds) Mixed agreements revisited. Hart, Oxford, pp 187–207

Handoll J (2006) Capital, payments and money laundering in the European Union. Richmond, Oxford

Heliskoski J (2001) Mixed agreements as a technique for organizing the international relations of the European Community and its Member States. Brill, Leiden

Hermann C (2010) Die Zukunft der mitgliedstaatlichen Investitionspolitik nach dem Vertrag von Lissabon. Europäische Zeitschrift für Wirtschaftsrecht 21:207–211

Hindelang S (2009) The free movement of capital and foreign direct investment: the scope of protection in EU law. Oxford University Press, Oxford

Hoffmeister F (2010) Litigating against the European Union and its Member States—who responds under the ILC's draft articles on international responsibility of international organizations? European Journal of International Law 21:723–747

Johannsen S (2009) Die Kompetenz der Europäischen Union für ausländische Direktinvestitionen nach dem Vertrag von Lissabon. Beiträge zum Transnationalen Wirtschaftsrecht 90:1–46
Karl J (2003) The competence for Foreign Direct Investment. Journal of World Investment and Trade 4:413–448
Koutrakos P (2009) Legal basis and delimitation of competence in EU external relations. In: Cremona M, De Witte B (eds) EU foreign relations law-constitutional fundamentals. Hart, Oxford
Krajewski M (2005) External trade law and the Constitutional Treaty: towards a federal and more Democratic Common Commercial Policy? Common Market Law Review 42:91–127
Kuijper P (2010) International responsibility for EU mixed agreements. In: Hillion C, Koutrakos P (eds) Mixed agreements revisited. Hart, Oxford, pp 208–228
Lykotrafiti A (2011) Consolidation and rationalization in the Transatlantic Air Transport Market—prospects and challenges for competition and consumer welfare. TILEC Discussion Paper 2011–2033
Rosas A (2000) The European Union and mixed agreements. In: Dashwood A, Hillion C (eds) The general law of E.C. external relations. Sweet and Maxwell, London, pp 216–236
Rubins N (2004) The notion of investment in international investment arbitration. In: Horn N (ed) Arbitrating foreign investment disputes. Kluwer, The Hague, pp 283–324
Shan W, Zhang S (2010) The Treaty of Lisbon: half way toward a Common Investment Policy. European Journal of International Law 21:1049–1073
Tietje C (2009) Die Außenwirtschaftsverfassung der EU nach dem Vertrag von Lissabon. Beiträge zum Transnationalen Wirtschaftsrecht 93:1–32
Tudor I (2008) The fair and equitable treatment standard in the international law of foreign investment. Oxford University Press, Oxford
Woolcock S, Kleinheisterkamp J (2010) The EU approach to international investment policy after the Lisbon Treaty. European Parliament Directorate General for External Policies, Brussels
Yala F (2005) The notion of investment in ICSID case law: A drifting jurisdictional requirement? Journal of International Arbitration 22:105–126

Index

P. J. Cardwell (ed.), *EU External Relations Law and Policy in the Post-Lisbon Era*, DOI: 10.1007/978-90-6704-823-1, © T.M.C. ASSER PRESS, The Hague, The Netherlands, and the authors 2012

MIX
Papier aus verantwortungsvollen Quellen
Paper from responsible sources
FSC® C105338

If you have any concerns about our products,
you can contact us on
ProductSafety@springernature.com

In case Publisher is established outside the EU,
the EU authorized representative is:
Springer Nature Customer Service Center GmbH
Europaplatz 3, 69115 Heidelberg, Germany

Printed by Libri Plureos GmbH
in Hamburg, Germany